THE BOOK OF
SPORTS CARS

Charles Lam Markmann • Mark Sherwin

FOREWORD BY BRIGGS S. CUNNINGHAM

FREDERICK MULLER LIMITED

LONDON

First published in Great Britain in 1960 by
Frederick Muller Limited

Printed in Great Britain by Spottiswoode, Ballantyne & Company Limited
London and Colchester
Bound by The Leighton-Straker Bookbinding Company Limited

To MARY and INGA

Foreword

This is a book for which lovers of the automobile have waited a long time: the most comprehensive text-and-picture history of the dual-purpose car since it came to life more than sixty years ago.

As the authors of *The Book of Sports Cars* point out, "in the beginning they were all sports cars". The automobile began its active life, whatever the intentions of its creators, as a new instrument of sport. Because the increasing demands of this sport imposed an ever-growing burden of technical development, the sports car and its achievements have never stopped forwarding the improvement of the everyday automobile. Here at last, evolved from years of painstaking research, is a record of what the world's motorists owe to the dreams and the daring of the men and women of motor sport.

It was, for example, the Grands Prix of the early years of this century that begot the demountable rim—an invention that was necessitated by the incalculable time losses when clincher tyres blew out in races. The races and rallies and trials of those early days also made inevitable the rapid development of the pneumatic tyre from the fail, brittle casing no stronger than a bicycle tyre to the magnificent, durable shoes that every car can wear today as a matter of course.

So, too, we can trace virtually every advance in automobile design and construction to the demands and ambitions of the builders and drivers: the vast improvements in ignition systems, in fuel and carburation, in steering and suspension, in solving the problems of weight distribution and of power/weight ratios, in engine economy and efficiency, in braking—one has only to remember that the first four-wheel brakes were developed by Isotta-Fraschini in 1910 to meet the emergencies of fierce competition—and in coachwork, both aerodynamically and aesthetically.

In arranging the history of the outstanding marques by countries of origin, the authors have made it plain how first one nation, then another took the lead in developing the automobile as a sporting instrument and hence inevitably as a thing of greater common use and benefit. First Germany led the world, then France, then Great Britain and Italy and the United States. Not the least of the services rendered by *The Book of Sports Cars* is to point out the valuable contributions of other, smaller countries that might easily be overlooked in the grand sweeping picture—the Netherlands, for instance, which gave birth to the first four-wheel drive, four-brake car just after the turn of the century; or Belgium, which produced such impressive marques as Métallurgique and Minerva and Excelsior; or Austria, the home of Austro-Daimler and Steyr.

The Book of Sports Cars is a magnificent tribute to the glorious past and the exciting present, a fascinating record of the history that points to the challenging future. A book to be read for pleasure and profit, it will be an invaluable addition to the library of every enthusiast of motoring history.

Briggs Cunningham

Contents

Foreword by Briggs S. Cunningham   3

In the Beginning They Were All Sports Cars   7

THE CARS

Great Britain:

A.B.C.	10
A.C.	10
Allard	12
Alvis	14
Aston Martin	15
Austin, Austin-Healey	18
Berkeley	19
Bentley	20
Bristol, Arnolt-Bristol	23
Crossley	24
Dellow	25
Doretti	26
Elva	26
Fairthorpe	26
Frazer Nash	27
G.N.	30
H.E.	31
Healey, Nash-Healey	32
H.R.G.	33
Invicta	35
Jaguar	36
Jensen (Avon Standard)	39
Jowett	40
Kieft	41
Lagonda	42
Lea-Francis	45
Leyland Thomas	46
Lotus	46
M.G.	48
Morgan	53
Napier, Hutton	54
Peerless	57
Riley	57
Rolls-Royce	60
Singer	62
Siddeley Special	63
Squire	63

Straker-Squire	64
Sunbeam, Talbot, Sunbeam-Talbot	65
Triumph, Vale	69
Turner	71
T.V.R.	71
Vauxhall	71
Wolseley	73

France:

Amilcar	75
Ariès	76
B.N.C.	77
Ballot	77
Berliet	79
Bignan	79
Bugatti	80
Chenard & Walcker	84
Cottin et Desgouttes	86
Darracq	87
D.B.	88
de Dion-Bouton	89
Delage	90
Delahaye	92
Derby, Vernon-Derby	94
Gobron-Brillié	95
Gordini	95
Grégoire	96
Hispano-Suiza	97
Hotchkiss	99
Georges Irat	100
Lorraine-Dietrich, de Dietrich	101
Mors	102
Panhard	103
Peugeot	105
Renault	107
Rolland-Pilain	109
Salmson	110
S.A.R.A.	111

Talbot, Talbot-Lago	111
Tracta	112
Voisin	114

United States:

American	116
Auburn	116
Biddle	117
Chadwick	118
Chrysler	118
Cord	120
Corvette	121
Crosley	122
Cunningham	122
Duesenberg	124
du Pont	127
Ford	128
Kissel	129
Locomobile	129
Lozier	130
Marmon	131
Mercer	131
Packard	133
Peerless	133
Pierce-Arrow	134
Scripps-Booth	134
Simplex	134
Stutz, H.C.S.	135
Thomas	137
Wills Ste. Claire	138

Italy:

Abarth	139
Alfa Romeo	140
Ansaldo	143
Cisitalia	143
Diatto	144
Ferrari	144
FIAT	148
Isotta-Fraschini	151
Itala	153
Lancia	155
Maserati	159
Moretti	161
Nardi	162
O.S.C.A.	163
O.M., Züst	164
S.I.A.T.A.	165
S.P.A.	167

Germany:

Adler	168
Benz	168
B.M.W., E.M.W.	170
D.K.W.	172
Horch	173
Mercedes, Mercedes-Benz	173
Porsche	178
Wanderer	180

Belgium:

Excelsior	181
F.N.	181
Impéria	182
Métallurgique	183
Minerva	185
Nagant	185
Pipe	187
S.A.V.A.	187

Russia:

Russo-Baltique	188
Soviet Russian Sports Cars	188

Austria:

Austro-Daimler	189
Denzel	191
Steyr	191

Spain:

Pegaso	192

The Netherlands:

Spyker	193

Sweden:

SAAB	194
Volvo	194

Japan:

Datsun	194

BUILDERS

Sydney Allard	195
W. O. Bentley	195
A. C. Bertelli	197
Marc Birkigt	198
Ettore Bugatti	198
Colin Chapman	200

Louis Coatalen	200	Eugenio Castellotti	245
Briggs Cunningham	201	Louis Chiron	246
Albert de Dion	203	Peter Collins	247
Fred and August Duesenberg	204	René Dreyfus	248
Enzo Ferrari	205	S. F. Edge and Charles Jarrott	249
Amédée Gordini	207	G. E. T. Eyston	251
J. A. Grégoire	208	Luigi Fagioli	252
Donald Healey	209	Juan Manuel Fangio	253
Ernest Henry	211	Giuseppe Farina	254
Antoine Lago	212	John Fitch	255
Vincenzo Lancia	213	Froilan Gonzales	257
Albert Lory	215	Masten Gregory	258
The Maserati Brothers	215	Fritz Huschke von Hanstein	259
Wilhelm Maybach	216	Mike Hawthorn	260
Laurence H. Pomeroy	218	Philip Hill	263
Ferdinand Porsche	219	Hermann Lang	264
Georges Roesch	220	Christian Lautenschlager	265
Harry C. Stutz	222	Onofre A. Marimón	266
Rudolf Uhlenhaut	223	Stirling Moss	267
Gabriel Voisin	224	Luigi Musso	269
		Felice Nazzaro	270
		Alfred Neubauer	272
DRIVERS		Tazio Nuvolari	273
The Bentley Boys	225	Reg Parnell	275
Woolf Barnato	225	Alfonso de Portago	276
Dr. J. Dudley Benjafield	226	Dario Resta	277
Sir Henry R. S. Birkin	228	Bernd Rosemeyer	278
S. C. H. Davis	228	Harry Schell	279
Bernard Rubin	229	Richard J. B. Seaman	280
Glen Kidston	230	Raymond Sommer	281
John Duff	230	Piero Taruffi	282
Frank Clement	231	Maurice Trintignant	283
George Duller	231	Achille Varzi	284
Clive and Jack Dunfee	231	Luigi Villoresi	286
The Bugatti Drivers	232	The Women	286
Robert Benoist	233	Camille du Gast	286
Meo Costantini	234	Some French Women Drivers	287
Williams	234	Gwenda Hawkes	287
Jean-Pierre Wimille	235	Elisabeth Juneck	288
Antonio and Alberto Ascari	236	Dorothy Levitt	289
Jean Behra	237	Denise McCluggage	289
Clemente Biondetti	238	Evelyn Mull	291
Prince Bira	239	Kay Petre	291
Georges and André Boillot	240	Dorothy Turner	292
Felice Bonetto	241	Sheila Van Damm	292
Jack Brabham	242	Elsie Wisdom	293
Manfred von Brauchitsch	243	Venues: Races, Rallies and Hill-Climbs	295
Gastone Brilli-Peri	243	Acknowledgments	316
Rudolf Caracciola	244	Bibliography	320

In the Beginning They Were All Sports Cars

The automobile did not come into being as a utilitarian vehicle for the transport of men and goods. It began as an instrument of pleasure: a working model of a spring-driven vehicle was one of the amusements of Leonardo da Vinci. When the internal-combustion engine became a practical reality, its first application to transportation—and indeed its major application for a long time thereafter—was the provision of pleasure.

But perhaps we should do well to define a sports car before we go farther. A precise and dogmatic definition cannot be drawn for any category whose components are so highly individual and particularized, so we must of necessity start with a general principle. A sports car, then, is an automobile designed for the enthusiast to whom pleasure is its paramount potential: pleasure in its performance and pleasure in its design. The sports car is a dual-purpose car: it is equally at home in city traffic and in all-out competition, and it requires no essential modification to convert from the one use to the other. It is, in short, a car that is meant to be driven to a race, in the race and back home from the race—and to make any kind of driving exciting.

All the early cars fell into this category. Their designers and builders raced them as soon as they were sure they would run; their buyers, in the main, never thought seriously of doing much else with them (except, perhaps, dazzling the neighbours). One bought an automobile, in the early years of this century, as one bought a hunter: *pour le sport seulement*. If the vehicle turned out to be really useful in conveying oneself and one's friends or one's chattels from place to place, that was a bonus: but it did not really matter. What did matter was that here was a new form of sport.

This sport enjoyed a number of virtually simultaneous sires in widely separated places: in Austria it was fathered by Siegfried Marcus; in Germany, by Karl Benz and Gottlieb Daimler; in France by Panhard and Levassor, the Marquis de Dion, Louis Renault and others; in Great Britain by F. R. Simms, Percy Riley, the Hon. C. S. Rolls, S. F. Edge and many more; in Italy by Senator Giovanni Agnelli, the Ceirano brothers, Vincenzo Lancia; in the United States by the Duryea brothers, Elwood Haynes, Henry Ford—the list of pioneers is limitless. All these men, whether the cars they made were large or small, were producing (whatever their ultimate dreams) essentially a luxury item whose price made it available only to a few. And most of those few bought it to have fun with it; when there was serious travelling to be done, they relied on the horse-drawn carriage or on the railway.

It was principally in the United States, in the years immediately preceding the First World War, that the initial concerted effort was made to transform the automobile from a sporting luxury to an everyday adjunct of living. After that war, Great Britain, too, saw the motor car become a tool as well as a toy; but in Europe it remained for the most part the monopoly of the sporting rich. True, some small "economy" or "family" cars were made and marketed on the Continent; but they were always relatively few and even the least expensive were well beyond the reach of the majority of the population.

Sports motoring developed variously according to geography and economics in the first half of the century. In the beginning, the road race was as common in America as in Europe and ultimately, through special Acts of Parliament, got a foothold in some parts of the British Isles; indeed, there was at first no other racing. Manufacturers—and in some cases private owner-drivers—sent their German Benzes, their British Napiers, their French Panhards, their Italian FIATS to compete on American highways, and the American Locomobiles and Thomases and Simplexes were shipped over the ocean to return the compliment. But the mushrooming of the utility or family car in the United States soon clogged its roads, and its makers no longer produced automobiles that could race as well as relax; competition became, in the United States, the monopoly of cars specially built for racing under extremely limited artificial conditions: the circular or oval track, which bore no resemblance to actual road work. Today only one round-the-houses course exists in the United States, and it was created less than 10 years ago: Put-In Bay, an island on Lake Erie where once each year the Cleveland Sport Car Club and the Northeast Ohio Region of the Sports Car Club of America stage a day of racing on the narrow farm roads and village streets of a resort community, whose terrain makes it necessary to limit entries to cars of under two-litres capacity.

The same situation developed in the British Isles. The famed Tourist Trophy, which for almost 50 years was run on public roads, first in the Isle of Man and later in Northern Ireland, is now held on a closed circuit. But in Europe the public highways have remained the race courses, and the cars that compete on them have remained (except for grand-prix racing) substantially the same as those offered for sale to such Europeans—or Americans—as have the money to buy them. Even today there are few closed courses in Europe, though apprehensions for spectator safety are beginning to bear ominously on such renowned highway racing circuits as those of Le Mans, Monaco and the Mille Miglia.

American automobile designers were the first to stop building competition characteristics into their general products. This was not a sudden unanimous change: into the 1930s models of several American production vehicles fully merited the classification of sports cars: the Auburn, Cord and Duesenberg, for example, or the Marmon or the Kissel, or the du Ponts, Chryslers and Stutzes that ran at Le Mans. But, as the opposition to road racing increased, manufacturers who wanted racing products began to build them for the only type of racing that the country would countenance: on an enclosed track. Such cars, because they were designed exclusively for this one purpose, had and have little or nothing in common with road cars of any kind: they are generally single-seaters, they lack lights and tops and mudwings, they have no starters or fans and at most two forward gears, their braking, steering and suspension are adapted exclusively to a flat course on which the only turn is left. In sum, they are single-purpose cars fully as much as the family saloon or convertible is a single-purpose car of quite another type.

In Europe, however, road racing has never been threatened with extinction. A manufacturer who wishes to enter his cars in competition there knows that they will have to race on exactly the same kinds of highways that he drives daily between home and office; he knows that they will have to race at night, that they may have to stop—and start again—many miles from the pits with their service crews; he knows that they will encounter every possible type of corner; and he knows, too, that a large number of his customers, while they may want to race their cars, must also depend on them for other uses.

What he also recognizes, unlike his American counterpart, is that a substantial proportion of the motoring public, while it may never enter a formal race on any kind of course, wants a thoroughbred. Perhaps these people drive only to get from A to B: but to them the process of getting there is as much—perhaps even more—to be enjoyed as the arrival. Hence the sports car has always formed a much higher percentage of British and Continental than of American production; and hence the American who drives for the fun of driving has found increasingly that he must import his fun. It can be categorically stated as of the time of publication that only one American manufacturer has seriously sought to challenge foreign supremacy in the field. That is General Motors' Chevrolet division, which, after some false starts and foredoomed compromises, is beginning to approach fulfilment of all the criteria of a sports car with its Corvette.

What are these criteria? We have said that first of all the sports car must satisfy the need for pleasure in motoring performance and design and that it must be able at a moment's notice to switch from carting groceries to capturing trophies—and back again. Now let us try to be specific, to isolate and identify the qualities that make for this ideal dual personality.

Primarily, of course, the sports car must be capable of any kind of normal use. It must be licensable, able to endure all the irritations of traffic and suitable for normal needs: that is, for bad weather, for darkness, for all kinds of roads, for carrying one or more passengers and for sustained driving. It must be immediately responsive: to a tap on the accelerator, a ten-degree flick of the steering wheel, a toe on the brake pedal. It must be matched in its components: steering, brakes, suspension, weight, ignition, gearing and power plant must be designed each in terms of all the others. One does not find, for example, 60-mile-an-hour brakes or undulant springing on a 130-mile-an-hour sports car: every part is designed with every other part—and the ultimate function of the whole—in mind, and all superfluity, whether of bulk or of weight or of gadgets, is outlawed. Hence the true sports car is the most roadable and the safest of automobiles: it is built not only to stay on the road whatever the road may be but also to stay on course—with one big *if*. The sports car demands to *be driven*: it will not take you out and do the thinking for you.

It represents, whatever its size, the maximum performance that can be wrested from that particular combination of volume, weight and thrust. Hence it is devoid of non-functional addenda that sap horsepower (and the driver's attention to his business), and it is rich in all those safety features that are, in reality, functions of performance: maximum road-holding, maximum deceleration as well as acceleration, the greatest controllability with the least fatigue. The last is achieved not through the piling on of costly, delicate, power-wasting delegations of the driver's functions but through the tightening of the steering ratio—expressed in greater proportion of road-wheel turn to steering-wheel rotation—and the retention of driver control of road speed by virtue of individual selection of gear ratios to fit changing driving conditions.

The sports car, too, has another trait: it knows superbly what to do and is magnificently capable of doing it—but it requires a master who also knows its qualities and is capable of making it show them. The man who has a sports car, and knows it as intimately as the passionate equestrian knows his horse, rides Pegasus every day.

And now let us see what forms and evolutions this 20th-century Pegasus has presented to the nations and the generations that have learned to mount him.

THE CARS

Donne e motori,

gioie e dolori.

—Italian proverb.

GREAT BRITAIN

The 1920–4 A.B.C. is exemplified by this 1922 model

The 1925 A.B.C. super-sports

A.B.C.

One of the most successful light cars ever made had a production life of only seven years. The A.B.C., designed by Granville Bradshaw and first built by A.B.C. Motors at Walton-on-Thames, came out in 1920. For four years the cars were unchanged; in 1925 various improvements were introduced that, according to experts, made this superb little vehicle even finer. Production ceased in 1927 after about 8000 cars had been built. Of these, according to G. de Jongh, only five survive.

The earlier model, which won 58 gold medals in various contests and finished seventh in a field of 18 at Brooklands with a fastest-in-class (1500 c.c.) speed of 86 m.p.h., was a flat-twin overhead-valve engine of 1203 c.c. capacity. Air-cooled, it had a close-ratio 4-speed gearbox with shaft drive to a spiral bevel rear axle. Quarter-elliptic springs were fitted all round and two sets of brakes operated on the rear wheels only: one internal expanding (foot) and the other external contracting (hand).

The 4-cylinder, with E-13 A.C. engine, four overhead valves per cylinder. This engine set the light-car record of 82·73 m.p.h. for 300 miles

Cylinders were of steel and all bearings, except one in the timing gear, were either ball or roller. Weighing less than 12 cwt. fully laden, the car developed 35 h.p. at 3500 r.p.m. In 1925 A.B.C. changed to cast-iron cylinders, enclosed overhead valves lubricated from the engine and stiffer crankshaft and timing gear. In this year the company introduced the super-sports, bored out to 1320 c.c. and developing 40 h.p., and claimed a 0–50 acceleration of 15 seconds. De Jongh, who has owned five of both models and is still racing his super-sports, considers the latter unquestionably superior because of bad engine vibration in the earlier model and loss of power when the engine heated. The super-sports had double Zenith carburation. Both models were long and narrow—102-in. wheelbase and 47-in. track.

A.C.

The unbeatable leader of the 2-litre sports cars owes its origin to a meeting almost 60 years ago between an unusual butcher and an inspired engineer. John Portwine's chain of meat shops was prospering and he was caught up in John Weller's dream of a superior light automobile. From the Weller car that they produced in 1900 came the firm of Autocar & Accessories Ltd., maker of the Autocarrier and for the past 35 years of the A.C. It is now known as A.C. Cars Ltd.

The Autocarrier was a commercial vehicle; the company's first passenger cars were the then popular three-wheelers. Weller had the design for a four-wheeled car almost completed when the outbreak of the Kaiser War prevented production beyond prototypes, which had transverse front springs and semi-elliptic rears. Three-speed gearbox and worm-drive rear axle were combined in an aluminium casing, and

[Photograph by John K. Milner]

The 6-cylinder of 1926, 56 h.p. This car set a 24-hour record of 82·58 m.p.h. at Montlhéry

Courtesy of A.C. Cars Ltd.]

The 1927 sports, 6-cylinder, covered 15,000 miles at Montlhéry in two days less than the previous record, driven by the Hon. and Mrs. Victor Bruce and J. A. Joyce of the works

the 4-cylinder engine was the French Fivet. The whole car weighed just under 10 cwt. and in 1913 at Brooklands hit 45 m.p.h., then a feat for any light car.

As Fivet could not meet the engine demand A.C. changed over to the well-known Anzani unit while Weller experimented with a light 6-cylinder engine. S. F. Edge, oriented to competition, became a director of the firm and then chairman, and in his first year the A.C. broke 57 records, using its own new overhead-valve engine with four valves per cylinder. It entered the 100-m.p.h. class that year, with an engine under 1500 c.c.

One of the first to use aluminium bodies, A.C. was the first British car to enter the Monte Carlo Rally (1925) and the first to win it (1926), driven by a private owner. In 1925, too, A.C. broke the world's record for a one-man 24-hour drive, averaging 82·5 m.p.h. at Montlhéry. In 1931 the company joined the dominant trend of building gearbox and engine as a unit. Two years later the Earl of March (now the Duke of Richmond and Gordon), an eminent racing driver, became coachwork designer for A.C. In the 1930s A.C. adopted triple S.U. carburation and synchromesh gears.

The shortened sports chassis, nicknamed The Flea, was introduced in 1937, when exports to the United States began. Wilson pre-selector gearboxes were also made available. A special sports engine with 7:1 compression, compared to the normal 6·5:1, was offered. An Arnott-supercharged engine was also, unenthusiastically, available. New designs were again shelved for war production in 1939, and the first post-war cars appeared with bronze main bearings, better engine cooling and bigger brakes, hydraulic at the front and mechanical at the rear.

The tubular chassis was introduced in the mid-1950s, when the A.C. was offered with a new choice of engines: A.C.'s own 1991-c.c. 6-cylinder, with an 8:1 compression ratio, or the 1971-c.c. Bristol engine with 8·5:1 compression, a much faster power plant developing 120 h.p. compared to 90 from the bigger

Courtesy of A.C. Cars Ltd.]

The March tourer, designed by the then Earl of March, retained the gate-change 4-speed crash box. It was a favourite car for touring and tough rallies

Courtesy of A.C. Cars Ltd.]

The current Aceca coupé, a four-seater gran turismo machine weighing only 16·4 cwt. and independently sprung all round. Available with A.C. or Bristol engine

engine. In further stages of tune, the Bristol unit has been raised to almost 145 b.h.p. A.C.-Bristols, both open and closed, have taken more first places than any other production 2-litre car.

ALLARD

The love of speed, the gift of innate engineering talent and the lack of money may fairly be called the reasons why there is an Allard marque. It is one of the few production cars of quality that developed from a back-yard "special".

Courtesy of A.C. Cars Ltd.]

The Ace roadster, which with the Bristol engine out-classes all production cars under 2 litres, weighs little more than 15 cwt.

Courtesy of the Allard Motor Co. Ltd.]

The first Allard, rebuilt from a Ford wreck, is still in use, though with a new body. It is shown with some of its trophies

The first Allard was built in the late 1930s by Sydney H. Allard from a wrecked Ford V-8 saloon. In one week it became a Bugatti-tailed roadster and inaugurated its maker's career by winning its first trial so handsomely that demands for replicas poured in on the owner.

Allards are happiest in competition: racing, sprints or hill-climbs. The firm builds no engines: the customer chooses his own power unit for the frame and body he buys from the Allard Motor Co. Ltd. Initially, Fords, Chryslers and Cadillacs were most in demand and Chrysler- and Cadillac-powered Allards, with the remarkably favourable power-weight ratio of 4·5-litre engines developing several hundred horsepower in very light installations, have scored many notable successes: the Monte Carlo Rally, Le Mans, Prescott Hill-Climb, the Tour of Sicily and a number of American courses.

Photograph copyright by Louis Klemantaski; courtesy of the Vintage Car Store]

A J-1 Allard in its favourite event: a hill-climb

12

[Photograph copyright by James Brymer; courtesy of the Vintage Car Store

The so-called "tail-wagger" Allard, nicknamed for obvious reasons

Photograph by Daniel Rubin; courtesy of Everett L. Poorman]

A J-2 Allard leads through a turn on the old Bridge-hampton road course

[Photograph by David Klein

One of the last J2X Allards, at its best on hills. Body was re-designed for Le Mans after FIA banned cycle wings. This example has Oldsmobile 88 engine with Offenhauser heads, delivering 310 h.p. and 145 m.p.h. at 4500 r.p.m. It weighs 20½ cwt.

Photograph by R. A. Woolf]

This Allard L tourer with modified 1948 Mercury engine weighed 20 cwt. and accelerated from rest to 50 m.p.h. in 5·5 seconds

Starting with open two- and four-seaters, the Allard Motor Co. was formed in 1946 and for some years offered coupé, drop-head and saloon bodies as well. In 1952 Allard adopted the tubular chassis and de Dion rear axle, and also introduced a smaller car using Ford Zephyr rear and Zephyr or Consul engine. The earliest Allards were "J" models; the more refined and longer two-seater was labelled "K", the four-seater "L", the drop-head "M", the saloon "P". Coil springs had replaced transverse leaf front springs in 1949, when two-leading-shoe front brakes were added.

The J2, or Palm Beach, was very popular in the United States with coil springs all round and de Dion rear. The J2X was Cadillac- or Chrysler-powered, as was the J2R, with tubular frame. The P2 was also tubular, deriving from the saloon that won the Monte Carlo Rally, driven by Allard.

Since 1956 only two models have been in production: the Palm Beach Mark II, available with either Ford Zodiac or Jaguar XK-150 engine, and the new Gran Turismo, for which the Jaguar is the recommended engine although the chassis is designed to take any American motor.

Courtesy of the Allard Motor Co. Ltd.]

Exquisitely bodied gran turismo has 3·5 litre, 210-b.h.p. Jaguar engine with double overhead high-lift camshafts and 8:1 compression

The unpretentious 10/30 was 10 years ahead of its time. It had a 4-speed gearbox and forced-feed lubrication

The 12/50 that saved the company's life. This car still competes

ALVIS

The red triangle of Alvis first gained glory in 1923 with what has justly been called "the immortal 12/50"—it cannot be worn out. But, before the 12/50, Alvis began with the 10/30—the figures refer to rated and developed horsepower—which appeared in 1920 with such refinements of later years as forced-feed lubrication. A 60-m.p.h. car, it had a 4-cylinder side-valve engine of 1460 c.c.

Hill-climb and race victories were garnered by this first Alvis as by its successors. The 12/50's 1923 victory in the 200-mile Brooklands race at 93·29 m.p.h. was enhanced by the defeat of the favourites, two supercharged FIAT 403s, one driven by Sir Malcolm Campbell. It was this victory that assured the company's survival, for its finances were at best tenuous when the decision was taken to risk everything on the race.

Alvis, created by T. G. John, a civil engineer and naval architect, with a clergyman's son, G. P. H. de Freville—joined in 1922 by Capt. G. T. Smith-Clarke, creator of the 12/50—originally made its own drive shafts. It also pioneered planetary valve springs that eliminated surge. It was one of the first English firms to employ 4-wheel brakes, in 1924, the year in which the marque broke 39 class records in one day at Brooklands.

Its front-wheel-drive racing car was brought out in 1925. The engine was essentially a 12/50 reversed in a duralumin frame with a de Dion front axle and beam rear axle, but the front suspension was soon changed to an independent system with unequal-length upper and lower transverse springs on each side. Three years later these cars, independently sprung all round, finished first and second in class at Le Mans. Production of a 6-cylinder car (later to be known as the Silver Eagle) began in 1927. Eight-cylinder f.w.d. cars were produced for factory teams' use only.

Four-cylinder front-wheel-drive two-seater, unlike 8-cylinder f.w.d. car, was available to the public. Examples survive in Britain and U.S.

Speed 20 corners hard in a hill-climb. Alvis was remarkably stable

The most luxurious of Alvis sports cars, the very fast Speed 25

Short-chassis 4·3 litre topped 105 m.p.h. in standard form with this Vanden Plas tourer body

Perhaps the best-known Alvis, the Speed 20, was produced in 1932 with a 6-cylinder, overhead-valve 2·5-litre engine and three carburetters. With a sports saloon body it was capable of 90 m.p.h. The next year Alvis led the industry in creating a 4-speed gearbox with synchromesh on all four gears despite the many cries of "Impossible!" Also in 1933 independent front suspension was offered on some models, using a single transverse spring above and wishbone links below.

The Speed 25 appeared in 1937 with its companion, the 4·3-litre, which achieved 105 m.p.h. in a road test by *The Motor*. After the war Alvis produced a sports tourer called the Speed 14, but the firm now confines itself to highly superior family cars that maintain the tradition of first-rank craftsmanship that has always characterized the marque.

TB-14 was Alvis' last sports car, built for a short time after Second World War

ASTON MARTIN

"Excel the best" might almost be said to have been the unspoken credo of Aston Martin, through all its changes of ownership and management, from its foundation in the Edwardian era to the present. The founders, Lionel Martin and Robert Bamford, were determined to beat Ettore Bugatti at his own game; today, under David Brown, Aston Martin has succeeded in conquering Enzo Ferrari.

The first car ran in 1913. It was compounded of a 1908 Isotta-Fraschini chassis and a 4-cylinder side-valve Coventry Simplex engine of 1400 c.c., which propelled it at 70 m.p.h. War in 1914 prevented full production, and after the war Bamford retired and Count Louis Zborowski, a famous amateur racer, recapitalized the company.

While experiments were made in the early 1920s with a twin-overhead-camshaft engine of 65-mm. bore and 112-mm. stroke, which was raced successfully, production was concentrated on a side-valve sports tourer with 70-m.p.h. sustained speed and a remarkable record for freedom from adjustment. In 1927 the firm was taken over by a racing driver, A. C.

The first production prototype, 1921, with Lionel Martin (centre) and H. Kensington Moir (left)

The short-chassis International of 1930s, which won Le Mans Biennial Cup

The record set at the 1935 Le Mans by the Mark II Le Mans stood for 15 years

Bertelli, who designed a new 1·5-litre engine with a single overhead camshaft and, later, dry-sump lubrication: i.e. the oil was carried in a tank separate from the crankcase, which was supplied by one pump and drained by another.

This car became the famous International, sometimes known as the Le Mans model. A compact four-seater, with an aluminium-on-ash body, it had cycle mudguards all round and was one of the prettiest cars of its period. Its looks, coupled with phenomenal road-holding and outstanding steering, helped to establish the sports-car trend. Bertelli not only ran the company, designing bodies as well as mechanical components, but also successfully raced his cars at Le Mans and Ulster. The 1·5-litre speed record of 75·5 m.p.h. set by Aston Martin at Le Mans in 1935 with a Mark II Le Mans stood until 1950. The Ulster model, despite its weight, carried a 100-m.p.h. guarantee.

The 2-litre Ulster (Speed) Model

16

The 2-litre sports drop-head of 1948–9 derived directly from the Spa car. Its 4-cylinder overhead-valve engine developed 90 h.p.

The post-war 2-litre winning at Spa in 1948

The first DB Aston-Martin, a gran turismo whose lines changed very little. It had the 2·6-litre Vantage engine

DB3S coupé winning at Silverstone, 1954

The company was taken over by R. G. Sutherland in 1932; in 1935–6 it brought out a 2-litre engine with a hollow crankshaft, developing over 100 b.h.p. to propel less than 18 cwt. These cars continued to distinguish themselves until the Second World War, which halted work on a prototype model with independent front suspension and the then almost unknown integration of body with tubular frame.

After the war simplicity of maintenance gained emphasis and Aston returned to pushrod valves in a 2-litre four. In 1947 the company passed to David Brown, who had also acquired Lagonda. For two years the only Aston available was a two/four-seater drop-head, one of which won the 24-hour sports-car race at Spa outright in 1948. Two years later the Aston and Lagonda engines were made interchangeable: this was the birth of the 6-cylinder 3-litre series ($82·5 \times 89$ in the current model, Mark III) with 8·2 compression, d.o.h.c. and 140 b.h.p. at 5500 r.p.m. It offers a choice of fixed- or drop-head four-seater coupé on a tubular frame with independent front suspension. It may fairly be said—as the Nürburgring and other races have shown—that no British car can match the Aston for handling at high speed. Regardless of coachwork, it will take the hardest 90-degree corner at otherwise frightening speeds without any "lean". Aston's successes include not only the German course but also four at Le Mans, two in the Mille Miglia and one in the Tourist Trophy, as well as innumerable wins and seconds in less important races on both sides of the Atlantic.

The experience of the racing-bodied 3·9-litre DB3S led to the introduction of disc brakes, when overdrive was also made optional. In 1959 the DB4 was added to the other models—one might almost call it a detuned DB3S with its 263-b.h.p. 3·7-litre (92×92) engine whose cylinder head and crankcase are of aluminium alloy. Disc brakes are standard on all wheels, with servo assistance. Cylinders are wet-lined. Track is 54 in., wheelbase 98 in.; the rear coil springs are mounted behind the axle. Top speed for this 26-cwt. car is around 140 m.p.h.

3-litre DBR1 of 1957 driven by Roy Salvadori. It has been succeeded by 3·9-litre car of very similar appearance that made an excellent record in 1958

1959 DB4 supplements continued DB3 fixed- and drop-heads. This gran turismo car will clock 26 seconds from rest to 100 m.p.h. to rest

AUSTIN
AUSTIN-HEALEY

Solid, workaday vehicle that it has been for so many years, the Austin has nevertheless a sporting background. The Austin 7 first appeared in 1922 as an economy car with an engine derived from a motorcycle, but two years later a pointed-tail sports model was offered. Weighing less than 9 cwt., it was driven at a top speed of 52 m.p.h. by a tiny 4-cylinder engine developing 10 h.p. In 1928 it was offered with a supercharged 747-c.c. engine and in 1930 the Ulster model, blown or unblown, was available. It ran creditably in the Tourist Trophy (whence its name) and, with a close-ratio 3-speed gearbox, could readily exceed 70 m.p.h. By the mid-1930s the Austin Nippy had captured a loyal following.

Austin dropped out of sports-car production then, until in 1952 Donald Healey came around with a proposal to build an economical but high-quality sports car, with one eye on the American market, around available components. He quickly adopted Austin's 2·6-litre (87·3 × 111·1) four and various other components and designed a steel-and-aluminium body of pleasing grace for the era of envelope coachwork. The 3-speed gearbox was retained. Front suspension, of course, was independent. Overhead valves were pushrod-operated.

The 19·6-cwt. Austin-Healey with 7·5:1 compression soon set records, being driven by Healey at 113 m.p.h. in Belgium. The 100-S, a later development 200 pounds lighter, utilized the same engine with 8·3:1 compression, a 4-speed gearbox and disc brakes all round, being good for almost 140 m.p.h. Normally equipped with a full-width racing screen, it required a certain body-making skill to convert quickly to bad-weather road use. In addition, Austin-Healey offered the 100-M with a so-called Le Mans kit consisting of the 4-speed gearbox, 8·1:1 compression, high-lift camshaft and larger carburetters with a special cold-air box. All the Austin-Healeys used two S.U. carburetters and acquitted themselves excellently in New Zealand, California, Sebring, the Mille Miglia and Le Mans.

In 1957 the 100-6 appeared: 102 b.h.p., six 79·4 × 89 cylinders, 8·25 compression. A modification to 117 b.h.p. at 4750 r.p.m. was soon added: it consisted of a 6-port cylinder head and special pistons for the 2·6-litre engine. The first cars offered two auxiliary seats of debatable comfort and practicality in a forlorn attempt to revive the true four-seater sports car of the vintage and post-vintage era; but these were later made optional with pleasing effects on body appearance and a slight gain in the very poor luggage accommodation. The 100-6 continued the optional overdrive on the two top gears. A detachable hard top was made available; when it was fitted with the sliding-panel sidescreens that became standard with the 100-6 the car could run in gran turismo races with fixed-head sports cars, and gave a very good account of itself. Top speed with the so-called Le Mans cylinder head and pistons is in the 120s.

In mid-1958 a totally new Austin-Healey appeared: the Sprite. Evidently designed to reach that part of the market that was being shut out by rising costs, the Sprite is a sports car stripped to essentials yet lacking nothing in performance. Powered by a 948-c.c. four (62·9 × 76) with 8·3 compression and pushrod o.h.v., it produces 45 b.h.p. at 5500 r.p.m. to propel its 12½ cwt. at 80 m.p.h. Its rack-and-pinion steering is 2¼ turns lock to lock and handling is markedly superior to that of the bigger Austin-Healeys. The engine is a modification of the standard Austin unit: Austin, like the various Nuffield marques, having been gathered into the embrace of the giant British Motor Corporation.

Courtesy of Austin Motor Car Co. Ltd.]

The 100-h.p. 1908 racing car that ran in the French G.P. and at Brooklands

Courtesy of the Vintage Car Store]

Supercharged Austin Ulster won the Brooklands 500-mile race in 1929 and later exceeded 100 m.p.h. on that track

The unblown Nippy of the 1930s developed from the Ulster. Side-valve 747-c.c. engine promised 75 m.p.h.

Four-cylinder Austin-Healey. Its high-speed sister, the 100-S, had a lower, unframed windscreen and a large quick-filler petrol-tank cap

Austin-Healey 100-6 in gran turismo trim with removable hard top. A similar car set a record of 10,000 miles in four days at 97·13 m.p.h. at Montlhéry

Austin-Healey Sprite. Top stows under rear deck with spare tyre, tools and luggage, accessible only from inside car. Headlight treatment (a money-saver) recalls TR-2

BERKELEY

Introduced in 1957, the Berkeley is the smallest sports car currently marketed. Front-wheel drive and all-round independent suspension are up to the minute; the use of a Dynastart (combination generator and starter) recalls Edwardian and Vintage cars. The 328-c.c. 2-cylinder engine was offered with a 3-speed motor-cycle-type transmission, the 3-cylinder 492-c.c. model with a 4-speed gearbox. Both are air-cooled two-stroke Excelsior power units developing respectively 18 b.h.p. at 5000 r.p.m. and 30 b.h.p. at 5500 r.p.m. For 1959 the 4-speed gearbox was made standard for both models. The ratios are 15·21, 9·18, 6·35 and 4·64.

Originally offered in both roadster and fixed-head coupé form, the Berkeley, like the Corvette, has a glass fibre body, into which the headlights are faired. The smaller car weighs 6 cwt., the larger one slightly more. They are built by Berkeley Cars Ltd., a leading trailer caravan maker, and evolved from the combined planning of Charles Panter, Berkeley's director, and Laurie Bond, originator of the three-wheeled Bond Minicar.

Only opening bonnet shows which model a Berkeley is

Twin-coil ignition and the absence of valves are noteworthy, the cylinders being fed on the two-stroke system. Braking is excellent and the steering is unusually quick: $2\frac{1}{4}$ turns lock to lock. Top speed was not much above 60 m.p.h. The Berkeley has won many awards in competitions in Britain and the U.S. For 1960 it is offered with a 2-cylinder, 692-c.c. engine.

The 3-litre touring Bentley that finished second in the 1922 Isle of Man T.T.

The 1924 Le Mans car, the first with 4-wheel brakes

The 3-litre Red Label Speed Bentley developed 88 b.h.p. at 3500 r.p.m.

BENTLEY

Ettore Bugatti once called the Bentley "the fastest truck in the world", but it has always been a great deal nobler than that would imply. From the first 3-litre to the 8-litre, and even into the Rolls-Bentley period, Bentleys have justly been ranked among the world's premier sports cars.

Of the 3061 cars built under W. O. Bentley, the 3-litres made from 1922 through 1929 accounted for 1639. The first car was built in 1919, the last in 1931; more than 1000 are still in regular use throughout the world, and many of them are still adding to the incredibly long record of Bentley wins. Now, of course, they race chiefly against their contemporaries in vintage events.

No. 1 Bentley was ready for test in 1919: a 4-cylinder engine with dual ignition, overhead camshaft and a main bearing between each pair of crank throws. For three years the prototype was subjected to the most critical testing before the first cars appeared for sale in 1922, on a short wheelbase of $117\frac{1}{2}$ in., the 130-in. chassis resulting from a demand for more general-purpose construction. In that same year a Bentley ran at Indianapolis, in the Isle of Man Tourist Trophy and at Brooklands, and the marque's glorious career of record-setting began with 87·42 m.p.h. for 12 hours in the then Class D.

In 1923 Bentleys inaugurated their association with Le Mans, finishing fourth. These early Bentleys had 2-wheel brakes; it was in 1924 that all-round braking was fitted, and Bentley, for which the best was barely good enough, was already experimenting with hydraulics. The Speed, or Red Label, car, which had been sired by the T.T. car, introduced dual carburation, and this year Bentley scored the first of its five wins at Le Mans. In the same year the marque took the 1000-mile record at 97·4 m.p.h. and the 24-hour record at 95·03.

Bentley's legend at Le Mans was established in 1927, when the entire Bentley team of three cars hurtled into a frightful multiple crash. Dr. Benjafield's Old No. 7 of 1926, which had also crashed in the last hour of the race that year, was seemingly twisted out of all roadability in 1927—wings and lights shattered, brakes and steering distorted and the heavy chassis itself wracked out of shape—but S. C. H. Davis and Benjafield held her on the road somehow for the next 20 hours and won the race outright at an average speed of 61·36 m.p.h.

In 1927 the famous $4\frac{1}{2}$-litre appeared; one of these was knocked out at Le Mans in the White House crash after setting a lap record of 73·4 m.p.h. At the same time, the $6\frac{1}{2}$-litre car was in full production. Meanwhile a good deal of carefully planned experimentation had evolved a succession of gearboxes from the close-ratio A type used on the first 3-litres through wider ratios and back to the close spacing of the A gearbox. These were crash boxes, of course, but were notable for retaining their silence for long periods even in competition.

[Courtesy of W. A. Hawkins]

**The first Vanden Plas sports tourer on a 4½-litre chassis.
Maximum speed was 92 m.p.h.**

Le Mans was a Bentley triumph again in 1928—the victor was the 4½-litre car that had been knocked out of the 1927 race, and it gave Woolf Barnato the first of his succession of triumphs in this race. Virtually the same models appeared there again in 1929, backed up by the new Speed Six, which, again driven by Barnato, this time with Tim Birkin, led the team home to capture the first four places—an accomplishment that Britain did not equal until Jaguar's 1956 sweep. Fifty of the 4½-litre cars were produced with Amherst-Villiers Roots-type superchargers, hung between the dumb-irons and driven by the crankshaft at engine speed. A few others were specially supercharged for racing by Barnato and, after Rolls-Royce absorbed the company in 1931, six unblown 4½-litre cars were built.

The 6½-litre car was intended as a more dignified Bentley, but its dignity in no way impaired or was impaired by its sporting potential. In 1930, once more driven by Barnato, it took first over-all at Le Mans and a sister Speed Six took second. These cars retained the 100×140 bore and stroke of the 4½-litre, adding two cylinders to the block and retaining dual valves, all 24 being driven by a single overhead camshaft that ran on a coupling rod from the crankshaft. The system incorporated compensation for expansion and contraction. Another interesting feature of the 6½-litre was the dynamo, which was driven from the crankshaft at one-half engine speed at first, as on the 3-litre, but later sixes were modified to take engine-speed dynamos powered from the front of the crankshaft. Mechanical brakes were retained on the sixes, but from their introduction in 1926 they were fitted with servo assistance as standard.

The competition record of this dignified automobile is still the envy of dozens of other marques: two Le Mans victories, each of which added the unusual achievement of taking the Rudge Cup as well; the Six-Hour Race at Brooklands, second place in the Irish Grand Prix, a Double-Twelve win at Brooklands, and, almost 20 years later, a continuing string of victories in vintage events. Some of these winners today are the identical cars that ran at Le Mans so long before the 1939 war.

It was in the last year of W. O. Bentley's régime, when world-wide depression had virtually eliminated the never-great market for cars of such quality, that the gigantic 8-litre appeared. It was never raced privately or as a works entry. The biggest Bentley carried on the camshaft gear of the Speed Six and the stroke was unchanged, but bore was raised to 110 mm. and either 5:1 or 5·5:1 compression ratio was offered, giving 200 and 225 b.h.p. respectively. One of these cars, owned by Forrest Lycett, broke the British record for a standing-start mile in 1939 by turning in a time of 92·9 m.p.h., after which the owner, a former president of the Vintage Sports-Car Club, continued in it to his office to start the morning's work.

[Courtesy of the Bentley Drivers' Club]

**Woolf Barnato at the wheel of the Speed Six, victor at
Le Mans, 1929 and 1930**

The long-chassis blown 4½-litre at Brooklands. Supercharger lies between dumb-irons

One of the few 8-litres

The 4¼-litre Bentley at Prescott; appearance was almost identical to the 3½-litre

Just 100 of the 8-litres were produced. In a desperate effort to compete with the small Rolls, Bentley offered a 4-litre car on the 8-litre chassis, the engine reverting to the conventional two valves per cylinder and—designed by Harry Ricardo—introduced pushrods for the first time in the marque's history. Performance was vile, according to W. O. himself, despite unquestionable longevity, and no one bought the cars. The repeated transfusions that Barnato had given the company in past years had come to an end. A receiver was appointed and the company's assets were offered for sale. Just when a deal seemed certain with D. Napier & Sons, a solution that appealed to W. O. not only because he would be retained as chief designer but also because he had always held Napier cars and aeroplane engines in the highest regard, an unidentifiable syndicate upset the bidding and only through a chance remark overheard by Mrs. Bentley at a cocktail party did W. O. learn that Rolls-Royce had bought him out.

Rolls, of course, faced the same depression problems that had beset W. O., but R.-R.'s resources were considerably greater. The new owners increased their famous 20/25-h.p. engine to 25/30 and dropped it in the chassis of a proposed 2¾-litre Rolls that had never got past the prototype stage. This became the 3½-litre Bentley of the 1930s, a lovely car to look at, a pleasant car to drive and a post-vintage thoroughbred that is still occasionally used in V.S.C.C. and similar competition. But many buyers loaded it with unsuitably heavy coachwork and the engine had to be enlarged to 4¼ litres to approximate, with the bodies then in demand, the performance of the 3½-litre. Nonetheless it did not disgrace its ancestry in the Irish Tourist Trophy races.

The 4¼-litre Bentley went out of production with the Second World War. The present Bentley, a luxury car of eminently respectable performance, is in all specifications identical with the current Rolls-Royce, the only difference being in the shape of the radiator shell.

The Bristol 450 finished first, second and third in their class at Le Mans in 1954 and appeared in limited production. Note wing fillers for petrol and oil

The Type 402, using cross-pushrod engine developed from BMW, coupled front treatment of 400 and 401 with more graceful, lower-drag coachwork

The 405 was a true sports saloon, enlarged from the 404 coupé. Left front wing opens to give access to the spare wheel; right holds the battery

The 2-door 406 is roomiest of Bristol's gran turismo cars. Dunlop servo-assisted disc brakes are fitted on all wheels and the engine is 2·2 litres

BRISTOL
ARNOLT-BRISTOL

A relatively new name in the motor industry, the Bristol first came on the market in 1946–7 when the Bristol Aeroplane Co. decided to produce high-performance cars of superior quality on Continental basic principles: domed combustion chambers, overhead valves and other advances that were at that time relatively infrequent in British manufacture. The primary model was the pre-war BMW type 328.

The first Bristol, called the 400, set a reputation for top performance coupled with fuel economy that has persisted. The 400, however, suffered from too much body weight and too little room at the rear, but both these faults were corrected in the 401, which was designed by Italian coachmakers. Simultaneously with the production of sports cars, Bristol entered the Formula 2 field, supplying engines of 140 b.h.p. for many of Britain's best racing cars, such as the Lister-Bristol and the Cooper-Bristol. By the time the 404 Bristol was ready, the company was offering a choice of engines of 105 or 125 b.h.p. Through the 405, a choice of bodies was also offered: a four-seater saloon or a four-seater drop-head, both of which have been found suitable for gran turismo competition.

Bristol bodies use varied materials according to needs: steel for high stress, wood for lighter framing and aluminium alloy for panels. The combination assures a good power-to-weight ratio. Rack-and-pinion steering, anti-slip clutch, Alfin brake drums (until the 406 introduced disc brakes all round), torsion-bar rear suspension and telescopic shock absorbers front and rear are characteristic of this car. The engines carry three Solex down-draught

The Arnolt-Bristol roadster ready to race. These cars finished first, second and fourth in their class at Sebring

The Arnolt-Bristol coupé

carburetters, and manual ignition control is available in addition to the conventional automatic. A rather high kerb weight of 26·9 cwt. is competently handled by the lively engine.

This 2-litre power plant has also been employed in A.C. and Frazer-Nash sports cars. In addition, Bristol, in co-operation with S. H. Arnolt of Warsaw, Indiana, and Chicago, has developed a special export car in the 2-litre class, the Arnolt-Bristol. First offered in 1954, the Arnolt-Bristol was shown in a stark competition model, open, and a more touring roadster and coupé. All three bodies are designed by Bertone of Italy.

Virtually all the mechanical characteristics of the Bristol are retained, but the weight is cut to 17·9 cwt. The rack-and-pinion steering gives three turns, lock to lock. Headlamps are sunk close together, flanking the long, narrow grille, behind which the 1971-c.c. Bristol engine, raised to 9:1 compression from the standard 8·5:1, develops 130 b.h.p. at 5000 r.p.m. Overhead valves, pushrod-operated, are inclined at 80 degrees, and the crankcase carries a special cooling scoop. A close-ratio 4-speed synchromesh gearbox drives a 3·9 rear axle.

CROSSLEY

When Crossley Motors Ltd. was formed in 1904 to produce 20- and 40-h.p. cars, it was in many respects 20 to 30 years ahead of its industry. Pump cooling was standard on its engines, which used extra-light pistons and high-tensile steel connecting rods; carburetters were fully automatic and brake shoes expanded within the drums. The engines were cast in blocks of two cylinders each and final drive was by chain. In 1907 Charles Jarrott had broken the London–Monte Carlo record with the Crossley produced by the parent company, the Crossley Oil Engine Works.

Crossleys ran in the Tourist Trophy as early as 1905, but never successfully. After 1910, the 20- and 40-h.p. cars gave way to 12- and 15-h.p. models and

the latter, in "Shelsley Model" form, was distinctly sporting. During the First World War the 4½-litre Crossley 25/30 was extensively used by the British Army and so impressed a visiting Russian military

The bull-nosed Shelsley Model Crossley in a competition before the First World War

The 20/70 was identical in appearance to this Model 2 except for knock-off Rudge wheels

24

mission that its members arranged to build the cars at home.

The 2·6-litre side-valve engines and solid chassis demonstrated their reliability in repeated competition successes.

After the war, Crossley built both small utility vehicles and the distinctly sporting 20/70. This decidedly long-stoke engine (90 × 150 mm.) with side valves delivered 75 b.h.p. from its four litres. Unlike the earlier cars, it had a 4-speed gearbox with fairly close ratios and a 3·3 top gear which provided 75 m.p.h. So high was the firm's reputation for quality that Ettore Bugatti licensed Crossley to build his cars in England. But the only Bugatti influence that infiltrated Crossley cars was the clean detail, the fine workmanship and the square gearbox.

In 1926 the 20/70 was discontinued and the company reluctantly began to build the 6-cylinder cars for which demand was growing. The 3-litre 20·9, while not designed as a sports car, is used as one still, particularly in the Antipodes. It had aluminium crankcase and oil pan, unit construction of engine and gearbox and a 1:1 top-gear ratio—so close were the ratios that bottom was 3·53:1! Heavy at low speeds, the steering lightened quickly with acceleration, and lock to lock was only one and a half turns. Four-wheel brakes were employed to stop the

Courtesy of W. B. Easterbrook-Smith]

The 2-litre Silver Crossley

26¾ cwt. of 3·2-litre car: bore and stroke had been reduced to 75 × 120 mm.

The last sporting Crossley—though by no means the last Crossley link with motor sport—was the 1930–1 Silver Crossley, powered by the virile 15·7, a 2-litre 6-cylinder engine still devoted to the long stroke (65 × 100). By the time of the Second World War the company had abandoned all car production and was manufacturing only commercial vehicles. In the mid-1930s, however, its 2-litre engine was enthusiastically adopted by Lagonda.

DELLOW

A pioneer in post-war British automobile manufacture, Dellow produced its first car in 1947, employing rigid tubular chassis construction and coil springs, built around the 1172-c.c. British Ford 4-cylinder engine and axle. The whole is enclosed in bodies built up from tubes of welded steel that, welded to the frame, form a very strong integral structure. Panelling is of aluminium, and over-all weight is about 11½ cwt. in the Mark II. The basic Ford engine was offered with alternative compression ratios of 6·16 and 7 and corresponding b.h.p. of

31 and 36. These cars are especially favoured for trials, a largely British form of competition entailing much cross-country running through fields, roadless hills and other rough terrain.

The Mark V Dellow, which appeared in 1957, offered only the 7:1 Ford engine in a total weight of about 9¾ cwt. The body, like that of the Mark II, is little more than the essentials. Rather more comfort and less harsh lines characterize the current Mark VI, which also offers only the 7:1 engine with choice of single or dual S.U. carburation. The 3-speed gearbox is very widely spaced—top, 4·429; bottom, 16·23. Full weather equipment is standard and fair luggage space is provided.

The business-like Mark II

[*Photograph by Michael P. Clapham*

The current Mark VI is only 7 in. longer than the 6 ft. 11 in. wheelbase of the Mark II and weighs about 11½ cwt.

Courtesy of Dellow Engineering Co. Ltd.]

DORETTI

One of the most promising of British medium-sized sports cars had a production life of only two years because of the high cost of manufacture. The Swallow Doretti was based on Triumph (TR-2) mechanical components, which were identical with those in the TR-2. But, in contrast to the conventional chassis and body construction of the latter, the Doretti utilized a tubular chassis to which fabricated body sections were welded. Independent coil-spring front suspension with telescopic shock absorbers and semi-elliptic rear suspension with piston-type dampers, as on the Triumph, were employed. Body finish was of very high standard, necessitating a much higher price than that commanded by the TR. The Doretti was in production from 1954 to 1956 but had no chance to earn the kind of competition reputation that still sells sports cars as it did in the 1920s.

ELVA

For some years specializing in single-purpose competition cars, the Elva Engineering Co. Ltd. made its first try at dual-purpose machines in 1958 with its new Elva Courier, derived in great part from its racing machines.

Utilizing the standard MG-A engine and gearbox, the Courier mounts them in a light large-tube frame suspended on double wishbones and coil springs at the front; at the rear, coil springs link the frame to a one-piece rigid axle. Coachwork is of glass fibre, on which paint is sprayed after moulding to obtain a first-class finish. The Courier is virtually the only sports car in current production still using a V-shaped windscreen (of laminated glass) and this is attributed primarily to supply problems in obtaining the high type of curved one-piece screen that Frank Nichols, the designer, demands. The Courier appeared late in 1958.

Photograph by E. C. Barker]

The Triumph-based Doretti developed 90 h.p. from its 2-litre engine. It weighed 19¼ cwt. fully laden

FAIRTHORPE

Even smaller than the Berkeley, the first Fairthorpe coupé entered the market after the war with a 1-cylinder engine of 248 c.c. Known as the Atom Mark I, this plastic-bodied, rear-engined coupé held three adults. Headed by Air Vice-Marshal D. C. Bennett, Fairthorpe Ltd. soon offered the Atomota, a 2-cylinder coupé of 646 c.c., weighing 8¾ cwt. against the 8 cwt. of the Mark I, and moving the engine to the front of the car.

Far more sporting, the Electron and the Electron Minor have run creditably in club competitions on both sides of the ocean. The Electron Minor anticipated the Austin-Healey Sprite with a Standard 4-cylinder engine of 948 c.c., in which overhead valves and an 8·25 : 1 compression ratio produce 38 b.h.p. at 5000 r.p.m. to propel 8 cwt. of car. Like the Atomota, the Minor has a widely spaced 4-speed gearbox. It is good for 75 m.p.h. at peak r.p.m.

The Electron is the biggest Fairthorpe, with a dry weight of 10¼ cwt. and a 1098-c.c. Coventry-Climax engine of four cylinders, overhead camshaft and 9·8 : 1 compression. Developing 84 b.h.p. at 6900 r.p.m., it has a top speed in three figures and a much more closely spaced gearbox than the Minor. All the Fairthorpes have all-round independent suspension by wishbones and coil springs. Only the Electron has 15-in. wheels; the other models use 13-in.

Racing derivation shows in Courier lines

[*Photograph by Lewis M. Schulz*]

Sliding windows help keep the Atomota's weight low

Courtesy of Fairthorpe Ltd.]

The Electron Minor

The Electron, Fairthorpe's biggest and fastest car

FRAZER NASH

In every country and every period in which motor sport has thrived, certain marques have inspired cults. In almost every case, the members of such a cult not only ignore the existence of all other marques but even form sub-cults that bar all but one or another model of the major cult's marque. An outstanding example is the Frazer Nash. One of the marque's sub-cults recognizes only the chain-driven models.

The direct ancestor of the Frazer Nash was the G.N., a 2-cylinder car that excelled in trials and hill-climbs and on road and track. In 1922 Capt. Archie Frazer-Nash parted with H. R. Godfrey, his partner in the G.N., and built the first Frazer Nash, marketed as a Frazer Nash G.N. The first Frazer Nash *pur sang* appeared in 1924 with a 4-cylinder overhead-valve engine in a frame derived from that of the G.N. but better adapted to high speeds. It had, of course, chain drive to a rigid rear axle, and no differential, which contributed substantially to the marque's cornering reputation. The transmission had three speeds, which, because of the chain drive, were easily varied to suit differing driving conditions. Two-wheel brakes were standard on the first cars but a year later 4-wheel braking was adopted. With the quarter-elliptic springing of that time, front-wheel braking torque often tended to fold front axles under cars, but Frazer Nash eliminated this by considerably stiffening the already Spartan front springs.

Initially the engine for the Frazer Nash was the French Ruby. In 1925, however, the famous Anzani side-valve 1496-c.c. unit was made normal equipment, tuned to deliver 40 b.h.p. at 3600 r.p.m., quite enough to propel the 13½-cwt. car at 70 m.p.h. The Anzani's outstanding characteristic was no mechanical innovation but a combination of lightness with durability and the ability to retain high tune for long periods. Four-speed transmissions were soon adopted, but the chain drive persisted through the 1930s, by which time it had become unique.

The pushrod overhead-valve 4ED Meadows engine supplanted the Anzani in 1929. Both had the same cubic capacity but the Meadows developed 50 b.h.p., making the Frazer-Nash Boulogne one of the fastest cars of the 1930s. A quirk in the gearing gave the car a faster lap time at Brooklands in third gear than in top, though in either gear it lapped at 80-plus. The road-racing Frazer-Nash Shelsley, built in limited numbers, used the single overhead camshaft Gough engine of four 69 × 100 cylinders; designed for use with a blower, it was believed safe up to 6000 r.p.m. and offered 70 b.h.p. The Shelsley car had a tubular front axle and cantilever front springs; 105 m.p.h. was guaranteed and in 1937 one of these cars set the Shelsley Walsh hill-climb record. This model was also the basis for a single-seater "Mountain Record" car that topped 120 m.p.h.

Another popular engine with Frazer-Nash owners was the Blackburne, a 6-cylinder available in either 1496 or 1667 c.c. These had double overhead camshafts, one being driven by a roller chain and in turn driving the other through helical gears. The valves were set at 90 degrees into hemispherical combustion chambers; two carburetters were standard and three were sometimes used. The cars by now weighed about a ton but were still good for 90 m.p.h. Very few were built with a twin-camshaft R1 Anzani 1½-litre engine developing 70 b.h.p.

The hyphen entered the name on the transfer of the company to two brothers, H. J. and W. H. Aldington, in 1928. Under their auspices the marque continued the successes begun with its founder, distinguishing itself in the Tourist Trophy—one of the most popular models was the T.T. Replica— at Brooklands and in hill-climbs. In 1933, while continuing the chain-driven cars, the Aldingtons bought the British rights to the German B.M.W.

The Anzani-engined Boulogne Frazer-Nash at Silver-stone. Outside exhaust was standard through 1939. Dead accurate steering with one turn, lock to lock

Capt. Frazer-Nash in the 1928 Super Sports

The T.T. Replica with 1½-litre Meadows engine

The 1934–5 Colmore with d.o.h.c. 6-cylinder Blackburne engine—the archetype of the unfortunately defunct family sports car

The Frazer-Nash-B.M.W. 328, almost indistinguishable from its German counterpart

The Le Mans Replica Mark II

and were to offer, in late 1934, Frazer-Nash-B.M.W.s, first with the German Type 55 engine and then with the famous Type 328. This model of the Frazer-Nash-B.M.W. was the first sports car to cover 100 miles in an hour. But the Aldingtons, while filling special orders for the old chain-gang cars right up to the outbreak of the Second World War, were more interested in current design. It is worth noting, at this point, some of the successes of the chain-gang car, the sight of whose outboard exhaust system, hand brake, gear lever and ignition control is rich with motoring history.

In 1925 Frazer Nash won the Boulogne Grand Prix des Voitures Légères and twice broke the lap record. In 1926 the marque scored 300 first-class awards. In 1927 and 1928 it set new records at Shelsley Walsh. In the next few years Frazer-Nash took more gold medals at British courses; in 1932 it took two Glacier Cups in the Alpine Trial; in 1933, four entered the Junior Car Club race at Brooklands and four finished in the first four places. It becomes almost monotonous to chronicle the un-broken succession of victories throughout the life of the pre-war Frazer-Nash. It is not unremarkable to record that in 1936 the full touring model, the Colmore, was timed from zero to 50 m.p.h. in 10·6 seconds and to 60 m.p.h. in 14 seconds!

When the Second World War ended, the Aldington brothers, still doing business under the name of A.F.N. Ltd., formed a connection with Bristol to produce the Frazer-Nash-Bristol, which was based on the pre-war B.M.W. design. Adopting torsion-bar suspension at the rear, transverse leaf in front and rack-and-pinion steering, and adapting the post-war Bristol engine in various tune from 95 to 150 b.h.p., Frazer-Nash produced each car by hand, often substituting de Dion-tube rears on order and maintaining the flexibility of the chain-gang era by

Photograph by Michael P. Clapham]
Roadster of the 1950s

Photograph by Michael P. Clapham]
The latest Le Mans coupé

offering a wide choice of gear and axle ratios. The first post-war cars were offered for sale in 1948 as the High Speed Model and the Fast Tourer; a slightly modified High Speed, a private entry, finished third at Le Mans in 1949 and was the basis for the sub-sequent Le Mans Replica cars.

In 1951 Frazer-Nash performed a feat never before accomplished by a British car: outright victory in the brutal Sicilian Targa Florio. Two years later A.F.N. ran a coupé at Le Mans, averaging 95 m.p.h. for the 24 hours but finishing thirteenth. Some experiments had meanwhile been made with the 2·6 Austin engine, but the attachment to B.M.W. triumphed and Frazer-Nash has now committed itself to the rigid tubular frame of B.M.W., with full independent suspension, de Dion tube and the Bavarians' V-8 engine in both its 2·4- and its 2·6-litre forms. Both a fixed-head coupé and an open two-seater are available, but externally neither of these envelope bodies offers the slightest visual hint of its illustrious ancestry.

[Photograph by Temple Press Ltd.; courtesy of H. R. Godfrey]

H. R. Godfrey in a 1920 hill-climb aboard the 1914 Vitesse model, belt-driven, which made fastest time of the day. G.N. radiators are dummies

G.N.

As high an authority as John Bolster contends that the G.N. is one of the two outstanding cars of the vintage years (the other being the 30/98 Vauxhall). As Cecil Clutton pointed out ten years ago, some of the G.N.s were still competing successfully 40 years after the firm was founded; at the half-century mark they are still in action. Experts call it the finest of the cycle-cars.

H. R. Godfrey and A. G. Frazer-Nash first met in 1905 as engineering students and served their apprenticeships together. Right from the beginning they talked of producing an automobile, but in those days the market was limited to the very rich. On the other hand, the motor-cycle was available to a much wider market; but it was considered extremely perilous. The solution devised by Godfrey and Frazer-Nash was to unite the prince and the pauper.

As early as 1906 they were building experimental models, using twin-cylinder air-cooled motor-cycle engines with the belt drive then popular. In 1910 they went at it seriously with the idea of possibly selling a few vehicles, but a report on their activities in a cycling magazine brought a relative stampede of buyers. With two lathes, a drilling machine, hand tools and £50, they were in business. Insistence on a one-third deposit with every order made it possible to

[Courtesy of H. R. Godfrey]

Capt. Frazer-Nash at the wheel of a 1921 car, stripped for racing, that won its class in the first Brooklands 200-mile race

Courtesy of H. R. Godfrey]

Godfrey still considers the 1919–21 car the peak of G.N. accomplishment. Separate chains were employed for each gear

purchase materials. A year later, a satisfied customer persuaded the partners to let him invest £1000 in their enterprise.

The motor-cycle engines of those days were designed for one-gear, clutchless operation and could not idle. G.N. therefore designed its own engine: a 90-degree twin with a big flywheel and automatic inlet valves. On its first test it proved itself the solution, but inlet pushrods were added because they were demanded. Chains were adopted for primary drive, but the rear belts, being trouble-free, were retained. Top speed was 45 m.p.h.

This was the birth of one of the most famous of cycle-cars. Competition events were multiplying and a maximum engine size of 1100 c.c. was established. G.N. enlarged to meet the standard, added more fins to the cylinders and mounted the engine across the frame with the exhaust side forward for better cooling. The transfer of the clutch—the single-plate mechanism that remained standard on both G.N. and Frazer Nash—to the flywheel made it possible to fit either 3- or 4-speed gearboxes and top speed was raised to 55 m.p.h., still employing V-belts for final drive. The First World War, of course, interrupted production, but not experiment; by the time of the Armistice, G.N. was ready to produce its first chain-driven car. (Three years later G.N. was making special modifications for disabled drivers: 25 years ahead of Detroit.)

Acceptance was immediate; in France, Salmson clamoured to build the car under licence, which was granted. Competition successes piled up, especially in 1921, when G.N. scored 112 firsts in speed trials, 11 fastest times and 28 gold medals in reliability trials. No other vehicle could touch its fuel economy, which in one test reached 94 miles per gallon. Both Godfrey and Frazer-Nash were their own chief competition drivers. The partners separated in 1922 and, though the company continued for some years thereafter, its cars were of the family type rather than the Légère and Vitesse that crowned the final year of the partnership.

Throughout production the G.N. had a one-bearing crankshaft and overhead inlet valves. The wooden chassis of the first models gave way to channel-section pressed steel, but no differential was ever employed. The heaviest sports G.N. ever built weighed less than 9 cwt. and was quite capable of 60 m.p.h. In full racing trim 74·41 m.p.h. has been clocked. The earliest models were steered by wires wound around the steering post—"cable and bobbin"—but this gave way to a bevel gear.

[Photograph by Michael P. Clapham

On the H.E., as on many other two/three-seater vintage sports cars, the rear seat was protected only by a tonneau cover when the hood was erected

Courtesy of R. Radford]

The last 14/40 H.E., built in 1927. Detachable brass valve caps in cylinder head were standard

H.E.

Like many other marques, the H.E. was a First World War baby. The Herbert Engineering Co. Ltd. had a fine reputation for accuracy in its sub-contracting for the British aircraft industry and turned to car production when peace came.

Proclaiming its avoidance of "objectionable" racing traits, the first H.E., announced in 1919, had side valves, overhead worm final drive and three-quarter elliptic rear springs. Basically, until the depression killed it, the marque did not change, despite the addition of front-wheel brakes and some variations in wheelbase and swept volume.

The first sports model, prototype of the 14/40 offered to the public, broke class records at Brooklands in 1921 at 87·63 m.p.h. Weighing about a ton, the 4-cylinder 75 × 120 (2120-c.c.) engine developed 40 b.h.p. when compression was raised to 5:1. A multiple-disc clutch carried power to the rather widely spaced 4-speed gearbox.

The 4-wheel brakes were added in 1925, with an

adjustment accessible from inside the car that enabled the driver not only to take up on all brakes but to alter as he chose the ratio of deceleration as between front and rear wheels. A 75-m.p.h. speed was guaranteed by the works.

Meanwhile, a 2000-c.c. model had been introduced by dint of reducing the bore to 72·5 mm. This was known as the 13/40; there was a 13/45 with an aluminium cylinder head. In 1927 the 14/40, having become a 14/60, was dropped. As was common at the time, there was no water-pump, heat being relied on to cause the water to expand and pass through the radiator and jackets; but, unlike many contemporary sports cars, the H.E. did have a fan. Early models had magnetos; some later ones had dual coil ignition. Pump and splash engine lubrication was the general rule. The most popular H.E. wheelbase was 9 ft. 9 in., representing the contemporary average in sporting and semi-sporting cars.

In 1929 H.E. produced a 6-cylinder car known as the 16/60-h.p. The wheelbase was cut by 3 in., bore and stroke were reduced to 65 × 115 and gear ratios were brought slightly closer. The crash box was retained. Like its 4-cylinder predecessor, the 16/60 was widely acclaimed for its excellent road-holding under all conditions; long, flat semi-elliptics made for a rather harsh ride at low speeds but softened greatly as acceleration mounted. Two important changes in the 16/60 were a single-plate clutch and the option of a Cozette supercharger. The sports coupé had a fabric Weymann body, but, although it did appear at Brooklands, there is little other record of any sporting participation by either the coupé or the tourer, though both were apparently planned for such activity if one may judge by the 6:1 compression and the fitting of quarter-elliptic springs all round with radius arms for both axles, as well as servo-assisted braking.

[Courtesy of the Donald Healey Motor Co. Ltd.

The 1948 Mille Miglia cars

HEALEY
NASH-HEALEY

Long before he produced a car under his own name, Donald Healey had been a leading creator of sports cars. Immediately after the war he teamed with A. C. Sampietro, who had long been associated with Thomson & Taylor, a firm specializing in high-performance cars and particularly Alfa Romeos, to design the Healey, which appeared in 1946 using a 2·5-litre 4-cylinder Riley engine measuring 81 × 120. This engine dated back to 1938; Healey doubled the single carburation and modified the manifolding to produce 100 b.h.p. at 4500 r.p.m. The engine was built in a unit with the clutch and a close-ratio gearbox.

Using the classic box-section frame with independent front suspension, the car weighed just over a ton and, at over 100 m.p.h., was for a brief time the fastest closed car on sale. A roadster and a gran turismo coupé were entered in the 1948 Mille Miglia, in which Healey himself drove the open car, finishing ninth over-all. The coupé finished first in the touring class. In 1949 Healeys took first and fourth in the touring class.

In 1949 Healey introduced the Silverstone, which weighed 200 lb. less than the Mille Miglia cars and, using the same engine, was about as fast. Placed first and second in class and third over-all at Sebring, and finishing first and second in its class in the Alpine Rally, it carried on the record established by its predecessor, which had also achieved class wins in the

32

[Copyright by J. E. Reynolds; courtesy of Motor Sport

The Healey Silverstone at Rest-and-be-Thankful. Head-lamps are set inside the radiator grille

Photograph by Richard A. Manley]

Nash-Healey coupé

1947 and 1948 Alpine Rallies and first in the un-limited touring class in the 1948 Targa Florio. Unlike the Mille Miglia roadster, which had a fairly respect-able rear seat, the Silverstone was a strict two-seater. The V-windscreen of the Mille Miglia car had given way to a flat one-piece screen that could be wound down out of sight into the scuttle. Headlights were mounted close together inside the grille.

Two new cars were introduced by Healey in 1951. The first, built almost wholly with an eye to dollar sales, was the Nash-Healey, powered by the American Nash Ambassador overhead-valve 6-cylinder engine of 3847 c.c. with 8:1 compression and seven main bearings. Double S.U. carburetters were fitted, but Nash's 3-speed gearbox with automatic overdrive was retained. The car had servo-assisted hydraulic brakes and weighed 21·4 cwt., for which the engine developed 125 b.h.p. Bodies, designed by Farina in Italy and built in England, were of two kinds: roadster and coupé. The chassis was slightly modified from the Silverstone's and the engine was later increased to 4·1 litres and 140 b.h.p. in racing tune. In 1952 the Nash-Healey took third place over-all at Le Mans, the automatic overdrive having been modified for racing to prevent reversion to normal drive when the driver "put his foot in it".

For no discernible reason, however, the Nash-Healey was not a commercial success and production ended fairly soon. Meanwhile Healey had presented still another car, this one a sports drop-head with a slightly modified 3-litre Alvis engine. Almost square at 84 × 90, the 6-cylinder power plant developed 106 b.h.p. at 4200 r.p.m. Healey's own trailing-link suspension with coil springs was used front and rear.

While both these cars were in production, Healey was at work on the development of the Austin-Healey, prototypes of which had run at Le Mans in 1952 with his Nash-Healey. But in the following year motor sport suffered a hard blow when Donald Healey announced his withdrawal from competition because international regulations were fostering the racing of prototypes that would never go into pro-duction. Undoubtedly Healey was thinking back to

Courtesy of the Donald Healey Motor Co. Ltd.]

Donald Healey (left) with George Mason of Nash-Kelvinator Corp. in a Nash-Healey roadster. Alvis-engined drop-head used virtually the same body

the years when only series cars could run at Le Mans and the race was still what it had set out to be: a test of production motor cars.

H. R. G.

The most vital half-century of automobile develop-ment is exactly spanned by the creative career of H. R. Godfrey, who in 1906 began the experiments that resulted in the legendary G.N. After he severed his connection with that marque and engaged in other ventures, he returned in the mid-1930s to the design of sports cars, feeling that at that time the sports car was too often merely a family car with a so-called sports body and a loud exhaust, as well as excessive weight, what he himself called soggy steering, poor roadability and inadequate braking.

With two other veteran competition drivers, E. A. Halford and G. H. Robins, Godfrey opened a work-shop to begin the creation of a contemporary car of full sporting character. The result was a 14¼-cwt. car powered by a 50-b.h.p. 1½-litre engine in a deep-channel frame slung on wide springs for rigidity, a

[*Photograph by The Motor; courtesy of H. R. Godfrey*
Courtesy of H. R. Godfrey]

The classic H.R.G. as produced for 20 years, 1936–56

The fixed-head coupé

low centre of gravity, accurate steering geometry and very low unsprung weight through the use of a tubular front axle and 11-in. brakes of magnesium alloy.

The famous Meadows 4ED engine was adopted, with a thicker crankshaft, and a 4-speed crash gearbox. A beautiful, pure vintage two-seater aluminium body was mounted and from its début in 1936 the H.R.G. exceeded its makers' expectations, with a top speed of 92 m.p.h. and 0–60 acceleration in 13·6 seconds. A smaller engine was also made available— 1100 c.c., 60×95, and 1180 c.c., 63×95—in the same body and chassis as the 1500. By 1939 synchromesh gears were in use. At Le Mans in 1937, H.R.G. was placed thirteenth over-all and was the second British car in its class; the next year it was the first-placed British entry regardless of class. Trophies were won at innumerable British races and hill-climbs. A pretty sliding-roof-and-window two-seater coupé was available, as well as a Bugatti-tailed Le Mans open two-seater.

Just before war began in 1939 a 1½-litre Singer engine, modified by Godfrey to produce 10 additional horsepower, was tested and found equal to and quieter than the Meadows unit. The Singer unit was also available in 1100-c.c. form, but war halted further tests.

In 1946 Lord Selsdon and T. A. S. O. Mathieson, a well-known competition driver, joined the firm and production was resumed with the Singer engines in short-stroke form. But in 1952 work began on a more modern power plant, resulting in the introduction of a d.o.h.c. engine in 1956 consisting of a Singer

Photograph by Michael P. Clapham]

The last H.R.G.

block and a new H.R.G. head. This was mounted in an all-independently suspended tubular frame on wide, thin-leaf transverse springs and equipped with disc-braked magnesium wheels reminiscent of Bugatti's alloy wheels.

The prototype, with double the original horsepower at no increase in weight, gave exceptional performance. But the absorption of Singer by the Rootes Group cut off the supply of engine blocks and other components and the company was not financially equipped for the extensive re-designing and experimentation that would be entailed in putting the new model into production. Lacking the resources of the great combines for both experimentation and distribution, the H.R.G. Engineering Co. Ltd. has had to limit itself to general engineering work.

[Courtesy of Donald Monro

The N.L.C. Invicta of 1929–30. All Invictas enjoyed liberal use of light alloy bearings

[Courtesy of Donald Monro

The 1½-litre Invicta was a consistent concours d'élégance winner

[Courtesy of Donald Monro

The standard 4½-litre low-chassis car. Raymond Mays' lightened model defeated a Tourist Trophy Mercedes-Benz SSKL at Shelsley Walsh

INVICTA

High quality and low production marked the Invicta, a surprising number of which are still used for daily transport and in competitions. The first cars were produced in 1925 and marketed in 1926 by the Invicta Car Co. Powered by a 2½-litre Meadows 6-cylinder engine of rather virile character, one of these cars in the hands of Violet Cordery covered 5000 miles at Brooklands at an average of 73 m.p.h.

The next year the engine was bored out to 3 litres, mostly for long-chassis (L.C.) cars, though there were some special short chassis. Both frames tended to whip because of their immense strength, according to Donald Monro, president of the Invicta Section of the Vintage Sports-Car Club. These 3-litre cars ran up to 60 m.p.h. from rest in 20 seconds—and they weighed 26¾ cwt.

In 1928 Invicta began mounting the 4½-litre dual-ignition Meadows in the same chassis, and the 0–60 time immediately shrank to 15 seconds. Top speed was 86 m.p.h., the engine developing 95 b.h.p. at 4000 r.p.m. Two years later a stronger chassis, the N.L.C., was developed, offering much greater rigidity at top speeds of 85 and 90 m.p.h., but a 103-h.p. engine was required for a car that weighed 31¼ cwt. with open coachwork.

Probably the most famous Invicta was the 100-m.p.h. low-chassis car inaugurated in 1930. Invicta connoisseurs recognize it on sight by its lower, square radiator, chromium exhausts and one-door front (on the passenger's side). While its top speed was not phenomenal for its time, handling had so far improved that the low-chassis Invicta was virtually synonymous with high-speed cornering.

Invictas were favoured by many well-known drivers even before Miss Cordery outshone her 1926 feat by driving a 4½-litre Invicta, with her sister, 70,000 miles in the same number of minutes. Donald Healey won the Alpine Rally outright with an Invicta in 1931 and led a team of them to the Glacier Cup. Raymond Mays, Invicta-mounted, broke the sports-car hill-climb record at Shelsley Walsh. S. C. H. Davis and George Abecassis also were very much at home in Invictas.

An Invicta Club Team was formed for competition in 1936, before the club was absorbed into the V.S.C.C. Led by Monro, these drivers specialized in hill-climbs, for which they lightened their cars, known as the Red Gauntlet model, by extensive chassis drilling, lighter coachwork and cutting 4 in. off the 10-ft. frames.

The Red Gauntlet two-seater

This 4½-litre coupé, built in 1933, still holds the class record for Prescott Hill-Climb—52·13 seconds, compared with Sydney Allard's 1958 time of 52·76 in his new gran turismo car powered with a C-type Jaguar. Shutler's car, using pre-selector gearbox, reached 107 m.p.h. for the standing kilometre

However, the depression had not spared Invicta any more than it had passed over any of the other quality machines. In an effort to reach a new market, the company introduced a less expensive model in 1933, using the 1½-litre Blackburne engine employed by Frazer-Nash. But in the 22¼-cwt. Invicta the Blackburne could not be expected to approach its feats in the Frazer-Nash chassis, and by 1934 the Invicta Co. had to yield to economics. It was bought up by Railton, which built about a dozen low-chassis 4½-litre cars from the remaining parts inventory. Of the total of 77 of this model ever made, 45 survive, several of them in the United States, where they command almost as high a price as when they were new.

A second firm bought up the old Invicta parts depot and played with plans for a new Invicta that would be based on the 2½-litre Darracq, but only one car was built and the venture was abandoned.

After the Second World War a new Invicta company was formed to produce a purely luxury car, known as the Black Prince. Equipped with independent suspension and automatic transmission, the Black Prince was an Invicta only in name, and its life was brief. Even farther from the true Invicta is the Buick series to which this name was given for 1959.

JAGUAR

Few marques have had as meteoric a rise as Jaguar. But Jaguar has accomplished a feat impossible to the meteors of the solar system: it has matured into an established planet.

William (now Sir William) Lyons entered business in 1922 with, in his own words, "a partner (William Walmesley), an idea, a heap of enthusiasm and an overdraft". The business was that of building motor cycle sidecars; but the partners had their eyes on automobiles. They called their firm the Swallow Sidecar & Coachbuilding Co., and they soon persuaded the Austin works to allow them to build shapely, luxurious bodies for the Austin 7. Swallow prospered in Blackpool, where it had been founded, and the partners grew restive for the capital of the British motor industry: Coventry. They moved there in 1935, and it was then that Jaguar was born.

Four years previously, Swallow had persuaded Capt. (now Sir) John Black, who had hauled the Standard Motor Co. from pit to peak, to build two special chassis for Swallow coachwork. The 109-in.

wheelbase mounted Standard's 1·7-litre 6-cylinder engine and a special gearbox; the 90-in. car was powered by the 1·6-litre 4-cylinder plant. These cars were known as the SS-1 and the SS-2, the initials representing the names of their parents: Standard Swallow. Both were immediate successes and a new company, S.S. Cars Ltd., was formed to concentrate on them. More power was demanded, however, and in a few months the SS-1 was being offered with a 2·6-litre engine, while Lyons began thinking of better and better performance: the 75-m.p.h. SS-1 looked much faster, and Lyons wanted it to live up to its appearance.

Among his engineers was W. M. Heynes, late of Humber, to whom the task fell. He took the faithful L-head 2·6-litre engine, raised its compression, substituted an aluminium head and new manifolding with dual carburation and put it in a new, shorter chassis designed by Lyons. This SS-90—that was its top speed—was the sire of today's XK cars. Light for its time—19½ cwt.—it was fitted with a high-lift camshaft but it fell short of the 100 m.p.h. at which Lyons was aiming. Fewer than 100 were made.

Heynes then changed to overhead valves with pushrods and higher compression, giving about 95 b.h.p. Cautiously, Lyons sub-contracted the manufacture to Standard and the christening to his own publicity department. From some 500 names of creatures both living and legendary, Jaguar was selected, and the SS-Jaguar bowed to the public in 1936. A beautiful car then and now, and competitively priced; also it did produce 100 m.p.h. Heynes, however, enlarged bore and stroke to 3½ litres for an alternative engine that would deliver 105 m.p.h.

The company did no racing before the war, but its clients did not share its fear of losing money. Wins and high places showered on private Jaguars in the Alpine Trial, the Monte Carlo Rally, Brooklands races and other contests. Meanwhile the company had brought out a 1608-c.c. car in two- and four-seater closed bodies. From 1936 to 1939 the company consolidated its position; Walmesley sold out and new capital came in. By the time war began, Jaguar knew it had gone as far as it could with the existing engines and new designs were shaping.

On the return of peace the company changed its name to Jaguar Cars Ltd., and re-introduced the 1939 saloon and drop-head as the much-prized Mark IV—the last classic-line Jaguar. Experiments on the "X" engine began, successive models being labelled "XA", "XB", etc. It was the eleventh modification that was finally adopted; hence the XK designation. Touring cars continued to be developed, but we will concern ourselves only with the sports machines, except to note that the Mark V touring car, restyled to a not too happy cross between classic line and post-war bulk, introduced independent torsion-bar front suspension and two-leading-shoe hydraulic brakes.

The new XK-120 was first shown at the end of 1948 in open two-seater form and was an instant success. Six months later, officially observed on a normal Belgian road near Jabbeke and using ordinary fuel, an XK-120 roadster clocked 132·6 m.p.h. This assured the success of the new 3442-c.c. d.o.h.c. engine. The rest of the road-testing was in effect done at a profit to the works by the rush of enthusiastic buyers.

In 1951 Jaguar entered racing. An XK120-C with raised compression and other modifications won at Le Mans, setting new records for average speed— 93·5—distance covered—2244 miles—and fastest lap —105 m.p.h. Jaguar won the Ulster Tourist Trophy and took second and fourth as well (in 1950 it had taken the first three places); it won at Spa, took three team prizes in the Alpine Rally and won the Liège–Rome–Liège rally outright; another Jaguar finished second, assuring the company of the team prize, as well as being the first car ever to complete the 3000-mile run without the loss of a single point. Jaguars were also first and second that year in the Tulip Rally.

Courtesy of Jaguar Cars Ltd.]

The ancestor, the SS-1

Courtesy of Jaguar Cars Ltd.]

The first sports car was the SS-90, identical in appearance to the SS-100 shown here. Four-seater bodywork was also available

Courtesy of Jaguar Cars Ltd.]

The 120 coupé was one of the most beautiful cars produced since the war. The 120-M had dual exhaust and ⅜ in.-lift inlet and exhaust camshafts. Standard 120 offered wire or disc wheels

[Courtesy of Jaguar Cars Ltd.

The XK-140 roadster could be distinguished from XK-120 only by latter's grille, which had more and thinner vertical bars

Courtesy of Jaguar Cars Ltd.]

Both 120 and 140 were available in drop-head form. This is the 120

[Photograph by Dr. Ian R. Entwistle

The C Jaguar attained 148 m.p.h. at 5800 r.p.m. Some of these cars were also used for normal road work

[Photograph by Fred C. McPhearson; courtesy of Jaguar Cars North American Corp.

The XK-SS was essentially a D-type detuned for road use with similar frontal appearance

Le Mans was almost a Jaguar monopoly for the better part of the decade. In 1953 they finished first, second and fourth with a record average of 105·85 m.p.h.—the first winning average to top 100—and another new distance mark. In 1954 a works car finished second, a private 120-C fourth. In 1955 the magnificent D Jaguar, with 9:1 compression and 250 b.h.p., set new average speed and distance records as well as a lap speed of 122·39 m.p.h., and a privately entered D finished third. In 1956 Jaguars were first, fourth and sixth; in 1957 they swept the first four places and another Jaguar finished sixth.

Rheims, Ulster, Silverstone, Sebring, Spa—every famous venue was the scene of a new Jaguar victory, a new record for the course set by Jaguar, sometimes both. The world's outstanding drivers wanted to pilot these cars, and Mike Hawthorn, the 1958 world's champion, did particularly well with them, as did Stirling Moss. Meanwhile more and more of the C and D modifications were being built into the dual-purpose cars. The 160-h.p. XK-120 was offered in modification as the 190-h.p. 120-M with stiffer suspension and dual exhaust. Fixed- and drop-head coupés became available, and these as well as the roadsters scored heavily in road-racing throughout Europe and America. The XK-120 was succeeded by the 190-h.p. XK-140, with rack-and-pinion steering, and a 210-h.p. version known as the XK140-MC. Rather paradoxically, these were often beaten in club racing by 120-M's, which have the reputation of somewhat better roadability. Overdrive was optional on the 140.

A special dual-purpose version of the D, known as the XK-SS, was produced briefly but was killed off by a tragic factory fire. Weighing under 18¼ cwt. dry, it was propelled by a 262-b.h.p. engine with 9:1 compression and top speed was estimated at 146 m.p.h. Top gear was direct drive, and the gear ratios were very close.

The XK150 coupé was the world's first production car to offer all disc brakes as an option. Dual exhaust is standard. Front seat is 4 in. wider

The 150 and 150-S roadster are identical in appearance. Half-elliptic rear springs are damped by telescopic shock absorbers. Steering is 2¾ turns lock to lock. Like all XK's except SS, car weighs about 26¾ cwt.

In 1957 Jaguar introduced the XK150 in fixed- and drop-head form only. These cars had 8:1 compression (7:1 was optional) and optional servo-assisted Dunlop disc brakes, and in standard form developed 190 b.h.p., 210 b.h.p. being available on special-equipment models. Like the 140's, they offered the choice of overdrive or automatic transmission. In appearance, they carried farther the decline from the elegance of the 120 that began with the 140; the 150 has little line and depends for its aesthetic appeal much more on the treatment of masses, which tend to fuse into one another, whereas every feature of the 120 was sharply defined. Some observers note a very marked resemblance, in profile, between the open 120's and the 1940 B.M.W. Mille Miglia roadsters.

Jaguar introduced a roadster into the 150 line in 1958, its most powerful dual-purpose car to date. The standard model has a special cylinder head and high-lift camshafts and standard output of 210 b.h.p., or 1 b.h.p. per cubic inch. It has twin S.U. carburetters, a chrome-iron block, domed combustion chambers in an aluminium-alloy head, aluminium-alloy pistons and steel connecting rods. Manual or automatic transmission is optional. The side-screens of the 120 and the 140 have given place to wind-up windows. The car weighs 27¼ cwt.

A special version, the 150-S, has already shown its qualities in racing, frequently vanquishing the much bigger-engined Corvettes. While most of its specifications, including weight, are those of the standard roadster, power and torque outputs have been raised by a straight-port cylinder head combined with three S.U. carburetters and 9:1 compression, resulting in 250 b.h.p. at 5500 r.p.m. A heavier clutch, lead-bronze bearings and twin fuel pumps are fitted, and only manual transmission with overdrive is available. Some idea of the performance of this fully dual-purpose car may be obtained by comparing its timed top speed of 136 m.p.h. with the racing D's maximum of 162. The 150-S accelerates from 0 to 60 m.p.h. in 7·3 seconds, the D in 4·7 seconds. The 150-S was timed for the standing quarter-mile in 15·1 seconds, against the D's 13·5. The XK-SS lay nicely between the two with its estimated top speed of 146 m.p.h., 0–60 acceleration of 5·5 seconds and standing-quarter-mile time of 14·1.

JENSEN (AVON STANDARD)

Like the Allard, the Jensen evolved from a "special": in this case, based on an Austin 7 in the hands of the Jensen brothers, Alan and Richard, while they were still in their teens. This car, second-hand, was a present from their father when Alan was 19 and Richard 16. The first thing they did with it was to

Alan (at wheel) and Richard Jensen in their first car, based on an Austin 7

39

[Photograph by Michael P. Clapham

The Jensens' Avon Standard used the side-valve 4-cylinder Standard engine

[Courtesy of A. E. L. Mash & Associates

The 541-R is a full four-seater high-performance car

strip it to its smallest components. When they had put it back together in their own fashion, it was one of the fastest cars on the road.

One car that they had out-run finally flagged them down: its driver was the chief engineer of the Standard Motor Co., and he wanted to inspect this fleet enigma. When he had done so, he asked whether they could build something similar on the Standard chassis. Thereafter they built the Avon Standard to order, in both roadster and, in 1930, coupé form, but their names did not appear in connection with it.

The name of Jensen first became known hyphenated after Patrick. The Patrick-Jensen was custom built on a modified Wolseley Hornet chassis. Their reputation spread to Hollywood and a film star sent them a chassis from Detroit to be finished to their criteria of perfection. The first standard Jensen appeared in 1936: the first car in the world on which overdrive was stock equipment, with a Ford V-8 engine and the imprimatur of the late Edsel Ford.

From the time of Munich to VE Day the Jensen brothers devoted themselves to war work by day, fire-watching at night and planning all the time. The result was the Jensen Interceptor, a fast luxury saloon that preceded today's 541-R model, capable of 125 m.p.h. with the new 4-litre Austin DS7 6-cylinder engine using three carburetters (the standard 541, like the *de luxe*, uses the Austin 130). The 541

de luxe was the first production car to make disc brakes on all wheels standard equipment. Dual exhaust is also employed.

While no record of Jensen competition is available, not only its performance but its high quality warrants its classification as a sports car. The welded platform chassis utilizes coil-spring front suspension. The body is glass fibre and the total weight is about $26\frac{3}{4}$ cwt. Twin electric fuel pumps and rack-and-pinion steering add to the performance and manœuvrability, and a servo-assisted hydraulic system doubly assures quick action from the discs. Despite the size of the engine and the total weight, fuel consumption is moderate, helped by the optional overdrive.

JOWETT

The first Jowett was produced by two brothers of that name, William and Benjamin, with a flat-twin water-cooled engine. They built it in 1906 but it was not publicly sold for four years, pending further developmental work. The cylinders were horizontally opposed and the final drive was by worm gear. The

Courtesy of Jowett Engineering Ltd.]

The first Jowett weighed less than $6\frac{1}{4}$ cwt. and, 50 years ago, carried engine and gearbox in unit. Thermo-siphon cooling was used

An exemplary vintage Jowett, developing 17 b.h.p.

Photograph by J. D. Rogers]

basic principle of the engine was continued by the company until production of cars ceased in 1953.

Few Jowetts were of full sporting calibre, though they did well in the Scottish Six Days' Trial of 1921. In 1928 a specially built 8-cwt. car took the 12-hour 1100-c.c. record at Brooklands at 55 m.p.h. Until almost the end of the vintage period, Jowetts used 2-wheel brakes: the foot-pedal operated a contracting band on the transmission and the handbrake contracted bands on the rear wheels. In 1929 4-wheel brakes were fitted and, for the first time, detachable cylinder heads were used. The first cars were of 802 c.c., later enlarged to 907 c.c. in 1922. Only in 1936 was a 4-cylinder engine attempted. The 3-speed gearbox of the early cars was controlled by a cone clutch wound with boned asbestos cord.

The 4-cylinder Jowett Javelin continued the principle of horizontal opposition of cylinders. The 1½-litre engine had two carburetters and transmitted its power through a 4-speed synchromesh gearbox. This car was the basis for the truly sports model known as the Jupiter, which appeared in 1949 with a tubular frame designed with the help of E.R.A. Ltd., a firm of racing-car specialists. The Jupiter utilized torsion-bar suspension all round and, like the Javelin, had pushrod overhead valves. Though it weighed about a ton, it was good for a steady pace of 80 m.p.h.

In 1950, 1951 and 1952 Jowett won its class at Le Mans, breaking the course record for 1½-litre cars in 1950 with an average of 75·8 m.p.h. That, by the way, was the Jupiter's first race. In 1951 it was first and second in its class in the Monte Carlo Rally and won a number of hill-climbs and races, including

Watkins Glen. While it incorporated rack-and-pinion steering, weighed only 16·9 cwt. and was good for better than 90 m.p.h., both the Mark I and the Mark I-A—the chief difference being access to luggage space: internal in the Mark I, external in the I-A—had bench seats and steering-column gear levers. The fuel tank, as on the current Triumph, was mounted as close to the middle of the car as possible to minimize changes in weight distribution between front and rear as petrol was used.

KIEFT

Enough Kiefts have seen road use to warrant the inclusion of the marque in a book on dual-purpose cars. Designed and built by Cyril Kieft in limited numbers since 1954, these very fast 1100-c.c. Coventry-Climax-engined cars weigh about 10¾ cwt. Compression of 8·8:1 enables them to top 110 m.p.h.

Photograph by the authors]

An early Kieft

[Courtesy of Motor Sport

An early Jupiter roadster

The Jowett Jupiter roadster in final form. The windscreen was easily removed for replacement by racing screen

[Courtesy of the Henry Ford Museum

Courtesy of Kieft Sports Car Co. Ltd.]

The 1955 model

The latest Kieft has a full-width screen and transparent headlight fairings for road use

Courtesy of Kieft Sports Car Co. Ltd.]

With tubular chassis, rack-and-pinion steering and full independent suspension—wishbone and coil in front, transverse leaf and wishbone behind—they are extremely roadworthy and 11-in. brakes are fitted with 15-in. wheels whose rims are detachable. They have taken class prizes in races in six countries.

Kieft employs moulded plastic bodies that do not dent and have unusually high resistance to damage by impact or fracture through fatigue.

LAGONDA

An American who wanted to be an opera singer, a creek in Ohio bearing an Indian name that means "smooth running stream" and the favour of the Romanoffs combined to make one of the finest of British sports cars.

Wilbur Gunn, a native of Lagonda Creek, Ohio, was supposed to go into his family's sheep-shearing machinery plant and was educated accordingly. But he went to England instead and, though he never became an opera singer, he did begin building 3-wheeled twin-cylinder cars around the turn of the century, naming them after his birthplace. A perfectionist, he made every part, down to nuts and bolts, except the carburetter. The reward was a series of successes in reliability runs, in which Gunn himself frequently drove. His other hobby was civic and public affairs.

About 1910 he produced his first four-wheelers: a 20-h.p. 4-cylinder and a 30-h.p. 6-cylinder. Virtually the whole output was sold to Russia, where again they scored high in reliability tests. One of the outstanding features of this car was its rear suspension, anticipating today's trailing-link suspension and, like it, limiting axle movement to the vertical. The axle was supported by four rods—two above and outboard, two below and inboard. Just before the First World War, Gunn built an 1100-c.c. 4-cylinder of relatively short stroke—67 × 78—with overhead inlet valves and side exhaust valves, both working from one camshaft. Again Gunn far anticipated modern practice by welding body and chassis into a unit. (David Scott-Moncrieff, in *Veteran and Edwardian Motor Cars*, attributes this advance to an interest in economy rather than an insight into the monocoque technique.) These cars had probably the quickest steering ever produced—one-third of a turn lock to lock! The 3-speed gearbox was built in unit with the engine and worm drive was used.

Though Gunn died shortly after the war, this model was continued in essence through 1925. It was not a sports car, though it did occasionally turn up at Brooklands and, in 1921, took the one-hour record for light cars at 80 m.p.h.

[*Courtesy of the Henry Ford Museum*
The 4½-litre Rapide won Le Mans outright in 1935

42

Courtesy of E. B. Watson]
The first real sports Lagonda was the radically new 2-litre of 1926. This car, still in daily use, has clocked 265,000 miles

Courtesy of F Lt. C. G. Clarke]
The high-chassis model of 1928. Low-chassis version of this year was timed at 95 m.p.h. at Le Mans

In 1926 this Edwardian concept was abandoned for a radically different one. From the outset the 2-litre 4-cylinder engine had chain-driven double overhead camshafts and a high compression ratio, somewhat offset by very complicated manifolding. The chassis was very strong, though heavy, the steering good and the brakes more than adequate. Without reducing the weight—fabric-bodied tourers weighed about 26¾ cwt.—the chassis was lowered for full sports use. At the end of the 1920s a supercharger was introduced with the claim that it would increase

top speed from 80 to 90 m.p.h. in the 14/60 Speed Model. These long-stroke—72 × 120—engines had a close-ratio gearbox but are considered by experts to have been over-geared, hampering acceleration from rest. In 1928 an option of a 3-litre 6-cylinder Meadows engine was introduced.

In 1932, as we have seen, the 6-cylinder Crossley engine was made standard in the Lagonda, now known as the 16/80 and equipped with still better brakes. At about the same time, Lagonda took two exciting steps: re-entry into what used to be called the *voiturette* class and a full plunge into the very big engine.

The *voiturette* was the 1100-c.c. Lagonda Rapier, of which relatively few were ever produced—the survivors are eagerly sought today. It used twin camshafts and 62 × 90 bore and stroke, with a comfortable maximum of 6000 r.p.m.; 50 b.h.p. at 5000 r.p.m. was supposed to be normal. Weight was a problem, partly because economy thwarted the original intention of using an alloy head and block with dry cylinder liners. Instead, both components were iron and the engine alone weighed close to 400 lb. An E.N.V. pre-selector gearbox was used, enabling the driver to move the lever to the gear he wanted without engaging it until he kicked his pedal; this was coupled with a three-quarter floating E.N.V. axle. Some of the finest body-builders supplied the coachwork, including A. C. Bertelli, designer of the Aston-Martin International (a historical omen, perhaps), and the Earl of March, now Duke of Richmond and Gordon and owner of the Goodwood circuit. Both Sir Malcolm Campbell, the speed hero, and Tazio Nuvolari were delighted with the Rapier. The one-ton kerb weight was cut to just over 15 cwt. with the right kind of open two-seater bodies, and in 1934 at Le Mans the Rapier qualified in both the Biennial Cup and the Rudge-Whitworth Trophy. A few blown versions were produced with top speeds around 130 m.p.h. and in 1951 one of these defeated a C Jaguar, mainly because of better cornering.

The other Lagonda innovation was the 4½-litre, using a wholly conventional chassis and the same 6-cylinder Meadows engine so well exploited by the Invicta. Though the Lagonda was heavier, it could stay with the Invicta and in 1935 a 4½-litre Lagonda Rapide was the over-all winner at Le Mans. Within the same period, Lagonda had produced a special Continental model for the Alpine Rally, a 3-litre Speed Model bored out to 75 mm. and two 3-litre "selector specials". The first of these had the Maybach pre-selector gearbox containing four silent gears and four lower, less silent ones: the latter's three upper ratios roughly corresponded to the three lower ones of the quiet gearbox, so that in effect five speeds were available. Four reverse ratios were also provided by this transmission. Ultimately this was supplanted by the Wilson pre-selector.

By 1935 Lagonda had a multiplicity of models at the same time: the Rapier, the 16/80, 3-litre, 3½-litre, 4½ and 4½ Rapide, which was timed at 100

Courtesy of D. Exner Baumann]

The 3-litre tourer of 1932

Photograph by J. R. D. Barker]

The Abbott-bodied Lagonda Rapier

Photograph by J. O. Cooper]

The 1935 tourer used same body (Vanden Plas) and chassis for 3½- and 4½-litre. This 3½ exceeded 90 m.p.h.

The short-chassis 6-cylinder drop-head of 1936–7 looked like the V-12 except for length

The 4½-litre Rapide. This car won at Watkins Glen in 1948. In 1939 the Rapide was also offered with the 12-cylinder engine, which reached 112 m.p.h. A drop-head body had full-skirted front wings and rear wheel-spats. Front suspension was independent

The last of W. O. Bentley's great designs: the 4½-litre V-12 Lagonda, with special coachwork

m.p.h. and carried the same body as the 3-litre. But, perhaps because of this diversification, the company found the going hard and had to reorganize. The Rapier was sold outright and its new makers followed Lagonda's designs except for a 90-m.p.h. blown car introduced in 1936. The outbreak of war ended the Rapier's career.

The chief stockholder in the new Lagonda company immediately hired W. O. Bentley as chief designer. W. O. lost no time clearing out all the smaller models and concentrating on the 4½-litre. He improved the chassis to the highest luxury standard and certified safe 100-m.p.h. speed. The fastest British-built car of its day in 150-b.h.p. form, it scored the best lap in the 1936 Tourist Trophy.

But Bentley knew the day of the big, long-stroke six was rapidly ending; in 1937 he introduced the V-12 Lagonda in a chassis that had already been tested with the 4½-litre. The stroke was very short, top speed well over 100 m.p.h. and only the slow 0–50 acceleration—10 seconds—bothered Bentley. It was, however, the first production closed car to top 100 m.p.h. In 1939 the 12-cylinder ran at Le Mans against blown Bugattis, Talbots, Delages, Delahayes and Alfas, and finished third to Bugatti and Delage. Stripped of their wings at a Brooklands meeting, Lagondas lapped at 128 m.p.h. But the outbreak of a world war interrupted Lagonda's career for a second time.

In 1947 the David Brown Companies acquired Lagonda, which had a new 2½-litre 6-cylinder under development. This overhead-camshaft engine was based on the 12, and it was dropped into an all-round-independent-suspension chassis, on which an aluminium body was mounted. The whole car was hand-made and was one of the finest luxury cars of the post-war period. It made no pretensions, however, to sports classification or character. Since 1955 Lagonda and Aston Martin have shared the same engine, of 8·2:1 compression and 140 b.h.p.

Lagonda's competition successes go back to the 1921 car that was not even supposed to race. Class wins at Brooklands were numerous; in 1928, though the cars were not placed at Le Mans, they were touching 95 m.p.h. In 1936 they won their class at Montlhéry.

LEA-FRANCIS

The first Lea-Francis was made in the 19th century. But for the first quarter of this century the company was best known for its motor-cycles, until it re-entered the automobile field in 1922 with an air-cooled twin-cylinder car and two small fours, with side valves. Intended to be no more than pleasant economy vehicles, they were soon dropped.

The 4-cylinder overhead-valve Meadows engine, developing about 20 b.h.p., made the Lea-Francis a very sprightly machine. It did very well in the tough light-car trials of the R.A.C. in 1924 and shone at Brooklands in the flying mile. In 1925 the 4ED Meadows, used in so many fine sports cars, was adopted for the Lea-Francis in a model known as the 12/40, which was guaranteed to do its 60 m.p.h. in full touring trim and tune. A year later it was timed at 70, and it had the brakes to go with its speed.

In 1927, too, Lea-Francis became Britain's first production supercharged car. The Cozette blower was mounted vertically in the Hyper-Sports Model, which was quite capable of 90 m.p.h., a most unusual speed for 1½-litre cars in the 1920s. Meanwhile Lea-Francis was experimenting with 6-cylinder d.o.h.c. engines of its own design, as well as transmissions embodying free-wheeling, but these never got very far.

The marque had its greatest period from 1927 to 1930 with the Hyper. In 1928 the new Tourist Trophy races in Ulster were inaugurated and Kaye Don, who later held various land-speed records, drove a Hyper to victory by the incredible margin of four one-hundredths of a mile per hour over the very potent front-wheel-drive Alvis. Privately entered Lea-Francis cars ran most respectably at Le Mans, finishing eighth in 1928 and sixth in 1930. In both the 1920s and the 1930s they won their class at Brooklands several times; in 1927 a Lea-Francis topped all the 1½-litre cars at Shelsley Walsh.

The company went into receivership in 1930 and was inactive for several years thereafter. Production was resumed in 1933 with the 12/40 4-cylinder in both blown and unblown versions and a 2-litre six. Engines, road-holding, steering and brakes were generally praised. But there was another hiatus in production until 1937, when the "Leaf" began to eye competition again. In 1938, a Lea-Francis was first in its class in a long handicap race at Brooklands track in Surrey.

By this time the 2-litre engine had been abandoned for two 4-cylinders, one of 1496 c.c. (69×100) and the other of 1629 c.c. (72×100). Both engines had twin camshafts, driven by chains and helical gears, and hemispherical combustion chambers. Valves were actuated by pushrods. A synchromesh close-ratio gearbox was fitted. These cars were manufactured up to the beginning of the war in 1939. The engines had been designed by R. H. Rose, formerly with Riley, who followed the Riley pattern as closely as he could without incurring a lawsuit for infringement.

After the war these engines re-appeared as 1800-c.c., 78-b.h.p. units and later as 2496-c.c. 100-b.h.p. power plants, being bored out successively to 75 and then to 85 mm. and the stroke ultimately being lengthened

Courtesy of the Lea-Francis Owners' Club]
The 1902 Lea-Francis tourer

Courtesy of the Lea-Francis Owners' Club]
Kaye Don in the Hyper Sports that won the 1928 Ulster Tourist Trophy

The Lea-Francis 12/40 salonettes of 1929–30 were distinctly sporting. These cars are shown racing at Oulton Park in 1956

Copyright by Richmond Pike; courtesy of the Vintage Sports-Car Club]

**This Westland-bodied 2½-litre roadster is the only one in
existence. It closely resembles the standard model that
was the company's last car**

to 110 mm. Meanwhile Lea-Francis was edging into
the dollar market with a 1½-litre engine specifically
designed for American midget racing, in which the
valves were inclined at 90 degrees and compression
was raised to 14:1. On methanol-benzole-castor oil
fuel these engines developed 120 b.h.p. at 5500 r.p.m.

The post-war sports cars scored no notable successes, though their performance was quite respectable.
The 1800-c.c. engine was the basis for the Connaught
grand-prix engine when these cars were first made,
but by 1953 Lea-Francis had abandoned building
private cars.

LEYLAND-THOMAS

In the middle of the First World War, Leyland
Motors was dreaming of producing the finest luxury
car in the world. While J. G. Parry Thomas was
busy designing Leyland's aeroplane engines, he was
also working on the dream car, whose prototype was
displayed at the Olympia Show in London in 1920.

Its eight cylinders in a row were cast integrally
with the top half of the crankcase—89 × 146 or 7266
c.c. Like that of the later 6-cylinder Bentley, the
overhead camshaft was driven by connecting rods
and operated the normal two valves per cylinder, set
at a 90-degree angle and equipped with cantilever
springs to obviate bounce. With two carburetters,
this engine developed 145 b.h.p. at 3000 r.p.m. The
4-speed gearbox was linked conventionally to a unique
axle held in place by a torque tube. There were
two spiral bevel gears and the half-shafts' angle to
each other could be altered to compensate for high-
crown roads.

The brakes, however, were the old 2-wheel type,
with servo assistance, vacuum operated. Steering
was, surprisingly, three full turns lock to lock; the
rear springs were quarter-elliptics on torsion bars
within the frame, and anti-roll bars were fitted at
front and rear. The wheelbases, to choice, were
10 ft. 6 in., 11 ft. 9 in. and 12 ft. 6 in. In full touring
condition the Leyland-Thomas exceeded 90 m.p.h.;
at Brooklands, stripped, it achieved 115 m.p.h. first

time out. By dint of fine tuning and fitting a streamlined
body, Thomas got the car up to a Brooklands lap record
of 129·36. This figure is only 15 m.p.h. less than the
existing record set in 1935 by John Cobb in his
specially built Napier-Railton.

Only 18 Leyland-Thomases were built in its five
years of production—hardly surprising in view of
the extremely high price of the chassis alone. One,
formerly owned by David Scott-Moncrieff, is now in
Leyland Motors' museum; it is not known whether
any others survive.

One of the last Leyland-Thomases built

LOTUS

A civil engineer out of the University of London
and the R.A.F., Colin Chapman started competition
motoring after the war, in spare time from his job
as a structural engineer with the British Aluminium
Co. Today, well under 30, he has made his cars a
legend in a few years.

Trials were his first competition, in an antique
Austin 7, originally a saloon, which he rebodied
into an open two-seater. Modifications to engine
and chassis produced a 100-m.p.h. car that was a
consistent winner on the steep, muddy trials courses.
This car he called the Lotus.

The Mark II used both a Ford Ten and the Austin
engine, while the Mark III, which was never beaten,
monopolized the 750-c.c. class with the same Austin 7
engine, modified by Chapman to take a double-choke
carburetter. Those who saw him drive the cars he had
built wanted replicas, and by 1954, instead of making
components at night, after work, he was established
in his own business.

Road-testing had been carried out—an aero-
dynamics expert strapped himself to the bonnet of

Colin Chapman and his wife in a hill-climb with the
first Lotus

The Mark III Lotus

**The Lotus Seven weighs only slightly more than 6¼ cwt.,
develops 40 b.h.p. from 1172-c.c. Ford engine raised to
8·5:1 compression and has worm-and-nut steering**

The Lotus Club Eleven in full road trim in New York

an experimental car that was then driven over an airfield at 110 m.p.h. so that he could analyse the problems involved—and at 23 Chapman offered the Mark IV for sale. This was still a trials car, using the Ford Consul engine, much tuned. The projected Mark V, Austin-based, was never produced.

The car that really gave Lotus its impetus was the Mark VI, which was made available in either assembled or kit form. Chapman's major contribution to it was the very light but very strong multi-tubular frame and the body, the rest of the components being standard mass products. Most buyers of these cars installed either Ford or M.G. engines, and they are true dual-purpose machines like the current Lotus Seven.

Lotus introduced its fully streamlined dual-fin design with the Mark VIII in 1954. Originally it used the 1172-c.c. Ford engine but this was soon sup-

planted by the 1100-c.c. Coventry Climax, over-square (72·4 × 66·6), which delivered 84 b.h.p. at 6900 r.p.m. with 9·8:1 compression. It has linered cylinders and an overhead camshaft and is of light alloy, with aluminium pistons and head. On such fast, light cars the fins are functional, serving as stabilizers like those on aeroplanes.

Numerous competition successes crowned the Mark VIII, which was followed by the Mark IX, with slight body modifications and the same engine. The Mark X is its 2-litre version. But by far the most successful Lotus to date has been the Mark XI, which is available in 750-, 1100- and 1500-c.c. versions. The 1100 won its class at Le Mans in both 1956 and 1957, when it was also second in the Index of Performance—first place having been taken by the 750. Two 1500-c.c. Coventry-Climax engines are used—one of 1460 c.c., 9·5:1 compression and

100 b.h.p. at 6200 r.p.m., the other of 1475 c.c., 10:1 compression and 141 b.h.p. at 7000 r.p.m. Disc brakes and de Dion rear suspension are used on the Le Mans 85 and Le Mans 150 versions of the Mark XI, while the Club 75 and sports have drum brakes and live axles. The 75 employs the 1500-c.c. engine, tilted 10 degrees; the sports uses the Ford Ten, as does the Lotus Seven.

In 1958 Lotus offered its first coupé, the Elite, a gran turismo car with an over-square 1220-c.c. Coventry-Climax engine—76·2 × 66·6—disc brakes and strut-type rear suspension created by Chapman and including a doubly articulated drive shaft assuring lateral location. This was developed from the Formula II racing car and allows changes in rear-wheel camber with varying load to maintain handling. Like all current Lotuses except the Seven, the Elite has rack-and-pinion steering. It weighs only about 10¾ cwt. against the Le Mans model's 7¾. The chassis, in all open models, is composed of both round and square tubing in which the drive-shaft tunnel and floor are integral; the coupé has no independent frame but chassis and body are integral in construction.

The strut-type rear suspension also appeared on the Mark XV, introduced in 1958 with excellent results at Le Mans. Here the engine is inclined 60 degrees from the vertical to reduce height and frontal area. It is again a 1475-c.c. Coventry-Climax d.o.h.c. unit, 81·2 × 71·1, with 10:1 compression and 150 b.h.p. at 7200 r.p.m. A twin dry-plate clutch, hydraulically actuated, controls a 5-speed gearbox,

The Elite's integral body-chassis construction is entirely of plastic

with Chapman's own ratchet shift, in unit with the final drive. The car has a limited-slip differential and weighs 8¾ cwt. The disc brakes are mounted outboard at the front but inboard at the rear to decrease unsprung weight. An interesting engine feature is the double duty imposed on one of the gears driving the twin overhead camshafts: this gear also operates both the delivery and scavenge pumps that circulate oil between the engine and the separately mounted oil reservoir. Wet cylinder liners are also used. Either a 2- or a 2·2-litre Coventry-Climax engine may also be fitted.

Lotus successes, listed individually, would fill a respectable pamphlet. In a typical year of national and international meetings, they included 143 firsts, 121 seconds and 91 thirds. Class marks have been set in virtually every division of records.

M.G.

No one who has ever owned an M.G. can think of it again, however long afterward, whatever the *bolide* he may be driving, without nostalgia. It would be impossible to count the enthusiasts and the competition drivers who went to school with M.G.; nor can one estimate the debt that the whole world of motor sport owes to Abingdon-on-Thames. It might be added that no other British car has done so much for its native country's dollar balance, for M.G.'s acceptance in the United States was instantaneous and has never stopped growing.

The first M.G. was nothing more than a highly tuned Morris Oxford, which the gifted Cecil Kimber took in hand in 1923, naming it from the initials of the original Morris corporate name, Morris Garages. Mounting a Hotchkiss engine with pushrod overhead valves in an Oxford chassis and stripping the body down to essentials—even staggering the seats to lower width—Kimber produced an 80-m.p.h.-plus car that took a gold medal in the 1925 Land's End trial. This was followed—there has never been any attempt to explain the numerology—by the Mark IV, with a maximum output of 35 b.h.p. from an 1800-c.c. 4-cylinder engine. The Mark IV carried a 3-speed gearbox, which did not prevent it attracting a large market.

The demand for more speed resulted in the 2½-litre 6-cylinder Mark I with overhead camshaft. The 3-speed gearbox was retained for reasons of weight-saving, but its second gear was designed to provide speeds above 50 m.p.h.; top speed was around 75. This 18/80, as the Mark I was sometimes called, had only one carburetter. Wheelbase was 9 ft. 6 in. and track was just 4 ft. In 1930 the Mark II appeared, 4 in. wider, better braced in the chassis and fitted with dual carburation and servo brakes. For the first time, M.G. was building with an eye on road-racing; and, simultaneously with the Mark II, it developed the rather fierce Mark III, nicknamed the Tigresse.

Both these cars were intended to provide a machine ready to race at a price that would not strain buyers' pocketbooks. The Mark III had down-draught carburation from its two S.U.s on a 6-cylinder engine of just under 1100 c.c. that produced 100 b.h.p. The crank and connecting rods were fully machined. Manifolding was divided, inlet ports being set on the right and exhaust on the left. The 4-wheel brakes were cable-operated and fully adjustable from within the car even in the heat of the race. A close-ratio crash gearbox housed four gears. The first car appeared in the Junior Car Club's Double Twelve at Brooklands in 1930 and was soon lapping at 86 m.p.h. until some

The first M.G. and its creator, Cecil Kimber

The famous M, ancestor of all the M.G. Midgets

The Mark III Tigresse set the pattern for the marque's successes

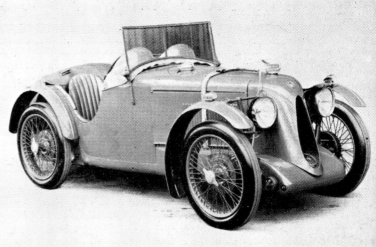

The radiator shrouding of the C-type Montlhéry was later removed; supercharger was mounted directly in front of radiator

The doorless J-4 Midget carried blower between dumb-irons and carburetter beside it

The famous K-3 Magnette continued the outboard carburetter but shrouded it and the supercharger in wire-mesh stone guards

[Courtesy of Nuffield Exports Ltd.

A sporting Magna four-seater

carburetter screws loosened and the butterfly was macerated by the valve gear. The Mark III never raced again, but for the next six years its basic features triumphed on both road and track.

While the Marks II and III were under development, Kimber was also working on a totally different M.G. This was the first of the famous Midgets, the M, an 847-c.c. 4-cylinder car that was never—at first—thought of in the same breath with racing. A more unlikely competition car would have been hard to imagine: petrol carried up next to the engine and fed by gravity, fabric universals, a body designed with little thought of drag. In June of 1929, when the Morris Minor-based M was just two months old, Kimber sent three of them to the J.C.C.'s High Speed Trial at Brooklands, in which certain minimum distances had to be covered in an hour to qualify for awards. They got the awards.

When the Mark III turned out for the Double Twelve the next year, the M went along too, but very little attention was paid to it. Eight teams started, only two finished: M.G. and Austin, and Austin finished second to the M's, whose best average for the 24 hours was 60·23 m.p.h. What impressed everyone—just as it still impresses everyone 30 years later—was the remarkable cornering. On the strength of this, F. H. B. Samuelson (now Sir Francis Samuelson, Bt.) entered his own M at Le Mans, where it lapped for eight hours at 55 m.p.h. until an oil pipe broke. Sir Francis repaired the damage, drove the car to Brussels and, after minimal practice on the complex, hilly Spa course, finished fifth in class in the 24-hour Belgian race.

It is not within the scope of this book to discuss the experimental cars built by M.G. from then on for attacks—generally successful—on the land-speed record. This story is told in detail in *Maintaining the Breed*, Lt.-Col. John W. Thornley's fine history of M.G. But from the successes of the M to the present decade, M.G. record cars have been making history.

From the 57 × 83 M the designers proceeded to the C, or Montlhéry Midget, still adhering to the original aim of building only dual-purpose cars for sale. In

the C, the stroke was shortened to 73 mm.—total volume, 746 c.c.—and for the first time M.G. adopted the dry sump, oil being fed, under float-chamber control, from a reservoir on the firewall. In the 1931 Double Twelve, the late Major Goldie Gardner drove his first race for M.G.; another member of the team was the Earl of March; and Sir Francis was back. In the first day of the race they made a great deal of trouble not only for their own class, lapping at 65 and 70 m.p.h., but also for the big cars. Despite a number of pit stops on both days, chiefly because of valve-spring failure, the C types took the first five places over-all, the team prize and all class awards.

For the Irish Grand Prix the C shed the radiator shrouds that had helped to give it its French nickname, for these had been adapted from its experimental predecessor, EX 120, which had lapped the French course in practice at 106 m.p.h. and had exceeded its goal of ticking off 100 miles in a timed hour. The shrouds had been required then because of the weather; but Brooklands had shown they could be a handicap as well. Better cooled, the C's won easily in Ireland and were turned toward Ulster and the T.T. For this race the C was supercharged, the blower taking the space immediately ahead of the radiator that had been occupied by the shrouds, and the single carburetter rode outdoors next to the blower. Thus modified, the little C, stripped of its touring impedimenta, could lap Brooklands at 96 m.p.h., and it won the T.T. handsomely at 67·90 m.p.h. for five hours' racing.

The next star in M.G.'s galaxy was the J series, which had four members: J-1, open and closed four-seaters; J-2, the open two-seater sports; J-3, essentially a supercharged J-2, and J-4, the racing car. The J-2 set the cut-down door pattern that remained standard for M.G. until the post-war A type arrived. The pointed tail was cut away and a slab fuel tank appeared, also to remain until the A was introduced. J-1 and J-2 were 847-c.c. engines—57 × 83—while J-3 and J-4 were only 746 c.c.—57 × 73. While the first three models developed the customary 36 b.h.p. around which unblown M.G.s had generally hovered since the Mark IV, the J-4 produced 72·3

The P series was the direct forerunner of the T cars and the last with overhead camshaft. Many think it superior to any later M.G.

Courtesy of Nuffield Exports Ltd.]

50

b.h.p. at 6000 r.p.m. (compare the supercharged C's output of 52·5 at 6500). The C having shown itself too fast for its brakes, 12-in. sets were fitted on the J, all models of which had a single overhead camshaft. The J-4, even with standard axle ratio, distinguished itself in hill-climbs as well as races.

Simultaneously with the J the company was producing the 6-cylinder type L Magna, preceded by the type F, both very fast high-performance tourers. Nor were these all: the K series of Magnettes had already been begun, reaching its peak in the 120-b.h.p. supercharged K-3, a 1087-c.c. 6-cylinder car of beautifully functional appearance. Nuvolari, who spoke next to no English and had had no experience of M.G.s at all, won the T.T. on a K-3, to which a J-4 finished a close second. The latter ran sixth over-all at Le Mans in 1933 and third in the Isle of Man Mannin Beg race. The T.T. J-4, incidentally, maintained an average for the whole race, 73·46 m.p.h., that exceeded the previous year's lap record. The "non-racing" J-3 won a Coupe des Alpes in 1933 and a mountain race in Liechtenstein, as well as helping to give M.G., at Montlhéry, all international Class H records.

Even more formidable was the record of the K-3, some of which has already been recounted. It includes first in class in the Mille Miglia of 1933, victory in the French Grand Prix 1100-c.c. race and all international Class G records from the flying mile to one hour. Six inches wider and eight inches longer than the J Midgets, the K introduced a secondary steering arm, to take up road shock, and a pre-selector gearbox. In the Mille Miglia these cars exceeded 110 m.p.h. in the hands of such drivers as Earl Howe, Count Lurani, George Eyston, Tim Birkin and Bernard Rubin; on the other hand, plugs oiled constantly and Eyston and Lurani made 157 plug changes in the 1000 miles.

Where the K had magneto ignition, the L used a coil, and this car too proved itself in racing, finishing second to the K-3 in the 500-mile race of the British Racing Drivers' Club with a 92·24 average; at Montlhéry it took the 200-mile record with an average of 80·49. This, be it remembered, was an

Courtesy of Nuffield Exports Ltd.]

The TD is known all over the world. Its top speed of about 80 m.p.h. is raised slightly in Mark II modification, which usually has cycle wings

unsupercharged car in the early 1930s. It was succeeded by the N Magnette, a 1271-c.c. 6-cylinder whose NE modification, weighing about 16 cwt., gave M.G. its third T.T. victory, despite the very fierce threats of Rolls-Bentley and Lagonda.

In contrast to the J engines' 2-bearing crankshafts, the K and L cars had intermediate main bearings. Now M.G. was ready to revert to a Midget, which was to be designated the PA, and for this, as well as for the Q and R types, a cut-down K engine was designed—four 57×83 cylinders, 847 c.c., in which the ball race used in the front main bearing of the J was replaced by white metal. The PA had 6·2:1 compression, giving 35 h.p. at 5600 r.p.m. Side by side with the PA the company made a 6-cylinder counterpart, the 1271-c.c. NA Magnette.

The PA was immensely popular because of its speed, durability and exceptional handling, but more power was wanted and it was bored out to 60 mm. in the PB model, raising compression to 6·8 and horsepower, with wider rings, to 43·3. While both P cars were ostensibly not racing cars, the PA was sent to Le Mans in 1935 in custody of an all-woman team, whose members drove the cars from Abingdon to Le Mans and without exception qualified the cars for the biennial Rudge-Whitworth Trophy, all cars averaging over 53 m.p.h. and, among them, requiring throughout the race only the replacement of one tail-light bulb. However, the qualifications were never brought to maturity because in 1935 M.G. withdrew from racing.

Before that, however, the works had laid down the Q racing Midget, with K-3 wheelbase and 3 ft. 9 in. track. Its 746-c.c. engine was almost as powerful as the previous year's 1100-c.c., and it was fitted with a Wilson pre-selector gearbox with a safety clutch designed to slip automatically when that was desirable on shifts. The Q was built without road-racing equipment, being designed solely as a track car. Experiments with independent suspension developed this into the monoposto R.

The company's withdrawal from racing, however, did not mean the end of the marque in competition.

The TC, shown here, was identical in appearance to TA and TB. It was the last model to use large wire wheels as standard equipment

[Courtesy of Nuffield Exports Ltd.

51

Private owners continued to race their cars and to score one victory after another. And the company stayed on in the lonely world of land-speed record runs, building and modifying experimental cars for George Eyston and Goldie Gardner to race against nothing but time and death on the Autobahnen of Germany and the salt flats of Utah.

Hence the successor to the P types was the sports T series, which began in 1936 with the TA, a less austere but still very elegant version of the P in coachwork, with hydraulic brakes. Its wheelbase was just three-sixteenths of an inch shorter than that of the K-3 and its track, in the first three series, through TC, was 3 ft. 9 in. These cars, weighing close to 18 cwt., carried a 1250-c.c. engine, $66 \cdot 5 \times 90$ (1292 c.c. and $63 \cdot 5 \times 102$ in the TA) with pushrod overhead valves and $54 \cdot 4$ b.h.p. (50 in the TA). Like the P type, the first to abandon bucket seats, they had bench backs. All were open two-seaters and the TB also offered a two-seater drop-head. And all had synchromesh gearboxes with well-spaced ratios.

The TC was the first M.G. to become widely known in the United States, where it is still loved despite its undeniable mechanical inferiority to the TD, which has an even better gearbox and very much superior steering and comfort. The TD, introduced in 1950, was the first M.G. to adopt box-section chassis, independent front suspension and rack-and-pinion steering. (The so-called Mark II TD, with extra fuel pump and other modifications, developed 57 b.h.p. at 5500 r.p.m., against the standard T output of $54 \cdot 4$ at 5200.) It was also the first M.G. to adopt disc wheels—at first virtually solid, then altered to perforated design for better brake cooling. In 1954 the TD's lines were softened somewhat for the TF, but it still retained the vintage emphasis on line rather than mass—undoubtedly an important factor in its sales. The TF, using at first the Mark II power plant, was in turn stepped up to 1500 c.c.— 72×90—and 63 b.h.p. at 5500 r.p.m., and wire wheels were offered as an option.

The TF ceased production in 1955; but four years earlier the prototype of its successor, the A, was running at Le Mans, for M.G. had returned to the races, determined to regain its old prestige. The new car, without regard for the nostalgia of the classicists, scrapped the last vestige of T styling, with its incontrovertible high drag, for a new, low envelope body designed by Sydney Enever, who had so much to do with the experimental record cars. This was first fitted on the TD chassis, but a new engine was designed for it and appeared at Le Mans in 1955. Both 1955 cars, using 73×89 engines developing 68 b.h.p. at 5500 r.p.m., finished well up in general classification.

Technically, both TF and A types race in the same class with such other 1·5-litre-and-under cars as Porsche, and TD's against Alfa Romeo Giulietta. But in each instance the Continental car consistently runs rings round the M.G., and in 1958, to redress the balance, M.G. brought out a twin-camshaft variant of the A. Its 1589 c.c., delivering 97 b.h.p. at 5000 r.p.m. and 108 at 6700, puts it on theoretically equal terms with the Porsche 1600, and its Dunlop disc brakes all round effectively counter its approximate top speed of 120 m.p.h. Like the standard pushrod A, it is available as either a roadster or a fixed-head coupé, both of which are relatively heavy —18 cwt., a weight that to some extent militates against the high b.h.p. and 9·9:1 compression. It was followed a year later by the 1600—a pushrod engine of the same capacity.

The TF was the last of the classic-coachwork M.G.s. Knock-off wire wheels were optional

This new twin-cam M.G.-A is identical in appearance with the standard A except for this car's knock-off disc wheels. Standard car offers bolt-on discs or knock-off wire wheels, retains drum brakes all round

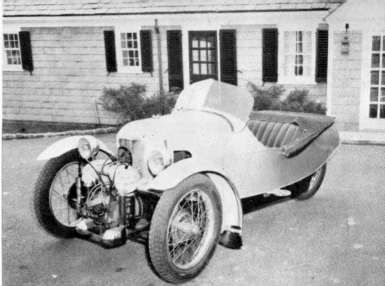

[*Courtesy of Morgan Motor Co. Ltd.*

Photograph by Clinton Martin]

H. F. S. Morgan in his first car. The sliding-pillar front suspension, still in use 50 years later, is clearly visible

A characteristic three-wheeler of the between-wars period, powered by 1000-c.c. air-cooled J.A.P. engine

MORGAN

Two admirable and endearing facets of British national character are exemplified by the Morgan: disregard for what the rest of the world may be up to, and loyalty to a proved pattern of simplicity.

H. F. S. Morgan founded the Morgan Motor Car Co. Ltd. in 1909 after thorough schooling and practical experience in engineering. His first car, a three-wheeler, was immediately successful in tests because of its rigid frame, light weight and independent front-wheel suspension—a type that is basically still in use on today's Morgans. It consists of a sliding pillar with special spiral springs and steering dampers. Only Lancia has stayed so long with this type of suspension; and both marques have amply demonstrated its worth.

The first Morgan was built solely for its designer's pleasure, with no idea of sales; but everyone who saw it wanted a replica and, with the help of his father, a minister, Morgan began to build commercially. He received his first patent in 1910 on the basis of drawings supplied to his order by a young man who is now Sir John Black of Standard Motors. Though the first cars were single-seaters, Morgan soon changed to two-seaters and won a gold medal in a 1911 reliability trial.

Shortly before the First World War the company entered cycle-car racing, with considerable success. In 1913 Morgan himself broke the 1100-c.c. one-hour record with just under 60 miles; in the same year another of his cars won the Grand Prix d'Amiens against a number of four-wheelers.

As early as 1915 Morgan produced an experimental four-seater on his tricycle chassis, notable for having its single wheel, which was the driving wheel, at the rear. Initially this was also the only braked wheel, but trials experience showed the wisdom of front-wheel braking as well. For the first 22 years of its existence the Morgan had only two forward speeds and no

reverse, but in 1931 it adopted a conventional three-speed-forward-and-one-reverse gearbox and initiated detachable wheels.

Two years later the marque established a number of world records, including a one-hour record of more than 100 miles. But by this time the competition of the four-wheeled car had become much more intense and Morgan was virtually alone in continuing to build the tricycle. It was powered with a twin-cylinder air-cooled engine mounted ahead of the bonnet, which covered only the front part of the cockpit. Morgan had experimented with a conventional chassis as long ago as 1914 but had put it aside in view of the proved performance and popularity of his current design. By 1936, however, the three-wheeler had become wholly obsolete, though Morgan continued to build it until 1950, with a Ford engine.

In 1936 the first rectangular Morgans were shown in Paris and London, designated the 4/4 to describe the change in the number of cylinders as well as wheels. The first cars mounted a 1100-c.c. Coventry-Climax engine, 63×90, with overhead inlet valves and side exhaust. This shot it along the roads at honest 75-m.p.h. speeds and it handled, then as now, admirably. Spurred by the three-wheeler's record of 350 first prizes in speed and reliability trials, the new car had something to aim at.

After the 1939–45 war Morgan at first used a Ford engine and later adopted a 1200-c.c. engine specially built for it by Standard, but it was soon outclassed in competition and in 1950 it changed to the 2088-c.c. (85×92) Standard engine, which produced 70 b.h.p. at 4200 r.p.m. With this engine Morgan continued to use a separate close-ratio 4-speed gearbox, centrally situated; and the 17-cwt. car ran very fast. The specially-designed chassis featured Z-shaped side members with five cross-members, of which the rear one was tubular. Inside this the semi-elliptic springs slid on specially designed blocks.

In 1954 Morgan offered optionally the Triumph

53

engine, at that time the 90-b.h.p. TR-2 (it is now available with the 100-b.h.p. TR-3), which not only put it in the 2-litre class but gave it a very honest 100 m.p.h. In this form it immediately began to defeat Triumphs in racing because of the Morgan's advantage in lightness—about 300 lb.—and it continued to dominate Class E production cars until the advent of the A.C.-Bristol. It is still not uncommon to see a well-prepared Morgan, in the hands of an outstanding driver, finish ahead of even the A.C.

Body styles became more varied and the Morgan was made available not only in the standard two-seater form but also as a four-seater tourer, a two-seater drop-head and a four-seater d.h.c. In these cars the windows slide along the doors and are not removable. Despite these changes, basic line remained unchanged and even today, when the handsome flat radiator that often made one think of some of the Bugattis has been sloped and softened into something more nearly approaching contemporary trends, the Morgan retains the true classic line—and it is indeed the only marque left anywhere that has not succumbed to envelope styling. Rather interestingly, it seems not to have suffered aerodynamically, for the cars it defeats today are all envelope-bodied.

In 1955 Morgan, while retaining the Triumph engine option, also reverted to a smaller class by giving, in the Series II, the choice of a virtually standard 1172-c.c. Ford engine in the two-seater. A side-valve power plant measuring 63 × 92, the Ford is principally noted for its durability. The 2088-c.c. Standard Vanguard engine was also maintained as an option for all body styles.

[*Photograph by Inga M. Naylor*

The Morgan Plus Four changed little from its introduction in 1936. This is the two-seater. Folding windscreen was standard

Courtesy of the Long Island Automotive Museum]

The current Morgan offers only the rigid windscreen, easily removed for racing. Radiator sweeps back into bonnet. Knock-off wire wheels are available as an extra

NAPIER
HUTTON

Among the many distinctions of the Napier are three interesting firsts. Napier was the first British car to race abroad; it was the first to build a 6-cylinder production car; and it introduced Napier green as Britain's racing colour: this as a tribute to the Irish in 1903, when the Gordon Bennett Race was run in their country.

D. Napier & Sons was a firm manufacturing weighing machines of such quality that the Bank of England designated the company to make the machines with which it weighed its coins. Young Montague Napier became interested in S. F. Edge's Panhard, which had finished second in the 1896 Paris–Marseilles race, and not only converted it from tiller- to wheel-steering but also built an engine for it; this unit was so excellent that he was soon being asked for more.

By 1900 Napier was building cars. Edge and the Hon. C. S. Rolls drove a 16-h.p. Napier in that year's Paris–Toulouse race but dropped out because of mechanical failure. However, Napier continued to build all-out racing cars and tourers as well; and Edge became his chief salesman. To Edge, the best weapon in the salesman's arsenal was competition successes; and he was as good a driver as he was a salesman.

Their first car was a 2-cylinder that, despite a break in its aluminium carburetter, won its class in the 1000-mile Trial of 1900 and finished second over-all. The first 4-cylinder Napier was the Paris–Toulouse car; this was followed by a giant of 165 × 190 mm. intended for the 1901 Paris–Berlin and Gordon Bennett races, but it destroyed its tyres and the engine was later adapted to marine use. In 1902 Napier returned to the Gordon Bennett with an untested 30-h.p. car of the then strange square proportions of 127 × 127. The course lay from Paris to Innsbruck; the Paris–Vienna race was being run concurrently.

Disaster was their truest companion: *en route* to Dover, a cylinder head cracked (it was replaced during the Channel crossing); in France, second gear failed because the pinion had not been hardened, and Napier straightened the teeth by hand and hardened the gear in a local workshop; the next day the gearbox had to come out again because a spacer had been left out. Despite three days and nights without sleep, Edge and his cousin, Cecil, set out at the appointed time, but their brakes failed in the Arlberg Pass. Nonetheless they completed the course, the only competitors to do so, and won the Trophy.

Another Napier began an equally remarkable accomplishment in the same year. Mr. and Mrs. Charles J. Glidden—the founders of the Glidden Tour—ordered a 24-h.p. 4-cylinder car for a world tour and in the next few years rolled up 46,000 miles with no more trouble than a half-hour roadside repair. At one point he fitted flanged wheels to his car and drove it some 2000 miles on the Canadian Pacific tracks to Vancouver; in all he ranged from the Antipodes to the Arctic Circle in his 1902 Napier.

While Glidden was crossing the Arctic Circle, Napier was preparing a new machine. He had always scorned hot-tube ignition, and as early as 1902 he had insisted on live rear axles rather than chains; in 1903 he introduced the first production 6-cylinder car, of 18 h.p. It did well in Continental hill-climbs and set a new land speed record in Florida at 104 m.p.h.; as soon as Brooklands opened, S. F. Edge took the six out with a pledge to average 60 m.p.h. for 24 hours. Everyone laughed, but Edge completed his mission with a 24-hour average of 66 m.p.h. This feat also did much to popularize the detachable wire wheel. In 1908 Napier won the Isle of Man Tourist Trophy race, though for various reasons the car was then called the Hutton.

Unfortunately, the company abandoned racing in that year, though it continued to build high-quality automobiles into the mid-1920s and, as we know, very nearly brought out a Bentley-designed car. During the First World War Napier built first-rate aeroplane engines of 12 cylinders in an unusual arrangement: they consisted, in effect, of a V-8 engine with a third bank of cylinders set into the V. These engines were dropped into special record cars for Sir Henry Seagrave and John Cobb, the first of whom achieved 231 m.p.h. with his Napier Lion-engined Golden Arrow in 1929. Linking two Lions in a Railton-designed car, Cobb set a still-unbroken record of 394·196 m.p.h. in 1948. The last passenger cars built by the firm were in the Rolls-Royce class and cost even more.

Napiers were never small cars. The 1901 machine withdrawn from the Gordon Bennett had a 16-litre engine and weighed three and a half tons; it developed 102 b.h.p. at 800 r.p.m. and 85 m.p.h. was claimed for it. It had no throttle, ignition adjustment being the sole means of regulating engine speed. The

Courtesy of D. R. Grossmark]

This 2-cylinder 1900 car is the earliest surviving Napier. Still used in Veteran Car Club (G.B.) events, the 8-h.p. model has four reverse as well as four forward speeds, using two ring gears and only one pinion. Both pistons are on the same crankshaft throw but fire alternately. Note chain drive and solid tyres

Courtesy of D. Napier & Son Ltd.]

The first 4-cylinder car appeared late in 1900. Horizontal radiator tubing was employed

The 16-litre car built for the 1901 Gordon Bennett; S. F. Edge at wheel. Note over-the-shoulder hand brake behind him

Courtesy of D. Napier & Son Ltd.]

The 30-h.p. winner of the 1902 Gordon Bennett was the first Napier to use live axle. Edge is at the wheel, Montague Napier beside him

Samson—the 6-cylinder L48—in original form. Changing these clincher-rim tyres—wheels were not demountable—was a bugbear in competition

The over-square (127 × 102) 60-h.p. sporting 6-cylinder car of 1907, photographed in 1958 at Napier's 150th Anniversary Rally. Radiator is not original

aluminium cylinders had triple automatic inlet valves and, for the first time, the clutch was all metal, in contrast to the leather-cone type used earlier.

The 1902 Gordon Bennett winner was incredibly lighter: complete, it weighed less than one ton and the engine was 6·4 litres developing 44·5 b.h.p. for 75 m.p.h., with quadruple valves. The chassis was

of wood, armoured with steel, a practice followed in the 1903 Gordon Bennett cars of 7708 c.c. and 45 h.p. (the increase was in cylinder bore, which was raised by 12·7 mm.). Three-speed gearboxes, as in 1902, were used, and the cars weighed very little more. One of the 1903 cars was of 80 h.p., with a 13-litre engine in a pressed steel chassis; tie rods and radius arms strengthened the rear axle; 85 m.p.h. was claimed. It is hard to believe that this giant weighed only 200 lb. more than the 45-h.p. cars.

Only in 1904 did Napier yield on automatic valving and adopt mechanical operation, though the valves remained overhead. The so-called 100-h.p. car, of the same over-square dimensions as the 1903 80-h.p.—165·1 × 152·4—was clocked at 82·26 m.p.h. for the flying kilometre and was supposed to be capable of 90 m.p.h. Though no Napier car finished the 1904 Gordon Bennett, which was run in Germany's Taunus Mountains over an 87-mile circuit (four laps), Edge's car lapped in 1 hour 37¾ minutes. The L48 racing car of six cylinders, produced this year, relied on a 2-speed gearbox and an engine of 158·7 × 127, with tubular radiators running vertically on either side of the bonnet. This car, after excellent performances in Britain and on the Continent, set the land-speed record in Florida. Known as Samson, it ran a private match race at Brooklands against an 18-litre FIAT called Mephistopheles. Samson reached 70 m.p.h. in its bottom gear and scored a lap speed of 113 m.p.h., with a handsome lead, but the crankshaft broke at the end of the third lap.

The last Napiers to race in major competition did not even wear the maker's name, so the victory was chalked up to Hutton in the records. The (Napier-) Huttons were of two models for this race, the only specified limitation of which was a 101·6 mm. bore. One car had a 177·8 mm. stroke, the other 203·2 mm. The 4-cylinder engines were cast in pairs, and the traditional Napier pattern of inlet above exhaust valves was abandoned for straight side-

The 1908 Napier-built Hutton, driven by Cecil Clutton in a recent Anglo-American Rally. Detachable wire wheels are those that caused 1908 Napier to be banned from 1908 Grand Prix de France

56

valve construction. Ignition was by coil and magneto, multiple-disc clutch was fitted and there were shock absorbers at all corners. Wearing detachable Rudge-Whitworth wire wheels, the complete car weighed about 26¾ cwt. Despite the furious rivalry of two Darracqs, the shorter-stroked Hutton won the race at 50·25 m.p.h.

PEERLESS

One of the newest marques in sports cars, the Triumph-based Peerless was introduced with a flawless Le Mans appearance in 1958. Making no effort at a class win, Peerless Cars Ltd. looked on the 24-hour classic as an excellent means of testing its new car for all the world to see. The result justified the firm's confidence: the car ran without trouble for the full 24 hours, averaging 84 m.p.h. and 22 miles per gallon at this speed.

One of the few full four-seater gran turismo cars on the market, the Peerless uses the TR-3 engine and gearbox (overdrive on the three top gears is an option) in a tubular space frame with de Dion tube at the rear. Front suspension, of course, is independent; semi-elliptics are used at the rear with double-piston shock absorbers, in contrast to the telescopic type at the front. Disc brakes are fitted on the front wheels. A true dual-purpose car, the Peerless has very adequate luggage space without interfering with the passenger compartment. Instrumentation is virtually the same as that of the TR-3.

The body is all glass fibre and, unlike those of

Photograph by Michael P. Clapham]
Even bumpers are plastic on the Peerless gran turismo. Knock-off wire wheels are optional; bolt-on discs are standard

many G.T. cars, the rear quarter windows swing open. Evidence of the race-bred design may be found in the mounting of the fuel tanks: one in each side of the body, just behind the door. Each tank holds about nine gallons and feeds separately to the two carburetters; a switch on the dashboard permits the driver to select which tank he wishes to use. Wheelbase is 7 ft. 10½ in., track is 4 ft. 3 in., and total weight is about 18 cwt.

The space frame and the aerodynamic coachwork enable the TR-3 power unit and drive train to deliver a top speed of 117 m.p.h. and to accelerate from rest to 50 m.p.h. in 6·8 seconds, to 80 m.p.h. in 17·5 seconds.

RILEY

Though the Riley Motor Co. started building automobiles before the turn of the century, its first sporting vehicle did not appear until 1924, when the 11/40 Redwing of 1½ litres came as a kind of precursor of the fine cars in store. It was in 1926 that Riley displayed at Olympia the first of that series of sports cars that in many respects showed the way to the designers of today's high-performance machines. This engine was the creation of Hugh Rose, who, as is set forth earlier, duplicated it as closely as he could for Lea-Francis.

This first Riley sports was an 1100-c.c. unit with two camshafts set in the cylinder block, both being exhaust camshafts in order to achieve higher engine speeds. The valves were set at 45 degrees in hemispherical combustion chambers and the crankshaft, though having only two bearings, was exceptionally solid. The first tourers were quite heavy for this engine—they weighed almost a ton—and could barely reach 60 m.p.h. Fabric-bodied Monaco saloons were also mounted on this chassis and, though they were never intended for sporting use, some of them are raced today in vintage events.

The Riley 9, as it was known, aroused the interest

of J. G. Parry Thomas and he was well advanced on modifications when he was killed in 1927 while attempting a new speed record on Pendine Sands. Reid Railton took over and evolved the famous Brooklands (its true designation was the Speed Model, though virtually no one calls it that) that produced 50 b.h.p. at 5000 r.p.m. and was a genuine 90-m.p.h. car. The Brooklands appeared at a time when the 1100-c.c. class was a virtual Continental monopoly; but the shortened and lowered Brooklands version of the Riley took the international six-hour record at 85·2 m.p.h. in 1928 and two years later won its class in the Tourist Trophy, finished first over-all in the Irish Grand Prix and became the first unsupercharged car to clock 100 miles in the hour.

These achievements arose out of the combination of a 9·8-cwt. car with well-chosen gear ratios to exploit the potential of the 4-cylinder 60·3 × 95·2 engine to the maximum. Worm-and-wheel steering and firm semi-elliptic springing all round contributed to exceptionally precise cornering. The 19-in. wheels had 13-in. brake drums; the wheelbase was just 8 ft.

[Courtesy of the Automobile-Club de l'Ouest

E. Duggan Kehoe's magnificent Brooklands ready for the start of the 1958 Rétrospective at Le Mans. This car finished sixth over-all and second in its class at Le Mans in 1934, when the first four 1100-c.c. cars home were Rileys

Copyright by Charles Dunn; courtesy of Capt. R. F. E. Baker]

The March Special, another creation of the then Earl of March, was a first-rate dual-purpose car. This 26-year-old Riley is in daily use and averages 1000 miles a month, in addition to competition use. Light aluminium body contributes towards a maximum speed of 78 m.p.h.

[Courtesy of Nuffield Exports Ltd.

The 6-cylinder Grebe was the direct ancestor of the M.P.H.

Courtesy of the Riley Register]

The 6-cylinder M.P.H.

[Courtesy of the Riley Register

The Kestrel shown here is the 1½-litre 6-cylinder model. It was one of the few closed sports cars of the 1930s

Photograph by Michael P. Clapham]

The famous Imp, still very much in demand today

[Photograph by Dr. A. T. Birmingham

This Ulster Imp, 24 years old, with pointed tail and external exhaust system, is shown at the old Riley works in 1957. It could top 90 m.p.h.

Courtesy of Nuffield Exports Ltd.]

The Ulster Sprite, which touched 90 m.p.h., carried a token passenger door to comply with F.I.A. regulations. Brake backing plates and 17-pint sump were in magnesium. Sprite was the only sports Riley whose brakes were not adjustable from inside car

In 1928 Riley offered a 6-cylinder engine which was in effect the 9½. In the short-lived M.P.H. model this engine was offered with a 95·2-mm. stroke and a choice of three bores ranging from 57 to 62 mm., swept volume accordingly varying from 1458 to 1726 c.c. Compression on all these engines was 7:1 and a 3-bearing counterbalanced crankshaft was used. Like the Imp, the M.P.H. had a 4-speed pre-selector gearbox (Wilson) and multiplate automatic clutch. But the Imp was a 4-cylinder car using the regular 1087-c.c. engine mounted in the Brooklands. Its more advanced version, the Ulster Imp, used the 1087-c.c. engine too, but for this model the compression was raised to 8·25:1 and the crankshaft was fitted with detachable weights. The capacity of the sump was doubled to 14 pints, a more powerful oil pump was supplied and only a conventional manual 4-speed gearbox was fitted. All these Riley gearboxes, by the way, were in unit with the engines; the Ulster Imp had probably the closest ratios, from 11·78 in bottom to 4·77 in top; the clutch, naturally, was foot-operated and was of the single-plate type.

The September, 1929, Shelsley Walsh climb was a Riley monopoly: they won all seven categories. A saloon set a class record for 1000 miles at 65·83; in the London–Edinburgh Reliability Trial of that

year the marque took 19 gold medals, five silver and two bronze. In the next year six Rileys entered the Monte Carlo Rally and all finished excellently. It was in 1930, too, that a Brooklands was driven from New York to Los Angeles over all kinds of roads in five days and 20 hours for an average speed, including all stops, of 41 m.p.h. The final 130 miles were covered in exactly two hours.

Riley was one of the few makes of its period to produce a closed car of sporting character. This was the Kestrel, which appeared variously with the 1100-c.c. engine, the smallest and largest 6-cylinder units of the M.P.H. model and the enlarged 4-cylinder Sprite engine, the last made by the company before it passed to Nuffield in 1938. This Sprite engine, 69 × 100, produced 54 b.h.p. from its 1496 c.c. with a compression ratio of only 6·8:1; it was fitted to choice with manual or pre-selector gearbox and, like the M.P.H., boasted three main bearings.

All these variations on the Riley theme amassed honours on British and foreign courses. Like the M.G., the Riley has been the school for many of today's top drivers; the 1958 world champion, Mike Hawthorn, started with an Imp in his teens and remained an active member of the Riley Register until his death. Today, as in their prime, Rileys of

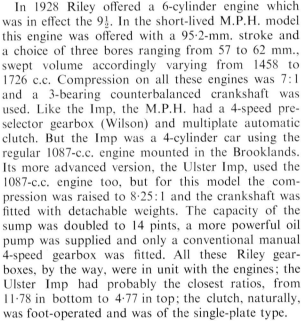

The last Sprite was the last real sports Riley. Like all the sports models, it had steering fully adjustable for wear

[Courtesy of the Riley Register

The 1950 car, retaining the twin cams high in the block and the inclined overhead valves, tried to marry post-war and vintage coachwork

Photograph by Loring Chandler]

all sizes prove themselves time and again the masters of larger and even of more powerful cars, thanks to their magnificent handling and more than adequate brakes. It is small wonder that they served as the springboard for one of Britain's most successful G.P. cars, the E.R.A.

After the 1939–45 war, Nuffield attempted to put Riley back into the sports category with a 2½-litre 4-cylinder (80·5 × 120) roadster and four-seater drophead, but this was a heavy model that lacked the bite and the handling of its ancestors and was withdrawn after a very few years despite a 1950 class win at Le Mans. Today's Riley is little more than the old radiator design on an M.G. Magnette body shell, chassis and engine, merely one more of the numerous products of the giant British Motor Corporation, born of the marriage of Nuffield and Austin.

The 1910 Silver Ghost, mechanically similar to the 1911 car that ran from London to Edinburgh and back in top gear in that year, then went at once to Brooklands and was timed at 78·26 m.p.h.

ROLLS-ROYCE

The aloof, sedate Rolls-Royce has been for so many generations the very symbol of detached *hauteur* and untroubled perfection that it is quite easy to forget how rugged a career the marque has had.

The Hon. Charles S. Rolls was a wealthy amateur of the mechanical arts when, in 1904, he first encountered the experimental 2-cylinder cars designed and built to an exceptionally high standard by a Manchester electrical engineer, F. H. Royce. Almost immediately the two men formed their partnership; and very nearly as quickly their combined names achieved that identity with the ultimate in excellence that has persisted ever since.

Their first cars were of bewildering variety: 2-, 3-, 4-, 6- and 8-cylinder engines, all with overhead inlet and side exhaust valves. In 1905 one of their 4-cylinder

cars finished second in the Isle of Man Tourist Trophy; the next year Rolls-Royce won outright. Their most successful model up to this time was the 30-h.p. six, whose speed was matched by its silence; and Claude Johnson, who had become their right hand, proposed that thereafter they standardize production on one model, the 40/50 shown at Olympia in 1907.

Soon to be known as the Silver Ghost, this was a 7-litre 6-cylinder engine of perfectly square proportions—114 × 114—with side valves; it developed 48 b.h.p. at 1200 r.p.m. and its compression ratio was only 3·2:1. The wet clutch was a fabric-lined cone type, controlling a 4-speed gearbox whose third gear was direct, top being an overdrive. The chassis was herculean; it had semi-elliptics all round. Royce himself designed both the single-jet carburetter and the coil and distributor that worked with the magneto. Even in those days of unpredictable drip lubrication, Royce's crankshaft was drilled and the engine was oiled by pressure. It was cast in two blocks of three cylinders each, and was silent and smooth at any speed in any gear.

Like H. F. S. Morgan, Royce was impervious to fads and novelties; he was, with Rolls, simply dedicated to the best. That this was not always, in the case of his engines, the most aesthetic was evident in another designer's appraisal of the Silver Ghost unit as "a triumph of workmanship over design". The distortion implicit in the comment was underlined by the ability of the Silver Ghost to move at a walk in top gear or to accelerate as effortlessly as a locomotive to its 55-m.p.h. maximum.

Such imperfections as disturbed Royce were soon eliminated: the noisy overdrive was abandoned in 1909, when the stroke was lengthened 7 mm. and the engine grew to the 7410-c.c. volume that was to characterize it for the next 17 years. The rear springs were made three-quarter elliptic about this time and altered to cantilever in 1912. Rolls-Royce has always refused to divulge the horsepower of its cars (and to explain its reticence), but experts estimate that late Edwardian Ghosts developed about 65 b.h.p. at 1750 r.p.m., giving a top speed around

The original Silver Ghost that made the famous 15,000-mile non-stop run. Still in service, it has completed over 500,000 miles

65 m.p.h. In 1911 a streamlined wingless car clocked 101·8 over a flying half-mile at Brooklands.

The punishing Alpine Trial naturally attracted the makers of a car that had done so well in the T.T. and had completed a non-stop 15,000-mile 1907 reliability run at a total mechanical replacement cost of £2 2s. 4d. Rolls, who had loved competition enough to ride as a mechanic if he could not get a drive, had been killed in an aeroplane crash in 1910; but in his tradition the firm prepared several cars for the Alpine contest by substituting 4-speed gearboxes, aluminium pistons and modified camshafts. They scored brilliantly against much larger cars and in 1914 the lone Rolls-Royce entry was the only one of the 75 starters to make a non-stop run. These were the famous Alpine Eagle cars that were the basis for the post-war Silver Ghost.

This car was very little different from its pre-war ancestor. The brakes, which had previously acted on the transmission, were now fitted into huge rear drums; Royce designed a new dynamo and starter motor. Compression rose to 3·8:1, horse-power and top speed to about 75 each at 2200 r.p.m. in a monobloc casting. Despite its undeniable weight, one of these cars triumphed over both a 30/98 Vauxhall and two 37·2-h.p. Hispano-Suizas in a Biarritz hill-climb in 1921.

This is about the last authenticated record of a Rolls-Royce in competition, though there are tales —which we have been unable to verify—of a barnstorming tour of United States tracks by a works team in the early 1920s. In 1924 the Ghost added front brakes, with mechanical servo operation; and right to the end of the model the car was equipped with a governor that could be set at any desired speed and depended on to maintain it regardless of external circumstances.

The Silver Ghost and its successors, the Phantom I and Phantom II, were built in Springfield, Mass., as well as in Derby for about 10 years, but, though these cars were constructed to the same exacting specifications as the British originals, they have never enjoyed the same repute—or resale value. The P-I, like the "baby" Rolls 20, was never considered particularly sporting, though its open models could clock 80 m.p.h., and it was not really a new design. The P-II, however, raised compression to 5·25:1 and, for the first time, mounted engine and gearbox in unit; it abandoned the cantilever springing and fitted semi-elliptics all round. One 1931 P-II with aluminium tourer coachwork, on a test in 1958, left a new MG-A far behind at a traffic light, and some P-II's were capable of considerably better than 90 m.p.h. These, however, were the last Rolls-Royces that could be said to have sporting qualities.

Photograph by Arthur Schuh;
courtesy of the Library of the Automobile Manufacturers' Association]
The 1913 Rolls during the 1947 Glidden Tour

Courtesy of Rolls-Royce Ltd.]
The 1914 Alpine Eagle, alone among the 75 starters to make a non-stop run. In the 1913 Alpine Trial the Rolls-Royce team took seven prizes

Photograph by Fred H. Sills]
This aluminium-bodied P-II tourer was built in 1931. This car is regularly driven between Illinois and Florida

61

[Courtesy of Rootes Motors Ltd.

The 1912 Singer 10 finished first in that year's R.A.C. Standard Car Race

Courtesy of "Motor Sport"]

Rare 1½-litre 6-cylinder Le Mans model

SINGER

The Singer began, like so many other makes, with a three-wheeler at the turn of the century. By 1909 it was offering four models, from a 7·9-h.p. 2-cylinder to a 24·8-h.p. 4-cylinder, and won its class in a 2000-mile reliability trial.

In 1910 and 1911 it had a number of triumphs, such as the 15-h.p. class at Brooklands with a 77-m.p.h. average, the flying half-mile having been covered at 81·25 m.p.h. Singer took three firsts in various Brooklands races and one each at Aston Hill-Climb and Shelsley Walsh. In a novel contest, a Singer raced an Henriot monoplane at Brooklands and won with 78 m.p.h., the plane finishing flat out at 40 m.p.h.

Brooklands was again Singer's arena in 1912, when the company introduced the famous Singer 10. This was a 1096-c.c. 4-cylinder engine—63 × 88—and the 3-speed gearbox was incorporated in the differential housing. This car lapped Brooklands at 64 m.p.h. and a team of three scored a number of wins there in that year. In 1913 the marque introduced an overhead camshaft and inclined valves on the 14, and the cylinders were cast in one piece. Another innovation was the integration of engine and rigid chassis: common practice at this time dictated the provision of a sub-frame to mount the engine firmly while the chassis proper whipped and flexed at the will of the terrain.

During most of the vintage period Singer was not outstanding. In 1928, however, the Singer 8 appeared, bringing the overhead camshaft into virtually the lowest price class. Properly tuned, this car could be propelled at better than 65 m.p.h. and in December of that year a Singer 8 set out to put a year of hill-climbing into one day at the steep Porlock ascent. Under Royal Automobile Club observation, it shuttled up and down all day, making 100 round trips in 15 hours and averaging eight minutes for each, chiefly in bottom gear. Thereafter known as the Porlock model, it was followed by the Kaye Don (after the famous driver) and then by one of the best known of all its models, the Singer 9.

Introduced in sports form in 1932, this 972-c.c. car won a Coupe des Glaciers in the Alpine and qualified at Le Mans the next year with a completely trouble-free run at 50 m.p.h. The 60 × 96-mm. engine could run safely up to 6000 r.p.m. with its solid 2-bearing crankshaft, but the gear ratios were considered remarkably inappropriate—5·57 top and 24·4 bottom in the Le Mans Speed Special! Nevertheless the marque was building its reputation with a succession of victories. In 1935, however, three Le Mans Singers had the same accident at the same place in the Ulster T.T.: the steering drop-arms broke. It was definitely ascertained that this was not the result of any inherent fault in the cars: the drivers had

62

The 1937 Singer Le Mans at the French circuit's 1958 Rétrospective

[Courtesy of the Automobile-Club de l'Ouest

The post-war SM1500 was last sports Singer and one of last British sports four-seaters

Photograph by Michael P. Clapham]

attempted a last-minute modification to improve the steering and had removed one part too many. Nonetheless the blow to the model's standing was severe.

Among Singer's pioneering innovations were independent front suspension as early as 1934 and, in the same year, a fluid drive permitting clutchless gear-shifting. After the Ulster disaster the company built a number of fast 6-cylinder 1½-litre cars, but its popularity had already begun to decline. The post-wat 1½-litre SM1500 continued the overhead camshaft design that had done so much to establish the marque earlier, but it never regained its former stature and in 1955 the company was absorbed by the Rootes Group.

SIDDELEY SPECIAL

In limousines, aircraft engines or armaments, Armstrong-Siddeley has always stood for top quality. The Siddeley Special that was offered to the sporting motorist from 1932 through 1937 was not an exception.

The 5-litre engine—88.9×133.4—was built very largely of light alloy, on the pattern of the company's successful aero engines. Fully counterbalanced and machined all over, the crankshaft ran on seven bearings and was fitted with a friction vibration damper. Overhead valves were pushrod driven and the six cylinders had wet liners. A 4-speed Wilson pre-selector gearbox was used with an automatic clutch. Both hand and foot brakes controlled all four wheels with servo assistance. The 35¾-cwt. tourer was clocked at 93 m.p.h. and would run smoothly in top gear at 6 m.p.h. A four-seater gran turismo coupé was also offered in coachwork that showed considerable appreciation of aerodynamic problems.

While the earlier Siddeley Specials were extensively used in rallies, there is no record of the car's having been raced. The Mark II, which appeared in 1936, was lengthened, the gear ratios were lowered and the car as a whole lost its sporting characteristics to an emphasis on luxury.

SQUIRE

One of the most expensive 1½-litre cars ever built in England was the Squire, which was in production only from 1934 through 1936. Adrian Squire was determined, like so many other Britons, to produce a sports car in British racing green that would be a match for Alfa Romeo and Bugatti, and every one of the very few cars he made was delivered with a 100-m.p.h. guarantee.

Powered by a supercharged Anzani engine with double overhead camshafts, the Squire employed the 4-speed Wilson pre-selector gearbox with fairly close ratios, separately mounted. Acceleration from rest to 60 m.p.h. was 10·5 seconds, a remarkable figure then and a sound one now. Compression was 6·8 : 1. Two chassis were offered throughout the life of the marque:

Courtesy of Armstrong Siddeley Motors Ltd.]
The Siddeley Special tourer was popular for rallies

102- and 123-in. wheelbase; the track was 54 in. on both models, and the short-chassis two-seater weighed 22½ cwt. The parallel channel-section frame members were cross-braced, by both tube and I-beam, in eleven places. Extra-wide semi-elliptic springs were pivoted at their inner ends and slid in trunnion rollers at their outer ends; radius rods were used to locate the front axle, and all shock absorbers were hydraulic.

Photograph by Charles J. McManus, Jr.]
One of the two Squires in the United States. Crankshaft-driven dynamotor is shrouded ahead of radiator. Double water-pumps compensate for lack of fan

Finned light alloy brake drums virtually filled the 18-in. wheel diameter and the hydraulic cylinders were fed with cooling air. Cockpit hand-brake adjustment also acted on the main brakes. The cam-and-lever steering was two turns lock to lock. An auxiliary oil reservoir kept the sump at the proper level, feeding through a float chamber. The valves were reciprocally inclined at 90 degrees, the camshafts were chain-driven. With all these advanced features, Squire used the outmoded dynastarter.

Performance was very nearly what was claimed. The Squire was almost as adhesive as a Bugatti, and, when the windscreen was folded, could reach a genuine 100 m.p.h. in the flying half-mile. Besides the two-seater, a long-chassis tourer and drop-head coupés on both chassis were offered. Only some 20 Squires were ever made, of which nine are believed to survive in Great Britain and two in the United States.

**The 15-h.p. runabout of 1909, ancestor of the 15/20 of
1914 and early 1920s**

**The Brooklands car as it is today; original paint was
diagonal black and white stripes. Only coachwork
differentiated it from standard models**

STRAKER-SQUIRE

Straker-Squire both derived from and contributed to aircraft engine development. The first cars built by Sidney Straker (uncle of the famous racing driver, H. Kensington Moir) and R. L. Squire, in 1906, were a licensed British version of the Cornilleau-Ste.-Beuve, a 25/30 side-valve six notable for the quality of its construction. In the following year the Straker-Squire offered two models, a 12/14 and a 16/20. Surviving the world-wide 1907–8 depression, Straker-Squire decided thereafter to build only one model at a time.

One of the first over-square engines, this was a 4-cylinder 14/16 of 87 × 85 mm., the cylinders being cast in pairs. Its lubrication system was probably unique: exhaust gas was put to work to blow oil from the scuttle-mounted tank into a drip-feed lubricator. The live-axle drive had three speeds, of which the top was direct.

The appointment of A. H. R. Fedden as chief engineer was responsible for the Straker-Squire's sporting reputation. He very quickly replaced the 14/16 with the 87 × 100 monobloc 15-h.p., soon lengthening the stroke to 120 mm. In 1914 Fedden developed this engine into the 3-litre 15/20 of 90 × 120, a special version of which, retaining the side valves that characterized the car, took several class records at Brooklands, clocking 98·74 m.p.h. for the flying half-mile. For the 1914 Tourist Trophy, however,

Fedden went to a 3·3 engine with a single overhead camshaft, driven by gears; this car produced 83 b.h.p. at 3200 r.p.m. and, though one of the two entered in the T.T. broke a piston, the other finished a good fourth in this extremely destructive race. It was these engines that contributed substantially to the Allies' aircraft engines in the First World War.

Early in 1919 Straker-Squire took a lesson from aviation and introduced an unusual 3920-c.c. engine of six separate cylinders measuring 80 × 130. An overhead camshaft was gear-driven from the front and, while the rocker lay-out was encased in aluminium, the valve springs were exposed. This unit produced 90 b.h.p. at 3750 r.p.m., using a balanced 7-bearing crankshaft, plate clutch and a separate 4-speed gearbox of excellent ratios. Long cantilever springs were employed in the rear. Engine bearings were scraped in by hand and each engine was bench-tested.

But it was three years before production models of the new car were on the market, though Kensington Moir had many successes with the prototypes before joining Aston Martin. The Straker-Squire held the test-hill record at Brooklands; it lapped the course at 103 m.p.h. Costs of so fine a car were high and the firm lacked the capital for intensive production and marketing of this 24/80. Straker's death in a hunting accident in the mid-1920s abruptly ended the marque's promising career.

**The windscreen, wings and running boards of the 6-
cylinder roadster were designed for quick removal for
competition**

**The 6-cylinder sports tourer had a self-starter, but
retained a starting handle in case of emergency**

[Copyright by Charles Dunn; courtesy of Sir Francis Samuelson, Bart.

Sunbeam's 1914 T.T. winner at Silverstone 40 years later, driven by Sir Francis Samuelson, its owner. Clutch is leather cone, crankshaft runs on ball bearings. Oil tank alongside drive shaft feeds crankcase by pump

The 3-litre 12/16 of 1914 in touring form

[Courtesy of Rootes Motors Ltd.

[Courtesy of the Library of the Automobile Manufacturers' Association

Sultan Ibrahim of Johore in his 24/60 Sunbeam of 1921

The 3-litre car that finished second at Le Mans in 1925, despite broken chassis, driven by S. C. H. Davis and Jean Chassagne. Normal wings were fitted for this race. Dry-sump lubrication, pioneered by Sunbeam, was standard

[Photograph by Anthony S. Heal

SUNBEAM
TALBOT
SUNBEAM-TALBOT

One of the oldest and most glamorous marques in Britain, the Sunbeam was first built in 1899 by John Marston and Thomas Cureton in Marston's cycle factory at Wolverhampton. Even then Sunbeam was pioneering: when virtually every other maker was using horizontal engines, its one-cylinder unit was vertical. From this Sunbeam went on to two cylinders; it was the second British marque to offer a 6-cylinder car, and a four was also made. But it was the advent of the famous Louis Coatalen as chief designer in 1909 that launched Sunbeam's renown.

Coatalen had learned his profession with Panhard, Clément, de Dion, Humber and Hillman. His first creation for Sunbeam was the famous 4-cylinder 95×135-mm. 16/20, which he raced himself very creditably. In 1911 he reduced this to the 80×120-mm. 12/16, with a T-head—i.e. inlet and exhaust valves on opposite sides of the cylinders—revising the engine in 1912 to an L-head—both valves on the same side—and a 30-mm. longer stroke. His 1911 streamlined racer, the Nautilus, lapped Brooklands at 77·54 m.p.h.; the next year it was developed into an 80×160-mm. 4-cylinder engine with overhead camshaft and four valves per cylinder. The 1911 six of 90×160 and 25/30-h.p. took 17 Brooklands records, lapping at 75·66 m.p.h. for 12 non-stop hours.

Until 1911 Sunbeam owners had the choice of chain or shaft drive; but then the former was discontinued. The firm made its first serious racing effort in that year's Coupe de l'Auto at Dieppe; the next year it swept the first three places in that race and third, fourth and fifth in the French Grand Prix against much larger cars. The Sunbeams were virtually standard 3-litre (80×149) 12/16's, with side valves (one of them, in monoposto form, took the 12-hour world record by covering just short of 911 miles—better than the 6-cylinder car's Brooklands record). With increased performance, the 12/16 finished third in the 1913 Coupe de l'Auto, making the only non-stop run, and Coatalen felt ready for the Tourist Trophy, especially after his $4\frac{1}{2}$-litre sixes, driven by Jean Chassagne and Dario Resta, finished third and sixth to huge Continental cars in the 1913 Grand Prix de l'Automobile-Club de France. An experimental 9-litre V-12 Sunbeam was also built at this time: it topped 120 m.p.h. and took the one-hour record at 107·95. This was the start of Sunbeam's many assaults on the land-speed record.

The 12/16 was redesigned for the 1914 T.T. along lines laid down by Ernest Henry's successful Peugeot engines. Coatalen switched to overhead valves with twin overhead camshafts, using four valves for each of the four $81·5 \times 156$ cylinders. Driven by Kenelm Lee Guinness (who originated the K.L.G. spark plug), the new car won the Isle of Man race at an average speed of 56·4 m.p.h., covering 600 miles in 10 hours 37¾ minutes and taking a trophy for the 16 fastest mountain road climbs. It was not raced again by the works; a new owner installed a standard tourer body and used it in this form for many years until it was purchased by Sir Francis Samuelson, who restored the original bodywork and successfully competes with the 1914 car today.

Sunbeam also made a number of Indianapolis appearances during the First World War, generally with pre-war cars except for a 4·9 six that was somehow built just in time for the 1916 American race, in which it finished fourth. The list of Sunbeam triumphs, then and since, would very nearly make a book of its own and is set forth in detail in Ian Nickols' and Kent Karslake's fine history, *Motoring Entente*.

The first post-war high-performance car was the 4½-litre 24/60 of 1921, which used the old 25/30 engine with pushrod overhead valves in a very much lighter frame. But one of the greatest Sunbeams ever built came just four years later: the twin-cam 3-litre with six 75 × 110 cylinders—the first d.o.h.c. car to be offered in production except for Ballot's 50 cars of 1923. The new Sunbeam delivered 90 b.h.p. at 3800 r.p.m. and would exceed 90 m.p.h. in road trim and tune. Servo brakes were standard and gearbox and steering were excellent. The chassis, however, was quite long—the wheelbase was 130 in.—and disproportionately narrow—54 in.; with the long cantilever rear springs the Sunbeam earned a certain notoriety for dubious control at high speed that tended to nullify the advantages it otherwise boasted over the 3-litre Bentley. The 3-litre Sunbeam finished second at Le Mans in its first year and won various Brooklands contests; the blown 1928 model delivered 138 b.h.p. at 3800 r.p.m. Blown or unblown, the 3-litre was for many years the identification of the enthusiast. As late as 1956 all the original cars of this model were still running.

In 1920 Sunbeam had combined with the French Talbot-Darracq firm, a fact that has done nothing to ease the task of the historian or the connoisseur. A few years later Sunbeam's racing department was exported across the Channel; but before that Coatalen once more tried his hand at improving on Henry's design for the 3-litre G.P. of 1921. This car, modelled

The 1913 Talbot 25/50 excelled in hill-climbs. Cylinders were cast in pairs; 4½-litre engine exceeded 70 m.p.h. This model was continued into the 1920s

on Henry's Ballot, was a 65 × 112 eight-in-line, with dual valving and twin cams: its advantage over the Ballot lay in the use of plain bearings and pressure lubrication. It did not start in the G.P. after all, but it won the next year's T.T. In that same year Ballot abandoned racing, so Coatalen was able to hire Henry; but the only innovation he could produce was a 68 × 136 four using a 3-speed gearbox, and this combination was not even spectacularly unsuccessful.

Coatalen's admiration swooped farther south, to FIAT's Vincent Bertarione, whom he lured to the S.T.D. complex and who produced a smaller (67 × 94) 1922 FIAT that Coatalen mounted in his 1922 Henry-designed chassis, which still employed an engine sub-frame. This car took first, second and fourth in the French G.P. The ingenious Bertarione supercharged it for 1924—he was the first engineer to compress the mixture of air and fuel, as is done today: previously the air alone had been compressed—to be the year's swiftest car with 138 b.h.p. at 5500 r.p.m., achieving 125 m.p.h. Experts consider the Italian's 1926 1½-litre straight eight—which was labelled a Talbot—his finest design, aided by an extremely stiff chassis. But in 1927 S.T.D. abandoned racing and the car was never exploited.

Much of the racing development was carried over into the sports car: for example, both the 24/60 and the 16/40 (the post-war development of the 12/16) could be had with overhead cams and dual valves, though very few were built in this form and no survivors are known, according to *The Vintage Motor Car*. These were joined by the 14, a 72 × 120-mm. 2-litre four using overhead pushrod valves and an aluminium block into which cylinder liners were shrunk. The block was later changed to cast iron, and the coil ignition gave way to a magneto, hand control replacing automatic. The gearbox had three speeds. One of the first British firms to offer 4-wheel brakes, Sunbeam made them optional as early as 1923.

A new sports Sunbeam arrived in 1924: the 75 × 120-mm., 2120-c.c., 4-cylinder 14/40, which gave 50 b.h.p. at 3000 r.p.m. But three years later all the Sunbeam models, including the many out-and-out touring cars of unexceptionable but also unexceptional performance, began to decline in achievement

The A-12 Talbot of 1918 of 1750 c.c. was Roesch's first design for this marque. Pressed steel box that was rear cross-member of chassis carried tools and spare out of sight

[Photograph by M. R. M. Porter

The 14/45 Talbot designed by Roesch weighs about 25 cwt. Three fan blades on flywheel rim supplement cooling; no radiator fan is fitted. This 1927 car is in daily use in India

Courtesy of "Motor Sport"]

The Talbot 105 sports saloon evidences Roesch's insistence on visibility. At that time sports cars were expected to use heavy chassis built for saloons

[Photograph by Bryan Smith

This 105 Brooklands tourer, now used daily in Johannesburg, is one of the team that won first three places in Brooklands 500 Miles. In recent years it has beaten an XK-120 Jaguar

Photograph by Bryan Smith]

This is the 105 driven by Mr. and Mrs. Tommy Wisdom in the 1934 Alpine Trial and later fitted with 110 engine to lap Brooklands at 129·7 m.p.h. It, too, is now in daily use in South Africa, with 110 engine. Owner has nick-named it Cassius for its "lean and hungry look"

and quality. The post-vintage cars scored few successes, though the vintage models kept the marque's honour high right up to the start of the Second World War. In 1935 the Sunbeam company was so deeply in a financial slough that it had to be pulled out by the Rootes Group, in which its identity was soon submerged; only the name remained.

A few months earlier, Rootes had also purchased Clément-Talbot Ltd., which had been a part of the original Sunbeam-Talbot-Darracq complex. The French branch remained independent and is discussed in the section on French cars. But Talbot's international character had been established as early as 1903, when D. M. Weigel, who held the British concession for Clément-Bayard cars, persuaded the Earl of Shrewsbury and Talbot to set up the British manufacturing firm of Clément-Talbot Ltd.

Adolphe Clément, born in France in 1855, had studied engineering, gone into the bicycle business and made a fortune by acquiring the French rights to the new Dunlop pneumatic tyre. After investing

some of this wealth in the manufacture of motor-cycles and rear-engined cycle-cars, he determined to build full-size automobiles and produced his first in 1901 with an engine designed by a Commandant Krebs, one of Panhard's directors. Clément's next car ran in the Paris–Berlin race; but he could not market under his own name for, during one of his many ruthless financial campaigns, he had sold the right to do so. Since his factory was in Mézières, which was graced by a statue of the legendary Chevalier Bayard, he added that name to his own.

The first Clément-Bayards, some of them square (160 × 160) and over-square (185 × 160), ran creditably for a half-dozen years in such events as Paris–Vienna, Paris–Madrid, the Argonne and Ardennes Circuits and the French G.P. They were all shaft-driven 4-cylinder cars ranging from 18 h.p. in 1903 to 135 in 1908. While Clément continued to build his own cars in France until about 1912, he supplied designs and patents for the Clément-Talbot products, and from the beginning of British production the French

[Courtesy of Valerie Motors Inc.

The Talbot 110 3½-litre of 1937 employed Wilson pre-selector gearbox. Coachwork had softened from stark sports cars of early 1930s

Courtesy of Sheila Van Damm]

The Alpine, the last sports incarnation of Sunbeam-Talbot. Windscreen is removed, racing cowl mounted

cars were known as Bayards, while the English bore simply the name *Talbot*.

The Talbot's Dewar Cup victory in 1904 and its record 2000-mile trip across the Australian wastes in 1908 were preludes to the 1913 feat of becoming the first car of any class to cover 100 miles in an hour, at Brooklands. Its best lap was 109·43 m.p.h. The 4½-litre 4-cylinder engine (101 × 140), with side valves, developed 132 b.h.p. at 3500 r.p.m., according to its makers (authorities seriously dispute the claim), and was one of the most efficient then known. The production version, the 25/50, was known for its hill-climb victories.

But in the early vintage period Talbot lost considerable ground with quite prosaic machines until Georges Roesch was brought back from another S.T.D. factory as chief engineer in 1925. At this time Talbot had a vast range of models; Roesch's first move, characteristic of his unorthodox thinking, was to sweep all the eggs into one new basket. Discarding all the old Talbot designs, including his own 1750-c.c. of 1918, he created entirely new ones for a car that remained the firm's basic pattern until it was absorbed by Rootes.

A brilliant engineer—he is currently developing industrial gas turbines for the British Ministry of Supply—Roesch was dedicated to following the simplest path to maximum efficiency. His first Talbot, the 14/45, was a small six—1665 c.c.—with pushrod overhead valves and coil ignition; high compression and light moving parts enabled it to develop 48 b.h.p. in a solid chassis. One of his innovations was to mount the radiator directly and rigidly on the engine block, eliminating perishable hoses and vibration-affected connections. The bodies were inclined to be heavy, and starting was never easy, even with a 24-volt battery, because of the dynastarter; on the other hand, routine maintenance was much easier than on most cars then. From the beginning, too, Roesch introduced such refinements as upward-sweeping windscreen wipers and electric direction indicators as standard equipment.

The 14/45 was the direct ancestor of the Talbot 75, enlarged to 2 litres and retaining the tulip-shaped

valves, fulcrum-pivoted rockers and 7-bearing crankshaft. Valve-gear and compression improvements developed the 75 into the 90, which gave 93 b.h.p. at 4500 r.p.m. in a 2·2-litre engine whose cylinders measured 69·5 × 100 against the 61 × 95 of the 14/45. Running like watches in the 1930 Le Mans, they finished third and fourth behind the much larger—and noisier—Bentleys; in addition, they swept the first three places in their class in the T.T., Irish G.P. and Brooklands 500 Miles.

Roesch's greatest achievement was the 105, a 3-litre 75 × 112 car whose normal 100 b.h.p. could be boosted to 140 for racing. Its top speed in touring form was over 90, a high figure for so comfortable a car. Brakes were increased in size and power. A 105 finished third at Le Mans in 1932 and for the first time in 19 years gave Britain the team prize in the Alpine Trials, last won by Rolls in 1913. One 105 was fitted with a 110 engine, of which very few were made, and lapped Brooklands at 129·7 m.p.h. This engine, whose 3·3 litres (80 × 112) produced 140 b.h.p. with 10·2 : 1 compression, could top 125 m.p.h. The impressive itemized table of Talbot victories in *Motoring Entente* is evidence of the designer's talents; a four-seater won a 500-mile race at 104·7 m.p.h.

From the mid-1930s until the 1940s the names of Sunbeam and Talbot appear rarely in motor-sport annals. After the Second World War the Rootes Group offered the Sunbeam-Talbot as a saloon and a drop-head coupé, but no serious claim of sports-car character was made for them. In 1953 Sunbeam-Talbot attempted to re-enter the sports-car field with the Alpine model, a fairly heavy 4-cylinder two-seater of 2267 c.c. (81 × 110) developing 80 b.h.p. at 4200 r.p.m. It was clocked at 120·125 m.p.h. in Belgian record trials, driven by Sheila Van Damm, who also drove Alpines to win various trophies with Stirling Moss in several Alpine Rallies. Moss set a one-hour average of 116 m.p.h. with the Alpine at Montlhéry. The Alpine also won the Manufacturers' Team Prize in two Great American Mountain Rallies, but the model did not sell well and was soon discontinued—to date, the last inscription of these two glorious names on the roll of sports cars.

TRIUMPH VALE

The nickname *Trusty* earned by the Edwardian Triumph motor-cycles was an accurate if fortuitous epithet for the sports cars that bear the Triumph name today.

The Super Seven pioneered hydraulic brakes in Britain

Like so many British automobile makers, Triumph started with two-wheelers in Coventry. After the First World War the company attacked the light-car market with indifferent results; it was not until 1927 that the Super Seven made a definite impression on drivers. While it used a side-valve 832-c.c. engine, a 3-speed gearbox and worm drive, it also incorporated such advanced features as hydraulic brakes and dual connecting rods. The 1929 model was accused of following American radiator styling.

The 6-cylinder vogue of 1930 brought the 1203-c.c. side-valve Scorpion, a two-seater, which vanished unobtrusively in a couple of years. It was succeeded by the marque's first real sports car when Donald Healey was retained as experimental manager and designed the Southern Cross, which used both the 1203-c.c. engine and a 2-litre Coventry-Climax with overhead inlet and side exhaust valves. These cars scored impressively in trials and rallies, notably the Monte Carlo, and were continued into 1937.

In 1934 they were joined by the Gloria and in 1936 by the Vitesse. The Gloria had four 66 × 90 cylinders (1232 c.c.) with the F-head and a 3-bearing crank. With 6·2:1 compression the single-carburetter model developed 42 b.h.p. at 4500 r.p.m. The 4-speed gearbox was complemented by free wheeling; final drive was now by spiral bevel gears. The 1½-litre Gloria engine, with dual carburation, was a 69 × 100 four with 7:1 compression. The Vitesse was the first Triumph to use an engine built by the company. This was not unlike today's Triumph engines and all valves were overhead. The tuned 1767-c.c. engine produced 62½ b.h.p. During this period Triumph was virtually ignoring the family car for the sports; but from 1937 until the war the reverse was the case.

The 2-litre Southern Cross, designed by Donald Healey

The Gloria tourer

The 6-cylinder Dolomite coupé-roadster had "waterfall" radiator grille

The post-war semi-sports looked faster than it was

During those years, however, the firm did produce one outstanding sports model, the Dolomite—one version of which almost led to international litigation. The 4-cylinder car was engined much like the Vitesse; the 2-litre six (65 × 100) with 6·8:1 compression had a close-ratio 4-speed gearbox on the drop-head (the closed cars were fitted with wider ratios) and could be tuned to 72 b.h.p. Dual carburation was standard. To the naked—or even the aided—eye, the d.o.h.c. 2-litre 8-cylinder Dolomite looked as if it had come right out of the Milan works of Alfa Romeo, whose protests could be heard in Britain without electronic assistance. Only six of these cars were made; one, driven by Healey in the 1935 Monte Carlo Rally, was demolished by a train.

Just before the war, Triumph was sold to a firm of toolmakers, which retained Healey as chief engineer, but only about 40 cars were built before armaments production took over. In 1945 this firm sold Triumph to the Standard Motor Car Co. Ltd. and under this aegis Triumph re-entered production in the late 1940s with well-made but uninteresting sedans. In 1949 a semi-sports drop-head was offered with 1800- and later with a 2000-c.c. engine—one of the more successful efforts to marry vintage and contemporary coachwork concepts and certainly much more attractive than the Jaguar Mark V or the 2½-litre Riley roadster. This was also one of the few two-seaters of our period to continue a rumble seat (which had a folding windscreen).

The introduction of the TR-2 in 1954 brought the firm back to the front rank of sports cars. Headed by Air Marshal Lord Tedder, Triumph offered a solidly built 2-litre overhead-valve engine of 83 × 92, with wet cylinder liners, that developed 90 b.h.p. at 4500 r.p.m. (raised to 100 at 5000 in the TR-3). The chassis is exceptionally strong, at some sacrifice in lightness; and the weight of the body is an added handicap; but the current 19-cwt. TR-3 will accelerate from rest to 50 m.p.h. in six seconds in high tune; top speed in racing form is close to 125 m.p.h. Compression is 8·5:1. Disc brakes on front wheels were added late in 1957. One of the most comfortable lower-priced sports cars for both driver and passenger, it is also one of the few to provide visible luggage space. Steering is 2·3 turns lock to lock and fanciers of Italian sporting machinery admit the TR is the only British car that takes a corner like an Italian. Another aspect of its true dual-purpose character is its economy: not only will the engine hold its tune for very long periods, but on long fast journeys the overdrive-equipped standard car will give as much as 40 miles to the U.S. gallon. (The overdrive operates on the three top gears of the delightfully spaced gearbox.)

The Triumph's racing record has been dimmed since its engine has been made available in the much lighter Morgan and since the much more expensive A.C.-Bristol entered the 2-litre field. But Triumphs have scored heavily for several years in such high-speed events as the Alpine Rally and

Courtesy of Standard Triumph Motor Co.]
The TR-2 during Liège–Rome–Liège Rally

Liège–Rome–Liège. In the latter event in 1957 they were beaten only by special Porsche and Mercedes-Benz speed cars; in 1958 Triumph won the cup for the fastest climb of the Stelvio Pass in the Alpine Rally and placed first and second for the whole rally in the unlimited class. It was also first in class in the Monza speed trial phase of the rally with an

Courtesy of Standard Triumph Motor Co.]
With detachable hard top, a TR-3 won the team prize at Sebring in 1958

average of 100·7 m.p.h. To take full advantage of the class—unlimited over 1600 c.c.—these cars used Vanguard cylinder liners bored out to about 2200 c.c.

A limited marque called the Vale was built around older Triumph components from 1933 to 1936. A very handsome machine based primarily on the Super Seven, it has left no outstanding performance records.

The Vale was based on the Triumph Super Seven
Photograph by Michael P. Clapham]

TURNER

Like many manufacturers of the vintage period, Turner uses a proprietary engine—in this case, the 948-c.c. 4-cylinder Austin with 8·3 : 1 compression. It is in the forefront of modern design principles, employing full independent suspension, magnesium wheels and drums and a tubular chassis bent into A-shape in the middle. The differential is welded to the frame and the suspension is by transverse leaf springs front and rear. Rack-and-pinion steering gives firm control of this 11½-cwt. car.

Originally the Turner was offered with a choice of engines: two by Vauxhall, one by Lea-Francis and one by M.G. With the Lea-Francis unit it was clocked at 112 m.p.h. on 80-octane fuel. The current model with the Austin engine has a drilled chassis for lightness and has become fairly popular in American club racing, where it performs well in class.

Photograph by Michael P. Clapham]

The Turner has 6 ft. 8½ in. wheelbase and 3 ft. 9¼ in. track

Functionalism marks T.V.R. coachwork

Courtesy of T. V. R.-Jomar Ltd.]

T.V.R.

Really Anglo-American rather than British alone (it is marketed in the United States as the Jomar), the T.V.R. consists of engine and chassis built in England and an American glass fibre or aluminium body built by Ray Saidel in Manchester, N.H. Mounting the body on Trevor Wilkinson's chassis, powered by the well-known 1100-c.c. Coventry-Climax, Saidel took the cars to the Thompson Raceway in Connecticut and pounded them around this beautiful, trying course until he and his staff had eliminated all "bugs".

Side by side with the coupé, T.V.R. Engineering Ltd. and Jomar offer a competition roadster. The coupé, however, is a true dual-purpose car in any of the forms in which it can be ordered. These include aluminium coachwork for racing (the glass fibre body is intended for touring but is often raced) and a choice of engines: the normal 1172-c.c. Ford, the same engine supercharged, the 1100-c.c. Coventry-Climax and single or double overhead camshaft

1500-c.c. Coventry-Climax. The Climax-engined cars fit alloy brake drums as standard equipment. All are equipped with standard interior touring accessories and the 1172-c.c. coupé will exceed 120 m.p.h. In 1958 the marque had its best racing year, scoring victories at Bridgehampton, Lime Rock, Thompson and many other courses.

VAUXHALL

A 30-year-old car that can cover 107 miles in one hour on an unusually rough circuit must come of good stock. The Vauxhall 30/98 that accomplished this in 1953 at Montlhéry represented the acme of a long breeding period that followed an almost accidental conception.

The first Vauxhall was designed by F. W. Hodges, a marine engineer in the Vauxhall Iron Works. Having tried a single-cylinder engine with opposed pistons in his boat, he built a 5-cylinder radial engine 10 years before the Wright Brothers got off the ground. It drove a car, but not very well, so Hodges designed another single-cylinder car that in 1903 had coil springs all round. This air-cooled auto-

mobile was reinforced the next year by a water-cooled 3-cylinder. All these were chain-driven.

In 1905 one of the greatest of all automotive engineers joined Vauxhall. Laurence Pomeroy, Sr. (father of today's automotive authority), gave the marque its first live-axle car, a 12/16-h.p. 4-cylinder; in 1908 he produced the first sporting Vauxhall, a 20-h.p. four (90 × 120) whose competition record was so impressive from the start that it was kept in production right up to the start of the war in 1914. With modifications, its 39 h.p. was raised to 52·6 at 2370 r.p.m.—a fantastic engine speed in those days —and the streamlined car reached 88·6 m.p.h. in the flying ½-mile at Brooklands. In the 2000 Miles Trial

[Courtesy of Vauxhall Motors Ltd.

The outstanding 1908 2000 Miles Trial car

Courtesy of the British Travel Association]

L. H. Pomeroy's (Jr.) Prince Henry in 1954

of 1908, which ran from London to Glasgow and back—via a 200-mile speed test at Brooklands—the standard car driven by Percy Kidner, a director, outclassed everything in its category in performance and capped this by making no involuntary stops for any mechanical reason: it did not even add oil or water.

Hill-climbs were the early Vauxhall's meat and it was strong in the Prince Henry Reliability Trials; however, Vauxhall did rather badly in the speed sections. Hence Pomeroy produced the renowned Prince Henry car, retaining the dimensions of the 20-h.p. It is interesting to note here that these cars were both popular and successful in Russian racing—driven by Russians and by company directors. One was given to Pomeroy's son by the original owner; another, discovered in a field, beat all the American entrants in the 1954 Anglo-American Vintage Rally.

The 3-litre Prince Henry, with its 38 b.h.p. and 50 m.p.h., sprang from Pomeroy's interest in high engine speeds. He had given special study to problems of lubrication, camshaft and piston design to obtain 2500 r.p.m. and by 1910 was developing 60 b.h.p. at 2800. Like Roesch, Pomeroy was a disciple of simplicity; he called it immoral to use four parts where two were enough. His Prince Henry cars, incidentally, were the first in Britain to adopt the so-called "torpedo" styling then fashionable. But their relatively small engines put them under considerable disadvantage against the huge Continental cars. Nonetheless, by 1911 they were guaranteed to do 65 m.p.h. In 1913 the engine was enlarged to 3969 c.c. (95 × 140) for 75 b.h.p. at 2500 r.p.m. and put in a much heavier chassis that it propelled at more than 70 m.p.h.

Meanwhile Vauxhall was building some 6-cylinder cars, but its mainstay was the 4-cylinder 25 (like the Crossley, it became a standard British staff car in the First World War), with special racing versions for the Coupe de l'Auto and the French G.P., in which they defeated the Lion Peugeots. In 1913 a man named Higginson, inventor of a new method of feeding petrol to engines, asked Vauxhall to build him a special car for hill-climbs, and this was the origin of the world-famous 30/98. There are con-

flicting stories as to the reason for the designation: one version has it that the first number represented the increased horsepower of the 25 engine, the second its increased bore (it measured 98 × 150—4525 c.c.); the official works history accepts the first part of this legend but attributes the second number to the intended maximum horsepower.

Mounted in a light chassis, the engine had a good power-weight ratio and did all that Higginson desired, including a Shelsley Walsh climb, carrying four people, in 55·2 seconds. It also lapped Brooklands at 100 m.p.h. and was the constant racing rival of Sunbeam and Talbot. At the same time, its 25-h.p. ancestor was winning races at home and abroad and setting new Brooklands records, including 87·74 m.p.h. for 700 miles and 83·31 m.p.h. for nine hours.

The original 30/98, the E type, was given better brakes after the war and in 1922 was converted to pushrod overhead valves and designated the OE. The stroke was cut to 140 mm., resulting in 4224-c.c. volume. The front brakes added in 1923 are generally called sketchy; the last cars, made in 1927, were given balanced crankshafts that enabled them to produce 120 b.h.p. at 3500 r.p.m. and the brakes became hydraulic. About 200 E and 300 OE cars were built and a good many survive in both ordinary use and competition today; one of the best known belonged to T. W. Carson, secretary of the Vintage Sports-Car Club. The very last 30/98's also adopted a closer-ratio gearbox used on other Vauxhall models, which included a sleeve-valve engine. Pomeroy had left for America in 1920, his plans for a single overhead

A 30/98 OE now in Massachusetts; it was formerly used in India

Courtesy of Edgar L. Roy]

camshaft 30/98 still in the experimental stage, where his successor, C. E. King, abandoned them.

In 1921 Vauxhall returned to the light-car field with the 14/40 Princeton, a side-valve 4-cylinder of interest chiefly because of its close resemblance in appearance to the 30/98. But General Motors, which had got control of Vauxhall in 1925, had no interest in high-performance cars and within three years their production had ceased.

WOLSELEY

The younger son of a field marshal and viscount from Staffordshire and a farmer's son from Buckinghamshire first met in Australia, where each had gone to make his fortune. From that meeting grew two of the oldest automobile companies in Britain.

Young Herbert Austin, the farmer's son, was a first-rate engineer and got a job in Frederick Y. Wolseley's works for building mechanical sheep-shearers. Austin made a number of improvements, patented them and, returning to England, sold the patents to his employer in return for a share in the ownership of the business. Young Austin was fascinated by horseless carriages but could get no backing from his firm. On his own, he constructed—like so many pioneers in various countries—a three-wheeler with a flat twin engine enjoying an overhead camshaft. A year later, in 1896, he built another, and this time the Wolseley directors were interested: their own business had fallen off. They gave the new car their blessing and the company's name.

The third Wolseley was the first to have a wheel at each corner, and Austin himself drove it in the 1000 Miles Trial of 1900 to win first in class. The inventor was also helping Sir Hiram Maxim, a director of Vickers, on the latter's project for a steam aeroplane, and Vickers took over the Wolseley firm. Austin got Wolseley into racing in 1902 with a 30-h.p. square (127 × 127) horizontal 4-cylinder engine. Entered in the Paris–Vienna race, the car broke its crankshaft twice: from then on Austin adopted forced-feed lubrication. In 1903 he entered three cars in the notorious Paris–Madrid, driving one himself. His and another broke down; the third, driven by Capt. Leslie Porter, later of the Royal Flying Corps, missed a turn, hit a house and burned. The mechanic was thrown out and killed.

By 1905 Wolseley was building quite huge cars for racing. The 181 × 152·4, rated at 96 h.p., was still a horizontal four, however. It was mounted in a well braced chassis of rather disproportionate size: wheelbase was 9 ft. 1 in., track 4 ft. 6 in. One was driven in the 1905 Gordon Bennett Race by the Hon. C. S. Rolls, who had to lap the 85-mile Auvergne circuit four times. He fought a furious duel throughout with a 6-cylinder Napier and finished just 47 seconds ahead of it, beating a 120-h.p. Mercedes at the same time to finish second over-all.

The first 4-wheel car, a star of the 1000 Miles Trial of 1900. Still usable, it is in the company's private museum

Wolseley withdrew from competition in that year and not long afterward Austin left to start his own works. For the next quarter-century Wolseley produced a varied range of well-built but totally uninteresting cars, except the 1914 Stellite, an excellent light car that was the basis of the Wolseley 10 of the 1920s. The Stellite was a vertical four (62 × 89) with two or three forward speeds, to choice. In the early 1920s it acquired a single overhead camshaft

Capt. Porter in his 1903 Paris–Madrid car

The Hon. C. S. Rolls at wheel of 1905 Gordon Bennett car

and was enlarged to 65×95. The single-seater set many Brooklands class records, including 500 miles at 80 m.p.h., and the two-seater Moth was good for better than 70.

In 1926 the Wolseley company went into bankruptcy and Lord Austin, for obvious reasons, tried to buy it against the competition of General Motors and Viscount Nuffield, who still held the Wolseley dealer franchise that he had acquired when he was a garage owner in Cowley. Nuffield won, and it was through him that Wolseley returned, however briefly, to sports cars. His Wolseley Hornet of the early 1930s was a 6-cylinder version of the o.h.c. Morris Minor (57×83, 1271 c.c.); but this quickly became the Hornet Special with a special manifold, raised com-

pression, domed pistons, an oil cooler, dual carburation and a 4-speed gearbox. Further modifications, such as cast-iron cylinder liners and a better balanced crank, gave it a 75-m.p.h. maximum with the strengthened chassis and suspension. It was sold as a bare chassis and coachwork was to the customer's order.

In 1935 the engine was enlarged to 1604 c.c. (61·5×90) and, like its predecessor, it was very often pitted against far more expensive machinery with considerable success. Two years later the Hornet won its class in the 12-hour Donington sports-car race. It was never raced by the works and all its achievements are owed to private owners. Hornet production ended in 1937.

[*Courtesy of Nuffield Exports Ltd.*

The Stellite's promising career was aborted by the 1914 War

Courtesy of Martin Johnson]

A typical Wolseley Hornet sports of the post-vintage thoroughbred era

FRANCE

AMILCAR

The major contestants in 1100-c.c. motoring in the vintage period were Amilcar and Salmson, and many examples of both marques are still racing today. Amilcar was born in 1920 and named by producing an anagram of the names of the two chief financiers, Lamy and Akar. Though its first goal was the production of economy cars, a sports version was introduced as a by-product in 1921 and was immediately successful. Like most Continental sports machines of that period, it was uncomfortable, the seats being staggered so that the passenger rode about 6 in. behind the driver and had to share his leg-room with the gear-shift lever (and, on some cars, with the clutch pedal).

The first Amilcar engine was a 55×95 side-valve engine in unit with a 3-speed gearbox in a very fragile chassis on quarter-elliptics. A 58-mm. bore was also obtainable. Its lubrication system was the optimistic one of mounting dippers on the flywheel to throw oil into a gallery that fed the bearings. An Amilcar won the 24-hour Bol d'Or Race in 1922, and the firm developed the Grand Sport model the next year. It had a much stronger chassis, half-elliptics and 4-wheel brakes. The engine was bored

out 0·05 mm. and British drivers, including the late Goldie Gardner, became enthusiasts of the marque. It was especially good in hill-climbs. Like the C4 Petit Sport, the C.G.S. had no differential.

Delage inspired the next development, which remained in the 1100-c.c. class with a 6-cylinder (55×77) engine mounting twin overhead camshafts and a Roots supercharger and developing 83 b.h.p. at 6000 r.p.m. This G6 was virtually a Formula II racer; in road trim with detachable cylinder head and plain instead of roller bearings it gave 65 b.h.p. and was guaranteed for 100 m.p.h. In 1927 it was the first car of its class to top 125 m.p.h. on the road and only very much larger cars could beat it in racing. In 1926 the G6 appeared in a lowered chassis, known as the Surbaissé, which had the added advantages of more scientific lubrication and better brakes. Its total weight in full touring trim was well under $12\frac{1}{2}$ cwt., despite a larger sump. The G6 wheelbase was 6 ft. 2 in., track 3 ft. 8 in.

A touring Amilcar appeared in 1926 with a 1580-c.c. engine (67×112). Its 9 ft. 6 in. wheelbase contrasts with the 8-ft. Petit Sport and it had a 4-speed gearbox and semi-elliptics. Another touring version was the

[Courtesy of the Henry Ford Museum

One of the early road cars

From the collection of Jacques Rousseau]

Morel, one of its designers, in the 1924 car

75

The 1925 C.G.S. accommodated third passenger in hatch behind front seats

[Photograph by Clinton Martin

The dual-purpose Surbaissé was raced by its owner and also used for his honeymoon

Photograph by G. H. Fisher]

G, with the side-valve 4-cylinder engine and wheelbase of 8 ft. 6 in., track of 3 ft. 11 in., to take four-seater open and closed bodies. The stroke was increased twice, to 105 and to 110 mm., while the bore remained at 60; the volume rose to 1187 and 1244 c.c.

Vintage Amilcars piled up an impressive record: first and second in the Italian G.P., first three places and fifth in the 200 Miles at Brooklands, flying kilometre at 128·55 m.p.h., 3000 kilometres at 84·95 m.p.h. (they were durable as well as fast, as present racing owners will attest) and 24 hours at 85 m.p.h.

During the 1930s Amilcar made some interesting 2½-litre 4-cylinder cars and a single overhead cam straight-eight of 1980 c.c. (63 × 80). Late in that decade, when the firm had been taken over by Hotchkiss, the Amilcar Compound was announced with a light alloy frame and front-wheel drive developed by J. A. Grégoire.

Copyright by Richmond Pike; courtesy of G. H. Fisher]

Of the six G6 Amilcars imported into Britain, four are still racing. This 33-year-old car will still exceed 100 m.p.h. Auxiliary hand pump helps mechanical fuel pump

The front-wheel-drive Amilcar Compound, so-called because of its multiple springing

From the collection of Jacques Rousseau]

[Courtesy of the Société des Ingénieurs de l'Automobile
The two-seater of the 1920s followed "torpedo" styling

The 3-litre Coppa Florio winner of 1927

[Courtesy of the Automobile-Club de l'Ouest

ARIÈS

The Ariès, whose sporting appearances were rare, was the child of Baron Charles Pétiet, president of the Chambre Syndical des Constructeurs d'Automobiles for almost 40 years until his death in 1958. Pétiet designed the 160 × 98 engine with which the Ariès ran unsuccessfully in the 1907 Kaiserpreis and it 4-cylinder 1908 with four desmodromic valves per cylinder.

Under his guidance in the 1920s the Ariès developed into a first-class sports car with a 3-litre 4-cylinder engine of 80 × 140, which won the Coppa Florio. Its single overhead camshaft carried a link through the middle of the radiator to which the crank was attached. The marque disappeared a few years before the Second World War.

The 1930 B.N.C. team at Le Mans. Brake drums were ribbed

The 1931 Le Mans car had lost the smokestack-like radiator filler

B.N.C.

Such little recollection as the B.N.C. still enjoys is limited to its competition cars and its larger touring models are completely forgotten.

Of the same class as the Amilcar, the B.N.C. began as a light car with a filigree chassis and the sketchiest of two-seater bodies. In 1929 B.N.C. absorbed the Lombard as its own competition department and built some very fast light cars on this design, which had originated from a very advanced 750-c.c. car.

The production Lombard, which appeared in 1927, and the B.N.C. after 1929 mounted an 1100-c.c. 4-cylinder engine of 61×92 in which every bearing was either ball or roller. Twin overhead camshafts were fitted, though the valving was the conventional two per cylinder. Unsupercharged, the engine delivered 45 b.h.p. at 4800; the Cozette supercharger increased this to 70 b.h.p. at 5500 r.p.m. Outboard semi-elliptic springs front and rear supported the chassis; unlike the Amilcar, the B.N.C. was fitted with a differential. The 4-speed gearbox was coupled to a multiple-plate clutch.

B.N.C.'s touring cars of 1930 and 1931—the marque vanished in the economic abyss—had larger 4-cylinder engines that would deliver 80 m.p.h. in contrast to the 100 guaranteed for the sports cars. The luxury model, the Eagle, was an eight in a choice of four or five litres with side valves and mechanical servo brakes. It was one of the earliest cars to be delivered with all-round independent suspension as standard and it anticipated today's Citroën by offering a choice between springs and air suspension.

BALLOT

Having done extremely well making engines for Delage and for his own taxis up to 1914, and stationary engines for his Government during the war, Ernest Ballot resolved to go racing and at the end of 1918 entered a team for the 1919 Indianapolis. Then he decided to find someone to design the cars for him.

His choice was the Swiss, Ernest Henry, who had been so successful with the Peugeot. One hundred days later the new Ballots were being road-tested. Under that year's 4917-c.c. formula, Henry abandoned the 4-cylinder competition fetish that had obtained so long and produced a straight-eight of 74×140 mm. with gear-driven twin camshafts and four valves per cylinder: the spark plugs were let into the dome of the hemispherical cylinder head between the cams. Two large-choke carburetters were employed.

Henry was said to have been rather less brilliant in designing the lower parts of his engines: these had roller main bearings, floating bronze bushings between the small journals and the connecting rods, and lubrication from a dry sump by centrifugal crankshaft action. Because the bushings would not fulfil his expectations by revolving at half the crank speed, the bottom of a Henry engine frequently limited the high potential of the top. In accord with his usual practice, this engine was mounted in a sub-chassis, leaving the main frame all but unbraced. Nonetheless, weight was so skillfully shared between front and rear that both these 5-litres and the later 3-litres handled beautifully.

The Indianapolis experience was an ironic failure. The cars were too high-geared and no spare ratios had been taken along, so smaller American wheels and tyres were installed. They gave so much trouble that Ballot lost the race; the irony lay in the identity of the victor: Henry's 1914 Peugeot. But Henry and Ballot returned for 1920's 3-litre race, with in effect a scaled-down 1919 car of 65×112 mm. and front brakes. At 2500 r.p.m. the engine gave 82 b.h.p.; it could reach 107 b.h.p. at 3800, but the rod bearings could not endure that speed for more than an instant. The close-ratio 4-speed gearbox had a bottom ratio of 7:1; the clutch was a leather cone and the design lacked low-speed torque, so that the cars made a very poor start. Although they were the fastest of their class at that period, they finished well back both at

Indianapolis and in the G.P. of Europe; their major victory was the Brescia G.P. in 1921.

Ballot therefore abandoned racing but not some of its lessons. His first production car was a 2-litre four (70 × 130) with twin overhead cams that easily topped 90 m.p.h. Only 50 were made, however, and no survivors are known. This engine, giving 75 b.h.p. at 4000 r.p.m., had ball-bearings for the crank but Henry's floating bushings were retained. Ballot's next try was the 2LT, of the same dimensions as the twin-cam car but with side valves; it would not go much over 65 m.p.h. because of its great weight, so the very strong vacuum-operated 4-wheel servo brakes were rather wasted. The 2LTS of 1925 had, on the other hand, excellent performance characteristics despite heavy bodies and an inadequate gearbox; it was especially admired for its flat cornering.

In 1927 Ballot returned to the overhead cam for the 2LT6, followed by the 3-litre RH2 with eight 63 × 105 cylinders which were bored out successively to 66 and 68 mm. The final version of the straight eight was an 80-m.p.h. car but suffered frequent bearing collapse. In 1931 Ballot was absorbed by Hispano-Suiza.

[*Courtesy of the Long Island Automotive Museum*

Ballot's first Indianapolis car, now owned by Briggs Cunningham, finished fourth and averaged 84·35 m.p.h.

Photograph by B. B. Whitehouse]

With this square sports-saloon body the inclined-valve 2LTS could cruise without trouble at 65 m.p.h.

[*Courtesy of "Motor Sport"*

A 2LT Ballot still in daily use in England, 35 years after it was built

Courtesy of the Société des Ingénieurs de l'Automobile]

Among the prettiest Ballots was the o.h.c. 2LT6

A Berliet in the Prince Henry Trial of 1909

Berliet's sporting Silver Arrow ran at Le Mans in 1923

Bignan team at work next to Bugatti pit at Le Mans in 1924. Note large-ribbed brake drums—a cooling device many years ahead of its time

BERLIET

Built in France for some 30 years, the Berliet had only sporadic sporting outbreaks. Early Berliets with their T-head engines were the models for some of the Sunbeams in the first years of this century but ultimately the Berliet car was copied almost completely by the British marque for a brief time.

From 1907 into the First World War Berliet built a 2½-litre 4-cylinder engine of 80×120 mm., its cylinders being cast in pairs. Ignition was by magneto and cooling was by the unassisted thermo-siphon principle: i.e. expansion caused by heat forced the water to circulate through the engine. A multi-plate clutch governed a 4-speed gearbox. Suspension was by semi-elliptics at the front, three-quarter elliptics at the rear. Though the detachable wheel was gaining in popularity, Berliet did not adopt it until after the war; the 1909 Prince Henry Trials car was thus at some disadvantage. This 40-h.p. machine was built under licence by the American Locomotive Co. and sold in the U.S. as the Alco.

In the 1920s Berliet appeared at Le Mans with a 2-litre six of delightful if conservative lines. The water pump had now become standard and the clutch was a single plate. Four-wheel brakes were not adopted until past the middle of the decade.

While Berliet never made a competition record under its own name, it was a high-performance car built carefully to exacting standards. Its American licensee, the Alco, won the Vanderbilt Cup in 1910.

BIGNAN

The French have always been known as a nation of individualists *à l'outrance*: hence it is not surprising that theirs is the only country in which anyone ever thought of taking 2-wheel brakes off the rear of the car and putting them on the front.

Two French firms, however, did exactly that in the early 1920s. One was Bignan, which in its eight-year career from 1920 to 1928 did not compete often but always scored high. It has left a reputation that many more active and longer-lived marques may envy.

As early as 1922 Bignan developed a 2-litre engine that delivered 75 b.h.p. at 2000 r.p.m., but it was never put into production. The series cars had a 2-litre 4-cylinder engine (75×112) in which a single overhead camshaft actuated four desmodromic valves in each cylinder. In 1923 a Bignan tied for fourth place at Le Mans with the 3-litre Bentley; in 1924 the French marque won its class in the gruelling 24-hour race at Spa. The Bignan Grand Sport was good for 85 m.p.h. and it was a Bignan that broke S. F. Edge's 17-year-old Montlhéry record for 24 hours by clocking 74 m.p.h.

BUGATTI

There will never be another Bugatti. The prohibition imposed by Bugatti's daughter on any attempt to continue the marque is solidly grounded in her incontestable belief that no modern designer can produce a car entitled to bear the immortal name of Le Patron.

Ettore Bugatti first built cars in Italy at 17. He was a consultant engineer to de Dietrich before he was 21, and he is generally believed to have had a major part in the design of the 1908 Isotta-Fraschini, with which de Dietrich was associated. The first Bugatti was a 1327-c.c. miniature that finished second to the 10½-litre FIAT in the 1911 Grand Prix de France. Even this primeval Type 13 had the uncannily precise steering and gear change that were to characterize the marque throughout its history; in that era of heavy, slow-turning engines the Type 13 ran like a watch at 3000 r.p.m.; in short, Bugatti revolutionized the automobile industry and created the light sports car single-handed.

This was a tiny car with two valves for each of its four 65×100 cylinders, operated by a single chain-driven overhead camshaft. It had a 4-speed gearbox whose ratios were almost ideally spaced: 3·43, 4·5, 6·25 and 11:1. Its engine developed 25 h.p. to propel 10 cwt., and the final drive was by shaft. The clutch was the wet multiple type that the marque employed throughout the vintage period. In 1914 the Type 13 was given dual valving and evolved into the Brescia model, which could top 95 m.p.h. in contrast to its predecessor's 60. These were the cars that Bugatti buried at Molsheim when the Germans struck in 1914 and that he exhumed to embark on an incredible career of victories in 1919. From 1920 to 1925 they were the world's fastest light cars. The Brescias were bored out to 69 mm. and finished in the first four places in the 1921 Brescia race, which gave them their name. It includes, popularly, the medium-wheelbase Type 22 and the long-wheelbase Type 23.

Bugatti's models were bewilderingly numerous and their designations offer no clue to their dates, for often several of them would be in simultaneous production. In 1915 Black Bess, a chain-driven 5-litre car that had actually been designed in 1908, ran in the Vanderbilt Cup. Its four cylinders measured 100×160 and each had three valves: two inlet, one exhaust. Basically an expanded Brescia, it was capable of 105 m.p.h. One of these cars built for Bugatti's great friend, Roland Garros, the aviator after whom Bugatti named his younger son, is still running in England.

Two Brescia engines were coupled to produce Bugatti's first 8-cylinder car; his first true straight eight was the tank-bodied car that was clocked at 117 m.p.h. at Tours in 1923. Its touring version was the 1991-c.c. Type 30, with 60×88 cylinders, and had a 3-bearing crank as well as the three valves per cylinder. Like all Bugattis before and since, it was made with integral cylinder head and block; in order to grind the valves one had to start from the bottom and work up. The Type 30 was among Bugatti's slower products.

The Types 35 and 43 were produced together, the 43 being a production version of the blown 35B. This was a grand-prix car, but virtually all grand-prix Bugattis are also used as road cars and may be considered dual-purpose (more than one Type 37, for example, is used as a going-to-work car). The 43 was one of the first 100-m.p.h. cars offered to the general buyer and marked a great improvement in Bugatti braking. Like all Bugattis, the 35 had an excellently spaced gearbox. There were four manifestations of the 35, which in its original form was unsupercharged, with eight 60×88 cylinders—a 2-litre car.

The 35A, which appeared in 1926, two years after the basic 35, was a slightly modified version, still unsupercharged; the supercharged 2-litre car was

[Photograph by John Caperton

The Type 43 with Belgian body

Photograph by Derek Smith; courtesy of the Montagu Motor Museum]

The magnificent Type 44. Similar car won 1958 Bridge-hampton vintage race

[Photograph by D. W. H. Scott-Moncrieff

Black Bess, the 5-litre car of 1913, was designed in 1908. Built for Roland Garros, this example belongs to C. W. P. Hampton

Photograph by D. W. H. Scott-Moncrieff]

C. W. P. Hampton's 1914 Brescia exemplifies the stark simplicity of Bugatti design

[Courtesy of the Société des Ingénieurs de Automobile

Type 22 was marketed in stripped form as Brescia Modifiée

Photograph by Clinton Martin]

The three-seater Type 23 accommodated one passenger in the tail

[Courtesy of the Henry Ford Museum

Part of the Targa Florio legend: the 35B

Photograph by Inga M. Naylor]

This Type 37 finished third in 1958 vintage race at Bridgehampton

[Courtesy of Scuderia La Manovella]

The Type 49 is a study in functional beauty

Hollow front axle and reversed rear springs were fitted to this very fast Type 50, ancestor of Type 54 grand-prix car

[Photograph by John Caperton]

The Type 54 spoke wheels lack the studs of those on the Type 35B

[Photograph by Ben Johnson]

the 35C of 1927. In the same year Bugatti made the 35T, a 2·3-litre car (60 × 100), and the 35B, which was the blown edition of the 35T, and officially designated the Targa Florio, where it starred. There was also a 4-cylinder version for 1½-litre racing, with a bore and stroke of 52 × 88; this was replaced in 1927 by the Type 39 of 60 × 66 cylinders and its blown version, the 39A. All these cars used roller bearings throughout. It was the 35 that introduced Bugatti's famous alloy spoke wheels, which were of cast aluminium integral with the brake drums.

Road-holding was a major part of the Bugatti legend, and even in comparison with the most advanced modern designs it is fantastic. Bugatti used the engine and the wide-flanged gearbox supports to brace his chassis, emphasizing front-end rigidity and obtaining the same effect in the rear with reversed quarter-elliptic springs. Unsprung weight was held to the minimum. To have driven a Bugatti is an experience that becomes a lifelong criterion.

Cooling was not helped by the cylinder heads, which allowed little room for water circulation; Bugatti relied on cast iron to dissipate the heat. In contrast to standard practice of placing spark plugs at the hottest part of the engine—i.e. close to the exhaust valves—he located them on the inlet side. Maximum speed was sacrificed to low-end torque.

Between the Types 35 and 35A came the 37, a 4-cylinder (69 × 100) 1½-litre car with plain bearings; its supercharged version was the 37A. It appeared in 1927 and was followed three years later by the Type 47, which consisted of two 39 engines side by side on a common crankcase (like the 16-cylinder Bugatti aircraft engines built under licence by Duesenberg in the 1914 war) and fitted with two superchargers. The 4-litre version of this car had a lengthened stroke of 88 mm., and was the second most costly Bugatti ever built (exceeded, of course, by the famous luxury Royale, which had no sporting propensities).

The 1926 Type 40 was the touring edition of the 37—the cheapest and simplest Bugatti, almost the Model T of the marque. With its 75-m.p.h. top speed it competed with the contemporary Frazer Nash. Two Type 40 blocks were coupled to produce the Type 44, a 3-litre eight with a single carburetter. This car, whose prototype was shown in 1919, came on the market in 1927 and was continued well into the 1930s; many consider it the peer of the renowned Type 57. With 99 b.h.p. at 4500 r.p.m. it would hit 90 m.p.h. and is frequently raced by private owners, who have exceeded 100 with multiple carburation.

Little known outside France, the Type 49 was introduced in 1930 as a 3·3-litre 72 × 100 straight eight with dual ignition and, on the later models, a dry-plate clutch. Its reliability earned it the sobriquet of "the doctor's Bugatti" and one car used for 10 years by Cecil Clutton clocked 750,000 miles without a breakdown. It produced 92 b.h.p. at 4000 r.p.m.

Reversing general procedure, the 4·9-litre Type 50 of 1930 was the ancestor of the 1931 grand-prix Type 54. The 50 had eight 86 × 107 cylinders developing 200 b.h.p. at 4000 r.p.m. and would exceed 115 m.p.h. The gearbox was cast with the rear axle and, unique among Bugattis, had only three close-ratio speeds. The relatively high compression ratios of all Bugattis could be altered—while one was removing the crankshaft to get at the valves—by either changing pistons or inserting spacers between the block and the flange of the crankcase.

In 1931 Bugatti adopted twin overhead cams in both the Type 51, which was a 180-b.h.p. version of the 35B with a domed combustion chamber and a shorter crank, and the Type 54, the 300-b.h.p. car developed from the 50 and the all-independent Type 53, which had 4-wheel drive and clocked 133 m.p.h. at the Avus in Germany. One of the most beautiful of all Bugattis was the Type 55 roadster, which consisted essentially of a 51 engine in a 54 chassis (108-in. wheelbase). With its body, designed by Jean Bugatti, it weighed less than 22½ cwt. and in standard trim attained 124 m.p.h. at Brooklands (it reached 98·9 in a standing quarter-mile). Launched in 1932, it abandoned the 3-valve layout for two and developed 135 b.h.p. at 5000 r.p.m. Two years later, still clinging to cable brakes, Bugatti introduced his last real production model, the Type 57.

The 3257-c.c. engine (72 × 100) gave 125 b.h.p. at 4500 r.p.m., but plain bearings were substituted for the rollers of the 55; saloon-bodied 57's are still raced. In 1935 it appeared in the sports version, the 57S, in which the compression rose to 8:1 from 6·2; Earl Howe drove one to third place in the 1935 Tourist Trophy, averaging 79·7 m.p.h. A similar car, developing 175 b.h.p. at 5500 r.p.m., set a one-hour record of 135 m.p.h. and a 24-hour record of 124 at Montlhéry in 1936; the next year a tank-bodied version won Le Mans at 85 m.p.h. That was the blown 200-b.h.p. 57SC, which could reach 130 m.p.h.; a 57C won Le Mans again in 1939 with an 86·5 average, a record beaten only when the C Jaguar appeared. In 1938 hydraulic brakes were finally adopted. Jean Bugatti was killed in 1939 while testing the 57C.

In 1934 Bugatti's Type 59, driven by René Dreyfus, won at Spa; the car was timed at 168 m.p.h. and was estimated to have a potential of 180. It was variously equipped with engines of 2·8, 3·3 and 3·8 litres and it is generally considered the peak of

Photograph by Miles Coverdale]

The front springs of the Type 55 pass through a circular-section axle, eliminating brake stresses. Shock absorbers were controlled from the dashboard

The characteristic Type 57 coupé

Courtesy of G. S. Cesari]

Copyright by Richmond Pike; courtesy of William Nock]

The coach-bodied Type 57 at a Prescott Hill-Climb organised by the Bugatti Owners' Club

Bugatti's genius. The split front axle was joined in a threaded collar to duplicate the characteristics of independent front suspension. Its weakest point was its transmission, in which, as in chassis design and suspension (he clung to leaf springs), Bugatti's competitors were at last beginning to outdo him.

The first post-war grand-prix race in France was won by a 4·9-litre car whose only departure from

[Photograph by Albert de Lay

The exquisite Type 57SC with Gangloff drop-head body

We have deliberately avoided any listing of Bugatti competition achievements: there were 4000 major victories in 20 years, and they deserve a book of their own. Virtually every major driver of the vintage period was associated with Bugatti at one time or another, and the list of his pilots reads like the honour roll of the two decades between the wars.

This Type 59 that René Dreyfus drove to victory at Spa in 1934 is the treasure of Francis H. Ludington

Photograph by Kurt H. Miska]

Bugatti tradition was hydraulic brakes. But competition and personal misfortune, as well as years of injustice, were taking their toll of *Le Patron*. After his death in 1947, the factory attempted to produce a new car, the Type 101 and 101C, based on the 57 and 57C, but it never reached full production and outwardly resembles any other expensive post-war car.

CHENARD & WALCKER

Chenard & Walcker began with a motor tricycle built by Chenard in 1895, for which he was paid £2500 by an Englishman. With this as capital, he built others, one of which was sold to a mining engineer named Walcker, who liked it so well that he proposed to Chenard that they go into business together. Chenard later confided that he accepted the suggestion because, though Walcker had no money, he did possess not only considerable business acumen but also a new bride with whom he was very much in love.

Their first car was shown in 1901—a 2-cylinder. This was soon developed into a four, which won the Gaillon hill-climb in 1904; from then on the marque scored a series of victories through the 1937 Bol d'Or. Chenard & Walcker developed its own carburetter and, in 1911, it was the first marque to fit aluminium pistons in production cars. Forced lubrication through a drilled crankshaft was begun a year earlier. Like the Bignan, the Chenard & Walcker of the early 1920s carried brake shoes only on the front wheels, with ribbed drums for cooling. They were augmented by an external band contracting on the transmission and controlled by a hand lever. This was useful but took a high toll of rear axles. The gearbox drove a mechanical servo for the wheel brakes.

A 3-litre four (80×150) scored successes just before the First World War. In 1923 the marque finished first and second in the inaugural Le Mans race with a 3-litre four (79×150) employing a single overhead camshaft (later doubled), and set a new world record by covering 1372 miles in 24 hours at 57 m.p.h. Several victories in the Coupe Boillot followed, as well as another in class at Le Mans and a first in the Belgian 24-hour race with a 4-litre straight eight. This was replaced by a d.o.h.c. 2-litre four (69.5×130), to which, after the absorption of the Sénéchal cycle-car, was added an 1100-c.c. car that, with a supercharger, vanquished even the blown 7-litre Mercedes eights in the 12-hour San Sebastian race in 1926, again setting a world record. In the same year, Chenard & Walcker finished one-two-three in the Coupe Boillot.

Noted for its advanced experimentation, Chenard & Walcker followed Bugatti's example by introducing a tank type of coachwork on its very fast 1100-c.c. cars (100 m.p.h.) in 1925, which featured faired front wheels, flush sides not unlike modern slab-sided design, and three-quarter aproned rear wheels. Closed and drop-head bodies were also built in the same style, and 4-wheel brakes were added a few years later. Known even to its admirers as the Wart Hog, the tank model was nevertheless impeccably finished in every detail. Handling was outstanding and for almost a decade the smaller cars continued to compete, some being fitted with 1500-c.c. engines.

Public reaction to the early experimentation in aerodynamic coachwork forced a return to conventional—and more aesthetic—lines. In 1930 a Chenard & Walcker side-valve 2200-c.c. two-seater (74·9 × 110) set a 24-hour mark of 82·5 m.p.h. at Montlhéry. Like most of the marque's later sports cars, it carried the chassis below the rear axle along the underslung lines developed in the United States many years earlier by Harry C. Stutz. The 2½-litre 1932 car (85 × 110) adopted independent front suspension. Chenard & Walcker now makes transmissions and components for industrial and agricultural machinery.

Courtesy of the Société de Constructions Mécaniques Chenard & Walcker]

The 1905 car won an endurance contest

Courtesy of the Société de Constructions Mécaniques Chenard & Walcker]

The 1909 sports

[Courtesy of the Société de Constructions Mécaniques Chenard & Walcker

The 1914 "torpedo"

From the collection of Jacques Rousseau]

The 1924 eight at Le Mans. Note front-wheel brakes only

[Courtesy of the Automobile-Club de l'Ouest

Tank-bodied 1100-c.c. car repeats Le Mans run in 1958 Rétrospective

Courtesy of the Société de Constructions Mécaniques Chenard & Walcker]

The 1930 record car refuelling during its Montlhéry run

COTTIN ET DESGOUTTES

In its 27 years of existence (from 1904 to 1931) the Cottin & Desgouttes brought no laurels to the works in Lyons. It was, however, a superior high-performance car that, while it rarely won a major event, was always a worthy competitor to the more prominent marques during the 1920s, the only period of its sporting activity.

A conventional 4-cylinder car of 3 and 4 litres, it was extremely partial to the so-called torpedo body styling of the day, in which both two- and four-seater open coachwork was brought to a more or less gradual point at the rear. Probably its outstanding achievement—with a pushrod overhead valve engine—was to come second in the G.P. de France in 1924. Several such models were raced at Brooklands during the 1920s without leaving any entry in the records. Four-wheel brakes were adopted fairly early in the decade; at the very end, all-independent suspension was offered.

Photograph by Michael P. Clapham]

The overhead valve model did well in the 1924 French G.P.

[Courtesy of the Automobile-Club de l'Ouest

The four-seater torpedo of 1925 carried a large oil radiator alongside the bonnet for racing

From the collection of Jacques Rousseau]

The 1926 3-litre provided a hatch for an occasional third passenger

[Courtesy of Automobiles Talbot-Darracq S.A.

The 9-h.p. voiturette of 1902, competitor in cross-Europe races, had a brake on the differential as well as on the rear wheels

Courtesy of the Société des Ingénieurs de l'Automobile]

The over-square 4-cylinder of 1904 was a pioneer of overhead valves and scored successes in France and U.S. with Louis Chevrolet, founder of Chevrolet

DARRACQ

The original Darracq company, like so many others, developed from bicycles through motor-cycles. Alexandre Darracq showed light cars as early as 1895, but no sale is recorded. His luck with an electric was comparable, and his monster 70-h.p. racer acquired a few buyers but no racing drivers.

Darracq's own interest in racing was limited to its publicity value for the cheap cars he hoped to build and sell in volume: the first New York and London taxis were Darracqs. His cars appeared in the Paris–Berlin, Paris–Vienna and Paris–Madrid races, the Argonne and Auvergne competitions, the Targa Florio and some German races before 1910. All had cone clutches and gilled tube radiators and most had coil ignition, the exception being the 1904 over-square 160 × 140 4-cylinder of 100 h.p., which had a magneto. As early as 1901 Darracq abandoned chain drive for good. Perhaps the outstanding difference between his cars and most others

of the period was their relatively short stroke; after 1903 he built only one—the 1907 Targa Florio car—that was not square or over-square.

Close relations were established very early with the Talbot firm and in 1919 the two companies merged, later absorbing Sunbeam in Britain—a combine that continued until it was swallowed in England by the Rootes Group in the middle 1930s and Lago bought the Suresnes works. The Talbot-Darracq was generally labelled *Darracq* in England, probably to avoid confusion with the British-built Talbot.

As early as 1900 Darracq had pioneered the tubular frame, but he went backward to wood, armoured in steel, and then in 1903 adopted pressed steel. In that year his cars were offered with engines of one, two and four cylinders, ranging from 1103 to 5122 c.c.; his first six, in 1907, was 5652 c.c., and this grew a year later to 8143. For a couple of years before

87

The big Darracqs won the Vanderbilt Cup twice

[From the Lazarnick Collection; courtesy of the Library of the Automobile Manufacturers' Association

The 1914 Darracq weighed 23½ cwt. This side-valve 3-litre 4-cylinder engine, with 4-speed gearbox, can still reach 55 m.p.h., "given sufficient room"

Photograph by Frank Smith]

the First World War he employed sleeve-valve (sometimes called "valveless") engines, in which a concentric sleeve between the piston and the main cylinder slides up and down with the piston to open and close the inlet and exhaust ports.

The vintage Darracqs were fours and eights (one, in 1920, a V) until 1926, when a six was introduced. Some of the early vintage racing cars were built without differentials. Almost without exception Darracq's greatest vintage successes were scored with 1½-litre fours with overhead camshafts. His lighter cars, too, accounted for the early successes like the victories and high places in the Paris–Bordeaux, Paris–Vienna (a one-two-three sweep for the marque), Paris–Madrid, Coppa Florio. The big car won the Vanderbilt Cup in 1905 with an average of 61·5 m.p.h. for 283 miles and repeated in 1906; it also finished second in the St. Petersburg–Moscow. Darracq was second and third in the famous "4-inch" Tourist Trophy—so-called because the bore limitation was the only regulation imposed.

The vintage Darracq sports tourer

In the vintage era, class victories at Le Mans, the T.T. and Brooklands were almost monotonously regular. The last Darracq achievement was second place in the 1927 Coppa Florio, with a 3-litre 6-cylinder of 75×110 bore and stroke.

D.B.

Although the firm of Deutsch & Bonnet was established in the late 'thirties to engineer automotive improvements, it is only in this decade that it has begun to produce cars under its own marque, D.B., and these have immediately sprung to the forefront in their class. For years it was almost inevitable that they would win on index of performance at Le Mans.

The D.B., which weighs less than 13½ cwt., is based on the air-cooled flat-twin four-stroke 850-c.c. Panhard engine with overhead valves. This unit develops 56 b.h.p. at 5700 r.p.m. with 8:1 compression in the over-square cylinders (85×75). All suspension is independent: by transverse upper and lower leaf springs in front and by torsion bars in back. Third gear, which, like second, is synchronized, is direct drive and fourth is overdrive. One double-barrelled Zenith carburetter is used and the

tuned D.B. will top 90 m.p.h. with standard two/four-seater coupé coachwork. A 750-c.c. Le Mans edition ($79·5 \times 75$) was offered for several years. Roller bearings are used throughout the engine.

Both the engine and the driving unit are mounted in the front, with special U-joints of D.B.'s own design. Cornering is superb, though understeer will naturally appear first if the car is taken beyond the limit of adhesion. It is quite understandable, therefore, that D.B. has made an impressive record of wins in class and on index at Sebring, Le Mans, Montlhéry, the Mille Miglia and the Mont Ventoux hill-climb, where it has out-run all gran turismo cars regardless of class. Its 89½-in. wheelbase and 4-ft. track give it an unbeatable advantage on narrow or twisting courses that carries over into normal traffic driving and helps to make it a highly desirable dual-purpose vehicle.

88

The 1952 Le Mans team car: the 750-c.c. drop-head stripped of hood and windscreen

The 1957 coupé, like American Cord 20 years earlier, mounted retractable headlamps to maintain air-stream

Le Mans roadster of 1957 had headlights faired into its wings

The current coupé continues faired headlights and adds transparent roof panel that can be covered from within. Rectangular wheel slots help to cool the brakes

DE DION-BOUTON

Count Mechanic, his relatives and friends derisively called the Comte Albert de Dion (he became the Marquis after his father died) when he began to be interested in making automobiles in 1883. A crack duellist and the scion of a very ancient Belgian family, he had been enthralled by a toy steam engine built by the petit-bourgeois Georges Bouton and the latter's brother-in-law. De Dion tracked them down and together the trio built a 4-wheeled steam car that steered with its rear wheels.

The family objected so strongly that de Dion *père* sought unsuccessfully to have the courts enjoin his son from continuing what seemed a ruinous waste of the family's fortune. But the Count pushed on and the Marquis mellowed; by the time he died in 1901 he was quite fond of riding in his son's cars. The Count was increasingly attracted by the internal-combustion engine and Bouton went along with him; the brother-in-law had to be dropped.

Some of the earliest de Dion-Bouton engines were rotary units of 4 and 12 cylinders, but what really established the firm was its single-cylinder engines installed in its own motor-cycles and light cars and also sold to any rival who wished to buy them. The first of these units, in 1899, was a water-cooled 80×80-mm. engine of $3\frac{1}{2}$ h.p., which was soon enlarged to 90×110 mm. and 6 h.p. Racing models developed 8 and 10 h.p., and de Dion engines were used all over the world. They powered the early American Pierce-Arrow and Peerless.

Though he was one of the founders of the Auto-

mobile-Club de France, de Dion was not much interested in racing and the firm did very little of it, though it was always ready to help customers who were interested. The single-cylinder car was available almost up to the First World War, alongside many other models ranging to a 50-h.p. eight. One de Dion, driven by an anonymous amateur, finished fourth in the 1908 Targa Florio. In the famous New York–Paris race of the same year a 30-h.p. 4-cylinder car with demountable rims got as far as Vladivostok before it was withdrawn. This was a large machine—its cylinders measured 109·5 by 130·2 mm.—of 128-in. wheelbase and 57-in. track, a virtually stock double phaeton, as it was catalogued, with a top speed of about 50 m.p.h. In contrast, the 8-h.p. 2-cylinder de Dion had finished second and third the year before in the almost equally destructive Peking–Paris race.

It is generally held that the only true sports de Dion-Bouton cars were those of 1909–11 known as the B.V. and C.P., though certainly the achievements of the touring models entitle them to at least honorary admission to the category. The B.V. was a single-cylinder (100×160) car of 12 h.p. with three speeds, shaft drive, magneto ignition and forced lubrication. Like the New York–Paris car, it used detachable rims on wooden wheels and was good for 50 m.p.h. Semi-elliptic springs were fitted all round. The 8-h.p. C.P. was also a single-cylinder car, of 90×150.

De Dion-Bouton continued building automobiles into the depression of the 1930s but from the beginning of the 1914 war none of them would qualify as sports machines.

89

In the 1900 de Dion-Bouton occupants faced each other, steering was by tiller and engine was under rear seat. Note starting-handle on side

The detachable rims of New York–Paris car were new in 1908

De Dion-Bouton C.P. of 1911, almost identical in appearance with B.V. of 1909; these are the only models marketed as sports cars. Note radiator's resemblance to that of early Packard

The world's first V-8 production engine was this 1911 de Dion-Bouton

This de Dion-Bouton 1913 tourer was one of first with electric lights

DELAGE

One of the many marques that got its start with a de Dion-Bouton engine was the Delage, established in 1905 by Louis Delage, a workman's son who struggled for his engineering diploma and started his career in a government job.

In 1908 he won the Grand Prix des Voiturettes, using one of the single-cylinder de Dions; the next year he turned to fours, using both de Dion and Ballot units and very soon building his own engines. One of these, driven by René Thomas, won at Indianapolis in 1913. This was the first of Delage's departures in valving: in this car the valves were horizontally opposed and the exhaust manifold came out of the top of the engine. In 1914 he adopted twin overhead camshafts and—one of the first to do so—4-wheel brakes.

Vintage grand-prix Delages are historic—as early as 1925 the blown V-12 ($51 \cdot 3 \times 80$) with two camshafts for each cylinder bank produced 195 b.h.p. and 140 m.p.h. at 7000 r.p.m., using ball or roller bearings wherever possible. This was succeeded by the straight eight designed by Lory, a $57 \cdot 5 \times 75$ engine with integral block and head and valves opposed at 100 degrees. With a $6 \cdot 5 : 1$ compression ratio and 7-lb. supercharger it yielded 170 b.h.p. at 8000 r.p.m.; it had five speeds, top being overdrive. New rules allowed cars to run without riding mechanics, so, to balance weight, Delage angled the engine across the frame. Placing the exhaust manifold on the driver's side cost a number of races because of foot burns. A 10·7-litre V-12 was built for the land-speed record, which it set at 143·24 m.p.h. in 1923; it is now in England, where it has seen both race and road use.

One of the first sports Delages developed from the 80×149-mm. 3-litre based on the pre-1914 War cars with horizontal valves and a 5-speed gearbox in which fifth was overdrive. Among the finest models was the 14/40, which had a number of variants. Preceded by a $3\frac{1}{2}$-litre six for which 80 m.p.h. was claimed in 1919, the side-valve 2·2-litre machines of 1921 established the foundation for the great vogue enjoyed by the pushrod overhead valve cars that followed a few years later. The first of these 14/40's, which were said actually to develop 50 b.h.p. for a maximum of 75 m.p.h., was the DI of 1923, with four 75×130 cylinders, 4-speed gearbox with fairly wide ratios, single-plate clutch, pump lubrication operated from the camshaft and the then current dynastarter, an American-made unit.

This was followed by the 1925 DIS, with larger valves and a modified cylinder head. The chassis was lowered the next year for the DISS, which had a closer-ratio gearbox and torque-tube drive; but, to confuse the issue, the 1927 car was renamed DIS. It was the first Delage to add a water-pump; previously the thermo-siphon method of cooling had been relied on. All these cars had about the same top speed as the DI; a DISS in England is still running with well over 100,000 miles on its odometer.

[Courtesy of Charles Stich]

As early as 1914 Delage used 4-wheel brakes

[Photograph by James P. Mulvanny; courtesy of William Galbraith]

The 14/40 DI of 1923 at the 1958 Ulster Spring Rally

The DIS with two-seater Kelsch body; third seat in tail hatch

[Courtesy of the Vintage Sports-Car Club]

The straight-eight engine of 4 litres was adopted in 1930, known as the D8; it retained the pushrod overhead valves and, offered in Grand Sport form the next year, was guaranteed for 100 m.p.h. This model set several distance marks at Montlhéry and averaged 112 m.p.h. for 12 hours.

Its most sporting manifestation was the short-chassis D8/120, with 7·25:1 compression for the 4744-c.c. engine and a top speed just under 100. By the time this model appeared the company had encountered financial problems from which it was rescued by Delahaye, and the latter name appears on many of the D8/120's components. It used the Cotal electric gearbox favoured by Delahaye, which eliminated the need for a clutch pedal except for stopping and re-starting. It developed 142 b.h.p. for its 38 cwt. Like the crankshaft, the camshaft had five bearings. Lock to lock, the steering took 2½ turns.

The D8/120 was followed in 1936 by the D6, an 80×99 six of 3 litres with independent front suspension by a transverse leaf spring. The competition version won the 1938 Tourist Trophy. With 7:1 compression it developed 100 b.h.p. Like the D8/120, it also had the Cotal gearbox.

Both Delage and Delahaye attempted to resume production after the Second World War but could not survive long in a radically changed market.

Copyright by Charles Dunn; courtesy of B. L. C. Angell]

The DISS in four-seater form

One of the first finned cars: a 1937 D6-70

Photograph by "The Autocar"; from the collection of George A. Moffitt]

91

[*Photograph by "The Autocar"; from the collection of George A. Moffitt*   *Courtesy of V. F. Mashek*]

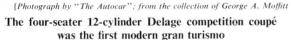

**The four-seater 12-cylinder Delage competition coupé
was the first modern gran turismo**

The D8/120 drop-head coupé was not supercharged

DELAHAYE

One marque that owes nothing to the bicycle is Delahaye: it sprang from a factory making agricultural machinery. From the time Delahaye began to make cars, in the mid-1890s, it took an experimental approach. A member of the Delahaye family drove a 6-h.p. single-cylinder car in the Paris–Marseilles–Paris race of 1896 and fitted it with pneumatic tyres. These single-cylinder cars had belt drive and 3-speed gearboxes; but from the beginning they were all-tubular chassis. In the 9½-h.p. 2-cylinder of 1900 water tubes ran the length of the frame to aid in cooling the engine. Unlike other cars of that period, Delahaye enclosed as much of its mechanism as possible.

The horizontal engine mounting was dropped in 1902; a 4-cylinder engine appeared the next year, using chain drive. "The gear lever", D. W. H. Scott-Moncrieff drily notes, "was, as in many cars of its day, in a position just rediscovered by the modern designer—horizontally under the steering wheel." Another Delahaye experiment was water cooling of the silencer, based on the theory that rapid cooling would diminish noise. In the same year, 1904, the marque was using the magneto. Delahaye also engined the first petrol-driven White car for the American company. The first Delahaye six, in 1911, was cast in a V at a 30-degree angle.

During the greater part of its life the marque was not considered a sports car, though its vintage models were outstanding for strength and performance. It was only in the last years of peace that Delahaye made its mark in motor sport; but that impression will prove lasting. The 1936 car appeared with two 6-cylinder engines, each with three car-

buretters: the 3·2-litre Coupe des Alpes and the 3·5-litre Competition, both of which were said to derive from Delahaye trucks. The Competition (135M), which soon replaced the 3·2 engine (Coupe des Alpes remained as a model designation with no relevance to engine size), delivered 160 b.h.p. at 4200 r.p.m. and the car was good for better than 110 m.p.h. with pushrod overhead valves, accelerating from rest to 60 in 13·7 seconds. The cars were delivered with close-ratio Cotal or synchromesh gearbox as desired; front suspension was independent, by transverse spring and radius rods, and steering was only 1¾ turns lock to lock—an ideal combination for the Alpine Rally for which these cars were designed. One of these cars won a Brooklands match race to determine the fastest car in England in 1939: the losers were a 2·9 Alfa Romeo and a Talbot-Darracq. A slightly modified version was also available with 8·3 instead of 7:1 compression; in this car the valves were transposed to allow larger inlet valves.

Delahaye won the Monte Carlo Rally twice and Le Mans once, in 1938, setting a lap record the next year. In 1937 the first V-12 Delahaye was built, to compete for a prize of 1,000,000 francs for the fastest time for 200 kilometres at Montlhéry. Driven by René Dreyfus, the 4½-litre (75 × 84·7) Delahaye with three overhead cams defeated J. P. Wimille's modified 4½-litre Bugatti to win the prize with an average of more than 90 m.p.h. The same driver won the Grand Prix de Pau with a six in 1938.

Just before the war several 200-h.p. 12-cylinder cars were built with sports bodies by Figoni, designed by the painter, Géo Ham, whose weight precluded their exceeding 130 m.p.h. Two of these are now in the Kremlin, one having been seized from King Michael's palace when the Russians overran Rumania

[Courtesy of the Société des Ingénieurs de l'Automobile

The first Delahaye was driven by its maker in the Paris–
Marseilles–Paris race. Several of this model are still
runnable

Courtesy of the Société des Ingénieurs de l'Automobile]

The 1927 car followed the classic pattern. All Delahayes
are known for their durability and performance

and the other having been taken by them in Berlin;
a third belongs to Adrian Conan Doyle, son of the
creator of Sherlock Holmes.

For a few years after the war Delahaye offered the
6-cylinder cars in a 4-litre version (94×107); horsepower varied from 140 to 185 dependent on carburation and compression ratio. These cars had coil-
spring front suspension and semi-elliptics with a
de Dion tube at the rear. Known as the 175, 175S,
178 and 180, they varied chiefly in wheelbase—112
to 130 in.—and maximum speed—106 for the 175S
and 90 for the 178 and 180. Early in the present
decade Delahaye ceased manufacturing automobiles.

From the collection of Jacques Rousseau]

Mme. Lucy Schell, mother of 1958's fourth ranking
driver, in her 135 roadster, with her husband

The 135MS at Le Mans Rétrospective of 1958

Courtesy of the Automobile-Club de l'Ouest]

[Courtesy of L. Oliver Cook]

This Coupe des Alpes d.h.c. with Chapron body won first prize at the 1938 Paris Salon de l'Automobile

Photograph by Helen Harvie]

Miss Harvie's 1926 roadster is the only completely original Derby surviving in either Britain or Australia

[Courtesy of Adrian M. Conan Doyle]

The 12-cylinder Delahaye's windscreen winds down into scuttle. Note streamlining covers for front as well as rear wheels

[Courtesy of the Long Island Automotive Museum]

One of the last Delahayes. Small grilles conceal headlights

DERBY
VERNON-DERBY

Almost as forgotten as the B.N.C., the Derby was in its day one of the finest of the French cycle-cars and, like most machines in this category, its earlier models were built with solid rear axles. The Derby has always enjoyed a certain esteem in Australia, where it is universal practice to replace the original rear axles with Model T Ford differentials.

The Derby first appeared in 1921; it lasted barely 15 years. Proprietary engines were used for the most part, the favourite choices being the Ruby, the S.C.A.P. and the Chapuis-Dornier, all in the 1100-c.c. class. All these were overhead-valve fours; the Chapuis-Dornier used a good bit of aluminium, especially in the crankcase, clutch housing and gearbox. Until 1928 all Derbys had 3-speed gearboxes. Wheelbase varied between 94 and $94\frac{1}{2}$ in., track between $43\frac{1}{2}$ and 44. Magneto ignition was standard, as was thermo-siphon cooling. The wire wheels were integral with the brake drums, which formed the hubs and to which the rims were spoked direct.

Four-wheel brakes were introduced in 1929, when a 1500-c.c. six (60×88) was also offered, with pump cooling. The pressed-steel frame was continued with its cross-bracing, though no diagonal members were used. The six had 102-in. wheelbase and 48-in. track; in 1931 it grew larger in all areas, the engine measuring 1847 c.c. (66×90), wheelbase 106 or 123 in. and track 48 or 50. Single dry-disc clutches appeared and for 1932 the gear lever was mounted on the dashboard and spiral-bevel front drive was adopted, continuing to the end. In the next year the popular English 4-cylinder Meadows engine (1496 c.c., 69×100) was used. Many of these cars had been imported into England and modified by Vernon Balls, who raced Amilcars and Salmsons as well as Derbys and whose cars were known as Vernon Derbys. These 12/50-h.p. cars had all-independent suspension and coil ignition. The last Derby was a 2-litre V-8 (65×75) with exhaust over inlet valves and spiral-bevel front drive. Only at the end of its career did the marque attempt Le Mans: in 1934 and 1935, failing to finish both times.

GOBRON-BRILLIÉ

A less successful pioneer than Delahaye was Gobron-Brillié, which for the 30 years of its existence was probably the only car to carry two pistons in each cylinder, firing together.

This revolutionary design coupled the bottom pistons by a crankshaft, the uppers by a cross-shaft that was in turn linked to the crankshaft by long connecting rods. The 4-cylinder block was cast in pairs. In each cylinder the top and bottom pistons drew apart simultaneously; at the same time fuel was drawn into the cylinder. The return of the pistons compressed the gas and it was fired electrically. On the next upward stroke the exhaust valve carried off the burned gas in the conventional fashion.

The unusual engine was mounted vertically, though, in the early cars, at right angles to the chassis. The Gobron-Brillié did well in many of the early races until the 1908 formula excluded it; no effort was made to conform to the new rules. In 1904 the 4-cylinder (140 × 220) car, with the tubular trellis-work chassis characteristic of the marque, set a world speed record of 88·7 m.p.h.

Until it went out of business in 1929, Gobron-Brillié continued to use its opposed-piston design in engines ranging from two to six cylinders. For the last 11 years of its life it offered a conventional proprietary engine as an alternative.

Courtesy of the Société des Ingénieurs de l'Automobile]
Partly stripped for speed, opposed-piston Gobron-Brillié with chain drive set 1904 speed record

GORDINI

When Amédée Gordini founded his own marque in 1951, he characteristically paid no attention to what was "being done". His designs were the result of his racing and mechanical experience, which had made short work of doubters. Gordinis, like Roesch Talbots, represent the optimum coupling of simplicity and efficiency.

Working with 4-, 6- and 8-cylinder engines, Gordini set a high power-weight ratio as his goal and achieved it with all three types. Using aluminium extensively in engine and transmission, he built his tubular chassis of chrome molybdenum steel: the heaviest of his sports cars weighed $14\frac{1}{4}$ cwt. with its 220-h.p. 2982-c.c. straight-eight engine. The smallest Gordini, the 130-h.p. 1490-c.c. four, weighs $10\frac{3}{4}$ cwt. His chassis are suspended by a torsion-bar system of his own design, on which he holds a patent, and stabilizing bars are mounted front and rear.

Gordini engines are now all square: 78 × 78 for the 1490-c.c. four, 75 × 75 for the 150-h.p. 1987-c.c. six and again 78 × 78 for the eight. Balanced crankshafts of exceptional rigidity run in six main bearings in the 4-cylinder engine, in eight mains in the 6-cylinder and in 10 mains in the 8-cylinder. All cylinder heads are hemispherical and surmounted by two camshafts, the valves being set at a 45-degree angle. Maximum speeds are sufficient to give serious competition to much bigger machines: almost 150 m.p.h. for the four, 5 m.p.h. more for the six and better than 165 m.p.h. for the eight. Compression ratios range from 7·8:1 to 9·5:1, though the earlier grand-prix cars have gone as high as 11·5:1 and 12:1. Ignition is generally by coil, but magneto is available as an option.

Full synchromesh 4-speed gearboxes are employed on all Gordinis, in unit with the engines. Like many other marques used extensively in competition, Gordinis are fitted with right-hand drive, which offers

[Courtesy of Automobiles Gordini
The $1\frac{1}{2}$-litre coupé

The $2\frac{1}{2}$-litre six at Le Mans
[Courtesy of the Automobile-Club de l'Ouest

a number of advantages to the racing and fast-rally driver even in countries that drive to the right: better visibility on mountain roads and better balance on tight inside corners. The Gordini made its mark early with its outright victory in the first leg of the 1952 Carrera Panamericana in the hands of Jean Behra, who scored another victory for the marque the following year in the Tour de France.

Normally fitted with two carburetters, Solex for the gran turismo cars and Weber for the sports-racing, the 8-cylinder Gordini used four Webers at Le Mans, where a 2½-litre six (80×82) with three Webers and 1095-c.c. four (75×62) with two also appeared. Gordini finished third on index in 1953 and first in class with the 2½-litre six, no longer in production. An equally short-lived six was the 2261-c.c. (80×75) of 1955, which produced 125 b.h.p. at 5000 r.p.m. for 150 m.p.h. The later Gordinis turn slightly faster—6000 r.p.m. for the 1½-litre four and 5500 for the six and the eight. From time to time Gordini has offered such options on his cars as dry-sump lubrication and gear- or chain-driven camshafts to the customer's choice.

Coachwork has always been limited. Most of the sports Gordinis are open two-seaters, but a dramatically aerodynamic coupé was for some time available on the 1½-litre chassis. The longest wheelbase is the 92-in. eight, with 50-in. track; the six has the same wheelbase but the track is 4 in. less, while the four has an 86-in. wheelbase with the 50-in. track.

Courtesy of the Automobile-Club de Nice

Jean Behra takes the victory tour in the Gordini eight after his triumph in the Tour de France

Photograph by H. N. Vachon; courtesy of Automobiles Gordini]

The 1½-litre roadster and the 2-litre six are almost identical in appearance

[Photograph by J. Harris Reed

This 1912 Coupe de l'Auto car is still used by its British owner, whose father bought it in 1913

GRÉGOIRE

The two French cars that have borne the name *Grégoire*, like America's two Cunninghams, are completely unrelated.

The earlier Grégoire dates back to the turn of the century and was continued until the death of its creator in 1923. It was a much favoured sports car in the years just before the First World War, when it had its greatest successes.

Earlier 4-cylinder models had engines cast in pairs, though monobloc design superseded this in 1913, when the exhaust manifold was cast in a unit with the cylinders. The 3-bearing crankshaft was drilled and was lubricated by pressure. Aluminium was extensively used, even at this early date, and both crankcase and pistons were of this light metal. The 16/24 had enclosed side valves and a 4-speed gearbox, with cone clutch and torque-tube drive. Springs were semi-elliptic at the front and three-quarter elliptic at the rear.

There was also a 14/16 (65×130, in contrast to the larger car's 80×120) with a separate exhaust manifold and semi-elliptics all round. After the war the company made a 3-litre car with six 80×120 cylinders; but its outstanding products were the 16/24 and the 1912 model that gave the Hispano-Suiza so much trouble in the Coupe de l'Auto.

This was a 3-litre (80×149) with a T-head and caps on the exhaust valves. The 3-bearing crankshaft was made in two sections and bolted together; it was lubricated by centrifugal force, oil being fed by gravity to the dry sump from a 6-gallon tank under the scuttle. The wet multiple-disc clutch controlled a 3-speed gearbox transmitting power to an early form of overdrive that in effect gave six forward speeds: the rear axle held two ring gears in constant mesh each with its own pinion; the choice was made through a lever at the driver's left hand.

Today's Grégoire is the creation of J. A. Grégoire, whose dedication to front-wheel drive dates back more than 30 years. Using a 2188-c.c. flat 4-cylinder engine (90×86) with water cooling, he built the Hotchkiss-Grégoire Grand Sport saloon in 1949, an 80-b.h.p. car capable of 93 m.p.h. in its overdrive fourth gear. All wheels were independently hung on coil springs and the front wheels were fitted with Grégoire's patented Tracta joint, enabling them, though they were driving wheels, to turn in a radius comparable to that of the conventional car. The variable-rate suspension is also a Grégoire design: a horizontal coil spring for each front wheel is hung under the A-frame. Extensive use of aluminium kept

Photograph by J. Harris Reed]
The 16/24 tourer was a popular sports car in 1912–13

Courtesy of J. A. Grégoire]
Today's Grégoire, designer at the wheel

weight to about $17\frac{3}{4}$ cwt. but the aerodynamic five-seater body was not pretty.

Grégoire's latest car, available as either fixed- or drop-head sports, utilizes the same engine with a Roots supercharger offering 125 b.h.p. at 4500 r.p.m. and a 110-m.p.h. top speed.

HISPANO-SUIZA

Like Bugatti, Hispano-Suiza is a magic name. Its adherents, like those of Bugatti or Alfa or Mercedes, recognize no rival; and it is easy to understand why this should be so.

Hispano-Suiza was the creation of a young Swiss electrical engineer, Marc Birkigt, who started his career in Spain and named his car after the two countries that contributed its design and its financing. His first automobile appeared in 1904 and in the next 10 years he built, as was the custom of the time, some 35 different models. Birkigt was an originator rather than a follower, and Hispano-Suiza was first with the T-head motor cast *en bloc*, the misnamed Hotchkiss drive through the springs, low ratio of bore to stroke and, especially, the fast-turning engine. In his first racing attempt, the 1910 G.P. de France at Boulogne-sur-Mer, his 69×200-mm. 4-cylinder car was placed first among the light cars. The next time out, in 1912, Hispano was the first car to use a supercharger successfully: it was mounted

between the engine and the radiator of a 3-litre four and not only supercharged the mixture on inlet but also scavenged the burned gas by means of a third valve in the head.

One of the most famous and most beautiful Hispanos—the European equivalent, as a symbol of the excitement of the motor car, of the American Mercer and Stutz—was the 15·9-h.p. Alfonso model. Light, short in wheelbase (it was built in both two- and four-seater models), it derived directly from the 1912 Coupe de l'Auto car and its four 80×100 cylinders (3614 c.c.) produced 64 b.h.p. at 3200 r.p.m. As on the earlier cars, the engine was built in unit with the 3-speed gearbox (some Alfonsos had four speeds); it could be tuned to deliver 90 m.p.h. The King of Spain was so delighted with the car, which was built in Barcelona until the First World War, that he allowed his name to be given to it.

Birkigt also was an early advocate of the square engine. His 1907 sixes had a bore and stroke of

[Courtesy of the Montagu Motor Museum

The 1907 Hispano-Suiza in a recent rally

Courtesy of the Henry Ford Museum]

The exquisite Alfonso

[Courtesy of Charles Stich

The 4½-litre (90 × 180) finished first in the 5-litre class and second over-all at Anjou in 1914

Courtesy of Alec Ulmann]

Weymann at the wheel of the Monza model with which he defeated Stutz at Indianapolis; relief driver, Robert Block, is beside him

115 × 115 and 130 × 130 (later changed to 100 × 120 and 130 × 140) and these were accompanied by two 4-cylinder cars of 100 × 120 and 130 × 140, the cylinders cast in pairs.

At the start of the 1914 war, in which Spain remained neutral, Birkigt volunteered to aid France and for the next four years built the magnificent V-8 aircraft engines used by all the Allies and still admired by many engineers. When peace returned he remained in France, with which he has been identified ever since.

His first post-war car derived directly from the plane engine, with its steel cylinder liners screwed into an aluminium block, and overhead cam acting directly on the valve tappets. Its six 100 × 140 cylinders produced 135 b.h.p. at 3000 r.p.m. with dual ignition and a double-barrelled carburetter. It was built in unit with the gearbox and had a single dry-plate clutch, as well as torque-tube drive and 4-wheel brakes with mechanical servo. Known in France as the 32-h.p., it has become famous in the rest of the world as the 37·2 (methods of measuring horsepower

vary among countries). Like the Alfonso, the new 6597-c.c. car emphasized lightness; it weighed 22 cwt. Inertia was harnessed to power the servo, driven by a clutch shaft from the transmission, so that the decelerating force available was always proportionate to the speed. The brake drums were finned aluminium castings into which heat-resisting metal liners were shrunk. Large cross-members helped assure extreme chassis rigidity in a day when flexibility was more often the rule. The gear-change was reputed to be the easiest of all the crash boxes, and 85 m.p.h. was easily reached, even with the low compression ratio of 4·5:1.

This car's 2½-turn steering was ideal for sports use, and two short-chassis models were introduced on a 133¼-in. wheelbase. The first of these was known as the Monza, bored out to 102 mm. for 90 m.p.h. Two years later, in 1924, an 8-litre version (110 × 140) with 6:1 compression, driven by André Dubonnet, won the Coupe Boillot at Boulogne and was thereafter known as the Boulogne. This was an honest 100-m.p.h. automobile.

[Courtesy of Alec Ulmann

The boat-tailed Monza formerly owned by A. E. Ulmann, founder of Sebring; now in Briggs Cunningham's collection

Photograph by Michael Boys; courtesy of L. G. Albertini]

Incredibly, this Tulipwood Boulogne (named for its bodywork) was driven to fifth place in the 1924 Targa Florio by André Dubonnet

In 1928 Hispano and Stutz staged a famous 24-hour match race at Indianapolis. This grew out of the late C. F. Kettering's $25,000 bet that a Cadillac could beat a Rolls from Detroit to Dayton. By a logical process too obvious to trace, C. T. Weymann, inventor of the fabric body so widely used on all the best vintage marques, converted Kettering's original challenge into the Hispano–Stutz race, and a well-used Monza model proceeded to idle round the oval at 70 m.p.h. for the full time while the Stutz came apart. After 19 hours the American car could no longer be repaired; the Hispano was as fresh as at the start.

Hispano had continued to build its 4-cylinder car in Spain, where eventually production ceased and the factory ultimately passed to Pegaso. But the Flying Stork's fame rests solidly on its French products, which in 1930 were supplemented by the $9\frac{1}{2}$-litre V-12 with 100×100 bore and stroke. On this engine pushrod overhead valves replaced the overhead cam in the interests of silence; with 6:1 compression it gave 220 b.h.p. and 100 m.p.h. even with heavy coachwork, accelerating from rest to 60 m.p.h. in 12 seconds. Big as it was, its handling was utterly sporting.

It is a sad conclusion that must be written to the story of the Flying Stork. Like so many other embodiments of the tradition of quality, it was stifled by the

Courtesy of the "Carriage Cavalcade"]

The 1934 V-12 had seven bronze-bushed main bearings, aluminium crankcase, tubular connecting rods, oval alloy pistons

depression of the 1930s and today the name remains alive only as a supplier of aviation components, advanced armaments and textile machinery.

HOTCHKISS

When the War of 1870 broke out, an American engineer named Benjamin T. Hotchkiss happened to be in Paris. He offered his knowledge of mass production of rapid-fire guns to Napoleon III; after that, Hotchkiss remained in France and developed a vast armaments business that was eventually called on to make components for automobiles. In 1902, Hotchkiss produced its own car, a 50-h.p. In the next few years it also made a few 100-h.p. racing cars that were not too successful; in 1907 the firm abandoned racing. Hotchkiss is generally credited with having introduced the torque tube: a casing attached to the gearbox at one end and the differential at the other to take up the torque of the drive shaft.

The almost-circular radiator of Hotchkiss disappeared from competition after 1907

[From the Lazarnick Collection; courtesy of the Library of the Automobile Manufacturers' Association

99

Requisitioned by French, German and British armies, this Paris-Nice drop-head was salvaged from an army-surplus dump to run in three post-war Tulip Rallies. Windscreen can be folded flat

During the vintage period Hotchkiss continued the emphasis on ball bearings that had marked the earlier cars. Its cars were big (wheelbase was 12 ft.) and unusually robustly built. They were powered by a 6½-litre (100 × 140) overhead-cam six that gave 130 b.h.p. at 3000 r.p.m., comparable to the 37·2 Hispano's output. In the 1930s the 6-cylinder engine was reduced to 3½ litres (86 × 100) with pushrod overhead valves, and the chassis shrank to a wheelbase of 10 ft. 1½ in. and a track of 4 ft. 8 in. About the middle of the decade a Grand Sport chassis of 9 ft. 2 in. was also offered; this was often fitted with the so-called Paris–Nice engine, with 7 : 1 compression and dual carburation, good for 115 b.h.p. and 100 m.p.h. with fairly heavy closed or drop-head coachwork; it would reach 60 m.p.h. from rest in 13·7 seconds.

While the Hotchkiss was not raced, it starred in rallies that were the next thing to races, winning the Monte Carlo five times. Hotchkiss and Bugatti were the last French marques to give up beam front axles—Hotchkiss adopted coil-spring independent front suspension only after the 1939 war, and hydraulic brakes only a little before that war. The post-war car also had the Cotal gearbox. Combining with Delahaye and working with Grégoire, Hotchkiss went out of automobile production a few years ago.

GEORGES IRAT

Georges Irat was one of the first Frenchmen to produce a modern car after the First World War. A 2-litre 4-cylinder, it was built to the utmost simplicity consonant with efficiency and without regard to cost. As a result, the Georges Irat never sold well, but it set a pace for other French marques.

Appearing in 1920, the Georges Irat stressed overhead valves, 4-wheel brakes with servo, aluminium pistons and a dynamically balanced engine. It was one of the first French cars to position the driver on the left. Georges Irat was an important contender in the first Le Mans race, though it did not win a place. During the 1920s and well into the next decade it continued substantially unchanged; then, a few years before the war, it introduced a front-wheel-drive car that adhered to the same high standards that had characterized the previous model. A smaller car had been added to the line and this too was equipped with front-wheel drive; like the 2-litre, it adopted Citroën's designs.

The outbreak of war cut the life of the Georges Irat to less than two decades.

The 1923 Georges Irat at Le Mans

The front-wheel-drive small Georges Irat of 1936. Like many drop-heads of that period, it retained the advantage of a fold-flat windscreen

The 2-litre f.w.d. Georges Irat, the last model, with less frontal area to reduce drag. It was powered by a 2-litre (78 × 100) Citroën 4-cylinder engine

This type of de Dietrich finished third in the Paris–Madrid

The big de Dietrich raced at Anjou on eve of First World War

Lorraine-Dietrich still had chain drive in 1908

The 1926 car that won Le Mans in that year was privately entered often thereafter. It won 1958 Rétrospective

LORRAINE-DIETRICH DE DIETRICH

Not the least element of the record of de Dietrich, which was later to become Lorraine-Dietrich, is the fact that in 1905 the company gave his first job to Ettore Bugatti. De Dietrich had been in business only a few years, but it had already shown a taste and aptitude for racing, having a 24-h.p. car driven by Mme. du Gast in the 1903 Paris–Madrid and finishing third with a 45-h.p. driven by Charles Jarrott. This was the ancestor of the famous 60-h.p., a 12-litre car of four 146 × 108 cylinders that actually gave 70 b.h.p. at 1200 r.p.m. One of its outstanding features was its L-head—i.e. all valves on the same side—in an era when the T-head was believed to be the only kind that would provide adequacy of both valve area and cooling. This 70-m.p.h. car, which finally abandoned armoured wood for pressed steel frame, scored well in the Targa Florio, broke the Paris–Nice record and won the Moscow–St. Petersburg race. Its cylinders grew to 15 litres by 1912, when a Peugeot half its size, designed by Henry, opened

the industry's thinking to the smaller engine and twin overhead camshafts with inclined valves. Chain final drive, however, was favoured by de Dietrich almost into the vintage period.

Lorraine-Dietrich, as the firm became known about this time, did not come back to the sport until the mid-1920s. In 1924 the marque finished second and third at Le Mans with 3½-litre sixes of 75 × 130 mm. designed by Marius Barbarou. These had undetachable cylinder heads and overhead valves driven by completely exposed pushrods, which were most brittle. Their other fittings included dual ignition and carburation, three-speed gearboxes and cantilever rear springs; they were capable of 95 m.p.h. Servo brakes were fitted to the Le Mans cars. In 1925 they won outright and also took third place; in 1926 they made a 1-2-3 sweep and that year's No. 1 car was privately raced again and again at Le Mans without much to show. The marque vanished during the depression.

101

[Photograph by J. W. Haughton]

The 1898 Mors still in use in England is a flat twin (70 × 110)

Courtesy of the Société des Ingénieurs de l'Automobile]

The 70-h.p. 4-cylinder (145 × 175) winner of Paris–Madrid was fitted with shock-absorbers

MORS

Contrary to the statement of a fanatical M.P. in the House of Commons, the Mors car was not named for death, nor did its drivers believe they had the right to kill whatever got in their way.

Emile Mors began building cars for enthusiasts, rather like Bugatti later, around the turn of the century. A few years later he perfected one of the first dependable self-starters: unlike Kettering's, it worked by compression rather than electricity. As early as 1902 he employed shock-absorbers. Mors dominated the competition arena for less than five years; but then, no one knows quite why, the marque was abruptly shorn of its sporting character. It expired quietly in the early 1920s.

Mors was Panhard's great rival in the early years of the century. In 1901 the 60-h.p. 2-cylinder Mors won the second Paris–Bordeaux race with an average above 50 m.p.h.; it was second and third in the Belgian Circuit des Ardennes, the No. 3 car being driven by William K. Vanderbilt, founder of the Vanderbilt Cup, who was to set a world speed record of 76·5 m.p.h. with a Mors in 1902. In 1903 a Mors capable of 80 m.p.h. averaged 60 m.p.h. to win the bloody Paris–Madrid. The Mors attained 100 b.h.p. during its brief sporting career but never again did so well as in these first few years.

From the Lazarnick Collection;
courtesy of the Library of the Automobile Manufacturers' Association]

William K. Vanderbilt set world speed record on Mors

102

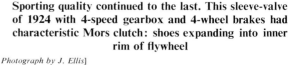

Sporting quality continued to the last. This sleeve-valve of 1924 with 4-speed gearbox and 4-wheel brakes had characteristic Mors clutch: shoes expanding into inner rim of flywheel

The 24/32 Mors of 1904 was a 4-cylinder car

[Photograph by J. Ellis   Photograph by J. Ellis]

[Courtesy of the Société des Ingénieurs de l'Automobile

The 1891 tiller-steered car built for Hippolyte Panhard

Courtesy of D. Napier & Sons Ltd.]

Charles Jarrott (at wheel) with S. F. Edge in Panhard that finished second in 1896 Paris-Marseilles Race. Montague Napier installed wheel steering and pneumatic tyres

[Courtesy of S. A. Panhard et Levassor

The 6-h.p. 2-cylinder (90 × 130) car of 1897, at Le Mans 60 years later. Tubular radiator, in front of this car, was sometimes rear-mounted

Courtesy of the Henry Ford Museum]

The 1904 Panhard

PANHARD ET LEVASSOR

If the Daimler was the father of the automobile, its second child, the Daimler-engined Panhard, was the father of the sports car, and at that by a second marriage.

Gottlieb Daimler had sold the French rights for his engines to an old lawyer-friend, Edouard Sarazin, who commissioned Emile Levassor to build them. Levassor was a partner with René Panhard in the manufacture of woodworking machinery, and it was he rather than Panhard who was primarily interested in cars.

However, before Levassor could complete the engine, Sarazin died. Daimler had met Mme. Sarazin, for whose acumen he had so much esteem that he transferred to her the rights he had sold to her husband. Levassor had also met the lady and had as much regard for her other qualities as Daimler had for her business ability. Mme. Sarazin soon became

Mme. Levassor, and her husband devoted his labours entirely to the automobile aspect of Panhard et Levassor.

At this time—1890—it was usual to make an automobile by mounting an engine and its auxiliaries in a carriage, the engine generally being put at the rear. Levassor started out by designing the vehicle for his engine, which he located at the front after two rear-engine experiments. To test his cars, he drove them himself in competition, beginning with the world's first race, the 1895 Paris–Bordeaux–Paris, for which he entered a 4-h.p. air-cooled V-twin (80 × 120) with automatic inlet valves and hot-tube ignition. A double leather cone clutch controlled the 4-speed gearbox and final drive was by chains. The wooden wheels had iron tyres. Levassor's co-driver overslept and so the builder had to start alone. He spent 48 hours and 47 minutes at the tiller of his car to beat the entire field with a speed of 15·38 m.p.h. for the 750-mile race. But, since the rules stipulated that the prize would go to the first four-seater to finish and the Panhard et Levassor was a two-seater, Peugeot got the trophy.

Panhard won the Paris–Marseilles–Paris the next year with its first 4-cylinder, of the same cylinder dimensions as the twin but with 8 h.p. Levassor, however, crashed, suffering internal injuries that proved fatal in 1897. The firm was then re-capitalized and the Chevalier René de Knyff, a famous gentleman driver, became a director. In the 17 years between Levassor's first car and the outbreak of the 1914 war the firm made almost 40 different models, all fours from 1899 on.

Panhard, which had produced the world's first vertical four, was in the forefront of racing at and after the turn of the century: second to sixth inclusive in the 1901 Paris–Bordeaux with 40-h.p. fours (130 × 140), coil ignition replacing the hot platinum tube heated by an external burner; first in the light-car class with a 12-h.p. four (90 × 130), which duplicated this win in the Paris–Berlin; first in the 1902 Circuit du Nord with the 70-h.p. car of 130 × 140; second in the 1903 Gordon Bennett with a 160 × 170-mm. 70-h.p. driven by de Knyff; first in the 1905 Vanderbilt Cup with a square (170 × 170) 90-h.p.— the first Panhard to adopt magneto ignition and shaft drive. The biggest Panhard—a 130-h.p. four of 185 × 170, or 18 litres—was left far behind in the 1906 G.P. de France.

But, if the marque's popularity was rising with every race, so was the cost of competing. These two factors caused Panhard to gradually diminish its racing activity, but the 40-, 50- and 60-h.p. cars that it continued to build were indisputably race-bred. In 1911 Panhard also offered two smaller cars with sleeve-valve engines made under the patents of Charles Y. Knight of Wisconsin.

After the First World War Panhard paid little attention to competition, though its products were considered well above the average. A 1925 car catalogued as a sports set a one-hour record of 116 miles, but enthusiasts were not attracted in any great numbers. Capt. G. E. T. Eyston's 125-m.p.h. record in a special Panhard in 1932 did nothing to gain it repute as a true sports car; it was only after the Second World War that the marque won new acclaim in the sports category.

The post-war Panhard was at once radically new and another argument in support of the old adage about history's repetitiousness. Once again Panhard was an opposed twin, air-cooled; but now the final drive was in the front, the differential and gearbox were built in unit, valves were overhead and suspension was independent in front by transverse leaf spring and semi-independent at the back by torsion bar. The new 2-cylinder engine was only 850 c.c. (85 × 75).

This Dyna-Panhard (so-called because of the turbine-like cooling system that is employed also for interior heating and defrosting) weighs only 13·4 cwt. with its wheelbase of 8 ft. $5\frac{3}{16}$ in. and track of

[Courtesy of Automobiles D.B.

The aluminium-bodied 1950 coupé had D.B. coachwork

Photograph by the authors; courtesy of Norbert Guillaume]

The Dyna Junior drop-head weighs 11·6 cwt. It has a simple longitudinal frame with two cross-members

104

The 1957 Le Mans coupés were not unlike D.B.

[Courtesy of S. A. Panhard et Levassor

The 4-door saloon is a frequent class winner in races and rallies

Courtesy of S. A. Panhard et Levassor]

4 ft. 3 $\frac{3}{16}$ in. Even the bulge-sided saloon is a true sports car, having proved itself in innumerable races and rallies since its introduction.

The Z-1 drop-head, known as the Dyna Junior, was available in the early 1950s with the standard 42-h.p. engine good for over 80 m.p.h., a slightly slower 745-c.c. engine or the 120 Sprint and 130 Sprint, developing about 40 and 42 h.p. respectively. Almost a half-dozen times these post-war Panhards have been first on index at Le Mans; twice they have done so at Sebring. They were first in their class in the Francorchamps G.P. for production cars, the Mille Miglia, the Monte Carlo Rally and the Alpine. In the Liège–Rome–Liège Rally they took the first three places in class; in the G.P. de Rheims, the first two. They have also been the basis for the highly successful D.B.

PEUGEOT

Peugeot was a name known all over France before Armand Peugeot was born almost 100 years ago; it is still seen on old coffee and pepper mills. The original Peugeots were ironmongers; Armand was trained for engineering and commerce in England. A business friend of Levassor, he was easily persuaded of the future of the self-propelled vehicle, but he distrusted petrol. However, experience with steam sent him back to Levassor, and in 1890 the first Peugeot appeared with Levassor's air-cooled V-twin engine. Unlike Panhard, Peugeot mounted it horizontally. Since he had been a bicycle builder before going into automobiles, he entered the car in the Paris–Brest bicycle race: it averaged 9½ m.p.h. to clinch last place.

Peugeot began building his own engines in 1896; from the first he favoured the long stroke. All his engines until 1902 were 2-cylinder, but he adopted water cooling in 1898 and battery ignition two years later. His first engine was a 4-h.p. of 84×126; other favoured proportions were 115×160 (10 h.p.) and 140×190 (30 h.p.). In 1902 he departed from this formula to build a 4-cylinder 50-h.p. engine measuring 155×150 and a 16-h.p. four of 120×94. These were his first cars with magneto ignition and honeycomb radiators; the earlier coolers were tubular.

Returning to the long stroke for his famous racing *voiturettes*—which were anything but light or little cars by later standards—Peugeot deepened his cylinders to as much as 300 mm. A number of races were run by Jules Goux on a 3-litre four whose bore and stroke were 65×260. Ernest Henry was retained to design a 7·6-litre engine for the big cars, producing as much as 200 h.p. at 3500 r.p.m. with light steel pistons. His designs were at their best over 2500 r.p.m., and he created low chassis of excellent weight balance to make the most of the engines and the close-ratio gearboxes that they required. Henry was the first to exploit the double overhead camshaft and inclined valves—he used four per cylinder in his 4-cylinder monster, which was copied almost item for item by Sunbeam.

Courtesy of the Société des Ingénieurs de l'Automobile]

The 1891 Peugeot, chain-driven, was no match for bicycles. It steered by tiller

Photograph by C. A. Oakden]

The 1902 twin-cylinder (95×95) was first with header-tank radiator, supplied by Mercedes. Speed was controlled through ignition rather than throttle

It was Goux, Georges Boillot and Paul Zuccarelli, all engineers as well as Peugeot works drivers, who persuaded the management to retain Henry, and they worked with him on the design of the 1913 car that pioneered dry-sump lubrication. Weighing 15 cwt., the 3-litre machine produced 90 m.p.h. at less

The 5650-c.c. car (100×180) at Amiens, 1913; Georges Boillot at wheel

Courtesy of S. A. des Automobiles Peugeot]

[Courtesy of S. A. des Automobiles Peugeot

The 7·6 car in road-race trim, Boillot at wheel. Similar car won twice at Indianapolis

Courtesy of the Société des Ingénieurs de l'Automobile]

Rated at 6 h.p. outside France, this tiny 4-cylinder car seated two people in tandem. It was favoured for voiturette races of the early 1920s

than 3000 r.p.m. and was quite capable of 100 m.p.h. The big car that won at Indianapolis that year and the next had a bore and stroke of 110 × 200; a 4½-litre (92 × 69) d.o.h.c. engine good for 115 h.p. at 2800 r.p.m.—almost 115 m.p.h.—tried for the G.P. de France in 1914 but lost so much time with tyre trouble that it was defeated by Mercedes. This was the first Peugeot to race with 4-wheel brakes. Finally, a 2½-litre (75 × 146) of 85 h.p. was prepared for the Coupe de l'Auto but the beginning of war cancelled the race and the car was not used until peace returned.

Peugeot was much less active in competition thereafter; increasingly its rôle was limited to private owners who entered true dual-purpose cars (the distinction between racing and sports cars, which had begun to manifest itself before the war, became unmistakable in the 1920s) at various French courses. The Peugeots of the 1920s, like the Panhards, had adopted the sleeve-valve principle (which is more correctly denominated *valveless*) and were to prove the exception to the rule that the greater refinement of such engines had to be paid for in performance; the 4-litre Peugeot of this type could very nearly hold its own with the 3-litre Bentley. Two of these Peugeots appeared at Le Mans in 1926: one did not finish and the other, when lying second, was disqualified for a broken windscreen. The marque's last Le Mans

Courtesy of the Société des Ingénieurs de l'Automobile]

The valve-less 1926 car set Montlhéry record, ran at Le Mans. André Boillot and Louis Rigal drove it in the 24-hour race

appearance was a 2-litre car that finished fifth in 1938.

Since then Peugeot has made its name with a remarkably dependable, if completely undistinguished, family car of medium price and high quality.

106

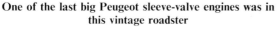

One of the last big Peugeot sleeve-valve engines was in this vintage roadster

[Autocar photograph from the collection of George A. Moffitt]

The last Le Mans Peugeot was this 1938 Darl' Mat' with Cotal gearbox, which ran again in 1958 Le Mans Rétrospective

Courtesy of the Automobile-Club de l'Ouest]

First sports Renault was this 1899 "torpedo", steered by tiller

Szisz at wheel of 90-h.p. car that won 1906 French G.P.

By 1910 the "torpedo" had acquired this shape, with 20/30-h.p. 4-cylinder engine (100 × 140)

The high-performance 45-h.p. was marque's vintage sports car

RENAULT

Like many a modern business man's son with leisure and money, Louis Renault enjoyed tinkering with machinery. In 1898, when he was 20, he bought a $1\frac{3}{4}$-h.p. de Dion three-wheeler but was displeased with its handling, so he built a four-wheeler, with pneumatic tyres and wheel steering, in which he mounted the engine at the front, a shaft drive and a differential. He patented the car and tried to sell the rights, but his friends wanted him to make replicas for them; suddenly he was a manufacturer.

In a year his brothers, Marcel and Fernand, were in partnership with him and Renault was racing. Emphasizing smallness and lightness, the Renault frequently beat the more prevalent monsters, still using the single-cylinder de Dion engine. Having sold 350 cars in 1900, the brothers enlarged their plant and looked for an enlarged engine as well. De Dion-Bouton's biggest was a 2-cylinder, but Bouton's brother-in-law made fours and Renault turned to these in 1902, winning the Paris–Vienna Race with a 16-h.p. engine of 120 × 120 (in contrast to the 100 × 130 single-cylinder car that won the previous year's Paris–Berlin). Orders poured in and Renault again had to enlarge the plant. The pattern had been set for Renault's next 26 years.

The 1903 Paris–Madrid car was a 30-h.p. four of 124 × 130. It won the light-car class with an average speed of 62·3 m.p.h. but the victory was tragic for Louis Renault. Marcel, to whom Louis was devoted, tried to pass another car on a curve after miles of running hub to hub at better than 60 m.p.h.: taking the dirt shoulder of the road, he skidded into a tree, turned over twice and was killed almost instantly. Renault withdrew from racing at once.

However, he did build a car for the Hungarian driver, Szisz, to use in the 1905 Vanderbilt Cup. This was a 60-h.p. four (160 × 150) with a leather cone clutch, like all Renault's high-performance cars up to the 1914 war; it did not place. In the 1906 French G.P., run near Le Mans, Szisz (who used to drive railroad locomotives) drove a 90-h.p. (166 × 150) car—one of the first with demountable rims—to victory over 18-litre machines whose engines took up the greatest part of the weight allowance of 18 cwt. Reversing the proportions of bore and stroke, the 1908 G.P. car had four 155 × 160 cylinders and developed 100 h.p. While Renault had passed the peak of its racing career, which soon ended, the firm was profiting handsomely by the royalties on the 1899 patent for a direct-drive gear.

The last pre-war sports model was the Vivagrand

The workmanlike-looking 4CV can reach 80 m.p.h.

One of the first 4CV modifications was the two-seater
V.P.

Rosier modification of 4CV is one of a few open versions

108

The Mille Miglia saloon has aluminium cylinder head

The Dauphine family car's excellent road-holding gives
it advantages for race and rally use

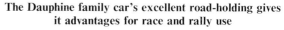

War brought the legendary Renault feat of the first Battle of the Marne, when the taxis of Paris saved France by becoming troop transports. Peace, however, did not alter the purely utilitarian character that the marque had assumed, continuing to build 4-cylinder cars on the foundation of the Paris–Vienna 2-cylinder. But in the middle 1920s a high-performance luxury car was added to the line—the 45-h.p., which was a radical departure from Renault's original reliance on small engines in light chassis. The 45 was a 9123-c.c. six (110×160) with one carburetter and magneto ignition—only 4-wheel brakes with mechanical servo indicated any advance from the pre-war thinking. The dynastarter was hopelessly unmatched to its task, and a starting button was mounted outboard next to the crank. Renault clung to thermo-siphon cooling and the behind-the-engine radiator; vanes on the rim of the flywheel were supposed to help cool the engine. The wheels were wood, with detachable rims. Horsepower was supposed to be 140 at 3000 r.p.m., though 2750 was the maximum allowed, and the $44\frac{1}{2}$-cwt. car with its 12 ft. 6 in. wheelbase was good for 90 m.p.h.

The 1925 sports version, still side-valve, had a 3-speed gearbox and external oil cooler. The wire-wheeled four-seater set a number of records at Montlhéry, from 103·9 m.p.h. for 500 miles to 87 m.p.h. for 24 hours. But this was virtually the marque's last important sporting effort until our own period, though a fairly sporting car was produced just before the Second World War. In the post-war period, however, Renault has returned to motor sport with a zest and an accomplishment that would hardly be expected from the very un-sporting aspect of most of its current products.

Even in its homely standard guise, the little 750-c.c. 4CV has participated effectively in races and rallies throughout the world; in the Little Le Mans at Lime Rock in 1958, a 10-hour endurance race for production sedans under $1\frac{1}{2}$ litres, a privately entered 4CV—its volume just half the maximum—finished high in class against the astonishing SAAB and covered 600 miles at top speeds with only two pit stops, both for driver change and fuel. Weighing well under $13\frac{1}{2}$ cwt., it has a 3-speed gearbox; bore and stroke are $54·5 \times 80$. These cars, in whose rear-engine design the late Dr. Porsche had a major part, were all built after the company was nationalized by the French Government as a result of collaboration charges made against Louis Renault, who has since died.

Various modifications of the 4CV have also appeared, with coachwork by Rosier, as well as the Alpine version. Many of these include aluminium cylinder heads and glass fibre bodies on the standard all-independent chassis; the Alpine offers the option of a 4- or 5-speed gearbox. Like the stock 4CV, these versions have removable cylinder liners. They have scored well in their class and even in higher classes in both Le Mans and the Mille Miglia.

The slightly larger Dauphine, also a 4-door saloon, has an 845-c.c. engine and has made an equally high reputation, winning its class at Le Mans, in the Mille Miglia and in many of the hardest rallies, such as the Monte Carlo and the Tour de France, and averaging close to 70 m.p.h. for the full 24 hours at Le Mans. New versions modified by Amédée Gordini, the famous designer of racing cars, offer a 4-speed gearbox and vastly increased horsepower: from the stock 32 to about 45. Very few have been built to date; production will be undertaken for the most part at Renault's English works.

ROLLAND-PILAIN

In its 25 years of manufacture, the Rolland-Pilain enjoyed its best time near the end. Established in 1907 and killed off by the depression, the marque was another of those that stressed quality rather than economy of construction. Six- and 8-cylinder engines of 2- and 3-litre capacity and relatively high r.p.m. even today—in the neighbourhood of 5000—roller-bearings for crankshafts, overhead camshaft, disc rather than plate clutch, 4-wheel brakes, were characteristic of the Rolland-Pilain in the early and middle 1920s; but the marque was always dogged by bad luck. At Strasbourg in 1922 the long crankshafts of the eights could not endure the vibration; at Le Mans, where Rolland-Pilain ran every one of the first four years, it could never finish among the first half-dozen cars. It was always just below the highest level, yet well above the average.

Courtesy of the Automobile-Club de l'Ouest]
An early 4-cylinder (95×140) Rolland-Pilain

Elegance of line was equal to mechanical quality of 1926 car at Le Mans. Note headlights reversed to lower wind-resistance

From the collection of Jacques Rousseau]

109

SALMSON

Originating as the French licensee for the G.N., Salmson began to build its own cars in 1921 with a startling unorthodoxy. The 1100-c.c. 4-cylinder side-valve engine had only four pushrods: the cams were recessed for double duty so that a second spring could close the valves. The chassis and weight were comparable to those of the Amilcar and the two marques were great rivals for a decade.

In 1924 Salmson introduced its Grand Prix model, 62 × 90, with twin overhead camshafts. This and the AL-3 type had a wheelbase of 8 ft. 1 in. and a track of 3 ft. 7 in.; steering was one and a quarter turns lock to lock. Since the Salmson, like the Amilcar, had no differential, cornering could be tricky as well as excellent. Maximum speed was only about 65 m.p.h. but excellent acceleration gave these cars an advantage in all their races. From the 1921 car's first race to the triumphs of the blown 50 × 78·8 straight-eight at the end of the 1920s, the marque scored 1200 firsts—85 of them in 1925 alone. The four was the first 1100-c.c. car to reach 100 m.p.h. in 1924, 110 m.p.h. in 1925 and 120 m.p.h. in 1926. The eight could attain 135 m.p.h. and twice won the Biennial Cup at Le Mans, as well as class prize in the Targa Florio.

An interesting feature of the early cars was the 2-wheel brakes. The foot brake operated only the right-hand wheel, the hand brake governing only the left. To some extent this compensated for the lack of a differential on tight corners. Front springing was semi-elliptic, rear was cantilevered quarter-elliptic, and the early cars had friction shock absorbers, but only at the rear. The 3-speed gearbox was controlled by a leather cone clutch; the Grand Prix model had four speeds.

During the 1920s Salmson built no sports cars. In that period a British Salmson was also marketed but it was essentially the same as its French contemporary. After 1945, however, the marque re-entered the sports-car field with a 2½-litre d.o.h.c. six of British design with 7·5:1 compression and 110 b.h.p. In gran turismo and drop-head form the car was continued until mid-1957, when the company abruptly ceased automobile production. In many of the hard, fast European rallies it scored high, winning the Coupe des Alpes, finishing second in class in the Liège–Rome–Liège and the Monte Carlo and winning the latter's speed test outright (its maximum is well over 100 m.p.h.), and later finishing second over-all in the Liège–Rome–Liège.

[Photograph by John Geary]

The 1924 roadster with side valves and aluminium body. Brake cables run through radius rods

Photograph by Michael Sedgwick]

The 1928 touring Grand Sport

The post-war drop-head

[Photograph by Michael P. Clapham]

The Salmson that finished second over-all in 1955 Liège–Rome–Liège had one of the more beautiful envelope bodies

Photograph by R. Cotton]

SARA

The distinction of the slowest time ever made at Le Mans belongs to the air-cooled SARA, which covered 609 miles at an average of 25·4 m.p.h. in the inaugural race of 1923. In the marque's last appearance there, in 1933, it was disqualified for failing to complete the minimum distance stipulated for its class. In the years between, however, it performed quite creditably.

One of the multitude of cycle-cars that sprang up in France after the First World War, the SARA was originally quite similar to the others with its light chassis and body and its 1100-c.c. 4-cylinder engine. After the 1923 fiasco, the marque managed to finish at least one car of its entry in the upper third or better. In 1927 SARA was third in the competition for the Biennial Cup—rather oddly, with its 1100-c.c. engine, for in that year the marque had also gone to a 1498-c.c. unit. In the next two years its 1800-c.c. engine again brought the car into contention for the cup, though the marque never won it.

The 1927 SARA team at Le Mans: 1100-c.c. car at left, 1500 at right

TALBOT
TALBOT-LAGO

Any attempt to clarify the history of the Sunbeam-Talbot-Darracq combine is dangerous. After Talbot-Darracq bought Sunbeam, the Darracq works in Suresnes continued to build Darracq's designs and added some from the British Talbot line. In 1933 Sunbeam sent one of its officers, the French-born Antoine Lago, to Suresnes to head the plant there while continuing his management of the Wolverhampton factory. When the Rootes interests took over in England, Lago, an outstanding engineer, bought the Suresnes establishment to build his own cars.

Earlier, Lago had developed a combination of friction clutch and Wilson pre-selector gearbox that could be worked with one pedal. With a free hand in Suresnes, he immediately turned this gearbox to racing and took first and second in the 1936 Tourist Trophy with a 4-litre six mounting three carburetters. The hemispherical combustion chamber resembled that of the B.M.W. and later Bristol; extra transverse pushrods enabled the single camshaft to operate the inclined valves. This was replaced by two camshafts high up in the block, on the Riley pattern. These cars won a number of other races before the war, the team being managed by René Dreyfus.

The same engine, developing 160 b.h.p. at 4200 r.p.m., was soon used for gran turismo cars with daringly beautiful bodies on a 104-in. wheelbase; even weighing $29\frac{1}{2}$ cwt., these coupés were capable of 118 m.p.h. Bored out to $4\frac{1}{2}$ litres, the engine was also mounted in G.P. cars and in some rather sketchily bodied sports types for the 1938 and 1939 Le Mans, without too much success. After the war the $4\frac{1}{2}$-litre cars ran up an impressive record of G.P. victories all over Europe, including an outright win at Le Mans in 1950, beating every course record in the hands of Louis Rosier and his son, who have made so many improvements in the performance of the tiny Renaults.

This victory was all but duplicated in 1952, when Pierre Levegh stubbornly insisted on driving his own $4\frac{1}{2}$-litre six without relief, stopping at the pits only

The 1937 drop-head by Figoni & Falaschi on an early Lago chassis

The Figoni & Falaschi coupé was raced at Le Mans before the war and at Watkins Glen in 1950. It has $4\frac{1}{2}$-litre engine

The 1939 Le Mans car at 1958 Rétrospective

The car that almost won at Le Mans in 1952

long enough for the car's needs to be filled while he took a hasty sip or bite to keep going. At the end of the 23rd hour it looked as if Levegh and Talbot would be the first combination ever to win Le Mans without a driver change; but Levegh was by now reacting automatically. Hours earlier his pit crew and even his wife had given up their vain attempts to persuade him to accept a co-driver; on his last pit stop he did not even recognize the people in his crew. At 23 hours and 30 minutes he was invincibly ahead of the second-place Mercedes; but then, undoubtedly because he was too dazed to control his movements, he broke his crankshaft—probably by over-revving. Too far from the finish to push the car there in time, even if he had had the strength, Levegh sat immobile as the whole field flashed by.

The car in which this was done had two carburetters for its 93×110 cylinders (the 8-cylinder version had three carburetters) and 8:1 compression. The transverse-leaf independent front suspension of Lago's first car had given way to coils; the rear springs remained semi-elliptics. At each corner of the car a friction shock-absorber was mounted as well as a hydraulic.

The Grand Sport coupé is available on a 4½-litre chasiss or with 2½-litre engine of six $74 \times 104 \cdot 5$ cylinders and 85 b.h.p.—the 100 m.p.h. "Baby Talbot"

Talbot production is limited by its market, for the cars are expensive. Every Talbot (marketed in some countries as Talbot-Lago) is race-bred and, if the owner wanted to risk his investment, could be raced almost as it stands. The Wilson gearbox remains standard.

TRACTA

Perhaps it was his intellectual reactions to the physiological processes involved in attaining front rank as a runner in the 1920 Olympics that first oriented J. A. Grégoire toward front-wheel drive. While the notion was neither new nor untested, it had not proved itself—aside from the American Miller track car and the British Alvis—until Grégoire built the Tracta.

A graduate in both engineering and law, Grégoire had opened a garage in Versailles in the 1920s and begun competing in races and rallies with everything from Amilcar to Bugatti. His friend and backer, Pierre Fenaille, was insistent on front-wheel drive and Grégoire not only became its leading apostle but was the first to design a method of overcoming the then insoluble problem of eliminating vibration and drag in wheels that did both the driving and the steering. Fenaille suggested a double enclosed universal joint in the pivot of each front wheel, and this became known as the homokinetic Tracta joint because of its constant velocity governed only by the driving shafts.

Tracta made its début at Le Mans under the worst possible circumstances. Fenaille's chauffeur, Armand Bourcier, was driving Grégoire and the rest of the team to Le Mans in Fenaille's Panhard when it crashed at Arnage. Only Etienne Boussod, a former aviator who was to drive one of the Tractas with Fenaille—Grégoire and the chauffeur were to drive the other—was unhurt; the others were taken to a hospital in an ambulance. Grégoire, his head bandaged, insisted on racing and, arrived at the course, appealed through the public-address system for a co-driver: anyone with a competition licence.

Grégoire, head bandaged, in Tracta's first Le Mans. Gear lever was dash-mounted. Car weighed about 17¾ cwt.

A mechanic named Lemesle volunteered; Grégoire explained to him the mysteries of front-wheel drive. Lemesle and Grégoire alternated driving and pitting: there was no other crew. Despite the addition of heavy rain to these handicaps, the car qualified for the Biennial Cup.

The first Tracta used the 55-h.p. 1100-c.c. S.C.A.P. engine with a Cozette supercharger. The Lancia type of front suspension—coil springs and vertical pillars—was adopted, with a de Dion-Bouton steering box. Brakes fitted to the differential—foreshadowing the inboard brakes of a later period—eliminated front-wheel brakes. The tubular rear axle was carried by semi-cantilever springs fixed above the chassis. Low centre of gravity and remarkable road-holding contributed to the top speed of almost 90 m.p.h.

In the following years Tracta adopted the 1600-c.c. S.C.A.P. engine and with this unit came second in class at Le Mans. The 1100-c.c. car, which was continued, placed both first and second in class in 1929 and 1930. Later a 6-cylinder American Continental engine was offered, and in the final years—the marque disappeared in 1934—a 6-cylinder Hotchkiss was used. These were virtually hand-made cars; Grégoire himself says: "I do not think that Tracta ever managed, whatever the price was, to sell a chassis or a car for more than the actual cost!" Thanks to the further backing of Fenaille's wealthy banker father, Maurice, the firm was enabled to survive and develop during its eight years of production. Though Tracta could not hold out in a world of growing conformism, its experience enabled the designer to develop a theory and practice of engineering that have since been adopted with success in a number of other countries.

The 1600-c.c. car of 1928 had cycle wings, improved cooling arrangements and shrouded supercharger

This impressive sports coupé of 1933 used the 6-cylinder engine

The first Voisin carried a fuel tank above the bonnet

The Voisin tourer of the early 1920s. Sports and touring coachwork were always virtually identical in this marque

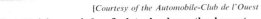

VOISIN

A pioneer in aeroplane construction, Gabriel Voisin, who was in his way as much an artist and eclectic as Ettore Bugatti, carried over his aviation thinking into automobiles when he began building cars after the First World War.

His first engine, shown in 1919, was adapted from a Citroën and fitted with the Knight sleeve that remained standard on all Voisins until their disappearance in the late 1930s, except for one model introduced in 1938 that had a supercharged Graham engine from America. His first car had four 95 × 140 cylinders (3970 c.c.) cast *en bloc*. As in most Knight designs, each cylinder had its own head, though for neatness a top cover hid all. The crankshaft was balanced and had five white-metal bearings in an aluminium crankcase. The cylinder sleeves were operated by a chain-driven shaft. The engine was pump-lubricated, ignition was by magneto and 80 b.h.p. was claimed at 2600 r.p.m. A single-plate clutch governed a 4-speed gearbox, in unit with the engine. Cantilever rear springs were later replaced by semi-elliptics as on the front. Brakes were optionally 2-wheel, 4-wheel or 4-wheel with vacuum servo.

This was followed by the C-4, which was to take the first three places in the 1922 G.P. de Tourisme. Reduced to 62 × 110, it had a 2-bearing crank in a crankcase made in a unit aluminium casting with the clutch housing and gearbox, which had only three speeds. No servo was allowed for the 4-wheel brakes. In contrast, a modified C-3, considered the sports model and designated C-5, had lighter pistons, additional oil for the sleeves at high speed, and a 10 ft. 11½ in. wheelbase compared to 11 ft. 8½ in. In the 1923 French G.P. the 70-h.p. C-4 finished fifth to cars of 100–110 b.h.p. A wind-driven propeller mounted ahead of the radiator cooled the oil. The C-5 developed almost 100 h.p. at 3000 r.p.m. for 75 m.p.h. The C-7 was a C-4 bored out 5 mm.; both used dynastarters and coils.

Voisin showed a prototype 12-cylinder in 1921. This was a V-engine, angled at less than 60 degrees, in contrast to the later monobloc 12 that ran well back into the driver's compartment. The 7240-c.c. V (80 × 120) had hydraulic brakes, the fronts being fed through the axle instead of by individual exterior lines; and rear semi-elliptic springs were hydraulically assisted. In 1927 a Voisin broke the 45-h.p. Renault's 24-hour record at Montlhéry, averaging almost 115 m.p.h.

About this time Voisin started building sleeve-valve sixes of 67 × 110 (2330 c.c.). These were the C-11, -13, -14 and -15, varying slightly from model to model. They all shared double sleeves as against the earlier single sleeve per cylinder; machined crankshafts; unit aluminium crankcase, clutch housing and gearbox; forged steel connecting rods; slightly rounded magnesium alloy pistons and exhaust manifolds that looked like motor-cycle cylinder heads. These cars had a dry multi-plate clutch, 3-speed gearbox and 2-speed rear ends, with a choice between vacuum-servo and electro-magnetic operation: in effect, they thus had six speeds. Vacuum servo was standard for the brakes.

Mixed with these cars were the 4530-c.c. C-12 (86 × 130) with dry-sump lubrication, pump instead of thermo-siphon cooling, single-plate clutch and 4-speed gearbox; the C-16, which was the same car enlarged to 5829 c.c. (94 × 140); the C-23 of 2994 c.c. (76 × 110), very like the C-14, and the C-24, which was a 23 with higher compression, lowered frame and longer wheelbase. In 1929 another V-12 appeared. The angle was just 60 degrees and both blocks were bolted to a cast-iron crankcase. Measuring 3860 c.c. (64 × 100), the engine powered a 4-speed gearbox through a single-plate clutch; final drive was taken by a torque tube. This car set a number of world's records at Montlhéry.

Two of the last Voisins were of special interest.

[Photograph by R. A. Pilkington

The C-3 tourer of 1924

Courtesy of Gabriel Voisin]

The 60 × 120 (later 67 × 110) four of 1922–6 developed 30 h.p.

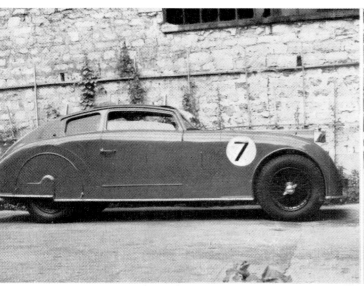

[Courtesy of Gabriel Voisin

The aerodynamic sports saloon of 1936 was available with a 3-litre 6-cylinder engine or the in-line 12

From the collection of George A. Moffitt]

One of the last cars. War killed the marque in 1939

The 12-in-line was a 6-litre engine, basically two C-23's bolted end to end, for which 180 b.h.p. at 4000 r.p.m. and 125 m.p.h. were claimed. Some authorities believed its great length was based on the desire to bring the centre of gravity nearer to the geometrical centre. Fuel was carried in two tanks flanking the drive shaft. One of the last production cars was a 75-b.h.p. 3·8-litre (76 × 140) with the Cotal gearbox. Bodied in aluminium, the car had a sliding roof operated by a vacuum motor of two oscillating cylinders. Like virtually all Voisins, it was designed with the frame included in the body.

Voisin held a number of records at various times —48 in 1932, ranging from 100 miles at 128 m.p.h. to 30,000 miles at 74 m.p.h. and from one hour at 128·5 m.p.h. to seven days at 75 m.p.h.

UNITED STATES

AMERICAN UNDERSLUNG

Even before he went into business for himself, Harry C. Stutz made a lasting reputation by creating the prototype of a basic design that is vital to any successful high-speed car 50 years later.

In creating the American Underslung for the American Motors Co. of Indianapolis in 1905, Stutz was concerned primarily with achieving maximum road-holding at top speed under all conditions. He began his Underslung by inverting the usual chassis so that it hung from the axles instead of riding on them. Semi-elliptic springs front and rear were anchored above rather than below the frame, and outboard of it. The resulting low centre of gravity and high stability had many imitators and was continued in all American Motors models until the company went out of business in 1920.

Stutz used chrome vanadium steel—quite rare then—for his 4-speed gearbox, which had all ball bearings and was integral with the differential. For the 102 in. of wheelbase, 36 in. represented front springs and 47 in. rears. The vertical 4-cylinder engine was cast in pairs; bore and stroke (all American

Courtesy of Francis H. Ludington]
The 1911 American Underslung tourer

cars are measured in inches rather than metrically) were $5\frac{3}{8} \times 5\frac{1}{2}$ and swept volume was about 285 cu. in. At the rate of approximately 60 cu. in. to the litre, this would be $4\frac{3}{4}$ litres, just slightly under the European average for the time. The car was rated at 46 h.p.

AUBURN

Although the Auburn Motor Co. was founded in 1900, it was not until E. L. Cord gained control in 1924 that the marque could make any claim to being a sports car. Cord was responsible for two of the most exciting American cars of the late 1920s and 1930s: the Auburn Speedster and the Cord.

The first Auburn Speedster appeared in 1929 with an 88-h.p. side-valve 8-cylinder Lycoming engine ($2\frac{7}{8} \times 4\frac{5}{8}$) and a 3-speed crash gearbox. It was in the 5-litre class and this model 88S won the Pike's

[*Courtesy of Leonard Peterson, Jr.*
The 1929 Speedster had a detachable top stowed behind the seats

Peak Climb in its inaugural year with a record that stood until 1955. Like most American cars, it had 6-volt ignition (in contrast to the almost universal 12 volts of British and Continental cars) and single carburation. All suspension was semi-elliptic. Unlike foreign marques, most American engines are relatively slow-turning, and Auburn was no exception. It was also a pioneer of the long wheelbase, running 125 to 130 in. when other American cars were averaging 115.

In the early 1930s Auburn experimented with a V-12 Speedster that sold for the incredible price of $1845 for a 160-b.h.p. car. The 90 m.p.h. of the standard saloon at 3500 r.p.m. could be considerably increased with the optional 2-speed rear axle (ratios of 4·55 and 3·04:1). The 6·3-litre engine, again a Lycoming, used horizontal valves actuated by a single camshaft lying in the V; six individual water-jacketed castings bolted to the cylinder heads made it possible to work on the valves without removing the heads.

The classic X-frame of the earlier Auburns became X with A-shaped bracing on the blown 1936 straight-eight, which dropped back to $4\frac{3}{4}$ litres and 150 b.h.p. Brakes were hydraulic all round. In completely stock form this car did five miles at 104 m.p.h. on the Utah salt flats, in comparison to the stripped V-12's top of 118·32 and ran 1000 miles at 109·33 m.p.h. The 1936 car clung to the solid I-beam front axle, semi-elliptics, single carburetter. The cylinder head was aluminium. Like most Auburns, the car weighed between 31 and 36 cwt.

Very few Cabin Speedsters were built. European influence is obvious

BIDDLE

In its five-year career the Philadelphia-built Biddle had little opportunity to prove its mettle. European influence was apparent in its exterior styling, especially in the first models of 1917. Mechanically, it followed the prevalent American pattern of a large, slow-running engine mounted in a heavy chassis and bodied with equal disregard for weight. The power plant was the detuned 16-valve 4·8-litre (4 × 6) four from the early racing Duesenbergs.

Not a mass-produced automobile, the Biddle was built with primary emphasis on quality. The result was a product far too costly for a competitive market, and in 1922 the marque appeared for the last time.

The Speedster of early 1930s was available as an 8 or 12

European coachwork influenced the bodies of the 1917 Biddles

The blown 1936 Speedster was last of the Auburn line

The later Biddle roadster was more conventional. Bolt-on wheels replaced knock-off hubs

The Great Chadwick Six introduced the supercharger to the U.S. This is the 1909 car

CHADWICK

The first American attempt at supercharging was represented by the Chadwick, which originated as a 4-cylinder car in a Philadelphia stable. The spun-copper water jacket of this car was characteristic of the high quality that Lee F. Chadwick sought to put into his products.

The four was superseded in 1906 with what he called the "Great Chadwick Six", whose epithet proved eminently justified. Demand for these cars grew rapidly and the factory moved to western Pennsylvania. No expense was weighed in the search for perfection; D. W. H. Scott-Moncrieff says the Chadwick's lubrication and cooling were probably the best of its time. Dual ignition was standard, as was a 4-speed gearbox in which chrome-nickel steel was used exclusively. Dissatisfied with contemporary coachwork, Chadwick started a body firm of his own that ultimately became General Motors' Fleetwood division.

In 1908 Chadwick built his supercharged 60-h.p. sports car, which could do 100 m.p.h. in standard road tune and trim. When Indianapolis was a dirt track the Chadwick won a 5-mile race at 67·66. In the same year, 1909, a Chadwick set a new record of 1:38½ for the agonizing Giant's Despair hill-climb, smashing by 11 seconds the previous record, set by a 1908 Chadwick. The marque won a number of other races and trials until economics caused its death in 1914.

The 1908 Vanderbilt Cup car was characteristic of Chadwick machines. It could be driven without strain at as little as 5 m.p.h. in top gear, yet it could withstand the stress of a 3-stage supercharger. Scott-Moncrieff ranks it with the Stutz, the Simplex and the Mercer.

CHRYSLER

The first American manufacturer brave enough and confident enough to match his product against the best of Europe at Le Mans was Walter P. Chrysler, former president of General Motors.

Chrysler had left G.M. when he was in his forties to reorganize Willys-Overland and then, at 46, he decided to retire. Idleness, however, wore him out quickly and in 1921 he bought up Maxwell and Chalmers. Two years later, having liquidated the liabilities acquired with these two marques, he devoted himself to the car that was to carry his name. His primary interest lay in producing a quality 6-cylinder car with high compression and performance at relatively low cost. Initially, there was also a 4-cylinder Chrysler, the 50, but it made no sporting pretensions.

Chrysler was one of the first American marques to fit hydraulic 4-wheel brakes as standard equipment. In 1925 it sent a completely standard 6-cylinder car to Le Mans. Though it finished the 24 hours, it was not qualified because it fell two laps short of the 119 its class was required to complete. It was a side-valve car of relatively long stroke—3 × 4¾—in the 3·3-litre class; this was the Model 70.

In 1928 Chrysler returned to Le Mans with four cars, one of which, driven by Louis Chiron, did not finish; another also dropped out. The two others, however, placed third and fourth over-all, the leader averaging close to 65 m.p.h. for the 24 hours. These were somewhat larger-bore cars than the first contestant, with 4076 c.c. Only Bentley and Stutz finished ahead of them. The next year Chrysler fared somewhat worse with two entries, both of which finished but were beaten by four Bentleys and a Stutz to finish sixth and seventh over-all and third and fourth in the final of the Biennial Cup, at virtually the same speed as in 1928. Chrysler's final appearance at Le Mans was in 1931, a bad year for the other American entrant, Stutz, as well. Neither Chrysler—a 6·3-litre Imperial driven by Raymond Sommer and a 4·6-litre—completed 15 laps.

The 70, 72, 75, 77, 80 and 88 (Imperial) Chryslers of the 1920s and 1930s were the only high-performance cars of that marque that would qualify as sports machines. From about 1933 until the war they lost appeal; the 300 series offered in post-war years, while undoubtedly endowed with excellent engines (adopted by Briggs Cunningham for his own cars), are far too big, too un-roadworthy, too slow in handling and too automatized to compete with even the stick-shift Corvette.

[From the collection of Jacques Rousseau

The Chrysler 75 (left) and 77 at Le Mans in 1929. They differed slightly in cubic capacity.
Like all Chryslers, they had 3-speed gearboxes

[From the collection of Jacques Rousseau

Chrysler's first Le Mans car, the 70 of 1925. Wire wheels, Marchal lights and lighter wings were French replacements

Photograph by Alfred B. Reimer]

A typical Chrysler roadster of the late 1920s

Raymond Sommer in the 112-h.p. 1931 Imperial at Le Mans

One of the last sporting Chryslers was the 1933 Imperial phaeton

[From the collection of Jacques Rousseau

Courtesy of Chrysler Corp.]

[*Photograph by K. R. Graham*]

The L-29 drop-head was truly elegant

[*Courtesy of K. R. Graham*]

The 1931 L-29 in rare roadster form

[*Courtesy of the Henry Ford Museum*]

**The late Cord was the first American car to employ
drilled wheels**

CORD

Two basic prejudices—one apparently universal,
the other peculiarly American—militated against
the Cord's ever proving itself to the full. The universal prejudice, which might be broadly characterized as the fear of whatever is new, was directed
against front-wheel drive; the national prejudice
prevented the marque from displaying its dual-
purpose character in sports-car competition because
virtually the only racing tolerated in the United
States between the wars was that of specially built
cars on specially built tracks. (One of the authors
used to race a borrowed L-29 in some highly illegal
events on the bridle paths of New York's Van Cort-
landt Park, but as far as is known no international
notice was taken.)

Cord missed being the first production front-
wheel-drive American car by one month, having
been preceded by the short-lived Ruxton. Cord
lasted from 1929 almost until the 1939 war and is a
collectors' item today, but it never really caught on.

The L-29 used a straight Lycoming eight of just
under 5 litres ($3\frac{1}{4} \times 4\frac{1}{2}$), with 5·25:1 compression
and 125 h.p. at 3600 r.p.m.: the same engine used in
the Auburn 8. It was not turned round for the front-
wheel drive; instead, the crankshaft was extended
at the front to take the flywheel, thus making it
difficult to reach the timing chain. The combustion
chamber of the L-head was the best of its time.
But the weight of almost $42\frac{1}{2}$ cwt. and the ill-chosen
three speeds and differential limited top speed to
barely 80 m.p.h.; acceleration figures were 10 years
or more behind the times. However, weight distribution was far above average, unsprung weight was
minimal, thanks in part to inboard front brakes,
and cornering was incredible despite the four turns
lock to lock and the $137\frac{1}{2}$-in. wheelbase. Cord,
indeed, pioneered the long, low look that was to
become so popular in all automobile-making countries: the bonnet was half the total length of the car.

Public indifference was so strong that production
ceased in 1932. But three years later Cord was back
on the market with a car designed by August Duesenberg with a low body by Gordon Buehrig, former
Duesenberg stylist. The new car had a 125-h.p.
Lycoming V-8 in a 125-in. wheelbase, the whole car
weighed 31·2 cwt. and, with a 4-speed gearbox—in
which third was direct and fourth was overdrive—
was capable of almost 100 m.p.h. Frame and body
were built together, front suspension was independent
by transverse leaf and longitudinal arms, and rear
springs were semi-elliptics supported by a tubular
axle. Front brakes were now outboard. Headlamps,
when not in use, were reversed and folded into the
wing silhouette, motive power being provided by
hand cranks on the dash.

The coffin-nose bonnet, as it was called, was horizontally louvered all round for ventilation. The gear lever was mounted on the steering column but, since the actual shifting mechanism was electrical, an H-gate box instead of a lever was used and changes were made by merely flicking the lever into position. Transmission and differential were built in unit. The 4·8-litre engine ($3\frac{1}{2} \times 3\frac{3}{4}$) peaked at 3200 r.p.m. with 6·25:1 compression; a single dual-throated carburetter was used.

Coachwork was limited to two- and four-seater drop-heads and a reasonably aerodynamic 4-door saloon in which line as well as mass was employed to aesthetic advantage as well as economy of repair. Wings were quite discrete from body panels and, if destroyed in collision, could be replaced without buying 25% of a new body. At the same time, the body design allowed the engine an accessibility unknown in American cars since.

The new Cord represented a tremendous advance over the L-29 but it could not overcome the public's resistance to what had not been seen before, and the marque disappeared before the Second World War.

CORVETTE

It was most fitting that the first all-out U.S. attempt at a dual-purpose car in 25 years should be made by Chevrolet, which owes its origin to the Darracq racing driver, Louis Chevrolet, who, stranded in the United States after an accident to his car, decided to remain and build his own automobiles.

The first Corvette appeared in 1953 with a plastic two-seater body. However, in weight, width, length, multi-turn steering and soft suspension, to say nothing of automatic transmission, it had virtually no sports-car characteristic other than speed. It was a 150-h.p. six of almost 4 litres with the traditional Chevrolet overhead valves, plus such features as three carburetters, high-lift cams, extra alloy steel exhaust valves. Luggage space was almost as big as a saloon's, and still is. Much was made of simulated knock-off wheels, in the American automotive tradition of pretending (compare the landau irons on fixed-head coupés in the 1920s and 1930s).

Corvette soon found it necessary to offer a manual transmission. This was a close-ratio 3-speed gearbox, and a 225-h.p. V-8 was added; but horsepower, weight and space were wasted on power-operated top and windows (the original Corvette had excellent removable sidescreens). Detachable hard tops have been featured by Corvette almost from the start.

By 1959 Corvette had improved and widened its range of options to provide a car of tremendous acceleration and speed, benefiting to some extent from the experimental SS model tested at Sebring. There are now four engine choices, standard equipment being a 4½-litre V-8 ($3\frac{7}{8} \times 3$) with 10·5:1 compression, developing 290 b.h.p. at 6200 r.p.m. Other valuable options include fuel injection, choices of multiple carburation, heavy-duty clutches, special cams, limited-slip differential and a good close-ratio 4-speed gearbox. In road trim and tune the Corvette will give close to 130 m.p.h. and will reach 60 m.p.h. from rest in 6·6 seconds. Steering has been accelerated to 3·2 turns, lock to lock, but weight is still high, at 30 cwt. Unimpressive racing performance in past years has also resulted in the option of heavy-duty brakes and improved suspension offered in kit form.

Top speed and acceleration are unquestionably exciting and impressive and can be matched by only a few of the most expensive but smaller-engined British and Continental machines. However, in any competition in which manoeuvrability and road-holding are dominant factors, rather than brute force, much slower cars will regularly defeat the Corvette (Austin-Healey 100-6's have done it); even drivers accustomed to winning in Corvettes are wary of the car on twisting circuits (wheelbase is 102 in. and minimum track is 57 in.). The marque's appearance at Le Mans in 1960 reversed the skeptics: Corvette finished eighth and tenth over-all.

121

The early Corvette on a tight corner

[*Courtesy of the Chevrolet Division, General Motors Corp.*

The dual headlights detract from improvement in Corvette's looks

Courtesy of the Chevrolet Division, General Motors Corp.]

CROSLEY

The easiest way to go wrong in buying a sports car, as J. A. Grégoire points out in his autobiography, recalling youthful enthusiasms, is to be seduced by the sweep of a wing or the song of an exhaust. Neither of these allures ever sold a Crosley, because it lacked both; it was one of the ugliest cars ever built and, in the 750-c.c. class, one of the best.

First built just before the 1939 war, the Crosley entered competition in 1949 and the next year finished first on index of performance at Sebring. The first cars had 12-in. wheels, 8:1 compression with 18 h.p. or 10:1 compression with 26 h.p., disc brakes (later abandoned because of jamming caused by mud), 85-in. wheelbase, 40-in. track and a total weight of 9·6 cwt. The four cylinders were square ($2\frac{1}{4} \times 2\frac{1}{4}$) and total volume was only 721 c.c. Coil springs were used at the rear but semi-elliptics at the front carried an I-beam axle. Telescopic shock absorbers were fitted all round. Although top speed was not much over 70 m.p.h., the Crosley's cornering was so fantastic that it more than compensated in competition for the relatively low maximum.

The chassis was very much like that of the M.G.-TC, except that it was largely supported by the body, which weighed $4\frac{1}{2}$ cwt. The engine, built in unit with the gearbox and clutch, was sited well behind the front axle so that the weight distribution of the fully loaded car was exactly 50-50. The early models (on which doors were optional) had two bucket seats, very heavy matting, individual air vents for the driver and passenger, undercoating, good weather protection and excellent driving position, all controls being right where the hand would fall on them. The pre-war car was air-cooled; but thereafter all Crosleys were water-cooled until Powel Crosley dropped the marque in 1952.

Oven-brazed sheet steel was used at first in the monobloc engine, whose cylinder head was fixed; this was replaced by cast iron for economy. Pistons, pumps, intake manifold and bell housing were aluminium. The crankshaft ran in five main bearings; the single overhead camshaft, shaft-driven, acted directly on the valves by way of barrel-type cam followers. The crankshaft was safe up to 7500 r.p.m.

Crosley always used a 3-speed crash gearbox, in which top was direct drive, and was fitted with a racing clutch. A standard Crosley ran at Le Mans in the early 1950s and was forced out only because the voltage regulator failed and burned out the dynamo. These engines are readily adaptable to 4-speed transmissions and have frequently been mounted in foreign cars, notably S.I.A.T.A.s; but the standard Crosley will out-handle the best of these hybrids. Some of the original Crosleys are still used as hunters' cars in the Ozarks, and many a new sports special is still built round the Crosley Hot-shot engine.

Courtesy of George Sanderson]
The Super-Sports at Sebring. A coupé was also made. Late engines developed 26·5 b.h.p. at 5400 r.p.m.

CUNNINGHAM

For 20 years one of the finest cars in the United States was the Rochester-built Cunningham. Like the quality European makers of that day and this, James Cunningham & Sons ignored annual model changes and offered new cars only when the firm felt that sufficient advance had been made to warrant them.

As far as is known, the Rochester Cunningham was never raced, but Ralph de Palma, the famous Indianapolis driver, made a number of speed trials with a stock roadster in 1919, when *stock* meant "right off the showroom floor at random". In full road trim, these long-wheelbase cars (132 and 142 in.) averaged 98·5 m.p.h. The engine was a 90-degree 7-litre V-8 ($3\frac{3}{4} \times 5$) typical of the relatively slow units then favoured; it produced 90 h.p. at 2200 r.p.m. It had a counterweighted crankshaft, cast-iron pistons, pump cooling and a water-jacketed intake manifold. The 4-speed gearbox of the 1920s had direct drive on third and overdrive on fourth. Steering was by worm and sector; later cars employed 4-wheel brakes of three shoes each. Outstanding for workmanship, durability and handling, the old Cunningham was a victim of the great depression.

The name was revived with added glory in the 1950s by Briggs S. Cunningham of Connecticut and Florida, who was determined to see an American driver in an American car win at Le Mans.

His first attempt, in 1950, was made with two cars entered as Cadillacs—one an almost standard 2-door saloon, the other a much-modified roadster known as Le Monstre, which finished 11th, just behind the saloon. Then Cunningham determined to build an entirely new car around a proprietary engine. Except for his very first and last cars, that engine was a Chrysler. The C1 Cunningham utilized a standard Cadillac engine in a tubular chassis equipped with a de Dion rear axle. The C2, which looked almost identical, had a de Dion rear and 180-h.p. $5\frac{1}{2}$-litre Chrysler engine with 7·5:1 compression turning over at the high figure—for an American power plant—of 4000 r.p.m. This car placed 18th at Le Mans

Elegant simplicity marked the 1920 Cunningham roadster

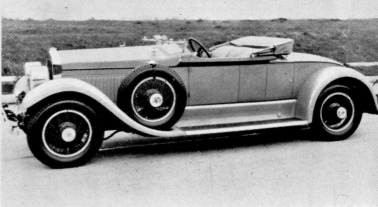

The 1929 roadster was rather more opulent in the best classic tradition

Briggs Cunningham's C1 and C2 looked almost identical

The C3 coupé was sold in small numbers at a great loss

Some C4R's had four dual Weber carburetters. Cylindrical oil cooler was mounted at extreme right of cowl

Like roadster, C4RK coupé used knock-off magnesium alloy wheels

The C5R was the marque's best Le Mans contender, finishing third in 1954

For Le Mans, C6R's nose was lowered to Ferrari-like air scoop

in 1951; others finished first, second and fourth at Watkins Glen the same year.

The C3 was a Vignale-bodied coupé—the chassis was sent to Italy for coachwork and returned to Cunningham's West Palm Beach factory for finishing. Two inches longer than the C2's 105-in. wheelbase, it retained the 58-in. track, but the original 3-speed synchromesh gearbox with over-drive was replaced by a semi-automatic transmission with torque converter. The $3\frac{3}{10} \times 3\frac{5}{8}$ engine gave 220 b.h.p. at 4000 r.p.m. with four Zenith down-draught carburetters and the luxurious coupé was good for 140 m.p.h. Brakes, as on all Cunninghams, were hydraulic drum-type. The C3 returned to a conventional rear end but with coil springs. Like the previous cars, it weighed 25 cwt.

A 5-speed transmission was tried in the 1952 cars —C4R roadsters and a C4RK coupé—but at the last minute before the start of Le Mans it had to be replaced by a standard 3-speed Cadillac gearbox. The same Chrysler engine was now developing 300 h.p. at 5200 r.p.m. With a solid rear axle, the C4R finished fourth at Le Mans; the C4RK coupé did not finish. Ten more horsepower was pulled out of the engine the next year, when it was mounted in the C5R, which used torsion bars front and rear

on solid axles, in contrast to the various independent suspensions on all previous Cunninghams. A S.I.A.T.A. 4-speed gearbox was adopted and Cunninghams finished third, fifth and tenth at Le Mans, clocking 154·81 m.p.h. over the timed section. Where the C4R had weighed $21\frac{1}{2}$ cwt., the C5R was up by 180 lb.

The final brave effort was the C6R, which was radically different from all Cunningham's other cars in many respects. Abandoning the big power plants, he employed a 16-valve 4-cylinder d.o.h.c. 3-litre Offenhauser ($3\frac{31}{32} \times 3\frac{5}{8}$) that put out 260 b.h.p. at 6000 r.p.m. with 8:1 compression. Dual-throated Weber carburetters were used and, for the first time, a multiple-disc clutch governed the 4-speed synchromesh gearbox. Coil springs and ball joints were used in the front suspension and the de Dion rear came back with coil springs. Like the C4R and C5R, the new car had a 100-in. wheelbase; track was 52 in., against the respective 54 in. and 55 in. of the immediate predecessors. Dry, the C6R weighed 17 cwt. But it lacked the speed of the earlier cars and at both Sebring and Le Mans in 1955 it could not make the checkered flag: a sad ending to a gallant and costly effort to bring America back into motor sport.

124

DUESENBERG

The Model A and Model X roadster looked virtually identical. This is a 1922 car

A re-bodied Model J on Mount Equinox hill-climb, A. J. Hoe at wheel

Two American cars contributed new words to the language. When the little boys of the authors' youth cried out in admiration: "That's a doozy!" they did not know the origin of their catchword; but it derived from probably the finest car ever built in America, the Duesenberg.

Fred and August Duesenberg were building successful racing cars before the First World War; then they made Bugatti aircraft engines under licence. After the Armistice they turned to commercial production as well, and nothing could have been more auspicious than the introduction of their Model A in 1921. A virtually standard version of this 88-h.p. 4-litre straight-eight ($2\frac{7}{8} \times 5$), fitted with a racing body, won the French G.P. with the then record speed of 78·5 m.p.h., finishing 15 minutes ahead of the second car, a Ballot. The single overhead camshaft, balanced crankshaft, bronze main bearings and 15-in. ribbed-drum hydraulic 4-wheel brakes of both the touring and G.P. cars were years ahead of the rest of the American industry. The G.P. car's hydraulic brakes were operated by water.

Two years later a standard Model A tourer covered 3155 miles in 50 hours and 21 minutes on the harsh bricks of the Indianapolis Speedway—an average of 62·63 m.p.h. The only stops were for tyre changes: driver changes and refuelling were done from a supply car at a minimum speed of 50 m.p.h. These were heavy cars; they were not lightened when E. L. Cord bought the marque in 1926, retaining the Duesenberg brothers to design for him the finest and fastest car in the world. The result, which came remarkably close to the perfection demanded by Cord, was the Model J: a complete break from the Model A and the few Model X's derived from it, which differed chiefly in having longer wheelbases, timing chains instead of gears and various types of headlights.

The 7-litre Model J appeared in 1929, claiming 265 h.p. at 4200 r.p.m. with two carburetters. The 50-cwt. car carried a d.o.h.c. straight-eight, with four valves per $3\frac{3}{4} \times 4\frac{3}{4}$ cylinder, in a deep chassis with numerous tubular cross-members. It would accelerate from rest to 60 m.p.h. in 8·6 seconds and to 100 m.p.h. in 20 seconds. Top speed was close to 115 m.p.h. in fine tune, and 95 m.p.h. could be exceeded in second gear—there were only three speeds. The compression ratio was 5·72:1. Steering was among the best ever produced in America, with $3\frac{1}{2}$ turns from lock to lock; the wheelbase was $153\frac{1}{2}$ or $142\frac{1}{2}$ in., to choice. The Duesenberg was the only American car that fitted a tachometer as standard instrumentation; the panel was almost as complete as an aeroplane's, including even an altimeter and a brake-pressure gauge: booster adjustment from the dash was possible.

In 1932 the supercharger was added and the model was designated the SJ. The maker claimed 325 b.h.p. at 4750 r.p.m.—a very high engine speed in America then and now—and the blower, of the centrifugal vane type, turned at $6\frac{1}{2}$ times the engine speed. The SJ reached 100 m.p.h. in 17 seconds—

125

Courtesy of A. J. Hoe]

Le Baron built this phaeton body on the J chassis

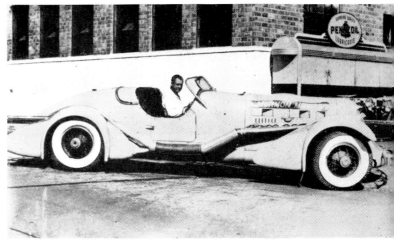

Courtesy of A. J. Hoe]

The Mormon Meteor reached 160 m.p.h. on Utah salt flats

The J drop-head at speed

Courtesy of A. J. Hoe]

The SJ drop-head bodied by Rollston

The SJ sports phaeton by Le Grande

**French coachbuilder gave this roadster its unusual
folding V-windscreen**

it could top the century mark in second gear—and its maximum was in the 130's. Some few SJ roadsters were built on 125-in. wheelbases. While the SJ was undoubtedly the fastest car in the country, A. J. Hoe, the ranking expert on the marque, has encountered J's with raised compression (8:1) that produced 390 b.h.p. and comparable performance.

Though Duesenberg had long since abandoned racing when the J was made, Ab Jenkins, then known as America's Speed King, set many new records on the Utah salt flats in 1935 with a 142-in. SJ weighing 42·8 cwt. and known as the Mormon Meteor. For 24 hours he averaged 135·47 m.p.h. on a 10-mile oval, covering 3253 miles. This included time taken for the standing start and for refuelling and tyre checks at 400-mile intervals. The highest speed reached was 160 m.p.h. and the best one-hour average was 152·145, a new record. This was 17 miles an hour faster than Hans von Stück's record in an Auto-Union special at the Avus.

In addition, many Duesenbergs have been privately entered in various forms of competition, including post-war hill-climbs. Prince Nicholas of Rumania drove an SJ at Le Mans in 1933 and 1935: the first time he was disqualified for refuelling illegally, the second run ended with retirement after the 38th lap, when lying sixth. Among the very wealthiest Europeans, Duesenbergs (which cost from $8500 for

126

**The 1934 SJ with Rollston torpedo roadster body, one
of the last cars with that designation**

Prince Nicholas of Rumania in SJ at Le Mans in 1935

the J chassis, bare, to $11,750 for the unbodied SJ in the United States) were favoured for the Paris–Nice and similar rallies. Both J and SJ chassis were the delight of the finest custom coachbuilders in both hemispheres.

Of the 650 Duesenbergs built between 1921 and 1937, 250 are still running. Ten years after the last car was built, an effort was made to revive the marque, but comparable quality would have cost a minimum of $25,000 in 1947. So the world still awaits the second American sports car to win an international grand prix.

From the collection of Jacques Rousseau]
Moran in du Pont at Le Mans, 1929

DU PONT

In the 12 years of its life, du Pont never made a cheap or a bad car. From the beginning, almost all the bodies were custom built of aluminium. E. Paul du Pont established the firm in 1919 in Moore, Pa., moving it later to the du Ponts' stronghold, Wilmington, Del.

The first of the 700–800 du Ponts was a four, with du Pont's own engine: monobloc L-head, $3\frac{15}{16} \times 5\frac{1}{8}$, or 4·3 litres, producing 75 h.p. Thermo-siphon cooling was employed; a single-disc clutch governed a 4-speed gearbox (top being overdrive) and the rear axle was full-floating. In 1923 a 6-cylinder side-valve engine appeared developing 75 b.h.p. at 3000 r.p.m.; it was soon changed to overhead valves, the cylinders being reduced to $3\frac{1}{8} \times 5$ and centrifugal pump cooling being added. Wheelbase lengthened from 124 to 136 in., 4-wheel hydraulic brakes were introduced and for a brief time a 3-speed gearbox was used.

When the straight-eight Continental motor was adopted in 1928 and modified by du Pont to produce 140 b.h.p. from 5·2 litres ($3\frac{3}{8} \times 4\frac{1}{2}$), the semi-floating rear axle of the six was retained, a multiple-disc clutch was introduced and a fuel pump replaced the vacuum fuel feed. The speedster models were guaranteed for 100 m.p.h. and in 1929 Charles Moran, Jr., now a financier and American representative of the F.I.A., drove one at Le Mans. He was lying eighth when the rear-seat ballast required by the rules came adrift and broke through the floor, striking the propeller shaft and breaking the gearbox casing. In 1930 Moran qualified a two-seater for Indianapolis at 89 m.p.h. but after 22 laps he hit an oil patch and slid into the wall.

Du Pont went out of production in 1931.

Courtesy of the British Travel Association]
The 1929 two-seater speedster

From the collection of George A. Moffitt]
The four-seater speedster

The Model K speedster's rear seat was removable. Weather equipment was extra

The 1910 Ford 999, capable of 103 m.p.h.

FORD

When Henry Ford inadvertently contributed *flivver* to the Anglo-American language he had already built—and abandoned—a first-class sports car, as well as outright racers. The sports car was the 1907 Model K, which, according to its publicity, had such flexibility as to "enable the driver to accelerate from zephyr to a cyclone speed almost instantly".

The 40-h.p. 6-cylinder engine ($4\frac{1}{2} \times 4\frac{1}{4}$, or $6\frac{1}{2}$ litres) was individually cast—that is, each cylinder was separate—with side valves, pump cooling, a chrome nickel-steel crankshaft in an aluminium case, dual (coil and magneto) ignition, multiple-disc clutch, the same two gears that later appeared in the Model T (though with hand control), nickel-steel frame and vanadium-chrome-manganese longitudinal springs: semi-elliptic at the front, full elliptic at the rear. The foot brake operated on the transmission. With 120-in. wheelbase and 56-in. track, the car was stable at well over 70 m.p.h.

Very few of these were made and from 1909 Ford limited his production to the famous 3-litre Model T with its four $3\frac{3}{4} \times 4$ cylinders, transverse springs and uniform black—an outgrowth of the Model R of 1908, which was virtually the same. However, there was one exception to this limitation of production: the 1910 revamping of 1903's Old 999, the famous Ford racer that had been clocked at 91·30 m.p.h. in 1903. The 1910 version covered a mile at better than 103 m.p.h., using the T-engine as a base. In a way

The Model R was direct ancestor of the Model T

it was the ancestor of the $10\frac{3}{4}$-cwt. 1912 Model T torpedo, which had higher than normal compression, a light flywheel and a very light body. In Britain and Europe isolated enthusiasts raced Model T's up to the 1914 war, and in the United States they formed the basis for hotted-up specials for many years after that; but the K remained the marque's ultimate sporting achievement to this day.

128

The 1912 torpedo had sharply raked windscreen and steering column. It was Model T's high-performance version

The 1911 Model T as it was raced in France

KISSEL

From 1906, when it began production, until 1917 the Kissel was a staid quality car. Just before the United States entered the First World War, the marque produced its first speedster, a model that was to be continued almost until its demise in 1931.

In its original form as planned by Conover T. Silver, Kissel's New York distributor, the speedster had more sporting looks than performance. Five dummy exhaust pipes swept out of the bonnet, there were no doors and the steering wheel was flat at the top. The two-seater body terminated in a well-curved boat tail. Very soon the pretence of the exhaust pipes was dropped and one door, then two, were added. Running boards gave way to step plates in 1921.

Chassis and engine were conventional, the latter being a $3\frac{5}{16} \times 5\frac{1}{2}$ (later $5\frac{1}{8}$) six developing 61 h.p. and capable of 70 m.p.h. A dry multiple-disc clutch preceded the 3-speed gearbox; the rear axle was fully floating. The heavy car—few American cars have ever been really light, except the Model T Ford—had a wheelbase of 124 in. and a track of 56 in. In 1924 a big 2-flywheel straight-eight appeared, capable of 90 to 100 m.p.h. with the speedster body. The later $30\frac{1}{2}$-cwt. "Economy Eight" ($2\frac{7}{8} \times 4\frac{3}{4}$) could reach 80 m.p.h. on 65 b.h.p. at 3200 r.p.m. Kissel, like most American cars after the early years, used a bench seat; a jump seat pulled out from either side of the tail, just ahead of the rear mudguards, until optional rumble seats appeared in 1924. Suspension was semi-elliptic in front, three-quarter-elliptic behind prior to 1921.

LOCOMOBILE

There was really only one year of glory for Locomobile in all its three decades from 1899 to 1929. That was 1908, when the 1906 car that had made

Courtesy of E. E. Husting]

The Silver Special Kissel Speedster's windscreen frame extended only two-thirds up

Courtesy of E. E. Husting]

The late Kissel Speedster had eight cylinders. Note the step plate

George Robertson and Glenn Ethridge, driver and mechanic in the 1908 victory, aboard Old 16. Peter Helck still drives this car

Courtesy of the Long Island Automotive Museum]

129

the fastest lap in the Vanderbilt Cup of its birth year became the first American-built and -driven car to win an international road race.

Old 16, now owned by the famous artist, Peter Helck, was a 90-h.p. car based on the standard Type F of 45 h.p. A square four ($7\frac{1}{4} \times 7\frac{1}{4}$), cast in pairs, it had pushrod overhead valves, a 24-in. leather cone clutch for the 3-speed gearbox and chain drive. To save weight and horsepower, the fan was replaced by radial cooling vanes on the flywheel. On a 100-in. wheelbase, the car had a pressed steel frame, drilled for lightness, and semi-elliptics all round. In the 1908 Cup it duelled hub to hub with an Isotta-Fraschini at 100 m.p.h. to clinch its victory at an average of 64·38 m.p.h. for the 258 miles.

Locomobile had begun production with a four and a $12\frac{1}{2}$-cwt. 9-h.p. 2-cylinder. The four, like Old 16, was cast in pairs, but it used the F head: overhead inlet valves, side exhaust valves; maximum r.p.m. was 2000 and it carried an aluminium body. Its top speed was 67 m.p.h. The coil radiator was soon abandoned for the cellular type. In so-called toy tonneau form it was one of the most sporting American cars in the first decade of the century. A direct derivation from Old 16 was the Gentleman's Speedy Roadster made in the next few years, a really fast car with a minimum of non-essentials. The company continued building quality cars until the depression, absorbing Mercer.

Courtesy of T. J. Lester]

A Model 72 Lozier identical to this was second at Indianapolis in 1911

LOZIER

More fortunate than Locomobile though only half as long-lived, the Lozier packed achievements into its 15-year career from 1901 to 1916. In 1909, when the company was building $5\frac{1}{4}$-in.-square fours and $4\frac{5}{8} \times 5\frac{1}{2}$ sixes, rated at 50 h.p., one of the latter, wholly standard except that it was stripped of its body, ran in the first Indianapolis race.

This model changed very little during the rest of the marque's life and appeared identically, except for bodywork, on road and track. Cast in pairs, the 9·3-litre engine could reach 2300 r.p.m. and over 90 m.p.h. The T-head's two camshafts ran in six ball bearings each, the crankshaft in four ball-bearing mains: ball bearings were used throughout the $43\frac{3}{4}$-cwt. car. Aluminium was employed for the entire body and bonnet, crankcase, oil pan and transmission housing. Third gear was direct drive, fourth was overdrive; the clutch was multiple-disc. From hub to hub the car measured 131 in.; track was 56 in.

In 1911, the standard Lozier came second to a Marmon special in the first 500-mile Indianapolis race, having been plagued by 14 tyre changes. Later that year Lozier was first and fourth in the Grand Prix of Savannah against the best of Europe and America. From then until the marque retired, it continued to pile up victories throughout the country.

Still favoured by collectors, Lozier proved itself again in 1957 in the Anglo-American Vintage Rally, beating a Le Mans Bentley and Sunbeam and a 30/98 Vauxhall at Thompson Raceway: the Lozier was the only American car among the 10 competing to win any performance firsts in the whole rally. It was the fastest pre-1916 car on the hill-climb and over-all was second only to the Vauxhall.

[Courtesy of the Long Island Automotive Museum

The 4-cylinder 1908 toy tonneau (5 × 6, almost 8 litres) had four speeds, 40 h.p.

130

The Locomobile Gentleman's Speedy Roadster sometimes mounted monocle windscreen on steering column

[Courtesy of Valerie Motors Inc.

The four-seater 1913 Lozier sports starred in 1957 Anglo-American Vintage Rally

Courtesy of the British Travel Association]

MARMON

For the generation that came too late to dream of Mercer, the goal of boyhood was a Marmon speedster. Marmon, which was another of the depression victims, started in 1904 and made its first racing appearance in 1909 when Indianapolis opened as a dirt track. When the race was halted at 235 miles because of the rapid deterioration of the track and the heavy casualties among competitors, a Marmon lay third. In 1911, however, Marmon won the first 500-mile race in the hands of Ray Harroun, who set a precedent and created a universal safety factor by driving alone and relying on a rear-view mirror instead of a mechanic to tell him what was behind his $4\frac{3}{4}$-litre six.

At this time Marmon was making a four and a six, both cast in pairs. The $4\frac{1}{2} \times 5$ four was rated at 32 h.p., the six, of the same dimensions, at 48. Both used magneto ignition, cone clutch and a 3-speed transmission, and both had the same wheelbase and track—120 and $56\frac{1}{2}$ in. The longer-stroke (6-in.) Wasp that won Indianapolis developed 100 h.p. at 2300 r.p.m., could exceed 80 m.p.h., and a few roadsters identical to it were sold publicly. Like Lozier, Marmon made extensive use of aluminium to produce a relatively light car. The two marques were close racing rivals for several years.

In the 1920s Marmon produced another fast car, the Model 34 speedster. Its six cylinders were cast in blocks of three ($3\frac{3}{4} \times 5\frac{1}{8}$); a dry-plate multiple-disc clutch controlled the 3-speed box and the rear axle was three-quarters floating. Wheelbase was 136 in., track 56 in.; the very pretty boat-tailed two-seater, with its spare wheel lying flat on the curved, sloping deck, was capable of at least 80 m.p.h. The model was made for seven years. In the 1930s Marmon attempted to revitalize its sales—which had been hit as hard as those of the other quality cars—with a V-16, but it did not catch the public taste and the company went out of business in 1933.

The 1911 Indianapolis car was almost identical with the 1913 runabout

The speedster of the 1920s, in 1958

Photograph by Richard Sherwin]

MERCER

If the Stutz was, as Harry C. Stutz said, "the car that made good in a day", the Mercer—its bitter rival—was the car that became a legend in its lifetime. There are those who think the greatest achievement of the name of Roebling was Brooklyn Bridge; and there are those, completely ignorant of the bridge's creator, who know only that Roeblings made Mercers.

The marque barely reached puberty: born in 1909, it died in 1925. But the years after its entry into competition in 1911 are studded with victories and records. A curious facet of the marque is the fact that F. R. Porter, the designer, used 3-speed gearboxes for the early sports cars and 4-speed gearboxes for the lower-performance tourers. Though 25,000 of these machines were built to the highest standards, fewer than 100 survive to perpetuate what is frequently called America's finest sports car.

The first sports Mercer Raceabout (the Runabout had a windscreen and some other amenities) was the Type 35-R: four $4\frac{3}{8} \times 5$ cylinders, just under 5 litres, with single magneto ignition and carburation and about 60 h.p. at 2000 r.p.m.: peak r.p.m. was about 2500. On a 108-in. wheelbase, the car weighed $21\frac{3}{4}$ cwt. Valves were in T-formation; every car was guaranteed to cover a mile in 51 seconds. Frequently, Mercers taken at random from a showroom set distance records without having been run in or specially prepared: one such car in 1912 covered 150 miles on the road in 130 minutes.

The 35-C introduced dual ignition by magneto. All the cars had 44 steel-to-steel clutchplates in oil, chrome vanadium springs, sub-frame engine mounting and shaft drive. The 35-C weighed $20\frac{1}{2}$ cwt., the almost identical 35-J 22 cwt. All 35 Mercers would easily hold 75 m.p.h., with matching road-holding

[Courtesy of Charles Stich

Peter Helck and son, Jerry, in a Type 35 Mercer. Some cars had monocle windscreens

Courtesy of the Henry Ford Museum]

The 22-70 tourer of 1916. An identical car is in everyday use by a New York lady doctor many years its junior

[Courtesy of the Long Island Automotive Museum

The 1920 L-head Raceabout

Courtesy of the British Travel Association]

The 1922 Raceabout was the last. Note outboard fuel-pressure pump, twin fuel-tank fillers

and steering, which was just $1\frac{1}{4}$ turns lock to lock. The foot brake worked only on the transmission; the steel chassis tended to flex, putting some strain on the aluminium engine and gearbox mounts. These 35's were the most-prized Mercers; some of them averaged as high as 95 m.p.h. in their racing victories.

In 1915 Eric R. Delling replaced Porter as chief designer. He abandoned the engine sub-frame and introduced an L-head four ($3\frac{3}{4} \times 6\frac{3}{4}$) of 4·9 litres on a 115-in. wheelbase. The total weight of the new 22-70 series was 22·3 cwt. This car returned to single magneto ignition and won the Giant's Despair Hill-

Climb with a new class record in 1916.

By 1918 the last of the Roeblings had died, and Mercer was bought up by Locomobile and Crane-Simplex, which continued Delling's designs until 1922. For the next three years the Raceabout—by now fitted with some weather equipment—was sold, in rapidly dwindling volume, with a 6-cylinder overhead-valve Rochester engine of $5\frac{1}{2}$ litres ($3\frac{3}{4} \times 5$) and a 3-speed gearbox. To say that these are the least desirable Mercers is hardly to deprecate them, for they are still Mercers; and to many people any Mercer is more to be coveted than the prime example of any other marque.

The 30-h.p. 1907 runabout showed much European
influence

The boat-tailed 7-34 speedster had choice of staggered
or conventional seats

PACKARD

"Ask the man who owns one" was Packard's slogan;
for the run-of-the-mill Packard, it is also the authors'.

William D. and S. W. Packard became car makers
principally because, when they visited Alexander
Winton to make some suggestions about their Winton.
he rather brusquely suggested that, if they thought
they could do better, they should do so. So they did.

In 1902 they hired Charles Schmidt, formerly an
engineer for Mors, and for the next dozen years or
so Packard had really sporting characteristics,
whether in 25- or 40-h.p. 4-cylinder or 38- or 48-h.p.
6-cylinder form. Schmidt had not only designed but
driven the record-breaking 1904 Gray Wolf, which
did a mile in 46·4 seconds and could exceed 90 m.p.h.
as a result of Schmidt's concentration on making
limited power produce maximum performance. The
engine was a four of $4\frac{3}{16} \times 5$, about 4 litres, developing
26 b.h.p. at 1000 r.p.m. Schmidt abandoned previous
armoured wood frames for pressed steel, with an
aluminium racing body. From this car came the
Model L, cast in two pairs, and the famous 30-h.p.
with four $5 \times 5\frac{1}{2}$ cylinders cast in pairs, magneto
ignition and three speeds. Both foot and hand brakes
worked the rear wheels. The wheelbase was 108 in.,
the track $56\frac{1}{2}$ in.

The Packards of the 1920s gave more attention

to luxury than to performance. While their coachwork was probably the most beautiful in the country
in design, its execution tended toward the slip-shod
in paint and mating of surfaces, and late vintage
Packard engines were considered rather soft in the
light of their frequent need for reboring. Generally,
they were held in much higher esteem abroad than
at home.

One Packard produced at the very end of the
vintage period, however, was superior to almost
anything made in America at the time. This was
the 7-34 speedster of 1930, a 6·3-litre straight-eight
($3\frac{1}{2} \times 5$) whose 145 h.p. at 3400 r.p.m. could drive
its 41 cwt. at almost 95 m.p.h. in five-seater form.
It had the then high compression ratio of 6·3:1, a
4-speed gearbox and a wheelbase of $134\frac{1}{2}$ in. with a
59-in. track. The option of a lower-ratio rear axle
enabled the speedster to just top 100 m.p.h. It was
offered with a variety of open and closed bodies.
Mechanical refinements included separate inlet and
exhaust manifolds, the latter being finned for cooling;
dual-choke carburation and cooling fins on the brake
drums. Externally, the speedster was narrower than
normal Packards, the running boards were shorter
and the windscreens, contrary to contemporary
Packard practice, could not be folded.

PEERLESS

It was the first decade of Peerless's 32-year span
that produced its most interesting cars. In 1900 the
company began producing under de Dion licences
in Cleveland; two years later it was making its own
engines of one and two cylinders. In 1903 an 80-h.p.
four was built for the Gordon Bennett Trophy but
was wrecked soon after the start.

Peerless achieved its greatest fame from its Green
Dragon racer, driven by Barney Oldfield. This car,
like Bugatti's Type 54, was developed from a touring
car, the 24-h.p. 1905 Peerless, which had a fine
sporting record of its own: 1000 miles in less than
26 hours, class record at Mt. Washington, and a
number of racing victories throughout the United
States. It had an overhead-valve 4-cylinder engine
($4\frac{1}{8} \times 5\frac{1}{4}$), cast in pairs and mounted in an unusually

short wheelbase: 109 in. (track was the usual 56 in.).
The 60-h.p. Green Dragon was an enlarged version
of the 24-h.p. and its four $5\frac{1}{4} \times 5\frac{3}{4}$ cylinders subsequently went into the 60-h.p. touring car. All Peerless
cars at this time used a 4-speed gearbox.

The 1906 roadster had both external contracting and
internal expanding brakes on rear wheels

The Green Dragon, at once the product and the progenitor of touring cars, set innumerable records on dirt, boards and roads and defeated a number of larger European machines. It never raced outside the country. By the time of the 1914 war, Peerless had settled down to making a line of unexciting quality vehicles that continued until 1932.

PIERCE-ARROW

Pierce-Arrow, which was born with the century and absorbed by Studebaker in the mid-1930s, was always synonymous with the ultimate in dignity. It is perhaps less well known as one of the easiest of all American cars to drive, with its finger-light steering even in 1909, its easy gear changes and the smooth, silent engine.

One of its many models was of definitely sporting character: the 1916 raceabout, which was built on the largest of the year's chassis, a wheelbase of $147\frac{1}{2}$ in. and track of 57 in. The cone clutch controlled a 4-speed gearbox that transmitted power to a semi-floating rear axle; braking was on the rear wheels and was both expanding and contracting. The six 5×7 cylinders were cast in pairs; the $13\frac{3}{4}$-litre engine developed 60 b.h.p. Unlike other Pierce-Arrows, it carried the headlights mounted between rather than in the front wings. It was notable for its exceptional handling at high speeds.

SCRIPPS-BOOTH

One of the shortest-lived marques anywhere was the Scripps-Booth, which appeared in 1915 only to be swept into General Motors a few years later. Its 1916 V-8, which showed considerable evidence of European influence, was its one sporting manifestation; thereafter the marque subsided into prosaic sixes.

Cast *en bloc*, the 90-degree V-engine had a bore and stroke of $2\frac{5}{8}\times3\frac{3}{4}$ (about 2·3 litres), closer to Continental trends of the period than to the dominant American one. Rated at 22 h.p., the engine was mounted in a conventional frame of 120-in. wheelbase and 56-in. track. A dry multiple-disc clutch controlled the 3-speed gearbox, and the spiral bevel drive, the prevalent pattern, drove a three-quarters-floating rear axle. While no competition records exist, the marque is reputed to have had excellent road-holding at all speeds.

[Photograph by Air Commodore N. R. Buckle, M.V.O.
The Scripps-Booth roadster in England

Courtesy of the Long Island Automotive Museum]
The 1916 Pierce-Arrow raceabout starred in 1954 and 1957 Anglo-American Vintage Rallies

SIMPLEX

One of the first of the international cars may be said to be the Simplex. Carlton R. Mabley and his brother-in-law, Proctor Smith, were New York agents for the Mercedes in 1903 when Mabley was inspired to become a manufacturer as well as an importer. Smith was amenable, and the car they produced used chrome nickel steel manufactured by Krupp in Germany, who also built the entire chassis for the Simplex. In fact, for a number of years many Simplex components were interchangeable with Mercedes parts.

In 1909 Simplex came into its own as a sports car, winning the 24-hour Brighton Beach track race in Brooklyn, where it covered 1091 miles, and the Fairmount Park road race in Philadelphia. This car was a 10-litre four ($5\frac{3}{4}\times5\frac{3}{4}$) cast in pairs, with side valves in T-arrangement; it developed 50 h.p. at 1200 r.p.m. and its chain final drive was good for well over 75 m.p.h. As on most chain-drive cars, a variety of front sprockets was offered to afford varying final-drive ratios. The foot brake worked bronze shoes on the shaft of the front sprockets—the jackshaft or countershaft—and the hand brake operated directly on the rear wheels.

Smith & Mabley had got into financial trouble and the firm had had to undergo reorganization. A 90-h.p. four ($6\times5\frac{3}{4}$) won a great number of road races, dirt-track competitions and hill-climbs, and set a 10-mile standard-car record of 90·9 m.p.h. in 1910. These cars were designed by Edward Franquist, who also produced a 7·8-litre shaft-driven Simplex in 1912 as well as a 75-h.p. in 1914, the last American car to have chain drive. It was good for 80 m.p.h.

In 1914 Henry M. Crane replaced Franquist as chief engineer; two years later the fours were abandoned for a 9·9-litre L-head six ($4\frac{1}{4}\times6\frac{7}{8}$) known as the Crane-Simplex. This car was so exactly planned and built that, as long as it remained in its original ownership, it was unconditionally guaranteed for life. In 1917 the factory converted to aviation engines and, when the war was over, never returned to automobiles.

[Courtesy of the Henry Ford Museum

The 1909 Simplex tourer still exceeds 75 m.p.h.

Courtesy of the Long Island Automotive Museum]

One of America's finest: the 1910 Simplex Speed Car

The 75-h.p. 1914 car was the last in the U.S. with chain drive. Electric lights and starters were made standard in 1913

The 1912 car carried two fuel tanks for racing or long-distance touring

[Smithsonian Institution photograph; courtesy of Alec Ulmann

Courtesy of the British Travel Association]

STUTZ

Only the irredeemably Mercerised will deny equal rank to the Stutz in the American motor-sport legend. Harry C. Stutz built the first car bearing his name in 1911 as a test-bench for the rear axles he sold to other manufacturers, and sent it into the first Indianapolis 500-mile race. Finishing 11th at 67·75 m.p.h. without one stop for mechanical adjustment, it wrote a glorious first chapter.

Stutz's first cars used the $4\frac{1}{2} \times 5\frac{1}{2}$ Wisconsin four, but by 1913 he was building his own engines, a four and a six. The $6\frac{1}{2}$-litre T-head four was the more powerful, developing about 60 b.h.p. at 1500 r.p.m. from its $4\frac{3}{4} \times 5\frac{1}{2}$ cylinders cast in pairs. Wheelbase was 120 in. (alternatively 130 in.), track was 56 in. and weight was about $26\frac{3}{4}$ cwt. Springing was semi-elliptic all round. The engine was lubricated by pressure through a hollow crankshaft and dual ignition was by magneto. Transmission and differential were in unit; a double-knuckle universal joint and

H.C.S.

torque tube carried power from the cone clutch to the 3-speed gearbox. The six was identical in volume, its 4×5 cylinders being cast in threes, and in all other specifications. The 4-cylinder Bearcat was continued until 1924, by which time it had changed to mono-bloc engine, left-hand drive and inboard controls.

At the same time Stutz was building a smaller car that he called the H.C.S. Unlike the Stutz, which offered a number of open and closed bodies in addition to the Bearcat, the H.C.S. was available only as a two-seater on an 108-in. wheelbase (the track remained 56 in.). Its 4-cylinder L-head engine used the hollow crankshaft of the Stutz; its $3\frac{3}{4} \times 5$ cylinders gave a volume of about 1·8 litres. When Stutz left the Stutz Motor Car Co. in 1919 to build only the H.C.S., a full line of bodies was produced on 120-in. wheelbases and the power plant became an overhead-valve four, enlarged to $3\frac{5}{8} \times 5\frac{1}{2}$ giving 50 b.h.p. and 70 m.p.h. despite its $28\frac{1}{2}$ cwt. weight.

[Courtesy of the "Carriage Cavalcade"]

Eighty m.p.h. was well within the reach of the original 1913 Bearcat

From the catalogue of the Stutz Motor Car Co.; courtesy of Alec Ulmann]

The early H.C.S. roadster

[Courtesy of the Long Island Automotive Museum]

The Series G Bearcat of 1919 had dual valves, monobloc engine

[Courtesy of the Henry Ford Museum]

The Speedway Roadster of mid-1920s used dual-valve Bearcat engine or o.h.v. six ($3\frac{3}{8} \times 5$, 4·4 litres) giving 75 b.h.p. at 3200 r.p.m. and 80 m.p.h.

In 1923 the H.C.S. was given a 4·2-litre six ($3\frac{1}{2} \times 5$) with overhead valves, pushrod-operated and made of silicone steel. Producing 80 b.h.p. at 2850 r.p.m. for a 32½-cwt. car, it was not phenomenally fast. The wheelbase was increased to 126 in. and vanadium steel was used in 2½-in. wide springs. Stutz's original idea of an economy car, obviously, could not be realized on these terms, and at the end of 1924, when it was producing a fine-quality machine (which, incidentally, looked from the front almost exactly like an Hispano), the company turned all its production facilities to taxis.

Before the founder left the Stutz Motor Car Co., the marque had already run up an impressive record: third at Indianapolis (finishing in a literal blaze), fourth in the Vanderbilt Cup, first several times in Fairmount Park and Brighton Beach and innumerable other firsts all over the country, frequently beating Mercer and the best of the imports. In 1916, when a disgruntled Bearcat owner turned up at the factory to complain that his car was sub-standard, it was turned round without being touched and driven across the country to set a new transcontinental speed record. In 1915 a Bearcat won a 350-mile race at 102·56 m.p.h.

Before Stutz's departure he introduced the first of the marque's dual-valve cars, a 4-cylinder ($4\frac{3}{8} \times 6$, or 6 litres) T-head Speedster based on the Bearcat. The cylinders, however, were cast *en bloc* and, as in the Bearcat, pistons and crankcase were of aluminium. There were also a Bulldog tourer on the Bearcat chassis and a Bulldog special on the 130-in. frame.

In 1924 the Stutz Co. introduced its Speedway Six on a 130-in. chassis: an 80-h.p. 4·7-litre overhead-valve unit. For the first time, Stutz appeared with a gearbox built in unit with the engine. But there was another reorganization and the new president of the company, F. E. Moscovics, felt that sporting emphasis had prevented the company from developing its sales; thereafter it was to emphasize comfort and safety. Moscovics, however, departed from his own credo long enough to enter a Black Hawk roadster—designed by Paul Bastien, one of the creators of Belgium's Métallurgique—at Le Mans, where it finished second to Barnato's Bentley; in the

[*Courtesy of Alec Ulmann*]

The Black Hawk roadster before the start of a duel with Hispano in 1928

Courtesy of the "Carriage Cavalcade"]

The close-coupled 1933 DV-32 Super-Bearcat, last of a proud line

same year the Black Hawk made its unsuccessful bid to out-run an Hispano for 24 hours at Indianapolis. This was a 4·7-litre eight developing 90 h.p. with single overhead camshaft and underslung worm drive, which was rare in the United States. Four-wheel hydraulic brakes, of course, were now standard; of Stutz design, these were supposed to be self-adjusting. With a balanced crankshaft and nine main bearings, the Black Hawk turned at 3200 r.p.m. A Black Hawk 6 was also offered: 4 litres and 85 b.h.p. at 3200 r.p.m. Like the eight, it had a single overhead camshaft, a 4-speed gearbox and 2½-turn steering. American and foreign coachbuilders liked to work with the Black Hawk, and many of the cars were sold to royalty and nobility.

In 1929 Stutz returned to Le Mans with a 5·2-litre edition of the Black Hawk, one of which had a Roots supercharger supposed to give it 143 b.h.p. at 3800 r.p.m. Two of the cars did not complete the course; the third finished fifth. Again in 1930 the marque appeared at Le Mans, with what was to be the last Stutz model, the DV-32 Super-Bearcat. It was a straight-eight whose two overhead camshafts controlled four inclined valves per $3\frac{3}{8} \times 4\frac{3}{4}$ cylinder (6·3 litres). Though both entrants failed to finish at Le Mans, the Super-Bearcat was of top sporting quality. Guaranteed for 100 m.p.h., one of the cars held 103 for six hours. Engineers noted a marked resemblance between its cylinder head and that of the J Duesenberg.

The DV-32's standard chassis was 134½ and 145 in.; the Super-Bearcat had a 116-in. wheelbase and a two-seater Weymann fabric drop-head body, well designed to stand up to the 156 b.h.p. at 3900 r.p.m. Cost, however, put these cars beyond the reach of all but the wealthiest, and in 1935 the Stutz Motor Car Co. was interred in a bankruptcy court.

THOMAS FLYER

Unquestionably the greatest achievement of the Thomas was its victory in the incredible New York–Paris race of 1908, a feat whose only parallel is the similar heroic triumph of the Itala in the Peking–Paris race of the previous year.

Founded in Buffalo in 1902, the E. R. Thomas Motor Co. first made a sporting name with its Thomas Flyer of 1907, which won the 24-hour race at Brighton Beach, covering 997 miles at 41·55 m.p.h. without a single replacement. This was a 60-h.p. monster four ($5\frac{1}{2} \times 5\frac{1}{2}$, or 8·7 litres) with a 118-in. wheelbase and 56-in. track. Chain-driven, it had brakes on the rear wheels and also on the forward sprockets, a multiple-disc clutch and four speeds. Dual ignition was provided by magneto and dynamo.

Montague Roberts, who had set the Brighton Beach record, was chosen for the 1908 car's Paris run. His car was the new 6-70, a 70-h.p. six with the same bore and stroke as the four but with a total volume of over 13 litres. Its wheelbase was cut 4 in. and the sprocket brakes were shifted to the jackshaft but the other specifications were the same as those of the Brighton Beach car, and the 6-70 could run at 5 or better than 70 m.p.h. in top gear with an aluminium seven-passenger body (the speedometer went optimistically to 100). Its 11-in. ground clearance made it ideal for the New York–Paris run, which was made by a standard car whose only modifications were to the wheels, to provide for a possible dearth of tyres; an extra-large petrol tank

The New York–Paris car early in the race. Original car is preserved in Long Island Automotive Museum in state in which it arrived in Paris

From the Lazarnick Collection; courtesy of the Library of the Automobile Manufacturers' Association]

The 6-70 tourer of 1910

The 6-40 runabout of 1912, as it appeared in 1953

and a winch coupled to the engine so that the car could pull itself out of ditches.

The epic victory, whose story is told in a later chapter, gave the marque a solid reputation that was borne out by its subsequent competition record of wins and respectable places in races all around the country. But the Thomas Co. was absorbed by the United States Motors combine, which disintegrated in 1912, when the Thomas was offering two sixes, the 70 on a 140-in. wheelbase and the smaller, shaft-driven 6-40 ($4\frac{1}{4} \times 5\frac{1}{2}$, or 5·2 litres). Unlike the 6-70, whose cylinders were cast separately, the 6-40 had them in pairs. Its wheelbase was 134 in. and rear brakes were inner and outer.

WILLS STE. CLAIRE

The American car that made an outstanding impression on European experts in the 1920s was probably the shortest-lived of the country's finest: the Wills Ste. Claire.

Its designer was an engineer before he was a business man. C. H. Wills had worked for Henry Ford almost from the latter's start; he had concentrated on Ford's racers as long as they were made. When Ford bought out his Ford Motor Co. stock in 1919, Wills was a multi-millionaire; but he remained an engineer and a perfectionist.

Two years later he introduced a high-performance car that was one of the most advanced in the country, the 60-degree V-8 Wills Ste. Claire with a single o.h.c. for each bank. The 6-litre engine ($3\frac{1}{4} \times 5\frac{1}{2}$) produced 65 h.p. at 2700 r.p.m. It was full of refinements. The crankshaft ran on seven main bearings; at the front it drove a vertical shaft that controlled the cooling fan and the overhead camshaft. The cooling fan was equipped with an automatic clutch that cut out its operation when not needed, thus allowing that horsepower to be utilized for driving the car. Wills, a metallurgist, was extremely partial to molybdenum and aluminium, his connecting rods being made of the latter material.

The Gray Goose roadster and phaeton were offered on two wheelbases, the longer (127 in.) becoming in 1924 the standard. At this time Wills introduced a $4\frac{1}{2}$-litre six of the same dimensions as the eight but some 200 lb. heavier (the Gray Goose six roadster weighed $31\frac{1}{4}$ cwt.) and developing 66 b.h.p. at 3000 r.p.m. Both cars could reach 75 m.p.h. and Wills Ste. Claire made several record cross-country runs, climaxed by a New York–San Francisco time of 83 hours and 12 minutes in 1926, the final year of production. Despite their size, the cars were known also for their extreme adaptability to Alpine roads and were highly esteemed in Switzerland. No one who owns a Wills Ste. Claire today will accept any price for it.

The Gray Goose roadster

The Type 205A of 1951 was in the 1100-c.c. class

In 1952 Abarth moved up to the 1500-c.c. class

Abarths are available with standard bodies of basic maker or coachwork such as this by Bertone

The Zagato-bodied 750-c.c. coupé is latest Abarth. Two parallel crests in roof allow comfortable seating without vitiating low silhouette

ABARTH

Carlo Abarth founded Abarth & Co. just after the Second World War to supply specialized speed equipment for Continental and British sports cars, but the firm soon became interested in making modifications so extensive that the results were virtually cars of a new marque. While the first Abarths were built impartially on FIAT, Alfa Romeo and Lancia foundations, the marque has become identified in recent years with FIAT alone, and has specialized in a 750-c.c. car based on the FIAT 600. Abarth has also built out-and-out racers, as well as record cars based on the FIAT that have amassed scores of records for Italy, of which the outstanding one is 25,000 kilometres in 10 days at an average of 72·3 m.p.h. on the brutal Monza track.

Abarth's most desired car is the 750-c.c. Mille Miglia Grand Touring model, which develops 44 h.p. at 6000 r.p.m. with 9·8:1 compression; special versions are also available with 46 h.p. and with 47 h.p. at 6200 r.p.m. on 10:1 compression. All internal parts of these units are polished and specially prepared, and exhaustively tested before delivery, being torn down and reassembled midway in the tests. The basic FIAT engine is enlarged to 61 × 64 mm., single carburation and dual exhaust systems are used, crankshaft and camshaft are replaced and clutch, transmission and differential are modified to exploit fully the added horsepower. All these rear-engined cars employ all-independent suspension.

Abarth cars have brought Italy the mountain-climbing championship as well as long-distance records, and are at the head of their class in every major rally and race in Europe as well as the United States.

ALFA ROMEO

The history of Alfa Romeo is hardly less romantic than the lineage of its serpent crest that traces its design to an 11th-century bronze replica of the brazen serpent made by Moses in the wilderness, modified by the Crusaders.

In 1906 Alexandre Darracq established a branch factory in Milan, but it did not prosper and in 1909 it was sold to the Società Anonima Lombarda Fabbrica Automobili (Lombard Automobile Manufacturing Co.), whose initials soon gave it the local nickname of Alfa. Two years later, the new company was taken over by an engineer named Nicola Romeo; it was reorganized after the war under the name of Alfa Romeo.

The first sporting Alfas appeared in the early 1920s, when the company made its mark in racing with victories in the Targa Florio—taking the first three places the second time. This was achieved with the 3-litre sports RLSS 22/90, developed from the 2-litre P-1 racing six. Pushrods operated the overhead valves for its six 76×110 cylinders; maximum engine speed was 3500 r.p.m. and some cars could reach 90 m.p.h. From the first, Alfa had the unbelievably true, quick steering that has characterized almost all Italian cars and become a standard by which every other machine is judged.

In 1924 Alfa's racing car was the P-2, a 2-litre d.o.h.c. eight that covered 10 kilometres at 125 m.p.h. and starred in that year's Grand Prix de l'Europe. In 1925 that race was run at Spa, where thousands of Frenchmen were cheering their own blue cars and jeering the three red Alfas of Antonio Ascari, Giuseppe Campari and Count Gastone Brilli-Peri. The race was well under way when the team's manager, Vittorio Jano, set up beautifully laid tables in the pits, flagged all three drivers in and treated them to a sumptuous, leisurely meal (with the proper wines) while the mechanics washed the cars and the rest of the field thundered by time after time. When the drivers had had all they wanted, Jano sent them back to the course, and the red cars finished first, second and third. From then on the list of Alfa's victories and drivers reads like the golden book of racing.

A $1\frac{1}{2}$-litre (62×88) six had meanwhile been put into production and in 1929 this was enlarged into the famous 17/95 (horsepower) or 1750 (c.c.). This 6-cylinder car (65×88) was available with either one or two overhead camshafts and blown or unblown to choice. The Gran Sport version gave 95 h.p. at 4400 r.p.m. and could exceed 100 m.p.h. It was generally fitted with one of the most exquisite bodies ever made: an open two-seater by Zagato, who is still making magnificent Alfas that almost cause one to forget the restrictions imposed on beauty by envelope coachwork. Roadholding was phenomenal, in the Italian tradition, and brake drums were ribbed. A dual-choke Memini carburetter fed the engine. Magnificent as these cars were—and are—to see and to drive, they required considerable attention: superchargers, for example, must be repacked with petroleum jelly every 1000 miles; cooling water must be replaced every 1500 and carbon removal and valve grinding are recommended at 8000-mile intervals. Yet this is not too high a price to pay for cars that swept the 1930 Tourist Trophy in one-two-three order—No. 1 being a completely standard model that beat works Bentleys—and went on to win the Mille Miglia and Targa Florio.

This car was produced until 1934. It compared on even terms in every respect with the contemporary Bugatti; and in the 1930s Alfa succeeded to Bugatti's place at the pinnacle of racing. As early as 1920 Enzo Ferrari had won the Targa Florio on an Alfa; in the 1930s he formed his own Scuderia Ferrari, using only Alfas. From 1930 to 1935 the Targa Florio was an Alfa monopoly; in the last year the first eight cars in the Mille Miglia were Alfas. Their rigid chassis and orthodox suspension, according to Stanford, represented the highest development of these systems. By this time the 1750 had been superseded in competition by the 2·3, which was its 8-cylinder version. Bore and stroke were the same; a 10-bearing crankshaft was fitted and gears were employed to drive the two camshafts. The 2·3 won the Targa Florio, driven by Nuvolari; Lord Howe and Tim Birkin won the Mille Miglia at 78 m.p.h. in 1931 with a similar car. The P-3 racing car—the

The 2·9 that won the 1951 Swiss G.P.

[Copyright by "The Autocar"; courtesy of C. C. Wakefield Co. Ltd.

The 6-cylinder Disco Volante had 3-litre ($82 \cdot 5 \times 92$) and $3\frac{1}{2}$-litre (87×98) versions with 8:1 compression, three or six carburetters, 200 and 230 h.p. and 150-m.p.h. maximum. The coupé weighed about $17\frac{3}{4}$ cwt.

Works photograph from the collection of Kurt H. Miska]

[Photograph by D. Fulluck; courtesy of F/Lt. P. M. A. Hull

The 22/90 tourer of 1924, the first sports Alfa

Courtesy of R. H. Blum]

The 1750-c.c. roadster, Gran Sport

[Courtesy of the Automobile-Club de l'Ouest

The 2·3 Le Mans car of 1931 at 1958 Rétrospective

Courtesy of Scuderia La Manovella]

Nuvolari won 1933 Mille Miglia in this 1931 8C Monza model, now owned by Rome's Venturi Museum. Note filler for oil tank; dry sump was standard

[Photograph by Dr. Ian R. Entwistle

The P-3 converted into highly roadworthy two-seater sports. Crankshaft and camshafts were made in halves, cylinder head was non-detachable; engine was essentially two fours in line on common crankcase

Photograph by P. S. de Beaumont; courtesy of Everett L. Poorman]

The 105-h.p. 2½-litre at Bridgehampton, 1951

[Photograph by Julian Apley]

Courtesy of S. A. Alfa Romeo]

The aluminium-bodied 1900C Super Sprint is a four-seater, admirable for touring or gran-turismo racing

The Giulietta coupé is adaptable as the 1900C

designation appears in the factory's own historical sketch—used the same engine bored out to 2·9 litres (68 × 100) with a dry sump. It developed 180 b.h.p. and could top 130 m.p.h. with two blowers, one for each cylinder bank. Like the other Alfas, it was designed by Jano, who abandoned the solid front axle for wishbones and torsion bars in 1938, when he also fitted a transverse leaf spring and swing axles at the rear. The car that won the Mille Miglia that year weighed 25 cwt. At that time, too, he introduced the 2500-c.c. six that was to be raced both before and after the war, as well as the 1½-litre eight known to its admirers as the Alfetta. This is strictly a grand-prix car, outside the scope of this book. Victory after victory was rolled up by Alfa in all categories right up to the war.

Perhaps the marque's record year was 1950: 11 races entered, 11 races won, including the world's championship. The pre-war 2·9's were still competing, alongside the 2500-c.c. cars. Then Alfa began drastic reductions in engine size. The 1900C Super Sprint is a very light d.o.h.c. four capable of better than 130 m.p.h. with a closed touring body and a 5-speed gearbox; it may be called the current analogue to the 8C 2·3 despite its having only four cylinders (84·5 × 88). There is nothing in today's Alfa line to

take the place of the 8C, of course, with its open four-seater Le Mans bodies and two-seater Mille Miglia roadsters, the first on a 122-in. wheelbase and the second on 108 in.; and certainly nothing matches the 104-in. Monza version with its special camshafts and then high compression ratio of 6·5:1, giving 153 b.h.p. at 5400 r.p.m.

In the early 1950s Alfa brought out the Disco Volante (Flying Saucer), a 3- and 3½-litre car with which even Fangio could not attain success. By all odds the best known of Alfa's current cars is the amazing 1290-c.c. Giulietta and its higher-powered Veloce sister, which is identical in appearance but not in performance. Both are fours of 74 × 75 developing respectively 70 and 90 h.p. at 6000 r.p.m. The Giulietta will top 100 m.p.h., the Veloce has 10 more m.p.h. and the Special Sprint coupé, with 100 h.p., is good for 125 m.p.h. It has a 5-speed gearbox with Porsche synchromesh. None of the Giuliettas exceeds some 15 cwt. (compare the 16 cwt. of the blown 1750); some have dual carburation (the Veloce uses Webers, the other Giulietta one Solex), opposed to the six Webers of the 3½-litre Disco. Their truly remarkable performance combines with excellent detail and finish to make them ideal dual-purpose cars.

The Special Sprint Giulietta, a two-seater

The Giulietta roadster has wind-up windows, easily removed windscreen

[Courtesy of S. A. Alfa Romeo

Courtesy of S. A. Alfa Romeo]

ANSALDO

Little known today even in its birthplace, the Ansaldo was a hand-made automobile of high quality in the 1920–30 decade. Its most sporting manifestation was the 4CS of 1923–6, a 1928-c.c. (72·5 × 120) four with 5·5:1 compression, a single overhead camshaft, 48 h.p. at 3000 r.p.m. and 70 m.p.h. top speed. Both sump and crankcase were cast in aluminium, and the sump was heavily ribbed for cooling. The single dry-plate clutch governed a 3-speed gearbox integral with the engine. On its 9 ft. 1 in. wheelbase it had, like virtually all Italian cars, almost magnetic adhesion to the road under all circumstances. The sporting version weighed about 14¼ cwt.

Unfortunately for today's amateurs of the marque, virtually every Ansaldo was hand-made and of individual design, so that cannibalizing an Ansaldo in order to keep another one going is next to impossible because of differences in connecting rods, camshaft covers, body mountings, etc., even in cars with the same year and model designation.

CISITALIA

Developed to prototype form just before the Second World War, the Cisitalia was the brain-child of Piero Dusio, who used a good part of his war-earned fortune to put the marque into production in the late 1940s and early 1950s, until his financial collapse forced him to emigrate to Argentina, where

An Ansaldo tourer of 1926 still in use in New Zealand

he is now building industrial vehicles. It is notable that a large part of the post-war Cisitalia profits was used to supply the bond that freed Dr. Ferdinand Porsche from a French war-crimes prison.

Dusio relied on FIAT power plants; his 1939 prototype was built round a blown 1500-c.c. unit. He also used some of the smaller FIAT engines and chassis, notably the 1100 chassis with a 1258-c.c. engine having 8·4:1 compression and two dual-throated Weber carburetters. Developing 72 b.h.p. at 5500 r.p.m., it was capable of 105 m.p.h. and had competition brakes and 4-speed transmission. The 1089-c.c. FIAT engine was put into another Cisitalia model that gave 90 m.p.h. from its 53 h.p. at 5200 r.p.m. All these are o.h.v. engines.

What contributed largely to Dusio's failure was the attempt to develop a Porsche-designed 12-cylinder

The Spyder was known as the Nuvolari competition model

The 1500-c.c. coupé bodied by Farina

One of the latest Cisitalia coupés

One of the rare drop-head Cisitalias

rear-engined grand-prix car with five forward speeds and selective 4-wheel drive. Its estimated top speed of 230 m.p.h. caught Nuvolari's imagination and he hoped to race it, but it was never brought to competition readiness. When Dusio went to Argentina the prototype car followed him and made one or two brief appearances in that country as the Autoar but it never completed a race.

[Photograph by R. O. Barnard]

A 1926 Diatto tourer, in daily use in England

DIATTO

Diatto was building automobiles in the early years of this century, many of them under the name of Diatto-Clément as a result of adaptations of the designs of Albert Clément. In 1907, for example, the Diatto-Clément was a 25-h.p. four with dual ignition, pump cooling and side valves operated by two camshafts. Chain-driven, it had a 4-speed gearbox and multi-plate clutch.

In the vintage decade the Diatto was a 2-litre four with a single overhead camshaft and achieved some distinction in its period, despite its conventional chassis and suspension. Like many other Continental marques, Diatto was fitting 4-wheel brakes as standard equipment long before they became general in Great Britain and the United States.

FERRARI

The Bugatti *mystique* of the between-wars decades has passed in our day to Ferrari, ten times winner of the world's championship for constructors and producer of as bewildering a variety of models as ever came from Molsheim.

Enzo Ferrari's first cars, two 2500-c.c. 8-cylinder prototypes, ran in the 1940 Mille Miglia; war interrupted their development and it was not until 1947 that the Prancing Horse of Modena and Maranello reappeared. Like Bugatti, Ferrari derived most of his hand-made dual-purpose cars from his grand-prix designs. The first sports car to wear the sign of the Prancing Horse was the 1500-c.c. (55 × 52·5) V-12 known as the 125S. The cylinder banks were

set at the 60-degree angle that only the grand-prix V-6's abandoned (for 65 degrees); 100 b.h.p. was developed at 7000 r.p.m., reaching over 100 m.p.h. (150 in G.P. form); dual overhead cams were used and ignition was by a single magneto (many earlier Ferraris used only magneto ignition). This 13·4-cwt. car formed the foundation for all the Ferraris that have followed. Tubular chassis and independent front suspension have been used from the beginning.

The 125S was followed by the 166S, a 2-litre V-12 (60 × 58·8) with 230 b.h.p. at 7000 r.p.m. Horsepower rose again to 270 with the 3·3-litre 275S (72 × 68) and to 330 for the 4·5-litre 375S (80 × 74·5). Speeds of 125 to more than 130 m.p.h. became commonplace for Ferraris with these models, followed by the 212 Inter, a 2·5-litre car (68 × 68·8), developing 190 b.h.p. at 7200 r.p.m. This was one of the heaviest of the marque to its date, weighing 17·8 cwt. In 1951 the first 250 Europa gran turismo appeared: a 140-m.p.h. coupé weighing about 19½ cwt. that is still essentially the same: 2953 c.c. with 12 cylinders of 73 × 58·8 developing 240 b.h.p. at 7000 r.p.m. with 9:1 compression and 157 m.p.h. The 1958 Testa Rossa version of the 250 has 60 more horsepower and some 30 more m.p.h.

Two 4·1-litre cars were added to the line: the 340 Mexico (86 × 68), with 280 h.p. at 6600 r.p.m.,

James Kimberley, former president of the S.C.C.A., in his 4·5 that ran in the Mille Miglia

From the collection of Kurt H. Miska]

a 175-m.p.h. machine, and the 340 America of the same dimensions but with the usual Ferrari 8:1 compression against the Mexico's 9:1: it gave 220 h.p. at 5000 r.p.m. and something under 150 m.p.h.

In a kind of shadow-land between dual-purpose and purely competition machines, two fours departed from the V-12 tradition. The 500 Mondial was a 2-litre car (90×78) of 170 b.h.p. at 7200 r.p.m., with 9·2:1 compression, good for 150 m.p.h.; the 750 Monza was a litre bigger (103×90) and, with the same compression, produced 250 b.h.p. at 6000 r.p.m. for 10 more m.p.h. Both these models have an interminable list of victories, added to by the record of a third four introduced in 1956: the 2-litre Testa Rossa with the same bore and stroke as the Mondial, 8·5:1 compression, and 180 b.h.p. at 7000. Weighing some 100 lb. less than the 13·4-cwt. Mondial, the Testa Rossa was also good for 150 m.p.h.

The most magnificent of all Ferraris—the analogue to Bugatti's Royale—is the 4·9-litre Superamerica. Essentially a detuned grand-prix machine, it has the usual V-12 engine (88×68), which produces 340 b.h.p. at 6000 r.p.m. (360 in the competition version, in which compression is raised from 8·5 to 8·6:1), good for 165 m.p.h. in $22\frac{1}{4}$-cwt. touring form and for 180 or better in the competition model, $4\frac{1}{2}$ cwt. lighter.

For Le Mans Ferrari has also built a $2\frac{1}{2}$-litre machine, the 625. This 220-h.p. four (94×90) is one of the few Ferraris outside the grand-prix category with dual magneto ignition and easily attains 160 m.p.h. There were also two 6-cylinder Le Mans cars: the 280-h.p. 3·7-litre 118 (94×90) and the 4·4-litre (102×90) 350-h.p. 121. Unlike the G.P. sixes, these engines were arranged in line. In 1959 Ferrari returned to a V-6 that had already been used in G.P. machines, adapting it to the sports car. Called the Dino after his son, Alfredo, who had designed it just before his premature death, this is a 60-degree 1983-c.c. engine (77×71) developing 200 b.h.p. at 9·8:1 compression and 7200 r.p.m. Each cylinder bank has its own overhead camshaft; fuel is fed to three dual-choke Webers by both mechanical and electric pump, as on most Ferraris, and an oil radiator is standard.

The tubular steel frame has a stiff rear axle with lateral rods and triangulated reaction arms. Coil springs and telescopic shock absorbers are fitted at all four wheels, as are disc brakes. The open two-seater weighs about $12\frac{1}{2}$ cwt., giving a weight-power ratio of 7:1.

Ferrari victories since full production began in 1947 are innumerable in both sports and G.P. categories. They include Argentina, Le Mans, the Nürburgring, the Mille Miglia and every major course in all countries where sports cars are raced. Indianapolis is probably the only G.P. course where the Prancing Horse has never cut the tape.

Courtesy of Comm. Enzo Ferrari]

The 125 makes its début in 1947, driven by Franco Cortese. Rear semi-elliptics are still used by Ferrari

Photograph by Kurt H. Miska]

The 166S with Motto body. Dual hydraulic brakes are standard on all models

Courtesy of the Henry Ford Museum]

The 2·9 Mille Miglia roadster

145

The Mexico competition coupé

The Vignale sports body on 4·1-litre chassis

The 4·5-litre 375 America in drop-head form

The Mondial, like all Ferraris, is fitted with dual exhausts

The 3-litre Monza roadster

The 4·5-litre Mille Miglia coupé by Farina

The Superamerica is Ferrari's biggest car

The 3·5-litre Mille Miglia roadster was one of most successful Ferraris

Famous Testa Rossa of 1956–7 kept these lines in 1958 3-litre version

Farina's competition body for the gran turismo Europa

Today's Europa in standard body; it is often raced in this form, which is barely distinguishable from the first Europa. Porsche synchromesh is standard

The California Spyder on the 250 Europa chassis

147

FIAT

Two wealthy young cavalry lieutenants stationed in Verona in 1892 were bosom friends who shared, among other qualities, an insatiable intellectual curiosity and a keen interest in science and technology. Cavaliere Giovanni Agnelli and Giulio Gropello also shared an orderly named Scotto, who had been a smith; and these three, finding an old Daimler oil engine in a scrap heap, laid the foundation for today's giant FIAT works.

But six years elapsed after the trio's experimentation with the discarded engine before Agnelli returned to motors; then it was with the fixed idea that automobiles should be mass-produced in a limited range of models. At the same time Agnelli was concerned with the problem of training the kinds of specialists that the new industry would demand. What he had observed and experienced as an army officer on frequent strike duty led him to base all his plans on what even today would be described as an enlightened and, in some opinions, dangerous policy of industrial democracy.

With Count Carlo Biscaretti di Ruffia, later the head of the Museo dell'Automobile in Turin; his father, Count Roberto; Count Emanuele Cacherano di Bricherasio, Socialist heir to one of the oldest titles in Italy and father of his country's traffic laws, and a half-dozen others, Agnelli formed the Fabbrica Italiana Automobili Torino, whose initials gave the future car its name. From the beginning Agnelli was keenly aware of the value of racing as a sales promotion.

F.I.A.T.'s first cars were 6-h.p. flat twins, the engine being mounted in the centre of the metal-armoured wooden frame and driving the rear wheels by a single chain without a gearbox. Top speed was close to 40 m.p.h. In 1901 these cars, driven by Vincenzo Lancia and Felice Nazzaro, won a road race whose hills were too much for all the competitors. These models were succeeded by an 8-h.p. two and then by a multi-geared 12-h.p. four, which defeated a 24-h.p. Panhard in a private bet race and beat a Mercedes in a hill-climb. All these early F.I.A.T.s were water-cooled and chain-driven.

In 1904 F.I.A.T. began to hit its racing form, when Lancia won the Coppa Florio with a chain-driven 75-h.p. four that introduced the all-steel chassis for this marque and exceeded 100 m.p.h. In the next year a 120-h.p. 16·2-litre four (180 × 160) appeared with pushrod-operated overhead valves set at a 90-degree angle to each other. It finished second in the Gordon Bennett and the G.P. de France, in which F.I.A.T. was among the first makers to use the detachable rim. The 90-h.p. four (165 × 165) was less successful. Though shaft drive had been introduced on some models in 1906, chain drive was retained on the 16-litre and other sports cars; the big machine took first and second in the Targa Florio. At the same time a "light" T-head six was being marketed; as in the bigger cars, much of

148

The 509 Mille Miglia with Bateau body (990-c.c., 57 × 97) weighed 10¾ cwt. on a 100-in. wheelbase. The overhead camshaft engine with 8 : 1 pistons and blower (509A) won its class in the 1928 Targa Florio with a faster average than a bigger Bugatti despite its 3-speed gearbox. Ignition was by magneto

The 509S of 1928 had a 92-in. wheelbase and 47-in. track and was capable of 78 m.p.h. unblown

the engine mechanism was still exposed but casting was now monobloc. In 1908 FIAT—the periods were dropped in 1906—won the American G.P. at Savannah with Wagner and the Coppa Florio with Nazzaro, whose team-mate, Lancia, set a lap record of 82 m.p.h. From 1908 to 1917 FIATs were manufactured under licence in Poughkeepsie, N.Y.

The marque's racing had passed its peak by 1909, though victories continued at a lesser rate, with the 90-h.p. S61, the 120-h.p. 130 × 190 and the 200-h.p. 150 × 200 of 1912. The 120-h.p. car featured an

The 3·7-litre 80-h.p. 6-cylinder 525S was an 85-m.p.h. tourer. Felice Nazzaro is at the wheel

The 12-h.p. F.I.A.T. in the first Tour of Italy, 1901, with Felice Nazzaro

Nazzaro on the winner of the French G.P. at Dieppe, whose four 180 × 152 cylinders produced 130 b.h.p.

The 1907 6-cylinder roadster

The 200-h.p. S74 of 1911, capable of 140 m.p.h., won at Savannah

The 1500-c.c. Tipo Spinto 501 owned by Baron Giorgio Franchetti. An identical car was the first racing vehicle for Piero Taruffi

A 519S tourer from John Ellis's collection

[Photograph by Capt. G. Liston Young

The 508S Mille Miglia Balilla, introduced in 1933, won its class in that race; stripped and tuned, it can exceed 100 m.p.h.

[Courtesy of FIAT

The Balilla coupé used the roadster's 995-c.c. (65 × 75) 36-h.p. engine

[Courtesy of FIAT

The Balilla was bored out to 68 × 75 (1089 c.c.) for the 42-h.p. 1938 508C Mille Miglia car, capable of 90 m.p.h. in road trim

overhead camshaft and dual valving; the 1914 G.P. car had 4-wheel brakes. FIAT had also produced a monstrous record car some years earlier, a 28·4-litre (190 × 250) 300-h.p. four timed at 143 m.p.h.

After the 1914 war FIAT built both G.P. and sports cars. One of the former followed the Gobron-Brillié principle by opposing two pistons in each of six cylinders; one set of pistons opened the inlet ports, the other controlled the exhaust. This engine gave 174 b.h.p. in bench tests but was never raced. One of the most interesting of the vintage FIATs was the Tipo 501, first produced in 1919. This long-stroke side-valve four was of such high performance that it served as a trainer for many of today's top racing drivers. The 509S, which first appeared in 1925 and was continued for some years thereafter, was an overhead-cam 990-c.c. four (57 × 97) that, like the 501, boasted excellent steering and very good 4-wheel brakes on a 90-in. wheelbase. Top speed was 78 m.p.h.

The 501, which was continued until 1929, was never intended as a sports car but has won over 1000 races in private hands. Its 1460-c.c. engine (65 × 110) could be had in an o.h.v. version—the 501S—good for 68 m.p.h., and its 104-in. wheelbase and 49-in. track added to its handling quality. The car had pump cooling and a multiplate clutch. The standard car won its class in the 1921 Targa Florio and was only 3 m.p.h. slower than the winner, a 4½-litre 1914 FIAT.

Quite as big as the 1914 car, the 4766-c.c. Tipo 519 of 1922–30 was a pushrod-o.h.v. six (85 × 140) developing 80 b.h.p. with drilled aluminium pistons and a fully balanced crank in five main bearings. It could reach 85 m.p.h. and had exceptional hydraulic servo-assisted 4-wheel braking. Its wheelbase was 130 in., its track 56 in.; while the 501 used semi-elliptics all round, the 519 fitted them only at the front, employing full cantilevers at the rear.

FIAT rejoined the 1-litre class with the Balilla of 1933 and following years. Weighing only 12 cwt., it was quite lively with its 36-h.p. 65 × 75 engine with pushrod overhead valves and could cover a quarter-mile from rest in 20·2 seconds. Its aero-dynamically experimental development into the 1100, with a 90-m.p.h. top speed, foreshadowed the post-war low-drag closed coachwork.

During most of the post-war period FIAT has given little attention to sports cars, though its products have formed the basis for a number of smaller, specialized marques. Recently, however, FIAT has modified its work-horse 500-c.c. car for sports use. The tiny four-seater has a rear engine of two 67·4 × 70 cylinders, 21·5 h.p., 8·6:1 compression, a high-lift camshaft and a top speed of 68 m.p.h. Despite its unquestionable ugliness the 500 is not only admirably useful in daily traffic but rewarding to drive in race and rally with its quick acceleration and characteristic adhesion and cornering. Introduced in 1958, it won its class in the Hockenheim 12-hour race and in the Liège–Brescia–Liège.

150

[Courtesy of FIAT

Courtesy of FIAT]

The short-lived 2-litre V-8 of 1953 was better known as a base for S.I.A.T.A. cars. Its 105-b.h.p. engine was capable of about 115 m.p.h.

Like the American Crosley, the new sports 500 belies appearance with performance

ISOTTA-FRASCHINI

Bugatti's magic is believed by experts to have influenced the early Isotta-Fraschini, when the firm founded in 1900 by Cesare Isotta and Oreste Fraschini was closely linked to de Dietrich a few years later during Bugatti's tenure as designer for de Dietrich.

The first Isottas were single-cylinder cars; the 1906 model was the first with multiple cylinders—it had six—and launched the firm on its career of pioneering experimentation. The first six had a water-cooled emergency brake; its 1907 successor had a compressed-air starter. In 1910 Isotta was the first production car in the world to standardize 4-wheel brakes, and its 1920 straight-eight was the first such production engine.

Like most Italian firms, Isotta-Fraschini entered racing fairly early with a 120-h.p. overhead-camshaft car that was unsuccessful in 1905. In 1907, however, Fernando Minoia scored the marque's first major victory, winning the Coppa Florio with a 145×120 car that retained the o.h.c. The next year Isotta brought out a 1200-c.c. o.h.c. car whose design is generally credited to Bugatti, and one of these 62×100 fours with 4-speed gearbox won the G.P. des Voiturettes at Dieppe. This model, according to Karslake and Pomeroy, was in effect the prototype of Le Patron's own Type 13. In 1908, too, the big Isotta won the Targa Florio and finished second to Old 16 in the Vanderbilt Cup.

From 1910 on the marque produced a 100-h.p. 10·6-litre four (130×200) with four valves per cylinder. Pump-cooled, the engine was cast *en bloc* and none of the mechanism was left exposed. The cylinder head was non-detachable and the cylinder bases were individual. The 4-wheel braking introduced on this model was never abandoned; rods operated the shoes inside the large finned drums. This car had a smaller 27/80 version of 6234 c.c. (105×180). By 1913 the sports model was producing 140 b.h.p. Still chain-driven, the 1913 Isotta had six brake

drums: one on each wheel and two on the jackshafts to which the forward sprockets were fixed. On its 130-in. wheelbase the car weighed 45 cwt.; an excellent example is maintained in running order by Fred H. Sills of Byron, Ill.

Isotta's sporting career dropped off sharply after the 1914 war, though in both 1925 and 1926 the marque won the rugged 230-mile Targa Abruzzo on public roads. By now Isotta was building only the straight-eight that it brought out in 1919: an 85×130 80-b.h.p. 6-litre soon enlarged to a 7·3-litre (95×130), using pushrods for its overhead valves and developing 120 b.h.p. at 2400 r.p.m. The Tipo Spinto used dual carburetters and, with other changes, gave 140 b.h.p. at 2600 r.p.m. Like the Hispano, it had only a 3-speed gearbox, not too well spaced. Two wheelbases were available: $134\frac{1}{2}$ and 145 in. The crankshaft ran in nine main bearings and tubular connecting rods were fitted. The 1919 Tipo 8 became the 8A when the first Spinto modifications were incorporated: dual exhaust manifolds and 5:1 compression. The chassis alone, however, weighed over $27\frac{1}{2}$ cwt.

Where the 8A was capable of 85 m.p.h., the 8B, which is the collector's prize, could exceed 90 m.p.h., since better breathing and valving allowed 150 b.h.p. at 3000 r.p.m. Like the earlier eights, it was a favourite chassis of all the major custom coachbuilders and some remarkably beautiful cars were turned out on it. Production declined sharply during the 1930s but after the Second World War a final attempt was made to revive Isotta-Fraschini with a $3\frac{1}{2}$-litre V-8 mounted in the rear and driving independently sprung rear wheels (front suspension was also independent). Known as the 8C or Monterosa, it had a 5-speed gearbox and its road-holding was extravagantly praised. Sufficient capital to produce it in salable quantities could not be found, however, and by 1950 Isotta was merely another name in motoring's Valhalla.

A 1908 Isotta finished second in the Vanderbilt Cup

A big 4-cylinder tourer of 1909

The 140-b.h.p. 1913 sports has a laterally braced chassis, inboard brakes on jackshafts

The 1914 racing runabout with 120-h.p. engine, unlike earlier cars, had enclosures for its chains

A 1926 Tipo 8A Spinto with boat-tail body

This late 1928 tourer, with English coachwork, is still in daily use

152

An 8B Spyder

A Castagna-bodied 8B tourer. Both sections of V-wind-screen fold flat

The last Isotta had a rear engine, undistinguished envelope coachwork

153

ITALA

When Giovanni and Matteo Ceirano began building cars, using their family name as the marque, they were immediately successful. The brothers' personal relations, however, progressed in inverse ratio and two years later, in 1903, Matteo opened his own small plant in Turin and named his own cars Itala. A year later he triumphed so brilliantly in a hill-climb that a group of financiers offered a brilliant capitalization, justified in 1905 when Itala won the Coppa Florio. It is suspected that Vincenzo Lancia had a hand in the design of this 112-h.p. chain-driven 16·6-litre four (185×155), which lapped at over 70 m.p.h. A much smaller 40-h.p. sports car won the first Targa Florio, whose rigours are indicated by the winner's average of less than 30 m.p.h.

Itala's name was made in 1907 when Prince Scipione Borghese piloted the shaft-driven 8-litre car to victory in the incredible Peking–Paris race. This was the 40-h.p. engine, each of whose cylinders had almost the same volume as a whole modern sports-car engine. Dry-sump lubrication depended largely on gravity and pressure; there was no provision to return oil to the reservoir, whence the name of the "total-loss" system of lubrication. The crankshaft ran in three main bearings; each connecting rod weighed 7 lb., each piston $7\frac{1}{2}$ lb. Exhaust pressure was employed to feed petrol to the single carburetter; a 33-plate metal clutch governed the 4-speed box, riding in a constant over-supply of oil. Primitive as the car may sound today, it was capable of over 65 m.p.h. and its durability is attested to by the Peking–Paris victory and by the survival of a similar car in running order in England.

The epic of two continents was followed by the shaft-driven 100-h.p. and 100-m.p.h. G.P. car of 1908, now owned by Cecil Clutton. Unlike the general run of Italas, which employed a T-head, this car used the F-shape for its four cylinders, cast in pairs (12 litres, 155×160). The engine turned at only 1800 r.p.m.; the camshaft had a sliding mechanism to permit valve arrangements to be modified from the driver's seat. In 1958 it was still able to meet its original performance standards in a run at Silverstone.

The Coppa Florio winner of 1905

Works racing dropped off and most Italas in competition were private entries. In 1913, however, the marque entered a team of rotary-valve cars in the French G.P., but because of chassis and transmission troubles none finished. The rotary valve was Itala's answer to the problems entailed by the poppet valve: the rotary valves were driven from the camshaft, but at one-quarter of engine speed, and each one served two cylinders. Each valve was in effect a ported plug rotating in an extension of the cylinder to permit inlet and exhaust. They were first installed in a 35-h.p. 4-cylinder engine having a bore and stroke of 105 × 150.

Financial troubles brought on by licencing arrangements for building Hispano aviation engines during the 1914 war severely handicapped Itala in resuming automobile production in the 1920s. Ceirano had long since left the company to start another, S.P.A., and bankers moved into management. In keeping with the general trend, Itala now directed its efforts to small engines, producing a 2-litre overhead-valve six (65 × 100) with magneto ignition on a 126-in. wheelbase, which continued into the 1930s, and scored notably in Alpine tests. Its Type 51 was at one time modified by Sir Malcolm Campbell as his first Blue Bird. In 1926 Itala developed a 60-degree V-12 racing car with front-wheel drive and a choice of engines: 1100 c.c. (46 × 55) or 1500 c.c. (50 × 55). They were believed capable of sustaining 8000 r.p.m. but were never officially raced.

Photograph by Cecil Clutton]

The 12-litre G.P. car of 1908 as it is today

Courtesy of Charles Stich]

The same model in 1908 Coppa Florio, with Cagno at the wheel

[Courtesy of FIAT

Prince Borghese at the wheel of the Peking–Paris car

Photograph by Torino Motori; courtesy of FIAT]

The 1909 racing car

[Courtesy of FIAT

The 1924 Itala six that won the Australian championship

Photograph by Torino Motori; courtesy of FIAT]

Itala torpedo six of the late 1920s

LANCIA

When young Vincenzo Lancia, bored by the tinning of soup that had made his father rich, apprenticed himself to F.I.A.T., his two greatest pleasures were music and motors. Less than a decade later, having progressed from apprentice to test driver to racing driver, he left to make music with motors of his own.

Though Lancia hardly ever allowed his own cars to be raced and his successors still insist the machines are built only for touring, their record of sporting distinction goes back almost to their origin. Lancia adopted shaft drive on his first cars and, up to the 1914 war, built various conventional side-valve fours and one six that are large by present standards but represented his initial determination to get away from the monsters then fashionable in the industry. Longer and lower chassis have been a Lancia characteristic since 1907. For the first few years of his new venture he occasionally drove for F.I.A.T. In 1908 he won his class with his own car, a 14-h.p. four; in 1910 he set a class record for the mile with a time of 49·4 seconds on a 20/30-h.p. four.

The glory of Lancia began with the opening of the vintage era. Fond of naming his models after letters in the Greek alphabet, he developed his pre-war 5-litre 4-cylinder Theta (110×130) into the Kappa, which differed from it only in that the Kappa's cylinder head was detachable. The Dikappa was virtually identical; the Trikappa was a $4\frac{1}{2}$-litre V-8 (75×130) that has been described as a reduced version of the 1919 prototype 6-litre V-12 (80×100) that was never put into production but that set the pattern for the famous Lambdas by establishing the 22-degree angle of the V, which remained unchanged in all Lancia engines for 20 years.

The prototype of the Lambdas was tested as early as 1919; production began in 1922 with the first independent front suspension to be employed on series cars. This consisted of an enclosed coil spring, containing a hydraulic telescopic shock absorber, on either wheel, and it is still used on today's Lancias. There were in all nine series of Lambdas, varying

in detail. The first series had 3-speed gearboxes and 3-plate dry clutches instead of the 9 plates on earlier Lancias. Peak r.p.m. of the 50-h.p. o.h.c. 4-cylinder engine was 3250 r.p.m.; bore and stroke were 75×120 and total volume was 2120 c.c. Both banks of the V were cast in unit. With a four-seater body the car weighed less than $15\frac{1}{4}$ cwt. and could easily exceed 70 m.p.h.; when faster light cars were built by other makers, Lancias could generally out-run them by virtue of remarkably superior road-holding, though the narrowness of the engine's V created breathing difficulties that made themselves felt in long competitions.

Tubular connecting rods were employed on the first six series; the seventh and eighth had H-shaped rods. In 1926 the bore was increased to 79·37 mm. and volume to 2370 c.c.; in 1928 the bore was widened again, to 82·55, volume rising to 2570 c.c. Though 4-speed gearboxes were introduced on the 1925 cars, the 3-plate clutch was retained throughout the Lambda's history. As series numbers went up, changes included the integration of body and chassis—though some chassis were made for special coachwork—and the use of finned cast aluminium brake drums. Horse-power rose to 65.

One of the earliest cars, a 1909

Courtesy of Lancia & C.]

155

[Photograph by Arthur Schuh;
courtesy of the Library of the Automobile Manufacturers' Association

The 1914 Theta was an ancestor of the Kappa

Photograph by Vincenzo Lancia;
courtesy of Air Commodore N. R. Buckle, M.V.O.]

The prototype of the Lambda under test at Sestriere late in 1918

[Photograph by Clinton Martin

The first series Lambda of 1922. Note clearly visible front suspension

[Photograph by Hayden R. Shepley

The fifth series Lambda on long wheelbase

Contemporaneously with these high-performance light cars, Lancia built the luxurious Dilambda, a pushrod 3960-c.c. 100-h.p. V-8 (79·37 × 100) in an X-frame, in which rigidity was stressed and single-plate clutch became standard. In the 1930s came the luxury-sports Artena, a 1925-c.c. 55-h.p. V-4 (82·55 × 90) and Astura, a 75-h.p. 2604-c.c. overhead-cam V-8 (68·85 × 85); this was later enlarged to 2972 c.c. (74·61 × 85) in an integral body-and-frame construction that was also used for the Artena. A host of other Lancias were also evolved during the 1930s—Augusta, Aprilia, Ardea—but all these highly dependable cars were unfortunately as dull as they are durable. An aerodynamic experiment of 1928 was called by Clutton and Stanford "perhaps the ugliest car ever made until the inception of the Chrysler Airflow models of 1934".

The post-1939-War Aurelia was noted, like the Lambdas, for its peculiarity in showing maximum performance only after some 10 miles of hard driving. Much shorter than the shortest-wheelbase Lambda—which exceeded 120 in., in contrast to the Aurelia's 104 and 96½ in.—the 2½-litre Aurelia is a 60-degree V-6 (78 × 85·5) with 8·4:1 compression, developing 118 b.h.p. at 5300 r.p.m. and capable of up to 115 m.p.h., depending on coachwork. It is offered with a two/four-seater gran-turismo coupé body or a two-seater drop-head that has replaced the earlier Spyder two-seater. The rather heavy car—it weighs 25½ cwt. —has been raced by private entrants with indifferent results but is nonetheless in the upper bracket of sports cars by reason of its durability under stress.

The rare 9th series Lambda at Prescott in 1952

A special-bodied 1932 Artena roadster

its lively responses and its excellent adhesion. The sliding-pillar front suspension of 1919 is still in use, though the beam front axle of that day has disappeared; rear suspension is by semi-elliptics with telescopic shock absorbers. Gearbox and differential are integral. Aside from suspension, it is an entirely new design by Jano of Alfa Romeo renown.

Special V-6 racing engines have been built for Ferrari's G.P. cars. Lancia itself made an abortive foray into competition in the early 1950s, sending an Aurelia coupé and a specially bodied open sports car bored out to 3100 c.c. to the Carrera Panamericana, which Juan Manuel Fangio won for Lancia, and entering a 3-litre coupé and an open car in the Mille Miglia, which Ascari won for the marque.

In 1959, after some years of planning and postponement, Lancia introduced the sports version of its Flaminia. The Aurelia's V-6 was changed to 80×81.5 (total volume remaining the same), the wheelbase to 108 in. and horsepower to 131 for a 19·6-cwt. Zagato-bodied coupé. Body and chassis are integral but an elastic auxiliary frame carries the engine, suspension and steering unit. The suspension of the Aurelia was retained, as was the rear-end unit, with inboard disc brakes.

The economy Appia series joined Lancia's sports machines in this year with a two-seater coupé bearing a Zagato body almost identical to the Flaminia's. In this 1090-c.c. V-4 (68×75), producing 53 b.h.p. at 5200 r.p.m., the gearbox is built in unit with the engine, and 90 m.p.h. is claimed.

The 1932 Astura V-8

The 1934 V-8 Dilambda

157

The early Aurelia coupé; appearance has not changed

The Farina-bodied 3-litre sports

The 3-litre coupé leaves Brescia at the start of the 1953
Mille Miglia

The first Aurelia Spyder had aluminium head and block
with cast-iron cylinder liners, as well as de Dion rear
end. Sidescreens fastened on doors

The current Aurelia drop-head on $96\frac{1}{2}$ in. wheelbase has
swing half-shafts and wind-up windows

The Zagato coupé body is virtually identical for sports
Appia (shown here) and new sports Flaminia, except that
the latter has twin roof-crests

MASERATI

None of the five Maserati brothers who established the marque of the trident in 1926 has any connection with it today. Carlo and Alfieri have been dead for decades, Ettore withdrew from the company in the early 1930s and Bindo and Ernesto build the O.S.C.A. (Mario, the sixth brother, was an artist.) Krupp and Thyssen bought Maserati in 1959.

The brothers, several of whom were racing drivers, opened their factory in Bologna and the very first car they built was entered in the 1926 Targa Florio, finishing ninth in a field of 33. Alfieri drove the 1500-c.c. (60 × 66) 125-h.p. straight-eight that was to win so many races in the hands of Ernesto and of numerous others before the marque entered *monoposto* G.P. racing to compile an even more illustrious record. The greatest part of Maserati's limited output up to the Second World War was in fact G.P. cars—a d.o.h.c. 16-valve 78 × 78 blown 1500-c.c. four, a 4800-c.c. (69 × 82) 16 that took the world's record for 10 kilometres at almost 160 m.p.h.; a 1500-c.c. 185-h.p. six (65 × 75) and, after Bindo and Ernesto sold the factory to Commendatore Adolfo Orsi, a d.o.h.c. 3-litre straight-eight (69 × 100) that gave 355 b.h.p. supercharged. This engine was revised by Ernesto to measure 78 × 78 and gave 420 b.h.p. with 6·5:1 compression. Independently sprung in front, it used trailing quarter-elliptics at the rear. It was with this car that Wilbur Shaw won at Indianapolis in 1939 and 1940.

After the Second World War Maserati returned to racing as gloriously as before, but the marque was also seen more often on the road. Bodied by Farina, the A6 1500 appeared in 1948 with six 66 × 72·5 cylinders that produced 65 h.p. and close to 100 m.p.h. at 4700 r.p.m. with 7·8:1 compression. The tubular frame was suspended on coil springs all round and the whole car weighed about 17¾ cwt. This 1½-litre car was the sire of the potent A6 series that followed, the first of which was a 12½-cwt. 2-litre sports car (72 × 80) putting out 130 b.h.p. at 6000 r.p.m. with three Weber carburetters, for a top speed of 125 m.p.h. Scanty bodywork made the car easily convertible to current Formula II requirements.

Orsi retained G. Colombo, Alfa's chief engineer, who had designed Ferrari's V-12, to produce a better engine for the trident emblem. His solution was the d.o.h.c. A6GCS, with twin magneto ignition, three dual Weber carburetters and six 76 × 72 cylinders in a light alloy block, giving 165 b.h.p. at 6750 r.p.m. The design featured nickel-chrome steel connecting rods, a 7-bearing crank and dry-sump lubrication with front-mounted oil radiator. This was soon enlarged to 2½ litres (84 × 75) with 8·78:1 compression and 210 b.h.p. at 7500 r.p.m. The wheelbase was 89·8 in., front track 51 in. and rear 49 in.; the car weighed 14¾ cwt. Rear suspension was altered to a transverse leaf, the de Dion tube was mounted in unit with it and the gearbox was moved back to the differential.

Reversing current practice, Maserati expanded the engine to 3 litres by lengthening the stroke: cylinders now measured 84 × 90. Putting out 245 b.h.p. at 6200 r.p.m., the 300S was placed third and fifth at Sebring in 1955. Aluminium was used for the clutch, which, with the flywheel, weighs about 15 lb. Many of the refinements of the 2-litre car were retained, but the de Dion tube was moved forward of the gearbox-differential unit. The brakes were huge and well finned.

Maserati went both up and down from the 300S: up to a 4½-litre 450S and down to a 1½-litre 150S. The 150S is a d.o.h.c. four (81 × 72) realizing 130 b.h.p. at 7500 r.p.m. with 8·75:1 compression in a tubular chassis. Twin coil ignition is fitted, with two dual-choke Webers; suspension is identical with that of the 300S, but the wheelbase is 3·2 in. less. Its racing record, except for one win at the Nürburgring, has been mixed on both sides of the ocean. The 450S is a V-8 with two overhead cams to each bank of 93·8 × 81 cylinders; it develops 400 b.h.p. at 7000 r.p.m. with four dual-choke Webers, and magneto and coil ignition are employed. Alloys are used extensively and the whole unit weighs only 4¾ cwt. Colombo moved the de Dion tube behind the gearbox-differential unit and, for the 1957 Mille Miglia, in which Stirling Moss drove the car,

A Maserati in the 1926 Targa Florio. It won its class

[*Courtesy of Officine Alfieri Maserati, S.p.A.*

The blown 230-h.p. 3-litre eight of early 1930s owned by the late Sir Henry Birkin

From the collection of Kurt H. Miska]

The early post-war A6GCS at Thompson Raceway

The 1500-c.c. A6 gran turismo by Farina. A drop-head body was also available

The A6G2000, a later development of the first A6GCS

The A6G2000 competition coupé by Farina

The 3-litre car in full road trim is not designed for snugness

Jean Behra drove 150S to victory at Nürburgring. Top speed is almost 150 mp.h.

160

a 2-speed transfer gearcase was mounted just behind the clutch so that the 5-speed gearbox (most Maseratis have only four) was doubled to 10 speeds for the steepest mountains and the flattest straights, where the car was capable of 190 m.p.h. It accelerates from rest to 100 in 11 seconds. In racing its record has been spotty: brakes forced it out of the Mille Miglia, but it won at Sebring and in Sweden and has scored a number of victories on lesser courses.

Maserati's current series car is the 3500T gran turismo, developed from an experimental 3½-litre Mille Miglia machine. In fixed- or drop-head body (the former seats four, the latter two) on a tubular chassis, it is capable of 145 m.p.h., its six 86 × 100 cylinders producing 240 b.h.p. at 5500 r.p.m. with 8·5:1 compression. Air-cooled brakes have servo assistance; front suspension is independent by coil spring and torsion bar; rear uses two semi-elliptics with torsion bars. The wheelbase is 102 in.; track is 54·7 in. at the front and 53·5 in. at the rear.

From the collection of Kurt H. Miska]

The 4½-litre V-8 has had a mixed record

The drop-head on 3500T chassis virtually repeats silhouette of fixed-head coupé. Front brakes are discs

Courtesy of Officine Alfieri Maserati]

[Courtesy of Scuderia La Manovella

The 1953 gran turismo with 750-c.c. engine

MORETTI

Giovanni Moretti began building trucks and motorcycles in the same year when the Maseratis made their first car. But it was not until the present decade that Moretti turned to sports cars in the 750- and 1200-c.c. categories, whereupon the marque established its place as a leading contender, in its class and sometimes over-all, from Monza to Palm Springs, including Montlhéry, the Mille Miglia and several European mountain championships.

The 750-c.c. sports cars—Moretti builds other models as well—use a d.o.h.c. four (60 × 66) producing 75 b.h.p. at 8000 r.p.m. with two dual-choke Webers and are good for about 115 m.p.h. Frequently known as "baby Ferraris" because of their exhaust note and fine styling before 1959, the fixed-head bodies suffer from immovable windows except for side vents in door windows. Engine and gearing are flexible enough to permit smooth running at 15 m.p.h. in top gear.

The 1200-c.c. sports engine also has double overhead camshafts. Its four 72 × 74 cylinders develop 80 b.h.p. at 7000 r.p.m. Top speed is about the same as that of the 750-c.c. cars.

The 1200-c.c. gran turismo of 1954 abandoned the
quarter window

The 750-c.c. Bialbero model of 1956 was marque's most
beautiful car

The 750-c.c. sports of 1957 won the Italian mountain
championship

The current 1200-c.c. gran turismo has yielded to
commonplace styling

The "Barchetta" is a graceful example of envelope
coachwork. It weighs 7½ cwt.

NARDI

Though Crosley has disappeared as a marque, it
survives in the power plant of the 750-c.c. Nardi, a
two-seater car available with either closed or open
body weighing at most 9 cwt. But the 63×48 four,
which develops 42·6 b.h.p. at 5500 r.p.m., with
pushrod overhead valves, cannot exceed 100 m.p.h.

Nardi follows the current trend toward tubular
chassis and independent front suspension; but the
rear springs are quarter-elliptics and only third and
top gears are synchronized. Interesting and graceful, the Nardi has made little impression by its
performance.

[Photograph by Kurt H. Miska

**An early 1500 O.S.C.A. Similar bodies were often used
on all chassis**

Photograph by Kurt H. Miska]

The 1100-c.c. car of early 1950s

O.S.C.A.

When Bindo and Ernesto Maserati sold out to the Orsis, they remained for some 10 years as consultants. Then they went back to Bologna and opened the Officine Specializzate Costruzioni Automobili, where they still do special work for such makers as Lancia and Ferrari. In addition, they build the 750-, 1100-, 1500- and 2000-c.c. O.S.C.A., named from the initials of their company. The brothers work side by side with their 40 craftsmen, and for all them quality is the sole criterion.

The 750, which won the Index of Performance at Sebring in 1958, is a 76-h.p. d.o.h.c. four (62 × 62) with 9·5:1 compression. The whole car weighs about 8 cwt. and will exceed 115 m.p.h. Its chassis is tubular, front suspension is by coil springs and unequal wishbones and rear springing is by coils and trailing links. Only the two top gears are synchronized.

The rear suspension of the 1100, on the other hand, utilizes the torsion bar. It too has d.o.h.c., a tubular frame and synchromesh on only third and top gears. The four 71 × 70 cylinders, with 9:1 compression, develop 94 b.h.p. at 6800 r.p.m.; valves are inclined in the hemispherical combustion chamber. Two dual-choke Webers feed the engine and ignition is by a single coil. With an aluminium body on a 90-in. wheelbase with 47·5-in. maximum track, the 9-cwt. machine will exceed 120 m.p.h.

Courtesy of the Automobile-Club de l'Ouest]

**An 1100-c.c. O.S.C.A. coupé won its class at Le Mans
in 1953**

While the 1500-c.c. car is a hundred pounds heavier, it is also 20 m.p.h. faster, its four cylinders with d.o.h.c. developing 130 b.h.p. at 6300 r.p.m. Like all O.S.C.A.s, it can be revved up to 9000 and raced again; and, like its sister cars, it has the fantastically expensive and efficient ZF gearbox from Germany.

O.S.C.A.'s 2-litre is its heaviest (11·6 cwt.) and fastest car: 160 m.p.h. from a 165-b.h.p. six with double overhead cams. The six is notable for its extremely favourable weight-to-power ratio: only $8\frac{1}{2}$ lb. per horsepower.

**The 750 identical to 1958 Sebring Index and Class H
winner**

The 1500-c.c. car for 1959

[Courtesy of Bindo Maserati Courtesy of Bindo Maserati]

The sire of O.M.: the Züst reaches Paris in 1908

The 1925 O.M. six

O.M.
ZÜST

There are probably more marques composed of initials in Italy than anywhere else. O.M. is derived from Officine Meccaniche, a Milanese firm that was originally an iron foundry, then a builder of loco- motives and heavy railway equipment and, during the First World War, an aeroplane manufacturer. Before that war it had absorbed the old Züst firm, which had built a number of huge cars in the Edward- ian style. One of these was placed second in the New York–Paris race of 1908 despite successive mishaps. This was a 40-h.p. four, chain-driven, with a top speed of 60 m.p.h. For that period, its wheelbase was short: 114 in.; track was 66 in. In its few years of car-making, Züst (sometimes called Brixia-Züst because it was based in Brescia) built a 10/15-h.p. 3-cylinder car and a 50/70-h.p. four in which each cylinder was cast separately and the gearbox had its own oil pump. Roberto Züst, originally a Swiss hydro-electric engineer, stamped all his chassis out of a single block of metal, fitted brakes on the dif- ferential and supplied water-cooling to the wheel- drums.

By the late 1920s the six had been enlarged to 2350 c.c.

O.h.v. car of 1933 had sloping radiator. It weighed about 16 cwt.

Last O.M. was built in 1935; radiator was once more vertical

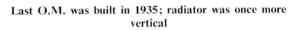

O.M.'s first cars appeared in 1920. The 1500-c.c. 4-cylinder 12/15-h.p. car (69 × 100) won the Coupe des Alpes several times, as well as the Gran Premio d'Italia (when grand-prix and sports cars were more or less the same); the 2-litre 25/30-h.p. six (65 × 100), in various developments, was even more successful. Both were side-valve engines and neither car was so light as some of its rivals: the four weighed 12 cwt. but finished second, third and fourth to a 9-cwt. Bugatti in 1921.

O.M. took a number of speed records and the dual-carburetter sports six won the first three places over-all in the 1927 Mille Miglia, as well as the Biennial Cup at Le Mans in 1926. All the cars had balanced crankshafts; clutches were multiple-disc. Early in the 1930s overhead-valve versions were made optional, but a few years later the Italian Government compelled the company to abandon making cars. Today, as part of the giant FIAT complex, it builds trucks and industrial machinery.

It is an interesting footnote that present-day O.M. owners report that the cars have a tendency—most unusual in Italian machines—to slide on wet surfaces.

S.I.A.T.A.

The Società Italiana Auto-Trasformazioni-Accessori started as a specialist in conversions and modifications, with emphasis on transmissions of its own design and manufacture. By far its most frequent foundation is one of the many FIAT models.

S.I.A.T.A.'s marque began before the war with a 569-c.c. competition coupé whose 52 × 67 engine was derived from the FIAT 500. It produced 30 h.p. at 5500 r.p.m. for a 75-m.p.h. maximum and set a class record in 1938. Ten years later a 750-c.c. engine (60 × 65) with the same base won the Italian championship, clocking 95 m.p.h. with 42 b.h.p. at 6000 r.p.m. and a 5-speed gearbox. While S.I.A.T.A.s have often been equipped with various American engines, including the Crosley and the Ford and Chrysler V-8's, the marque has been notably successful with its own adaptations of FIAT's V-8, which has found its optimum sports-car application under the S.I.A.T.A. emblem.

This is a 2-litre unit (72 × 61·3) whose 115 b.h.p. at 6500 r.p.m. will guarantee a road speed of 125 m.p.h. and better in S.I.A.T.A.'s 208S with a 5-speed gearbox. Like most of the other models, the 208S is bodied by Bertone. S.I.A.T.A.'s own refinements of independent suspension make even legendary Italian road-holding still better.

[Courtesy of S.I.A.T.A.

The 1938 coupé set a 24-hour class record at 70 m.p.h. average

The 568-c.c. Pescara model is good for 75 m.p.h. with 24-h.p. 568-c.c. FIAT-derived engine

[Courtesy of S.I.A.T.A.

Courtesy of S.I.A.T.A.]

The 1948 sports won the Italian championship

The Gran Sport was available with 1400-c.c. FIAT derivation but was sometimes fitted with American engines

Courtesy of the Henry Ford Museum]

[Photograph by David Klein   Courtesy of S.I.A.T.A.]

The Chrysler-engined car is relatively rare

The Daina coupé is a 95-m.p.h., two/three-seater with 1400-c.c. (82 × 66) FIAT-based engine giving 65 b.h.p. at 5000 r.p.m. It has 5-speed gearbox

[Courtesy of S.I.A.T.A.   Courtesy of S.I.A.T.A.]

The Barchetta uses same engine as Daina coupé but is a few miles slower in open form

The 208S coupé uses 5-speed gearbox with V-8 FIAT engine

166

The Spyder variant of 208S is slowed slightly by open-car drag and weight of $17\frac{1}{2}$ cwt. on 90·5 in. wheelbase

The Tipo America 208S is all-weather roadster, as fast as the Spyder

[Courtesy of S.I.A.T.A.   Courtesy of S.I.A.T.A.]

S.P.A.

The sporting career of the S.P.A. (Società Piemontese Automobili) was not spectacular. In 1909 the marque won the Targa Florio outright; in 1912 it scored a class first at Boulogne. The cars were typical of their time.

In the 1920s, about the time when the firm was absorbed into FIAT, it produced its Type 23S, which remained virtually unchanged for several years. This was a 2750-c.c. four (85 × 120) whose top speed was about 82 m.p.h., making it a theoretical competitor of the 3-litre Bentley. The inlet manifold was in the block, the ribbed exhaust manifold was separate; the detachable cylinder head carried bronze valve caps. Cased in aluminium, the gearbox was built in unit with the engine and the clutch was of the dry multi-plate type; a torque tube carried power to the rear wheels. The foot brakes operated on the front wheels and the transmission, the hand brake on the rear wheels. High-geared steering required only $1\frac{1}{4}$ turns lock to lock.

Courtesy of Charles Stich]

The S.P.A. in the 1908 Targa Florio

[*Courtesy of FIAT*

The 1912 car was first in its class at Boulogne

Courtesy of Capt. G. Liston Young]

The 23S sports of 1920s. This car is now in Museo dell' Automobile, Turin

GERMANY

The Adler Trumpf Junior of the 1930s

This 1938 Le Mans saloon is in regular use in Ohio

ADLER

Unlike the living eagle from which it takes its name, the Adler did its highest flying on the eve of its demise. The marque was born in the early years of this century and competed unsuccessfully in the 1910 Prince Henry Trial with a 5·2-litre four (105 × 150) producing 75 b.h.p. and a 3-litre car (85 × 130) of considerably less power. Adler also ran without success in the 1908 Tourist Trophy.

During the vintage decade the marque produced nothing of interest; but in 1932 it introduced a front-wheel-drive machine with full independent suspension, rack-and-pinion steering, all-synchromesh 4-speed gearbox and an all-metal body welded to a box-section chassis. The 40-h.p. 1700-c.c. engine had only 17·8 cwt. of car to propel and could well exceed 90 m.p.h. The final-drive and steering arrangements of this model, known as the Trumpf (the Trumpf Junior was a similar 65 × 75 four of 995 c.c.), were sufficiently like those of the Tracta to cause J. A. Grégoire to enter an infringement suit in the German courts. His victory proved purely moral, since the court stipulated in awarding damages that payment must be made in blocked marks. The Trumpf was built in France under licence as the Rosengart Supertraction.

The Adler Trumpf's roadholding and handling were so exceptional that the car was entered at Le Mans in 1937, 1938 and 1939 with aerodynamic closed bodies after the roadsters had proved themselves in races all over the Continent and the United Kingdom. The Le Mans saloons—full four-seaters, one of which survives in Ohio—were bodied in aluminium on tubular chassis in a Porsche design. Two carburetters fed the 105-h.p. engine, which ran up to over 4000 r.p.m. In 1938 the marque finished first and second on index at Le Mans, averaging 72 m.p.h. A top speed of 122 m.p.h. was made at the Nürburgring and in a 24-hour German test the average was 108 m.p.h. Bombed out during the Second World War, the company did not resume automobile production.

BENZ

Like many pioneers, Karl Benz built his first cars with engines at the rear. As much as possible he preferred, like Bugatti, to make his own components by hand in his own works. Initially he did not officially enter his cars in competition but in 1899 he built a racing car for his principal dealer, Fritz Held.

Externally it resembled his other products of the time, with rear wheels considerably larger than the front and a *dos-à-dos* body under the rear seat of which a flat 2-cylinder engine was mounted, the cylinder heads pointing toward the front. This 16-h.p. 100 × 100 car was good for 40 m.p.h. Since the engine was mounted behind the axle, power was carried forward to the 3-speed countershaft by belts and returned to the rear driving wheels by chain. The excess of rear weight handicapped the car, and in 1902 Benz engaged the Frenchman, Marius Barbarou, to revise his designs. Soon dissatisfied with Barbarou, Benz then hired Hans Nibel, who ultimately became a director of the company.

Nibel was responsible for the great Benz successes both before and after the First World War. These began with a second place in the 1906 Herkomer Trials with a 40-h.p. chain-driven four; the next year Fritz Erle finished first with a 50-h.p. car. These were factory-entered cars, in contrast to the privately entered machines that had raced earlier without notable successes though they almost always finished —in those days, a considerable achievement. Erle won the 1908 Prince Henry Trials with the 50-h.p. car (115 × 180) and a new 120-h.p. chain-driven four (chain drive was continued in Benz racers until the war) was driven to victory by Victor Hémery in the St. Petersburg–Moscow race—429 miles at an average of 51 m.p.h. over virtually non-existent roads. The car's maximum was 98 m.p.h. and it finished second to a Mercedes in the French G.P. at Dieppe that year. There were also 70- and 80-h.p. racing cars at this time.

Karl Benz's son, Eugen, at the wheel of a 1899 racing car

This Benz was placed second in 1906, first in 1907 in Herkomer Trials

The 120-h.p. was stepped up to 150 (15 litres, 155 × 200) and, driven by David Bruce-Brown at Daytona Beach, set a new record of 109 m.p.h.; it later set a 10-mile mark of 115. This was followed by the purely racing Blitzen Benz of 200 h.p. Cast in pairs, the 21½-litre four (185 × 200) turned 1650 r.p.m. and the car weighed 32·1 cwt. on a 112-in. wheelbase. Identified in America with Barney Oldfield and in Europe and Britain with Héméry, it set a mile record of 141·372 m.p.h. At the same time Benz was building sports cars of 60 and 75 h.p. that were piling up successes all over Europe in both races and hill-climbs. These were all fours, some of which, like the 5715-c.c. (105 × 165) 40-h.p., had dual magneto ignition, dual valving and shaft rather than chain drive. The 40 took a number of class records, being clocked at almost 104 m.p.h. In 1912 Benz returned to the rear engine for a racing four that was the ancestor of the post-war Teardrop car and was continued in production alongside it.

When peace returned in 1919 Benz began to consider a merger with Mercedes, but it was seven years before the marriage was regularized. A kind of liaison was brought into effect in 1923, however, when both companies were suffering the ravages of the German inflation, and the two marques were at once competitors and collaborators for the next three years. Benz was still building a small sports

This Benz finished second in 1908 French G.P. Note pits dug below level of course. Same car won the St. Petersburg–Moscow race

four and had begun to produce a 50-h.p. sports six. With the 1912 rear-engined racer, it formed the groundwork for the *Tropfenwagen* that appeared in 1922 and finished fourth at Monza in 1923 with an 85-m.p.h. average. This was a 2-litre (65 × 100) d.o.h.c. machine with aluminium alloy pistons, roller bearings, a 3-speed gearbox behind the engine, independent rear suspension with swing axles and inboard rear brakes. A similar car was placed first in the 1926 Freiburg hill-climb.

The 80-h.p. rear-engined Teardrop, last racing Benz, represented an early effort at applying aerodynamic theories. Front brakes were on the wheels, rear inboard flanking the differential

The Prince Henry Trials car (115 × 175, dual valves) had wide wings to meet required minimum body width

The first B.M.W. was a replica of an Austin 7

The Type 315/1 was the first full sports model

The 65-h.p. Type 319/1 reached almost 100 m.p.h.

The Type 328 ruled its class in Germany. V-windscreen folded flat

The coupé version of 328 at Le Mans

One of the streamlined 1940 Mille Miglia roadsters

B.M.W.—E.M.W.

The Bayerische Motoren Werke was organized in 1929 to build the Austin 7 under licence in Germany. Three years later Dr. Fritz Fiedler joined the company and it is he who has kept the marque at the forefront since.

Fiedler's first change was to design a 1·2-litre o.h.v. six that was soon increased to 1½ litres (54 × 94) with 6·8:1 compression and 40 b.h.p. at 4500 r.p.m. Equipped with three Solex carburetters, the Type 315/1 was driven to victory at the Nürburgring in 1935 by Ernest von Delius. It was soon followed by the 2-litre Type 319/1 (65 × 96), which produced 65 b.h.p. at 4600 r.p.m. with the same compression. The emphasis on lightness combined with strength was carried forward to the 327/28, the marque's pre-war peak of achievement.

Retaining the independent front suspension begun with Fiedler's advent, the new cars developed 80 b.h.p. at 4600 r.p.m. with 7·5:1 compression, bore having been increased exactly 1 mm. The 3-carburetter set-up was continued and Fiedler found a technique of obtaining all the advantages of overhead camshafts without the cost or disadvantages. The combustion chambers were hemispherical and the overhead valves were inclined; a single camshaft was set high up in the block. The 328 was good for 100 m.p.h. and accelerated from rest to 50 in 6·9 seconds 20 years ago. It soon made its mark with victories in the Mille Miglia, Le Mans, the Tourist Trophy, the Nürburgring and innumerable other races, as well as hill-climbs. B.M.W. itself did little official competing, most of the trophies being won by private owners. The Aldington brothers, who had acquired Frazer-Nash in Britain, obtained the British rights and marketed the car there as the Frazer-Nash-B.M.W. to the still unabated horror of chain-gang enthusiasts. One of these models was Stirling Moss's first car.

For the much-shortened 1940 Mille Miglia, run on a 100-mile circuit, the 328 was supercharged to produce 120 b.h.p. at 5800 r.p.m. In that race the 13¼-cwt. cars were good for almost 140 m.p.h. and won with an average of about 105. It was the first time that open-bodied B.M.W.s were raced without full touring equipment—a self-imposed rule that the works had always followed even when regulations did not require it. B.M.W. had revised its coachwork to minimize drag and the result was varied conceptions in both closed and open bodies, one of which is startlingly similar in profile to the first XK Jaguars of the next decade.

Eisenach, the site of the works, fell into Russian hands in the war and the East Germans made some efforts in the present decade to build their own sports cars there under the name of E.(for Eisenach)M.W. The output was limited to a few drop-heads using the old 327/28 designs and a very modern 1½-litre 140-b.h.p. six (73 × 66) with 10:1 compression, twin magnetos, full independent suspension by torsion bars and de Dion rear end. At the Nürburgring

Courtesy of Dipl.-Ing. Alfred Kempter]
Another 1940 car, whose profile is strikingly like that of the XK-120 Jaguar

Courtesy of Dipl.-Ing. Alfred Kempter]
The 1940 Mille Miglia coupé

Courtesy of B.M.W.]
The Type 507 with removable hard top in place weighs 25 cwt.

The 327 drop-head is copied by the East German E.M.W.

The 150-m.p.h. E.M.W. at Nüburgring

in 1955 it was clocked at 150 m.p.h. but it has run very little since.

The old company set up again in Munich. For a while one of its former engineers, Ernst Loof, produced a car he called the Veritas, using the 328 as a basis and departing only slightly from it. B.M.W. itself returned to production in 1953, having begun making motor-cycles a few years before. Fiedler introduced a V-8 engine in 1955 and this is still used. The 503 drop-head and the 507, available as either

fixed- or drop-head, are the high-performance B.M.W.s of today; though they are not often raced, they have scored victories in the Mille Miglia, the Eifel and the Alpine Rally. Both employ the 173-b.h.p. 3·2-litre V-8 (82 × 75), virtually all whose castings are in aluminium. Overhead valves are pushrod-operated from a camshaft in the base of the V. The 2·6-litre version (74 × 75, 100 b.h.p.) is used only in the family-type models.

D.K.W.

When D.K.W. decided to expand from motor-cycles to cars in the late 1920s, economy of conversion led it to build *Das Kleine Wunder* around its existing 2-stroke motor-cycle engine. At the same time the firm decided on front-wheel drive and adopted Grégoire's Tracta joint.

Later absorbed into the Auto-Union combine (which in turn became a part of Daimler-Benz in 1958), D.K.W. has only recently begun to make machines that may be considered sporting. They

retain the front-wheel drive, with rack-and-pinion steering, and the engine is a 3-cylinder development of the motor-cycle unit. Water-cooled and valveless, the 980-c.c. engine (76 × 74) develops 55 b.h.p. at 4500 r.p.m. with 8:1 compression and dual carburation and just reaches 100 m.p.h. It weighs 12 cwt. and is independently suspended in front by transverse leaf. Racing occasionally in Europe, it has performed creditably in the Mille Miglia and elsewhere.

The Monza coupé appeared on European courses

The Spyder is an exceptionally handsome small car

HORCH

August Horch was an early colleague of Benz, who at that time did not share his interest in making cars go faster. Horch's machines competed in the Prince Henry Trials, winning the 1906 event, but in little else, and, though the marque continued to produce fine automobiles until 1939, only these early cars and the very last models were in any sense sporting.

The Prince Henry winner was a 5·8-litre four (115 × 140) with ball bearings throughout and F-head valve arrangement with pushrods. This was a refinement of the design developed for the car that won the 1906 Herkomer. The 1906 car did not employ ball bearings for the connecting rods. In the 1907 Herkomer three gold medals went to Horchs, of which three models were then in production: a 22- and a 40-h.p. four and a 60-h.p. six.

The 22-h.p. car had 85 × 120-mm. cylinders; the 40-h.p. engine was bored out to 115 and shortened 20 mm. from the 1906 measurements. The crankcase was aluminium, ignition was dual, by magneto and coil, and the engine was pump-cooled. A leather cone clutch controlled the 4-speed gearbox, and final drive was by a shaft riding in a tube. Radius rods located the rear axle and suspension was by long semi-elliptics all round. Huge brakes expanded within the drums; these were hand-operated; the foot brake worked on the propeller shaft.

In its last years Horch built very heavy cars with in-line 4-litre eights and V-12's of 5 litres. These were fast machines comparable to contemporary Mercedes-Benz luxury cars. They had overhead camshafts, servo brakes and swing axles. Some were fitted with 8-speed gearboxes.

Courtesy of "The Autocar"]
Horchs lined up for the 1908 Prince Henry Trial

The last Horchs were magnificently finished
Courtesy of the Henry Ford Museum]

MERCEDES
MERCEDES-BENZ

It is a nice irony of history that Adolf Hitler's favourite car was named after the granddaughter of a Hungarian rabbi. Until 1901 the cars built at Cannstatt by Gottlieb Daimler bore his own name; in that year a rabbi's son named Emile Jellinek, who was Austro-Hungarian consul-general in Nice (and later in Mexico) and who had persuaded Daimler and Wilhelm Maybach to build a 6-h.p. racer for him, prevailed on the two Germans to re-design their sporting machines for greater speed and safety. He at once ordered 36, obtained sole distribution rights for France, Belgium, the U.S. and Austria-Hungary and insisted that the new car be named after his daughter, Mercedes.

What had particularly perturbed Jellinek was the famous Cannstatt-Daimler racing car known as the Phoenix. This 28-h.p. four (106 × 156), according to Scott-Moncrieff, "was one of the most dangerous and unmanageable vehicles ever constructed". It was ridiculously high and heavy—25 cwt.— on a 70-in. wheelbase and 55-in. track, and in the hill-climb at La Turbie in 1900 it crashed and killed Daimler's works foreman. Thereupon Daimler introduced a design by his son, Paul, for a 6-h.p. racer with integrally cast crankcase and 4-speed gearbox, steering-column gearshift and, unusual then, a pedal accelerator. From this car Maybach developed the first Mercedes, a machine that was to revolutionize the industry.

On a much lengthened chassis Wilhelm Maybach placed a unit making maximum use of a magnesium-aluminium alloy. Cylinders and head were all cast together; mechanically operated valves were arranged in T-formation and the four 116 × 140 cylinders developed 35 b.h.p. at 1000 r.p.m. The gearshift was situated in a floor gate, the radiator was the honeycomb type and the chassis was pressed steel. In the 1901 G.P. de Pau the car made a most inauspicious bow, retiring a few yards after the start. But two months later it ran away from the field on the hilly 280-mile Esterel course at Nice, averaging 36·63 m.p.h. It was 7·1 cwt. lighter than the car

The man-killing Phoenix racer

The first Mercedes, the 40-h.p. of 1901, was copied all over the world

Jenatzy in the borrowed 60-h.p. car with which he won the Gordon Bennett

that killed the foreman. After the race, it was driven round the countryside as an ordinary tourer.

Before Maybach left Daimler in 1907, he progressed to 60-, 90-, 100- and 120-h.p. racing cars. Often, too, the touring cars were raced, like the 40-h.p. that Count Eliot Zborowski drove to second place in the 1902 Paris–Vienna race. Chain-driven like its predecessors, it had four 118×140 cylinders and hollow axles. The 60-h.p. was bored out to 140 mm.—9·2 litres—and valves were arranged in an F. It won the 1903 Gordon Bennett and numerous other races and was the basis for the 12·7-litre 90-h.p. of 170×140. All these cars were destroyed by fire on the eve of the Gordon Bennett and it was actually a borrowed touring 60-h.p. that won. A similar car was third in the 1904 Vanderbilt Cup. In 1904 W. K. Vanderbilt set a world speed record of 92·3 m.p.h. in the 90-h.p. car.

The 90 became a 100-h.p. and emulated the American successes of its predecessors. Three 120-h.p. cars were entered in the 1905 Vanderbilt Cup but, though all finished, none were placed. During this period Mercedes cars were being built in the United States by Steinway & Sons, the piano maker, under licence; Maybach's elder brother had long been an executive in the piano company. It is also suspected that the marque had been duplicated earlier under licence by Simplex, many of whose designs show a close resemblance to those of Mercedes.

Paul Daimler succeeded Maybach as chief engineer and produced a very successful 120-h.p. car in 1908. Still a chain-driven four (155×180), it won the French G.P. at a 70-m.p.h. average. By now Mercedes was beginning to use shaft drive on some of its touring models, as well as experimenting with overhead valves on some and valveless Knight engines on others. Racing continued with the current and earlier cars; it was only in 1914 that a significant change was made. This was the $4\frac{1}{2}$-litre 115-h.p. racing car that was to sweep the French G.P. of that year, win at Indianapolis (where the bigger 1912 car had finished third) in 1915, win a half-dozen lesser American races and continue its triumphs into the Italian G.P. and the Targa Florio in the early 1920s.

Side by side with the $4\frac{1}{2}$ was the 28/95, an 8-litre six (110×140) developed from the 90-h.p. sports of 1912, a $9\frac{1}{2}$-litre four with three valves per cylinder —two of these being exhaust. The 90 introduced the pointed radiator; its next-of-kin, the 28/95, was the ancestor of the great sports cars of the 1920s. These were also influenced by an experimental 1913 car with aircraft engines having a single overhead camshaft, inclined valves and steel blocks. The 4-litre (100×130) Knight-engined cars were run at Indianapolis and in Belgium, though not too successfully. These and the 28/95 were the first cars built after the First World War; the 28/95's open valve gear was boxed in with aluminium. One of the latter was driven from Stuttgart to Sicily in 1921, when motoring in Germany was economically prohibitive, by Max Sailer, who then put the car into the

Coppa Florio and won. This last year of Paul Daimler's tenure was successful everywhere, and he retired without pangs of conscience.

Mercedes' glory really began to blaze when Daimler was succeeded by Dr. Ferdinand Porsche. While he was settling in, the firm built two blown fours: a 1½-litre (68 × 108) and a 2-litre. These were unsuccessful at Indianapolis; at Brooklands they could not exceed 80 m.p.h., at which speed the 2-wheel brakes were hopeless. Porsche checked them over, added front brakes and sent three into the combined Targa and Coppa Florio, which they swept. While Porsche was already developing a 2-litre G.P. eight, the real emphasis was being put on the big supercharged sports machines that were to be the symbol of road-racing for years to come. They benefited by the experiences of the 61·7 × 82·8 racer with d.o.h.c. and dual valving, which could run up to 8000 r.p.m. Its crankshaft ran in nine main bearings and dry-sump lubrication was used.

Porsche's first big-engine design for Mercedes was the blown 6-litre sports of 1925, known in Germany as the 24/100/140 and in England and the United States as the 33/140, which subsequently became the 33/180 or, in Germany, the K-Wagen. It was unofficially denominated The Death Trap because of its flagrantly bad cornering, roadability and brakes. The 94 × 150 six with wet cylinder liners was set in a 134-in.-wheelbase chassis; aided by the blower, it could just about reach 100 m.p.h. Though it had 4-wheel brakes, they were far from adequate for its weight. The K led directly to the magnificent S model, the 36/220 that appeared in 1927 after Mercedes had formally become Mercedes-Benz. On the same wheelbase as the K and with only slightly better brakes, the 6·8-litre six, bored out to 98 mm., topped 110 m.p.h. despite its 44½ cwt. and accelerated from rest to 60 in 14 seconds. As on many fast cars of that period, slightly more weight was at the rear than at the front, the engine being sited well behind the front axle. Steering was 2½ turns lock to lock.

The S won races with monotonous regularity, but authorities differ on its place in sports-car history. While Scott-Moncrieff calls it one of the finest sports cars ever built, Clutton and Stanford contend that, until the supercharger cuts in, performance is negligible and, when full-throttle pedal pressure engages the clutch actuating the blower, the result is more sound and fury than action, especially since the blower's use was hedged with many warnings from the works as to special fuel, duration of use —20 seconds maximum continuous application— and gears in which it was taboo. Scott-Moncrieff terms the S superior to its 38/250 successor, the SS, which was bored out to 100 mm. (7 litres) for 114 m.p.h. With each model change the gearbox improved, but the clutches remained danger-spots.

The SSK (Super Sports Kurz) was the same as the SS except for an 8-in. shortening of its wheelbase, and the SSKL (Super Sports Kurz Leicht) was

Courtesy of Charles Stich]

The 40-h.p. of 1905

Courtesy of Daimler-Benz A.G.]

The 1908 Dieppe victor, 120-h.p.

Courtesy of Daimler-Benz A.G.]

The 4½-litre 1914 car was victorious in half a dozen countries; first at Indianapolis in 1915

[Photograph by Clinton Martin
The 28/95 acquired front brakes just after 1914 war

[Courtesy of Daimler-Benz A.G.
The 2-litre Mercedes of 1922–3

[Courtesy of the Montagu Motor Museum
**Karl Kling (left) in the 1923 Targa Florio car, reputed
to reach 130 m.p.h.; Hermann Lang in the 2-litre sports
of same year and Lord Montagu of Beaulieu, chairman
of Montagu Motor Museum, in an S tourer**

simply the SSK lightened by extensive chassis drilling. The SSKL had 300 b.h.p. blown and a streamlined version was timed at 156 m.p.h. in 1931. It was the product of Hans Nibel, who had come to Mercedes in the Benz merger and succeeded Porsche as chief engineer. Rudolf Caracciola almost won the G.P. of Monaco in an SSK, losing his first place only because of time taken in refuelling; this sports car finished third in a field of full G.P. machines. But Caracciola redeemed its honour when he won the Tourist Trophy with a 72·82-m.p.h. average. The SSK was one of the best road-holding machines to come from Stuttgart in the between-wars period, and both the SSK and the SSKL were to go on winning races and hill-climbs for many years. Caracciola introduced the SSKL in 1931 by winning the Mille Miglia at 62·84 m.p.h., an average that included all stops along the 1000 miles.

In the early 1930s Mercedes-Benz made few sports-car changes. Two eights were introduced, including the *Grosser Mercedes*—7·7 litres, 95 × 135, with 280 b.h.p. unblown at 2700 r.p.m.—on a 148-in. wheelbase. Its X-shaped frame was composed of oval tubular members. This car and a six were fitted with a new 6-speed gearbox designed by Wilhelm Maybach at his Maybach-Zeppelin plant. But for the moment sports-car development was put aside, though much thought was devoted to grand-prix and record cars in preparation for the heroic duels with Auto-Union. A semi-sports car appeared in 1933: the 380K, a blown 120-h.p. 3·7-litre (75 × 100) eight with pushrod o.h.v. Hydraulic brakes and full independent suspension were introduced on the 123·5-in. wheelbase and the car was the precursor of the 500K and 540K that were to be the last pre-war Stuttgart cars with sporting pretensions.

These cars were a retrogression. The 5-litre 8-cylinder 500K (86 × 108) weighed 44½ cwt. and could be coaxed to 100 m.p.h., the gearbox was much inferior to those of the SSK and SSKL and, despite full independent suspension, steering was heavy and slow. The 180-b.h.p. 5·4-litre 540K (88 × 111) was bigger, heavier and only a few m.p.h.

faster. This car was developed under Sailer, the former driver, who had succeeded Nibel.

Mercedes-Benz was slow in returning to competition after the 1939–45 war. Its installations had been devastated, its organization dispersed. The first necessity was to earn money. For a few years production was concentrated on high-quality utilitarian cars and industrial vehicles and equipment; the only racing venture was the entry of pre-war G.P. cars in the Argentine race, where they finished second and third. But the new chief engineer, Dr. Rudolf Uhlenhaut, was hard at work on totally new sports and racing machinery, and, while ordinary Mercedes-Benz family cars were proving themselves with victories in the tough European rallies, he was developing the gull-wing 300SL coupé that made its début with a one-two victory in the 1952 Prix de Berne and repeated the performance at Le Mans when Levegh's Talbot failed a half-hour from the finish.

Since then the winning roster of the 300SL has paralleled those of all its predecessors. The first cars employed twin carburetters for 180 b.h.p. from the 3-litre six canted over sidewise to reduce frontal wind-resistance; current 300SL's have fuel injection and 240 b.h.p. The s.o.h.c. six (85×88) is set in a welded tubular frame with full independent suspension and huge brakes—the rear drums are inboard. Speeds of 160 m.p.h. can be obtained. The 300SLR, which Stirling Moss drove to a record Mille Miglia victory, is really an enlargement of the $2\frac{1}{2}$-litre grand-prix engine to 3 litres: eight 78×78 cylinders in line, with fuel injection, twin magneto ignition and 345 b.h.p. at 7500 r.p.m. The engine, which has no flywheel, delivers its power through a 5-speed gearbox with synchromesh by Porsche and, reaching 125 m.p.h. from rest in 22 seconds, can exceed 180 m.p.h. At Le Mans, to augment normal action of the Alfin brake drums with turbine-blade cooling and servo assistance, the cars were provided with a flap—like those of aeroplanes—that rose behind the driver at will and was slotted for rear vision.

Courtesy of Daimler-Benz A.G.]

The SSKL could hold its own with grand-prix cars

Courtesy of Daimler-Benz A.G. and A. J. Hoe]

The SS drop-head

Courtesy of Scuderia La Manovella]

The first 300SL coupé. Note door openings in roof

Dr. Uhlenhaut with the 300SLR coupé

The 300SLR roadster with magnesium body. A similar car figured in the 1955 Le Mans tragedy and the team was immediately withdrawn in mourning

The 300SL roadster is also available with a hard top

PORSCHE

Dr. Porsche established his company in the early 1930s exclusively for automotive research and development. There he evolved probably his most famous invention, torsion-bar suspension, and the designs for the Auto-Union racing cars, the early Volkswagen, the 12-cylinder Cisitalia and many other projects. Soon after his release from a French war-crimes prison in 1947, he began work with his son, Ferdinand, Jr., on the car that bears his name at the van of small sports and racing machines.

The first Porsches were 1100-c.c. machines with 4-cycle, 4-cylinder air-cooled opposed engines at the rear. Originally the Porsches worked chiefly with Volkswagen components. The engines were steadily enlarged: to 1290 c.c., to 1498 c.c. and to 1582 c.c. The flat 4 design gives a low centre of gravity and is known as the "boxer" type because to some German the sight of the swiftly moving pistons resembled that of fast sparring partners at work. While pushrod overhead valves are standard on some models, the exhaust valves being angled, d.o.h.c. units are optionally available, and the original 4-speed crash box has given way to an all-synchromesh transmission. The 550 Spyder, also known as the 1500RS and RSK (*Rennsport*—the K refers to the pattern of the front suspension) and now developed into the 718, has a 5-speed gearbox with synchromesh on the four top gears. All Porsches are aluminium-bodied.

The 44-h.p. 1300-c.c. car is primarily an economy version, to which a certain amount of performance has been sacrificed. Each of the other engines, however, is a virile unit in a chassis of narrow tubes with swing axles at the rear, torsion bars all round and a wheelbase of 83 in. against a track of $51\frac{1}{2}$ in. front and 50 in. rear, so that the car is almost square. Weights range from 10·6 cwt. for the Spyder to 17·8 cwt. for the cabriolet.

With the d.o.h.c. 1498-c.c. engine (85×66) in the Carrera version 100 b.h.p. is developed at 6200 r.p.m. with 9:1 compression. This rises 10 h.p. in the Gran Turismo engine of unchanged dimensions, and both give about 125 m.p.h. In the RS engine compression is raised to 9·8:1, horsepower to 135 at 7200 r.p.m. and road speed to 150 m.p.h. The 718 has been bored out 2·5 mm. and develops 150 b.h.p. at 7200 r.p.m. and road speed has risen accordingly. This engine employs all aluminium pistons, cylinder heads, cylinders and crankcase, and cylinder walls are chrome-plated. An oil-cooler with its own air scoop is placed beneath the car. On the 718 coil springs replaced the rear torsion bars.

The bigger engine, known as the 1600N (normal) and 1600S (Super), is less forceful, producing respectively 70 b.h.p. at 5500 r.p.m. and 88 at 6000 from identical $82·5 \times 74$ cylinders with pushrod o.h.v. The 1600N has 7·5:1 compression against the 8·5 of the 1600S; respective road speeds are 100 and 110 m.p.h. Both originally had roller-bearing crankshafts, but these were later restricted to the 1500 series and the 1600's had plain bearings. For 1959 the Carrera engine was increased to 1600 c.c. and 105 h.p.; the GT version to 115 h.p. The roller bearings were restored.

Whether Porsches race in production or modified classes, they are always an almost certain bet to win—1000 victories was the 1958 figure. It was specifically to break their grip on Class F that M.G. developed its twin-cam A engine. The 1500 Gran Turismo car has been known to defeat the very fast 2-litre A.C.-Bristol, and the Spyders harry the big Jaguars, Ferraris and Maseratis, aided by the remarkable Porsche road holding, cornering and braking. For both racing and touring, Porsches offer unusual comfort with their fine attention to interior detail.

Photograph by William E. Caldwell, Jr.]

One of the early Porsche roadsters. The V-windscreen was soon abandoned

[Courtesy of Dr.-Ing. h.c. F. Porsche K.-G.

The coupé, which was the same on all models. It will seat four

Courtesy of Dr.-Ing. h.c. F. Porsche K.-G.]

The two/four-seater cabriolet has a non-removable windscreen, quarter lights in door windows, and a typically German padded top for maximum snugness

[Courtesy of Dr.-Ing. h.c. F. Porsche K.-G.

The Hardtop has a removable plastic roof or an optional padded folding soft top. This plastic roof will not fit the cabriolet

Courtesy of Dr.-Ing. h.c. F. Porsche K.-G.]

Speedster was short-lived sidescreen model with removable windscreen and occasional rear seat

[Courtesy of Dr.-Ing. h.c. F. Porsche K.-G.

The D Convertible replaced the Speedster in 1958, retaining its removable windscreen for racing. Doors have wind-up windows of greater area than Speedster's screens. Top is austere and unpadded

Photograph by Kurt H. Miska]

The Spyder can be had with a rudimentary folding top and a full-width plexiglass windscreen

WANDERER

Affectionately known as the *Puppchen* in its early days, the Wanderer was one of the early tandem cars, the single passenger riding behind the driver. The Edwardian Wanderer was an 1162-c.c. four (62 × 95) with such advanced features, for its time, as pump cooling and lubrication. Its Zenith carburetter had two air intakes, one being for pre-heated air, and it was controlled by both a hand and a foot throttle. The 12-h.p. Wanderer ran up to 3000 r.p.m. and, with its 2·5:1 compression, was capable of 60 m.p.h. It weighed about 10 cwt. on its 89-in. wheelbase.

The engine was of the T-head type, with magneto ignition, and the cylinder head was fixed. The aluminium crankcase flared to join the U-section steel chassis, providing splash pans for the engine. Power was taken through a leather cone clutch to a 3-speed gearbox, thence to a shaft drive on which the foot brake operated. Springing was half-elliptic at the front and three-quarter-elliptic at the rear.

After the First World War, Wanderer resumed production at Chemnitz, where it had first been established, but the marque was undistinguished until the early 1930s. At that time Ferdinand Porsche had just set up in business for himself and he was called in to re-design the Wanderer for higher performance at a relatively low price. In this car Porsche made the first

Courtesy of Dr.-Ing. h.c. F. Porsche K.-G.]

The Type 718 was also available with a finless body

installation of torsion-bar suspension. While Parry Thomas had used torsion bars in conjunction with leaf springs in England in the 1920s, Porsche was the first to use the torsion bar alone; it was fitted at all four corners of the Wanderer, for which Porsche created a 6-cylinder engine of 1·86 litres, later enlarged to 2 litres. Its outstanding characteristic was the use of an aluminium block into which wet cylinder liners of cast iron were inserted. This engine was later enlarged to a 3·3-litre straight-eight that Porsche used as his personal car, but it was never put into production. A Roots-type supercharger was fitted to some of the 2-litre cars.

By the middle of the decade Wanderer had been absorbed into Auto-Union but production continued until 1939.

The Puppchen of 1910 was the first Wanderer. It had fixed wheels and detachable rims

One of the last Wanderers

[Courtesy of the Dansk Veteranbil Klub

Courtesy of William Scholes]

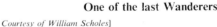

BELGIUM

[Courtesy of Charles Stich

Jeff Christiaens, long identified with Excelsior, at the wheel of 90 × 140 six in 1913

[From the collection of George A. Moffitt

A two-seater of the early 1920s

[Photograph by R. O. Barnard

The 1925 Excelsior at Oulton Park in 1956

EXCELSIOR

Having experimented with 2-cylinder cars, Arthur de Coninck brought out his first Excelsior six (110 × 160) in 1910. But his great basic design of 1911, developed to its peak in 1929, was the 85 × 130, with its unit construction of engine, clutch and 4-speed gearbox in an exceptionally rigid frame. It produced 66 b.h.p. at 1800 r.p.m., while its 4-cylinder sister of the same bore and stroke produced 34. The latter won a number of Belgian races in the years before the First World War.

Excelsior's racing six (90 × 160), also developed in 1911, weighed only 16 cwt.—less than many modern "light" sports cars. This 6-litre was driven in competition on both sides of the Atlantic, though without too much success. It was the 85 × 130 that made the greater impression. By 1920 this car had 4-wheel brakes of de Coninck's design—each brake worked in conjunction with that diagonally opposite—and his own stabilizer bar that was to be adopted almost everywhere for fast cars. The six led directly to the best of the Excelsiors, the Albert I, a 5·3-litre car whose 90 × 140 engine had a single carburetter and 115 b.h.p. in the touring model and three carburetters and 130 b.h.p. in the sports, which was an honest 90-m.p.h. car in the mid-1920s. It was marked by a single overhead camshaft, driven by a vertical shaft; alloy pistons, tubular connecting rods and a 7-bearing crank, and it was an easy one-two winner in the 24-hour Spa race of 1928. The Adex diagonal brake system was retained.

But the Excelsior was far too expensive a car for so small a country as Belgium (which, despite its size, has had almost 70 marques) and in 1928 the marque was absorbed by Impéria, which also swallowed Métallurgique and Nagant and itself was to be absorbed into the Minerva 10 years later.

F.N.

The Fabrique Nationale d'Armes de Guerre built its first car in 1900 in complete conformity to what everyone else was doing: a side-valve twin with chain drive, two forward speeds and cable accelerator handled from the wheel. In 1902 F.N. adopted shaft drive and by 1905 it was building a 40-h.p. four, cast in pairs, with four speeds; it followed the course of the industry by decreasing the size of its engines while occasionally adding to the number of cylinders, until it had an eight in the 1930s. Shortly before the Second World War, F.N. abandoned making automobiles and it has not returned to the field.

The marque's sporting achievements were few in the early years; in the 1920s it began to be a consistent winner in Belgian competition, a 1300-c.c. car winning over-all at Spa in 1926. Outside its own country the F.N. distinguished itself in the Monte

The 1925 F.N. team at Spa

The 1933 winners at Francorchamps

Carlo, Alpine and Liège–Rome–Liège Rallies. Its outstanding sports car was the 1300-c.c. (68 × 100), with four cylinders and four speeds, which brought a one-two victory at Spa in 1926. It was the model for the 2·2-litre 16CV and the later 1800-c.c. sport (75 × 100). Finally F.N. produced a 3·3-litre straight-eight, still using side valves, which was first over-all in the Liège–Rome–Liège of 1933.

IMPÉRIA

Nothing in the beginnings of the Impéria hints at the radical experimentation that was to mark the end of its career. The marque began in 1911 with a shaft-driven 16/20-h.p. side-valve four (90 × 120) with three speeds, a similar 4-speed 24/30-h.p. four (110 × 130) with dual pedal-operated brakes and a chain-driven 50/60-h.p. 150 × 150 four. All these led to the sports Impéria-Abadal (Abadal was a Spanish sportsman who inspired the design in 1913), originally an 80 × 180 four that had a great deal in common with the Alfonso Hispano-Suiza and was slightly faster.

After the First World War the Abadal was re-designed as an 80 × 140 straight-eight with s.o.h.c. and dual carburation—another machine too expensive for the country to support. Impéria therefore turned to 1100- and 1650-c.c. valveless engines. The first was a 27-h.p. four of 66 × 80, the second a 40-h.p. six of the same dimensions. Bored out to 69 mm., the six was a 70-m.p.h. car; the four set a national class record of over 80 m.p.h.

In 1935 Impéria began to build front-wheel drive cars under Adler licence, using full independent suspension by torsion bar. Neither the 1650-c.c. nor the 1-litre four was particularly fast. After the alliance with Minerva, the f.w.d. cars were equipped with a 3·6-litre V-8 slung transversely between the driving wheels. Built in 1936, these were the first production cars anywhere to eliminate the gearbox; they were good for almost 100 m.p.h. with their automatic transmissions.

Since the war Impéria has limited itself to assembling British cars in Belgium.

The first Impéria looked very much like a Mercedes

The Impéria-Abadal of 1922

[Courtesy of the Royal Motor-Union of Liège

The 1926 Impéria Grand Sport Six looked faster than it was

MÉTALLURGIQUE

In 1898 the Société Anonyme La Métallurgique decided to build automobiles as well as locomotives and rolling-stock. Two years later 25 cars were offered for sale—chain-driven, with two separate cylinders of 76 × 80—and these were immediately snapped up by the turn-of-the-century motor-sport enthusiasts. A four of the same dimensions sold as quickly.

In 1905 Métallurgique offered two new fours of 90 × 140 and 100 × 150, both with shaft drive. By 1908 five models were in production, of which the 84 × 110 was a monobloc. It was in this year that Métallurgique introduced the V-radiator that so many others were to emulate. By now all its cars were fours, with 4-speed gearboxes; probably the most famous was the 60/80-h.p. 10-litre (150 × 140), which actually developed 100 b.h.p. at 1400 r.p.m. and was timed at 99·5 m.p.h. In 1907 the marque was placed second in the Herkomer Trial; of the 170 cars participating only a Mercedes outdid it. For the 1909 Prince Henry Trial Métallurgique produced the 27/80-h.p. 105 × 160 with two camshafts and, unique in automobile history, five valves per cylinder. One camshaft rode on either side of the engine, and the inlet valves, almost as big across as the pistons, were in the cylinder head, one to a cylinder. Each cylinder had two exhaust valves on each side. The chassis alone weighed more than a ton but the car could exceed 80 m.p.h. on its 138-in. wheelbase (track was 56 in.), producing actually 100 b.h.p. The patent clutch had two bronze shoes, adjustable by separate screws; the foot brake worked on the drive shaft through the differential.

In 1910 more orthodox engine design resulted in the o.h.c. 85 × 145 in which aluminium was used for the crankcase, block, sump and cylinder head, as well as the pistons and connecting rods. Both crankshaft and camshaft ran in ball bearings; valves were

[Courtesy of the Royal Motor-Union of Liège

One of the first Métallurgiques, an immediate sporting favourite

[Photograph by Douglas FitzPatrick

The 1907 car, later fitted with a 21½-litre Maybach-Zeppelin six (160 × 170,) still exceeds 100 m.p.h. with twin camshafts in crankcase, four valves per cylinder, dry sump. Acceleration matches that of Jaguar XK-140

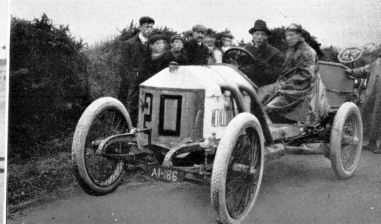

Courtesy of Raymond K. Wright]

Lord Brabazon at the wheel of a 1908 Tourist Trophy car

inclined at 75 degrees in the hemispherical head and compression was the then incredible figure of 7:1. This 90-h.p. unit was built for the Prince Henry Trial; otherwise the marque clung to side valves. All but two of the models were pump-cooled. A V-8 was begun in 1914 but interrupted by the war; however, a monobloc 85 × 145 four was built for racing, as well as a 90 × 150 four that attempted to replace valves with a rotary fuel distributor on top of the engine. This was quickly proved hopeless. Meanwhile the marque was establishing itself solidly in competition all over Europe, with particular success for its British distributor, J. T. C. Moore-Brabazon, now Lord Brabazon of Tara.

During the German occupation of Belgium the works was virtually stripped and post-war production had to start almost from scratch with the 80 × 130 and 90 × 140, which, like the rest of the line, had already had pressure lubrication. Detachable cylinder heads were introduced and, in 1922, front-wheel brakes were added, using the Excelsior's Adex system under licence. Paul Bastien, who had been with Métallurgique for many years and who was later to design Stutz's "vertical eight" and then to join Kaiser-Fraser, created the 2-litre 40-h.p. 70 × 128 four that was to be Métallurgique's sole model for the eight remaining years of its life. It had a shaft-driven o.h.c., magneto ignition, 4-speed gearbox, torque tube and half-elliptics all round. A 3-litre (80 × 149) sports, built briefly in 1922, was timed at 87 m.p.h. for the flying kilometre. But none of the post-war cars could match the record of their predecessors—the high-placed Herkomer and Prince Henry cars or the L-head 80 × 120 that finished one-two-three in 1912 in both the Tour de France and the Circuit du Maroc.

Photograph by Charles Lytle; courtesy of Raymond K. Wright]

Duke Ludwig of Bavaria at the wheel of his Prince Henry

Courtesy of Raymond K. Wright]

The 14-h.p. 1910 four (80 × 110) racing two-seater with rumble seat, built in Berlin under licence by Bergmann-Métallurgique Automobilwerke

[Courtesy of the Royal Motor-Union of Liège

The 80 × 130 car of 1913 was revived after the First World War

Courtesy of Raymond K. Wright]

Bastien's and Métallurgique's last design, a 2-litre four, superseded the 80 × 130 four of early 1922

184

[Courtesy of the Royal Motor-Union of Liège

The 6-h.p. Minerva of 1902

The Hon. C. S. Rolls at the wheel of the 1905 Tourist Trophy Minerva

[Courtesy of the Royal Motor-Union of Liège

MINERVA

Minerva is probably best remembered as a luxury car and then as one of the most successful exploiters of Knight's sleeve-valve principle, which is so favourable to well-shaped combustion chambers and high compression.

Sylvain de Jong switched from bicycles to motor-cycles in 1899, achieving instant success with his single-cylinder machines. He went looking for competition with his cars, winning Paris–Bordeaux in 1904, setting new records on the Antwerp–Ostend road and winning the Circuit des Ardennes in 1905. At that time his output ranged from a 635-c.c. 5-h.p. single-cylinder engine to a 6-litre 40-h.p. six of 105×120; he was still building conventional poppet-valve engines.

It was 1908 when de Jong adopted the Knight system for all his cars that was to help make them the millionaire's choice in a number of countries, including the United States. The 26-h.p. (100×140) of 1912–14 was also a sporting choice, as it showed by twice winning the Coupe des Alpes. It was, in fact, virtually the last of the truly sporting Minervas, for after the 1914–18 war the marque limited its production to high-quality automobiles from 2-litre fours up to the V-8 developed with Impéria.

Courtesy of the Royal Motor-Union of Liège]

The Minerva that won the Coupe des Alpes

NAGANT

Like the F.N., the Nagant was born in an arms factory, that of the brothers Nagant, Léon and Maurice. Before 1900 they had begun by building the opposed-piston Gobron-Brillié under licence, calling it the Gobron-Nagant. Their 8-h.p. four (with eight pistons) won a number of local races and on one occasion took 24 minutes off Panhard's time for the Spa–Bastogne–Spa race. As on the French original, the engine stood vertically under the driver's seat but at right angles to the chassis.

In 1907 Nagant developed its own L-head four in several sizes; the largest, a 40-h.p., drove by chains through a 4-speed gearbox. All the types—70×118, 12 h.p.; 90×120, 16 h.p.; 90×130, 24 h.p., and 106×150—continued the marque's local successes. In

1914 Nagant entered the G.P. de l'Automobile-Club de France at Lyons with a 4½-litre o.h.v. four $(95 \cdot 5 \times 150)$ that developed 130 b.h.p. at 3000 r.p.m. for a maximum above 85 m.p.h. One of the few cars to complete that destructive contest, the Nagant finished close to the top.

After the war Nagant offered virtually no sporting vehicles, though it did win the Belgian G.P. in 1925. Building well-made fours and sixes of reliable but undistinguished performance, it was absorbed into the Impéria complex.

The 1896 Gobron-Nagant

The 40-h.p. four of 1907 won many prizes

The 1913 "torpedo"

The 1914 Lyons racing car

The sporting tourer of the early 1920s

Early Pipe team ready to race

The 1907 *Kaiserpreis* car

The shaft-driven 1913 "torpedo"

PIPE

The Pipe was the most adventurous of Belgian sports cars in that it entered one foreign competition after another. First shown in 1900, it was raced that year at Spa; then it took part in the Paris–Berlin and the Paris–Madrid, the 1904 Gordon Bennett (finishing sixth) and the 1907 *Kaiserpreis*, in which it finished second. The last sporting appearance came in 1912, when Camille Jenatzy, Jr., drove a 160×180 four to second place at Boulogne behind his father on a Mercedes. This Pipe had six valves per cylinder, developed 175 b.h.p. and was timed at more than 125 m.p.h.

All the sporting Pipes were overhead-valve fours, the valves being inclined at 45 degrees and operated by pushrods from twin camshafts in the block. Most Pipes were chain-driven, shaft drive being adopted late in the first decade of the century and principally for touring machines. After the 1914 war the company turned to trucks and other industrial vehicles, which it still makes.

S.A.V.A.

A relatively late entrant in the Belgian automobile industry was the S.A.V.A., which began production in 1910 and competed actively from 1911 until the outbreak of war with a 3-litre four (82.5×140) that was remarkable for reversing the conventional F-head arrangement. The S.A.V.A. fitted the exhaust valves above the inlets. Using dual magneto ignition, it distributed the sparking plugs in equally unorthodox fashion, so that each cylinder had one plug at the inlet valve and the other at the top of the cylinder. Shaft-driven, these cars had 4-speed gearboxes.

After the Armistice S.A.V.A. continued this design in a 3·4-litre four (85×150) of monobloc construction and in a 2-litre (70×130) with conventional overhead valving. In 1923 the marque was absorbed by Minerva.

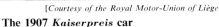

The S.A.V.A. at the 1913 Ostend speed tests

The 1909 Russo-Baltique after its victory

RUSSO-BALTIQUE

In 1909 Czar Nicholas II, who had obviously read Poor Richard's admonition, "If you want a thing well done, do it yourself", ordered Russia to produce an all-Russian automobile, no part of which must come from another country. The result was the Russo-Baltique, built by a locomotive firm of that name in Riga, which was then (as it is again) part of the Russian empire; and the Czar's restriction was breached in only two points. The engine was the design of Charles Fondu of Belgium and its development was the work of J. Potterat, a Swiss engineer at Russo-Baltique. The firm also built Hispanos under licence.

Two models were produced and both were successful in competition on the primitive Russian roads. The 24/30-h.p. 105×130 four, with three speeds and shaft drive, in full production form, finished third to a racing 70-h.p. Opel and a competition 50-h.p. Mercedes in the 375-mile Riga–St. Petersburg–Riga race in 1909. The 80×110 four won the same race in 1911, as well as the Duna competition and the Monaco Rally. Both engines had completely enclosed moving parts and lubrication lines.

SOVIET RUSSIAN SPORTS CARS

Production sports cars are unknown in the Soviet Union, where motor sport has only lately become significant. Some individuals have built *monoposto* competition cars from a combination of standard Soviet components and others of their own design and manufacture; a few have been made by state factories. Special emphasis has been put on engines under 350 c.c., and most racing has been on ordinary roads rather than on closed courses, which are rare and not particularly popular. Soviet Russia is probably the only country in the world where truck-racing is a recognized form of motor sport.

The Gorky Auto Factory has produced a highly tuned version of the Pobeda M-20, a 2150-c.c. four whose compression has been raised to 8:1 and to which four carburetters have been fitted. Aerodynamically bodied, this car has been timed at 125 m.p.h. The 3½-litre 90-h.p. ZIS six, with 6·7:1 compression, has been highly tuned and rebodied with open two-seater coachwork that is a combination of 1950 Studebaker front, early Thunderbird windscreen and 1954 Mercury rear quarters. From the 1220-c.c. Moskvich four, the Russians developed a 1360-c.c. championship machine on a 91-in. wheelbase, while Moskvich suspension and steering have been put into the record-breaking air-cooled Zvezda-5, whose air-cooled 492-c.c. twin is rear-mounted in unit with clutch, gearbox and final drive. Fully independent in suspension, it has independent hydraulic brakes for front and rear and is good for more than 100 m.p.h. A blown dual-ignition 3-litre V-8 was built from the GAZ; at the other extreme, Eduard Lorent has broken Count Lurani's Class J record with 135 m.p.h. in a 350-c.c. special. The 2-litre Kharkov-6 has been timed at 175 m.p.h. The 250-c.c. Zvezda-6, a 2-stroke four with 7·5:1 compression and one cylinder head for each pair of cylinders, weighs only 7 cwt. on its 98-in. wheelbase and is all-independently suspended, using swing axles at the rear.

Rally competition is becoming increasingly popular in the Soviet Union and the Russians are expected to enter international events in both racing and rallying.

The 2150-c.c. Pobeda M-20 in action
[Courtesy of the Embassy of the U.S.S.R.

The MZMA-2, built at the Moscow Bantam Car Plant
Courtesy of the Embassy of the U.S.S.R.]

The Zvezda-5 at speed. Zvezda-6 has opposed o.h.v. 4-cylinder 496-c.c. engine and, like other Soviet competition machines, a 4-speed gearbox

Russian trucks line up for the start of a race. Car at lower right with open door is a Pobeda that forms the basis for the Pobeda racing car and that is itself often raced

AUSTRIA

AUSTRO-DAIMLER

The Prince Henry Austro-Daimler that revolutionized the sports car

The 1913 car with contemporary American body

189

The 1100-c.c. Sascha was first, second and sixth in its class in the 1922 Targa Florio. At the wheel, Alfred Neubauer; at the radiator, Porsche (with cap and moustache)

Neubauer at the wheel of the first AD model

Hans von Stück, who later drove for Auto-Union, at the wheel of a 3-litre 1924 Bergmeister

The 19/100 in two-seater form

A 4-litre Bergmeister, now in daily use in South Africa

Another of the outstanding achievements of Dr. Porsche was the Austro-Daimler, which had the remarkable luck (good in one sense, appalling in another, in the light of his legendary personality) of twice enjoying his services as chief engineer.

The marque was founded shortly before the turn of the century and Paul Daimler was in charge at first. Until 1906 Austro- and Cannstatt-Daimlers were indistinguishable; but in that year Porsche's first arrival initiated radical changes. For the 1910 Prince Henry Trial Porsche designed—and drove to victory against more powerful machines—the historically important overhead-camshaft four that was to be virtually a model for high-performance cars. It was followed by two sister cars in second and third places, and all three were pure production cars in contrast to many highly modified machines that took part.

The 5·7-litre 27/80 had four separately cast cylinders of 105×165; the huge valves were set at a 45-degree angle in detachable cages. Dual magneto ignition and skilfully shaped combustion chambers contributed to the 95 b.h.p. and 80-plus m.p.h. of these cars, which were chain-driven at first but later fitted with shaft drive. Only the total-loss oiling system was to be faulted.

A most worthy successor was the Sascha, an 1100-c.c. four that performed creditably in the 1922 Targa Florio. Known as the AD, it was developed into the o.h.c 3-litre 6-cylinder 19/100 (76×100), which had some success in the 1928 and 1929 Tourist Trophy. A 100-m.p.h. car weighing $20\frac{1}{2}$ cwt. on a 109-in. wheelbase (short-chassis model), it had an aluminium alloy block with alloy cylinder liners and, of course, pressure lubrication. Porsche's influence is manifest, though he was by now at Daimler-Benz, from which he was to return to Austro-Daimler in 1928. The six was as good at hill-climbs as at races and was soon known as the *Bergmeister*. With a 4-litre 6-cylinder engine (85×115) in this car Hans von Stück set a new Shelsley Walsh time of 42·8 seconds in 1930, which was improved by only 6 seconds in the next 25 years.

Porsche had the capacity of making his own designs obsolete in record time. In 1930 he introduced the ADR, which had a straight-eight o.h.c. engine in a chassis with a central tubular member that carried the power train and was adapted from the Czech Tatra. Front and rear suspension were independent by transverse spring, and swing axles were fitted. With dual carburetters and magneto and coil ignition the 120-h.p. engine propelled the $26\frac{3}{4}$-cwt. car at 95 m.p.h.

Shortly thereafter Austro-Daimler was absorbed by Steyr and the marque disappeared.

190

[*Photograph by Henry Goldhann*

The 1951 Denzel roadster

The late coupé looks startlingly like a Porsche

[*Photograph by Henry Goldhann*

STEYR

Steyr began production in 1917, when the First World War was in full swing, with a 3·3-litre (80 × 110) six that put out 40 b.h.p. at 2400 r.p.m. This Type 5 became the Type 7 when front-wheel brakes were added in the early 1920s, but otherwise it remained substantially unchanged.

Once again Porsche entered the picture. Between stints at Daimler-Benz and Austro-Daimler, with which Steyr was closely connected for some time before the final merger, he designed an o.h.c. 4·4-litre six for Steyr that used roller bearings everywhere and coupled the swing-axle rear with a front beam axle. At no time did Steyr designate any of its products as sports or racing cars; it simply competed with normal production machines and did quite creditably with them.

The Type 12, a 1½-litre six (61·6 × 88), retained Porsche's chain-driven o.h.c. and developed nominally 30 h.p. at 3300 r.p.m. It was followed by 2- and 2½-litre sixes and a 995-c.c. four up to the 1939 war.

Courtesy of the Technisches Museum für Industrie und Gewerbe, Vienna]

The first Steyr

The Porsche-designed Steyrs at Montlhéry in 1925

Courtesy of Charles Stich]

DENZEL

Wolfgang Denzel is an Austrian who has learned to get more out of a Volkswagen than the Wolfsburg works is willing to put into it. His Denzel is an adaptation of the V.W. that has been timed at 99 m.p.h. and at 18 seconds for the standing quarter-mile, and its road-holding and cornering—steering is 2·6 turns lock to lock—are considerably better than the original's. The Denzel has made some impression in European racing but has not competed in the United States. From 1949 to 1956 it missed an Alpine Rally trophy only once.

Though a much-bored-out 1500-c.c. version with 98 b.h.p. and a claimed speed of 115 m.p.h. has been offered, the major production is the 1281-c.c. 78 × 67 four, opposed, air-cooled and rear-mounted as in the V.W. It is equipped with two Solex or Weber carburetters and 8·5:1 compression, and has a 4-speed crash gearbox.

SPAIN

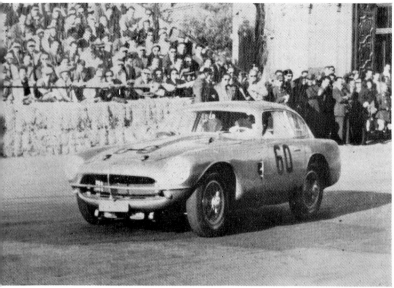

[Courtesy of E.N.A.S.A.

The smaller Pegaso coupé at Barcelona. All have inboard rear brakes

Courtesy of E.N.A.S.A.]

Prince Metternich at the wheel of the small roadster

[Courtesy of E.N.A.S.A.

The 3·9-litre (88 × 82) drop-head has hydraulic shock absorbers for all wheels

The big G.T. coupé, like most Pegasos, is Italian-bodied. Steering is 1·7 turns lock to lock

[Courtesy of E.N.A.S.A.

PEGASO

The Empresa Nacional de Autocamiones, S.A., in premises that used to be those of Hispano-Suiza's Spanish branch, may have hoped, in launching the Pegaso in 1951, to attain the place that Hispano held in men's esteem, and the product of the E.N.A.S.A. is certainly not unworthy of its predecessor.

Pegaso was intended from the first as a car that would be built to quality standards regardless of price, and there has been no defection from this criterion. However, the inherent costliness of such individual production today, even in as poor a country as Spain, combined with the expenses entailed by the factory's great distance from all major industrial supply centres, has made the Pegaso a machine that virtually no one can afford to buy, let alone risk in competition.

All Pegasos are dry-sump V-8's, ranging from the 2·8-litre (80 × 70) to the 4·7 (95 × 82); horsepower runs from 150 to 300. Originally Pegaso used two o.h.c. for each cylinder bank but later turned to pushrod operation for the overhead valves. Weber carburetters are favoured and compression ratios range from 6:1 to 9:1, lower ratios being preferred for the supercharged engines. The 92-in. wheelbase chassis is of the platform type, with torsion-bar suspension all round. The 5-speed gearbox is in unit with the German ZF limited-slip differential. Pegaso claims a top speed of 120·8 m.p.h. Like Rolls-Royce, it guarantees all its cars for three years.

THE NETHERLANDS

SPYKER

[Courtesy of C. Poel, Jr.

The first Spyker as it looks today. The front brakes were mounted inboard, at the differential

Courtesy of C. Poel, Jr.]

The Peking–Paris Spyker just before entering Moscow in 1907

Known in England as the Rolls-Royce of the Continent, the Spyker was built in The Netherlands from 1903 to 1925, the only sports car to come out of that country. It was created by two brothers, J. and H. J. Spyker, whose chief designer for the first decade was the brilliant Belgian, Joseph Laviolette.

Their first car was intended for H. J. Spyker to drive in the Paris–Madrid Race, but it was not completed in time. The world's first vertical six, it had separately cast 91×128 cylinders (8676 c.c.) whose pistons and connecting rods were splash-lubricated; the crankshaft and main bearings were fed by capillary lubrication through cotton wicks running from the lower part of the crankcase. Ignition was by low-tension magneto with make-and-break in each cylinder head. This first Spyker, which developed 50 b.h.p., was generally reputed to be much easier to handle than the contemporary Ford 999 and was used for touring for many years thereafter. It survives in the Museum van de Automobiel in Driebergen, The Netherlands: the world's first 4-wheel-drive car, with rear brakes on the jackshafts and front brakes on the front differential.

It successor was the 15/20 four that finished second in the Peking–Paris Race, despite rolling over twice in Siberia. This car continued the 3-speed gearbox and the huge leather cone clutch that had marked the first Spyker. All other details of its specification

have unfortunately been lost. It was followed by an experimental racer in 1910, an 80-h.p. four (180×140) that never competed. There were no further sports models until in 1918 J. G. Grootenhuis, one of the firm's directors, designed the so-called "aerocoque" on an 18/30-h.p. chassis. Drawing heavily on the firm's experience in building aircraft and engines for The Netherlands' armed forces, Grootenhuis produced a startlingly aerodynamic machine with a long undershield and aeroplane-type tail stabilizer; factory workers called it The Flying Hen. The axles and several other components were of American manufacture, but the engine and the body design were Spyker's. It was a 3560-c.c. four (90×140) with a dry multi-plate clutch and a 4-speed gearbox.

Spyker's last sports car, built from 1920 until the firm went out of business in 1925, was a rather international amalgam. It used a scaled-down 5-litre model of Wilhelm Maybach's Zeppelin engine, and all electrical equipment was made by Bosch. Both axles, the steering column, the 4-speed gearbox and parts of the chassis were French-built. The chassis was fitted with either a boat-decked two-seater body or a four-seater tourer; in the former coachwork it was driven from The Hague to Paris in a record time of 9 hours 23 minutes, reaching speeds of 85 m.p.h. with the 5472-c.c. 6-cylinder engine (95×135).

The under-shielded aerocoque Spyker, with airplane-type central fin

[Courtesy of C. Poel, Jr.

The last of the sports Spykers at a Dutch rally in 1958

Courtesy of C. Poel, Jr.]

SWEDEN
SAAB

The much-mourned full four-seater sports car of the vintage era came back almost unnoticed and in most unexpected guise when SAAB introduced its Gran Turismo in 1958.

Having started building automobiles some years earlier, the Svenska Aeroplan Aktiebolaget had produced a prototype roadster, the Sonett, that has yet to prove itself but that provided a first-class foundation for the G.T. Like Germany's D.K.W., SAAB uses a 2-stroke 3-cylinder engine of 748-c.c. (66 × 72·9), mounted in front in unit with gearbox and differential (the gear lever is on the steering column at a very awkward angle even though the box has four speeds). Acceleration from rest is not startling because the engine is at its best only above 3200 r.p.m. (maximum horsepower is 57 at 5000 r.p.m., or 50 with the detuned Sonett engine). The optional straight-pipe exhaust has as lovely a music as that of any small car on the road.

SAAB has established itself at the top of 750-c.c. production competition in both race and rally. Roadholding is excellent and the many small comforts provided in the G.T. emphasize its dual rôle. All seats are reclining and a number of stowage compartments are provided. The steering wheel is of the wood-rimmed racing type and an intricate time-speed-distance calculator eminently suitable for rallying is standard equipment, as are Italian racing tyres. A free-wheeling unit is incorporated in the gearbox.

VOLVO

It was in the 1920s that Aktiebolaget Volvo added the automobile to its many other machinery products, but it is only since the middle 1950s that the marque has made any sporting pretensions. Americans began to race the PV444 2-door saloon, a 1·6-litre o.h.v. four (79·4 × 79·8) that is basically a 2-carburetter derivation of the British Standard Vanguard engine.

As the 102½-in.-wheelbase car first appeared in the United States it was frequently mistaken for a slightly shrunken pre-war Ford. The 3-speed transmission that was standard has now become optional, having been replaced by a 4-speed full synchromesh gearbox on the PV544. Suspension is independent front and rear, coil springs and torsion bars being used

Courtesy of SAAB Motors, Inc.]
The Sonett experimental roadster

The Gran Turismo is a direct outgrowth of the Sonett. Top speed is close to 90 m.p.h.
Courtesy of SAAB Motors, Inc.]

for the rear axle. Producing 85 b.h.p. at 5500 r.p.m., the engine is reputed to propel the 19-cwt. car at 95 m.p.h. Unlike the SAAB, the Volvo has the gearbox and the differential in the conventional locales, and the gear lever where it belongs: in the floor. Roadholding is excellent despite the car's ostensibly disproportionate height, as innumerable competitions in both hemispheres have demonstrated.

The current PV544 has substituted a curved windscreen for the earlier car's V-type
Courtesy of Aktiebolaget Volvo]

JAPAN
DATSUN

Late in 1958 Japan joined the sports-car producers with its Datsun 1000, built by the Nissan Motor Co. Ltd., which started making motor cars many years earlier.

Obviously inspired by British models, the 988-c.c. sports four (73 × 59) produces 37 b.h.p. at 4600 r.p.m. with pushrod o.h.v. and a single Solex carburetter. Weighing under 17·8 cwt. on an 87-in. wheelbase, the two-seater is expected to reach 85 m.p.h. without undue strain. Conventional half-elliptics are fitted all round. The 4-speed gearbox, with synchromesh on the three top gears, is controlled from the steering column.

The new Datsun sports bodywork shows evidences of British derivation

[Courtesy of the Nissan Motor Co. Ltd.

BUILDERS

SYDNEY ALLARD

The accelerated progress of Sydney Herbert Allard from motor-cycle enthusiast to builder of an important sports car was based on the principle of one step at a time. It began with a family trait, his brothers, Leslie and Dennis, and his sister, Mary, having an abiding affection for powered transport. They became eager members of the Streatham Motor Cycle Club, which was distinguished for the abrupt endings of quiet meetings resulting from quick decisions to dash off to Box Hill, the last man there buying the beer. It is not unlikely that these young people contributed to the official decision to create a 30-m.p.h. speed limit, especially after some extra-legal races through the quiet lanes of Surrey.

Sydney, who with Dennis was a member of the committee, decided that more power was required and a Super Sports Morgan was obtained. Sydney drove it in his first race, a three-lap novice handicap at Brooklands. He won the first time and won again the following year. Meanwhile, back at Putney, his father had taken over a small garage and decided to place Sydney in charge. The young man worked according to regulations by day and experimented with special building at night. Hearing of a Talbot for sale in the Midlands, Sydney and his friends dashed north in an old truck, carrying tools and a hacksaw. When the sale was completed, the astonished seller saw the young men cut the chassis frame in half, load it on the truck and rush away.

Back at Putney, the chassis was shortened some more and, after a lot of work, there appeared a sort of special. The results were not too satisfying, but something had been learned. A 14-h.p. Ford tourer was stripped of trimmings, fitted with a 24-h.p. engine and sent out for some trials that fell short of success. Another Ford that had run in the Tourist Trophy was acquired and, with some changes, was run by Sydney Allard at Brighton in 1935, achieving the fastest time for an unblown sports car.

The next step was an idea for a V-8 special designed for mud trials; then came the purchase of a crash-damaged V-8 saloon and the first Allard special came into being. It was a Bugatti-tailed two-seater that won an award in its first event at Taunton and continued to make impressive showings at trials. Orders for copies came in and Allard began to build to order. In 1937, Allard took the car to the Ben Nevis Hill-Climb; the car turned over, rolling backward. It was stopped from a long drop by some friendly rocks and Allard escaped unhurt. It might have been this mishap that turned him toward speed cars. In any event, he built a lighter, more modern model that brought him success in sprints

Courtesy of the Allard Motor Car Co. Ltd.]

Sydney Allard

and hill-climbs and in 1939 won the Prescott sports-car record.

When the war broke out, Allard was put in charge of a large army repair depot at Fulham. Mrs. Allard looked after the canteen and the social life of 250 workers. When the fighting was over, Allard completed a body and chassis for his first appearance at the Bristol Club speed trials. In 1946, the Allard Motor Co. was formed. The next step was to refine all the experience and knowledge into a constantly improved car. Instead of remaining at a desk, Allard revived the old prototype with changes and improvements; then came one modern version after another. Advances are still being taken as the Allard firm continues. It seems a long distance from the days of illegal racing in Surrey and impromptu conclusions of meetings, but Sydney Allard and his men have worked so that distance is shortened by a speedy Allard sports car.

W. O. BENTLEY

When W. O. Bentley was asked to enter a car in the first race at Le Mans he said: "I think the whole thing's crazy. Nobody'll finish. Cars aren't designed to stand that sort of strain for 24 hours." But, when he was told that no British manufacturer was supporting this event, he permitted his patriotism, just this once, to outweigh more mundane considerations. He sent a 3-litre tourer with no intention of attending the race himself. At the final moment, however, curiosity won, and he went.

[*Courtesy of the Bentley Drivers' Club*]

W. O. Bentley

"After a few hours in the pit I decided that this wasn't at all stupid," he recalled. "It was in fact very exciting. Before darkness fell and the acetylene arc lamps at the corners were turned on, Le Mans was getting into my blood. By midnight, with the cars pounding past the stands with their lights on—my first sight of racing in the dark—I was quite certain that this was the best race I had ever seen."

The Bentley came in fourth on that 27th of May in 1923 and recorded the fastest lap. By the time that decade was over, W. O. Bentley's cars had won five times—the final four in succession. There were other races and other records during the 12-year life of Bentley Motors and, despite the prosaic distractions of business and finance, the serene and precise W. O., engineer and impresario, put glamour and excitement into the British green.

He was born of Yorkshire background on September 16, 1888, was christened Walter and showed an early inclination towards the mechanical. His best remembered toy was a stationary steam engine; his first fierce love was for the great locomotives that thundered past his home. After prep school and a reluctantly discarded ambition to become a great cricket player, W. O., or "The Bun", as he was called by his eight brothers and sisters, served a long apprenticeship in a locomotive works. During that time he discovered the joys of motor-cycling, winning among other awards a gold medal in the six-day trials over the hills of Wales.

When his student days were over, W. O. surveyed the railways as a career and found them sadly wanting. There seemed little promise of swift promotion and, besides, the petrol engine seemed more enticing. The transition from motor-cycles to four wheels was simple. He got his first job in automobiles as assistant to the second in command of the National

Motor Cab Co. of London. Here W. O. found himself in his true element, doctoring motors and outwitting wily cab drivers. When the time came for him to invest £2000 for the London agency of three French cars, Buchet, La Licorne, and Doriot, Flandrin et Parant, he was ready. In March, 1912, with his brother, H. M., he started the firm of Bentley & Bentley in New Street Mews off Upper Baker Street. "Seven years later," W. O. Bentley recalled, "in this same coach house, the first 3-litre Bentley engine, Ex-1, roared into life to the alarm of the local inhabitants."

It was at this time that W. O. formed the philosophy that was to guide his future. His favourite of the three cars he was selling was the Doriot, Flandrin et Parant—the DFP. Capital being too scarce to allow for any extensive advertising, W. O. decided that the quickest and most effective publicity came from racing. He won his first major effort—the Aston Hill-Climb. Bentley continued to drive the DFP in races and trials, scoring a respectable number of wins. Victories piled up and sales increased when suddenly war intervened. Bentley joined the Navy and made important contributions to the rotary engines that powered British planes over Germany.

When the war ended, W. O. decided to build a car of his own and in 1919 the Ex-1 3-litre was born. *The Autocar* published the first road test by Sammy Davis, who praised the speed, brakes and handling. He graciously forgave "the noise from the oil pump drive as inseparable from the first chassis of a new design".

Within a short time the Bentleys were making a name for themselves in road tests and races. W. O. explained the company's policy: "First, we never entered for a race unless we thought we would win and, if we won, we liked to do so at the lowest possible speed in order to preserve our cars and keep our true maximum performance from our competitors. We are in racing not for the glory and heroics but strictly for business."

Bentley vetoed all racing on winding or narrow roads where the small-car cornering showed his cars to a disadvantage. His uncompromising desire for the Bentley to perform outstandingly in all races made him set this unalterable formula: "Sound, painstakingly meticulous preparation—fast efficient pit-work."

The awesome success of the Bentley cars at Le Mans and in other major and minor competition admittedly sprang from the rules set by W. O. and the fine engineering and construction, but another grand ingredient contributed to the total. W. O. never hesitated to point to the Bentley Boys—the men who drove his cars—as the centre of legend and myth and great accomplishment.

Merely to list them at this point is to recall great moments in racing: Dr. J. Dudley Benjafield, bacteriologist and later Harley Street consultant; Sir Henry R. S. Birkin, Bart.—at the wheel with his silk scarf flying in the wind, twice winner at Le Mans;

Glen Kidston, Jack and Clive Dunfee, S. C. H. Davis, George Duller, J. F. Duff, Woolf Barnato, thrice winner at Le Mans; Dick Watney, Frank Clement, Baron d'Erlanger, Jean Chassagne, L. G. Callingham and R. C. Gallop.

Bentley, the cars and the Bentley Boys rolled merrily along through the wonderful twenties but, while there was almost constant joy at the race courses, there was deep brooding in the counting house. Finances were never W. O.'s strong point and, when the 1929 crash came along, the firm tottered and not long thereafter was taken over by Rolls-Royce. There followed a dismal stint with Lagonda, marked by heartbreaking litigation that hampered any further ambition W. O. might have had for creating a new car. He was not permitted to use the name of Bentley on an automobile.

A few years ago on the village green outside the Bentley cottage at Shamley Green, near Guildford, some 70 green Bentleys, many of them 30 years old, were assembled for a party to W. O. The air was thick with smoke, with technical talk, racing talk and vivid reminiscence. The members of the Bentley Drivers' Club were doing honour to their great patron and, in the words of W. O., "as the last booming Bentley exhaust note faded away that night and one or two of us settled down to some late-hour talk about the old days, I felt that it had all been worth while."

On his 70th birthday in 1958, he was among 400 guests at the 12th annual dinner of the Bentley Drivers' Club. Forrest Lycett, a founder-member who once interrupted his morning drive to his office in his 8-litre to set a new Brooklands record, rose to speak: to tell W. O. that the Bentley Boys of today could find no better way to show their gratitude for all the pleasure he had given them than to present Bentley with 1300 guineas and to dedicate almost as much to a fund for a W. O. Bentley Scholarship.

A. C. BERTELLI

The curtain raiser to the Coppa Florio of 1908 was the Circuito di Bologna, a tough race in which a driver had to select his riding mechanic with great care. Felice Nazzaro won the race, getting excellent assistance from his young Italian mechanic, Agosto Cesare Bertelli, who had started with the ambition of becoming a marine engineer, but had obtained a job with the FIAT concern in Turin. The idea of automobile racing remained with Bertelli and when the first war was over, he went to England, where he had spent his early years, obtaining a connection with the Enfield & Allday Co. Within a year he had made an important contribution to the design of the 10-h.p. 4-cylinder automobile.

He recalled that in the course of developing the car he came to the conclusion that racing does improve the breed. During the next two years he was a frequent contestant at Brooklands, competing in works cars in the J.C.C. 200-mile Race and the R.A.C. 1500-c.c. Tourist Trophy. Dudley Coram in his Aston Martin history said the little sports Enfield-Allday "was quite a notable machine of the period, and much of the experience gained in its development was undoubtedly embodied in the later Aston Martins when the marque was revived under Bertelli's technical supervision".

Bertelli's next assignment was for Woolf Barnato, who had not yet joined the Bentley team. In 1923, three cars by Bertelli were built in Barnato's private garage at Lingfield in Surrey. Barnato, Bertelli and Capt. J. C. Douglas drove the cars in the 200-mile Race, where they showed poorly. The next year Bertelli formed a partnership with W. S. Renwick in Birmingham with the intention of creating a new car, but the first 12 months were spent in experiments with a new type of cylinder head and overhead-valve layout. The firm finally did manufacture a car made up of its special engine, a modified Enfield-Allday chassis and a modest two-seater body. The car, nicknamed the Buzzbox, had a top speed of 80 m.p.h. and was registered as the R. & B. Before any other work could be done on this product, the partners became associated with the revived Aston Martin Motors Ltd., under the directorship of Baron Charnwood.

The combination of executive, engineer and racing driver, with a few turns as pit chief, gave Bertelli the sharp perspective needed in bringing the cars to the attention of the public. His own participation in races with the moral and financial encouragement of the other directors proved of great value. He had the distinction of having raced more than any other builder and it was no secret that he enjoyed that part of his duties more than any other. However, there were great production burdens to bear that tempered the satisfactions. S. C. H. Davis, in *The Autocar*, clearly stated the problem in discussing the 1929 output when he said: "What this car really needs is a thoroughly comprehensive system of manufacture, with a full works organization behind it. It is too good a machine to be produced in twos and threes."

Nevertheless the car went on to win many honours. Bertelli himself won the Biennial Cup at Le Mans in 1932. Other drivers got Gold Medals and achieved fine runs with Bertelli's Astons. In 1933, after a reorganization in the firm, Bertelli was able to devote his entire time to the engineering end. According to the critiques of the time, the newer models had lost none of the old charm, road-holding, cornering and braking while increasing their speed. Victories and credits continued to pour in, but the Great Depression was making itself felt more strongly every year. The sports car was becoming a luxury. Bertelli felt that he had done what he could for the firm and departed.

In 1956 it became historically evident that Bertelli had built and designed more than mere metal when the Aston Martin Owners' Club became of age.

The Grand Parade of Aston Martins was staged at Silverstone with the cars in age-places from vintages of 1921 to shiny new cars. One after the other they roared past the reviewing stand gleaming with pride of marque and maker. Among them were the old team cars—LM2, LM4, LM6, LM9, LM10, LM14 and LM15—and driving them were Maurice Falkner, R. C. Murton Neale, Pat Driscoll, T. G. Clarke, Charles Brackenbury, Jimmy Elwes, Mrs. "Bill" Wisdom as a passenger, and also Agosto Cesare Bertelli.

MARC BIRKIGT

Like so many men of genius, Marc Birkigt always felt that his work should be the story of his life. He gave few interviews; his writings were purely technical papers. Born in Geneva in 1878, he took his degree with honours at 20 in the École des Arts et Métiers. Electrical power fascinated the engineering world then, and Birkigt, seeking undeveloped territory, went to Spain to work on electric locomotives in Barcelona. But his interest was soon caught by the internal-combustion engine, and in 1904 he opened his Hispano-Suiza factory with Spanish financing. In the next 10 years he produced 35 different models, culminating in the Alfonso XIII.

When the First World War began, Spain remained neutral. Birkigt offered his services to France, for which he quickly created the V-8 engine that is still admired by all designers. These engines were built not only in France but also in Birkigt's Spanish works and, under licence, by Crane-Simplex in the United States. They were of aluminium block construction with steel cylinder liners and direct overhead-cam action on the valve tappets, and they helped to establish the reputations of such aces as Guynemer, Rickenbacker and Fonck.

As soon as peace returned, Birkigt went back to his first love, the automobile, and produced the famous *de luxe* six that was to bear Guynemer's stork insigne. The story of Birkigt's cars is very largely the story of the man. He was an indefatigable worker whose research and experimentation refused to recognize defeat; a problem was given up only when he was utterly convinced that he could find no solution. By the time he took up his pencil to start drawing, the whole design was complete in his mind, down to the methods of manufacture, the machines necessary and the ensuing assembly. It was his custom, once a design had been completed, to follow it through every step to final production, for he had learned long ago how persevering is the element of surprise. It is characteristic of the man that, having designed his aeroplane engine, which was all that was asked of him, he could not rest until he had also solved the problem of firing the plane's guns through the propeller shaft so that the pilot could aim directly. It is equally characteristic

Marc Birkigt

that, finding no machine tools capable of doing the work, he invented and patented them.

Even before the outbreak of the Second World War, Birkigt's factories were converted to armaments. When peace returned, he did not resume making automobiles but continued in armaments and aviation, adding textile machinery to his output. A man whose chief interest was his work, Birkigt had no hobbies. In the rare vacations that he permitted himself to take, he enjoyed hunting, boating with his family on Lake Geneva and, occasionally, tobogganing and bob-sledding. A *grand officier* of the *Légion d'honneur* and the holder of an honorary doctorate from the Zürich Polytechnic Institute, Birkigt died in 1953 at his estate near Geneva.

ETTORE BUGATTI

Ettore Bugatti was the aristocrat of sports-car designers. Like the Renaissance man, he was an individualist of many refined abilities.

The son and brother of artists, Bugatti was apprenticed to Prince Paul Troubetzkoy as a student of sculpture. But, aware of his limitations as well as his capacities, he recognized long before he was 20 that he was better endowed as a mechanical creator than as an artist. With his father's consent, he abandoned sculpture for automotive design. Without a day in an engineering school, he became a legendary creator of motor cars. At 17 he had built his first; at 19 he was retained by de Dietrich, one of the pioneer manufacturers, to design others—a contract that had to be signed by the senior Bugatti because Ettore was legally an infant.

Born September 15, 1881, in Milan, he was the son of Carlo Bugatti, painter, sculptor, mechanic, architect and silversmith. When Ettore Bugatti died in 1947, he had built some 9500 hand-made cars.

of which at the most 500 highly prized collectors' items survive.

Perhaps the secret of Bugatti's greatness lies in his obdurate perfectionism. From the time he established his first factory in Molsheim, Alsace (then under German sovereignty), around Christmas, 1909, Bugatti concentrated on making every engine, every chassis, every part a work of art in metal, emphasizing cleanliness of design and accessibility and disregarding the trend of others toward huge power plants in heavy frames. Bugatti strove for the small engine and the light vehicle that would represent the ultimate economy of energy and the optimum achievement in power.

To this end, Bugatti worked with every part of the car in mind, never losing sight of the complex interrelations of power plant, transmission, steering, suspension, brakes, chassis and coachwork, in which any one weak point must of necessity impair the functional unity of the whole. The true sports car, Bugatti wrote to Cavaliere Vincenzo Florio, who contributed so much to automotive competition, "should possess all the qualities required by the ordinary user. In the first place is security in its broadest sense. This means the absence of breakdowns either because of faulty material, poor design or construction . . . a really good car should give the impression of being held to the road." And a Bugatti, as Dennis May, the British motoring expert, has observed, will forgive its driver many mistakes: it is always working with him almost as if it were endowed with its own volition. As early as 1911 Bugatti demonstrated this in races in which his 6-cwt. voiturettes vanquished the giants of Europe.

When the First World War broke out, less than five years after the establishment of the Molsheim factory, Bugatti, who was still an Italian by passport though a Frenchman by conviction, acted decisively. Most of his 400 workers, being French, had to regain their own country at once. Bugatti arranged for the safety of his family, buried in the earth the vital parts of three racing machines under construction and, with an assistant, drove two completed cars into Germany. There Graf von Zeppelin intervened to obtain permission for Bugatti, despite his known French sympathies, to leave the country, and the Bugatti family, which by now included three children, arrived in Milan with total assets of two racing cars and a few trunks. Making his way to Paris, Bugatti devoted the next four years to vital assistance to the Allies' war effort, designing and building a synchronizer for aeroplane machine guns and, with Marc Birkigt, creator of the Hispano-Suiza, perfecting aviation engines superior to any then known. Many of these were in fact built under licence by the Duesenberg brothers in Elizabeth, New Jersey. The design of the double-eight engine —two parallel banks of eight cylinders each on a common crankcase in which two crankshafts were united by gearing—was carried from conception to completed blueprint in 24 hours!

Ettore Bugatti

In 1919 Bugatti regained possession of his factory, not too seriously damaged, and reassembled his old working force. With the five cars that he had secreted from the Germans in 1914, he launched a career of racing victories that few other designers could rival: five successive triumphs, for example, in the vicious Targa Florio with its 1200 curves in each 67-mile lap rising from sea level to 3000 ft. There were some failures: Indianapolis was the outstanding instance. Bugatti, wedded to the idea that automobiles were meant to be raced on roads, had not designed for the endless left turns of the American oval track; and his drivers there were amateurs. Nevertheless, in 20 years Bugatti scored almost 4000 major victories.

It is noteworthy that Bugatti himself, though a first-class speed driver, never competed or allowed his sons to race; but Jean, the elder, was permitted to test-run cars on the course that Bugatti laid out at Molsheim. In 1939 Ettore Bugatti suffered his greatest loss when a drunken postman bicycled on to this circuit in defiance of all warnings and Jean was killed in an effort to avoid harming him.

Always the master, Bugatti innovated where others were content to follow. His original conceptions of suspension, steering (every Bugatti steered flawlessly), and engines were unmatched; consequently, he was at times reluctant and even behind-hand in adopting or adapting the improvements of others, such as hydraulic brakes and the supercharger.

In his private life he maintained a reserve and an innate courtesy that were as characteristic as his creations in underlining his quest for perfection. He was affectionately feudal in his organization of Molsheim. He moulded it into a little principality almost entirely self-sufficient not only for the materials with which he worked but also for the maintenance of a high standard of living for every employee and for his own family. Farms, mines and subsidiary factories supplied virtually every need. Mild as he was in his bearing, Bugatti liked to be known as Le Patron; and Le Patron's home in Molsheim was a monument to gracious living, a high degree of cultivation and almost a cult of the thoroughbred horse. The maker of thoroughbreds could never have enough of them around him; even the inn he built to accommodate customers awaiting deliveries was named the Hôtellerie du pur sang.

The Second World War, engulfing Molsheim almost immediately after Jean Bugatti's death, sent his father back to Paris. Under the noses of the occupying Germans, Bugatti poured out aid to the Resistance (in whose service several of his best drivers were killed) and continued endlessly to design new engineering achievements; not only automotive but marine. His trawlers were to become the standbys of the Breton fishermen; he devised railway engines and marine engines; and he lived for the restoration of France and the revival of Usines Bugatti.

Ettore Bugatti died quietly at the age of 66. The man who almost became a journeyman sculptor bequeathed to the world instead the consummate artistry of his engineering design. The roar of his engines will forever challenge the drivers and designers of sports cars.

COLIN CHAPMAN

Bright and shiny Lotus aluminium bodies hang asymmetrically from the ceiling ready to be lowered on to the chassis. The slightest breeze sets them into feathery motion, turning the gloomy workshop into an entrancing mobile. Once completed, the Lotus cars are sent to eager buyers throughout the world, each purchase becoming a vote of utter confidence in Colin Chapman, builder-designer of the unorthodox, fiercely fast car.

Chapman, who was born in 1929 and still retains the rosy cheeks of youth, is England's youngest designer and builder. He began in the tradition of all builders of specials, putting together odd bits and pieces of this car and that and holding them together by faith in himself and the laws of mechanics. He was employed as a structural engineer by the British Aluminium Co., using his spare hours to experiment with cast-off remnants, giving free play to a rebellious trait to take nothing for granted. He carried many ideas back to prime principles, progressing by trial and error until he felt he had reached the design most suitable for his car.

After leaving London University and doing his share with the R.A.F., he took employment and worked in his spare time. His first car was fundamentally an Austin 7 with enough changes to make it capable of almost 100 miles an hour. Later editions

Colin Chapman

carried Ford parts and with this modification he competed successfully at club meetings. His reputation grew and so did demand for his components. At 23 he became managing director of Lotus Engineering and started to seek ways to reduce drag.

Experiments continued in wind-tunnel and road tests and the car finally took shape. By 1956 it had reached the stage where Stirling Moss and H. Mackay Fraser made five international records at Monza in class G. They covered 50 miles at an average of 132·77 m.p.h. Trophies and prizes have continued to pour in as Chapman continued to improve the Lotus. Chapman is suave and self-assured without being overconfident, and has not been overwhelmed by the growth of his organization. Having raced, designed, engineered, built and co-ordinated, he is familiar with all the problems at hand, thus attaining a degree of harmony of all department heads that would be the envy of General Motors. It is a question whether the rebel in him has not been lost in the increasing activity, but according to the best advices from the plant the experimenter is still very much in action.

LOUIS COATALEN

Louis Coatalen was a practical Frenchman who charmed the English by teaching them that there is nothing so sterile and frustrating as a designer of automobiles without a market. He worked on the theory that in his day cars should be built to fit the road, with an implied prediction that one day the roads would be built to fit the cars.

He came to England to join the Humber Co. in 1901, designing a new 12-h.p. chassis with a limou-

[*Courtesy of the S. I. A., Paris*

Louis Coatalen

sine body which featured curved windows of plate glass. The engine consisted of four cylinders cast in pairs; the car had electric and tube ignition and a 4-speed gearbox. It sold at the acceptable price of £300 and was considered excellent value.

Being a worldly man, Coatalen faced the frequent conflict of staying with the drawing board or making his practical ideas felt in the directors' room. He had performed nobly at Panhard, Clément, de Dion and several German concerns. When he left Humber he went to Hillman, where he married the owner's daughter; then, in 1909, in his late twenties, he joined the Sunbeam Co. as chief engineer. Here, it appears, he was able to merge his flair for design and business with highly satisfactory results.

He designed a new 16/20-h.p. 4-cylinder car (95 × 135 mm.) that he raced himself with considerable success. Working with other talented engineers, such as Hugh Rose, he produced a 12/16-h.p. T-head (80 × 120 mm.) in 1911, of which 650 were built and sold. The word *obsolescence* had not yet been coined by Detroit, but Coatalen had the idea. The T-head was followed by an L-head with a long stroke (80 × 150 mm.), of which almost 1000 were sold. Then came the 25/30-h.p. 6-cylinder (90 × 160 mm.) that created 17 records at Brooklands. Driven by Coatalen and T. H. Richards, it averaged 75·66 m.p.h. for 12 hours, the engine running without a pause for the 907 miles.

There have been critics who contend that Coatalen was more of a supervisor than an engineer at Sunbeam. He did have the affectionate title of *le patron* and he moved freely and with charm in his various capacities, expounding his philosophy that the automobile was a commodity that must show its maker a profit. Kent Karslake and Laurence Pomeroy, in *From Veteran to Vintage*, quote the following ledger figures for Sunbeam: Profit in 1909, £90; 1910, £20,700; 1911, £41,000, and, after the great Sunbeam

performance in the French Grand Prix of 1912, £94,909 on a capital of £120,000.

The year 1912 was truly a great year for Coatalen. In the Coupe de l'Auto over the Dieppe circuit, he, Dario Resta and R. F. L. Crossman came in first, second and third. In the Grand Prix they finished third, fourth and fifth, beating most of the bigger cars with their standard side-valve 12/16-h.p. models that had been clothed in narrow, streamlined shells. The same 3-litre side-valve engines were improved in 1913 so that K. Lee Guinness was able to make the only non-stop run in the Coupe de l'Auto, finishing third to Boillot and Goux in Peugeots. Always the innovator and willing to compromise for the sake of success, Coatalen admitted that his English engines could not compete with the special valve gear in the French cars. Thereupon he purchased one of the successful Peugeots, brought it to England and created a number of close copies that became Sunbeam racing cars. They were quite successful. Guinness won the 1914 Tourist Trophy and Resta got a fifth in the Grand Prix at Lyons. There were other victories, including a fourth at Indianapolis in 1916. Ultimately Coatalen hired the Peugeots' designer, Ernest Henry.

Coatalen had proved his point that good cars could be built and designed with profit as an objective. It was regrettable that the luxury market did not maintain its high level. Like so many other builders of luxury cars, Sunbeam had to yield to the morbid law of economics. Coatalen believed firmly in the commercial yield of successful racing. He admitted that designer and builders were important; that heroic racing drivers were picturesque; but he insisted that "the only thing the public remembers about a race is the name on the radiator of the winning car".

BRIGGS CUNNINGHAM

Briggs Cunningham, a living legend in motor sport and a master of every other sport in which he has shown an interest, has one massive ambition. He would like to see an American car win at Le Mans. This was at first a personal ambition and the car to win was to be a Cunningham. But after expending about a million dollars and tremendous personal effort, Cunningham hoped that "maybe somebody else can do the trick, starting us off by winning in a foreign car, until such time as an American manufacturer builds a winning car". In 1958, Phil Hill in a Ferrari fulfilled that hope.

With commendable national pride, Cunningham points out that "Americans have become tops at one time or another in just about every sport you can think of—but not in modern auto racing. We've been on equal terms in international boat racing, tennis, etc., but when was the last great American international racing car? Jimmy Murphy's win in a

Duesenberg at Le Mans in 1921. In Europe it's a matter of national pride to win at Le Mans. For instance, the Italians have subsidized Ferrari. But since American cars seem to be built for American conditions and driving habits, there's no real incentive for an American manufacturer to set up an international factory racing team. But you never can tell. After all, a Corvette or a Thunderbird could be the sire of an American throughbred at Le Mans. Maybe things are changing."

Enthusiasts who share these views regret that the great Cunningham has curtailed his activities. The Europeans whose entrenchment he has threatened admit that there is no American they'd rather see taking the checkered flag on the courses of the world than Briggs Cunningham. And thereby hangs the legend.

Briggs was born to wealth in 1907. His father had transmuted a profitable meat packing business in Cincinnati into a successful banking career. At 16, Briggs got driving lessons from the family chauffeur and was presented with a Dodge. Within two years the irrepressible young man was driving a Packard phaeton. The Cunningham family had a summer home in Southport, Conn., where Briggs met Lucie Bedford, daughter of an industrialist and an ardent boating enthusiast. While she waited six years Briggs ran the low hurdles and played football at The Hill School in Pottstown, Pa., and then went on to Yale, where he was an outstanding runner. After two years at college, Cunningham and Lucie were married. They honeymooned in Europe, taking with them his six-metre racing yacht. When they got to England Briggs purchased a supercharged Alfa Romeo and an SS Mercedes phaeton.

Many years later Briggs gained immortality in yachting circles when he sailed the *Columbia* in her successful defence of the America's Cup. He explained the philosophy of his life: "Some people like to do things with their minds. Some like to create or build. I like to do physical things, especially with my hands. I enjoy the feeling of power it gives to control things by touch." He refrained from mentioning that he did do things with his mind and that he had built—and built well. It was left to his opponent in the great races, Lt.-Comdr. Graham Mann, R.N., skipper of the badly beaten British yacht *Sceptre*, to pinpoint what others had felt about Cunningham. "He's charming, cheerful and wonderfully ingratiating," Mann said, "and he gave us the friendliest racing we've ever had."

Briggs and Lucie came back to Greens Farms, Conn., where they raced boats, collected historic automobiles and had three children. Among these activities he improved his tennis game considerably, brought his golf score down to the low seventies and served as brakeman in an Olympic bobsled trial. When the war broke out and the Air Force rejected him as too old, Briggs flew anti-submarine patrols for the Civil Air Patrol.

His love for cars, which prompted him to collect

Briggs Cunningham

almost 100, took him in 1948 to Watkins Glen, where he liked the action. Cunningham was the first in his country to drive a Ferrari, and as his racing ability developed he began to look to Le Mans as the ultimate in victories. His friendship with Phil Walters and Bill Frick resulted in the creation of a modified Cadillac called *Le Monstre*, which ran 11th in the 1950 Le Mans.

The race proved to Cunningham that only an American car of special construction had a chance at Le Mans. He therefore established his own factory at West Palm Beach, Fla., and built his first car, the C-1. It was modified into the C-2 and proved to be almost unbeatable on the airport circuits. This encouraged Briggs to build the C-3, a motor car of beauty and excellence with a chassis by Cunningham, an engine by Chrysler and a body by Vignale of Italy. The Cunninghams were wonderful cars and in their races throughout the United States they left behind them Jaguars, Ferraris, Allards and other top marques. A reason often presented for these successes was the fact that the Chrysler engine had a displacement of 331 cu. in.—$5\frac{1}{2}$ litres.

John R. Bond, author of *Sports Cars in Action* and founder-publisher of *Road & Track*, made the point that the Chrysler engine, originally designed for touring cars, was not the ideal sports-car power plant. The pushrod o.h.v. mechanism, he said, is not capable of attaining the r.p.m. of the single and double overhead-cam layouts used by other major sports cars and the engine, weighing $6\frac{3}{4}$ cwt., was relatively heavy for its output. In addition, there were peculiar production problems. For example, it was necessary to ship the unfinished cars to Italy for the master builder to put on the shells—with the usual agonizing delays—and the cars had to be sent back to Florida for the finishing.

In order to race at Le Mans Cunningham had to produce and sell at least ten of these expensive cars per year. He appeared in the 1951 Le Mans with a full team of C4R models. One car, driven by John Fitch and Phil Walters, was in second place for more than nine hours and finished 18th. This gave the marque a needed lift and a year later two open Cunninghams and one with an aerodynamic coupé body, designed by Dr. Kamm, who had worked on the Auto-Union, were on the starting grid. After the other cars were forced out, Cunningham himself drove one for more than 20 hours, gaining fourth place in one of the most historic displays of physical stamina, determination and sheer skill.

After the "heroic epic", as the European press described it, Cunningham took his cars to the major courses of Europe, including Rheims and Silverstone, as well as the United States, where they won more honours. But Cunningham frankly wanted Le Mans. He went back in 1953 with an open C4R, the C4RK coupé and the newest, the C5R. The C5R had remarkable road-holding qualities, having reverted to the rigid front axle. It passed the time traps at 154·81 m.p.h. There was no doubt about the cars' quality, but general misfortunes and unscheduled pit stops slowed them to finish third, sixth and ninth.

In 1954, Cunningham obtained a 4·5 Ferrari car and fitted the first water-cooled brakes ever used at Le Mans. It broke a rocker arm and retired. For the next and last year at Le Mans the C6R had an Offenhauser engine. Cunningham was in 13th place when he had to withdraw because of gearbox trouble. Among other problems with the 3-litre Offy was the matter of fuel. It had been developed to run on alcohol and other special fuels and the conversion presented a great difficulty. "We never managed to lick the problem of getting the Offy to deliver the performance we needed on pump fuel," Cunningham said.

When Briggs announced the end of his efforts, the post-mortems on the cars began to pour in. He took them cheerfully and replied factually wherever he could. He clarified the entire situation with one statement: "The people connected with Le Mans are there strictly for business. The foreign drivers get paid to win. We came over there primarily as sportsmen in 1950 and I like to think that before we were through we had made the Europeans take us as a serious threat . . ."

Shortly after he gave up building his car, he disclosed that he did not expect to do much more car racing. "I'm getting a bit too old for it," he explained. "But I hope to keep on sailing as long as I'm able to throw a leg over a rail." When he was asked how he could reconcile the speed of a yacht at 15 miles an hour with that of a sports car at 150 miles an hour, he said: "Essentially, they're one and the same thing, and I enjoy one just as much as the other. A boat and a car are both vehicles, each propelled by a power plant. In the case of the car the explosive force of gasoline is used; in the case of a boat, the often-changing force of the wind." The idea is that Briggs Cunningham likes to move.

ALBERT DE DION

There was something exquisitely entrancing about the model steam engine in the window of Giroux's toy shop on the Boulevard des Italiens that day in 1881. Comte Albert de Dion stood staring at it, observing its delicate workmanship, including the cylinder made of glass so that the piston could be seen at work. Within him a terrifying turmoil of emotions was taking place. He had come to the shop to purchase favours for the cotillion given by the Duc de Morny. This was part of his life as a Proustian *flâneur* in the finest of Paris society. On his way to the shop his mind was full of the frivolities he was to purchase when suddenly he was stopped by the sight of the engine. Perhaps it was because his grandfather, the Marquis Henri de Dion, had been a celebrated engineer, or perhaps it was his own secret longing for all things mechanical; in any case he purchased the steam engine after finding out that it had been made by Georges Bouton and his brother-in-law, Trépardoux.

Within the hour de Dion was knocking at the door of the tiny shed where Bouton and Trépardoux held forth. Bouton was friendly and articulate; Trépardoux was dour, dismal and morose, hiding behind a moist walrus moustache. Both complained that there was little money in the manufacture of this toy—say eight francs a day each. De Dion could hardly contain the turbulence within his soul. A dilettante all his young life, he realized that this might be the sesame to new life. He offered the two men ten francs a day each if they would work for him. They agreed cautiously, but were amazed when he set them up in an old house on the Rue Pergolèse and informed them that the real object of the new firm of de Dion, Bouton et Trépardoux was to be the manufacture of life-size steam carriages.

Two years later they had built their first steam automobile; a frightening contraption that belched smoke and cinders and shuddered as it moved, causing children and animals to scatter in all directions. De Dion's next step was to convert an English Rudge tandem velocipede with a one-horsepower engine into a self-moving vehicle. While beset by the mechanical problems and Trépardoux's obdurate hostility, de Dion faced an obstacle of a personal nature. His family was appalled by his activities. There would have been no objection if a young nobleman of his station maintained a race horse, a yacht or a *scuderia* of mistresses, but to work with his hands and spend money on this bit of "unsalable nonsense" was pure dementia. His father, the Marquis, even took court action to restrain de Dion, but nothing came of it. The charm and earnestness of the young man finally won his father to the idea and it is recorded that the elder de Dion eventually yielded and enjoyed trips in the horseless steam monsters.

When he realized that he had gone as far as possible with steam, that it was awkward, unwieldy and relatively inefficient, de Dion announced to his partners that henceforth they would concentrate on the petrol engine. Bouton yielded amiably, but Trépardoux was infuriated. He skulked back to his tiny steam models and was lost for ever in history. De Dion and Bouton went to work on the internal combustion engine and came up with a tiny model with a bore and stroke of 50×70 mm.—137 c.c. By 1895 they had a motor tricycle in production and during the following five years sold hundreds of them throughout the world. The engine started with a single horsepower and was increased as experimentation continued. By the time of the Tour de France of 1899 the horsepower had grown to $2\frac{1}{4}$. The fastest de Dion tricycle averaged 26·5 m.p.h. for 1350 miles, being beaten only by cars of 12 and 16 h.p.

The original 137-c.c. engine gave the plodding Bouton a great deal of difficulty. He had designed it to run at 900 r.p.m., considered quite fast in those days. However, a mystery developed. The engine worked poorly at this speed, but gave a fine performance when run at 3000 r.p.m. Bouton pondered and finally altered the normal speed to 1500 r.p.m. by creating a special coil with a contact breaker that gave "positively timed" ignition. This was the first time a true high-speed engine had been made. When de Dion marketed the 4-wheel voiturette he was able to increase the horsepower to eight and to give the car two speeds with constant-mesh pinions and expanding clutches, as well as a water cooling system that moved from the back to the front.

De Dion, who had succeeded to his father's title, believed that automobiles should be raced for the sake of sport as well as for testing under the most gruelling conditions. In the early days of the century, when the French government refused to allow road racing, he persuaded the Chamber of Deputies to legalize the sport in the sparsely populated Argonne area. David Scott-Moncrieff reports on this in his *Veteran and Edwardian Motor Cars*: "I have always heard that the Marquis de Dion said privately that if anyone seriously opposed the bill he would take it as a personal insult. The ready passage of the bill may not have been entirely unconnected with the fact that the Marquis was one of the most deadly duellists of his day."

The Marquis de Dion continued to improve his engine, building especially for anyone who wanted to race even though his own cars did not participate too often. His epitaph from the French press was "Father of the French Motor Industry", but historians have credited him with even greater achievements in the motor development of the world.

FRED AND AUGUST DUESENBERG

The two brothers who produced America's finest car worked with intimate co-operation to achieve their objective. Fred Duesenberg was the dreamer, the designer; August Duesenberg would bring the design into being, modifying where needed and nursing the project along. When tests would show that a change was needed from Fred's design, August would make it—but never without consulting his brother. Watching the two at work was an impressive experience. Each would be bent over his bench, intensely occupied with his own labour. When Fred reached a snag, he would pause, inhale deeply and mutter: "Mikes all critey!" This was followed by silence and then August would become annoyed by some unyielding problem and he would explode: "Judas priest!" Then they would smile and go on with their work, repeating their expletives from time to time. William R. Beckman, who was their chief engineer-draughtsman, said this was so much part of the pair that he and others who worked with them eventually acquired these expressions, using them to release pressure.

Beckman recalled that Fred "possessed the skill of proportioning which was uncanny. The question was raised as to the proper diameter of the shank for the tubular connecting rod and the size of the hole to be drilled through the centre for lightness. Fred picked up a steel scale and looked at it for a moment, after which he remarked that the rod should be made $\frac{11}{16}$ in. in diameter at the upper end, and should have a taper enlarging to $\frac{27}{32}$ in. in diameter at the lower end, and also should have a hole bored through the centre having a diameter of $\frac{17}{32}$ in. Here was one of the most important elements of the engine, and its size was nonchalantly being determined by a glance at the divisions of the scale." Beckman admitted he was sceptical and made a mathematical check. The result was a variation of a few thousandths of an inch.

Augie (no one ever called him August) frequently amazed his colleagues by on-the-spot inventiveness. One instance demonstrates this flair. In his day, the welding of seams in aluminium by acetylene torch was a new method, and many ugly seams were seen on the bodies of racing cars. Augie changed all that. He would sprinkle sawdust on the sheet near the seam to be welded and apply the heat to the underside. As soon as he noted the dust beginning to scorch he surmised that the surface was at the proper welding heat and the result was a thin, neat seam.

Fred and Augie were born in Lippe, Germany, moving to America in 1885. Their formal schooling ended early and whatever knowledge they acquired in the engineering field was through curiosity and work. Fred became a bicycle racer after they had opened a shop and repair business; he set two world records for paced sprints. When Des Moines, Iowa, got its first garage, the Duesenberg boys switched to automobiles. In 1903 they

August (*left*) **and Fred Duesenberg**

built their first racing car, the Mason, considered one of the finest of its time. Seven years later, Fred Maytag, later famous for his washing machines, purchased the Mason company, but the brothers did not go along with the deal. In 1912, the brothers failed to qualify with a car at Indianapolis, but Fred had fine results with it in the Algonquin hill-climb and later at Galveston, Elgin and Milwaukee. By this time they had moved their plant to St. Paul, Minn., where, among other achievements, they designed and built an engine for a speed boat, the Disturber IV, for Commodore J. A. Pugh of Chicago. In its trial run it did 60 m.p.h., a new record on water. The First World War prevented it from competing in the Harmsworth Trophy Race in England.

The fame of the two brothers and their fast cars had spread throughout the United States. Outstanding racing drivers sought an opportunity to run the cars and the Duesenbergs went along willingly. The impressive list includes Barney Oldfield, Eddie Rickenbacker (tenth in the 1914 Indianapolis), Peter de Paolo, Jimmy Murphy, Harry Hartz, Eddie O'Donnell, Davis Lewis and Tommy Milton, who won the 300-mile Elgin in 1919. A year later the Duesenbergs were third and fourth at Indianapolis. A special 16-cylinder Duesenberg driven by Milton set a world record of 158 m.p.h. at Daytona Beach; Murphy won the French Grand Prix in 1921, the first time an American had done this. The cars won at Indianapolis in 1924, 1925 and 1927. The over-all record is amazing, the car being placed 24 times in 27 major races.

Like so many designers and builders, the Dueser.-

bergs were not equal to the financial problems besetting the production of automobiles. The car bearing their name was in production about 16 years and ranged in cost from $6,500 to $25,000, which reduced their market considerably. They sold their interests to Willys and formed a new organization to build their famous racing cars. Their great masterwork was the Model SJ, which, Fred felt, was equal in every way to the Rolls-Royce or Daimler—but much faster.

Fred was a meticulous and daring tinkerer with engines, explaining that this was the only way to find any faults. His way was explained by an old friend, John W. Watson, who remembered one such tinkering job "when Fred perched himself out on the left front fender where he could reach into the motor to work with some test valves and watch the oil gauges which he had rigged up to show the pressures and temperatures. I think we did about 25 miles on that stretch and stayed at a speed of about 60 m.p.h. while Fred was on that fender."

Fred continued to work toward improvements until he died as a result of injuries in a highway accident in 1932. The cars he left behind are still cherished, many of them still with their original owners. Their reputation carried over so well that a strong attempt was made in 1947 to build them again in an enterprise backed by Marshal Merkes of Chicago and August Duesenberg. But to create them with their uncompromising quality was impossible at less than $25,000. There simply was no market. August Duesenberg died in 1955.

ENZO FERRARI

The man who has done more than any other since the war to make Italian automobiles the synonym for speed is afraid to ride in elevators. When he goes to the films, he insists on a seat as close to the exit as possible. Dedicated to speed throughout his adult life, both as a driver and as a builder, he regards his drivers as his sons but he has never seen his men or his machines race.

Commendatore Enzo Ferrari, the hermit of Modena, was born in February, 1898, to Adalgisa and Alfredo Ferrari in the town that is now his headquarters. His father had a little wood- and metal-working shop. There was another son, also Alfredo, who died during the First World War, in which Enzo Ferrari served as a member of an Alpine unit. Just before his military duty began, he had received his driver's licence, using a de Dion-Bouton.

Demobilized in 1919, Ferrari turned at once to the automobile industry for a livelihood and a career. Within a year he had joined Alfa Romeo and become a member of its racing team. He finished second in the 1920 Targa Florio and, the next year, had a first in the 4½-litre class. Thereafter his record was a series of over-all wins at various venues until he gave up driving in 1931.

Enzo Ferrari in the Targa Florio, 1923

But driving was by no means Ferrari's only interest in cars. He was constantly learning, not only on the course but also in the factory and the laboratory, soon becoming a member of Alfa's technical division and later finding out how cars were sold. Ultimately he became head of the marque's racing division, a post he held until Alfa Romeo withdrew from racing. In 1929 he founded his own racing team, the Scuderia Ferrari, and, while his favourite mounts were always Alfas, he also used Maseratis and other cars. His early drivers included Nuvolari, Baconin Borzacchini, Taruffi, Antonio Brivio and Count Trossi, later joined by Chiron, Dreyfus, Campari, Varzi, Caracciola, Farina—virtually every important racing name of the 1929–39 decade.

Even before the war Ferrari's influence crossed the ocean, when Nuvolari drove his Alfa to victory in the revived Vanderbilt Cup in 1936. Much of the Scuderia's consistent winning was the result of Ferrari's own constant experimentation with the cars he bought from the Alfa works, and his success was so marked that in 1938, when Ugo Gobbato, who was then managing director of Alfa Romeo, recognized the necessity for the factory to return officially to racing, Ferrari was entreated to resume his old post as racing manager. He brought back to Milan all his new developments of Alfa cars and a totally different 3-litre eight that he had begun to put through tests.

But by the end of 1940, when Italy was at war again, Ferrari had left Alfa for the second time and begun to build a car of his own. Two $1\frac{1}{2}$-litre 8-cylinder prototypes ran in that year's Mille Miglia. One was driven by Marchese Lotario Rangoni, the other by the son of one of Ferrari's best friends in his youth. The young driver was Alberto Ascari, who was to bring so many prizes to Modena and to do his best for the Prancing Horse at Indianapolis. But that was not to be until the war was over; meanwhile a series of troubles lay ahead for Ferrari. He had, of course, to forgo any further thought of building cars; his plant was moved from Modena to Maranello and turned over to industrial production. Of his staff of 100 workers, the majority were women. In 1944, the whole establishment was destroyed by an Allied aerial bombardment.

But, when peace returned the next year, Ferrari doggedly rebuilt his factory. To survive, he solicited contracts for the manufacture of machine tools; but his aspiration was the creation of a new V-12 that would bring the constructors' championship to Italy. Farina was testing the new 1500-c.c. car in practice for the G.P. di Piacenza in 1947 when he ran out of road and damaged the car so badly that it could not race. Franco Cortese had the second car and held the lead for 27 of the 30 laps of the race, until his fuel pump failed and he had to retire. But two weeks later Cortese took the same car out in front when the flag dropped for the Gran Premio di Roma and stayed there until the checkered flag signalled the first of the hundreds of victories that were to be inscribed on the records of Ferrari.

Every car that came out of Modena bore the famous Prancing Horse emblem. But Ferrari's adoption of this apt symbol goes back to his early races, and in fact even farther. When he won his first absolute victory, in 1923, a man and woman whom he did not know pressed forward in the admiring crowd around the young driver and asked a moment with him. Their eyes moist, they explained that they were the parents of Francesco Baracca, who had shot down 34 enemy planes in the First World War until his own machine hurtled him to flaming death. Among the wreckage there remained unharmed the crest he had always mounted on his planes, the Prancing Horse. Would not Ferrari, the couple implored him, carry their son's insigne thenceforward?

On every car Ferrari drove, the Prancing Horse rode high, and it was only natural, when he brought forth a marque of his own, that he should continue to use the embelm. Its victories since that day in 1923 have mounted almost a hundredfold above those of the slain hero it perpetuates. The cars of the Prancing Horse are Ferrari's whole life, especially since his only son, 24-year-old Alfredo, died of leukaemia in 1956, just when he was beginning to become a full colleague of his father. The new V-12 engine of 1958 was Alfredo's design and bears his nickname, Dino.

When those other sons of Ferrari, his drivers, lose one of their number to death, his grief is almost as great. He summons all his cars back to Maranello, locks himself away from everyone and agonizingly tries to determine whether what he is doing is morally right. Alberto Ascari's death while testing a Ferrari all but caused the Commendatore to liquidate his life's work. His anguish at the deaths of de Portago and Castellotti was hardly less. At such times it means nothing to him that he is his nation's pride, that other automobile makers voluntarily turn over to him their matériel. Even the devotion of his employees, who worked nights in their own time to build his cars while he made machine tools to pay their salaries, is all but forgotten.

"He is afraid for us," said his 1958 champion, Mike Hawthorn. "He cannot bear to see us take chances."

AMÉDÉE GORDINI

The man who has contributed perhaps as much as any other in history to the making of the great drivers of several generations enjoys the highest esteem in one of the smallest circles in the world, for only the most knowing of the *cognoscenti* seem to recognize the achievements of Amédée Gordini.

Nothing has ever been easy for Gordini; and, conversely, nothing has ever been strong enough to defeat him. Born June 23, 1899, in Bassano, near Bologna, in the Province of Emilia, he was one of five children whose father died when Amédée was 8, and just beginning to modify the few toys the family could afford. His other childhood pastime was repairing household utensils. It was at this time that he was introduced to the automobile, when the Giro d'Emilia went past his front door and the little boy could almost have touched Lancia, Agnelli, Nazzaro and the rest as they roared by. One of those contestants was a man Gordini was to know later: Charles Faroux.

Gordini was a wage-earner at the age of 10, when he was apprenticed to a mechanic in Bologna. At

Amédée Gordini

the end of his 12-hour working day, he ran home to gulp a hasty meal and spend the evening in a special class organized by the local schoolmaster for boys who could not afford the education to which their native endowment entitled them. These classes continued when Gordini entered the FIAT branch factory in Bologna, where his training consisted of cleaning parts and sweeping floors. But the boy's eagerness to learn won the attention of Eduardo Weber, who was to become famous for his carburetters. When Gordini left FIAT at 14 to join Isotta-Fraschini, he had the further good luck to become the *protégé* of Alfieri Maserati.

At 17 he became a soldier for the four years of the First World War, returning to Isotta, where in 1920 he built his first car. Somehow he had got hold of an abandoned Bianchi whose engine was restorable. Gordini built his own chassis for it and made it run well enough to attract the attention of Conte Moschi, a wealthy connoisseur of motor cars who promptly hired him. A year later Gordini, who was just 22, scored his first success with the help of a young motor-cycle rider who asked to be allowed to help him. The volunteer's name was Tazio Nuvolari.

Gordini had come upon an old Hispano-Suiza engine left over from the war. "It should put out about 160 h.p.," he told Nuvolari; but, when Gordini had reworked it, it produced 180 on the bench. Thereupon he designed a chassis and body for it, and Nuvolari, having found it satisfactory at Monza, took it to Brooklands. There the Hispano-Gordini was timed at just under 150 m.p.h. The builder, who had accompanied Nuvolari to England, stopped off in Paris on his way home, although he had already pushed his finances to the red line. It was a mistake Gordini made in Paris that was to give France one of her greatest car makers. Dining with friends, Gordini was charmed by some young ladies at a nearby table; he and his friends invited the girls to champagne, which is well known for its tendency to produce certain kinds of forgetfulness. As a result, Gordini had no money for his ticket to Italy, let alone the fine he had to pay after the *restaurateur* called the police.

In 1922 French law was more lenient than it is today concerning the employment of aliens, and he found a job with one Cattaneo, retired racing driver, aviation pioneer and Hispano expert. A close friendship sprang up almost immediately and survived when Gordini left in 1926 to establish a business of his own somewhat like those of such men as Porsche, Bindo and Ernesto Maserati and Abarth, which were created as firms that would make their names by devising modifications of existing machines. By this time Gordini had married and was already planning the education of his son, Aldo, who today is a frequent competitor in his father's cars.

With five men on his payroll, Gordini had no time to race and, what disturbed him more, no customers interested in racing. The closest he got to competition for some time was when he was asked to prepare a car to make the slowest possible time on Mont-Valérien. He found an old 6-h.p. FIAT that could be persuaded to run, worked it over and won the title of King of Crawling when the FIAT turned in the highest time for the 1500-ft. climb: $27\frac{3}{4}$ minutes, slower even than Prince Nicholas's Duesenberg, carefully prepared for the event by Gordini's friend, Cattaneo.

This new title gave Gordini no pride at all; now more than ever he felt compelled to prove that his talent lay in the other direction. He bought a 514 FIAT, modified and tuned it and entered it in the Paris–Nice Rally, losing because of the treachery of his chronometer. From then on he was interested only in racing. His budget limited him to a 995-c.c. SIMCA, which was a FIAT built in France under licence. Identical in appearance to FIAT's 508S Mille Miglia Balilla, Gordini's car was modified to produce 48 instead of 36 b.h.p. without adding a supercharger. It won the 1934 Bol d'Or against such specialized marques as Amilcar, M.G. and Salmson, all blown. But no one would pit for Gordini except his little boy, who was mechanic, timekeeper and pit manager for his dedicated father. Together these two went on to win their class at the 24 Hours of Spa, Rheims, Algiers and Provence.

His courage as well as his victories brought some change in the public attitude. José Scaron teamed with him for the 1938 Le Mans, where a refuelling infraction disqualified them, though another Gordini-SIMCA, a 500-c.c., won the first Annual Cup on the Index of Performance. The 1100-c.c. car came back the next year to win both the Index Cup and its Class Cup for Gordini and Scaron, and then people stopped calling Gordini the King of Crawling. Now he was the Sorcerer of the Automobile. He must indeed have had some magic, for he was able to conceal the 1939 car all through the war until he could freely bring it up to date for Wimille and Sommer to drive to fresh victories. These two men were his great friends and their deaths were heavy blows for Gordini. He himself stopped driving in 1947, handing over to his son; but he did not stop thinking in terms of competition. In 1951 Gordini abrogated his connection with SIMCA in order to be free to experiment without obligations; he began to work with *monoposto* grand-prix cars, which had engaged his attention five years earlier, as well as sports machines. Driven by such men as Fangio, Schell, Behra, Trintignant, the Gordinis made a name for themselves all over Europe and in Argentina; the little 1500-c.c. single-seater smashed the powerful Auto-Union's Mont-Ventoux record, storming the peak at better than a 60-m.p.h. average. In 1953 Gordini was made a *Chevalier de la Légion d'honneur*.

Like Georges Roesch, Gordini has always been a disciple of maximum simplicity coupled with maximum performance. His SIMCA modifications would add 25–30 per cent to horsepower by such means as altering cylinder heads and inclining valves without changing from pushrod to overhead-camshaft operation. Later he was to go to double overhead camshafts with adjustable tappets in all his engines; his crankshafts were to carry eight main bearings in 6-cylinder engines and ten mains in the 8-cylinder cars. The modifications that he conceived for the French Ford before it was taken over by SIMCA are equalled only by the 20–25 per cent power increase that he has made possible for the Dauphine.

Gordini's ingenuity is not restricted to engines. Much of his marque's coachwork is of his design, especially on competition cars; in addition, he has devised systems of both front and rear suspension that have been a decade in advance of his industry. The irony of Gordini's career has always been the invincible disparity between the capital of his intellect and that available to him at the bank.

J. A. GRÉGOIRE

Every Sunday morning, J. A. Grégoire, who is six months older than the century, appears at the Longchamps racecourse in Paris. He casts an appreciative eye at the familiar surroundings and then casually trots around the track for five miles. His muscles having been brought to their proper tone, Grégoire returns to his home and his other interests: building and designing automobiles; playing the piano; writing books; collecting fine art, and continuing his authoritative studies on wines and mushrooms. Each of these interests has its proper niche in the full life of Grégoire, who has been described by his intimates as reserved and aloof in the best Edwardian tradition.

Grégoire *père* was a railway engineer and a product of the École des Arts et Manufactures. He viewed

[*Courtesy of J. A. Grégoire*

J. A. Grégoire

the physical sciences as best for his son, and gave the young man a choice between studying at the École des Mines or the École Polytechnique. Young Grégoire selected the latter. After serving at the front in the First World War, Grégoire obtained his doctorate of laws and went to work in a textile factory. This palled on him soon, so he went prospecting in Madagascar. Tiring of that, he went back to Versailles and with some friends opened the Chantiers Garage. There he became acquainted with an Amilcar and a Bugatti, which he raced for fun, and developed an increasing interest in the motor car.

In 1926, he and his friend, Pierre Fenaille, built the Tracta racing car, which was one of the first front-wheel-drive cars ever made. The American Cord came two years later. The car was an immediate success. Grégoire drove it in many races, including four consecutive tries at Le Mans. From these experiences came his novel, 24 *heures au Mans*, which many reviewers considered semi-autobiographical. The car was also a commercial success. He sold patents of the front-wheel drive and Tracta joints to D.K.W. and Adler in Germany; Rosengart in France, who manufactured under an Adler Trumpf licence; André Citroën; the English Bendix Co., which during the Second World War equipped more than 600,000 Land Rover cars with the drive, and the New Process Corp in Syracuse, N.Y., which equipped about 300,000 jeeps with it, as well as many other military vehicles. In 1936, Grégoire designed the die-cast monocoque construction system that he mounted experimentally on an Adler. For Hotchkiss he designed the Amilcar Compound that created quite a stir during the 1937 Paris Automobile Show.

The Second World War found him as an artillery officer with a problem. The Hotchkiss people asked him to help in a programme of manufacture for the German army. He refused and was demobilized. During the occupation, he secretly designed the Aluminium Français-Grégoire, which weighed 8 cwt. and was able to carry four passengers at 60 miles an hour with a fuel consumption of 60 miles to the gallon. The designs of this car were sold to Kaiser in the United States and Harkness in Australia, and in France the Dyna-Panhard was based on this prototype. Grégoire continued to experiment and explore. In 1943 he surreptitiously built an electric car that set the world record, covering 160 miles at an average speed of 28 miles an hour without recharging. Seven years later, he designed a car with a turbine that won approval at the 1952 Paris Motor Show. In the years between he invented the Grégoire variable-rate suspension used in mass production by Renault, Berliet and Hotchkiss and by Cary Ltd. in England.

To the personal satisfaction of accomplishment was added the recognition of the industry. The Paris Academy of Science gave him the Montyon prize for mechanical engineering, and the Société Nationale pour l'Encouragement à l'Industrie gave him its gold medal, placing him in the company of Pasteur, de Lesseps and de Dion.

There is no connection between J. A. Grégoire and the earlier Grégoire car manufacturer, but J. A. confesses to a tiny falsehood during his school days. When his classmates would ask him whether his father made that car, rather than go into a long explanation he would reply: "No, it's my uncle."

The man who raced and the man who built has another facet that explains his Sunday romp around the track. He had a brilliant career as an athlete. He played a top game of rugby in the Stade Français and with school teams. In 1917 he won the national championship for the 100-metre race and in 1919 he represented France in the broad jump at the Inter-Allied Games. He is still an excellent tennis player. In addition to the Le Mans novel, in which he included his turbine car, Grégoire wrote a historical study and autobiography, *l'Aventure automobile*.

Grégoire's ramified activities may hold an excellent reason for his aloofness. Perhaps he is just too occupied to be otherwise.

DONALD HEALEY

The weather, the wind, the surface, the car and the driver were in historic harmony that day in August, 1956, on the Bonneville Salt Flats in Utah. Donald Healey, aged 57, expertly set the car of his own design in motion and proceeded to attain speed. He gripped the wheel with calculated calm as the friendly wind turned into a veritable gale. The needle climbed to 228 m.p.h. Healey held on

[*Courtesy of the Donald Healey Motor Co. Ltd.*

Donald M. Healey

as he sped through the timing device. When he completed his run he was told that he had been clocked officially at 203·06. This was perfectly satisfactory to him. He happily accepted the card that proved him to be a member (the 11th) in the 200-Miles-Per-Hour Club. Shortly afterward his firm announced that the supercharged and specially streamlined model he had driven for the record run was the prototype of the Austin-Healey 100-Six that became available to the public a month later.

Having tucked that achievement into the vast storehouse of his experience as a driver, designer and builder, Healey confessed that this was the biggest single thrill in his picturesque career: admission to the 200-Mile-Per-Hour Club. Thrills have been the fuel, the stinging stimulation in Healey's life. Starting at 16 with the Sopwith firm, he sought excitement in aeroplanes. At 17 he became a sergeant-pilot on anti-aircraft Zeppelin patrol. At 18, he was sent overseas with one of the first night bomber patrols and was shot down in error by British anti-aircraft, crashing behind his own lines and winding up with a severe case of shell shock. Invalided out after six months, he studied engineering and design and devoted his interest to automobiles.

After he had designed and tested racing cars, his enthusiasm for speed intensified as the effects of shell shock wore off. When he tried racing he found he had an immediate affinity for it and went at it with studied determination. After several casual rallies, he became a free lance and entered most of the important events in Europe. He won nine Alpine trials in succession and then went on to win the Monte Carlo Rally. The racing gave him the thrills he sought, but there was also the work at the drawing board and machine shop. His dual ability was appreciated by several firms for which he worked as a consultant in design and testing. He was technical director for Triumph, where his great creations were the Southern Cross and the legendary Dolomite eight. Driving one of these in a Monte Carlo Rally, he escaped unscratched when it was disintegrated by a train.

When the 1939 war broke out, Healey took charge of an aircraft carburetter for the British Ministry of Supply and later worked with the Humber Co. in the designing and testing of armoured cars. Meanwhile, deep in his mind, an idea and an ambition were forming. He felt that, when the war was over, the motoring public, or at least an intelligent section thereof, would be ready for an ultra-modern sports car, with a new type of suspension, light of weight and capable of 100 m.p.h. He had met a chassis designer, Achille Sampietro, at Humber, and they spent long nights orally creating their dream sports car, which took practical form not many years after. The Donald Healey Motor Co. was formed in 1945 and a shop was set up in an old R.A.F. hangar in Warwick. The car was quite successful, especially in America, where some 2000 were sold in four years.

But Healey loves to recall his greatest single sale. While driving one of his new cars near Oxford, he passed the local constable, who promptly gave chase and lost. Healey sent the chief constable a letter apologizing for the incident and enclosed a catalogue, suggesting the force might purchase such a car for the "speedier apprehension of criminals". The police force did not purchase such a car, but the constable did.

Healey continued to design and improve. The Nash-Healey was followed by the Healey 100, the Austin-Healey and the Sprite.

As a builder to drivers and a driver who builds, Healey has a philosophy toward the sport that should be a matter of record. "I don't think you could compete at record speeds," he holds, "unless you are a fatalist. I am. I know. If it's going to happen, it happens. That doesn't mean I think there is any great danger in racing. When a driver gets killed, it attracts a tremendous publicity which tends to exaggerate the incident of death. A car driver has as much chance of death travelling from London to Glasgow as he has in the Mille Miglia—which is the most hazardous race of them all." This is typical of his emotional approach to speed. After he broke the record at Bonneville, he remarked that "there is nothing particularly nerve-racking in going fast."

The oldest of his three sons is Healey's chief designer. The second son is in charge of the manufacturing of Healey speedboats and the third son is not in the business at all. Healey admitted that he would not have discouraged them if they had wanted to take up racing. "In fact," he reflected, "I am a bit disappointed none of them feels the inclination. In a way it would have been rather nice if one of them carried on the tradition—a Healey racing Healey automobiles."

ERNEST HENRY

The father of the modern competition engine died in obscurity, poverty and suffering. Those of his friends who had believed him dead and encountered him by sheer accident in 1950 after the six years of war—followed, for Henry, by five years in a hospital—barely recognized in the emaciated, one-legged man the creator of the immortal Peugeot and Ballot engines.

It was typical of Henry, in these months before his death on December 9, 1950, that he had made no effort to seek out old friends who might be counted on to help him. The modesty with which he had always viewed his own career was accompanied by a reserve that might well have been considered neurotic: not even the closest associates of Henry, the engineer, knew Henry, the man.

Born in Geneva on January 2, 1885, Henry completed his engineering studies there and served his apprenticeship in France. He was 27 before his name was known outside the factory where he worked: Peugeot. In 1912 appeared the first of the series of brilliant Henry designs that were to make Peugeot an almost monotonous victor on both sides of the Atlantic. The 1912 engine was considered too small for competition at 7·6 litres; but it was the brilliantly successful pioneer of the dual-valved cars with double overhead camshafts and valves inclined in hemispherical combustion chambers that were to set a pattern from which the Maserati and Ferrari engines of today have derived so much.

Convinced that the giant engine was doomed because of its cost, its weight and its fuel consumption, Henry was determined to equal or exceed its power potential with units only a fraction of its size. The 7·6-litre engine had given Georges Boillot victory in the 1912 Grand Prix de l'Automobile-Club de France. For the Circuit des Ardennes Henry conceived an engine less than half as big, the 2·9-litre (78 × 156) that René Thomas drove to victory in Belgium, that set a new Mont-Ventoux record and that established a number of other victories under Boillot and Zucarelli while Goux added to the lustre of the 7·6 car. With the 3-litre car Goux and Boillot went to Indianapolis in 1913 and came home with victory. During the next five years Mercedes and Peugeot were to carry on a long-drawn-out duel in the United States, the cars being privately owned by Americans. These Peugeots were enlarged to 4½ litres (92 × 169) but in all other respects they continued Henry's basic designs, including the multiple main bearings for the crankshaft and increased use of aluminium for greater lightness.

Henry spent the war years in France but, as a Swiss national, he was not subject to military duties. Throughout that period he was busy on the design of a new engine based on the principles of his Peugeots. Intolerant of any error in his calculations, he never spared himself at the drawing board, the desk or the bench, and he revised and tested

Jules Goux in Henry's 1912 Peugeot

constantly until he was confident of the new racing power plant. When racing resumed at Indianapolis, Thomas was invited to compete and asked Peugeot to provide a car. But in that first post-war year, 1919, Peugeot preferred not to risk the considerable investment entailed and Thomas cast about for another builder. He knew Ballot as a builder of robust engines for boats and planes as well as cars, but Ballot had never seemed interested in making automobiles other than taxis. Nonetheless, Thomas broached the subject to him and took Henry along as the convincing argument. Henry's new design was a 4·9 eight, within the Indianapolis formula, and Ballot decided to take the gamble. The ironic result we know: the Ballot's tyres could not sustain its speed and it was beaten by an earlier Henry creation, a 4½-litre Peugeot of 1914. Nonetheless, Henry's new Ballot set a new lap record of almost 110 m.p.h. before its tyres gave up.

Ballot had caught the racing fever and for 1920 Henry prepared a 3-litre eight, always holding fast to his inclined dual valving and twin overhead camshafts. He widened the space between inlet and exhaust valves, making it possible to fit the sparking plug between them at right angles to the piston crown. Bore and stroke were now 65 × 112, with dual magneto ignition. Ballot and Henry made the journey to Indianapolis to watch the cars. Some 30 miles before the end of the 500-mile race, when Ralph de Palma was far ahead of the pack in the new Ballot and two sister cars were among the next three contenders, Ballot was phrasing the cable he would send his office. Then de Palma ran out of petrol; when a mechanic poured in fresh fuel, the car caught fire. Chassagne, driving the second Ballot, was signalled to redeem the position, which had been seized by Gaston Chevrolet; as he swung out to pass Chevrolet, he hit a patch of oil and spun off the course. Thomas, on the third Ballot, did his best but Chevrolet had too great a lead to be overcome in the few remaining laps, and Henry returned bitterly to Paris.

He was perhaps too critical of himself and his creations. For the next few years, Henry's 3-litre and the new 2-litre four that was his last creation for Ballot were to dominate their classes in European racing and hill-climbs. For a long time Louis Coatalen of Sunbeam had held Henry in such high esteem that Coatalen's own designs were outspokenly called direct copies of Henry's; when Henry's 2-litre Ballots finished first and second in the 1921 Italian G.P. and broke the Gaillon hill-climb record, finishing one-two-three, Coatalen hired Henry to create a 2-litre Sunbeam for the Grand Prix de l'A.C.F. at Strasbourg. The result was a four in what was by now the classic Henry design, which the experts marked down as sure winner; but the cars failed to finish. Henry's 2-litre Ballot, however, though the works refused to compete any longer, was to go on for several years winning on numerous European courses.

Henry did not remain long with Sunbeam; nothing is known of his life thereafter, not even the date when he left the British firm, until his chance reappearance in 1950 just before his death. He loved to talk of his Peugeot and Ballot period with his friends; but the story of the next 30 years was his secret. At his death he was working in a Levallois engineering firm.

ANTOINE LAGO

Engineering and mechanics are so dominant a passion in the life of Major Antoine Lago—the rank dates from the First World War—that it is impossible to separate the work from the man. In his factory in Suresnes, he is as likely to be found working at a machine among his employees as hunched over a drawing-board or presiding at a directors' meeting. If he has a relaxation, it is hunting; but he would much rather be at Automobiles Talbot-Darracq S.A. or, as a close second choice, watching his cars at work in the hands of test drivers or racing pilots.

Lago was a director of Sunbeam-Talbot-Darracq in Wolverhampton in 1933 when the company asked him to take over at Suresnes while retaining the direction of the Sunbeam works. He had come to Sunbeam from the Wilson Self-Changing Gear Co. Ltd., of which he had been not only general manager but also a presiding technician. It was Lago who developed the Wilson pre-selector gearbox to one-pedal operation through the invention of a friction clutch operated by the accelerator, with a cam to keep the clutch disengaged when its use was not desired.

Racing and series production have always been closely related in Lago's view. When Rootes took over the S.-T.-D. combine in England, Lago retained control of Talbot-Darracq in France, free thereafter to combine racing activity and touring-car production as he thought they should be conducted. A firm believer in the theory that all makers benefit from the racing experiences—successes or failures—of any one, he aimed at creating cars that would require a minimum of maintenance and repair and that could be put back in top running order with the least expenditure of time, parts and money. His goal, in every car he has built, has been to obtain optimum performance in terms of speed, acceleration, roadholding, handling and braking. Therefore Lago has shied away from fully automatic transmission, preferring to exploit his touring and racing experience with the pre-selector gearbox that was equally successful for Georges Roesch's British Talbots. Yet his aeronautical background has impressed on him the potential of the turbine motor with its eventual elimination of the need for a gearbox of any kind.

His racing cars were derived directly from his 4½-litre production machines. By discovering weak-

Antoine Lago

nesses at high speeds, he believes, he has been able to perfect the vehicles he sells to everyday drivers, just as racing has enabled the metallurgist to improve his alloys and the rubber manufacturer to produce better tyres. "It is essential", Lago has declared, "to maintain a close and constant tie between the *bolide* and the customer's car. One is often tempted to break it in order to defeat a competitor whose sole concern is prestige and who therefore sends a monster to the track. But I have preferred to remain faithful to a principle that I believe to be essential: high performance has no true worth unless its results can be passed on to the average driver, who is not a virtuoso and can rarely command the constant services of a doctor of mechanics."

That is why Lago has refused to supercharge his cars. Always oriented toward increasing the market for the French automobile both at home and abroad, Lago has concentrated on producing quality cars at as low a price as high performance and durability will permit. "The goal to be attained", he believes, "is constantly higher performance with even smaller engines at continually diminishing costs."

VINCENZO LANCIA

When the fledgling F.I.A.T. company bought Ceirano & Co., there was no way of knowing that two of the most important assets purchased were a pair of young men. One was Felice Nazzaro, son of a small coal merchant; the other was his close friend and rival, Vincenzo Lancia, heir to a fortune.

Born in 1881, young Lancia had no desire to follow his father in the tinning of soup and meat products. The elder Lancia at last acquiesced, when Vincenzo baulked at entering the university, in his apprenticing himself to Ceirano. Disappointed as he was at his son's refusal to carry on the family enterprise, Lancia *padre* was himself a passionate inventor and must have been more than a little sympathetic.

Vincenzo Lancia was on Ceirano's payroll as a bookkeeper when F.I.A.T. took over; but, if a visitor wanted to find him, he would have wasted his time in the office. Lancia was in the shop, spending all his time in the fitting, testing and repairing of engines. As soon as Ceirano's Welleyes cars would run, Lancia test-drove them: his *flair* for both testing and exploiting a machine was notable from the beginning, and his ear was as sensitive to a false note from a noisy engine as it was to a mistake in the Wagnerian scores he loved so much. He was, by the way, an excellent singer.

F.I.A.T. at once appointed him chief tester. "In his hands", Count Biscaretti di Ruffia wrote, "every car either gave of its best or broke down under the strain." Whether testing on the road, thinking in the draughting room or driving flat-out on the course, Lancia had the power of intense concentration that for that moment completely cut off his normal joviality. His first racing victory was achieved on a 6-h.p. F.I.A.T. in 1900. His triumphs thereafter were numerous, but they were almost evenly matched by mechanical breakdowns, and Scott-Moncrieff observes that Lancia must have been the most frustrated driver of his time. Promoted to the post of technical adviser, he continued to test his theories and analyses on the course. In 1905 he finished fourth in the Vanderbilt Cup and made the fastest lap time; he was leading the field when a breakdown cost him 40 minutes of roadside repair and victory. The next year he set a number of records at Ormond Beach, Fla., and returned to the Vanderbilt Cup to finish second.

It was also in 1906 that he resigned from F.I.A.T. to set up his own works; but he continued to race for his former employers for the next two years. At the same time he occasionally raced his own new marque, scoring its first victory with a class win in a 20-km. record run in 1908; the time was 6 minutes 53·7 seconds. In 1910 he set a class record for the mile at Modena with a time of 49·4 seconds in the new Lancia.

As a driver no less than as a designer Lancia was an innovator. It was he whose style Nuvolari set himself to emulate: aggressive and fearless, Lancia went into a corner at maximum speed, repeatedly stabbing at his brakes and drifting to the very edge of the road before straightening. When he left F.I.A.T. to build his own cars, he turned his back on the

Vincenzo Lancia

prevailing trend to ever greater mastodons on wheels. "An about-face is essential," he declared; "I will lead it." Peak r.p.m. of his first 14-h.p. car was 1450 against the 800–1000 of most others; it had shaft instead of chain drive; a high-tension magneto provided its ignition; and it was light.

He fully expected a chilly reception, and he was not disappointed. Nor was he moved. He knew from the combination of racing experience and laboratory theory and experiment that he had chosen the correct track. By 1914 he had increased the horsepower of his "impracticable" cars to 35; a year earlier, again in defiance of industry-wide warnings, he introduced electric lighting as standard equipment. On the eve of the 1914 war he had the first automobile in Europe that was a complete integrally planned unit of engine, chassis and electrics into which his musical orientation helped him to infuse an infrangible harmony.

But for the next four years Lancia was restricted to war production. As soon as he could convert, however, he put into reality the dream he had perfected during that hiatus: his first V-engine, a 12 that could never be brought to fruition because of the taxation system then favoured all over Europe, which made multi-cylinder engines prohibitively expensive to licence.

He went back to the four, initiating a new method of model designations from the Greek alphabet. For no known reason, he began with Kappa (the modifications of the Kappa were to become the Dikappa and the Trikappa); but he was still absorbed with the promise that lay in his abortive V-12. And from this came Lancia's revolution of the automobile industry, the narrow V-4 Lambda with the world's

first production-car independent suspension—which is still in use on Lancia's products.

A restless perfectionist, Lancia could not relax his efforts to develop ever better machines, whether for pleasure or for burdens. His Omicron was the first light chassis powerfully enough engined to transport great loads of materials or large numbers of people; as truck and bus it became famous throughout Europe and the United Kingdom. Returning to the automobile, he doubled his Lambda into the 20-degree V-8 Dilambda, whose success began with the mere announcement of its coming, so accustomed was the world to Lancia's perfection by 1929. Constantly sensitive to the needs of the motoring world, he brought out the Artena and the Astura, less expensive machines that aimed to maintain the tradition of high quality even in a world-wide depression. At the same time he designed the huge Diesel-principled Ro, a great industrial vehicle fuelled with naphtha and endowed with an 8-speed gearbox so that it was equally adaptable to speed and weight.

The small car of today was foreseen by Lancia in the beginning of the 1930s, when he developed the Augusta, whose chassis and body were constructed as a unit. This was followed in 1936 by the 1350-c.c. Aprilia, large numbers of which in daily use today testify to the validity of Lancia's thinking in terms of the cheapest as well as the finest cars. With the Aprilia, Lancia brought full independent suspension within the range of even the most economical car owner, and these machines of the post-vintage period, even in their customary family-coachwork dress, are still capable of out-running many fast modern cars on roads where adhesion and cornering count for as much as acceleration and top speed.

Like Georges Roesch in England, Lancia believed in the maximum coupling of simplicity and efficiency; like Roesch, he was an aristocrat among engineers in his refusal to compromise with the highest standards. Deeply religious, he preferred actions to words as manifestations of his belief. Like Agnelli, Lancia was a pioneer in providing for the welfare of his employees not only in wages and working conditions but in establishing innumerable facilities for their enjoyment and benefit.

But all his life he had worked unstintingly, with that same untouchable concentration that had characterized his testing at Ceirano and his forceful driving in two worlds. His colleagues and his family begged him, in 1937, to take a holiday and a rest cure; they told him how ill he looked, how the strength was visibly leaving his huge body. He refused to believe them; he had too much to do; he was sure no one else would be as single-minded as he in carving out new ideas, safeguarding the growth of his company, anticipating the needs of his workers. Nonetheless the unflagging pleas began to move him; he would think about taking their advice, or at least seeking that of a physician. A week later, while he was still undecided, he died.

ALBERT LORY

The high-speed engine has been meat and drink and music and poetry to Albert Lory for most of his life. Born June 19, 1894, near Le Mans, he saw his first race at the Sarthe circuit when he was 12, and after that it was in vain that his parents tried to direct him to medicine as a profession and the violin as an accomplishment.

Lory was 20 when he was graduated from the École des Arts et Métiers in Angers as an engineer, just before the outbreak of the 1914–18 war. Rejected for military service because of his eyes, he worked briefly for Panhard and spent the rest of the war developing aviation engines for Salmson. For a short time after the Armistice he was connected with S.C.A.P. and then joined Delage, where his fame was to be solidly founded with the outstanding 2-litre and 1500-c.c. engines that won so many championships in the 1920s. Passionately devoted to solitude—even at his home in Vaucresson he spends most of his time alone—Lory had his own working quarters isolated from the rest of the Delage establishment.

When Delage was liquidated Lory joined the Société Nationale de Construction de Moteurs, for which, as France was falling in 1940, he was completing a 2000-h.p. aviation engine. But, when the Germans took over the factory, Lory resigned rather than contribute to their further successes, and for more than a year he was idle, spending his time in study at his birthplace. In 1942 he returned to work, concerning himself with the gas-generators that were adopted to propel the few automobiles still in use in France during the war. It was only in 1945 that he resumed work on internal-combustion units.

Joining the Arsénal de l'Aéronautique in 1945, Lory created a new 1500-c.c. V-8 racing engine, each block of which had two overhead camshafts. In bench tests it developed 266 h.p. at 7500 r.p.m. and, mounted in the short-lived car known as the C.T.A.-Arsénal, set a lap record at Montlhéry. Transmission problems remained to be overcome, however, and before the solution could be found the car was made obsolete by changes in the international formula. It was at the Arsenal that Lory met the woman who was to become his second wife and whose dominant impression of him is the intensity of his concentration on a problem. "When he works," Mme. Lory says, "no matter how great or how noisy the crowd around him, he is completely unaware of it."

The famous *Étoile filante* of Renault, which set a mark of almost 195 m.p.h. on the Utah salt flats, was another of Lory's creations. He had joined Renault in 1949 as a research director with special attention to turbines, and in 1956 he took his family to Utah to observe the tests. Both he and his wife have a distaste for flying and the 10,000-mile round trip was made entirely by surface transport. In the United States as at home, Lory kept largely to himself. He does not enjoy society—he visits Paris

[*Courtesy of Mme. S. Lory*

Albert Lory

perhaps twice a year—and he is not athletic, though he occasionally likes to watch tennis, European football or billiards; Mme. Lory attributes his aversion to the more brutal contact sports to his infinite gentleness of nature. His extreme individuality extends even to the cigarettes he smokes endlessly: he unwraps each and rerolls it in a paper of his own that pleases him better than the manufacturer's choice.

THE MASERATI BROTHERS

The six Maserati boys could watch their father every day from their native town of Voghera as he drove his powerful Krupp locomotive through the countryside. For five of them he was a symbol that was to determine their lives; Mario, fourth in order of birth, had no deep love for speed or machines and became an artist. But Carlo, Bindo, Alfieri, Ettore and Ernesto were dedicated to motors.

Carlo was the eldest. His favourite childhood game was the building of little machines of wood that ran only in his imagination. From these he progressed to a miniature steam engine that snorted formidably and occasionally shrilled a whistle. When he grew older, he got a job in a bicycle factory, to which he commuted on a horse-car. But to Carlo Maserati muscle, whether equine or human, was a poor source of power. In 1898 he obtained a loan from the Marchese Carcano di Anzano del Parco and used it to build his first engine, a single-cylinder unit intended

Ernesto Maserati

to be mounted in bicycles. So installed, it proved itself capable of some 35 m.p.h.

Admired and emulated by all his brothers except Mario, Carlo left the bicycle factory for a job with F.I.A.T. From there he progressed to Bianchi, then to Isotta-Fraschini and finally to Iunior, of which he became managing director. Meanwhile he had become a racing driver, and had won a German race in 1900 on a Bianchi. He was keenly interested in the early aeronautical experiments and was busy on designs for an aeroplane engine when he died at an early age, leaving to Alfieri, the third Maserati, his dreams and his injunction to continue.

Alfieri was then with Isotta as an engineer and racing driver. He had been a winner at Dieppe and he was eager to expand his activities. In 1910 he went to Buenos Aires to represent Isotta there with Ettore. For two years the brothers made and discarded plans for a racing car; in 1912 they returned to Italy and settled in Bologna, continuing their researches until war intervened. All the brothers served in the Italian army; after the armistice, Bindo, who was now the eldest, joined Alfieri and Ettore, resigning his post as chief test driver for Isotta. Ernesto, the youngest brother, who had also made a name as a technician and a racing driver, allied himself with the others. For years they worked together with the precision of Swiss watchmakers, outlawing all non-functional decoration from their designs, until in 1926 they had produced the car that won its class in the Targa Florio on its début, driven by Alfieri and Guerrino Bertocchi. Six years later Alfieri was dead, as the result of an accident in a later Targa.

Not long afterward, Ettore withdrew from the firm. Bindo and Ernesto continued to build the fantastic Maseratis until 1937, when Commendatore Adolfo Orsi bought them out and moved the factory to Modena. For the next ten years the two remaining Maserati brothers continued their connection with the marque as consultants, but in 1947 there was a rupture with Orsi and the brothers retired to Bologna. There they founded the O.S.C.A. firm, which they have developed into one of the premier builders of fast 750-, 1100- and 1500-c.c. cars. On their own once more, Bindo and Ernesto have returned to the meticulous perfectionism that marked the early years of the four brothers' co-operation in Modena, working among their 40 artist-mechanics with the constant motto: "Never hurry the job."

Beloved throughout the racing world, perhaps the Maserati brothers received their greatest tribute when they were asked to prepare factory-team Ferraris.

WILHELM MAYBACH

Wilhelm Maybach, the second of five sons of a master cabinet maker in the tiny industrial town of Heilbronn, Württemberg, was born on February 9, 1846. His parents died before he was ten, and he was taken to the larger city of Reutlingen under the care of the Gustav Werner Foundation. He yielded naturally to the friendly but firm discipline of the school, and, showing an easy aptitude for drawing, he was apprenticed to the draughting office of the factory to which the foundation was attached. When he manifested a modest ambition to advance himself, he was sent to an evening college where he took up languages and general engineering.

It may be speculated here that Reutlingen was a crossroads of destiny in the history of the automobile. It is a fact, however, that it was in Reutlingen that Maybach, the quiet and modest journeyman of the drawing board, met Gottlieb Daimler, a fiercely serious-minded young engineer who loved Schiller, singing and robust humour, and who had a firm feeling that the days of steam power were short in number. Werner, a social reformer, who ran the Bruderhaus factory on the lines of Fabian philosophy, attracted Daimler as general manager. Daimler stepped up production and showed a good profit for Werner, but, it is believed, at some sacrifice of the Fabian movement. There was a disagreement and Daimler resigned—not, however, before persuading Maybach to come with him to the Deutz Gas Engine Works of Otto & Langen as chief draughtsman. Thereafter, the association of Maybach and Daimler remained unbroken until the death of the latter. It was a clear case of two personalities dovetailing so finely that nothing could put them asunder.

Daimler was one of the early creators of the internal-combustion engine. Before him, in 1885, Karl Benz had conceived and constructed the world's first complete motor-driven vehicle, a 3-wheeled affair with a petrol engine, which he drove through the streets of Munich.

But the man generally credited with putting on the road a vehicle powered by an internal-combustion engine which ran on petroleum was Siegfried Marcus,

[Courtesy of Daimler-Benz A.G.

Wilhelm Maybach

a German-born Austrian, who tried out his machine on April 9, 1865, the day that the Civil War in America came to an end at Appomattox Court House. On the parade ground of Schmelz, in the western suburbs of Vienna, stood a wheelbarrow with a tall frame mounted over its high rear wheels and an awkward-looking contraption hanging inside the frame. Erwin Lessner, in his *Famous Auto Races and Rallies*, describes it as "reminiscent of a movable guillotine. Mr. Marcus began to crank one wheel. At first nothing happened, but then groaning sounds came from the gadget. Suddenly there was the sound of an explosion, and yet another, and then a chain of explosions. The wheels began to rotate of their own accord. A helper who had been holding the wheels in the air lowered them. Marcus jumped aboard and the wheelbarrow covered about 150 yards in two minutes."

Marcus, like Thomas Edison, was a practical inventor. A grammar-school graduate with a strong passion for the secrets of electricity, he was determined to invent an electric light. He was not aware of his momentous invention. He did have a photograph taken of his machine and then abandoned it in the courtyard of 107 Mariahilferstrasse, where boys from the neighbourhood used it as a rare toy,

gradually dismantling it. It is know that the engine was a two-stroke machine which was geared directly to the wheels. Perhaps what discouraged Marcus most was the cost of the fuel he used.

In 1874, after he had become a successful inventor, amassed a comfortable fortune and been appointed instructor in physics to Crown Prince Rudolf, he returned to the car as a hobby. He created a more complex design with a 4-cycle engine mounted on a wooden chassis and having a jet carburetter, a throttle and a workable electrical ignition system. He drove his "Strassenwagen" a year later in broad daylight and was swamped with public and police protests. It was ruled he could drive this weird vehicle only at night. Even though he was plied with praise and honours, Marcus was never impressed with the car, calling it a "waste of time and money".

It has been assumed that Daimler worked independently of Benz and Benz worked independently of Marcus in their quest for the internal-combustion engine. As Daimler progressed step by step in his search for a functional power plant, Maybach followed him. Daimler dreamed and drove himself and his workers; Maybach laboured quietly to bring these dreams to fruition. Their first success was a vertical engine of $1\frac{1}{2}$ horsepower, air-cooled, with tube ignition, which they attached to an ordinary carriage. It was a limited success. There followed construction of a tram road carriage and in 1888 a public taxi, the first in the world. These innovations brought commercial rewards, leaving Maybach more time for his ultimate design of a vehicle powered by an internal-combustion engine that would in no manner resemble the demented little carriage that ran without horses. Sheets with intricate drawings and diagrams rolled off his draughting board. He designed a motor for a boat that was quite functional and from which he learned a great deal. In 1898 and 1899 Maybach and Daimler came up with the Cannstatt-Daimler racing car, a 28-h.p. vehicle that was too heavy, ungainly, unmanageable and dangerous. Its wheelbase was too short; the body was too high; and before any modifications could be planned, a foreman of the factory was killed while racing it.

Paul Daimler, a son, had designed a small racing car of six horsepower which evoked a great deal of speculation in the motor car world. Its gearbox and crankcase were cast in one piece; it had four speeds and a reverse and the gear lever was on the steering column. It had a foot accelerator. Paul never quite finished the car because he left to take a job as manager of the Austrian Daimler Motor Co., and the development and other innovations were left to Maybach. The inspiration was patently present. Maybach started work on plans for a new type of vehicle—a dual-purpose car which could be used for racing and normal driving.

As Maybach wrought with tenacious travail, and the drawings went from his table to the machine shop, rumours were heard in France and in England that a wonderful machine, new and revolutionary,

Courtesy of Daimler-Benz A.G.]

Paul Daimler

was being created at Cannstatt and that it would be given the name of Mercedes. Paul Meyan, a leading motor-car historian of the time, wrote in *La France Automobile*: "The chief advantage of this car lies in its lightness. The metal used is an alloy of magnesium and aluminium termed magnalium. Further advantages are the long wheelbase, mechanically operated inlet valves, low tension electric ignition, a new and improved type of carburetter, and improvements in the cooling system in which only six litres of water are sufficient to cool the engine."

Maybach had truly wrought heroically. He created the spray carburetter, the honeycomb radiator and the change-speed gear, which are used in cars built today. The cylinder and cylinder-head of the Mercedes were cast in a single piece. The bore and stroke were 116 × 140 mm. and the horsepower was 35 at 1,000 revolutions. At the moment of its first appearance, the Mercedes made every motor car in the world obsolete, and it was not long before its design was copied by others who did not overlook the raked steering post and long, low sweep.

The quiet man from Heilbronn continued to labour at the drawing board of Daimler, who died in 1900. He designed the powerful 120-h.p. 4-cylinder racer of 1904 and a year later went to 123 h.p. He continued to improve the product until 1907, when he finally yielded to an almost forgotten ambition to have a small factory of his own. He had met

Count Zeppelin, the pioneer of dirigibles, through Gottlieb Daimler, and a strong bond of admiration had held the two after Daimler's death.

At the age of 61, he opened his factory at Schaffhausen with a contract from Zeppelin. In 1908 he designed the first engine for the dirigibles that were to become world-famous. He did not leave the field of motor cars, however, continuing to construct automobiles of superb quality in the class of the Hispano-Suiza and Rolls-Royce. The cars had two drawbacks in the commercial field. One was their too-generous size and the other was the complexity of the engines, which could be serviced only by specially trained mechanics. Shortly before Maybach's death on December 30, 1929, his factory at Friedrichshafen announced the creation of a new type of automobile fitted with a very versatile engine of 12 cylinders, based on experience gathered in building Zeppelin motors. The great economic depression that followed that fateful year prevented the new Maybach car from becoming a commercial reality.

Contemporaries have noted that Maybach's personality was always in the shadow of Daimler; that the two were inseparable, socially and professionally. Daimler was the more volatile, the man who got things done. But Maybach was the more articulate of the two when it came to the drawing board. He was able to take an ambitious idea and transmute it into a practical piece of machinery. Every automobile from the day of the first Mercedes attests to that.

LAURENCE H. POMEROY

In the early days of the motor car, when most of the designer-builders worked with elemental enthusiasm, mechanical instinct and inherent ability, trusting to arduous trial and error to bring them the desired result, it was rare to find among them a professional engineer. One of the first in the field was Laurence Henry Pomeroy, who became apprenticed at 16 to the North London Locomotive Works at Bow while starting a four-year engineering course at the East London Technical College. While Bugatti at 17 was building cars, Pomeroy applied himself diligently to his studies. How diligently is found in an excerpt from a talk he gave many years later to a group of young engineers.

"The ordinary apprentice, if he wants to become anything at all," Pomeroy said, "should be prepared to put in evening classes three nights a week for two or three hours each night, and on the remaining nights he should be prepared to put in two or three hours of homework. If he is up at 5 in the morning and knocks off at 6 at night and puts in this amount of work at evening classes, he will not have very much time left for himself when the hours of rest are taken into account, but unless a lad is prepared absolutely to devote himself to the profession he does not deserve to get on."

At 20, he took his first job with Humphreys & Co., civil engineers in London's Victoria Street, then went to Thornycrofts of Basingstoke, where he became acquainted with vehicles on a professional level. In 1906 he became assistant to the chief engineer at Vauxhall Motors, Luton, which had been making cars of indifferent quality, but was ready to improve the breed for the 2000-mile Trial of the Royal Automobile Club. While the firm's chief engineer was on vacation in Egypt, Pomeroy applied himself to a new design with 38 b.h.p. at 2500 r.p.m. (90 × 120 mm.).

In the 13 days of the R.A.C. Trial the car needed no stops for lubrication or tyres, averaged 26 miles to the gallon and showed a time of 37 seconds less than any car in its class during hill-climbs. Pomeroy went on with improved designs, using his engineering background to propound certain dogmas by which he wrought, such as: "Rolls-Royce is a triumph of workmanship over design", and, by inference, "no design is good unless it can stand a liberal dose of bad workmanship". By 1909 he was works manager of Vauxhall; two years later he became a member of the Council of the Institution of Automobile Engineers and won the Crompton gold medal. He was 28 then. Two years later he became a full member of the Institution of Mechanical Engineers, the youngest man to get that honour.

Pomeroy's son, Laurence, points out in his biography that the "social philosophy and negligible taxation of the Edwardian age made it possible for the successful man to earn and enjoy a substantial differential above the average salary. The chief engineers of the time lived on terms of financial equality with all but the richest of car users and could appreciate motoring from their customers' point of view. This led L. H. P. to build really fast cars which could be maintained by a new generation of young enthusiasts who did not enjoy the services of chauffeur-mechanics and which would also run for very large mileages without wear or the need for adjustment."

L. H. P., as his son called him, designed the important Prince Henry Vauxhall, named after the famous big Continental event that was won by Ferdinand Porsche in an Austro-Daimler. But the Vauxhall's beauty and performance were the talk of the trial. The Prince Henry was a souped-up old 20, made to turn at 2370 r.p.m., with the distinguished V-radiator. It won many victories for amateur drivers and the works team. As late as 1956 two of these old cars were still in use. One was discovered by Tony Brooke and was restored. The other was presented to Laurence Pomeroy, Jr., by the original owner. Brooke's discovery won over all American cars in the 1954 Vintage Rally.

Pomeroy left Vauxhall in 1920 after he had created the immortal 30/98, going to America, where he went to work for the Aluminum Company of America. He evolved a number of technically interesting automobiles that excited a great deal of speculation, but never reached the commercial pro-

duction stage. He went back to England in 1929 as managing director of Daimler, where he reorganized the design and introduced the fluid flywheel in conjunction with the pre-selector gearbox. He also replaced the Knight engine with conventional overhead valve units.

Excellence in design, performance and service were the guides in Pomeroy's career. It is truly fitting that the Vintage Sports-Car Club conducts a series of trials awarding the Pomeroy Memorial Trophy to the car that proves itself to possess the greatest all-round excellence regardless of age.

FERDINAND PORSCHE

Fundamentally, Dr. Ferdinand Porsche was an engine man. Those who observed him say they could see his eyes grow brighter as he listened to the purr or the roar of one of his creations, making mental notes of what had to be adjusted, changed or redesigned. Some have called him a martinet in his pursuit of perfection, but a listing of his accomplishments is enough to dispel any criticism of his method or manner. Porsche fathered the Volkswagen, Cisitalia, Porsche, Steyr, Austro-Daimler, the torsion bar and the swing axle. He designed and built buses and trucks, the Wanderer and the fabulous rear-engined Auto-Union.

He worked hard and faithfully at his drawing board, in the machine shop or even the pits to make certain that his machines performed as promised. He was a prim little man with an amiable moustache and a sharp twinkle that could become a bolt of electricity when he chose. His attire was almost a trademark. He would wear a loose-fitting tweed suit with giant patch pockets and a cloth cap pulled down to his ears. At races, a pair of binoculars would hang from his neck and a pair of goggles would be perched on top of his cap. His demeanour was one of intense dignity and concentration, a trait he might have inherited from his father, one of the gifted technicians in the textile field.

Porsche was born September 4, 1875, in Maffersdorf, near Reichenberg. By the time he was 22, the automobile fever had gripped the world and he gravitated toward that field. After serving an apprenticeship with Brown Boveri, he rose to a high position in the testing department. Five years later he joined the *Hofkutschenfabrik*, where he met Jacob Lohner, who was then interested in an electric automobile. Porsche went at the task with typical intensity and in 1900, when the vehicle was exhibited at the Paris Fair, it became the wonder of the day. Porsche then contrived a vehicle that was powered by a petrol engine coupled to a dynamo that sent current to a motor built into the back axle. This car, known as the Mercédès-Mixte or Lohner-Porsche, had an infinitely variable transmission; it was regarded as a clever piece of engineering, but according to

[*Courtesy of Wiener Technisches Museum*

Ferdinand Porsche

the other was Porsche's refusal to design a new type of racing automobile for France. The French made friendly and generous overtures to the prisoner, but, whether it was pique or patriotism, the little man from Maffersdorf remained obdurate. The authorities, pressed by political passions, decided to wait. The impasse was broken by Raymond Sommer, the great racing driver, who rated against the waste of keeping the engineering genius behind bars. He interested Charles Faroux, the creator of Le Mans, to use his formidable influence in the cause. The money was raised to pay the heavy fine and the ailing Porsche was released after almost two years.

He returned to Kärnten (Carinthia) in southern Austria near the Tyrol, where he built the Cisitalia with 4-wheel drive and a 1·5-litre 12-cylinder blown engine. He continued to toil at the drawing board and shops and after many months created a new sports car to which he gave the name of Porsche. It was the 1100-c.c. type 356, which became the forerunner of today's car. He continued to work on the improvement of his newest creation until his death on January 30, 1951.

Scott-Moncrieff, "its great weight and extreme complexity made it quite unsuitable for racing".

In 1906, Porsche became technical director of Austro-Daimler in Wiener-Neustadt, where, among other achievements, he built a car for the Prince Henry Trial of 1910 with which Austria carried off a sensational number of prizes. It is interesting to recall that at this time Porsche did some racing and road testing himself, and one of his mechanics was an able and cheerful young man named Josip Broz —better known today as Tito, the Yugoslav dictator. During World War I, he wrought patriotically for Skoda-Mörser, applying the principle of benzine-driven generators to heavy vehicles. When the war ended he became director-general of Austro-Daimler, being rewarded with an honorary doctorate by the Vienna Technical College. He got his next doctorate from the Technical College at Stuttgart five years later, when he went to work at Daimler, later Daimler-Benz. There he designed the blown 2-litre sports car that won the 1924 Targa Florio. After a short term with the Steyr works he returned to Stuttgart and set up a research bureau with a small but highly qualified staff of engineers. It was there that the first plans were made for the Volkswagen, the 1·86-litre and 2-litre Wanderer and the Auto-Union. One of the outstanding results of this concentrated research was the torsion-bar suspension.

When the second war broke out, the Volkswagen idea evolved into motor boats and service vehicles. Again Porsche worked hard for his country and at the end of the war he was arrested and imprisoned by the American authorities. He was soon released, but the French arrested him and sent him to a prison at Dijon. They had apparently two reasons for this: one was punishment for all who had aided Hitler;

GEORGES ROESCH

When the prosperity of the 1920s was at the height from which so many believed it could go only higher, Stuart Chase wrote a thoughtful magazine article devoted to the thesis that integrity was a luxury that few could afford. One of the few who refuse to compromise their integrity is Georges Roesch.

Born in Geneva in 1891, Roesch virtually grew up with the automobile. In the admirable Continental fashion—which is also the British—he not only took a degree in engineering but also served a rigorous apprenticeship. His mentor was his father, a pioneer in the field of the internal combustion engine. From Switzerland Roesch went to Paris, at that time the world centre of the automobile and aviation industries, and studied under Marius Barbarou and Louis Renault. Early in 1914 he went to England, where he joined Daimler; two years later he was appointed chief engineer for Clément-Talbot Ltd. After the war he returned to France, working with Talbot-Darracq, until he was recalled to England to create the great cars that culminated in the Talbots that won at Le Mans, Brooklands, the Tourist Trophy and the Alpine Rally. His connection with the marque was severed when it was absorbed by Rootes. During the 1939–45 war Roesch was chief mechanical engineer at Britain's National Gas Turbine Establishment, and subsequently he became a consultant on the development of small industrial gas turbines for the British Ministry of Supply. A widower, he finds motoring and mountaineering his most satisfying relaxations.

Simplicity and efficiency have been the two guiding principles of all Roesch's designs. His Talbot 14/45 of 1925 was based on applying fundamentals in the simplest way possible to produce maximum efficiency, and many of the innovations of those cars were to become standard after the war, while others are still far in advance of current practice—for example, Roesch's practice of mounting the radiator directly and rigidly on the cylinder block to eliminate perishable water hoses and the large relative movement between engine and radiator. Cooling problems interested him particularly and he was the first to employ pressurized systems in production cars, in 1929.

Roesch's genius extended to virtually every aspect of the automobile. Lubrication was of paramount importance in Roesch's designs, and parallel with it was protection against the intrusion of foreign matter. As long ago as 1916 he evolved the now universal sealed steering-rod ball joint; his rod was tubular and, once filled with oil, it needed no attention for 15,000 miles. His overhead valve chamber was in direct communication with the crankcase. A hand pump next to the oil filler made it possible, with a single stroke, to lubricate the entire front end, including springs and steering. The engine automatically oiled the clutch-withdrawal and brake mechanism as well as the gearbox and the transmission universal, these being enclosed in the torque tube.

Even the amenities were considered in Roesch's creations. As early as 1926 he fitted electric direction signals as standard. Long before others recognized the inefficiency of the windscreen wiper that pushed water up so that it must immediately fall back in the driver's line of sight, Roesch was mounting the

[*Courtesy of G. Roesch*

Georges Roesch

wipers at the bottom of the screen to eliminate the steady cascade on the glass. His sports cars of the 1930s mounted oil-level gauges on the dashboards.

His passion was engine design, and he was building standard cars with 10:1 compression when 6·5 was considered very high; on his 110 Talbot the ratio was 11·4:1. Roesch fully appreciated, according to experts, the advantages of operating at as high a compression ratio as possible, providing sufficient mechanical stiffness, rigidity and symmetry and giving meticulous attention to valve temperatures. Valves were staggered, to allow them to be larger, and their seats were well cooled. Pistons were short and light, being composed of cast-iron skirts united by the wrist-pins to aluminium crowns. Crankshafts were heavily counterweighted and large-diameter narrow bearings gave stiffness. The pressure-relief valve did not allow the oil pump to pull more from the sump than was necessary to go through the bearings. H-shaped connecting rods were very stiff.

Twenty years ahead of the rest of the industry, Roesch evolved a three-leaf-spring clutch design. His axle shafts with integrally forged flanges on which brake drums and wheels were mounted were equally in advance of most designers, who followed his lead only in the very late 1940s. Chassis design was also forward-looking, strictly defining the body space and providing for all wiring to outside lights to be completely concealed; the lights themselves were mounted on flanges rather than the prevalent forks.

The chief test driver was a man who loved speed under all conditions—the designer. When a 3000-mile Continental test revealed weaknesses in constant flat-out driving of a kind that no ordinary owner was likely to do, Roesch eliminated them before putting the car into full production. The resulting Le Mans cars, according to the late Charles Faroux, France's outstanding authority, were "absolutely stupefying and never seen before". Aluminium-ringed brake drums, for greater cooling, were again two decades ahead of time. Roesch not only adopted but adapted the Wilson pre-selector gearbox to give all the advantages claimed for fully automatic transmission while retaining the equally valuable characteristics of constant driver control.

Roesch's radical changes were reflected in Clément-Talbot's books as well as its machines. The moribund concern was soon the Hercules of the Sunbeam-Talbot-Darracq combine, and as such it was rapidly exploited to keep Sunbeam and Darracq alive. The result was inevitable, as we have seen earlier. The swallowing of Talbot in the current tide of uncreative mass production has deprived the automobile industry of a pioneer whose thinking was economic as well as scientific and who long ago recognized as basic truth that not only Detroit but also Coventry would seemingly prefer to ignore: that more cars can be sold more cheaply when their design is up to the needs and the potential of their times.

Play the game of word association with any American in his middle years or over; mention the word *Stutz* and the reaction will almost invariably be *Bearcat*. The player will then go into a nostalgic trance and conjure up visions of raccoon coats, hip flasks, college kids roaring over country roads in search of thrills, a soaring stock market, speeding tickets and Prohibition. Unless he is a true enthusiast, he won't know that the Stutz Bearcat was one of the most remarkable cars ever made and that its builder, Harry C. Stutz, was one of the truly outstanding designers America has produced.

When Stutz built this car in 1914, he had neither the intention nor the premonition that his product would come to represent an era. Actually it began only as a part of the Series E cars that Stutz produced in 1914. He found out about the public's reaction to his masterpiece one spring day that year when his sales manager, William D. Myers, told him: "We're so far behind in orders that the last Stutz was sold yesterday." Myers then showed him a newspaper clipping reporting a race between an aeroplane and a Stutz. "Who won?" asked Stutz. "I'll try to find out," Myers replied. "It doesn't matter," Stutz said. "No plane can get around a corner as fast as a Bearcat."

This uninhibited confidence was part of the man's charm. Lean, trim, well-dressed, favouring blue neckties and blue shirts, Stutz never smoked, rarely drank, loved seafood and steaks in good company and was, on superficial appraisal, the very epitome of a successful American business man. Beneath this, however, was Harry Stutz, the inventor, the innovator, the lover of good machines who devoted all his almost limitless energy to the making of great automobiles.

He was born in Ansonia, Ohio, September 12, 1876, the second of four children, to Henry J. and Elizabeth Snyder Stutz, second-generation Americans who owned a small farm near Dayton. His first job was at $1·75 a day, building pump engines for farmers. He went to night school to supplement a grade-school education, took a correspondence course and worked at the Davis Sewing Machine Co. and at the National Cash Register Co. It was a wide-eyed, Horatio Alger era in America, and young Harry Stutz was very much a part of it. Before he was 21 he announced that his life's philosophy would be based on the motto of the U.S. Marines: "The unbelievable we do immediately. The impossible takes a little longer." Then, a few months later, he put together his first car. "Old Hickory" was born in 1897. It had as outstanding features a water-cooled engine and a transmission modified from sprockets and chains from an old wheat-binding machine. His mother's backyard yielded the chassis, an old buggy with high wheels. "Old Hickory" was unbelievable, but it ran.

Clara Dietz was an attractive brunette, blue-eyed

and 18, when she went ice skating in Dayton and met Harry Stutz. They had many loves in common —a liking for good things, a zest for interesting experiences and a sense of humour. They were married in 1898. Five years later they moved to Indianapolis, where Stutz took charge of the G. & J. Tire Co. and later became sales engineer of the Schebler Carburetor Co., where he designed the car that was known as the American Underslung. Then he rose to the job of chief engineer and factory manager of the Marion Motor Car Co., where he put to good use his earlier experience, which included a spell with the Lindsay Russel Axle Co. The famous Stutz combination of rear axle and transmission was a direct result of this.

He left the Marion firm in 1910 to form the Stutz Auto Parts Co. with Henry Campbell. This firm combined with his subsidiary, the Ideal Motor Car Corp., to form the Stutz Motor Car Co. He set up his family in a spacious house in fashionable Washington Boulevard in Indianapolis, giving his school-age daughter, Emma Belle, the most acceptable surroundings. Emma Belle, friends observed, was much like her father, not only in looks but in temperament and mannerisms. He loved music; he played the saxophone and cornet (self-taught) and, to make up for his lack of virtuosity in these instruments, accumulated a large collection of recordings. These were semi-classical, the *Barcarole* from *Contes d'Hoffman* holding Number One position.

Stutz thrived under the compulsion to leave no minute of his day blank. He conducted his business affairs during every waking moment and filled in the empty spaces with intense play. He was an excellent shot, winning honours at trap shooting; he went fishing and big-game hunting, and found free moments to be an enthusiast of spectator sports like baseball and motorboat racing. His love for travel helped in the development of the Stutz car. During a trip through Europe he visited France, England, Germany, Belgium and Holland, noting the many motor car competitions and their relation to sales. When he learned of the new 500-mile Indianapolis Sweepstakes he decided to enter his car. "If the car wins," he told Campbell, "more people are going to hear about it than could ever be reached through an expensive advertising campaign. If it doesn't win, it will get lost in the shuffle and we will have learned more from this one race than we could from 10,000 miles of road testing." With Gil Anderson in the cockpit, the car finished 11th after making ten pit stops for tyres, but its reputation was made because it finished the race without any mechanical trouble.

Stutz sold the company in 1919 after insurmountable financial problems. He organized the H.C.S. Motor Co., leaving it in 1926 to go to Florida and retirement. Emotional problems also entered his life at this time. After 27 years of marriage, he met Blanche Clark, an accomplished harpist who appeared frequently with the Indianapolis Symphony Orchestra.

They obtained divorces and married. The first Mrs. Stutz took the matter gracefully, but Blanche Clark's husband, Herbert J. Miller, unsuccessfully sued Stutz for $50,000, charging alienation of affections. Stutz and his new wife settled in Orlando, where they divided their time between their citrus farm and their 88-ft. cruiser, *Bella*. But work was definitely part of his leisure. He designed a new air-cooled engine for aeroplanes and there was talk that he would be associated with the Bellanca Airplane Co. in a new venture. In June, 1930, he suffered an attack of appendicitis in Orlando and was rushed to Indianapolis for an operation. He appeared to be improving after the surgery when an infection set in. He died June 26, 1930, leaving lovers of good cars a heritage of glamour and accomplishment that has yet to be equalled.

RUDOLF UHLENHAUT

The dignified directors of Mercedes-Benz were fearfully agitated when they heard about the incident. With solemnity proper for the occasion they called Dipl.-Ing. Rudolf Uhlenhaut, who confessed that in a moment of exuberance he had taken the powerful W125 around the track, setting a better lap speed than any of the professional drivers testing that day. The directors thereupon subjected Uhlenhaut to a severe dressing-down, informing him in very certain terms that, while cars and drivers were replaceable, engineers of his stature were not. They admired his verve, but gave him clear orders not to repeat the offence. It is not known whether Uhlenhaut complied completely, because those who know him point to his lively affection for racing. Drivers and pit masters who have observed him during "sneak" tests say he is of grand-prix calibre.

Uhlenhaut is the man behind the victory. The cheering crowds on the courses of the world saw the famous Mercedes drivers and Alfred Neubauer. Not one whit of credit or glory need be taken from these men to point out that these victories could not have taken place without Uhlenhaut. It is he who begins the design for a racing car, develops it, brings it to the shop and turns the finished product over to the racing manager. Among the many outstanding cars he has developed are the 300SL and the W163.

He was born in London in 1906, the son of a bank director. His mother was English. His parents sent him to Bremen, where he attended high school, and later to Munich, where he earned his diploma in engineering at the Technical College. In 1931 he became a research engineer in the Daimler-Benz factory at Untertürkheim, applying himself to the secrets of the internal-combustion problems and the springs and chassis that go to make up the most important parts of the vehicle.

Dr. Hans Nibel had designed the W125, an 8-cylinder 5·6-litre engine that had to be reduced

Rudolf Uhlenhaut

because the big-formula cars were losing favour. Because of his interest in racing and his exciting achievements at the drawing board, Uhlenhaut was transferred in 1936 to be chief of the firm's racing division. With Max Sailer, Uhlenhaut created a new grand-prix car known as the W163. Although it kept the tubular chassis of the W125, it had softer suspension, hydraulic shock absorbers and more efficient brakes. A new 3-litre engine drove the car through a 5-speed gearbox. The engine had 12 cylinders in V-shape and four overhead camshafts working four valves to a cylinder. The W163 ran at Indianapolis with Duke Nalon at the wheel in 1947, but the car did badly because the American mechanics were unfamiliar with the fine points. John Bentley recalls that, during "the fitful occasions when the machine decided to run on all 12 cylinders, it looked like a race horse galloping through a pack of mules".

During the war, Uhlenhaut did his patriotic share, and, when the débâcle ended, he was working for a Belgian truck company, where Raymond Sommer found him. When the Daimler-Benz factories had been rebuilt from the rubble, Uhlenhaut returned, devoting his energies to passenger cars until he was restored to his position in the racing division. Working with Neubauer, he proceeded to re-create the Mercedes racing strength, experimenting boldly and achieving the satisfaction of success. He is known as a tireless and meticulous master of design; a clear-thinking supervisor in the factory and a chief who will not ask any driver to try a car that he himself has not already tested, the board of directors to the contrary notwithstanding.

Like most men who are heavily occupied with their vocations, Dr. Uhlenhaut is a busy hobbyist.

He can mellow the exhilaration of the sport with long and quiet hours in his garden, where he has gained some repute as a horticulturist. And, when this becomes too placid, he can dash off to some mountain top where his skiing is regarded as better than amateur, or a lake or seashore where swimming will restore his desire to get back to the racing cars.

GABRIEL VOISIN

Gabriel Voisin, who designed and built the first French aeroplane that flew more than a kilometre at a height of 25 ft., earning fame and fortune (£2000 in 1908) for the pioneer aviator, Henry Farman, faced a quiet inner conflict when he decided to start the manufacturing of automobiles eight years later. The field of popular cars was beckoning with reasonable assurance of wealth and stability. However, as an artist and a highly competent engineer, Voisin realized that he would be happy only if he turned out motor cars that would reflect his temperament and his personality. He had no feeling for stamping innumerable machines out of a single mould. He sought elegance and individuality, manœuvring his designs so that cars, even of the same series, differed from one another in some detail of engine and body.

To view a Voisin in its pristine beauty was an awesome and gratifying experience. Only the finest material went into its light but strong chassis. The whole car exuded luxury with a Spartan paucity of frills and unnecessary trim. Jean de Dobbeleer, a historian of the marque, describes one car as it left the shops:

"There would be two oil pumps for the sump. The gas flow in the inlet manifold was so calculated that an equivalent amount of mixture was delivered to each cylinder. Both the gearbox and the universal joints were lubricated by special oil pumps. Two 12-volt batteries were provided, the lights operating from one, but both were employed when starting up the engine. If you wished to adjust the brakes this could be done, without dismounting, from the driver's seat. To eliminate valve noise and thereby increasing passenger comfort still more, he used Knight-type sleeve valves. The modern conception of a door lock on a quality car of today bears no resemblance to the magnificent and smooth operation of one on a Gabriel Voisin car."

For 17 years, Voisin created luxury cars and some racing cars, especially constructed to compete for class records. He built 6-cylinder racers for the French Grand Prix at Tours in 1923, the first ones to show early streamlining. He had to wait five years, however, before his cars, with the Knight-type sleeve valves, took the international record at 214 k.p.h. for 10 miles and 183 k.p.h. for 24 hours at Montlhéry. Voisin's cars were in the class of the Rolls-Royce, Minerva and the Hispano. His most

Courtesy of Compagnie Aéromécanique]

Gabriel Voisin in 1916

successful models were the 6-cylinders of 13, 17 and 32 horsepower. The cars were unquestionably a mixture of luxury and realism. Voisin frowned on gold-plate bumpers and leopard-skin upholstery, but the engines of his cars were enamelled and his wheels were of polished aluminium. His steering was the essence of precision; his engines purred peacefully at all speeds and the Servo Dewandre braking created a fine sense of security.

The dark depression days of the mid-thirties made the building of quality cars an insupportable luxury. After his visit to the United States he returned with acrid criticism of the "cans on wheels", but he found it less costly to buy the supercharged Graham engine for his chassis. He faded from the scene for a while, but in 1945 he returned with a bi-scooter car powered by a 125-c.c. engine.

"The dead go quickly," Voisin told the authors with some bitterness over the world's three decades of indifference to the man whose daring automotive pioneering was to have been expected from his aeronautical achievements. Not only was a Voisin plane the first to be officially clocked for a kilometre of flight, in 1908; later that year one of his machines made the first city-to-city flight—Châlons to Rheims.

With Bugatti, whose 1500-c.c. cars he called the Queens of the Road, Voisin is at the top of the proud, uncompromising artists of the motor age. He built for the glory of turning out a perfect automobile and the few cherished Voisins that survive speak for his accomplishment.

DRIVERS

Woolf Barnato and Sir Henry Birkin at Le Mans, 1929

THE BENTLEY BOYS

"I think it all began with the coming of the Bentley Boys. Their arrival and the recognition and growth of their legend cannot be timed from any particular date; the corps grew slowly . . . gathering new recruits on the way as our racing activities increased. . . . The hard core was made up of only a dozen or so, and most of these were sporting men of independent means . . . they attracted the public's fancy and added a touch of colour, of vicarious glamour and excitement to drab lives. . . . The public liked to imagine them living in expensive Mayfair flats with several mistresses and, of course, several very fast Bentleys, drinking champagne . . . playing the horses and stock exchange and beating furiously around the racing tracks. . . . Of at least several of these, this was not an inaccurate picture."

—W. O. Bentley

WOOLF BARNATO

Foremost was Woolf Barnato. Three times winner at Le Mans, he represented the heroic age in racing—when, in addition to skill and daring, sheer animal strength was required to manage the wheel, work the brakes and change tyres. Barnato, called Babe, was mule-skinner and mother to the cars he raced because he loved to win and he loved the machines.

Indeed, he loved many sports. Before he discovered the racing car he took up cricket, reaching the heights as wicket-keeper for Surrey. He once wagered £500 to £100 that he would reduce his golf handicap from seven to scratch in 12 months. He won.

W. O. said Barnato's "consuming passion in life was to excel. He was a fair but unyielding competitor. His physique made him a natural heavyweight boxer. When horsebreeding struck his fancy he took over the Ardenrun stables and brought home an impressive number of winners. He was a successful speedboat racer."

Barnato's background was at once humble and spectacular, W. O. relates. "His grandfather, with the uncompromising name of Isaac Isaacs, was a shopkeeper in the east end of London. His father, Barnett, was a dashing fiery fellow, who changed

225

the name to Barnato, bought a claim in the Kimberley Diamond Mine and wound up in joint control with Cecil Rhodes of all the Kimberley mines."

Woolf was two years old when his father vanished forever from a ship off the African coast. Babe inherited his father's dash and daring as well as his wealth and business ability. He proved this when he became a director of Bentley Motors, but he never allowed his high post with the firm to influence his obedience and discipline when he raced under the direction of W. O.

At Le Mans in 1928, Barnato drove the slowest team car. He had been told by W. O. to maintain station just behind Brisson's Stutz in order to rattle the highly temperamental Frenchman. Brisson was aware of this and for lap after lap he managed to wag his tail in order to shower the pursuing Barnato with stones from the poorly paved track. At last Barnato could not stand this any longer and, as the two cars approached the stands, he squeezed past the Stutz, his offside wheels in the gutter splashing water. As the two cars sped by, Barnato made a taunting gesture with his hand. The spectators roared with laughter, but on the next lap Babe, true to the discipline imposed upon him, resumed his position. Barnato won that race because, as S. C. H. Davis explains, his speed during the night was so little less than that during the day.

Barnato's millions, which kept the Bentley firm alive for many years, were reflected in his mode of living. He was as enthusiastic and intense in his social life as on the racecourse. Prodigious parties at his Grosvenor Square flat or his vast red-brick mansion at Ardenrun in Sussex were the talk of London, which still remembers the party celebrating his second and Bentley's fourth Le Mans victory, when, as W. O. recalls, "inebriated Bentley Boys were being pursued by Eton-cropped flappers in short-length evening dress". He was married three times and managed to get through some £800 or £900 a week, indulging in his favourite private pastime—the dramatic wager. At one of his parties in Cannes he wagered he could beat the crack Blue Train back to London. Thereupon he set off in his 6½ Bentley, drove non-stop to Calais, took the next boat to Dover and was in his flat four hours before the boat train pulled into Victoria Station.

"I think the danger of motor racing is greatly overrated", Barnato once wrote. "It is not as dangerous as it seems." Yet he did not care for ordinary track racing and avoided the more dangerous events. W. O. points out that what made Barnato such an outstanding driver—he called him the "best driver we ever had and the best British driver of his day"— were his keen eye and judgment, his courage, discretion and self-discipline. "At Mulsanne Corner on the Le Mans circuit it took a stop-watch to prove that he was the fastest driver around and not the slowest as he appeared to be," Bentley said.

Barnato entered Le Mans only three times and Davis calls his third successive victory—in 1930—

his greatest race. He and his partner, Glen Kidston, outmanoeuvred, outdrove and outlasted the Mercedes team.

In the 1930 Double-Twelve at Brooklands Barnato was leading the field in his 6½ Bentley when the track was struck by a sudden, violent hailstorm. The hailstones stung his face until it bled and he could hardly see through his goggles. Davis recalls it might have been easy for Babe to invent a reason for a pit stop—but that might have cost the race. After he had won the close contest Barnato explained that a "driver existed solely to do his utmost for the car, whatever the difficulties he might encounter".

When Barnato died in 1948, Bentley wrote of him: "His appealing appearance, his vitality, his restlessness and his complete self-assurance gave him irresistible charm. As a sportsman he was a determined, almost dedicated perfectionist. He was the epitome of the international sportsman-financier-playboy and no one could have had more fun in living this rôle."

DR. J. DUDLEY BENJAFIELD

J. Dudley Benjafield, Harley Street physician and bacteriologist, was a gentleman with a delightfully dual personality, who was able to move without inhibition from his dignified vocation to his exhilarating avocation—sports-car racing. As a specialist in London's St. George Hospital, he was deeply immersed in experiments on the effect of dental infections on certain diseases. When not doing research, he was a practising physician and consultant; and, when not engaged in any of these pursuits, he was Benjy, the fun-loving, impassioned driver of Bentley cars and beloved fellow of the Bentley Boys.

W. O. recalls their first meeting, when a "tough, thickset and totally bald" man came to the showroom to purchase a long-chassis 3-litre Bentley with which he had been impressed after reading about the 1924 victory at Le Mans. "He placed on it a saloon body large enough to kill all performance," W. O. remarked, "and then obtained the red two-seater which Clement had raced in 1923. This provided him with the speed he wanted, and with it he raced with such energy at Brooklands that we invited him to share the seat of a 3-litre at Le Mans the following year. After that he drove for us at Le Mans in 1926, 1927, 1928 and 1929, in the Six-Hour and Double-Twelve at Brooklands and in a number of other events. Benjy was one of our steadiest drivers, one of our most reliable, and an equally strong supporter of off-duty fun and games."

Dr. Benjafield enjoyed himself thoroughly in the company of the Bentley Boys, frequently giving small dinners to which the better-known drivers of England were invited. These gatherings grew in interest until they evolved into the British Racing Drivers' Club, with Benjafield in charge of the club's finances and organization. During excursions into the realm of nonsense, he was affectionately referred to by his colleagues as "our bald-headed apothecary".

Benjafield, son of a London doctor, was educated at Marlborough, a public school, and learned medicine at University College Hospital in London. He loved the contemplative sport of fishing and eagerly pursued the craze for miniature, power-driven aircraft, spending hours coaxing a demented two-stroke engine to greater heights. Later he moved on to power-driven miniature boats, which, according to Davis, "seemed to run out of fuel consistently in the centre of lakes on the coldest day of the year". Chiefly, though, he loved driving cars and would spend hours fitting special gadgets on them. His hobbies were followed with deep interest by the other Bentley Boys. Once he gave up smoking and the entire Bentley ménage concentrated on urging him to take it up again to exorcise a fierce temper. His son, Patrick, did not follow Benjafield in either medicine or motor sports. He is a well-known photographer.

With S. C. H. Davis, Benjafield won his greatest race—the 1927 Le Mans. Davis called him "the stoutest-hearted driver I have ever known. He had practically no mechanical knowledge, but could drive and keep going no matter what the troubles". His colleagues recalled that he was wonderful fun at all times except during the hours before a race. He worried and fretted and became humourously confused in his mechanical ineptness. It has been said, by too many witnesses to be mere legend, that Benjafield never found out which way the wheel centre-locks should be turned on a Bentley. But when the race began he was of a single mind and purpose and he confined all his fun to the joy of speed.

The Bentley team at the 1927 Le Mans consisted of three cars: a new $4\frac{1}{2}$-litre driven by Frank Clement and Leslie Callingham; a 3-litre driven by Baron d'Erlanger and George Duller and another 3-litre, known as Old Number 7, which carried the number 3 and was driven by Davis and Benjafield. As the race progressed during the early hours, the Bentleys, with deliberate celerity, were running one, two and three, as was expected by a decidedly weak opposition. Callingham was leading at 90 miles an hour as he approached the White House corner in the dark just after a small French car had gone into a spin. He wrecked the big Bentley, blocking the road, but managed to escape injury. Duller in the number two car roared around the corner, saw the road block and crashed into the stern of Callingham's car. Duller was hurled into the air, described a perfect parabola and fell on a field on the far side of the hedge. He, too, walked away unhurt, but by this time the corner was strewn with wreckage and covered with oil. Duller ran back to warn Davis, but it was too late—or so it seemed. Davis, however, warned by some instinct, had seen the skid marks and the beams of askew headlights pointed in unorthodox

Dr. J. D. Benjafield

directions. He slowed to 20 miles an hour and struck the wreckage with a minimum of shock.

Davis backed the car and drove off just as another came round the bend and crashed into the wreckage. When Benjafield took over, he found the car had a bent axle, a broken headlight, a crushed running board and assorted breakage. Brakes, steering and rear wings were in questionable condition. A lantern was hung on the windscreen and Benjafield continued with Davis through a nightmare of wind and rain. They shared the wheel between them, resting in the pits, where they were fortified by champagne and cold fowl. Filled with enthusiasm, champagne, cold chicken and determination, they thundered into the welcome dawn behind Jean Chassagne in an Ariès. They had to make up 43 miles and they did, passing the cleaned-up wreckage at White House without a shudder because they knew no one had been seriously injured. Benjafield, Davis and the old Bentley won that race to the amazement and satisfaction of almost all. The two drivers were guests of honour at a dinner in London's Savoy Hotel and at the height of the celebration a sudden hush came over the assemblage. The big doors drew open and there, for all to see, stood Old Number 7, its engine purring, but still bearing the scars and mud of Le Mans.

Benjafield was the doctor, confessor and sometime historian of the team. He wrote *The Bentleys at Le Mans*, nursed the BRDC, and went along on all the wild parties staged by Barnato, Birkin and Rubin. During all those activities he managed to find time and energy for the more dignified duties at Harley Street. It seemed to all who knew him that the learned Dr. Benjafield had successfully solved the secret of a dual-purpose personality.

When Tim Birkin—Sir Henry R. S. Birkin, Bart.—got behind the wheel of a racing car he was faultlessly attired in a dark blue sports shirt, white overalls, a distinctive spotted scarf and a wide, multi-strapped belt. To W. O. Bentley he represented the ultimate in courage, excitement and glamour. Bentley called Tim the Bentley Boy *par excellence*.

Birkin's money came from Nottingham lace and during most of his life he did not seem to have to work for it. His fellow-drivers admired and liked him and were tolerant of his two outstanding weaknesses—his tendency to play to the gallery and his utter ruthlessness toward the cars he drove.

"I know of nobody before or since who could tear up a piece of machinery so swiftly and completely as Tim," W. O. said. "During his terrific duel with Caracciola in the early stages of the 1930 Le Mans, he threw a tread just after passing the Mercedes on the grass verge, and then, to everyone's horror, instead of coming in to change the wheel, continued on the canvas without dropping speed. When he was finally forced to come in he was down to the rim, with the mudguard smashed all over the place."

Tim won twice at Le Mans, once with Barnato in 1929 and again in 1931 with a 2·3 supercharged Alfa Romeo. As a driver, S. C. H. Davis says, he believed wholeheartedly in putting his foot down, reckoning to control the most difficult car by any other means than bringing back the throttle; and, if ever there was a man who deliberately took a calculated risk, Tim was the man.

Birkin drove his first Bentley in the Brooklands Six-Hour Race in 1927 and continued in W. O.'s cars through 1930 and then again in 1932 when he established a lap record of 137·96 at Brooklands. In 1931 he won the Irish Grand Prix in an Alfa Romeo and brought in a Maserati first at Brooklands.

During all his racing life he voiced his regret that no British firm could be interested in taking part in grand-prix competition. He came close to this ideal in the winter of 1928 when the late Hon. Dorothy Paget helped finance the supercharging of a Bentley 4½. The Bentley company was not prepared to create a team of cars especially for Birkin, and besides, W. O. did not approve of this modification. About a year later Birkin took a Le Mans type supercharged Bentley, only slightly modified, into the French Grand Prix at the snaky Pau course. The car had a maximum of 130 m.p.h. but was entirely too heavy for grand prix. When he came in second he had silenced a lot of scoffers who had referred to his car as a "magnificent lorry".

Tim went on to shatter records, startle racing crowds and earn the dubious title of "the Wild Man of Brooklands". His flying scarf was a constant source of worry to his friends lest it obscure his goggles at some inopportune time, but it added to his dash and derring-do and Tim never gave it up.

W. O. recalled that Tim lived equally furiously off the track. "Life was never dull with him around, even if only because of the abundance and wide variety of his girl friends."

However, by the time 1933 rolled around matters of the heart and the purse created a stress which, friends noted, left Tim in an unhappily depressed state. During the Tripoli Grand Prix that year he reached into the cockpit to retrieve his cigarette lighter and touched his bare arm against the hot external exhaust pipe. He took no notice of this. Some time after his return to London he was taken to bed with what appeared to be a cold. His fellow-driver and physician, Dr. J. Dudley Benjafield, was called in. Benjy noted the wound and upon examination found that Tim had blood poisoning. Tim resisted being sent to a nursing home and, according to Davis, asked Benjafield: "If I do go in will you promise I will be out again in time for Nürburg?" And Benjafield replied: "If you don't go in there is every possibility that you will not get to Nürburg or any other race." Shortly afterward Birkin was dead.

S. C. H. DAVIS

It is a singularly difficult problem to place S. C. H. Davis in a category in the realm of motor sport. As a driver, he was excellent, establishing some 250 records; as sports editor of *The Autocar*, he recorded the hurried history as it was being made on the racecourses of the world; as a student and scholar of the sport, he wrote innumerable books to be digested by enthusiasts on wintry days between races; as a riding mechanic, he drove with Count Louis Zborowski in the French Grand Prix of 1924; as a Bentley Boy, he won his greatest race, the 1927 Le Mans, and as a severe and celebrated pit manager he was regarded as one of the foremost authorities.

W. O. claims him for more reasons than the 1927 "miracle". It was Davis who wrote the first road test on the Bentley (it was full of praise and sympathetic understanding); it was Davis who encouraged the marque's early efforts, and it was Davis who took second place in a Bentley in the 1929 and 1930 Double-Twelves at a time when the team needed these honours desperately. He came second at Le Mans in 1925 and was in third place the following year when he crashed.

The career of Davis, called Sammy with admiration and affection by those who know him as well as those who never met him but have read him, spans that of the automobile. He was born in 1887, just two years after Karl Benz turned out the "complete" automobile, and obtained his education at Westminster, a public school, and at University College in London. He became an apprentice at the Daimler Motor Co. in Coventry, finding a strange affinity for the noisy and somewhat unreliable engines of the day. At the age of 20 he started competing on motor-cycles and until the First World War raced with mixed success at Brooklands.

Davis left Daimler to start *The Automobile-Engineer* in 1913, and when he returned from the war, where he saw action with the Naval Air Service, he obtained a job on *The Autocar*. This was an opportunity custom-built for Davis. He became the recording angel at Brooklands and other major tracks. He wrote and he raced and he studied the sport with scholarly enthusiasm that manifested itself clearly in his racing and his writing. Bentley wrote that "Sammy was a figure in the racing business for so long that a meeting at which one did not see him pacing about, sporting his inevitable black béret, asking questions, exchanging jokes, on familiar terms with everyone, was unimaginable".

S. C. H. Davis

His interests in racing were varied. Among his victories were the Six Hours at Brooklands in 1927 with an Alvis; the 1929 Tourist Trophy in the 1100-c.c. class in a Riley; the 500-mile cup race in Ireland the same year; the Shelsey Walsh Hill-Climb in 1937; then came the Mountbatten trophy race for motor boats in 1938, as well as innumerable trials and rallies, including Monte Carlo. In addition to his Le Mans crash, he had two more bouts with the ultimate—during a short race at Brooklands in 1931 and the Tourist Trophy race three years later. The scars that remained served to increase the sympathy and understanding that were always evident in his writings about the moment of truth and how other men reacted.

No matter what other cars he drove, Davis will forever remain enshrined among the Bentley Boys for his daring and magnificent performance during the fateful 1927 Le Mans after the White House corner crash. Two items must be added to the already voluminous details of the race. It is not known whether the idea originated with Davis or with Dr. Benjafield, but, in order to prevent W. O. from

retiring the car, Davis and Benjafield drove past the pits to shield the damage from W. O. And, while one was driving, the other was assuring W. O. that the car was in good running condition. The derring-do of the two Bentley drivers did not escape the spectators, however, and one gallant and appreciative Frenchman leaned over the hedge at a corner where the car had to reduce its speed and deposited a bottle of cool champagne in the driver's seat. The bottle had been uncorked and Davis made excellent use of it.

When the Second World War broke out he was given command of electrical and mechanical engineering workshops; then he was assigned to the Second Army, staying with it from the landing to the finish. Upon his retirement as sports editor of *The Autocar*, he was asked whether he contemplated a life of reduced activity. He answered that question to the authors some time later when he wrote: "I draw a lot, and paint, and write. I am particularly interested in history and archaeology. I usually enjoy wars. I am very fond of rifle shooting. I smoke like a steam locomotive, and enjoy long arguments and discussions on any subject on this earth. Also I like straying about the world seeing how people tick . . . and probably above everything else, a long, fast drive in an open sports car with the wife for company and as co-driver."

As an important participant and historian, Davis allowed himself the luxury of a philosophy of motor sport that he included in his first chapter of *Great British Racing Drivers*.

". . . In the racing world," he said, "as in the days when jousting was in fashion, fame, as we understand it, comes more from the verdict of the other drivers than from popular selections. A man can become apparently famous if some act he has done appeals to the imagination of news editors, but that is altogether different and usually transitory. But drivers know the difference between success obtained by driving a car so much superior to its rivals that it is almost bound to win, and the less spectacular, but infinitely more worthy, achievement with an inferior car against the strongest opposition."

BERNARD RUBIN

Another Bentley Boy was Bernard Rubin, the immensely rich Australian who was brought into the team by Horace Bentley, W. O.'s elder brother. Rubin, tall, rough and rather quiet, was the son of a pearl merchant. He was born on the rugged northwest coast of Australia and was educated among the native children, offspring of Chinese and Japanese pearl divers. He did not show an interest in his father's business affairs and took over an enormous sheep farm where he learned to ride horses while supervising an area that grazed 250,000 sheep. He welcomed a chance to go to England, where he and his brother were educated at Eton College. Horace

Bentley introduced him to Barnato, who guided him from horses to motor sports.

Because of his wealth, W. O. reflected, Rubin was in racing *pour le sport* and "enjoyed himself with great gusto". Rubin's finest race was with Barnato in the 1928 Le Mans, which they won. His worst was in the Tourist Trophy the following year, when, after a torrential rain, he forced the $4\frac{1}{2}$-litre Bentley into a turn too fast. The car flipped on top of him, but he was unhurt. Like Benjafield, he was not of a mechanical turn of mind and he was not at his best when the engine had to be nursed. His record for Bentley, however, did him credit both as a driver and as a sportsman.

With Barnato and Birkin, Rubin did well in the hedonistic department. They had adjoining flats in London and the parties they gave are still remembered by the survivors. But what really endeared him to his team-mates was his bravery during the 1928 Le Mans. He received a signal from the pit to increase his speed and he followed instructions without a protest, although he knew that the main frame had become weak to the breaking point. There were some in the pits who were aware of this condition, and they watched anxiously as Rubin continued to circle, knowing that the break could come at any time.

He gave the wheel reluctantly to Barnato for the final run and the car finished with the side of the frame completely broken through.

When he had had his fill of speed in automobiles, Rubin took to the air, going in for long-distance records. He and Ken Waller made a record flight from Australia to England and continued for some time testing aircraft for endurance. In the words of Ian Fraser, editor of Australia's *Sports Car World*, Rubin continued to resist the pastoral activities required by his father's business of wool and diamonds. He died in 1935 after a long illness.

GLEN KIDSTON

Death courted Glen Kidston four times, and thrice in his rough, tough, sharp and fearless fashion he would have none of it. He was the traditional naval officer type, silent and receptive to discipline. One brush with death is recalled by W. O. Bentley.

"I shall never forget the sight of the Speed Six in the 1929 Tourist Trophy", he wrote. "Kidston was straddled across the hedge after one of the longest and most incident-filled skids in the history of motor racing." The crowd held its breath and then broke into a long cheer as "Kidston stepped out without a scratch".

Kidston drove for Bentley at Le Mans in 1929. In that year he also recorded the fastest time in the Irish Grand Prix. He won at Le Mans the following year with Barnato. He also made excellent showings at Brooklands and other tracks on grand-prix straight-eight Bugattis and Salmsons. W. O. described

Courtesy of the Bentley Drivers' Club]

Glen Kidston

him as a born adventurer, of powerful build and handsome. As a driver he was not only fast but steady.

He was a passenger on one of the first London–Paris airliners when it became lost in a fog. Just before the plane hit the tree-tops, Glen, with the instinct of a racing driver, braced himself for the crash. He fought his way through the flaming fuselage with his fists and was the only survivor.

Another time, his submarine became caught in the muck of a seabed and, after all hope had been abandoned for him and his shipmates, the vessel freed itself and rose to the surface. For the third time in his life Glen had beaten death.

The final joust was over Africa in a little plane, The Moth. Kidston was on a tour and he ran into foul weather. Suddenly poorly strapped (or unstrapped) baggage came loose and the plane broke into pieces in mid-air. Kidston did not get a chance to get out in time.

Barnato wrote of Kidston: "He was the beau idéal of sportsmen. The word *fear* had been expunged from his dictionary . . . a resourceful and gallant driver with a flair for any kind of mechanism—a combination of tender hands and keen judgment, plus that indefinable will that means so much . . . the most perfect host . . . and a good talker and a better listener."

*　　*　　*

In a way, the man who started W. O. on racing was John Duff, a sports-car enthusiast who had become one of Bentley's London agents. He had originally purchased a short-chassis, 3-litre standard; he made some changes in the engine, stripped off the wings and took the car to Brooklands, where he tried to capture the D-class records.

Duff was described by W. O. as a man "with tremendous guts and determination". Driving single-handed on September 28, 1922, he took everything at Brooklands from the Three-Hour to the 1000 miles at speeds of about 88 m.p.h.

Even though this pleased W. O. greatly, he was less than enthusiastic when a few months later Duff told him he wanted to enter a new race at a place called Le Mans that was to last 24 hours. He wanted the Bentley people to back him, prepare the car, provide him with a mechanic and a co-driver and generally give him their blessing.

W. O.'s reply was discouragingly negative, but he hadn't counted on the persistence and persuasiveness of Duff. Not only did W. O. consent, but he went to Le Mans and watched, and was completely captivated by the race. Duff, with F. C. Clement, who was in charge of Bentley's experimental department and official works driver, wound up in fourth place and established a lap record. Duff drove for W. O. at Le Mans in 1926, 1927, 1928 and 1929, as well as in the Six-Hour and Double-Twelve at Brooklands. With Barnato he raised the world 3-litre 24-hour record in 1925 to 95·03 m.p.h.

* * *

Frank Clement was the Bentley professional, a full-time driver. While he lacked the amateur standing of the others, W. O. said, he matched their spirit completely and also drove consistently well, especially in the 3- and 4½-litre cars, and with great success and in more races than any of them.

"The short, squat, mischievous-faced Clement," W. O. recounts, "with his unmatched knowledge, was a tremendous asset to the team from the first win at Brooklands in 1921 to the 1930 Le Mans, and he was in the winning car in four major races. His pit work was the least spectacular, the calmest and the fastest. Frank was too methodical ever to get flustered."

The team enjoyed a good laugh when Clement shared a car with Dick Watney, who drove only once for Bentley. Clement was two feet shorter and a quick change in cockpit fit was difficult. Another one-time driver was L. G. Callingham.

W. O. speaks fondly of "dear old Jean Chassagne, who drove fast cars when Edward VII was on the throne", and of S. C. H. Davis, who with Dr. Benjafield brought home to victory the sole survivor of the 1927 White House corner disaster. He includes among the Bentley Boys Baron d'Erlanger, international banker and international playboy "whose wit and dry humour left an indelible mark in spite of his brief stay with us". And while not strictly a Bentley Boy, Bertie Kensington Moir is regarded as one of the stalwarts who "served Bentley Motors with distinction at the wheel, in the pits and in the service station".

* * *

George Duller had two loves—motor cars and horses—and, according to W. O., he was equally

F. C. Clement

happy with either as long as they went fast. He was bright, breezy and casual, and, during difficult moments when temperament troubled the Bentley Boys, it was Duller who with a quip and a chuckle was able to restore harmony.

He rode with Frank Clement in the "black" Le Mans of 1926 and was in the second car in the 1927 White House crash. He vaulted the hedge from the cockpit of his 3-litre in his finest steeplechase style.

In 1927, he and Clement in a 4½-litre won the Grand Prix de Paris at Montlhéry. There were eighteen starters and the 10·726-mile course, with many turns and hairpin corners, did not suit the Bentley. At the end of the first lap the Bentley had a clear half-mile lead and held it until the 18th hour, when the car caught fire through a petrol leak. Clement put out the blaze, but on the next lap another fire started. Clement got out and extinguished the flames, but by this time much of the lead had been lost. It took him and Duller three hours to regain first position and win the race. However, they got neither cup nor prize money because the promoters had gone bankrupt.

Bentley drivers met and conquered the moment of truth many times, but only one was ever killed in a Bentley. He was Clive Dunfee, who, with his brother, Jack, did some outstanding racing at Brooklands and in Europe in 3-litre Ballots and 2-litre blown grand-prix Sunbeams before racing for Bentley. Clive, "a shade quieter and also less experienced than the determined, irrepressible Jack, also drove an Austro-Daimler and an Alfa Romeo", W. O. recalled.

Jack and Clive were tall and handsome. They were the sons of Col. Vickers Dunfee, C.B.E., who created the City of London Police Reserve and was its commandant. Clive married Jane Baxter and gave up racing for a while. In 1932, very much out of practice, he entered the 500-mile race at Brooklands with his brother in "Old Number One", an 8-litre. The car had been lapping at 127 m.p.h. and, in spite of pit stops for refuelling and tyre changes, had averaged about 120 m.p.h. when suddenly the engine cut and was not heard again. Observers said Clive had gone too high on the banking in trying to pass another car, hit a tree and shot over the embankment behind the Members' Hill. Clive was thrown out and killed instantly. His wife and Jack were among the thousands who saw it. Jack never raced again.

THE BUGATTI DRIVERS

Ettore Bugatti was a feudal gentleman who loved people, reserving a special affection for those who drove his cars. Among the professionals were the greatest drivers of the day—men like Varzi, Nuvolari, Dreyfus, Benoist, Williams, Wimille, Chiron, Sommer, Eyston, Segrave and Campbell, and women such as Mme. Juneck and Hellé Nice. *Le Patron* enjoyed extending his lordly hospitality at Molsheim, where the professionals as well as countless amateurs would make frequent pilgrimages. He would assemble them in the small dining room of the villa, where they partook of good motor talk around a table laden with the finest dishes Alsace could produce and the excellent wines of the region. The conviviality was lubricated by enticing liqueurs that were distilled at Molsheim.

The memories of those pleasant *après-midis* are kept alive by the Bugatti Owners' Club, headed by The Right Hon. The Earl Howe and kept together by the common adoration of the marque and a sprightly quarterly publication, *Bugantics*.

Many drivers came to live at Molsheim, worked with Bugatti and departed for other interests, but all retained their admiration for and loyalty to *Le Patron*. Jean Chassagne was a guest for a number of years while he was with the team. One of his best races was the 1924 Grand Prix of France, even though he finished seventh because of serious tyre trouble. Count Conelli was another Bugatti regular. With Williams he won the Belgian race in 1931 that gave Bugatti the championship. When Albert Divo won the Targa Florio for *Le Patron* in 1928, Conelli came in third; he repeated his performance a year later. Divo won the Targa again in 1929. Ernest Friderich was one of the first drivers of the marque, appearing at Le Mans in 1911 with a small 4-cylinder car outlasting some 2-ton monsters. This race was held long before the endurance contest was

instituted, being run by a local club and given the semi-official name of Grand Prix de France. Friderich was an old steady with Bugatti. He served as mechanic; went to Elizabeth, N.J., during the First World War to help the Duesenbergs; won the Voiturette Grand Prix in 1920; drove valiantly in the 1922 French Grand Prix at Strasbourg until his magnetos gave out, and was the one who handed the diamond-studded cross to the Prefect for the official investiture of *Le Patron* into the *Légion d'honneur*.

Ferdinand and Pierre de Vizcaya were among the Bugatti regulars, braving the dangers of the Targa and Indianapolis, winning, cracking up or being placed, and enjoying all the thrills that went with the assignment. Jules Goux was another of *Le Patron's* steady drivers who won a number of races and was placed in several others.

The Right Hon. The Earl Howe

Perhaps the best illustration of Bugatti's popularity was the race staged by *Le Patron* at the Le Mans circuit in 1928. There were so many of his cars in the hands of private owners and drivers that the contest was held for them alone. Bugatti ruled that the cars could be driven by owners or professionals, provided they were not employed by the firm. He offered three new cars as prizes. After a number of elimination heats, the main race was held under handicap rules. The 2300-c.c. supercharged cars started from scratch, with time allowances for the others. The 1500-c.c. unblown had the largest edge— 34 minutes. André Dubonnet came in first and Philippe de Rothschild second—both on the 1500-c.c. unblown.

The drivers whose stories follow were not exclusively Bugatti men, but they made their greatest reputations with the marque.

Jean-Pierre Wimille, René Dreyfus, Robert Benoist and Antonio Brivio

ROBERT BENOIST

The most dramatic race that any Bugatti driver ever ran was not on a track, nor was it in championship competition. It was a race for life and the driver was Robert Benoist. After Williams was captured his place was taken by Benoist, who had been a leading member of the resistance group and had been in command whenever Williams, or Grover, was off parachuting behind the enemy lines. Benoist became a captain in the British army, where he was already well known for his devotion to the Allies in the 1914–18 conflict. He had been a fighter pilot and, when he offered himself for a similar task in the 1939 war, he was turned down because of age. When the Nazis overran France, Benoist, like many patriotic Frenchmen, joined the resistance.

Between the wars he had built a brilliant racing record, becoming a champion for Delage before joining Bugatti. He scored impressively for *Le Patron* and later became sales manager in Paris and race organizer for the works teams. Benoist was at Le Bourget airfield on the day the Nazis entered Paris. He was in his 57S Bugatti, hoping to drive it south, where he expected to rejoin his own unit. But an armoured division cut off his path. A German lieutenant, with more appreciation of a good motor car than simple decency, spotted the Bugatti and ordered Benoist to fall in behind the convoy. For an entire day the German convoy thrust southward, destroying everything in its path. When the order came to camp for the night, Benoist began to plan an escape.

At dawn, petrol was given to all the captured vehicles in the convoy. Benoist saw to it that his tank was filled to the brim. Just before the beginning of the day's run, the German lieutenant approached the Bugatti with some of his friends, opened its hood and pointed to some of the finer features. Benoist was certain that the German had plans to make the car his own, and Benoist was determined that no German would get the car. It was one man against a division. But this man was a French racing driver and his car was a Bugatti.

As the convoy lumbered along, Benoist, properly in line, noticed a secondary road forking to the left. As his car approached the fork, Benoist appraised his chances and acted. With the roar that only a Bugatti can make, Benoist dropped into first gear, accelerated, swung left, changed up and dashed down the road in a classic grand prix start. He was out of sight around a bend when the machine guns went off, and he was nowhere in sight by the time several of the Germans took up the chase in automobiles. Benoist remarked some time later that he was happy he had won that race even though it was an uneven contest.

Benoist went on to plague the Germans until June 18, 1944, when he was captured and tortured at Fresnes prison. On the walls of his cell were found the words: "Never confess." The Germans took him to Buchenwald, where he underwent more tortures in the infamous Block 37. On September 12, 1944, he and some 30 other prisoners—French, English, Belgian and Canadian officers—were hanged in an underground chamber.

Benoist was a man who preferred cheers to tears. His exploits against the Nazis and his exploits on the courses were the manifestation of an exhilarating outlook on life. A champion of the world on the track, winner at Le Mans and many other classic contests, he was a professional to whom the material rewards were secondary. He enjoyed the spirit of the chase whether he was leading or pressing the leader. The people of France knew him and loved him. During one of his hairbreadth escapes from the Nazis over the rooftops of Paris he found himself on the last roof and saw an open stairway. There was no other way, so he went down. At the foot of the stairs he saw the concierge, a club in hand. "I am not a housebreaker," he said quickly. "No," said the concierge, "but I believe you are Robert Benoist. Come into my room and have a drink." They had their drink, exchanged memories, and then the concierge explored the streets, found they were safe and Benoist went on his way.

MEO COSTANTINI

Meo Costantini was one of the loyal retainers of the Bugatti motor family. No one knew exactly what his official standing was, but that was not unusual because *Le Patron* was not one for handing out titles. Costantini did what the master required. He prepared racing cars and brought those same cars to spectacular victories. He was quiet and tall and carried himself with a simple dignity. Only when he was racing was his great value evident. His method was to avoid risks as he gripped the steering wheel with his big, powerful hands. He appeared to be willing to sacrifice the dramatic for tight precision, bearing down all the time with the single purpose of getting the most out of his car and eating up miles of road at greater speed than his competitors.

In the ten years he was with Bugatti, Costantini was credited with being the spearhead in a number of great victories for the works. He won the Targa Florio in 1925 and 1926, as well as two French Grands Prix, and made the fastest lap in the Italian Grand Prix at Monza with an average of 92·1 m.p.h. Of his many victories, those in the Targa Florio stand out in the opinion of W. F. Bradley, the authority on Bugatti. Recalling the advice given by Lancia that the essential condition for winning a race is to know how to keep on the road, Bradley points out that Costantini "knew with unfailing accuracy at exactly what speed and what manner each and every turn could be negotiated and nothing would tempt him to exceed that speed, or to change his tactics, in the hope of gaining a fraction of a second. As an engineer, he was immediately aware of the shortcomings of his car and the remedy was applied for the following race. Thus driver and machine developed together to the highest stage of efficiency."

Costantini was a household fixture at Molsheim, helping entertain visitors, dropping in at the quiet dinner parties and delighting all with his straightforward humour. He liked to tell how Bugatti had sold Costantini's Monza straight-eight to Capt. Eyston and how the great Englishman won the

Courtesy of René Dreyfus]

Meo Costantini

Boulogne light-car race at an average of 64·13 m.p.h. after a sporting run against Miss Ivy Cummings in a 4-cylinder Bugatti. Shortly after that, Costantini made his great bow before royalty when he won the San Sebastian Grand Prix and the praise of the King of Spain. When the amiable Meo finally departed from the Bugatti entourage, *Le Patron* confessed that he had left a deep void.

WILLIAMS

One summer day in 1926 at La Turbie, a young Englishman stepped into the cockpit of a Mercedes 28/95, eased the car to the grid and then proceeded without histrionics to win in his class. He was tall. He was quiet. He had a military dignity that seemed to murmur for the need of a monocle and a swagger stick to complete the portrait. The crowd took note of him with generous applause and the Mercedes people also took note of him—but the next time they saw him he was at the wheel of a Bugatti in the 1929 Grand Prix of Monaco.

Le Patron had many fine cars and many fine drivers—but in this one driver, whose racing name was simply Williams, he built a mystery which to this day has been only partly solved. Williams was a Briton who had spent almost all his life in France. He was regarded as a semi-professional competition driver because he occupied himself mainly with his kennels at La Baule. He had had an early connection with Rolls-Royce in France but little of it has been recorded. Bugatti related that Williams came to him for the purpose of driving. He never elaborated upon the matter and, when pressed about it, preferred to reply with a mystifying smile.

As a Bugatti driver, Williams was one of the best. In the Monaco Grand Prix, where he made his first showing, Williams was pitted against Rudolf Caracciola in the 6-cylinder supercharged Mercedes of more than 7000 c.c. His 2300-c.c. Bugatti was painted British green for the driver. Caracciola had the more powerful car and the greater experience, but as the cars started at the sea front, climbed the hill to the Casino, plunged down past the station to the seashore again, worked round a peculiar bend, paralleled the harbour, turned a hairpin and went flat out to the finish line, it was evident that Williams was going to win the race.

[*Courtesy of René Dreyfus*]

Williams

Williams won with an average speed of 50·23 m.p.h. He continued to drive and win for *Le Patron*, always under the single name of Williams.

The mystery of Williams was cleared up momentarily at the outbreak of World War II and then deepened more than ever. To the surprise of many of his friends, Williams appeared in a British army uniform as Capt. William Grover—his real name. Whether his driving had been a cover was open to speculation, but Williams—or Grover—remained in France during the occupation, having all the qualifications for the Intelligence Service.

With Benoist he organized and supervised a part of the resistance movement. His main job was the obtaining and distributing of guns and ammunition, explosives, radio sets and codes. He operated chiefly in the area to the west of Paris between Dourdan and Rambouillet. One day in the summer of 1943, Grover's headquarters was raided by the Gestapo

and he was captured with some of his colleagues. The Nazi curtain fell on all subsequent events. Some stories have it that Grover was taken to Germany and shot. Others say he died of tortures in a concentration camp. Still others say he lived through the war and was one of those unfortunates swallowed by the Russian army. His fate is still a mystery.

JEAN-PIERRE WIMILLE

Jean-Pierre Wimille, one of the steady drivers for Bugatti, who among other victories won twice for *Le Patron* at Le Mans—1937 and 1939—was the son of a Parisian newspaper man. The elder Wimille was so enamoured of motor cars that he passed the love on to his son by holding him on his lap and allowing him to steer the big, awkward and hairy cars of the day. When Jean-Pierre was sent to North Africa with the French army he showed an immediate affinity for speed. This seemed to be a solution for the volatility he had shown as a child because he apparently worked off his excess adrenalin in a motor car, becoming phlegmatic to the point of lethargy between races.

He began early on a borrowed Bugatti, as did hundreds of amateurs, but he handled his machine so expertly that Ettore gave him a job on the team. While his early efforts were laudable, he did not show his true professional calibre until 1936, when he won the Grand Prix of France in a 3300-c.c. Bugatti with Raymond Sommer at an average speed of 77·85 m.p.h. This event was for machines designated as sports cars, the Bugatti being converted into this class by the addition of mudguards and a windscreen. He took the same car a few days later to the fast circuit outside Rheims and captured first prize. Then he brought the car across the Atlantic and got second place in the Vanderbilt Cup race behind Nuvolari. He complained that the American course was full of "kinks and bends", which dragged his average down to 62·225 against 65·9 for Nuvolari. His complaint was that the "kinks and bends" were more of a nuisance than a peril.

In the 1937 Le Mans, which he won with Robert Benoist in a 3266-c.c. Bugatti with two tanks, covering 2043·026 miles at an average speed of 85·125 m.p.h., he had an uncomfortable meeting with death and disaster.

René Kippeurt, driving a Bugatti, had got into a mixup with a B.M.W., driven by Fritz Roth, the two cars blocking the road just beyond the White House corner. Jean Trémoulet's Delahaye bounced off the two cars. Raoul Forestier, roaring down the straight, saw the pile-up and, although he could not avoid striking the cars, he managed to avoid injury. What concerned him, after he had seen "a car literally flying through the air and, preceding it, the dismembered body of its driver", was the fact that Wimille was not far behind, coming out of the corner at about 125 m.p.h. Forestier leaped out to warn Wimille, fearing it was too late. But Wimille had seen the signal just as he was coming out of the turn and manœuvred desperately, barely missing the carnage. Kippeurt was killed on the spot, Pat Fairfield died during the night; Trémoulet lost the lobe of an ear, and Roth gave up most of his teeth.

Wimille did well for Bugatti. He, Williams and Pierre Veyron averaged 123·93 in a 5000-c.c. Bugatti in a 24-hour run at Montlhéry. Later, when he became the leading driver of the team, he admitted he enjoyed Bugattis more than any other car. This did not prevent him, however, from driving a 158 Alfetta, in which he came in second to Varzi at Turin by half a second, and beating Varzi on the Berne Circuit. He was at the height of his fame when he won at Le Mans in 1939 with Veyron, doing 2084·547 miles at an average speed of 86·855 to break all the records. Georges Fraichard, in *The Le Mans Story*, notes that Wimille can be considered the most consistently successful driver in the classic, having won the two races in which he entered. Two stands at Le Mans have been named in memory of Wimille and Benoist.

The end came, as it does for so many fine drivers, when Wimille was at the peak of his career. After a magnificent 1948 victory in the Alfetta, he plunged into the creation of a radically new car powered by a 2225-c.c. Ford V-8, situated in the rear of a three-seater gran-turismo coupé whose driver sat amidships. A Cotal gearbox took the power from engine to differential. A prototype was under test when Wimille entered the 1948 G.P. of Argentina.

As so many drivers have learned, Argentine crowd control is the shame of the racing world. In 1948, as before and since, the mob swarmed unmolested over the course, waving shirts at the oncoming cars as if they were so many bulls. Wimille was speeding into a corner when the *descamisados* completely cut off his view. He lost the line, crashed and was instantly killed.

* * *

ANTONIO AND ALBERTO ASCARI

It is unalterably scorched into the black grooves made by tormented tyres on racing courses that all drivers have their idiosyncrasies, which in other worlds and other sports are sometimes referred to as superstitions. Alberto Ascari had two of his own and one that he borrowed from the dogma of his profession. He had, with good reason, a horror for the 26th day of the month and a morbid fear of driving with another man's crash helmet. The third was the fixed rule that when a man is in a crash he should, as soon as possible, drive a racing car again.

It was on the 26th of July, 1925, that his father, Antonio, a world champion driver, had been killed in the French Grand Prix. Alberto was seven years old when he heard the news. He had adored and admired his father; he grew up surrounded by racing cars and racing talk and it was inevitable that motor-car racing would become his career.

The elder Ascari had left Alberto a fine heritage in the profession. Antonio belonged to the great years of Campari, Masetti, Brilli-Peri and Borzacchini. He had an abiding love for automobiles and pursued it with a simplicity and directness that gave wonderful warmth to those around him. He had no secrets and no jealousies. As an Alfa driver he was famous and he gave his complete loyalty to the Alfa Romeo. He owned a garage and an Alfa agency.

Once, shortly after winning the Italian Grand Prix at Monza, then a 600-mile race, he was testing a new Alfa when the cooling system cracked and he was badly scalded. Antonio, his face and arms covered with bandages, insisted upon completing the tests.

Antonio was an all-weather driver. He was noted for his skill on rainy days, when he seemed to handle his car with the delicacy of a violin virtuoso, knowing precisely when to slide into a corner on the wet road and pulling out without a skid. When the announcement was made at Montlhéry that his car had gone off the road and overturned there was a sudden silence, and, when it was followed by word that Antonio had been killed, 30,000 spectators rose in spontaneous tribute.

It was against such a background that Alberto Ascari entered racing at the age of 18 in the A.C. of Milano 24-hour race on a 500-c.c. twin-cylinder Sertum motor-cycle. He did well and many felt he would continue on the two-wheelers, but in 1940 Enzo Ferrari put out a new car under his own name and Alberto drove it in the Mille Miglia. He led the race before being forced out and observers felt that another Ascari was in the sport to stay.

In 1947, Alberto, married and the father of two children, returned to racing in an 1100-c.c. single-seater Cisitalia, which he ran at Cairo. Later he switched to a 2-litre Maserati, with which he won at Modena. In 1948 he entered his first major grand prix at San Remo with a new 4CLT Maserati and won. It was noted that his style had improved immeasurably and Alberto quickly gave credit for this to his good friend, Luigi Villoresi, who had imparted hard-won driving secrets to the younger man.

Alberto and Villoresi were in the Maserati team in the British Grand Prix the same year and Alberto came in 14 seconds behind his mentor. That winter Alberto finished ahead of Villoresi at Buenos Aires and thereafter victories continued to pile up.

With Villoresi he joined the Ferrari team for the long and exciting battle against the Alfas. They drove Ferrari's Formula 2 and scored many wins. In 1949, Alberto came in first in the European and Swiss G.P., the *Daily Express* Trophy, Bari and Rheims, and took second at Lausanne, Rome and Monza. A year later he attained grand-prix victories

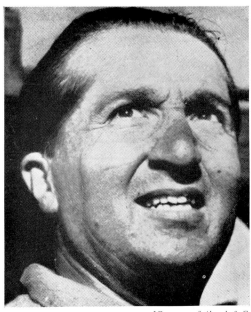
[*Courtesy of Abarth & C.*

Alberto Ascari

at Rome, Germany, Modena, Garda, Mons, Luxembourg, Penya Rhin, Buenos Aires and Mar del Plata.

Driving consistently under the 10-minute mark at the Nürburgring in 1950, he duelled with Fangio for the world championship and lost because of bad tyres. By this time he had gained a reputation as the safest and most careful driver in the top class, but this did not detract from his speed and daring. It was merely a matter of a proper mixture of skill and caution. He went on to win the world championship in 1952 and in 1953. In the intervening year he took firsts that included the Grands Prix of Europe, France, Holland, Germany, Britain, Italy, Pau, La Baule, Marseilles and Syracuse.

In the 1953 Nürburgring his right front wheel came off at 130 miles an hour, but Alberto held the car, riding on the large brake drum and coming into the pits in a rain of sparks. Everybody remarked about his charmed life and Alberto just went on racing and winning.

When the 1955 Monaco came round, Alberto was eager to compete against Fangio, who had just completed a lap at 1:41·1. Alberto went out and equalled the time. When the race was on, Alberto was riding a safe third behind Fangio and Moss when, on the 40th lap, Fangio's Mercedes gave out and Ascari lay second. He got into first place when Moss pulled into the pits in a cloud of smoke, but before he could adjust his speed his Lancia locked a wheel and hurled itself and him into the yacht basin.

He swam calmly until rescued by a boat and when he was brought out it was found he had a broken nose and considerable bruises. Alberto made light of it and allowed himself to be photographed with a fishing rod trying to hook the Lancia.

He had been scheduled to drive in the Supercortemaggiore before the Monte Carlo mishap had put him on the sidelines. He believed, however, that a driver should go back into a car as soon as possible after an accident, and his companions, Villoresi and Castellotti, agreed. They drove out to the circuit and Castellotti did a few laps. Alberto borrowed a helmet and got into a car, making several circuits and checking his time. In order to help him regain any confidence he might have lost (which was unlikely), the timers announced faster lap speeds than he was actually doing.

Suddenly, in the flat-out bend of Vialine, the car skidded sideways and turned over. Alberto died in the arms of Villoresi. The year was 1955. The month was May. The day was the 26th.

JEAN BEHRA

Few men were more obedient and devoted to the whip of speed when it was of the essence than Jean Behra. And still fewer could relax so absolutely when the urgency was over. Twice champion of France with all the attendant accomplishment, Behra had perfected the art of the pleasant hiatus. As a Ferrari driver, he lived in Modena, and of a quiet evening he would gather about him the faithful and regale them with French jokes told in Italian. The next plateau in the easy ritual was the playing of several hands of cards and then came the remembering of great events and the answering of leading questions.

"What did you do after crashing the Maserati during the Mille Miglia practice, Jean?" an enthusiast would ask. And Behra would smile his quiet, casual smile and reply: "I looked through the wreck, picked up my money, my cigarette lighter and my plastic car (a good-luck charm), and thumbed a ride to the nearest hospital."

This was the easy, off-track attitude of Behra, who for four successive years held the motor-cycle championship of France and then in 1950, at the age of 29, got into a 1500-c.c. Maserati for the Mont Ventoux hill-climb and was enraptured with the transition. That year he also drove a 4·5 Talbot at Montlhéry and a 1500-c.c. sports Gordini at the Bol d'Or, where he held more than an hour's lead when he was forced out by engine trouble.

Having impressed the professionals, he was soon invited to join the Gordini team, the only one representing France at Rheims. This team, which included Trintignant, Manzon and Simon, faced the redoubtable Ferraris, the great Alberto Ascari heading the drivers.

At the starter's motion the blue Gordini leaped ahead to the cheers of an amazed crowd. When, at the end of the first lap, Behra was leading the on-rushing Ferraris, the speed-wise spectators began speculating how long he could maintain that pace. But as lap upon lap continued to be eaten away it became evident that history was being witnessed.

The Gordini remained ahead, Ascari in his Ferrari so close behind that the two cars appeared to be attached to a string. There were breathless moments when only inches separated the cars.

Behra's driving was masterful. The other Ferraris were not even in the running and finally Ascari pulled into the pits with a dangerously overheated engine and the Gordini won its most dramatic victory.

When he discussed his career, Behra especially liked to remember his brief moment of victory in the 1952 Pan-American Road Race, which he entered with a 2·3 Gordini, the car with the smallest capacity in the race. He won the first and hardest part of the race from Tuxtla Gutierrez to Oaxaca, fighting off the frenzied pursuit of Lang's Mercedes and Bracco's Ferrari. He continued to lead on the following lap when suddenly his car skidded, teetered and plunged down a 60-ft. embankment. "It was the biggest bump, bounce and battering I ever got," he recalled, "but after a few weeks in the hospital I was fine again."

His casual approach to the ups and downs of the racing nobility brought him the gratitude of owners and pit managers. He signed with Maserati in 1954, did a lap at Monza in 1:59 and became the Number One driver for the team, proving at Aintree and Zandvoort that he could match the Mercedes aces, Fangio and Moss.

When Moss joined Maserati in 1956 he naturally took over the Number One position. Behra dropped to Number Two and kept up his share of the responsibilities with admirable spirit, doing splendid work as a tester of Maserati sports and grand-prix cars. The next year, Moss went to Vanwall, but first place was not for Behra because World Champion Fangio took the prime position. Behra reflected that, if he had to yield, it was no disgrace to yield to these two. Then he and Fangio won the 12 hours at Sebring in a 4·5 Maserati, both men displaying the utmost skill.

He was given a chance to drive a BRM at Caen and, after trying the car, announced: "I will win the race." He won that race and another shortly after in the same car—the Daily Express trophy. He won with Moss in the Grand Prix of Sweden and then drove the exciting 12-cylinder Maserati at Monza, trying to stem the Vanwall advance. He led for several laps but the car broke down. He outdistanced Musso and Collins at Modena, which was no surprise to Fangio, who had said earlier: "No one can beat Behra on the Modena circuit."

Behra went wherever racing excitement called. He won the 1958 Grand Prix of Venezuela in a 250 G.P. Ferrari, covering the 469 unattractive miles at a speed of 98·18 m.p.h. The contest, one of the last town-to-town races, was run from Palmarejo to Caracas over roads rutted and under repair, with terrifying twists and turns that took a heavy toll of drivers and cars. The Ferraris had a good day, too, taking the first four places. Behra did well with a Porsche during the year also. With Moss he

was third in the 1000 kilometres at Buenos Aires; with Scarlatti he was second in the 1008 kilometres at the Targa Florio; with Hermann he was third at Le Mans; he won the three-hour race at Rouen; he won the German Grand Prix at the Nürburgring; he was third at the Zeltweg Airfield in Austria; he was first at the Avusrennen over 332 kilometres; and he got a second at the Mont-Ventoux Hill-Climb and a third at the Schauinsland Hill-Climb.

The entire idea of racing was enchanting to him. Its joys and sorrows, its thrills and its breakdowns left countless scars on the body of Jean Behra, but his serene soul remained unharmed—and as he sat at sundown among his friends, he said in Italian spiced with a French accent: "I shall go on because I enjoy it." He was killed in a Porsche crash at the Avus in 1959 after Ferrari had discharged him for a breach of discipline.

CLEMENTE BIONDETTI

They called Clemente Biondetti the Monarch of the Mille Miglia. He had driven many machines over many courses and had scored many triumphs, but he won the Mille Miglia four times and he regarded it as his province—his strong suit.

Biondetti was a rugged man, square and solid, and seemed especially constructed in mind and body for the wracking stresses and strains that are called for in the long race. He never won a major grand prix—a condition he accepted without rancour; but on at least one occasion when he appeared to be unable to complete the Mille Miglia he showed a dramatic determination that is the talk of racing historians to this day.

It happened when his Lancia, slower than the roaring Alfas and Ferraris, was pressing hard to retain fifth place. The camshaft broke. The finish line was six kilometres away. Biondetti, then 54 years old, and his co-driver got out and pushed while the throng cheered. When the finish line was in view, only 800 metres uphill away, the co-driver collapsed. There was a dismayed hush from the crowd, but the intent Biondetti hardly heard it. He lifted the unconscious co-driver into the Lancia and pushed the car uphill himself. He crossed the line in eighth place and the plaudits of the onlookers drowned the sounds of the cars.

Biondetti was born in 1898 and was raised in Tuscany, where he learned to enjoy motor-cycles and raced them well. At 29 he purchased an 1100-c.c. Salmson sports and won the Italian championship in that class. He started on hill-climbs, winning many of them in a 2-litre Bugatti. He made only a fair showing in grand-prix racing and then entered the Mille Miglia in 1938.

It was as if a new world had been discovered. He set a record of 84·1 m.p.h. in a 2·9 blown Alfa. Eleven years later in his second Mille Miglia he beat Nuvolari; the next year he came in first again—this

[Courtesy of Abarth & C.

Clemente Biondetti

time with a lead of one and a half hours; and in 1949 he won again, beating Bonetto.

The man with a scar over his left eye and a cigarette in his mouth had become the acknowledged leader of the long race. He won the Tour of Sicily twice in succession and blasted his exhaust at rivals in other spectacular runs. In his final Mille Miglia at the age of 56, when a fatal disease was gnawing at his vitality, he was placed fourth behind Ascari, Marzotto and Musso despite heavy rain. During the same year he took fourth place with Masten Gregory in the 12 hours of Rheims. The following year, the endurance that had conquered thousands of miles at the highest possible speeds gave out.

PRINCE BIRA

When the eager young prince came out of fabled Siam and viewed the panorama of the Western world for the first time through a London fog there came to him the startling sounds of the internal-combustion engine. He had heard them before, but never in such concentrated volume—and he was impressed.

The 15-year-old prince was Birabongse Bhanudej Bhanubandh, of the direct royal line, a nephew of King Chulalonkorn, who reigned in Siam from 1853 to 1910. The young man had come to Eton to complete his education and from 1929 to 1933 he studied, played and was known to his fellows as B. Bira.

Showing an early aptitude for sculpture, he had the satisfaction of having some of his works exhibited at the Royal Academy of Arts. He also showed some promising ability at yacht racing—but the internal-combustion engine won out and, when he left Eton, he decided to remain in England and race motor cars.

Bira began with a Riley and a K3 M.G. Magnette, and was soon noted for a style that Hans Tanner, in *Great Racing Drivers*, called clean and polished; "and his temperament was suited to successions of brilliant performances".

The Automobile Club of Siam had not yet become a member of the F.I.A. so Bira drove under a British licence. When he acquired a 1500-c.c. supercharged ERA he caused quite a sensation among racing enthusiasts by frequently beating the works team drivers. Tanner reports that with Dick Seaman he was the most popular of the British drivers.

After the ERA came a 3-litre Maserati from Whitney Straight, with which Bira made the first 100-m.p.h. lap at Ireland's Phoenix Park. As a result he was asked to drive for the B.M.W. works team and became class winner in the Tourist Trophy and third over-all. Like most good British drivers he had to try Le Mans. In his first attempt in 1939, with Raymond Sommer, he drove a 2·5-litre Alfa Romeo coupé, but the car failed to finish. After the war he tried again with a factory Aston Martin, which crashed. Bira got out uninjured.

Bira switched his racing colours to blue and yellow—the mark of Siam, which was now in the F.I.A. He drove for a while for the Scuderia Plate in 4CLT Maseratis with Baron de Graffenried. He also made several runs in Amédée Gordini's SIMCAs. He was the first to get a 4·5 unsupercharged O.S.C.A. and won at Goodwood, setting a lap record.

During this time Bira had been racing his own cars, which was not only expensive but frustrating. As time went on the better equipped and staffed works teams made it increasingly difficult for private

Courtesy of Dipl.-Ing. Alfred Kempter]

Prince Bira

owners to compete successfully. Bira tried once more at Rheims in the French Grand Prix of 1954. He was in third place behind Fangio and Kling on the last lap when his fuel line clogged and he was beaten for his place by a Ferrari with Manzon aboard.

The Prince admitted that he had enjoyed his career in racing and with regal grace retired from the field and accepted his second love—yacht racing.

GEORGES AND ANDRÉ BOILLOT

France and Peugeot will not forget the Brothers Boillot, Georges and André, who did so much for the fame and fortune of their country and their marque on the racing courses of the world. Georges, the elder, was a champion of France, an exquisite virtuoso at the wheel, the idol of his countrymen, and, according to his critics, an insufferably vain man. He loved to play to the gallery and was overpowering in his esteem of himself. The Frenchmen loved him nonetheless because everything Georges claimed to be as a speed driver he truly was.

His long string of sensational tries and victories had won for him the unswerving affection of France. His failure to finish in the Targa Florio *voiturette* races of 1908 and 1909 only whipped his fans into frenzies when he won in the *voiturette* Targa of 1910. The Peugeot makers had designed a car for the 1911 Grand Prix, which they did not run. Georges took the same car for the 1912 Grand Prix and won handsomely, then repeated the feat a year later. Both times he had Jules Goux as a co-driver. They won at Indianapolis in 1913 and almost won the following year, losing because of repeated tyre trouble.

Georges approached the 1914 Grand Prix of France as the most glorious man on wheels in his country. He and his team-mates had become the masters of the new Henry Peugeot design with high-speed engines and overhead camshafts. He pressed his car to the utmost in an effort to beat Lautenschlager. Always the man of the magnificent gesture, he went beyond the capacity of his car during the last lap, causing it to falter and then stop. It has never been made clear what broke down —or whether anything broke down. Some observers called that ultimate thrust daring, if not reckless. Certainly his cornering during the final laps of that race had brought gasps of bewilderment from the experts and roars of approbation from the crowds. When his car stopped, Georges climbed out and wept.

When the 1914 war broke out, Georges became the driver for Marshal Joffre, a task full of easy honours and loathsome security. It was not for Georges. He obtained a transfer to the Flying Corps, where he faced the Germans in the air with much the same challenge as on the track. In a manner truly characteristic of him, Georges one day plum-

meted through the clouds to attack seven planes. He lost that one. When the wreckage of his aircraft was searched, they found him with a bullet in his head.

André, too, spent his war in the Flying Corps. After four years he returned to civilian life with a desire to race and a gnawing doubt whether he would ever equal his brother. He was young, romantic and daring, with a dash of his brother's vanity and recklessness. He went to America with a couple of Peugeots of questionable quality which lived up to their expectations, but he did persuade the Peugeot people to let him use a 1914 2½-litre for the tenth Targa Florio in 1919. It was the first post-war race and was accepted as a contest of men rather than machines. The straight-eight Ballot, driven by René Thomas, was the only post-war car with a maximum speed of 125 miles, having lapped Indianapolis at 105 m.p.h. and climbed Gaillon hill at 103 m.p.h. André's Peugeot had four cylinders.

The day of the race dawned under lowering clouds which erupted into thunder, lightning, hail, rain and snow. By the start of the race, nature's crescendo had given way to a howling gale which whirled the snow off the 3000-ft. hills. To make matters really sporting, the 67-mile course, which was to be circled four times, left the driver on his own, according to W. F. Bradley: "He has no pit manager to guide him, to signal him fast or slow, to call him in for fuel or tyres. If he is determined to win he must drive all out from the moment the start is given, only to find when it is too late to alter his tactics that he either has been outclassed or that he has made an unnecessary effort."

Thomas, the veteran, was making fine time during the first lap, while 50 miles behind André Boillot was tearing along trying to catch him. André had been off the road at least six times, but each time he got back and resumed his headlong speed. Near Cerda, on the left side corner, André's mount skidded, struck the bank and bounded three feet into the air. It teetered on the edge, but André and his mechanic did not wait for the laws of gravity to decide. They leaped out, pushed and pulled the car clear of the chasm, leaped in and roared up the hill spraying mud, stones and vituperations in all directions.

Intestinal fortitude was not sufficient in this wild race. Boillot had to think fast when he saw the capricious Sicilian sun suddenly come out brightly, drying up the roads. Even though he was ahead of Thomas, André stopped to change his non-skid tyres to smooth treads for greater speed. He achieved that speed, but, deeply fatigued by his battle with the elements, André applied his brakes too suddenly within sight of the finish line and the car skidded, spun and charged into the grandstand, causing several injuries. Willing and eager spectators pushed the car out of the splintered remains of the grandstand, tables, chairs and umbrellas, and dumped Boillot with his mechanic back into the cockpit.

The finish was 30 yards away and Boillot backed the car over the line.

The cry of "squalificato" was heard all about. Even though there was nothing in the rules that said a car had to win front wheels first, there occurred at this moment an act of sportsmanship worthy of the great. Ernest Ballot, the man whose car had lost, helped lift Boillot and his mechanic back into the car and instructed them to drive the 30 yards down the road and cross the line a second time—radiator first. It was an instant thick with drama. André fainted and his last words were: "C'est pour la France."

Boillot was on the road to greater glories, but never quite achieved the renown of his brother. In 1922 he won the Coppa Florio for Peugeot and with the same car got a fifth in the Targa of 1924 and a fourth in the Coppa the same year. He came in third in 1925 and fourth in 1927. As the plaudits increased, the vanity faded. But rarely did he win a race without murmuring or exclaiming, as the occasion required: "Pour la France, pour Peugeot."

Courtesy of Abarth & C.]

Felice Bonetto

FELICE BONETTO

In order to complete the 357·8 miles of the Short Madonie Circuit of the Targa Florio it is necessary to go around eight times. By the time the final lap is reached, the weary driver relies desperately on the swift reaction of his muscle memory to conquer every terrifying twist and turn. As he approaches the finish line he comes out of a bend into a steep straight and counts heavily on his hands and feet for those motions that will gun his car into the last burst of speed.

It was that way with Felice Bonetto as his Lancia came into the final climb that day in 1952, and his reactions were perfect; but the car sputtered, gasped and died. No fuel and the finish line 300 metres away at the top of the hill. But to Bonetto it was more than 300 metres. That distance represented thousands of frustrating miles on hundreds of courses, innumerable crashes, broken bones and some 20 years of pursuing the one grand victory. So, while the sun burned down upon him and the crowds cheered, Bonetto pushed the car to the finish line and collapsed. But the race was his.

Bonetto was a "pro" who could be found at almost every course in Europe constantly trying. He had given up motor-cycling because of too many crashes and made his first great run in the Mille Miglia with a 2·3-litre Alfa Romeo. The great drivers of the day—Nuvolari, Varzi, Chiron and Borzacchini—were also in Alfas, but Bonetto led them all until he spun over a stretch of water and bent his front axle. The shouts of "Who is this Bonetto?" still rang in his ears and gave him an inkling of what a great victory could do for a man.

He went on trying. On that fatal day at Monza when Borzacchini, Campari and Czaikowsky were killed, Bonetto performed a feat of driving that is still remembered. Czaikowsky's crash had flooded the south corner with flaming petrol and all the drivers cut across the grass—that is, all but Bonetto. He needed the time because he was driving a low-powered car. Lap after lap he cut through the flame and smoke and wound up in third place.

In 1948, broke and without a car, he got a job with the Cisitalia team and when the year was over he had won the Formula 2 championship of Italy for his company, fighting off Varzi and Nuvolari. With the same car he won at Mantua, Nuvolari's home track, against Nuvolari's 2-litre Ferrari, Ascari's and Villoresi's 2-litre Maseratis and Varzi's Cisitalia.

Bonetto's great compulsion to compete and win got him into so many crackups that after a while the enthusiasts described him as the man "with more crashes than kilometres". Ordinary crashes failed to deter him. Once during the Grand Prix of Bari his Cisitalia caught up with Chico Landi's Ferrari ten laps before the finish and, when Landi tried to pass on a corner, Bonetto's front wheels became entangled between the hedge and Landi's rear wheels. Bonetto's car flipped and he was taken to a cottage unconscious. He recovered rapidly and started to rush back to his car. Two persons who attempted to restrain him for his own safety were punched in the teeth. He ran back to the car, righted it himself, got it on to the track and took off. He won second place.

The road to the grand victory was strewn with more crashes and frustrations and misfortunes. But Bonetto persisted. The Targa Florio triumph was still fresh in his memory when he entered the Carrera Panamericana. It was his last race. Battling in his

Lancia for the lead against Taruffi, he lost control of the car.

JACK BRABHAM: WORLD CHAMPION

Ten years ago in Sydney, New South Wales, there was a very fast "midget" racer well-known on the tracks and at the hill-climbs, driven with joyous abandon by a dark-haired 24-year-old whose grin to this day brings the Mona Lisa to mind, suggesting that there is something we don't know about.

Jack Brabham was a byword in Australia. On the side of his midget he had painted, somewhat sheepishly: "N.S.W. Champ. 1948–1949." Today he could add, in bolder letters, "World Champion, 1959–1960"; but he would never dream of doing it.

The Champion, known everywhere in Europe as The Quiet Australian, is a shy, remote character, at a loss for words. He stumbles through the inevitable speeches at official receptions as briefly as possible in acute misery. But he handles tools, absorbed in his work on an engine, with the deftness and concentration of a brain-surgeon in the operating theatre. There are only two places where Brabham is happy and relaxed: one is his home with his wife Betty and son Geoffrey; the other is the cockpit of his Formula I Cooper Grand Prix car. Yes, there's a third—at the controls of his Cessna aeroplane.

The Champion made several forays into the world of sports-car racing, but he rapidly came to the conclusion that it was not his field, that, in fact, it frightened him. He much preferred the cut and thrust of Grand Prix racing and nice, safe speeds up to 180 miles an hour and record laps of 133 m.p.h. round the swinging curves of the Spa circuit.

He came to Europe literally to seek his fortune as a racing driver, lonely, vaguely known by name as some Aussie sport who drove midgets and 500's. Oh yes, didn't he finish fourth with a Cooper-Bristol in the New Zealand Grand Prix? Well, he teamed up with a better-known Australian, Tommy Sulman, who had bought a DB3S Aston Martin sports model, and partnered a fourth place in the 12-hour race at Hyères, in the South of France.

Then he acquired the not-very-good 250F Maserati that had been a sort of guinea-pig for the B.R.M. people, and had little joy from it—third place in the 1956 Aintree 200. Next, he went to John Cooper and never looked back, except to see how close the next man was behind him. He drove the two-seater sports model that year and then the new Formula II car and was always in the foreground of the picture. In 1957 he began winning with that car, which he practically built himself—London Trophy, Oulton Park Gold Cup and the Prix de Paris. He invaded the Continent and even drove a sports Cooper at Le Mans to take third place in the class, with Ian Raby.

Came 1958 and the Formula I Cooper, at first with the 2-litre engine. Historic was his mistake at Aintree

Jack Brabham

in the 200 miles when he slid wide and let Moss slip past on the inside of the last corner to win by just one length. But he won the Formula II race at Casablanca. Then he drove for the Aston Martin team and finished second, with Salvadori, on the DBR1 in the Tourist Trophy, exactly a length and a half behind Moss in the team.

His record in 1959 was remarkable, but the World Title was in doubt until the American race that December. The season of 1960 was in some contrast. Brabham won no marks in the first two races of the Championship series. Then he won five in a string and took the Championship with the irresistible onslaught of a Fangio—and now his driving style recalled that former master, for the exaggerated tail-skid, the hunched crouch over the wheel had vanished; now a new Brabham, faster, more polished, completely calm, was setting up fantastic lap speeds on every kind of circuit from the long straights of Rheims to the streets and tramlines of Oporto.

That season, too, when he was not winning *grandes épreuves*, Jack was driving Coopers in every available Formula II race and kept his hand in by winning at Brussels, Pau, Roskilde and Brands Hatch, although he was armed with the 1959 car.

In 1960 he won two trophies that presented a problem. One was a matter of 200 bottles of champagne at Rheims, the other was a silver cigarette box presented by his delighted rivals as a tribute to one of the most popular drivers ever to win a race. He drinks not, neither does he smoke.

Manfred von Brauchitsch

MANFRED VON BRAUCHITSCH

The peculiar occupation of running motor cars rapidly draws men from a limitless variety of backgrounds, but it is sometimes surprising when a hardcore family tradition is shattered by a new entry.

This is the case of Manfred von Brauchitsch, whose father was a Prussian colonel and whose grandfather and great-grandfathers were generals in the Prussian Army. Most famous of all was his uncle, Field-Marshal Walther von Brauchitsch, commander-in-chief of the German Army.

Young Manfred early manifested a distaste for the military and there might have been a family row had it not been for a fortunate skull fracture. Manfred was a cadet in a military school when he crashed on a motor-cycle. Since the German Army does not accept young gentlemen with cranial fractures as officer material, the field of motor-car racing was unopposed.

In 1929, in an SSK, he entered the Gaisberg Hill-Climb and won. He stayed with this Mercedes in the Eifelrennen and the Avus, where he got a third behind Caracciola and von Morgen. Three years later, in an SSK with a special streamlined body, he passed Caracciola to win by two seconds. The German press hailed him as the saviour of the Vaterland's prestige and he became the darling of the day. He was the star of a film and wrote a best-seller about the "Battle With 500 H.P."

Mercedes engaged him to drive in 1934, and he proved he was not outclassed when he won for his team in the Eifelrennen—its first victory in the 750-c.c. Formula class. He enjoyed the combination of Caracciola, No. 1 on the team, a steady driver,

and himself, more erratic but faster. He became pacemaker with the attendant risk of smashing up, but he liked the job.

Manfred made his fastest lap at the Nürburgring in 1938 in a 3-litre supercharged car—9:49. He almost won the Grand Prix of Germany that year but his car burst into flames and slowed him down. He leaped into the car after the fire was out but at the Flugplatz the scored steering wheel disintegrated at 120 m.p.h. and the car hurtled into a ditch. Von Brauchitsch was unhurt but Seaman won that race.

His last great race before the war was in the 1939 Grand Prix of Yugoslavia at Belgrade. Von Brauchitsch, who had been "dissuaded" by Neubauer from hopping a plane to Switzerland, made a magnificent run. In trying to avoid crashing with Bäumer, a teammate, he lost time and spun round dangerously until he could get set again. This, according to observers, was enough to enable the great Nuvolari to maintain his position to victory. Von Brauchitsch was second.

He did not resume his racing career after the war. Latest reports were that he had mysteriously disappeared in East Germany.

GASTONE BRILLI-PERI

One of the most dogged of drivers was Count Gastone Brilli-Peri of Tuscany, loved by all his colleagues and competitors and barely tolerated by whatever gods rule racing.

A big, good-humoured man whose face was virtually a map of the courses on which he had crashed, Brilli-Peri turned up at the Targa Florio in a Steyr in 1922, but a crash midway in the race finished it for him. In the same marque he failed again in 1923. But in 1924 he was placed 11th over-all on the Steyr, just behind Lautenschlager's Mercedes and the Alfa of Louis Wagner, who had made his greatest impact with his American victories before the First World War. It is not uninteresting to note that Brilli-Peri finished four places ahead of Neubauer in 1924; in the Coppa Florio, run concurrently, he finished 10th, again just behind Lautenschlager and four places ahead of Neubauer. When one reflects that the young Count was competing against such veterans as Werner on Mercedes, Campari on Alfa and Boillot on Peugeot, his showing is hardly discreditable.

Racing at home, Brilli-Peri used Alfa Romeos with somewhat better luck, notably in 1925, when Tommy Milton, flushed with Indianapolis victories, made a stab at the Italian G.P. at Monza. Brilli-Peri won that race at the wheel of a 2-litre Alfa. He did not try the Targa Florio again until 1928, when he was occasionally driving Bugattis, and he failed to finish. Brilli-Peri's biggest year was probably 1929, when he finished third in the Targa with an Alfa, behind Divo and Minoia on Bugattis. In the same year he earned the sobriquet of *l'africano* by winning the Grands Prix of both Tripoli and Tunisia

[Courtesy of Alfa Romeo

Gastone Brilli-Peri

on a Talbot. By this time other drivers had learned to keep their ears open when Brilli-Peri was behind them, for he had long since wearied of competitors who would not give him room to pass: he wore, from a cord round his neck, a piercing whistle that no one could pretend not to hear and that few could withstand.

RUDOLF CARACCIOLA

In 1935, after more than ten years of turbulence and travail on the racing courses of Europe, Rudolf Caracciola attained the championships of Europe and Germany. This is what he did to earn them: He came in second at Barcelona and first at the Eifelrennen. Then he won the Grands Prix of Tripoli, France, Belgium, Spain and Switzerland. Two years later, with an overwhelmingly powerful Mercedes, he won the two titles again, finishing first in the Grands Prix of Germany, Switzerland, Italy and Czechoslovakia, coming second at Monaco and the Eifelrennen.

There are many more statistics in the life of this great ace, such as the time in 1938 when he set a record of 268 m.p.h. in a giant Mercedes and a year later set four world records for the flying mile, the swiftest at 247 m.p.h.

But figures, no matter how conclusive, cannot tell the story of the eagerness and enthusiasm with which Caracciola started his career at the Berlin Stadium. Four funny little cars with funny little names were among the entries that day. They were the Omrikon, the Coco, the Grade and the Ego. Sitting alone and forlorn in the Ego was Caracciola. The car had been borrowed from a friend, and other friends had helped put it into condition. The Ego factory had pledged that, if Caracciola won

the race, he would get the parts free; if he lost, he would have to pay for them. Fiscally he was at his nadir, having just spent his last money on a bit of nourishment before the race.

He won that race, beating the larger Grade, and as a result worked up enough courage to apply to the Daimler-Benz firm. Christian Werner, the chief of the racing department, noted for his feats of speed and daring in the big Mercedes, offered the eager young man a job as a salesman for the company in Dresden.

When Caracciola showed his disappointment, Werner wagged a fatherly finger and said: "Patience, and perhaps one day you will be a driver." Shortly afterward he was given a 1½-litre blown Mercedes and won four events in the Muennerstadt Hill-Climb. When, some years later, he won the Avus despite heavy rain in which he skillfully manœuvred his car around the many accidents, Caracciola was counted as one of the regulars on the big courses. In the 1931 Grand Prix of Germany at the Nürburgring he won after a dramatic battle with Varzi, Nuvolari and Chiron. It was Chiron who pressed him closest and when the race was over the two men had a chat and began a lasting friendship.

Caracciola joined Alfa Romeo with wins of the Monza, Rome and German Grands Prix. When Enzo Ferrari took over the Alfa team, Caracciola, for reasons of his own, refused to race with him. Thereupon he and Chiron formed a private team, buying two Alfas and running as the Scuderia C.C. The association did not last long, although the friendship continued.

Then a series of strange events left Caracciola considerably shaken. Mercedes had prepared a special streamlined SSKL that Caracciola was to drive at the Eifel Races and the Nürburgring in 1933.

"Earlier that year Rudi was practising for the Grand Prix of Monaco", David Scott-Moncrieff recalled in *Three-Pointed Star*. "His attention was momentarily distracted and he left his braking too late and rammed a wall. He felt no ill effects, and it was only when he tried to get out of the car that he realized that his thigh was broken in several places. But worse was to follow. As Caracciola was now in the hospital, the SSKL was given to that most reliable works driver, Otto Merz. Rain had been falling heavily during practice and the surface was slippery in an unpredictable sort of way. Merz skidded at high speed, crashed and was killed."

Caracciola's greatest achievement in speed and endurance was his single-handed victory in the Mille Miglia of 1931. Scott-Moncrieff called it one of "the most epic drives in the history of motor racing, which ranks with Levassor's fantastic feat of 1895 and one or two more." Caracciola was driving the SSKL, a faster and lighter model of the SSK. Although he carried a co-driver, Wilhelm Sebastian, Caracciola drove the whole way.

Scott-Moncrieff wrote that "nearly all who witnessed this race say that the big white car did not

Courtesy of Daimler-Benz A.G.

Rudolf Caracciola

appear to be going fast. Caracciola gave the impression of taking it very easily. All around him was a swarm of Alfas with orders to catch him up and lure him on. But he took no notice and continued to run to schedule. And what a schedule! Over the 129 miles from Brescia to Bologna he averaged 95·8 m.p.h. Besides refuelling, even allowing for a stop because of a puncture, and another to fix his silencer, which was coming adrift, Caracciola completed the course nearly nine minutes quicker than the record of the previous year. Over a distance of 1000 miles he averaged 62·84 m.p.h., including all stops. Campari came in second in an Alfa, then Morandi and Rosa in an O.M. Ten Alfas followed in a row. The 4·9-litre Bugatti, in the hands of the great Italian, Achille Varzi, had been very much fancied as a winner. But Varzi retired, his car making very 'agricultural' noises".

Caracciola was not fully aware that he had won even after he was told. He was too numb. Later he confided to friends that the final miles were like some terrifying dream, endless and without purpose.

Caracciola had put off talk of retirement, but the matter was taken out of his hands in 1945 at the Prix de Berne. While leading his team, he crashed into a tree and broke his other leg. The limp of the first broken leg did not complement the limp of the second broken leg, Caracciola observed. Therefore, the quiet villa in Switzerland seemed more attractive than ever. He left the easy life in the Alps from time to time to be a spectator at races and it was

a great balm to hear the cheers whenever his name was announced. He died in a hospital in 1959.

EUGENIO CASTELLOTTI

Eugenio Castellotti's dexterity at the wheel was beautiful to behold as he swept around a bend in a graceful glissade, leaning ever so lightly into the direction of the turn and then with deft movements manœuvring his mount into an awesome burst of speed for the straight.

He was acknowledged to be one of the most brilliant drivers Italy has ever produced and he might have continued in the tradition of Nuvolari and Varzi had he not been burdened with one failing —carelessness.

Castellotti's consummate skill in the cockpit brought him a great victory in the 1956 Mille Miglia, where he showed Fangio, Musso and Collins the way to the finish line. That same year he also won the Italian championship in Ferrari's rebuilt Lancias. Before that he won an almost impossible third in Ferrari's Supersqualo at Monza, and had established a reputation for excellent performances in many other races.

Any sports-car enthusiast—from the most amateur rallyist to the slickest grand-prix professional—will testify that alertness and awareness are prime requirements in a driver before and during a run. Castellotti had them, of course, but with some outstanding lapses. Two will suffice to demonstrate the point.

In an important sports-car race at Monte Carlo which was being run over the full grand-prix distance, Castellotti was holding a comfortable lead over Marzotto when he became thirsty. He stopped his car for a drink—a soft drink—and, when the results were tabulated, Marzotto was first and Castellotti was second. He reflected that this was one of the most expensive soft drinks a parched man had ever enjoyed, and made a mental memorandum to be more careful during a race.

Before the 1954 Mille Miglia, Castellotti's racing manager carefully went through the routine count-down, pointing to the places where spare parts were kept and other such matters, and explaining that he had stored an extra can of oil just in case. Castellotti took off, cheerful and confident. When he ran into heavy rains he showed that he was a master of wet roads and his car was singing as he pulled into Pescara in third place in his Lancia behind Taruffi and Ascari. When he passed Pescara his oil pressure began to fail and he made his way cautiously toward Aquila, where there was more oil. Suddenly his engine seized and he just sat, watching the cars go by. When he was asked why he had not used the extra can of oil in his car, he looked astonished and explained that he thought the can contained petrol. It was a costly lesson of the elementary rule: when your racing manager talks— listen.

[*Courtesy of Ferrari Automobili*

Eugenio Castellotti

Castellotti began his racing career like so many young Italians by entering the Mille Miglia. His first was in a 2-litre Ferrari. He finished sixth in his class and 50th over-all. His first important victory came some four years later at Syracuse, when, with a 2·7-litre Ferrari, he brought the crowd to its feet with a brilliant exhibition of driving against Sighinolfi of the Scuderia Marzotto.

He became Italian champion, as predicted by an enthusiastic national press, and the road to greater achievements lay straight ahead. He confessed he had learned the bitter lessons of carelessness. One day, during a test at Modena, he crashed to his death in a chicane.

LOUIS CHIRON

Louis Chiron—the Fox, if you dealt with him on the racecourse, and the Debonair, if you saw him in white tie and tails at Maxim's—was on the starting grid for the French Grand Prix of 1950. He had won this race four times before, but this day was going to be more challenging than ever because arrayed against him were the more powerful Ferraris and Maseratis and driving against him were the incumbent masters of speed—Fangio, Villoresi, Farina, Bira, Sommer and Parnell.

Chiron was 51. His racing dated back to 1923, and, while in that time he had amassed a mountain of records and honours, he had to fight the depressing doubt that comes to every accomplished man in his middle years on the value of experience as a substitute for youth. Apparently his emotional alchemy churned up a successful mixture of the two because in a fiercely contested race he came home to his fifth victory.

A native of Monaco, Louis spent his early years working at the Hôtel de Paris in Monte Carlo and acquired all the hedonistic graces of the international set, with a definite appreciation of the better pleasures of the rich. Racing was one of them, and after some indifferent attempts he obtained a Type 35 Bugatti in which he finished second at Montlhéry in 1927, capturing the interest of Ettore himself. Chiron became a member of the Bugatti team and within two years with the Type 35 won the Grands Prix of Italy, Germany and, twice, Spain.

His successes encouraged him to try America, where he entered a 1927 Delage at Indianapolis and wound up seventh. He returned to Europe and Bugatti, and there ensued a series of victories that secured for him a place among the all-time greats. He defeated Varzi in an Alfa Romeo at Monza with an average speed of 98 m.p.h. and won at the Nürburgring 14 minutes ahead of the leading Mercedes. In 1930 he won the Grand Prix of Europe, got a second in the Targa Florio, and the Grands Prix of Rome and Monaco. A year after that he won at Lyons, Monaco, Czechoslovakia and the French Grand Prix, taking second place in the Grands Prix of Germany, Pescara and Montenero. The following year he got firsts at Nice, Dieppe and Masaryk and took thirds at Pescara and the Targa Florio.

After a short partnership with Caracciola in Monza Alfa Romeos, in which Caracciola smashed his leg during a practice run, Chiron went to the Scuderia Ferrari and drove the fantastic P3 Alfa, establishing another long and impressive record of victories.

Chiron's driving varied with his objective. With a good car and a chance to win, his actions at the wheel were superb. When he had superior cars

Courtesy of Nürburgring G.m.b.H.]
Louis Chiron

against him, he drove with cunning and caution that found him in the best parts of the corners as he nursed his machine into the most advantageous positions. He was not averse to using honest deception before a race in order to confound the opposition. Once, during a French Grand Prix, his followers noted with dismay that the Mercedes and Auto-Union were lapping Chiron's Alfa by five to six seconds. The deficit was observed by the opposition, too, and if five or six seconds can induce complacency, this tactic, coupled with Chiron's magnificent driving, won the race for him.

Luck, being a fickle companion, deserted him in 1936, when he did poorly with Mercedes-Benz. He concluded this association with a crash at 140 m.p.h. that forced him to remain away from the tracks until 1937, when he won the Grand Prix of France with a Talbot and promptly announced his retirement. He explained with a straight face that cycling was safer— even if it was done on a tight-rope across the Niagara Falls. His dictum was accepted with the proper solemnity—and no one believed him.

When the war broke out, it appeared that the retirement would stick. However, he began to frequent the courses in 1947, casting lustful glances at a gleaming 4·5 Talbot, and he was back on a whirl of victories once again.

He captured his fourth Grand Prix of France and continued through the next year for his now famous fifth win. He joined Enrico Plate's team of 2-litre Maseratis, where his string was halted by a heroic gesture. His car had caught fire and was heading for a crowd of spectators. Chiron could have leaped to safety and allowed the machine to continue on a path of death for the spectators. Instead, he remained with the car, steered it away and suffered burns that kept him in bandages for the remainder of the season.

He was back again in 1949 and the year after and so on, to the cheers of the multitude, which loved his resplendent attire and his immaculate manner at the wheel. At the age of 58 he drove a Citroën in the Mille Miglia with such skill and craftiness that he came in second in his class. The younger drivers bowed in admiration and respect before Louis, the Fox, the Debonair, the Perennial.

PETER COLLINS

Peter Collins was renowned for his daring performances as the chief driver for Ferrari, whom he joined in 1956. By the time he was 27 he had taken part in almost every sports-car race of his time. With Phil Hill he accounted for a record-breaking victory at Sebring in 1958. Some of his other wins include the 936-kilometre Targa Florio in 1955; the 360-mile Belgian Grand Prix in 1956; the 1000-kilometre Grand Prix Supercortemaggiore at Monza in 1956 and the Siracusa Grand Prix, the Naples Grand Prix and the Grand Prix of Venezuela in 1957.

Courtesy of "Sports Cars Illustrated"]

Peter Collins

His long record goes back to the days when he raced the little 500-c.c. Cooper and includes prodigious achievements with the 580-b.h.p. V-16 BRM. But the statistics can tell only part of the story of the eager young racer whose career ended abruptly on August 3, 1958. On that day, before a throng of more than 120,000 at the Grand Prix of Germany, Collins suffered a fractured skull when his red Ferrari leaped off the track.

At the time of his death, Collins, Stirling Moss and Mike Hawthorn formed the British Big Three in auto racing. He had started his Grand Prix career in 1950, competing against the top drivers of the world and learning his craft with amazing precociousness. Collins had a long and profitable association with Aston Martin, finishing second twice at Le Mans—in 1955 teamed with Paul Frère and in 1956 with Moss. He won the 1956 Tour of Sicily in a memorable duel with Piero Taruffi, the admitted master of the Sicilian mountains, becoming the only Englishman ever to win the event.

The son of a car dealer from Kidderminster, Collins was a clear-eyed, eager young man of medium build, whose modes of driving and living were identical: to the limit. Despite his devotion to his craft he was known to look lightly upon the rigid training régimes set by men like Juan Fangio, whom he loved and admired. He was throughly aware of the responsibilities of his profession—not only to the cars and to the throng, but also to his team-mates.

During the 36th lap in the 1956 Grand Prix at Monza, Fangio was sitting on the edge of the pit, having been forced out of the race with engine trouble. Collins, driving the only remaining Ferrari, pulled in for a check and saw Fangio. Collins leaped out of the car and motioned Fangio to get in. Fangio did and brought the car home in second place. The men in the pit fully understood the grand gesture. Collins knew that Fangio needed the extra points to win the world championship, but he also knew that he was giving up an assured second place in his own championship standing.

Legend was already beginning to grow about the young man who, as Fangio said, "drove like a demon and refused to accept defeat". In 1952 at the Sables d'Olonne he swept through a large oil patch and a nine-car crash with the virtuosity of a Nuvolari. Another time, at the Targa Florio, he picked up his driving turn with an eight-minute deficit and drove with such burning energy and daring that when he handed the car to Moss he had a one-minute lead.

In 1957 Collins married Louise Cordier, actress daughter of an assistant secretary-general of the United Nations, and she followed him devotedly round the racing circuits, keeping lap charts like a veteran pit manager. When he joined the Ferrari team, the Collinses moved to Italy and Collins, who took racing seriously, established himself in Modena. Unlike the traditional Englishman living abroad, he made a great effort to learn Italian as his second language, which greatly endeared him to the Commendatore and the mechanics.

Collins "carried success with dignity", William Boddy, editor of *Motor Sport*, wrote in tribute, and "died gallantly, driving a fine car to its limit of speed, and beyond. Musso died likewise. These accidents enhance the stature of the racing driver, who faces danger fearlessly, with open eyes. To use them as a weapon with which to bludgeon a clean and healthy sport is futile indeed."

RENÉ DREYFUS

The happiest years in the racing life of René Dreyfus were spent as a member of the Bugatti team. He esteemed his fellow drivers; he enjoyed the warmth and friendliness of *Le Patron*; he loved the atmosphere of the factory and he appreciated the cars. Yet the first time he asked Bugatti for a team job he was thrown out. Thirty years later he was made a *chevalier de la Légion d'honneur* for his contributions to French motoring glory.

The rebuff was emotional. In 1930, Dreyfus entered the Grand Prix de Dieppe with a 2·3 Bugatti and won. Later that year he purchased a 37A at Molsheim and drove it to Monaco. On the way he won the Grand Prix de St.-Raphael, beating the La Turbie record, and was the first to average more than 100 k.p.h. He entered the Grand Prix de Monaco as an amateur and beat Chiron, Nuvolari and the whole Bugatti works team. He did this by having an extra gas tank instead of passenger, four hours of straight driving without a pit stop, and working

Photograph by Richard Sherwin]
René Dreyfus

the oil pump, fuel pressure pump, auxiliary tank taps, gears and brakes. Bugatti was furious and failed to see any virtue in this *tour de force*.

After two unhappy years with the Maserati team, which were dogged by poor car preparation and slovenly pit work, Dreyfus finally joined the Bugatti team. It was a wonderful time for the linen merchant's son from Nice. Born May 6, 1905, educated at the Lycée de Vesoul and in two years of private tutoring, Dreyfus was groomed to enter the well-to-do business of his father. After learning to drive on his father's car, a Clément-Bayard, René fell in love with cars. He got his FIA licence at 18 and, in spite of family pleading, he divided his time between business and cars. He bought a Mathis 6CV in 1923 and won in local races. Later he bought a Brescia Bugatti and raced that, too.

The conflict of racing or the linen business came to a showdown when Dreyfus purchased the supercharged 37A. Racing came out ahead, especially since Dreyfus was being coached by Ernest Friderich, who drove for the Bugatti factory. Meanwhile the shadow of army service could not be ignored. But first his friend, Chiron, took him to the Targa Florio, where he ran as an amateur. He finished in 7 hours, 58 minutes, just behind Mme. Juneck, and wound up with the unalterable decision that racing was his life. After six months in the army, Friderich offered him a job in the Bugatti agency at Nice. Later he became chief salesman for *Le Patron* on the Riviera.

The statistics of Dreyfus's victories are impressive but an inner fire lights up his eyes when he remembers the incidents and not the figures in his career. In 1935 he joined Scuderia Ferrari, being teamed with Nuvolari, Chiron and Brivio. A year later he joined Talbot to develop new sports cars under FIA regulations. He brushes these tabulations aside with a gentle Gallic gesture to recount an incident with Nuvolari, whom he regards as the greatest of all time. Once the team manager asked Nuvolari to take over Dreyfus's car just to please the crowd—

the race was in Italy. Dreyfus had safely tied down second place and, when the race was over, Nuvolari refused to accept his share of the prize money because he said Dreyfus had already secured the position and deserved the full amount. "Nuvolari's eternal graciousness has contributed as much to the sport as his many victories", Dreyfus reflects.

In 1939 Dreyfus was at the front with the French army when his mother died. He returned for her funeral and was asked by the Écurie Schell (Harry's mother) to drive a Delahaye at Indianapolis the following year. Dreyfus reminded her of the war and laughed when she said she could fix everything.

In May, 1940, he was ordered to Paris, where he thought he would enter OCS, but Mrs. Schell had fixed it. With his co-driver, René Le Bègue, and Luigi Chinetti as chief mechanic, he sailed for the U.S. and Indianapolis. Knowing no English and less than that of the course, Dreyfus was ousted by a faster car in the qualifying trials and wrecked his own car in the requalifying run. He used Le Bègue's car in the race and was lying 10th when it started to rain. He swiftly began to pick up positions, one after another, until suddenly he was flagged down. He was told that at Indianapolis passing during rain was forbidden. Dreyfus was astounded at this because in European racing rain means no change in the rules.

After Indianapolis he tried to rejoin the French army but he was informed there was no France left. He joined the U.S. Army, where he learned English and became an interpreter in North Africa and Italy.

At the end of the war, Dreyfus wondered whether he was too old to race. He purchased the Gourmet Restaurant in 1945 and waited for racing to resume. Much to his amazement, he found that he loved business—the interplay and methodology—but seven years later a banker friend, Pierre Louis-Dreyfus, persuaded René to run with him at Le Mans in a 4·1 Ferrari. The car was forced out with a bad clutch. Later René captained the Arnolt-Bristol team at Sebring, finishing first, second and fourth. In 1957 he managed the Renault team at the Little Le Mans at Lime Rock.

As a racer, Dreyfus did not merely drive his car—he enjoyed it. "I always felt my car—like Fangio," he recalls. "I took pride in the fact that I could win and still bring in the car like new."

Dreyfus, who has not owned a car for years, now runs the Chanteclair Restaurant, a successful rendezvous for racing enthusiasts where cars and driving are the chief topic. At one table not so long ago sat an Englishman who was cynical about the Bugatti. "But they really weren't reliable," he insisted. Dreyfus, the inner flame again appearing in his eyes, pointed to his silver hair and said: "When I started racing for Bugatti this hair was black." Then, seeing the astonishment of those around him, he explained: "The cars were fast, exciting and reliable when properly driven."

At the circuits today Dreyfus seems content to watch, or to help in a pit. He confesses that, though he is prepared for that final uncontrolled drift for himself, he cannot take the chance of killing or injuring others. Asked directly whether he would race again. Dreyfus pointed to a face in a Bugatti team photograph on the wall of his restaurant. "That is a driver who has died," the French former champion smiled. "His name was Dreyfus."

SELWYN F. EDGE

CHARLES JARROTT

In the early days of British speed driving, when the sport was rough, rugged and "reprehensible", two loyally defiant men gave motor racing its greatest impetus. Selwyn F. Edge and Charles Jarrott launched the tradition of glamour and romance that rules the Green to this day.

"Few men have looked more like the traditional driver than Edge", Sammy Davis has written. "Tall, with a stern, determined face, thick, bushy eyebrows, a dominant nose, a firmly severe chin, he looked exactly the right type at the wheel of a racing car."

Edge was keenly aware of the publicity value of racing success and he was eager to increase the prestige and therefore the sales of the Napier. However, because of the British ban on racing, it was almost impossible to test a speed car in these islands. When he announced he was entering the Gordon Bennett Trophy race his friends were understandably appalled because the conditions were seemingly impossible.

Bennett, the excitable and eccentric newspaper owner, had stipulated that the race was to be nation against nation and each car had to be completely manufactured in the sponsoring country. There was a woeful dearth of ignition components and good tyres in Britain; sparking plugs were just making a start and gears were of questionable quality. France, on the other hand, was leading the world in everything automotive.

In 1902 confident French manufacturers had chosen the Chevalier René de Knyff on a Panhard, Fournier on a Mors and Girardot on a C.G.V. to carry the nation's honour. Edge took to the Paris–Vienna Race, which was run concurrently with the Gordon Bennett, a relatively small (127 × 127) 30-h.p. Napier with a cracked cylinder head and a soft second gear, both hastily repaired *en route* to the start. The car ran remarkably well as far as Belfort even though it refused to fire on all four cylinders. Edge, with his cousin, Cecil Edge, as mechanic, managed to use mostly first and top gears. Their spirits were buoyed when they learned that Fournier and Girardot had failed to reach Belfort; but de Knyff was miles ahead.

Then ensued a nightmare of racing tribulation

[Courtesy of D. Napier & Son Ltd.

S. F. Edge

and travail to try the physical and emotional stamina of supermen. Going down the twisting Arlberg Pass, their cornering seemed superb almost to the point of recklessness: those who watched could not know that the brake linings had burned away. At the bottom of the long hill, the Napier's shredded tyres doing a deadly tap dance on rocks and pebbles, S. F. and Cecil looked back and discovered that the entire rear of the body had vanished with every spare inner tube, all the tools and the jack.

This raised a fine problem. If they got a puncture they would have to proceed somehow because the purchase of a non-English tyre would disqualify them. Despair deepened, when suddenly Jarrott drove up to put a silver lining in their cloud: de Knyff's car had become disabled at a previous mountain. It was then only a matter of reaching the finish. "With their bare hands", Davis wrote, "they prised the tyre covers off the rims when punctures occurred, trundling the car forward to do so in the absence of a jack. The tube patched, they worked the cover back again on to the rim. By the fourth change neither man had normal hands; every finger, much of each hand, was torn, bleeding and covered with dirt. Even holding on to the wheel was an agony. Yet they went on, grimly. And so Napier won and Edge made a name in the world." He was the only Briton ever to win the Gordon Bennett Trophy.

When Edge decided five years later to give Napier a 24-hour world record, he surprised no one by driving the entire period. Two other Napiers, each with a relief driver, also entered the contest, but Edge got his record—65·9 m.p.h.—and it stood for 15 years until he himself broke it. The second record was made with a Dutch Spyker in two 12-hour stints because of changes in the rules governing the use of Brooklands, and the average was 74·27 m.p.h.

One of the earliest advocates of the 6-cylinder engine, Edge, who was born in Australia in 1868, joined A.C. as a director in 1921 and for the next eight years he was the driving force behind that marque's rise to fame. From 1922 on he was Governing Director and as such exercised final control over A.C.'s development of its light six. When the company went into voluntary liquidation in 1929, Edge severed all his ties with motoring and retired to his pig farm. For the next 11 years—he died in 1940—he devoted himself as single-mindedly to improving the porcine breed as he had to elevating the automotive.

In the heroic Edwardian era the peaked cap was the fashion for drivers, and Edge and Jarrott sported them more jauntily than all the others; but there the similarity ended. Edge was debonair, deliberate and wise in the ways of the world. Jarrott, with bulldog tenacity, maintained as his driving maxim the one word, *finish*. In his day British drivers did not rank high in racing and it was his unflagging persistence that got him a car from Panhard et Levassor to run in the 687-mile Paris–Berlin Race of 1901. After some 16 tyre changes in two days (including the repairing of punctures), Jarrott got to Berlin and earned a better Panhard for the next year's Paris–Vienna. Jarrott's mechanic in 1902 was his employer, Harvey du Cros, who held the Panhard franchise for Britain.

What followed was a historic peak of unswerving determination. On the second day of the race, one side of the frame fell away. Jarrott and du Cros, covered with dust and dirt, pitifully fatigued and unable to speak the local languages, got some bolts, "borrowed" the legs from a hotel table and created a cantilever support for the frame. They got to Innsbruck intact, but an earlier soldering of the water jacket was beginning to yield to the furious pressure.

In spite of it all, Jarrott had kept the car at full throttle. When water started to spurt from the radiator, du Cros spread-eagled himself across the bonnet, holding a towel round the water pipe. He was scorched and bruised and obtained questionable surcease only when he dismounted to repair inner tubes. Meanwhile the elements contributed further hardships. The men were alternately drenched by heavy rains and parboiled by searing sunlight, and a horde of insects stung them at every halt until they were covered with frightening bumps and welts.

Undaunted, they went on. The car steered strangely. The brakes were burned out. The engine was boiling. Four miles from the finish the car suddenly lost

[*Courtesy of D. Napier & Son Ltd.*

Charles Jarrott at the wheel with Montague Napier

power; a mile farther the greater part of the gearbox fell out. Du Cros leaped on a bicycle and rode back to find some Panhard mechanics, but they could do nothing. Some of the gears were still in the car, but the clutch could not be withdrawn. After some tests, Jarrott found that by engaging first gear and getting a push from the sympathetic onlookers he could make the engine run.

The Panhard moved forward slowly but evenly, giving forth frightful sounds and spurting flames from its exhaust and several unorthodox outlets. The silencer fell off; other parts of body and engine dropped amid clouds of dust, steam and sparks. And then, ever faithful to its master's motto, the car finished. It crossed the line and, with a gargantuan gasp, stopped. Jarrott had brought lasting glory to himself and Britain, and set an example for future generations of drivers.

He withdrew from racing before the First World War, though his interest in it remained acute and he was always ready to help any competitor to the utmost of his capacity. To the end of his life he was rich in anecdote, in counsel and in friendship.

GEORGE E. T. EYSTON

Wherever Capt. George E. T. Eyston appears it would be proper for an orchestra to strike up Sir Arthur Sullivan's anthem to W. S. Gilbert's classic reminder that *He is an Englishman*. For *in spite of all temptations to belong to other nations*, the tall, pink-faced gentleman with the bristling white moustache, who has driven an automobile at 357 miles an hour, *remains an Englishman*.

Eyston is symbolic not only of Stonyhurst, Trinity and Cambridge but also of the tenacity that has been the mark of British racing drivers. An incident early in his career illustrates this. During the Boulogne Motor Week in 1923, he damaged his car in a practice run and found himself in need of unavailable spare parts. Unable to get transportation from the track to Boulogne five miles away, Eyston, without bothering to remove his overalls, ran all the way to the coast, getting there just in time to board the boat. He reached London late at night, snatched a few hours' sleep and presented himself at the Aston Martin works, where he got what he needed. He returned in the same manner, worked on the repairs all night and turned up at the speed trials to win his class. Two days later he got third place in the Grand Prix de Voiturettes Légères in another car. Apart from being dishevelled he showed no outward signs of fatigue and strain.

How does one get into racing? "Well," says Eyston, "my father was a great friend of the editor of *The Field*, and we often stayed with him at his house overlooking the track (Brooklands). That was before the war. Afterwards—after Cambridge—I went to France to brush up my French, and stayed at an old château. It was overlooking Le Mans . . ."

During the 1914–18 war he served as lieutenant in the Dorset Regiment and became a staff captain in the Royal Artillery. He was wounded at Arras, won the Military Cross and twice was mentioned in dispatches. He returned to Cambridge for a B.A. in engineering and later established his own firm in the field.

After the first run at Boulogne, the city took him to its bosom and welcomed him enthusiastically the following year. In trying to avoid a wrecked car in his path on that circuit, Eyston, who had a 12-minute lead, crashed his machine into a telegraph pole after a prodigious spin that brought shrieks from the crowd. Controlling the car at speed seemed to come naturally to the young Briton even when the car was seemingly out of control. The Boulogne crash did not cause any great injuries and won him the affection of the French.

He had watched Segrave, de Palma and K. Lee Guinness at Brooklands and, when Lionel Martin suggested that he drive an Aston Martin at Brooklands, Eyston recalls, "I bought two chassis and one engine—so that I should be ready for everything—road and track racing." Late in 1926 he got a Bugatti and then he went to an M.G., a Panhard, a Delage, a Singer, a Riley and a Diesel car with an engine of the type that was used in London buses. He tried all cars in speed and course runs. He became a favourite of many nations. The Italians cheered him at the Mille Miglia, where he won his class, and the Americans stood in awe at his speed record on the salt flats in Utah. There is a photograph of him at Brooklands, where he scored so many victories, in a soapbox derby car. Brooklands was the course where, in the company of R. C. Stewart, Eyston made a lap record in an Alfa Romeo for 12 hours at

[*Courtesy of Nuffield Exports Ltd.*

Capt. G. E. T. Eyston

95 m.p.h. At Montlhéry with the Chrysler 72 he maintained a 72½-m.p.h. pace for 24 hours. In a Riley Monaco saloon he established nine international records during a 48-hour run.

If there were a key to any city in Belgium, Eyston would have been offered it after he raced sports cars and thrilled spectators with his deftness and sportsmanship at Stavelot, Francorchamps and Malmédy. Wherever he went, his austere grace and rugged charm captured the populace. France made him a Chevalier of the Legion of Honour. His home is filled with many victory cups, including the treasured Wakefield Trophy, which he won for capturing the world's land speed record for Britain. From being the first man to do 100 miles an hour in an M.G., he went to the fantastic 357-m.p.h. record in a Thunderbolt at Bonneville in 1938. The Thunderbolt, for the record, weighed six tons, had two 3000-h.p. Rolls-Royce engines and consumed five gallons of petrol a minute. In 1954, with Ken Miles in the Ex. 179 on the Utah flats, he captured seven international and 25 American records at speeds up to 120 m.p.h.

For a man born in 1897, Eyston has not muted this thunder as much as would be expected. He is a director of Wakefield's, the originator of Castrol, and a director of John I. Thornycroft & Co., which keeps in repair such vessels as the *Queen Mary* and *Queen Elizabeth*. He has been a broadcaster, an author of a racing book, *Flat Out*, and, in the finest sense, an international celebrity. He explains that

his hobby is work—"ordinary humdrum work", he reflects. But the man in the grey suit of casual cut and tie of club stripes who has represented England wherever he went gives away his secret when he confesses that one of his favourite cars, one which he named himself, was *Speed of the Wind*.

LUIGI FAGIOLI

The hobby of racing sports cars can be expensive; therefore it was a fortunate circumstance that the business of manufacturing spaghetti was prospering in Italy *circa* 1925. For it was in that year that Luigi Fagioli, who was in the enterprise with his brothers, and who had enjoyed a taste of speed on motorcycles, purchased a Salmson, then regarded as the finest 1100-c.c. car obtainable.

During the next two years he spent his weekdays attending to the problems of spaghetti and his Sundays taking part in small races. When the Salmson began to show the strain of constant racing, Fagioli went to the 1500-c.c. 8-cylinder supercharged Maserati that had captured great glory in the Targa Florio. He swiftly gained attention with it in two class victories and records in hill-climbs.

He got a Maserati factory car in 1931 for the Grand Prix at Tunis, coming in second behind Varzi's Bugatti. At Monte Carlo that year he came in second again with Chiron first and Varzi third. He liked the marque, which was fast and dependable, and the Maserati brothers showed their respect and affection for the young driver by offering him the Behemoth of the factory, the 16-cylinder supercharged machine, which had a known maximum speed of 160 m.p.h. He won with it at Monza and was rewarded with the job of Number One Driver for the team. The following year, as all Italy watched, he took the same car to victory in the Grand Prix of Rome.

He was borne to his hotel on the shoulders of cheering admirers and attained status as a national hero. Not long afterward Tazio Nuvolari decided to join Maserati and, there being no room for two heroes in the number one position, Fagioli accepted a post with the Alfa Romeo team.

Although there was no more than the usual rivalry between Fagioli and Nuvolari (they never drove in the same team) enthusiasts continued to speculate on the possible outcome of a knock-down-drag-out race between the two. It came in September, 1933, at Monza. Fagioli in a P3 Alfa went over the finishing line millimetres ahead of Nuvolari and set a new lap record for Monza at 108 m.p.h.

In 1934, the influence of the powerful Mercedes-Benz engine began to make itself felt on the courses of the world. With Caracciola on the disabled list and Brauchitsch not yet in the ace class, Neubauer favoured Fagioli, to whom he, like many others, referred as the "Abruzzi Robber". Luigi took to the 750-kg. formula cars with ease and scored victories in the Grand Prix of Spain, the Coppa Acerbo at Pescara and the Grand Prix of Italy and seconds in the Grands Prix of Germany and Czechoslovakia.

Fagioli was a big, raw-boned son of Italy's south, with all the warmth and friendliness that are built into the breed. The fast German cars suited him well, but the Teutonic discipline left him rebellious. He kept his peace for many days and many races, but Etna was boiling within him and all those concerned watched for the inevitable eruption. It came during a day when he was leading and was hailed into the pits for a vague reason. He was detained there by Neubauer, it is recalled, until Caracciola raced by to win.

The lid blew off and the fury burst forth. He consigned Neubauer, Mercedes and assorted crew members to permanent tortures in all the hells of motordom, and resigned. Those who witnessed the denunciation recall it was one of the finest examples of the sacred and the profane ever heard in a pit.

As the political turbulence in Europe increased, Fagioli's health seemed to decline. For a while he tried Porsche's Auto-Union but he did not take easily to the special technique required by this off-beat motorcar. The name of Fagioli was almost forgotten during the war years and afterward. But in 1950 the 52-year-old veteran got into the Mille Miglia with an 1100-c.c. O.S.C.A. and performed the neatest feat of the race. His average was 115 k.p.h. as against the leading Ferrari's 125 k.p.h. He won in his class and astonished everyone by coming in seventh over-all.

With his renewed youth at full swing, Fagioli was asked to join the Alfa Romeo team and was given a 500-h.p. 800-kg. to run in grand prix. Combining skill, experience and daring, he attained second place in the world championship. Two years later he got a remarkable third in the Mille Miglia, driving a Gran Turismo Lancia that had a top speed of 110 m.p.h. It was truly a satisfying race for Fagioli. He was behind Bracco's Ferrari and Kling's Mercedes—but he kept behind him, in fourth place, a Mercedes driven by Caracciola.

At the age of 54 he was riding high and enjoying moments that can be appreciated only by men of that age who have made a comeback. Then, one day at Monte Carlo, a circuit with which he was throughly familiar, Fagioli roared into the tunnel and never came out. His car had overturned and fourteen days later he was dead from the injuries.

JUAN FANGIO

Juan Manuel Fangio, five times world champion driver, is a gentle, friendly and modest man, who carries with dignity the adulation of his competitors. They have described him as the Picasso, El Greco and da Vinci of his craft. They have likened him to a god and, as one put it: "How can you be jealous of a god?" The press has heaped upon him such metaphoric descriptions as the "matador of motor sport", and the "Mercury of the Pampas".

Driving is Fangio's passion. He says so, simply and without elaboration. It is for others to point to incidents that demonstrate this. The Grand Prix of Monaco snakes along twisting, narrow streets and at one spot—the Boulevard Louis III—there is a sharp right-hand curve away from the bright blue sea into a tunnel, black and forbidding. Stirling Moss admits that even the most daring racing drivers instinctively ease their pressure on the throttle. "But", says Moss, "the Old Man doesn't. He has such amazing confidence." Other drivers recall a Fangio victory at the Nürburgring. In the final three laps he overcame the almost insurmountable lead of two Ferraris by driving two of those laps without once touching his brakes.

In the mad mix-up at Le Mans after the crash that killed 81 spectators and one driver, cars and equipment were scattered over the track. A lap later, with impeccable precision, Fangio steered through the cluttered section with such skill and artistry that other drivers said this approached the "quintessence of beauty".

Fangio is a casual man. He is subdued and plumpish and his hair is thinning. Fame and success kept him waiting until he was 30. He was born near Balcarce, a village in the valley of Argentina's table mountains, on June 24, 1911. He was the fourth of six children of an immigrant potato farmer and some-time plasterer. Among the usual boyhood

Courtesy of Daimler-Benz A.G.]

Juan Manuel Fangio

activities were many hours spent gaping at the mechanics in the local garage and, by the time he was in his early teens, he was a thoroughly efficient grease monkey there. He was basically shy and retiring until he had a near-fatal bout with pneumonia. Then, his neighbours recount, he blossomed forth as an eager participant in sports, showing great promise in soccer but maintaining his ardent interest in automobiles. After a year as an army cadet in the Campo de Mayor school, near Buenos Aires, where he was chauffeur for the commanding officers, Fangio returned to his home town with the fixed intention of becoming a racing driver.

Until he was 25, however, the best he could manage was to be a *corredor* (co-driver) because he was able to double as a mechanic. Then he acquired an old Ford and, with his brother, took it to their farm-yard workshop. By the time they had finished, only the engine block was intact. The car had been souped up and rebuilt for speed. "She may not have appeared very pretty," Fangio remembers, "but she stuck together well enough to last the three hours of a race."

Fangio showed even then that he was a stubborn competitor and an intent one. During one race in 1938 at Tres Arroyos, he was flagged down in the fifth lap. When he demanded to know why, he was told that five drivers had been killed in an accident. Fangio said he had not even noticed the pile-up.

He continued to race under the most primitive conditions, gaining priceless experience. In 1940 his friends helped him buy a Chevrolet coupé, which he entered in the Gran Premio Internacional del Norte, a tortuous, round-trip 6000-mile endurance contest from Buenos Aires to Lima. It was his first big victory. From that time on he won almost every long-distance race in Argentina, solidifying his reputation as a leading South American driver. However, World War II put an end to racing. Fangio went back to Balcarce and drove a taxicab for a living. He seemed destined for another discouraging uphill fight when in 1948 Juan Perón entered his life.

The dictator had been a casual racing enthusiast for some time, but in Fangio he recognized an opportunity for good publicity. He thereupon "hinted" to the millionaires in the Argentine Auto Club that Fangio needed help. They promptly outfitted him with a new Maserati and a year later Fangio justified their highest expectations. He won six grand-prix races and came home a national hero. The government gave him $30,000 and he got a spot on the works team of Alfa Romeo for 1950. In 1951, as captain of the Alfa team, he won his first world championship.

Fangio is a cautious soul. He has never allowed his generosity, which is ample, to exceed his income. Today he is a man of property. Racing alone accounted for $100,000 a year. He owns two service stations, a very large cinema and two automobile dealerships. But his greatest asset is his fame.

Whenever he raced in Europe, newspapers and wire services kept three trunk lines open to flash back to South America a "rev-by-rev" description.

The Old Man is probably the only racing driver who was ever kidnapped on the eve of a race. Just before the Cuban Grand Prix in February, 1958, Fidel Castro, whose forces were later to overthrow President Batista, ordered the arrest of Fangio and held him until the race was over. Castro made it plain that he bore no rancour against the Argentine but that it was Fangio's very fame that made his abduction a prime embarrassment for the dictator. Fangio himself said afterward that he had had a fine time listening to the race on the radio.

There have been countless analyses of Fangio's greatness on road and track. He has been called daring, but not reckless; confident, but not smug, and a great artist, but also a consummate craftsman. What is obvious is that he works with the same tools as the others, but he applies them so much better.

Fangio is a gallant opponent. Frequently, after winning a particularly close race, he will walk to the loser's pit and congratulate him on a good performance. Once, after defeating Mike Hawthorn and Peter Collins in a hairbreadth finish, he came to them and said: "You are both very fine and skilful and courageous drivers. It is a great honour for me to race against you."

Fangio admits he is forever aware of racing's "moment of truth", that speck in time when a driver hurls his machine into a curve and death stands waiting. He has seen many of his fellows pass over the line. At Monza in 1952 he had his only serious crash, suffering broken neck vertebra and head injuries. He vowed to his wife, Andrea, nicknamed Beba, that he would never race again. But he came back. However, he has kept his son, Oscar, away from racing.

An automobile has so much to give, his rivals explain, and Fangio seems to know just how much. He never drives a car beyond its capacity. It remains for Phil Hill, one of America's best road racers, to answer the riddle of Fangio's already legendary achievements: "With most of us," says Hill, "you can figure a ratio of 75 per cent car and 25 per cent driver. With the Old Man it's 40 per cent driver and 60 per cent car. He has us beaten by 15 per cent even before we start."

GIUSEPPE FARINA

When Giuseppe Farina stepped on the accelerator and his wheels did a lively scherzo around the course, he seemed to drive as if the devil were behind him and the angels ahead. He never denied the delightful habit of singing when at high speed, but those who watched his face in close-up through binoculars swore that he seemed to be cursing the devil and singing to the angels.

[*Courtesy of Abarth & C.*

Giuseppe Farina

This was Farina, the most famous introvert of sports-car racing, who enjoyed the amiable nickname of Nino but never made the slightest effort to acquire friends or even acquaintances. Hans Tanner describes him as an "ordinary citizen, a man without hobbies, indifferent to publicity, a man without excessive pride and, without doubt, Italy's most promising driver".

Observing Farina in the cockpit through a spyglass was educational, for, in the words of Enzo Ferrari, "he was the complete driver with all the attributes of a world champion". His style and manner, which have found many followers in recent years, were at once easy and commanding. He drove with outstretched arms, head back, eyes on the track in front but with sufficiently frequent side glances to obtain a rounded view of the entire field of action. During his rare moments of conviviality Farina would grimace his features into a rather cautious smile and explain that this style left him more rested and relaxed toward the end of a race, thus defeating fatigue, the archfoe of all drivers.

Statistically, this seemed to be a most desirable method because, among other honours, Farina became the world champion in 1950 after having held the Italian championship in 1937, 1938 and 1939. On the other side of the debate, however, records show that Farina was in a large number of accidents with the attendant large number of bone fractures, abrasions, lacerations and contusions.

After a rugged apprenticeship in the so-called monster cars of the early 1920s, Farina joined the Alfa Romeo works team under the masterful mentorship of Nuvolari. The prime rivals of the Italian cars in those days were the over-powered German machines and Nuvolari impressed upon his pupils that the only way to win or place was to snake between the Germans whenever a curve or bend presented itself. As Nuvolari pursued this perilous policy to the gasps and cheers of the crowds, Farina was almost always just behind him.

In the 1939 Grand Prix of Switzerland, Farina took the 1500-c.c. supercharged Alfetta, which after the war was developed into a faster car. But in this race it had 190 h.p. Farina held the little machine in the running against the 500-h.p. Mercedes just behind Hermann Lang but persistently in front of Caracciola and Brauchitsch in Mercedes giants and Muller and Nuvolari in Auto-Unions. Toward the end the remarkable little Alfetta finally gave way but the spectators were satisfied that they had witnessed a phenomenal display of driving skill and courage.

Farina seemed well on the way to another world championship in 1954—this one, according to his detractors, by default, for Ascari's Lancia was not ready and Fangio was delayed by his Mercedes. But misfortune was quite neutral that year. After Farina won at Syracuse by magnificent manœuvring past the burning wrecks of Gonzales' and Hawthorn's Ferraris, his luck deserted him in the Mille Miglia. He had set an average speed record of 126 m.p.h. through Peschiera when his car slid off the road. His injuries were sufficiently severe to keep him out of racing for several months.

When Farina took a Ferrari to the Argentine races in 1955 he also carried with him the torment that was the sum of all his injuries. He drove the race supported by morphine injections and came in second behind Fangio. Later that year he tried at Indianapolis but the car did not respond. A year afterward he went to Indianapolis again. Tired and depressed, he watched his car crash, killing the test driver.

It is to be noted that when Farina won the world championship he refused photographers permission to enter his house. He steadfastly refused to reveal in any manner his private life. When he was not driving, he worked quietly and intently in the coach-building shops of his uncle, Pinin Farina.

After the Indianapolis fatality he withdrew into his private world and never raced again.

JOHN FITCH

"Seldom is a simple man's sense of natural employment so completely gratified", says John Fitch of race-driving. "He has the hunt, the fight and the adventure all rolled into one experience . . . he strains his memory to retain each bump and feature of the surface, to mentally fix each cut-off point; he forces and cajoles his car, stretches his nerve, tests his skill and courage, spars for position . . . and, when and *if* he wins, enjoys a rare kind of satisfaction that enhances the value of every small thing in life, making senses more acute, thoughts more generous and friends dearer."

The man who wrote those words is anything but

[Courtesy of the Lime Rock Corp.

John Fitch

simple. Tall, spare, self-effacing almost to a fault, John Fitch has done more for motor sport than any driver in the United States. He has designed cars, built them with his hands, sold them, raced them—and written about them. Automobiles have been the dominant theme of his life from his birth in 1917 within exhaust-roar of the Indianapolis Speedway. His father, Robert Vanderbilt Fitch, was a designer who put the first closed body on a motor car.

John Fitch first saw sports cars, in the modern sense, in action at Brooklands in 1939. But he remembers, as a boy, "hanging on to the seat with everything I had" as riding mechanic while his stepfather punished a Stutz round and round the speedway in quest of new lap records. The stepfather was George Spindler, then president of the Stutz Motor Car Co.

Before Fitch's love for cars could find its expression, his country was at war. For four years his racing apprenticeship was served in the far more perilous cockpit of a fighter plane. Sent to England with the first U.S. combat units in 1941, he flew Havoc A-20's in low-level daylight attacks. Transferred to North Africa the following year, he captured a German ME-110 and crash-landed it behind his own lines in Algeria. From 1944 on he flew Mustangs escorting bombers over Germany, until he was shot down by anti-aircraft fire in February, 1945, parachuting into Germany and the hands of a village fanatic who attacked him with a knife.

Repatriated in 1946 after sitting out the rest of the war in a prison camp, Fitch settled in West-chester County. Remembering the brilliant British cars that had entranced him at Brooklands before he grew wings, Fitch opened an agency for M.G.s in 1948. He showed the cars wherever he could attract an audience, working night and day—and sold three that year. But 1948 was much more notable for John Fitch as the date of his first race.

He took one of his M.G.-TC's to Bridgehampton, which was still run on public roads, and finished fifth over-all. He had a wedding date, however, and off he went with the former Elizabeth Huntley for a New England mountain honeymoon in the same car. Suddenly remembering there was another race, in New Jersey, Fitch turned the car and dashed back to Linden Field, Mrs. Fitch's trousseau still strapped to the grid. Brusquely depositing bride and trousseau on a hay bale, Fitch took the TC to the line and came home third.

John Fitch was learning fast, and he liked what he learned. In September he entered another road race, the Watkins Glen classic, and finished second. When he finally took a first in class with the TC, he knew it was time to step up, and in June, 1950, Bridgehampton saw what was sometimes known as The Fitch Bitch take the first of its many second places. This roadster, laid out and built by Fitch, was based on a FIAT chassis, a Ford V-8 60 engine and a modified Crosley body. A magnificently road-worthy car, it was not fast enough for an over-all win, and so it was put aside.

It was in 1951 that Fitch really got his groove. Driving much more powerful cars than any he had handled so far, he entered 14 races, taking ten first-place trophies and four seconds, including a class win at Sebring with an XK-120. In the same year he borrowed a weary Cadillac-engined Allard in Argentina and trounced the cream of the international drivers for a first over-all and a new lap record. "The car fell apart completely the day after", Fitch recalls. Abruptly switching to the other extreme, Formula 3, Fitch won the first 500-c.c. race ever held in America, at Bridgehampton.

He had begun to build another special, based this time on the XK Jaguar, when Briggs Cunningham invited him to drive one of the new Cunningham cars at Le Mans, which had not been won by an American since the early 1920s. Here began the series of mechanical troubles that were so often to rob Fitch of a dream. By the end of the 18th hour the C-2 Cunningham was lying second over-all against the best that Europe's designers could produce; then the engine began to weary and little by little the blue and white car lost ground. But it finished; and, in spite of the mishap, Fitch and his team-mate, Phil Walters, finished first in their class.

Later that year, at Elkhart Lake, the Cunningham regained its old vigour and Fitch scored a flat win. Only a few weeks afterward, at Watkins Glen, came the incident that is characteristically John Fitch. Roaring around the course in a 2·3 Ferrari, John spotted the wreck of a competitor's car from which the driver could not free himself. Brakes and tyres screamed and smoked as he pulled his Ferrari off the road, slipped his safety belt and jumped from the car. Only when he was satisfied that his rival was uninjured did Fitch go back to his own car—and he finished a magnificent second. For this he was awarded the Sportsmanship Trophy.

In 1951 and 1952 Fitch increased his driving abroad, tackling the 2000-mile, five-day Carrera Panamericana with a stock Chrysler that failed the first day; returning to Le Mans for Cunningham (the car, a C-4, lay third when its engine blew up in the fourth hour of the 24); then competing in the Alpine Rally for Sunbeam-Talbot until a wheel bearing failed. Named S.C.C.A. national champion in 1952, Fitch got a drive in a 1500 Porsche at the tricky Nürburgring. He finished fourth; but he had caught the eye of Alfred Neubauer, the famous—and exacting—Kaiser of Mercedes-Benz racing. Neubauer asked him to test-drive the new 300-SL coupé on the Ring and, as a result, to drive the car in the Mexican race. (No other American has ever been invited to join the Mercedes team.) In return, despite five days of wrestling with defective suspension, Fitch finished third, making the fastest lap time on the final leg and being beaten only by Kling and Lang, his team-mates. But the third position was disallowed because on one leg Fitch had turned back to align a front wheel.

Back with Cunningham in 1953, Fitch scored an out-and-out win at Sebring to start the year. Going on to the Mille Miglia—called by many drivers the most dangerous race in the world—in a Nash-Healey, John was baulked again by mechanical trouble, this time brake failure. He tried Indianapolis, his boyhood workout arena, in a Brown Special but did not qualify: "Either I wasn't up to it," he reflects objectively, "or the car wasn't."

Returning almost at once to Europe for another go at Le Mans with Walters in a C-5 Cunningham, Fitch finished third over-all. He went on to Rheims and the worst accident of his career. The heavy Cunningham had barely taken the lead when it went completely out of control at 140 miles an hour and flashed end over end over end. That shook Fitch, and scratched him a little, too, but he was committed to Sunbeam-Talbot again for the Alpine that same month, and became one of the few Americans ever to win a Coupe des Alpes. The Tourist Trophy in Ulster—"a narrow, blind road built up on rain-swept mountains", Fitch calls it—and a faulty Frazer-Nash, and Monza and a seized engine, and he came home to win in California for Cunningham.

Another side of racing took hold of Fitch in 1954. He ran only four times, spending most of the year as technical adviser and driver for a Hollywood studio making a racing film. But in 1955 he went back to the road—to the most demanding of the roads, the Mille Miglia, as a Mercedes team driver in a 300-SL coupé. Determined to come in

first in the gran turismo category, John scored one of his greatest triumphs—a rare one for any American driver—by getting back to Brescia not only first in gran turismo but fifth absolutely. The memory of this, however, was overshadowed when, co-driving a 300-SLR, at Le Mans with Pierre Levegh, Fitch saw his team-mate crash in "the blackest moment in the history of motor sport".

After another creditable whirl at G.P. racing, in a car borrowed from Stirling Moss, Fitch teamed with the Englishman for the Tourist Trophy and they finished absolute first in a Mercedes 300-SLR. The credit belongs entirely to Moss, however, to hear Fitch tell it. But Mercedes left racing that year, and Fitch, for the first time, became identified with an American marque, Corvette. As team captain, he brought the car home first in its class at Sebring in 1956.

The following year, having spent months in helping to design the new course that was to win top rank in its first season, Fitch became racing director of Lime Rock Park. He still found time, however, to drive at his own and other courses in Maseratis, both 2-litre and 1·5, taking consistent firsts both in class and over-all. In 1958 his managerial and promotional duties at Lime Rock cut more deeply into his racing; in addition, he went into the automobile business again, opening a sports-car sales and tuning establishment in Lakeville, Conn., near his course.

In the past few years he has also begun to establish a name for himself as a writer, publishing articles in a wide variety of leading American magazines "for those", he says in his articulate autobiography, "who believe in the poetry of motion, as seen in the red blur of a screaming Ferrari in the Mille Miglia or the silver flash of a Mercedes-Benz on the Nürburgring . . . those who can understand that automobile racing is part of the human compulsion to do more than is necessary, or wise, or prudent in man's unending search for individual accomplishment".

FROILAN GONZALES

Some three hours by automobile from Buenos Aires (less if by sports car) lies the thriving little town of Arrecifes, where in 1922 was born to the owner of a Chevrolet agency a boy who was named Froilan. The family was named Gonzales and it boasted an uncle who raced cars and was killed in one.

Froilan grew into a sturdy, bright youth and his father sent him to the Monastery of San Nicolas to learn something. Whatever it was that Froilan was to learn may never be known, for the monks gave him a delivery truck to drive and he found great joy in it. He was attracted by competitive athletics, became an excellent swimmer and developed a goalpost shot in soccer that is still the talk of the community.

Like many drivers before him, Froilan had a strong interest in motor-cycles, taking part in the wild impromptu races that were the terror of the countryside. By this time he was making a livelihood in a trucking company while racing American stock cars.

Gonzales was, in a way, discovered by Fangio, who had supplied him with his first racing car, a 4CLT Maserati. This was in 1949, and a year later he raced at Palermo against Ascari, Fangio, Villoresi and Campos, finishing fifth. He went with Fangio to Europe, where he learned a great deal, and when he returned to Argentina he beat the Mercedes twice with a 2-litre supercharged Ferrari. This made him an undisputed national hero.

European drivers and spectators, pit crews and officials never failed to be astonished when Gonzales appeared on the scene. He was of gigantic girth and it seemed remarkable that he would fit into the tight cockpit of a Maserati, which attained the distinction of being a sturdy and robust car to hold Gonzales.

His body seemed custom-built to his manner. He was big, warmhearted and sympathetic. He took tolerantly to the nicknames that were created around him—*cabezon*, which means *big head*; the Bull of the Pampas or the Bull in the China Shop. His middle was compared with all the tyre advertisements that adorn race gatherings, but he continued to smile at all these and loved the name of *Pepe* best because that was what his close friends called him.

Gonzales ran his greatest race in the British Grand Prix at Silverstone, where his 4·5-litre Ferrari defeated the "unbeatable" Alfa Romeo 158. He had set the fastest practice lap, but, when the race began, Fangio leaped into the lead with a fantastic pace. The reason was obvious. Fangio knew he would have to stop for fuel, whereas the Ferrari could run through without a halt. The race was undecided up to the final minute, when Gonzales in one last burst crossed the finish line 50 seconds ahead of his fellow-Argentine.

He proved his massive skill and daring again at the Nürburgring when he became one of three to set a lap time of less than ten minutes. The others were Fangio and Ascari. In 1954, with Trintignant, he won at Le Mans, where it became generally known that despite his bulk he had a sensitive stomach. He admitted that he had been unable to take food during the entire 24 hours.

When two men come from the same country and both are great speed drivers, a natural rivalry can turn into a feud. In the case of Gonzales and Fangio it went farther, because, in addition to personality differences, they were in strong disagreement politically at a time when their country was in ferment.

The crowds fanned this feud, which halted abruptly when Gonzales was seriously hurt at Monza and was out about a year. The two men, however, had one common ground—that was Onofre Marimón, the young Argentine driver whom both had helped on the racing courses of their own country and Europe. Marimón was killed when his red Maserati plunged off the road at Wehrseifen during a practice run. Gonzales wept on the shoulder of Fangio and the old friendship was renewed. Gonzales was not the same after the incident. His health continued to decline and he suffered a severe accident in the Tourist Trophy. He retired to Argentina but cannot keep away from the sport altogether. He put a Chevrolet engine into a Ferrari and occasionally drives it in local races.

MASTEN GREGORY

The increasing American awareness of the beauties and skills of sports-car racing is bound to bring out a crop of young drivers some of whom may approach the successes achieved by men like Moss, Fangio or Nuvolari. Of the several regarded as such timber, one stands out. He is Masten Gregory, whose youth and record of brilliant performances have evoked a great deal of interest.

Gregory was born in 1932 in Kansas City and his earliest contact with motor racing was at midget races, where he watched Dale Duncan, his brother-

Masten Gregory

in-law. Hans Tanner reports that Gregory "got to know a great deal about midgets but openly admits to having been too frightened to take part".

At the age of 19 he got a Jaguar XK-120 and, after driving it about a bit, decided to start competition. Thereupon he telephoned Sidney Allard in England and asked that a new J2X Allard be flown to him at once. When the Allard arrived, Gregory put into it a souped-up Mercury engine he had removed from a very special Ford hot-rod that he owned. This attempt at playing mechanic and engineer came to an unhappy end when the combination failed.

The Mercury engine was replaced by a Chrysler especially prepared by Clay Smith. Gregory took it out at Caddow Mills, Texas, where he managed to stay just behind Carroll Shelby for five exciting laps. Then the engine blew up.

Smith created another engine, which Gregory took to Sebring. He was showing well, lying fourth in the field behind the Cunningham and two Aston Martins when his rods broke. The next car was a C Jaguar with which he set the fastest practice time at Chanute Field. He had brought no pit crew to the track and when he was low on fuel during the race he drove off the track to the petrol truck. He was promptly disqualified when he tried to re-enter the race.

The rough edges were beginning to wear round, however, as race after race added to the experience of this eager and alert young man. He took the C Jaguar to the 1000-km. in Buenos Aires, where he saw Maglioli and Farina win in a 4·5 Ferrari. When they crossed the finish line, Gregory bought their car and immediately took it back to the United States, where he wrapped it round a tree.

He liked the car enough to have it repaired and took it to Europe, where he began to attract attention. He drove the 12 Hours at Rheims with Biondetti and then in Portugal made everyone take notice by coming in just behind Gonzales and Hawthorn. His next race at Paris brought him in a tight second to Behra. Then he went to Nassau and won the top race.

A year later in a Monza Ferrari he won in Portugal; took third behind Musso and Behra at Bari and finished third at the Nürburgring behind Fangio and Moss in the 300 SLR Mercedes and ahead of the same type of car driven by Kling and a 3·7 factory Ferrari driven by Farina.

During 1956 Gregory and Temple Buell of Denver formed the Scuderia Buell, with Gregory as Number One driver and Buell supplying the machines. Gregory won the 2-litre class at Nassau with a Testa Rossa Ferrari. Then they went to Argentina with a 3·5 Ferrari and scored a dramatic victory over the factory cars. In succeeding years he was a mainstay of the Ecurie Ecosse.

The impressive records of young Masten Gregory continued to increase and racing circles on both sides of the Atlantic are watching.

FRITZ VON HANSTEIN

The dual rôle of racing driver and manager of the racing department for Porsche has presented to Fritz Huschke von Hanstein a climate of continuous

[Courtesy of Dipl.-Ing. Alfred Kempter

Von Hanstein, Dr. Fritz Fiedler, B.M.W. designer, and Bäumer after the 1940 Mille Miglia

challenge on which he thrives. One of the finest examples of this was the 1958 Grand Prix of Venezuela, one of the last town-to-town races, between Palmarejo and Caracas. As racing manager von Hanstein contemplated the 469 dreary miles of broken and rutted roads, awesome bends and corners, he must have shuddered at the thought of letting a man drive a Porsche at speed over them. In addition, the roads were under unsupervised repair by lackadaisical workmen who left spades and axes strewn about with criminal carelessness. Thereupon, von Hanstein, the racing driver, got into his car and covered the distance in 5 hours and 17·51 minutes for an average of 89·97 m.p.h., winning the 1500-c.c. class and coming in eighth over-all. *Motor Sport* ranked this as one of the high achievements of the season.

His interest in motor sport began during his school days in England. He was born in 1911 in Halle, a descendant of one of the oldest families in the German nobility. He inherited a large estate that had been in the family more than 1000 years. Because it was in the extreme eastern end of Germany, von Hanstein left the estate when the Russians took over. In England he studied law and drove motorcycles in rallies and hill-climbs. After becoming a lawyer, he decided to continue in motor sport, becoming the Number One driver for the Hanomag factory in Hannover. When Adler started racing its first streamlined sports saloon, von Hanstein became a member of the team from 1935 to 1938, running in the long-distance contests like Le Mans and Spa. In 1938, in a 328 B.M.W., he raced well enough to become champion of Germany. The following year he was in the lead for the title when the war interrupted his progress.

This did not prevent him from taking his saloon to the Mille Miglia, because Italy was not yet at war. He won the Mille Miglia in what has been called his greatest success. It was also the first time a closed car had won the race. Von Hanstein admits that he prefers closed cars and would rather run in the Carrera than the Porsche Spyder. When the war was over he did a good deal of racing in "home-made" cars from 760 c.c. to 2 litres. He joined Porsche in 1950 in his double job. In 1958 he won 12 races out of the 15 in which he started, including gran-turismo victories in the Targa Florio and the Ten Hours of Messina.

When he fled East Germany penniless, he was not disheartened because he had his racing to bolster him. He recalls only one incident with nostalgic regret and physical pain. In 1936 he looked forward to racing in the Auto-Union and he was given a contract. During a drive from a race, a mechanic who was at the wheel crashed the car, causing von Hanstein to suffer a severe shoulder injury. He had to give up Formula I racing and was forever reminded of the incident by a stiff shoulder. In his more than 25 years of racing, von Hanstein never attained the top ten, but his accumulated knowledge and experience in all kinds of competition—rallies, trials, hill-climbs, and long distance and scratch races—have assured him a position of respect among the racing managers and drivers of his time.

MIKE HAWTHORN

The first Briton to win the world championship gained his title in his eighth year as a racing driver; six weeks later he retired, and within two months he was dead—killed in an ordinary highway crash.

John Michael Hawthorn began racing in 1951, when he was under 22, under the tutelage of his father, Leslie, himself a racing driver of some note. Mike Hawthorn's first sports car was a pre-war Riley Ulster Imp, an 1100 c.c. car that had formerly been raced by the factory.

But the first time he drove was many years earlier, when he was 8. Hawthorn Senior, who was a first-class engineer as well as a good driver, owned a garage in Surrey (later his son's property) that was favoured by lovers of fine cars. In 1937, an army officer had left his Jowett at the Tourist Trophy Garage for repair; on his arrival to pick it up he was attracted by a grinding noise and, looking to see where it came from, he observed his car thumping over the lawn behind the garage and, at the wheel, a dirty-faced blond boy whose thumb was as if cemented to the starter button: he had the car in gear and was driving it on the battery.

During school holidays it was impossible for the elder Hawthorn to keep young Mike away from the garage. At 14 he bought a blown-up motor-cycle, repaired it, sold it and was given another. Not too much interested in school, Mike abandoned it when he was 17 and apprenticed himself to an engineering firm, meanwhile racing motor-cycles in his spare time. However, Mr. and Mrs. Hawthorn feared that, if allowed to continue motor-cycling to work every day, their son would not long be with them, and he was allowed to commute in a 500-c.c. FIAT, which was his introduction to fast cornering. From this he graduated to a Lancia Aprilia. In this car he soon found himself, at his father's instance, returning to school to become a proper engineer at Kingston Technical College and the College of Automobile Engineering. In Hawthorn's own words, however, "I never shone very brightly at mathematics and engineering theory. The driving-seat, not the drawing-board, was the place where I wanted to be."

In 1950 Hawthorn's father brought him the Riley Imp, which the boy put into proper shape under his father's guidance, adding hydraulic brakes and other modernizations. He entered a couple of sprints in the car in 1950 and spent the entire winter dreaming of his début in actual racing.

His first race was run against other Rileys at Gamston, and Hawthorn won. His father having

[*Courtesy of "Sports Cars Illustrated"*]

Mike Hawthorn

hurt his back, Hawthorn took over Leslie's 1500-c.c. Riley for the next race and took second in that. His greatest thrill in this first year of racing came at Dundrod, when, in a preliminary to the Tourist Trophy, Hawthorn pushed his Riley Imp ahead of an XK-120 Jaguar and was almost unnerved to realize he had just passed the great Louis Chiron. In this first season, Hawthorn ran 12 races, finishing well in all of them and spinning out enough in one to be called up for explanation to the great S. C. H. Davis, one of the stewards. He also accumulated enough points to win the *Motor Sport* Trophy for the year.

From then on Mike Hawthorn ran with the men, not the boys. In 1952 he decided to move up to Formula II racing in a Cooper-Bristol. This season taught the young driver a number of handy lessons: how a competitor can make one slide by pressing one's tail-lights and always threatening to pass; how turning one's head instead of using the mirror can send one right off the course. He soon found himself competing with Peter Collins, Jean Behra, Ken Wharton, Peter Whitehead and Harry Schell, as well as Gonzales and Fangio. In 1952, too, he drove his first Continental race, the Belgian G.P., in which he finished fourth, partly because of a faulty clutch and partly another mistake in conduct: seeing Taruffi walking up a hill from his disabled car, Hawthorn turned to wave consolingly and the next thing he saw was a telegraph pole coming up fast. It missed him, but the lesson did not.

At the end of the 1952 season Hawthorn went to Monza for the Italian G.P. and Enzo Ferrari invited him to try a Ferrari. Ascari and Villoresi took the car first, then Hawthorn followed: he had never experienced such fantastic braking and cornering. But then he went out on the same circuit in his Cooper-Bristol and made the mistake of handling it as if it were a Ferrari. He spun into the haybales hiding the concrete posts at about 70 m.p.h. and was flung out when the car overturned. His next stop was a hospital, where Ferrari repeated his invitation to the young Briton to join the team of the Prancing Horse.

However, a long siege of hospitalization in both Italy and England intervened, for fluid had gathered in a lung, and it was some time before Mike could return to Italy to sign the contract. During that trip he was introduced to skiing, but this was a sport he quickly rejected as being much too dangerous.

Hawthorn's first race for Ferrari was the Argentine Grand Prix in 1953. The team leader was Ascari, then world champion, and the other members were Farina and Villoresi. Hawthorn was under orders to stay behind them but ahead of everyone else, including Fangio and Gonzales on Maseratis. The spectator areas were crowded and the *descamisados*, under President Perón's benevolent eye, were allowed to swarm in and oust those who had bought tickets; as a result, the crowd bulged out on to the course itself, obscuring even the warning signs for the turns. A small boy ran across the track in front of Farina, who, swerving to avoid him, slid into the jammed throng. He collapsed among the dead and dying and, in the chaos, another child ran out and was killed by a Cooper. Farina's car had killed 15 people; the ambulances began rounding the course against the traffic and launched a grand prix of their own. As a result, one ambulance went out of control and killed two more spectators. The police tried to restore order with bull whips and one of them was kicked to death. Despite all this, Hawthorn finished fourth behind Ascari, Villoresi and Gonzales, Fangio's car having broken a universal joint.

After Argentina Hawthorn drove in two European races, finishing third in one and second in the other, and then came the Mille Miglia. He was not enthusiastic, feeling that this was a course that required months of learning; Hawthorn felt also that, since Ferrari had won the Mille Miglia the past five times, a good deal was expected of every member of the team. In his own Ferrari coupé, he spent three days touring the route and making as many mental notes as possible. His car for the race was a 3-litre V-12 and his riding mechanic had raced only once before, in a Tour of Sicily in which his driver had rolled the car several times. The long-drawn-out circus atmosphere of Brescia before the race began disturbed Hawthorn and even on his way to the starting ramp he could muster no enthusiasm; but, once off, he began to enjoy it despite the constantly recurring sight of wrecked competitors along the road. Brake failure ended the venture after less than a quarter of the distance.

After several lesser races in England Hawthorn returned to the Continent to drive a 4·1 Ferrari coupé at Le Mans. Again brake failure put him out, this time after only 12 laps. A few weeks later, however, Mike became the first Briton to win the French G.P. at Rheims since Segrave in 1923. At times he ran so close to Fangio that he could see the tachometer in the Argentine's cockpit. Reading about the race afterward, Hawthorn was most impressed to learn that the crowd and the commentators were yelling, beside themselves, and the other drivers were slowing down to watch the competition among the leaders; of none of this had he been even remotely aware. In fact, he had been afraid the crowd was bored.

He ran in the Nürburgring for the first time that year, and always liked the course, which he considered the toughest all-round test of car and driver because of its infinite variety of corners, its 5-in-1 gradients and its constant surprises. For spectator safety, however, he rated it much less highly. He finished third here and went on to Pescara for the 12-hour sports-car race, in which he won the new Tazio Nuvolari Cup in a 4·5 Ferrari G.T. Back at the Nürburgring, he was deprived of a drive when the engine was taken from his car for use in Ascari's; so Hawthorn spent the night before the race expertly putting a Frazer-Nash into proper shape for a pair of British drivers.

Hawthorn's worst year was 1954. He was disqualified in Argentina for being pushed by spectators; his engine broke and spun him out on the last corner when he was far ahead of the field; and the British press began to criticize him because he had not done his military service. While this question was being fanned into a minor scandal, Mike hit a wall in the Syracuse race and caught fire: he jumped out and rolled over and over in a field to smother the flames. He was particularly touched that Gonzales, seeing the blazing car, stopped to try to pull him out despite the certainty of an explosion any instant. Sent to a hospital on the Italian mainland, he missed many races but begged Ferrari to let him run at Le Mans. In a practice tour of Monza he found himself suddenly covered with petrol: a fuel-pipe junction had split and for a fraction of a second he relived the whole Syracuse experience.

Mastering the reaction, he went on to Paris, assigned to a 4·9 Ferrari for Le Mans. There he learned that his father had been badly hurt in a road accident and, before Mike could get a plane to England, the man to whom he had always felt he owed his whole career was dead. He had barely returned from his father's funeral when he was called for military service: but one look at the unhealed burns on his legs changed the army's mind. He went back to the Continent to race again but was still dogged by car faults, until he took second in the British G.P. at Silverstone. A number of other second-places followed—first frequently being Fangio —until the Tourist Trophy race at Dundrod. There it was a Hawthorn-Ascari duel lap after lap, each vying with the other in setting new lap records, down to 4:49 for the 7·4-mile course, or 92·38 m.p.h. Ascari's driveshaft tore loose toward the end and Hawthorn in his 750S Ferrari clinched the 1954 constructors' championship for the Commendatore. After a few lesser races, Mike wound up the season in hospital for a long-deferred kidney operation; ultimately this put an end to the military service question.

In 1955 he entered his first American race, Sebring, in a D Jaguar with Phil Walters and won, despite Ferrari's insistence that its Phil Hill-Carroll Shelby team had run the full 12 hours while Hawthorn and Walters had not. Ultimately Ferrari lost the battle and Hawthorn went back to England to drive for Vanwall. He also did well in Jaguar Mark VII's in saloon races. But the Vanwalls were not running well and, approached to drive for Lancia, Mike won his release from Vanwall only to learn that Lancia had retired from racing. However, he remained in green cars, for he signed with Jaguar for Le Mans. Hawthorn was clocking as much as 180 m.p.h. on the straights. At pit-stop time he passed Pierre Levegh's Mercedes and Lance Macklin's Austin-Healey with enough margin to allow him to turn in at his pit. He raised his hand in signal to Macklin, touched his brakes and cut inward, when a flying object flashed across his field of vision.

It was Levegh's Mercedes, in the worst accident in the history of motor racing: it cartwheeled over the safety barrier and disintegrated like a bomb; at the same time Macklin's Healey spun backward past Hawthorn, who had to overshoot the pit. Horror-stricken, he made another lap, because reversing is forbidden, and came into the pit, where he refused almost hysterically to return to the course. But he did return, to win, in an atmosphere of crowd fatalism that staggered him. There were official inquiries to be faced, and ugly irresponsible statements directed against several of the drivers; but in the end it was found that the tragedy was no one person's fault. Ferrari re-enlisted Hawthorn for various races in 1955, but the cars let him down frequently. And he had little better luck when he returned to a D Jaguar for Dundrod, where three drivers were killed.

But in 1956 Ferrari would not share Hawthorn, who became team leader for Jaguar. His car did not finish at Sebring. He also drove for B.R.M., with equally unsatisfactory results and one end-over-end crash that fortunately entailed no injuries. An accident at the Nürburgring, when Hawthorn's D Jag hit the back of a Porsche, stirred up much German resentment that had been latent since the tragic 1955 Le Mans, until Porsche's team manager declared unequivocally that the Porsche had been completely in the wrong. The rest of the year was a checkered record with Lotus and Vanwall and Maserati, as well as occasional Ferrari runs, ending with a Lotus flip off an embankment at Oulton Park.

Returning to Ferrari in 1957, Hawthorn began as usual in Argentina after the car's cockpit had been tailored to his height. The heat was at its worst and he had holes drilled in his crash helmet, but extreme heat cost him the lead. Then back to Sebring for a third place in a D Jag. Back in a Ferrari for the Monaco G.P., Mike found the steering undergeared and this gave him considerable trouble. More developed when another driver almost stopped in front of him between the tunnel and the chicane. Mike swung his wheel all the way over but could not prevent impact, which sheared off his right front wheel and brake drum. The car, completely out of control, drove on at about 50 m.p.h. for the sea wall, where Collins was standing up in his wrecked car. Collins ducked, the Ferrari jumped and landed on top of his car, and he and Hawthorn were unhurt.

Though he set a new lap record at Le Mans—3:58·7, or 126·2 m.p.h.—the 4-litre Ferrari could not go the distance and, when Musso was co-driving, the pistons blew; the same thing occurred in the Formula I G.P. of France. The rest of the year was full of frustrations and on the whole Mike was much more successful with his private plane, for by now he had acquired a pilot's licence and was flying a great deal for fun, as well as to save time getting from one race to another. He finished fourth in world championship standings and, with the rumours of Fangio's imminent retirement, it looked certain that Moss would be the 1958 champion after five successive years of finishing second to Fangio.

Still with Ferrari in 1958, Hawthorn was pressed for points by Moss from the opening of the season. Mike took more seconds than firsts, and ordinarily might have been expected to finish the season behind Moss had not Stirling, in a startling departure from previous years, had a remarkable record of cars breaking up under him. At Rheims Hawthorn set a new lap record in practice, almost 131 m.p.h., and a new record for the G.P. race itself, 125·3 m.p.h. This was his first victory in four years in a world championship race. But he finished second in the German G.P. at the Nürburgring, where his close friend, Peter Collins, was killed almost under his eyes. By the time the season reached its final race, the G.P. of Morocco at Casablanca, Hawthorn was four points ahead of Moss. But there was still more than a mathematical chance that Moss might win the championship: first place plus the extra points for a lap record would put him one point ahead of Hawthorn.

Moss did win the race, and he did make the fastest lap of the day, which gave him a one-point bonus. But it was not a lap record. Moss had scored nine points for a total of 41 for the year. But Hawthorn, who already had 36 points, finished second, gaining six more to give him a total of 42, after running fourth through most of the race. The answer lay in the sportsmanship of the American, Phil Hill, who, lying third, fell back deliberately to give the championship to the Englishman.

PHIL HILL

Phil Hill became America's top-ranking sports-car driver by building a strong foundation of experience on a succession of cars and an earnest willingness to rectify errors as quickly as possible. When he accepted, with proper modesty, his brilliant victory in the 1958 Le Mans, and heard himself praised as a driver who knows what his car can do and is adept at saving brakes and tyres in a long race, he paused to recall an incident of eight years before at Pebble Beach.

It concerned an XK-120 Jaguar whose engine he bored out to 3·8 litres and whose body he stripped of all excessive weight. In the process, it seems, there was slight neglect in the matter of brakes and clutch, but Phil won the race. "I drove like a madman," he confessed. "I look back on those days and shudder."

But the incident was part of the great accumulation of experience that began for Philip T. Hill, Jr., of Santa Monica, Calif., when he got a job as a mechanic with Walter Faulkner. He had spurned his studies in business administration to roar round the lonely canyons near Santa Monica in an old Ford; and later he had inspected with awe a collection of Alfa Romeos and Bugattis owned by a friend. While working on the Offenhauser engines and as a mechanic for Packard, Phil bought an M.G. and drove it to his first victory at Carrall Speedway, a professional track at Los Angeles.

Having extracted all he could learn from his first three cars, Hill bought a 2·9-litre Alfa Romeo that Biondetti had driven in the Mille Miglia. He scored too many seconds and sold the Alfa for an Aston Martin and later an M.G. with a Ford engine. In 1952 he got from Luigi Chinetti a 2·6-litre Ferrari that had won the Tour de France the previous year. This car, too, did not measure up, and Hill got a new 3-litre Ferrari.

Each car and each race added to the structure of the man. In 1952, Allen Guiberson of Dallas offered Hill a 2·6-litre Ferrari for the Mexican Road Race. Hill brought it in sixth. Then came his first Le Mans. He was leading his class in an O.S.C.A. when the rear axle failed. The European courses were fascinating and Hill went to Rheims and co-drove with Chinetti. They had to withdraw when the car started to buck and wobble whenever the brakes were applied.

In 1954, ulcers forced him to pause, but only briefly. He returned to the Mexican Road Race with an impressive second place and then went to Sebring with Carroll Shelby, and they wound up second again. The following year he won almost all

[Courtesy of "Sports Cars Illustrated"

Phil Hill

the U.S. events and was named S.C.C.A. champion in Class D Modified.

A truly gratifying second to Moss at Buenos Aires in 1956 brought him an invitation from Ferrari. He won the Swedish Grand Prix with Maurice Trintignant, got a third at the Nürburgring and won the nine-hour race at Messina, Sicily. A year later he teamed with Peter Collins. They gained second place behind the swifter Maserati with Moss in it. That was the beginning. Then they set a sports-car record by winning three prime international events in succession—Caracas that year and Buenos Aires and Sebring in 1958. With Olivier Gendebien, his Le Mans co-victor of 1958, he won Sebring again in 1959 for Ferrari.

Hill was now a member of the grand coterie of international sports-car aces. He removed all doubt as to his standing when he won the 1958 Le Mans with Olivier Gendebien of Belgium and, as a member of the Ferrari Grand Prix team, helped Mike Hawthorn win the world championship. He won the respect of the sport when he proved himself a loyal team man in Hawthorn's victory. He could have finished ahead of Hawthorn, but in true team spirit he held off so that his British partner could get the needed points. In recognition of his over-all achievement, Frank M. Blunk selected him as *The New York Times* sports-car driver of the year.

Hill is an intense young man, who has avoided marriage because "a wife would worry too much about my driving". He dampens his inner fires by relaxing at great speeds and listening to Vivaldi and Beethoven on a stereophonic combination that covers an entire wall of his lodgings. He is adept at several instruments, but admits that a finely tuned engine makes better music.

HERMANN LANG

Some of the chapter headings in the instructive autobiography of Hermann Lang reveal the emotional turbulence the great German ace experienced in his long ascent to driving eminence: *Racing Fever, Dark Shadows, Hard Times, Engine Fitter at Daimler-Benz, Racing Mechanic, Obstacles, Happy Days, Hopes, Disappointments, Catastrophe, Loss of a Friend, You Can Still Drive, Hermann; Try, Try Again, The Pitiless Race.*

Lang's life in racing may be regarded as the classic formula on how to learn, practise and finally succeed. The youngest of four brothers, he began as an apprentice mechanic in a motor-cycle repair shop and on his first ride smashed his machine into a tree. When he entered his first hill-climb, another tree got in the way and the family began to worry. After two of his four brothers were killed in road crashes, family objections became even stronger, but Hermann persisted and in 1931, at 22, he won the hill-climbs at Schauinsland and Ratisbona and became German hill-climb champion.

With an eye toward sports cars, Lang wrote to Daimler-Benz for a job as an engine fitter and was immediately refused by Neubauer, who felt that this youth had no real desire to be an engine fitter but was just another speed-happy lad who wanted to race for Mercedes. But Lang persisted and got the job. Before long his eagerness and ability were noted and he was given a chance as a racing mechanic with the grand-prix machines.

Neubauer, always in search of new drivers, questioned Lang closely one day about his motor-cycle experiences and shortly thereafter ordered Lang to drive the grand-prix cars to the circuit. He also hinted broadly that the young man might start observing the techniques of the works drivers. Lang watched, absorbed, memorized, practised and learned.

His next promotion was in the testing department of sports and production cars. In 1935, Neubauer announced that he would hold trials to choose the Mercedes works team. Lang had a trial run on the Autostrada at Milan and at Monza, where he showed so well that he was marked for more intensive training.

In his first race as a company driver, Lang landed in a ditch at the Nürburgring. In the German Grand Prix his car failed. Thoroughly disheartened, he entered the Grand Prix of Switzerland and finished sixth. Next year, in the German Grand Prix, he had passed Rosemeyer to go into first place, when, while

Hermann Lang

he was changing down rapidly, his hand struck the bodywork and he broke his finger. Caracciola took over, but, Lang recalls, "the spectators were very displeased with me and whistled their disapproval. A doctor bandaged my finger and on my return to the pits I saw Brauchitsch stop to hand over his car to Zehender, our Italian reserve driver. I asked Neubauer immediately to let me continue and he gave permission. I now endured unbelievable pain and do not even like to think of it. Every time I changed gear, the wooden splint on my finger touched the bodywork and I almost howled with pain. However, it had been my choice and I managed to finish. This time the spectators applauded heartily and I hoped that I had passed the acid test."

From there Lang went on to become one of the great attractions on the courses of Europe. In 1936 he won at Tripoli and hurled back the challenge of the Auto-Union at Avus with a victory and an average speed of 162 m.p.h. He moved right into the class of Nuvolari and Caracciola with his driving at Pescara with his 3-litre supercharged Formula I car. Just before the war he captured the European championship.

There were those who wrote him off after the war, but Lang came back as strong as ever. He entered many races and scored in an impressive number of them. He came third in Argentina in 1950, beating Fangio. During one practice lap he recorded 2·08 minutes against Fangio's 2·095. At Le Mans his Mercedes set a new course record,

covering 3733·78 kilometres in the 24 hours. He finished second in the Carrera Panamericana. Shortly before his retirement he drove a factory Maserati on the Nürburgring and took part in grand-prix racing in a Veritas.

Neubauer, the stern old taskmaster, summed up the career of his pupil this way: "Lang started out with considerable advantages. First and foremost, he possessed an inborn driving skill, allied to a first-class physique acquired through hard work and sport during his youth; tremendous will power; technical knowledge gained through his training as a mechanic, and, of course, his personal strength. . . . In spite of these assets, his road to success as a racing driver was a thorny one, by his own admission, because, like many others, he did not realize the difficulties and obstacles that lay ahead in this profession."

CHRISTIAN LAUTENSCHLAGER

The 1908 Grand Prix of France, which was held at Dieppe under a bright July sun, is noted for three important contributions to the history of motor sport. It was in this race that Christian Lautenschlager made his remarkable début as a driver. It was on this day that grand-prix cars were reduced to a mere $12\frac{1}{2}$ litres from the monsters of 18 litres and up. And it was on this day that the pit was created.

The reduction of engine size was a matter of evolution, good sense and expediency. Experience up to 1908 had indicated that the smaller car was more efficient in every department of racing and, while Dieppe still carried some giants, the "tiny" $12\frac{1}{2}$-litres were hailed for their general superiority.

As for the pits, everyone at Dieppe that day seemed astonished they had not been thought of before. In the beginning of racing, groups of mechanics and friends would refuel, change tyres and make other repairs at some specific place on the course, chosen in a rather haphazard fashion and remaining a constant source of worry for the driver trying to find it. For this grand prix, however, the sensible method was adopted. Shallow trenches were dug at the side of the road. A marker was placed so that the driver could always find his own pit. Inside the pit was stored all the matériel needed. Stirling Moss remarks in his *Book of Motor Sport* that "the sturdy pioneers would doubtless gasp at the sight of modern pits—drinks and snack bars attached; but the old name has stuck".

The début of Lautenschlager, however, was the most shocking event of the day, especially to the French. Lined up against his Mercedes were the French cars—Panhard, Gobron-Brillié, Mors, de Dietrich, Darracq, Brasier, Clément-Bayard. France was on the throne of racing. She had retained her triumphant place for many years all over the

Continent—and this was the Grand Prix of France. Her chances were excellent.

Lautenschlager, the newcomer, sat sullenly in his car watching the great aces like Hémery, Resta, Lord Brabazon and Rigal arrayed on the starting grid. There was a solemnity to the occasion, historians recall, and Lautenschlager apparently was deeply impressed by the task at hand. He flexed his powerful biceps, started the car over the bumpy roadway and pulled right behind Hémery, the leader, staying in that position for four laps.

The race was furious. There were 48 cars in the contest and at least 20 of these were timed at more than 100 m.p.h. over a long straight. On the fifth lap, Lautenschlager passed Hémery, both drivers remaining close to each other. Lautenschlager made nine stops for tyres and was not aware that after the ninth stop his pit had no tyres left. He was watched anxiously by his crew each time he roared by hoping that his tyres would hold. They did. He came in first with an average speed of 69 m.p.h.

The muscular, athletic Lautenschlager was a faithful Mercedes retainer from there on. With Teutonic grimness he pressed on impervious to the tricks and chicane of rival drivers. He proved this in the French Grand Prix of July 14, 1914, in which 47 cars and the manufacturers of six countries competed. On June 28 Gavrilo Princip had fired his momentous shots at Sarajevo and the furore, mounting to the ultimate hysteria, was at work even among the spectators of the race. Lautenschlager was hanging closely to Jules Goux, who was leading in his Peugeot. The canny Goux, knowing that Lautenschlager had brakes only on his rear wheels, tried to manœuvre the German into taking a hairpin corner too fast. Lautenschlager was aware of the trick and held back. He gave Goux the right of way on the corner and then went flat out to pass the Frenchman and win the race. There were no cheers.

When the war was over Lautenschlager returned to the tracks. He made a valiant attempt in a 2-litre Mercedes at Indianapolis in 1923, but at the age of 46 reactions were not so rapid. After 14 fierce laps he spun and crashed into a wall, wrecking the car but coming out unhurt. His mechanic's leg was broken. The year before, in the 13th Targa Florio over the Medium Madonie Circuit, 268½ miles, he came tenth. He went back to the same race in 1924 and came in tenth again. At the Coppa Florio, 335½ miles, he came in ninth. In both races, it was noted, the man who won the French Grand Prix twice did not take defeat gracefully or philosophically. W. F. Bradley reported that, when the German was sorely pressed, he roared into the pits "howling for everything and wanting that everything at once". But Bradley also recalled that Lautenschlager was one of the few drivers who mastered the engine "thrash" of the 6-cylinder, overhead-valve engine. The "thrash" was a periodic vibration which the tough and muscular Lautenschlager was able to tame. While he never

Courtesy of Daimler-Benz A.G.]

Christian Lautenschlager

worked under the discipline of Neubauer, Lautenschlager, aside from occasional outburts, was a well-disciplined driver and a man who set a pattern for Mercedes manner.

ONOFRE MARIMÓN

Onofre Augustin Marimón began his career in motor racing in a manner which would fulfil the fantasy of any young sports-car enthusiast. As a boy in Buenos Aires he watched his father, Domingo, race modified American stock cars and home-made racing cars. He decided early that he liked what he saw. His father was pleased—here was one parent who encouraged his son to follow his track marks.

Domingo Marimón had a friend, an up-and-coming young racing driver named Juan Fangio, who also liked the boy. When Onofre was just past 16 he took part in his first stock-car race with a few hints from Fangio. When, at 19, he entered his first big race in Cordoba, he was permitted to use the car that had helped Fangio on the path to racing glory—the modified Chevrolet *monoposto*.

Under the tutelage of Fangio he joined Froilan Gonzales in a 4·5-litre Talbot for Le Mans in 1951. They were forced out soon by engine trouble. It did not seem like a big beginning, and later at Rheims he ran into misfortune again when his Maserati blew up after two laps. After a fair run at Modena he returned to Argentina, where success again eluded him.

Fangio and Gonzales, then the two top Argentine drivers, brought Marimón back to Europe for the

Onofre Marimón

Grand Prix of Belgium, where the Ferrari opposition consisted of Ascari, Villoresi, Farina and Hawthorn. Ascari leaped to the lead when the cars of Fangio and Gonzales exploded. Toward the end the crowd was brought to its feet by the fierce driving of Hawthorn, Villoresi and Marimón. The race was decided in the final few minutes, with Marimón a close third behind Ascari and Villoresi.

Marimón, by this exhibition, had won for himself a place among the leaders in European racing. When Gonzales joined the Ferrari team in 1954 and Mercedes took Fangio, Marimón was signed by the Maserati firm. He made the fastest lap at Syracuse and scored a fantastic win in the Grand Prix of Rome. At Silverstone he came third in his outclassed Maserati behind Gonzales and Hawthorn and managed to come in ahead of Fangio.

Clear skies and a fine road surrounded by blue cornflowers made a wonderful setting for his next contest, the German Grand Prix. He went out for several practice laps and, when he did not return from the last one, they went out to look for him. At the Wehrseifen bridge they found the fatal skid marks, evidently made by locked wheels. Marimón had plunged to his death some 60 ft. below in a cornfield.

STIRLING MOSS

It is fortunate for motor sport that one of its great aces, Stirling Moss, C.B.E., is highly articulate, offering to the enthusiastic observer and to the eager amateur generous helpings of information and advice. Already an immortal on the racing courses of the world, Moss draws from his rich experience when he sets down this elementary philosophy:

"A race driver may not be an athlete, but his life depends on physical fitness. To succeed, he must keep himself in strict training, avoid all excesses and concentrate on the job; although of course he need not think and dream about motor racing all the time; on the contrary, a certain amount of mental relaxation is necessary.

"Obviously motor racing is dangerous, but its exponents do not run the risks that are so often supposed. Disaster results from the unexpected much more often than from any mistake on the part of the driver. As a result of practice, which must be thorough, he should know exactly what he can do. He should know the precise speed at which he can take a bend and he should know, to an inch, the most effective point for braking and acceleration. It is, in fact, almost a routine job. Personally, I think practice is more dangerous than the race, as the driver does more experimenting."

The unquestionable superiority of Moss as a driver, coupled with his warm and friendly sportsmanship, have made him a most popular driver, to the point where the fans hold him in proprietary affection. Win or lose, Moss can be counted upon to do his best to finish and to run a good race. He began a tradition in one of his early races when his car broke down near the end. He was well out of the running, but he waited until the checkered flag was down, then pushed his car across the line in order to be recorded as having finished. Some years later, during a race in Switzerland, his windscreen tore off, but he continued driving with one hand while holding his helmet with the other. He finished eighth—but he finished.

Moss was born into a motor-racing family. His father, Alfred, a dental surgeon of excellent reputation, had twice driven at Indianapolis in the Barber-Warnock Fords and had made the first 100-m.p.h. lap in a Ford at Brooklands. His mother, Aileen, was a highly respected trials driver, using Singers and Marendaz. Stirling recalls his earliest days at the wheel when he sat on his father's lap and steered.

At ten he was presented with a venerable 7-h.p. Austin. The lanes and pathways on the farm made a charming little circuit and young Master Stirling was having a high old time without realizing the agonies of doubt that were stirring his parents. They were naturally happy over his love for cars, but were tormented by qualms when he indicated firmly that he wanted to become a racing driver. Youthful determination won and at the age of 18 he got his licence. Then he got together with John Cooper, who was building 500-c.c. racing cars at Surbiton. He built one with a motor-cycle engine for Moss, who entered it in hill-climbs. It was 1948 and Moss got a third at Prescott, firsts at Stanner, Brough and Bouley Bay, a second at Great Auclum and Boscombe, and first at Silverstone, Shelsley Walsh, Dunholme and Goodwood.

This was a first year and the racing fraternity did not fail to take note. The young man was dextrous and daring and did not hesitate to experiment during practice. He would tackle a curve in several ways, repeating the manœuvre until he seemed satisfied that he had found the best way. Then, in the race, he would hold his throttle more open than most other drivers and gracefully pull ahead.

He was in his first race on the Continent a year later when he drove his special Cooper to victory. The remainder of his efforts that year was so impressive that John Heath, builder of the H.W.M. Formula II car, invited Moss to drive it. The machine was radically different in handling from the 500- and 1000-c.c. Coopers, but Moss managed. He shattered the complacency of Continental drivers, including Ascari and Villoresi, the stars of the Ferrari team, and the crowds murmured that the impetuous young Englishman seemed to be able to steer a car with all four wheels off the ground. He won his first British championship and went on to Maserati, becoming a factory driver after Fangio went to Mercedes. Later Moss went to Mercedes as the Number Two driver to Fangio, coming in second behind the Argentine most of the time and studying his technique all the time. Ultimately he beat Fangio in the British Grand Prix. An interesting rivalry had

sprung up between these aces, based on respect and affection.

Sheila Van Damm recalls a Mille Miglia incident in which Moss was leading Fangio. Moss had crashed through a barbed-wire fence. His car plunged down the side of a hill and was on its way to a drop of 300 ft. when it was stopped by a tree. Shaken but uninjured, Moss and his co-driver climbed up to the road just as Fangio came by. He screeched his car to a halt and backed up to Moss.

"Are you all right?" Fangio asked.

"Yes, thanks," Moss replied.

"Can I give you a lift to Rome?"

"Don't be crazy," Moss yelled. "You're wasting time. Go and get on with the race."

Before that race, Miss Van Damm recalls, she told Moss: "We've had an extra mirror fitted for the passenger so that one of us can see you before you come blinding past us. We don't want to get in your way."

"Nice of you to think of me," Moss said. "I suppose you'll weave over the road when you see Fangio coming up, too."

Miss Van Damm shuddered at the thought and then remembered that Moss had just ordered coffee before he was recognized. "The next moment", she writes, "our table was a mass of young struggling humanity armed with autograph books."

Of all the great years, 1955 will long be remembered by Moss. It began earlier in a discussion between Denis Jenkinson, a writer for *Motor Sport*, and John Fitch, the American ace. They agreed that the Mille Miglia might be won by a non-Italian if the problem of conquering the road were approached scientifically. If the driver could use a passenger who would be a mechanical brain it would help him considerably. Moss was driving a Mercedes-Benz 300 SLR in the race and invited Jenkinson to be his passenger.

"From four previous Mille Miglia races", Jenkinson wrote, "Moss had gathered together a good quantity of notes about bumpy level crossings, blind hill-brows, dangerous corners and so on, and as I knew certain sections of the course intimately, all this knowledge put down on paper amounted to about 25 per cent of the circuit."

The route that year was Brescia, Padua, Ravenna, Ancona, Popoli, Pescara, Aquila, Rome, Siena, Florence, Bologna, Modena, Piacenza and Brescia. Jenkinson and Moss logged all the difficult corners, grading them as "saucy ones, dodgy ones and very dangerous ones, having a hand sign to indicate each type".

Moss was deeply impressed by the scientific approach and worked at it with fierce application. He stressed to Jenkinson the importance of avoiding error. Their rehearsals were thorough, but, during their research, using a 220-A Mercedes-Benz saloon and a 300SL coupé, they had two accidents. Alfred Neubauer, the team manager, was more concerned with their safety than the damage to the cars. During

[*Courtesy of Officine Alfieri Maserati S.p.A.*

Stirling Moss

268

the long and sometimes tedious preparations one vital statistic stood out as a challenge. Up to then 23 Mille Miglias had been run and only one had been won by a non-Italian driver: Caracciola in 1931.

From the beginning, when the car rolled off the unique launching ramp and Jenkinson's chart unrolled, the signals worked. At Padua they saw Castellotti and passed him at Ravenna. Jenkinson lost his glasses, battled a queasy stomach and won when he went back to concentrating on the immediate task. Several straw bales were struck without damage to car or men, and at Pescara, where they refuelled they learned that Taruffi was leading. Somewhere around Aquila they passed Taruffi and at Rome they were leading. They were undisturbed by the sickening tradition that "who leads at Rome cannot win". They also remained calm when they landed in a ditch and Moss pulled out fast with only minor damage to the tail. They had no news of what was going on behind them and they forgot Jarrott's admonition that a leader in a race should feel like a hunted animal. What concerned Moss was keeping the car on the road while doing 170 m.p.h. in some spots and keeping the revs around 7,500. Jenkinson read the charts, faithfully and accurately gave signals and looked back now and then for the red fury that was Taruffi, who never caught up.

The average speed was recorded at 97·9 m.p.h. and Brescia witnessed the wildest demonstration in years when Moss was announced as the winner. He had begun that year with a fourth in the Argentine Grand Prix and a second in the Buenos Aires Grand Prix, He went on to win the British Tourist Trophy, the British Grand Prix and the Targa Florio and wound up second for the world championship behind Fangio. In 1957, at the European Grand Prix at Aintree, he won with a Vanwall at 86·8 m.p.h., became the first driver to lap the course at 90 m.p.h. and was the first Birish driver in 34 years to win that race.

Moss amassed British Gold Stars, prizes of great vareity and the adulation of the racing crowds. His single ambition was to win a world championship in a British car. The fact that he had beaten Fangio in single races but never managed to wrest the championship from him did not rankle with him; it merely increased the intensity of his drive. When Mike Hawthorn won it in 1958 there was no doubt that Moss was still the superior driver. In the New Year's Honours List Queen Elizabeth made him a Commander of the Order of the British Empire.

With all his spectacular victories, Moss has had to battle the jinxes of the racer such as bad weather, unexplained breakdowns and indifferent pit work. To those who have known him closely, he seemed to react to these difficulties with fatalistic cheer. Indeed, in the matter of weather, he appeared to enjoy the challenge of the elements. On a particularly raw and fearful day before a Tourist Trophy race, he is quoted by John Bentley as orating:

"The howling wind, like the wail of a banshee; the bending trees threatening to blow down on the course; the collapse of the press tent, torn down by the fury of the elements; what a day for racing! Would they abandon the race? No. We were off in good time."

Perhaps that expresses the philosophy of the great driver, who basically loves to race for the sake of racing. Moss has been asked often to delineate the art of driving. He says:

"Don't ask me what the essential ingredients are, because I don't know. Theorists say we must have a perfect sense of balance, superb sight, abnormally quick reactions so that our brains signal to our muscles in the briefest space of time. We must have cool, calculating minds and physical dexterity. Personally, I prefer to regard the ability to drive fast cars a little faster than most people as an intangible, almost abstract thing, like an ear for music, but with a motor car perhaps it's balance. It is something you cannot learn unless the fundamentals are inherent."

Moss, who is somewhat of a historian of his craft, also likes to play the prophet a bit. Recalling his Mille Miglia victory with Jenkinson unfolding the chart, he predicts that some day, perhaps soon, it will be possible to take motion pictures of a route and then unreel them in the cockpit for the driver to check. The film could be so inserted, Moss explains, as to depict the route as it will be several miles ahead. Another proposal would be telephone communication between driver and the pits. And the last, which he expresses with a shudder, is a driverless racing car controlled by radio from the pit. Yes, but who will be in the pit?

LUIGI MUSSO

The simplest way to explain the secret behind the success of Luigi Musso, one of Italy's great aces of road and track, is to tell the story of Joe DiMaggio, who in this book must be clearly identified as one of America's great baseball players. When DiMaggio began, as a lad, to learn the great national pastime, as it is occasionally called, he and his fellow-sandlotters (a sandlot is an impromptu baseball field laid out on any flat, unoccupied land, which, tradition has it, is the cradle of most professional players) were too poor to buy real baseball bats. Therefore they used cast-off oar handles, which were unwieldy, unbalanced and crude, and made striking the horsehide (euphemism for baseball) rather difficult. When DiMaggio finally was allowed to use a real bat, striking the ball seemed so simple that he became an immediate success in the big league (grand prix).

Musso, youngest of three sons of a wealthy Italian diplomat who spent many years in China, made his first automobile purchase in spite of the protests of his brothers. It should be pointed out here that

[Courtesy of "Sports Cars Illustrated"

Luigi Musso (left)

wealth is comparative. DiMaggio was too poor to buy a $4 bat, and Musso was not rich enough to buy a fine Maserati. So his first car was a 750-c.c. Giannini of venerable age.

The Giannini kept on shedding its tired old parts and Musso kept on putting them together. When he finally managed to keep them together during the 1950 Tour of Sicily, he had the misfortune to crash into a monument of Garibaldi and learned from the irresistible marble that day-dreaming is a costly luxury in a speeding car. He backed off from Garibaldi and went on, but found he could not climb the steep hills. Still trying, he climbed the hills in reverse, but while this demonstrated his admirable perseverance, it did not win the race for him.

A year later he tried the Tour of Sicily and the Mille Miglia, but the old Giannini just couldn't finish. Despite the handicap of the car, observers appreciated in the young driver the eagerness and ability that are needed for success at the track. The Maserati people recognized this. They had just put out their new A6GCS 2-litre sports and named three young men whom they were planning to groom for grands prix—Mantovani, Giletti and Musso. Each of the three was allowed to purchase his car on a finance plan.

Musso showed at once what he could do with a fine car. He drove brilliantly and almost unerringly, winning cheers, points and races. When the year was

over he was Italian champion in the 2-litre class. He won his class in the 1000-km. of Buenos Aires and the Tourist Trophy of Ireland. Maserati then gave him a grand-prix car, in which he won the Grand Prix of Naples and won his class at the Targa Florio.

In a fantastic seesaw battle with Vittorio Marzotto, Musso came in second in his class and third over-all. The two cars were never more than seconds apart and the lead changed constantly. Musso was delighted with a good car and the crowds were delighted with him. He went to Barcelona and was the only Italian driver in an Italian car to beat Fangio in his Mercedes. In 1955 he became the leading Italian of the Maserati grand-prix team.

A year later he was asked to join Ferrari. A crash at the Nürburgring laid him away for some time, but he got out of the hospital in time to drive brilliantly at Monza. Near the end of the race, with the lead safely tucked away, his steering wheel broke. This cost him the Italian championship, but a year later he shared victory with Masten Gregory in Temple Buell's private entry, a Ferrari, in the 1000 km. of Buenos Aires.

He tried for the Mille Miglia that year but illness forced him out. His place was taken by Portago. Then came a second at Naples with the Formula II Ferrari; a victory at Rheims, a second in the British Grand Prix, and a shared second with Hawthorn in the Grand Prix of Venezuela. Musso's driving thus clinched the world championship for Ferrari. When he attained the championship of Italy, Musso continued flat out for even greater achievements, lending support to an ancient adage that a good driver should have a good car and with a bit of good fortune the combination can be unbeatable. In the French G.P. of 1958 the bit of good fortune failed him. Musso's Ferrari went off the course at a tricky turn and somersaulted three times. He died of head injuries.

FELICE NAZZARO

Felice! Felice! Felice! This was the cry of love and adulation that resounded throughout Italy during the first ten years of this century whenever a tall and youthful man with fine, regular features and a coquettish moustache made his appearance. His income was 200,000 lire, three times more than that of a Cabinet Minister; newspapers vied for interviews; perfumed letters were pushed under his door; the Queen of Italy asked for a ride in a car driven by Felice, but not too fast, please, and the populace beamed with pride at its national hero.

His family name was Nazzaro, but the crowds discarded it for the popular single word, *Felice*. He was a driver of motor cars at great speed and he captured the imagination of the crowds by driving boldly and spectacularly. He was happy to be drenched with admiration and he responded by obliging and loving everybody—as a national hero should.

Felice Nazzaro

As all good heroes should, Nazzaro arrived at his peak not by birth or inheritance, but by hard work and from reasonably humble origin. He was born in 1881, the son of a lower-middle-class coal dealer of Torino, and remained unnoticed by compilers of scholastic honour rolls as he struggled through grammar school and three grades of high school. After an apprenticeship with a bicycle shop, he landed a job in the repair shops of a new firm, the Fabbrica Italiana Automobili Torino, which was called F.I.A.T.

He worked himself into a job as test driver and, after he had driven an 8-h.p. F.I.A.T. at 35 m.p.h., the factory naturally chose him in answer to Cavaliere Vincenzo Florio's request for a man to be sent to Sicily to teach Florio all about his new car. The Cavaliere's garage was full of interesting machines, including a 40-h.p. Panhard et Levassor that Nazzaro drove at 60 m.p.h. When it was time for him to return to Turin, Florio simply hired him away from the factory as his own chauffeur. It was a long time before Florio would release Nazzaro to his original employer.

He first came to national attention in 1901, when he won a 302-kilometre race between Turin and Bologna in a F.I.A.T. in a downpour that made the road dangerously slippery. The race was the result of a 5000-lite wager between the Duke of the Abruzzi, who said Italian cars were superior, and the Cavaliere Colitelletti, who backed the Panhard et Lavassor. The Duke lost the wager because his own entry, a F.I.A.T., skidded off the mucky road near Alessandria and broke an axle. But Nazzaro brought his own newly painted F.I.A.T. home, upholding the honour of Italy.

Nazzaro's interest in speed was first only to his interest in money, and, when he complained to the F.I.A.T. people that his salary was too small, he was promised bonuses. This delighted him because it supplied a single incentive for speed and material rewards. He went on to win at Mont Cenis and came second in the Gordon Bennett Race. In 1906 he came in sixth in the Vanderbilt Cup, but on his return to Europe scored many victories. The next year, his biggest, saw him taking first place in the Grand Prix of Italy, the Kaiserpreis and the Targa Florio, which consisted of three laps on the big Madonie Circuit, covering 277·3 miles at an average speed of 33·4 m.p.h. in a F.I.A.T.

Vincenzo Florio, who was a close friend, described Nazzaro as "quiet, thoughtful, very gentlemanly in manner. He had a wonderful mechanical gift and a delicacy of touch which amounted almost to fastidiousness, which enabled him to get the maximum out of a car without submitting it to any undue stress. He had an affection for his machine akin to that existing between human beings. No detail could be overlooked; everything must be perfect. He handled his cars as a violinist his instrument— perfectly attuned, but brought to life by a hidden fire. It was doubtless because of this combination that the cars handled by Nazzaro so rarely failed and so frequently crossed the line ahead of all others."

With his background as a mechanic and a test driver, it was a natural step for Nazzaro to plan for his own factory in Turin. He invested his fabulous earnings and entered the Nazzaro among the 37 cars in the Targa Florio of 1913. He prepared the car with great care because this time the Targa was in two stages around Sicily, covering 599·6 miles. He won, getting to the finish line more than an hour ahead of Marsaglia in an Aquila-Italiana and bettering the previous year's average speed of 24 m.p.h. to 31·04.

Nazzaro was a great racer and a great hero, but as a business man he was a failure. He built a fine car which suffered from lack of detail and finish. As a sales supervisor he had no ability. He entered his car again in the Grand Prix of France in 1914 and the effort resulted in an abysmal débâcle. Felice, who led his own team, was distraught by the details of running a race; his team-mates did not carry on for him; the pit work was miserably organized and the result was the destruction of whatever prestige the car had won at the Targa.

When the war was over, Nazzaro was almost penniless. FIAT gave him a chance in the 1922 French Grand Prix at Strasbourg. The great hero rose to the challenge and won the race, coming in 10 miles per hour faster than the second car, a Bugatti. He made two more casual appearances at the Targa and then faded into retirement. In spite of the many years since his name has been on the starting lists there are still those in Italy who raise their arms and pronounce with nostalgic awe the words: *Felice! Felice! Felice!*

[*Courtesy of Daimler-Benz A.G.*

Denis Jenkinson, Alfred Neubauer and Stirling Moss after the 1955 Mille Miglia victory

ALFRED NEUBAUER

Those to whom the pursuit of perfection represents the ultimate truth will understand Alfred Neubauer. His 280 pounds of overpowering personality was dedicated toward one end only—to win races by preparing for them with relentless thoroughness, thus leaving the irreducible minimum to chance. That he succeeded is racing history. During his three decades as racing manager of Mercedes, he was responsible for more victories in prime competition than any other man.

It has been said of Neubauer that his bite is worse than his bark—and that is more of a roar accompanied by lashes of lightning and temblors in the pits. He has been called rude, shrewd and uncompromising; a firm disciplinarian and a mountain of controlled wrath. Yet it should be pointed out to the uninitiate that all these appellations are meant as praise.

Neubauer offered no apology, but he did like to explain his attitude. "Racing manager," he said, "is no job that can be trained for. You must have been a racing driver yourself and experienced all his difficulties and problems, you must study them and combine experience with technical knowledge. Furthermore, every racing marque has a different

approach to racing, which gives their racing managers entirely different tasks. For Ferrari, the owner of a model workshop for racing cars, and for Maserati, a wealthy steel magnate, for whom racing is a hobby, problems are quite different from those prevailing for Alfa Romeo or our firm, where the experiences gained in races are finally used to benefit mass production."

The objective being clear, Neubauer proceeded accordingly. He began by never having fewer than three specially-built trucks capable of maintaining speeds of 70 miles an hour. His stock-in-trade was speed and he felt that everything he supervised must travel fast. The trucks contained enough equipment, including a turret lathe, to build a complete racing car.

Having established that all matériel was at hand, Neubauer's next move was to order tyre experts to examine the track during practice. These men measured the surface composition, tested temperatures, moisture and resilience. When they turned in their report, Neubauer knew to within a tiny percentage how long a certain type of tread would last and whether or when a tyre change would be needed for his racers. Meteorologists were then ordered to test barometric pressure, temperature and humidity on the day of the race so that Neubauer could adjust

272

the jet sizes on carburetters and determine the proper mixture of fuel.

With the persistence and precision of a drill sergeant, Neubauer had put the pit crew through its battle manœuving. He set a standard of one minute for refuel stops or tyre changes. During that time also the driver's goggles were cleaned, his thirst was slaked, the water in the car brought to its required level and the windshield was cleaned. The idea was to put the car back as close to its starting condition as possible. These actions called for such perfect timing and footwork that repeated rehearsals were held. Pit workers never farcically bumped into one another or tripped over themselves. At times like these, Neubauer operated with the artistry of a ballet master, cutting graceful arabesques to show how it should be done and then getting it done with the fierceness of a circus ring master wielding a whip.

Once, during a practice run in an English Grand Prix, Neubauer was caught with a flaw in his preparations. A leak had developed in the cooling system of one of his cars. He could have engaged a local artisan to weld the crack, but instead he sent word to Stuttgart that a specialist in the racing department be flown to England. The man arrived, made the repair in three minutes and was flown back to the factory.

His entourage was always gigantic. During the Mexican Road Race in 1952, Neubauer had with him 12 mechanics, two passenger cars, two aeroplanes and one special truck. The story goes that he cabled complaints across the Atlantic that his crew was too small, although, in spite of this handicap, Mercedes won first and second place in the major events. His crew, of course, was the largest of all at the event. Mexican racing officials are still murmuring among themselves about the Terrifying Teuton who celebrated the victory by roaring through the living room of the Mercedes agent wearing a huge sombrero and waving a magnum of champagne.

He treated his team as a family. He insisted that all Mercedes men eat together and well, with himself at the head of the table, pontifical and genial and in love with everybody. But, when anyone failed to adhere to the rules set down by the master, there was no compromise. During one race, the Italian, Fagioli, refused to yield to a team-mate in the battle for the lead. When Neubauer signalled for him to ease off, Fagioli spurned him. Neubauer scrubbed him from the race and from the team.

Only one man defied Neubauer successfully and it probably saved his life. Mercedes and Auto-Union were trying to set new speed records on the smooth German superhighway near Darmstadt. Caracciola had made one run at 268·5 m.p.h. He pulled into the pit and got out of the car, removing his helmet. Neubauer told him to get back into the car and try once more, pointing out that the Auto-Union with Rosemeyer would try for the record. Caracciola refused, saying it was too windy. Even the thunder of Neubauer would not move him. One hour later, Rosemeyer went out in the Auto-

Union and was killed. He was travelling at a speed greater than Caracciola's when the car was struck by a strong gust.

At the age of 67, in 1958, Neubauer retired officially. He continued to frequent racing courses in Europe, happily helping drivers and historians of motor sport. He recalled that at the age of 10 in his native Mährisch-Neutitschein he began collecting automobile catalogues. He was a dapper and slim cadet when he joined the Austrian army's first motorized detachment for World War I. When he was discharged he became chief of the test driving department for Austro-Daimler. In 1922 he finished 19th in the Targa Florio and was over-all winner in the Hungarian Tour with the famous Austro-Daimler Sascha.

He had a minor conflict between his love for racing and his natural ability as an organizer and a supervisor of racing problems. The matter was settled for him by Dr. Porsche in 1923. Porsche became chief engineer for the Daimler-Benz firm and offered Neubauer a job at Stuttgart-Untertürkheim. The job developed into the assignment of managing Mercedes racing.

In the years that followed, every great driver for Mercedes, including men like Fangio, Caracciola and Lang, was developed under the guiding hand of Neubauer. His own driving in Mercedes cars in the early 1920s was the foundation of his experience. His bulk and the two stop watches dangling from his neck were almost trade marks, as was the waving of his hat to the crowds when victory was his. Every race cost him the loss of several pounds, which he regained at the very next meal. Upon his retirement he had no cosmic parting word to the drivers and racing managers that came after him—simply because it is unthinkable that he will ever stay away from the racing of motor cars.

TAZIO NUVOLARI

"*A racing driver's talents must include first of all good judgment: he must be mature, he can never have enough experience. He must have nerves of stone, a sound heart, the ability to concentrate exclusively on what he is doing, a spirit of sacrifice, first-class distance vision and, above all, complete knowledge of the capabilities and limitations of his machine.*

"*I hope to continue racing until I have developed all these qualities.*"

> —Tazio Nuvolari at the age of 45, when he had won 100 major races and was the undisputed champion of the world.

Oil poured over the S-curve of the Monaco Grand Prix course as an engine blew up. Five cars hurtled into the rain-swollen pool, one after another: the first spun out of control and each of the others

[*Courtesy of Everett L. Poorman*

Tazio Nuvolari

crashed into it. Before any of them could be disentangled, a sixth car bore down at full speed and the crowd dared not look. But there was no crunch of metal on metal, not even a shriek of tyres. His foot still down and his wheel flashing back and forth, lock to lock, Tazio Nuvolari powered and steered his way unerringly through the mess of oil, water and machines without touching one of the six cars strewn across the road.

This virtuosity was no flash of luck. It was achieved by rigourous discipline in a burning pursuit of speed that had begun on a bicycle almost 30 years before, continued on flying motor-cycles and finally reached its acme in automobiles.

The son and nephew of Italian bicycle champions, Nuvolari, who was born on November 16, 1892, in Casteldario, near Mantua, soon outgrew man-powered motion. A lonely and arrogant child—perhaps because he was unusually short—he had exercised himself into great physical strength and assumed dominance of all his playmates. But in his mid-teens he felt ready to become a man, and for three years he plagued his father for a motor-cycle. He was 18 when he got it, and for the next 15 years he rode it faster than anyone in Europe, winning about 300 races despite an incredible number of bone-breaking accidents that first led his admirers to exclaim: "Tazio has a contract with the devil."

Nuvolari was 29 when he first drove a car in a race, finishing second in his class on the 122-mile Garda circuit. A year later he tried again, finishing second over-all in an Ansaldo. In 1924 he won his

first big-race victory. But for the next three years he stayed with motor-cycles exclusively.

In 1927, when Nuvolari was 35, he entered the Mille Miglia, one of the world's most gruelling races, in a Bugatti and came fifth. Thereafter, he never returned to two-wheel racing. In 1930 he won the Mille; almost 25 years later he was refused permission to run in this race because of a weakened heart. His last great victory was scored in 1950 at Palermo, when he was just short of 60. Three years later he died.

Nuvolari, who was only 5 ft. 2 in. tall and weighed 9 st. 8 lb. at his peak, lived an almost monastic life. He slept 14 hours a day, ate little meat and derived most of his nourishment from fruit, vegetables, cheese, eggs and milk. He did not drink, rarely smoked and favoured much walking to stay fit. Though he was married and had two sons, his real love was always his work: racing. And he called it his only diversion.

Equally adept in sports or grand-prix machines, Nuvolari was known as a car-killer. Always excitable in spite of the philosophy to which he strove to adhere, he would bang on the side of the car as he drove, and consistently proved the human body to be far more durable than any artifact. At Pau, for instance, in 1935, when his car caught fire, he decelerated to 100 m.p.h. and leaped. Three weeks later, despite a concussion and assorted fractures, he was racing again. In practice for the G.P. of Tripoli the following year, he burst a front tyre at 160 m.p.h. and was thrown 100 ft. through the air. Much against his will, Nuvolari was hospitalized overnight, but the next day he was back at the wheel.

Mostly he finished first; occasionally second, rarely third. When he did not finish among the first three, it was almost always because he had driven his car to death. His victories included not only the Mille Miglia but also the equally murderous Targa Florio, Le Mans, the Eifel, the Nürburgring, the Tourist Trophy (in a K3 M.G.) and the Vanderbilt Cup in 1936. After his victory he was besieged in New York to endorse dozens of products and refused. When his friends protested that he was throwing away money, he explained simply: "I know; but in this city there are so many Italians sweeping the streets, making roads, selling ice-cream, that we must let these Americans know we have some dignity."

Nuvolari's first big mount was a Bugatti, and he continued to drive for the French marque until he switched to Alfa Romeo in 1929. He remained with Alfa even after the factory had withdrawn from racing and its crest was being upheld by the Scuderia Ferrari, until 1938, occasionally driving also for M.G. and Maserati. In 1938 he signed with Auto-Union, which, with Mercedes-Benz, had proved far superior to the Italian machines. It is interesting to note that in the previous year, still driving Alfas, Nuvolari had decisively beaten both German teams despite far superior acceleration, top speed and braking. During his career he established six European speed records and in 1935 he set a world record for the flying mile: 200·8 m.p.h.

During World War II Nuvolari, who had always been a-political, was inactive (in the earlier war he had been an ambulance driver). In the mid-1940s he attempted a comeback despite failing health aggravated by the deaths of both his sons. He drove an Alfa for Ferrari; an open Cisitalia in which, despite a hailstorm that cut his face to ribbons, he finished second in the Mille Miglia of 1947; one of the then new Ferraris in the 1948 race, leading at Rome and gaining at Florence until the car succumbed, component by component, to the fantastic speeds imposed on it. It finally collapsed utterly near its birthplace, Modena.

Besides racing, Nuvolari's only great passion was his lifelong rivalry with Achille Varzi. Both men drove only to win, but Varzi was the more calculating. Nuvolari and Varzi once agreed over dinner that they were, in that order, the two greatest drivers then running. And in one Targa Florio when he was driving for Bugatti, Nuvolari cared less that he had lost than that he had finished ahead of Varzi.

Three superstitions persisted throughout Nuvolari's career. Early in his racing days, Gabriele d'Annunzio, the poet who loved *bravura*, had given him a silver turtle: it always hung from a chain round Nuvolari's neck. Whenever race regulations allowed a co-driver, Nuvolari preferred to have a hunchback, who he thought was a talisman. And, whenever he had signed to drive a race outside Italy, Nuvolari invariably bought a one-way ticket.

Courtesy of The David Brown Cos. Ltd.]

Reginald Parnell

REGINALD PARNELL

There is about Reginald Parnell a steadfastness of purpose and a solidity of manner that are universally admired among the members of the racing fraternity. He may not be sensational or dramatic, but his very persistence has given him the muted glamour that can be achieved only by driving ten different cars on 39 different circuits in 17 different countries and scoring 22 victories.

The people at Aston Martin, where he is racing manager, like to point out that the victories alone did not make the man. It was always Parnell who took the difficult job, tested the new cars, worried the opposition, tried out the strange circuit and gave inspiring leadership during his six years as captain of the works team.

He started it all at the wheel of a lorry when he was 14 and promptly was stopped by a policeman. Then in 1934 he visited Donington Park, where for the first time he heard the shattering arpeggio of the exhaust and discovered it to be his music. He purchased a vintage Bugatti G.P., found its maintenance too costly and switched to a K3 M.G. with which he did quite well at Brooklands, Donington Park and Crystal Palace.

Parnell recalls: "I kept on entering the races that seemed to pay the best money. I would have liked to have driven for a team, but nobody wanted

a man with my erratic and dangerous style." Others remember that he was so shy that he was unable to ask the advice of more experienced drivers. He simply had to learn by observation, trial and error.

In 1937 Parnell's racing licence was suspended after he crashed into Kay Petre's car at 105 m.p.h. during practice for the Brooklands 500. Mrs. Petre insisted that he had not been at fault, but the stewards were firm. Parnell accepted the verdict without complaint and spent the next season as a racing mechanic. His K-3 was the first car ever fitted with the two-leading-shoe front brakes that are now virtually standard. The R.A.C. reinstated his licence in 1939 and he went back to driving with a B.H.W. powered by a 4·9 Bugatti.

In 1939 Reg was a frequent entrant at Donington Park, Brooklands and the Crystal Palace, where more often than not he crossed the line first or close to it. When racing was resumed after the war he scored a number of successes in an E.R.A., including two firsts in the Swedish Grand Prix and a first in the International Trophy at Jersey in a 4-cylinder Maserati.

He joined the Aston Martin team in 1950 and wrote of his first important experience in *Motor Racing*: "At Le Mans the DB2 was a pleasant introduction to sports-car competition for me. The car handled remarkably well, and of course was much more comfortable than most of the racing cars I had driven, but it was a bit underpowered, I thought. We were sixth in general classification and second in our class."

One sensational race that Parnell won but that was never entered on the records was the International *Daily Express* Trophy race at Silverstone. He was driving a Ferrari, free lance, owned by Tony Vanderwell, and faced opposition made up of the Alfa Romeo team, with Fangio, Farina, Sanesi and Bonetto, and Ferraris driven by Ascari and Villoresi. When the race began, a torrential rain soaked drivers, cars and track, blinding spectators and pit crews. Sammy Davis recalls: "You could not see properly even from a stationary car and the racers went off in a blinding sheet of spray. In that screen of water cars were vaguely changing positions every few yards, the things that happened on curves had to be seen to be believed."

Parnell managed to remain in the lead, the world's finest cars and drivers unable to catch him. For 18 impossible miles, with inches of water covering the track, he held his first until the stewards decided that the danger was beyond reason and halted the race. Parnell was given the trophy, but the race was not recognized.

In his six years as captain of the Aston Martin team, for which among other successes he scored a fifth in the 1953 Mille Miglia, Parnell was regarded as one of the fastest yet most cautious drivers. When he became racing manager for Aston Martin he decided to pass on some of his experience to aspiring young drivers. Writing in *Motor Racing*, he pointed out that the best way to break into motor racing is through sports-car events.

"At every club meeting you will find somebody from one of the big teams watching drivers because there is always a shortage of really fine men for the job", he wrote. "It is a good idea to drive the same car or the same type of car for competition as you drive every day. It makes you perfectly familiar with every control and every peculiarity of the car.

"If you can't afford a sports car, probably the only way to break into racing is as a mechanic. The training is good . . . my own mechanical experience, I think, has accounted for at least 50 per cent of my good fortune on the tracks."

When Parnell retired from active racing they gave him a dinner at the Midland Hotel in Derby where everybody sang his praise. Davis pointed out that "truly you could not have a real race without Old Reg." Rodney Walkerly, at that time sports editor of *The Motor*, remarked that "we think of Stirling with awe, Mike with admiration, but we think of Reg with affection. He is the prince of sportsmen."

But Parnell, who has become a landmark in British motor racing, spoke for all when he said: "Some other sports may be more profitable than motor racing, and most are less risky, but the feeling of clean competition in first-class cars on high-speed circuits is enough to keep me in the game for a long long time."

ALFONSO DE PORTAGO

Alfonso Blas, 17th Marquis de Portago, whose mother had been a flaming-haired bareback rider and whose father on a one-man mission blew up two Spanish Loyalist submarines with a mine, lived in the tradition of danger and feasted on fear.

He was handsome, tall, dark and dashing. He was wealthy, his mother, an Irish girl from Chicago, having inherited a vast fortune from her first husband, Frank Jay Mackey, founder of the $550,000,000 Household Finance Corp., and with all that Portago had a deep, desperate need for danger.

His friends called him Fon and he lived every day as if it were his last. He was born in London and demonstrated the pattern of his life at 17 when he flew an aeroplane under a bridge to win a $500 bet. He moved on to horse racing and became the champion amateur jockey in France. Twice he rode the Grand National steeplechase in Britain and twice his mount fell under him. There was too much of him, however, at 6 ft. and 12 st. 4 lb., for professional horse racing, so he switched to boxing and swimming, where he excelled.

Then Edmund (Gunner) Nelson, who was to be his partner in the fatal Mille Miglia, introduced him to bobsledding. After less than 30 runs Portago came fourth in the Olympic two-man competition. While he was "idling" he played polo and jai-alai. His father, incidentally, died after a strenuous polo match that he had entered against the advice of his physicians.

Courtesy of Ferrari Automobili]

Alfonso de Portago

Meanwhile, the young Marquis did not neglect his social life. Fluent in four languages, he became a leader in the international set, where his wealth, position and natural grace should have brought great satisfaction; but the search for thrills continued until one day Nelson took him to see some automobile races and Portago found his true field of conflict. He won his first race and the second race. The third time he spun and lived through the moment of truth. This left him strangely exhilarated.

"I like the feeling of fear," he confided.

He accepted an invitation from Luigi Chinetti to ride with him in the 1953 Mexican Road Race. He was thoroughly shaken, vowing never to ride in a sports car with anyone again. Then he purchased a 3-litre Ferrari from Chinetti and with Harry Schell drove it in the 1000-kilometre at Buenos Aires in 1954.

He wrote an article for *Sports Illustrated* entitled "Racing Is a Vice", and reflected that "after a while a man becomes an addict (to fear) and has to have it. I think what frightens me most is that when I have actually lost control of the car there is absolutely nothing I can do except sit still, frozen with fear, and wait for events to take their natural course.

"Racing is a vice, and as such extremely hard to give up. All drivers swear that they will stop at such and such an age, but very few of them are able to do so. Racing drivers are inveterate gamblers and, like most of the breed, never know when to stop. Sometimes when a friend is killed you swear that you will never race again. The next day you think, well, this could never happen to me. By the third day you've got your gear together and you are off to the next race."

He got a Maserati 2-litre and entered Le Mans. At midnight he was leading in his class when a bearing went. He won with the same car at Metz. With Louis Chiron he entered the Rheims 12-hour race and was making a fine showing when the engine failed 15 minutes before the end. He observed, however, that he had learned a great deal from Chiron. He entered an O.S.C.A. at the Nürburgring and had a sensational practice run. In the race he started to compete with the Porsche team and wrecked the car. "They pushed me so I pushed back," he explained as he climbed out.

The Marquis had become a close friend of Chinetti and went back to Ferraris. He ran in the Grands Prix of Turin, Bordeaux and Pau and won two races at Nassau. He broke a leg at Silverstone but when he returned to racing a great reward awaited him. He was asked to join the Ferrari team and in his own 3-litre gran turismo he won at Nassau, Montlhéry and Castelfusano. He scored his great win in the Tour de France. He won classification as an ace in 1957 in Cuba when for three-fourths of the race he led Fangio, but fell back to third when a fuel line split.

Portago had always considered the Mille Miglia a "foolish race". He knew, like many other drivers, that to beat the Italians on their own roads would necessitate excessive risks. Yet, when Ferrari offered him the 4·1-litre, the finest and the fastest, he could not resist.

Some 3,000,000 fans and morbidly curious on-lookers crowded the thousand miles that day to watch the race. In the village of Castelgrimaldo thirty miles from the finish at Brescia the bright red Ferrari, with Portago at the wheel and Gunner Nelson as co-driver, was in third position when a tyre burst only minutes after they had disregarded a suggestion to change tyres. The car swerved across the road, into a telephone pole, bounced 20 ft. into the air, crashed into spectators on one side and then rolled to the other side, crushing others.

Portago and Nelson were killed with at least 12 spectators, including five children. Many more were injured. There was the usual indignation and outcry when the world heard of the tragedy.

Five women wept. There was his mother, from whom he had learned to love the life of danger; his younger sister, Solidad, whom he cherished and protected; his wife, the former Carol McDaniel of Charleston, S.C., mother of his two children; Dorian Parker, the celebrated cover girl and mother of his son, Kim; and the fifth—Linda Christian, the red-haired movie star who had kissed him that fatal day at the halfway mark in the race and who was the first to reach the scene of his death.

His intimates have reflected that Portago loved each of these women in his own special way—but he himself left no doubt that his greatest love—if that is the word—was his agonizing pursuit of fear.

DARIO RESTA

Dario Resta will be remembered as the only European driver to win the American championship. It came about because the English-born Italian did not care to bother with the war in Europe, where he had done creditably as a racer, having begun at the wheel of the great chain-driven Mercedes *bolides*. He crossed the ocean for the frank purpose of sweeping up some of the dollars that were said to be lying about on the American tracks.

He brought with him a 1913 Coupe de l'Auto Peugeot which he entered in W. K. Vanderbilt's 1000-guinea cup race. The prize was to be presented by Mrs. Vanderbilt to the winner of the 300-mile race to be run at the Panama-Pacific Exhibition. Among the competitors were Tom Alley on a Duesenberg, Ralph de Palma in a 1913 grand-prix Mercedes and Bob Burman in a Case. The fierce pace reduced the field of 31 to nine and in the beginning it appeared that the race would be between the Duesenberg and the Mercedes. The Duesenberg crashed and Resta won. The race is also remembered for a historic pit blunder. Harry Grant's Stutz was running well when he pulled into the pit for fuel. The crew members were so excited that they filled his big bolster tank with water instead of petrol.

Resta won another race in the Panama-Pacific series, which encouraged him to enter the 1915 Indianapolis. The race developed early into an open contest between Resta and de Palma. De Palma drove a calm and steady race while Resta pressed. He skidded into a wall just short of a major crash, damaging a wheel. The time cost him first place, but he came in a close second. Resta showed his style a year later at the new Chicago speedway when he beat de Palma, Eddie Rickenbacker and Barney Oldfield. His other victories continued to pile up and he won the American championship, which brought him the glory he sought and the dollars that went with it.

With a big bundle of newspaper clippings to bolster his ego and lots of dollars in hand, Resta made the error of trying to cash in on his popularity to sell the Sunbeam. He discovered that Americans rarely confuse their enthusiasms; besides, the Sunbeam was too expensive in comparison with American cars. He returned to Europe, where he had once led the Austin team. He wanted to get back into racing and got his chance at Brooklands, testing a new model Sunbeam which had been built for record trials. Resta was frankly happy with the rediscovery of speed. He got the youthful thrill of taking the car high up on the banked turn at Brooklands at high speeds. Apparently he had neglected to consider his long absence from this sort of activity and he was delighted by the admiring signals that came from the pits. He might have been dreaming of new records and a renewed career when the car went out of control. For one brief moment it teetered on one pair of wheels, overturned and charged through the corrugated iron fence on the Railway Straight. Resta was dead when the ambulance go to him.

BERND ROSEMEYER

Two steadfast beliefs ruled the short and spectacular career of Bernd Rosemeyer. One was pure fatalism and the other was the fixed determination that every speed record could be broken.

He demonstrated this one exciting summer afternoon at the 14-mile Nürburgring while driving the fantastic rear-engined Auto-Union. One member of the Auto-Union team, R. Hasse, had turned in a lap at 10:10. Tazio Nuvolari in a 12-cylinder Alfa did 10:08; Rudolf Caracciola in a Mercedes did 10:04; Manfred von Brauchitsch in another Mercedes did the lap in 9:55, and Hermann Lang in a Mercedes turned in the almost unbelievable time of 9:52. Then Rosemeyer went out and came back with a lap time of 9:46·2.

This phenomenal young German, whose entire car-racing career covered the brief span of three years, found his interest in the mechanical workshop of his father in Lingen. Motor-cycles were his early love and he had scored a respectable number of wins when Dr. Ferdinand Porsche heard of him. Suddenly Rosemeyer was plunged into grand-prix competition

because the Auto-Union, designed by Porsche, was such a difficult automobile to drive.

The position of the engine and the driver in the 400-h.p. Auto-Union presented a grave problem. Experienced drivers had approached the massive machine reluctantly because they would have to start learning all over again to handle this strange car properly.

After several unhappy incidents Porsche decided to engage men who had never driven racing cars before and start them from the beginning.

In his initial attempt with an Auto-Union in 1934 on the Nürburgring, Rosemeyer hurled the car sideways on the first corner and the breathless onlookers could not decide whether he was recklessly ambitious or a youth with the natural instincts of a master driver. He quieted the doubters in his first race as an official Auto-Union driver by crossing the finish line seconds behind the winner, the veteran Caracciola.

His victories mounted steadily until by 1936 he was the champion of Europe. Porsche was delighted to have found a driver who could show the utmost capabilities of his car. A strong affection grew between the two and Rosemeyer always sought out the older man for advice and criticism. He called him "Uncle Doctor".

It was Porsche who noted that "Rosemeyer never took any foolish risks. It was just that he drove faster than other people could."

The Auto-Union brought Rosemeyer to the United States in 1937 for the Vanderbilt Cup competition over the old Roosevelt Raceway. In what was probably the most spectacular automobile marathon ever wit-

Courtesy of the Nürburgring G.m.b.H.]

Bernd Rosemeyer

nessed in that country, Rosemeyer took the checkered flag. He flashed over the winning line only 51·3 seconds ahead of the Briton, Richard Seaman, who had battled him for the lead in the final 15 laps of the 300-mile race.

Rosemeyer, as more than 75,000 persons watched, covered the 90 laps at an average of 82·56, bettering the time of Nuvolari the previous year by 17 miles an hour.

It was on this occasion that Rosemeyer expressed the creed of fatalism through the lips of his wife, Elly Beinhorn, in her own right an international flyer. Because she spoke impeccable English Miss Beinhorn was named spokesman for the Auto-Union team.

"We are all fatalists," she said, "wives as well as drivers. We all know that many drivers who consistently do crazy things and tempt fate actually die in their beds, whereas silly incidents prove fatal to the most careful racing drivers. So fatalism is what we accept, and we live for the love our men have of their careers in automobile racing."

Then, as a footnote, Frau Rosemeyer added: "Of course there is no question that motor-car racing is more dangerous than flying, for there are so many mishaps even of a minor nature that can prove fatal to a driver in a racing car."

Rosemeyer was a quiet young man who made and kept friends. He was unassuming and carried lightly the honours heaped upon him in Europe and America. He preferred simple but calculated routines in his preparations for races. He had few professional peculiarities. His wife flew him to most of his races and when she was in the pit he would always raise his hand in salute to her as he passed.

January 28, 1938, was a cold and blustery day. Rosemeyer had decided it would be wiser for his wife to remain at home with their three-month-old son. A year earlier Bernd had established a new world speed record of 223·9 miles an hour for ten miles from a flying start and this day other drivers would compete for that record on the Frankfurt–Darmstadt Autobahn. True to his credo, Rosemeyer himself was determined to better it. But he soon learned he had a great mark to shoot at. Caracciola had just been clocked at 268·3 miles an hour.

Some said there was a sudden boisterous gust of wind. Others swore a front tyre was wreched from Rosemeyer's Auto-Union. Most said it was both. Travelling at tremendous speed, the car skidded 80 yards, somersaulted twice and was thrown 200 yards through the air. Rosemeyer was hurled out in midflight and landed in an embankment. He died instantly. He was 27.

Today on the Frankfurt–Darmstadt Autobahn where Rosemeyer died there is a simple monument.

HARRY SCHELL

Motor racing in Europe is ready for and in need of American drivers and automobiles, in the studied opinion of Harry Schell, the lonely American, who finished fourth for the world championship in 1958. Two years later he was killed in practice at Silverstone.

Schell felt that he was an unusual figure on the grand-prix circuits, surrounded by racing drivers of many nationalities, and, while a Fitch or a Gregory or a Hill appeared occasionally, there should have been more drivers from the United States.

He made his invitation attractive to the young man who wanted to race. "The grand-prix car is the ultimate in automobiles", Schell observed. "The car is designed to do everything as perfectly as it can be done. It must accelerate fast. It must corner fast. It must brake fast. It must do all these things continuously for hundreds of miles, its engine roaring at top speed all the time. It must be the finest piece of machinery man can put together."

Moving from invitation to challenge, Schell described a typical circuit—the German Grand Prix at the Nürburgring: "There is a corner coming up (it seems) every few seconds. Drivers make gear changes every 15 seconds. It is a 14-mile course with more twists and turns than a basket of pretzels. It climbs to a height of 2,000 feet and descends quickly to 600 feet. I've never counted them, though I have been told there are 180 curves in the course. But the amazing thing is that the lap record (set by Fangio) for 14 miles is an average of 87·74 m.p.h."

Schell spoke of motor racing with a natural affection

Courtesy of René Dreyfus]

Harry Schell

279

—natural because he was born into it. His father, Laurie, was a racing driver and patron of the Écurie Bleu, which ran Maseratis, Talbots and Delahayes. After he was killed in an automobile crash, his widow, Lucy O'Reilly Schell, also a racing driver, assumed the management of the team.

She sent René Dreyfus and René Le Bègue to Indianapolis with two supercharged 8-cylinder Maseratis. Schell recalled that his parents were behind the construction of the 4·5-litre unblown Delahayes that got first and third at Pau with Dreyfus and Comotti driving. He watched the preparations and the races and inherited the enthusiasm. Starting in 1946 with a 1500-c.c. Maserati, he had been in well over 300 races. Among them were many victories and many heart-breaking near wins that were spoiled by unco-operative clutches, axles, brakes and other vital parts strained beyond endurance.

After driving a succession of cars, Schell finally found the Vanwall, in which, with the encouragement of Tony Vandervell, he showed that he was the leading American driver in Europe. He recalled the Grand Prix of Rheims in 1956, when he was fourth in the first two laps against the Ferraris when his axle broke. While repairs were being made, Harry knew he could, at best, merely finish. Suddenly Mike Hawthorn in the other Vanwall roared past and signalled.

"I understood instantly," Schell recalled. "Mike was giving me another chance. He was right up there with the leaders and was offering me his car. What a magnificent gesture he was making. When I jumped into his car I was 52 seconds behind. The fantastic chase began and the crowds were beginning to sense the excitement. I moved into sixth place on the 17th lap; into fifth on the 20th lap; by the 21st lap I was in fourth; by the 23rd I was 24 seconds behind; by the 25th I was 12·5 seconds behind; and on the 30th lap I was right on the tail of Collins in the third-place Ferrari."

The man Schell wanted to catch was Fangio, but Collins and Castellotti were in the way. Schell planned to pass on the Thillois curve by going far into the corner without braking, taking Fangio on the outside. "Roaring along the straight at 180 miles an hour, Collins wouldn't let me by," he wrote. "At 400 yards from the corner I was still hitting 180. I kept my foot down until 300 yards. Then I jumped on the brake. I passed Collins and Castellotti when suddenly my brakes locked. I decided to go straight ahead; I couldn't make the corner. Suddenly the brakes unlocked and in an instant I was alongside Fangio, passing on the outside."

Fangio, however, would not let go. For one mile Schell stayed with the great champion and then a curve loomed. Fangio kept his foot down and Schell was forced to ease off. He pulled out of the race with a broken fuel-injection pump bracket and Fangio set a new lap record of 127·29.

Schell bemoaned the situation brought about by retirements and deaths. "Racing is not the same since the disappearance of Ascari, Portago, Castellotti,

Musso and Collins," he declared. He felt that was why Americans were needed in Europe and he pursued this propaganda when he presided over his Paris bar, *L'Action Automobile*, which he ran in the lulls between racing. If his own emotions could have been a guide for Americans who wanted to drive in Europe, he offered them with simple candour:

"As I plunge along the straight at Rheims at 180 miles an hour, or when I round a corner of Monza in a nice drift, I feel on top of the world. It is fantastic. I relax and I am unafraid, alert; and I know racing is my life. I am a hopeless addict."

DICK SEAMAN

Richard John Beattie Seaman had a great longing for speed. He overcame strong parental objections and surmounted political obstacles to achieve it— and then he sought more speed. His fixed ambition was to get into grand-prix racing, and he began at Rugby with fast motor-cycles. He was given a hand early in his career at Cambridge by Whitney Straight, who showed him how to ease into racing and gently appease his parents by running innocent-appearing M.G.s and Bugattis.

Since all team managers seem to be watching all drivers at all times, Dick Seaman was not long in creating a fine impression upon them. He learned much in the Varsity speed trials. A first at Berne, a third at Pescara and a second in the Nuffield Trophy brought him the reputation he needed to make a works team. In 1935 in an E.R.A. he took first at Pescara and he was on his way.

Seaman was not the kind of driver who would bring back the throttle the least part of an inch simply because he had achieved top speed. S. C. H. Davis points out that "on a fast bend or a relatively slow corner Dick never appeared to be fighting his car but to be coming around with it as one piece, and no driver before or since has ever got away from a curve back to speed more certainly or more quickly. Much of this was due to coming in comparatively slowly so that the car was not only steady but pointing in the right direction as it came out of the turn. And with all this he was a gentle driver, never unduly stressing the mechanism nor given to grasping and pulling levers hard."

Being the quiet type became Dick Seaman and also served him as strategy. When he discovered the Delage, with which he fell in love immediately, he raced it for the first time over the shorter course on the Isle of Man. Battling against powerful opposition, he achieved a spectacular victory despite a weird noise in the rear drive. He slowed down in the final few laps and the rattle vanished. But he confessed later that what pleased him most was the successful ruse of indicating in pantomime that he would have to halt for refuelling and then going the rest of the way without a stop.

Seaman's cool and masterful handling of M.G.,

E.R.A. and Delage finally won him the great reward and in 1937, at the age of 23, he was invited to join the Mercedes-Benz team. He was properly awed by the power of some of the cars. The ME 25 was producing well over 400 h.p. and after a preliminary test he admitted it was "rather a job to know what to do with so many horses".

In his first trial run for Mercedes he accelerated the car too quickly coming out of a corner and crashed into a tree. Dick took the blame manfully and was truly gladdened when Alfred Neubauer explained to him where he had gone wrong in coming out of the corner and then assured him that racing cars were (in moderation) more expendable than good drivers.

Neubauer, an inflexible disciplinarian, liked Dick from the start for his honesty, eagerness and team spirit. In the 1937 Vanderbilt Cup race, the first car, driven by Rudi Caracciola, got into difficulties early and Dick's was the only Mercedes left against the veteran Bernd Rosemeyer in the powerful Auto-Union. He made a magnificent run and, had it not been for fuel troubles in the last few laps, he might have come in first instead of second.

His greatest single triumph was the 1938 German Grand Prix. He and von Brauchitsch in twin super-charged Mercedes thundered around the course, the German holding a slight lead when both cars came into the pits. As Neubauer came over to von Brauchitsch's car, the German complained bitterly: "Seaman is hanging right on my heels and is driving me crazy." Neubauer, ever the autocrat, admonished

Richard J. B. Seaman

Seaman: "Hang back and let von Brauchitsch finish in first place." Then he promised that when the team ran in the English Grand Prix he would allow Seaman to try for first place. Seaman remained silent.

Suddenly there occurred one of fate's strange jests. A backlash in the pressure fuel apparatus caused a spark and in a moment von Brauchitsch's car was enveloped in flames. Neubauer dashed over and pulled the German out of the car safely, surveyed its ruins and swiftly turned to Seaman, who remained seated in his car, making no apparent attempt to get back into the race. "Drive on!" Neubauer screamed. Seaman looked calmly into his eyes and replied: "You told me not to pass von Brauchitsch."

Neubauer recalls vaguely that he made powerful pleas and some grandiose pledges to the young Briton. Seaman returned to the track and finished first for the team.

There were other victories and other races, but the joys and satisfactions were dimmed by the war clouds hanging over Europe. The situation of a British driver in a German team in 1939 was not a happy one since Hitler had taken a personal interest in the victories of German racing cars.

Seaman had met and fallen in love with a German girl and married her against the emotional opposition of his family. The pressures, domestic and political, were strong and unrelenting. He seemed to absorb them calmly, listening to advice, considering it seriously and finally determining what his course would be. He decided to remain with his friends, Neubauer and the German drivers.

And then there came a day of rain and heavy mist at Spa in the Belgian Grand Prix of 1939. Two years earlier at the same track Seaman had successfully avoided a high-speed skid of an Auto-Union by sweeping on to the verge and striking an iron stanchion. Thrown from his car, he had walked away with picturesque but minor injuries.

But this day was different. The track was tricky. Earlier Caracciola had crashed after an uncontrolled skid. With fifteen laps to go, Seaman took the lead, sliding on every corner with all four wheels but holding steady. At La Source corner the glide was longer than normal and recovery was impossible. The car crashed into a tree, the fuel tank burst and flames welled over the body. Seaman, stunned by the impact, was unable to free the catch that would have enabled him to get out past the steering wheel. Officials tried to help him but could not get to the catch in time. Badly burned, he died a few hours later.

RAYMOND SOMMER

When World War II broke out, Raymond Sommer, one of the best of all French drivers, was offered a properly deserved commission in the army. In keeping with his non-conformist philosophy, he rejected it and fought the Germans as a *poilu*, but even then could not avoid the life pattern of the dramatic and the picturesque. He shot down a low-flying enemy fighter plane with a rifle.

This was Sommer, called *Raymond Cœur de Lion*, who raced in the spirit of the true amateur and with the calculated daring and consumate skill of the perfect professional. He was born in 1906 to wealth and position, and during a lifetime of high adventure on the racecourses attracted a horde of bitter enemies who inflicted upon him the greatest hurt of all by making him a bitter man. The bitterness, however, came only toward the end. In between he was noted for his generosity and idealism. The end came on September 10, 1950, when his 1100-c.c. Cooper hurtled off the road at a curve on the perilous Gardours Circuit during the Haute Garonne Grand Prix. A seized wheel bearing was believed to be the cause. Today there is a plaque to his memory at that curve in the shadow of the Pyrenees.

His first exciting interest was aviation, but in 1930 he showed a curiosity in motor sport and began with a souped-up Chrysler in the 24 Hours of Belgium at Spa. He finished high in the money in his monster American car with eight carburetters, which was the centre of awe and admiration on the Rue Erlanger in the Paris suburb of Auteuil. However, Sommer himself cast admiring glances at a car parked near his home. It was a bright red Alfa Romeo sports 2·3-litre and its owner was Luigi Chinetti.

Sommer approached Chinetti with deference. "You plan to run this Alfa at Le Mans?" he asked. Chinetti said *yes*. "I would like to drive with you," Sommer said. When Chinetti told him the car was for sale, Sommer, with help from his father, a felt manufacturer, purchased the car. He entered it in the Marseilles Grand Prix of 1932 and there, according to John Bentley, "not only won the race, but by a combination of intuitive skill, raw courage and terrific determination he managed to beat the great Tazio Nuvolari. What was more, Nuvolari had a 2·6 Alfa of appreciably more power and speed than Sommer's machine."

As a result Chinetti was more than willing to have Sommer as a co-driver. They won the race against an Alfa Romeo factory team consisting of Campari, Borzacchini and Marinoni. The following year, Nuvolari selected Sommer as his co-driver and the two won at Le Mans in a new 2·3 Monza Alfa. The two were in rapturous *rapport* because they shared the same approach to driving: down on the pedal—all the way—and, if the car can't take it, that's just too bad. The automobiles might have suffered from this but between 1933 and 1939 Sommer recorded nine wins, six seconds and eight thirds, plus a sensational fourth in the Vanderbilt Cup of 1936. Just before the war he was named champion of France and had won a place as the most important independent driver.

Because of his money and his great ability and because he never showed any interest in becoming a member of a team, Sommer stirred feelings of envy and charges of snobbery among some of his fellows.

Yet he was acknowledged to be eminently fair in his dealings and a true sportsman during a race. He never hesitated to give aid and counsel to young drivers and generously imparted to them some of his hard-won tricks and secrets. His avowed distaste for the discipline of works teams was another factor that caused lesser men to suspect and resent him.

When the war was over and some of his racing friends were in need he never failed to give help. One of his most generous acts was his unpopular effort to free Dr. Ferdinand Porsche from prison at Dijon. The French government was furious because Porsche, designer of the Volkswagen during Hitler's reign, had refused to design a racing car for France. Sommer, aided by Charles Faroux, the leading automobile journalist of France, managed to raise the money needed for Porsche's freedom.

At the age of 40, when many drivers fear that their reactions are slowing down dangerously, Sommer returned to racing with the verve of youth. He scored first at the Marseilles Grand Prix, the Circuit de Trois Villes and the St.-Cloud Grand Prix. He got a second at the Nice Grand Prix and third at the Turin Grand Prix and the Brussels Meeting. He was named champion of France and champion of Europe. The cars he used that year were a Talbot 4·5, an Alfa Romeo 158 and the Maserati 4CL.

Before he reached that fatal curve, Sommer's record showed that he had competed in more than 125 major events and had won, placed or finished in more than 40 of them. Among his larger failures were the times when he allowed himself to run works cars, like the state-subsidized CTA Arsénal, a French grand-prix car, and the B.R.M., called by many a bundle of mechanical encumbrances and contradictions. His victories, frequently against more powerful cars, are attributed by Chinetti to his "boundless courage and great physical strength . . . he was not so much interested in finishing a race as in winning it."

Toward the end his bitterness mellowed. France gave him the Cross of the Legion of Honour "as the greatest driver in the country".

Sommer had a casual charm that the world likes to associate with the French gentleman; he had money and satisfying successes in his career, and he had honours bestowed upon him by his country and the racing profession, but those who knew him noted that his true happiness became evident only when he climbed into the cockpit of his car and hurled himself with spirit and abandon into the chase.

PIERO TARUFFI

Piero Taruffi, research engineer, designer and the most persistent pursuer of the Mille Miglia's checkered flag, retired from racing in 1957 at the precise moment when his car crossed the finish line at Brescia. He had been trying to beat the frustrating 1000-mile run countless times, flouting misfortune and vowing that one day he would win. As he was lifted out of the cockpit, he straightened slowly, waved grandly to the crowd and to the other cars and walked away proudly like a hero of old, his last dragon slain.

With the racing driver in permanent retirement, Taruffi, the engineer and designer for the Gilera Motorcycle Co., is still to be seen at all major motorcycle meetings and there is still a cheer from the stands whenever his name is announced.

He began with motor-cycles, setting 38 records, and then, just before the war, got into a 1500-c.c. Maserati and finished second to Villoresi in Palermo. His combined ability as a driver and engineer brought him to the Cisitalia firm, where he did a great deal to improve the product. He raced the 1100-c.c. car so successfully that he became champion of Italy in 1947. A year later, after winning at Berne, he came in second over-all in the Tour of Sicily with an 1100-c.c. sports Cisitalia.

While fighting bad weather, mechanical troubles and sheer hard luck in the many Mille Miglia races, Taruffi scored splendid successes elsewhere in a 158 Alfa Romeo and a Ferrari. One of his best remembered achievements was in a 4·5 Ferrari at Berne, where during an appalling downpour he came in a tight second behind Fangio, just passing Farina a few laps before the finish line.

He was approaching 50 and the Mille Miglia was still just a hope. In 1924, at the age of 17, he had won the Tourist Race at Rome in the family's 1500-c.c. FIAT, carrying his own cheering section as passengers. It consisted of his father, a distinguished Roman surgeon, and his young sister. He enjoyed the shouts of "Taruffi! Taruffi!" and made up his mind to continue in the sport—but with qualifications. Throughout his entire career on the track he remained a fine example of the European gentleman driver. During the 1954 Sebring race, in which he suffered a heart-breaking disqualification, he was brought to the microphone by Alec Ulmann, the race's founder. There was no shadow of rancour on Taruffi's face as he spoke in English to the multitude that had cheered him on. "After all," he said, "winning a race isn't the only thing in life."

But apparently it was. He piloted most of the leading cars—Alfa Romeo, Bugatti, Maserati, Ferrari, Lancia, E.R.A., FIAT—attaining 22 over-all firsts, 18 seconds, four thirds and at least ten class wins. As a doctor of industrial engineering, Taruffi speaks with added authority when he names the three chief ingredients for a good racing car: power, weight and shape. In a driver, he says, brain, body and heart are needed for success at speed. These three were highly necessary in the 1951 Pan American Road Race, lasting five days from the Mexican border at Guatemala to Juarez at the U.S. border. He won that race, finishing fresh and bright.

Taruffi's experience in the Mille Miglia did not go for naught. He became an expert in the long race and almost won the 1953 Targa Florio but for a matter of poor judgment in his pit. He returned to the Targa a year later in a Lancia and scored

Courtesy of Abarth & C.]

Piero Taruffi

a resounding victory, setting a record average of 55·8 m.p.h. for the vicious 357·8 miles over the Short Madonie Circuit.

The engineer in the man came to the surface quite frequently during his racing days. He built a "Tarf" for experimental purposes and then with a smaller version of it, powered by a 500-c.c. Gilera engine, he established the record for an hour run at Montlhéry.

Taruffi, always a popular driver, found himself suddenly in disfavour because he had refused to drive for Ferrari in the Targa Florio. Ferrari could not find a driver of equal stature and he lost that race as well as the world championship. Taruffi felt this keenly but managed to maintain his emotional equilibrium. He ran well at many tracks but his eye was on the Mille Miglia.

When he started his 13th try, even his detractors confessed to twinges of sympathy—and when he won it the cheers were genuine.

MAURICE TRINTIGNANT

The atmosphere that bright July day in 1948 at Berne was charged with tension and depressed by tragedy. Tenni, Varzi and Kautz had been killed in crashes, but despite some protests the racing had been continued. Speeding along in the SIMCA Gordini, Maurice Trintignant had good reason to enjoy his ride. He was in second place in a tight battle between his marque and the Cisitalias and his machine was purring along like a contented engine. Earlier in the race this had not been so, but somehow the ghosts and the gremlins had been exorcised by skilled mechanics, and an excellent chance for victory lay ahead.

Suddenly the car spun and looped. Somehow, Trintignant became detached from his cockpit and, as the car bounced away, he was left lying in the middle of the track—bruised but conscious. He lay there watching the startled drivers roar by him. How close he came to being struck is a matter of conjecture. He noted that Raymond Sommer just managed to slip under the SIMCA Gordini's second bounce. He was also aware that Manzon, Bira and Farina saw him and, rather than chance hitting him, plunged through the hedges, knowing that this would eliminate them from the race. When the shrieks of the horrified crowd died away, Trintignant did what he always did after a race. He returned to the sunny vineyards of his southern France and waited for the next race.

Trintignant's earliest recollection in the field of sports cars was a simple passion to drive fast. His background was purely pastoral: grapes, green fields and stately trees. No garages, no apprenticeship as a mechanic—only a desire to drive at speed. In his first race at Pau he came in fifth, watching René Dreyfus in a Delahaye run through non-stop to win. At 21 he won the Grand Prix des Frontières in Belgium with a Bugatti.

He was born in 1907, but it was not until after the war that he made his great showing and got his nickname, Petoulet, meaning "impolite noise" in the dialect of southern France. His car had stopped suddenly during a race and mechanics were mystified as to the cause until one found that a small bird had been caught in the intake of the supercharger. Jean-Pierre Wimille immediately applied the nickname, which has remained a label ever since.

Trintignant joined the SIMCA team as Number One driver, running the cars as they developed from the 1100-c.c. class to 1200, 1400 and the 1500-c.c. supercharged. But Amédée Gordini was unable, because of financial difficulties, to match the Alfa Romeos and Ferraris. During 1950, Trintignant drove the Formula 2 SIMCA to win a third in the German Grand Prix behind Ascari and Simon. In a 1500-c.c. SIMCA during the same meeting he established the fastest lap record regardless of class. By 1953 he was champion of France, and won an invitation from Ferrari. He brought the car to six firsts, including Le Mans with Gonzales. He crossed the finishing line in 19 races out of 21. That year he was in third place for the world championship.

The manner in which a man races is perhaps the best evidence of his outlook on life. An incident at Buenos Aires indicates what kind of person Trintignant is. He was in a fierce battle with Mike Hawthorn for the lead, trailing by 18 seconds. On the final lap Hawthorn's engine failed. Trintignant stopped, picked up Hawthorn, sat him on the tail of his car and drove on to victory.

His love of the sport is slightly modified by self-discipline. If he cannot win, he will not abuse the car. Rather, he would prefer to nurse the car so he can come to the finish line. He is precise. When he won the 1955 Grand Prix of Europe at Monte Carlo, he was clocked during the first 50 laps at 1:29·3 and the second 50 laps were recorded at an average of 1:29·6.

It is possible that Trintignant has found the *modus vivendi* for successful and happy living: enjoy the fury of fast driving on week-ends and relax among the vineyards of southern France during the week.

ACHILLE VARZI

In another time in history, Achille Varzi might have been a plumed knight on a spirited charger, enjoying a joust for the sake of the sport, rescuing fair ladies from ogres and leading the gracious life of a gallant gentleman. He might also not have been averse to accepting a gratuity for his jousting and, as for the damsels he rescued, he most certainly would have made romantic overtures to them.

However, he was born in 1904, too late for live dragons, into a family of prosaic textile manufacturers where finances were no problem, and a young man's whim to divide his portion of wild oats between girls and motor-cycles met no strong objections.

That the interest in girls would not diminish was no source of astonishment to his friends and family but the enthusiasm for the two-wheelers was expected to fade. It did not—mainly because of the existence of a young racer named Tazio Nuvolari. An intense rivalry sprang up between Varzi and Nuvolari that was continued with never-flagging fury in automobiles.

Nuvolari was volatile, earthy and dramatic. He loved motor cars and racing them—not caring too much how big or small they were or where the race was. Varzi was deliberate and selected his car with care and caution. He never went to a race without his private secretary. He would not join a team unless permitted to have his personal mechanic, Bignani. While there was a good deal of inward irony in his speech and manner, he was known as the man who never smiled. He did not care for the rough and tumble of a racer's life and lived only in the finest hotels, where he insisted upon the choicest foods and finest wines.

Varzi burst into motor racing flat out. In his own Alfa Romeo he entered the Grand Prix of Europe at Monza and came in second to Louis Chiron. He barely missed becoming champion of Italy in 1929, a title he achieved the following year and then again in 1934. In 1930, driving for Alfieri Maserati, he won the Grands Prix of Italy and Spain, the Coppa Acerbo at Pescara and the Targa Florio.

Varzi and Nuvolari were members of the Alfa team in the Targa, an unhappy situation that was watched anxiously by troubled manager and staff. Chiron in a Bugatti was pressing the leading Varzi and was on the verge of overtaking him when the cars reached the last eight miles of straightaway, where the Alfa had a strong advantage. But Varzi took no chances. He overworked the engine from 6000 r.p.m. to 6200 and 6300, roaring home at 6500. To everyone's amazement the engine did not falter or explode, but Nuvolari, who came in fifth, was infuriated. The Alfa team could not stand the strain of two such racing giants and Varzi, the younger, decided to leave.

At 26 he was the most talented and most promising ace on the roads and tracks of Europe. He had also broken the Bugatti spell over the Targa Florio, which *Le Patron* had held for five years in succession. Ettore spoke first among the designers and Varzi joined the team.

The next year he met Nuvolari again at the Targa. Bugatti gave him a car, but, in order to avoid any misunderstanding about his position, Varzi painted the car the Italian red, yet wore the blue French overalls to show he was attached to *Le Patron*'s firm.

It was a mad, wild race even without the feud. The high ground was shrouded in mist; heavy rains washed away entire stretches of roadway and each of the hundreds of blind turns was a blood-curdling gamble with disaster or death. W. F. Bradley in his biography of Bugatti recalls that "goggles became useless and were thrown away. Varzi drove through seas of mud, he sat in mud, he swallowed mud, he was blinded by mud just where the utmost precision was essential—but he hung on grimly." When it was over, Nuvolari was first and Varzi third.

That evening, Bradley reports, Vincenzo Florio met Nuvolari in the streets of Termini. "Where are you going?" he asked.

"Oh, just a walk, to get a little fresh air."

"Happy?"

"Well, I'm glad I beat Varzi."

By this time the bitter rivalry had become an obsession with Varzi. Manifestly sullen and brooding, he could not forget or forgive defeat and in the Monaco of 1933 the adrenalin content of his inner mechanism was at its highest. Historians of the day call the Monaco of that year the most thrilling and outstanding of all races in which a Bugatti figured. Varzi was ahead for three laps and then Nuvolari took the lead; during the next four Varzi was ahead, sometimes only by six inches. Then Nuvolari pulled up, only a second in time separating the Alfa and the Bugatti.

For 60 of the 100 laps they appeared like two cars on a string. Then for 17 long laps Nuvolari led, Varzi furiously trying to catch him. As Bradley says: "Champagne and flowers were being prepared for someone—but no one could tell which man would receive them."

With two laps to go, Varzi began that manoeuvre for which Nuvolari hated him so. He began to over-rev his engine, but by this time they were on the straight hill to the Casino and the Alfa showed its speed. On the last lap the cars were just a foot apart.

Courtesy of René Dreyfus]

Achille Varzi

Varzi, instead of changing up near the centre of the hill, kept his car in third. He took his last desperate chance and the rev counter climbed past the 6000 safety mark to 6500 and then 7000. The Bugatti, like a blue streak, passed the Alfa.

And then Nuvolari did an unusual thing. He, too, started to over-rev but his car caught fire. He was signalled to get out, but instead raised himself in his seat to escape the fumes. This was enough to slow him. There was some confusion at the pit and Nuvolari could have pushed the car 50 yards to the finish line to claim a position—but it didn't matter. Varzi had won the race.

Varzi went on to win more races, showing a grace and casual *hauteur* that seemed to set him above his fellows. He was living in the tradition of the grand knight. When he joined Auto-Union he swiftly showed he was the master of this eccentric car, driving it to its full limit as only two other men did—Bernd Rosemeyer and Nuvolari. His mechanic's most important job in those days was to have a lighted cigarette ready when Varzi came into the pits, reaching with a heraldic flourish for this little reward.

Then came the war and some problems of a personal nature. Varzi's name did not appear on the starting grids and there was talk of a permanent retirement. Suddenly in 1946 he returned and was put on the Alfa Romeo team. The following year he began to show his speed again and the crowds again cheered the old Varzi with his ever-present cigarette and his clean, carefully creased overalls.

It rained in Berne on the fourth of July, 1948, and the crowd was disturbed at the dismal news that Omobono Tenni, known as the Nuvolari of motor-cycles, had just been killed when his two-wheeler crashed into a tree. Two other events were scheduled for that day: one for small-capacity racing cars and a Formula I race for the Grand Prix of Switzerland.

Varzi had a lap to go on his practice session and the pits waited when suddenly Chiron, driving a Talbot, pulled up and screamed that Varzi was dead. He said that on the final turn he had seen the Alfa spin and turn over, hurling Varzi on to the track. He was dead when Chiron got to him.

One other thing of note happened that day. Varzi, like many other drivers, had worn a cloth cap. From that day on the FIA made it compulsory to wear crash helmets.

LUIGI VILLORESI

Luigi Villoresi, called Gigi, was an old pro, silver-haired before his time and bronzed of face, who in more than 25 years of racing probably covered more mileage in a Maserati than any other driver. With his brother, Emilio, he began racing in the early 1930s and continued through 1955, pursued by death on the track, which never caught up to him but took two who were very close.

Gigi became Italian champion in 1938 and 1939, driving a 1500-c.c. Maserati. In 1939 his brother was killed in a crash at Monza and for a time Gigi considered leaving the field, but his loyalty to Maserati won and he continued to race.

Villoresi entered the Targa Florio in 1939. The course had been shortened to 141·5 miles so it could be held in the Favorita Park on the western edge of Palermo. In a Maserati, Villoresi won over Taruffi and Barbieri; he came back in the same car the following year to win again, bettering his own time by almost four minutes.

By this time he had become the friend and tutor of Alberto Ascari, who seemed to have taken the place of Emilio in Gigi's affections. They raced together successfully and their victories over each other seesawed, but Ascari's youth manifested itself in the long run.

Between 1946 and 1948, Villoresi's career was at its apex. He again won the Italian championship and in the British Grand Prix beat Ascari home by 14 seconds. He went to Indianapolis and came third in a 3-litre Maserati. He won twice in the South American races and was gaining points toward a world championship when he crashed at Geneva. He might have been killed had not Farina hurled his own car aside, missing him by inches.

Villoresi recovered slowly. Just when rumours began to circulate that he was through, he entered the Mille Miglia in a 4·1-litre Ferrari and came in an over-all winner. Some time later, while his mechanic was driving him from Monte Carlo to Modena, the car crashed and Gigi was painfully hurt. He was placed in a plaster cast, but insisted upon racing and beat Gonzales by four-tenths of a second.

Courtesy of the Nürburgring G.m.b.H.]

Luigi Villoresi

Young men were beginning to crowd the field. There was Alberto, who was the winner in more races than ever; Stirling Moss and Fangio. Experts still remember Villoresi's run at Monza in 1954, when he took the lead from Fangio in a thrilling exhibition of skill and daring. Then came the death of Ascari, which hurt Gigi deeply. Not long afterward he was in a serious accident at Castelfusano and friends persuaded him that a man born in 1909 who had compiled a magnificent record had a right to retire.

THE WOMEN

CAMILLE DU GAST

In 1895 Camille du Gast heard that the men who manned balloons were experimenting with an umbrella-type contraption called a parachute and she decided she must try it. Jauntily ignoring the protests of everyone—government, family, friends—she went up with the aeronaut Capazza in his free balloon. At 2000 metres they tore up the bag and leaped from the basket. Both parachutes opened and Camille, having proved that a woman could do as well as a man, went on to explore another innovation in transport—the motor car.

Encouraged by her doting husband, M. Crespin, who made lots of money with another popular invention, the cinema, Madame, statuesque and delightfully vivacious, began her career in automobiles in the historic race from Paris to Berlin in 1901. Driving a 20-h.p. Panhard, she started in 122nd position and finished 33rd. Considering that her car was the smallest and only 22 of the heavy cars completed the 687 tortured miles, her accomplishment was regarded as somewhat of a miracle.

Feminine and tender-hearted, president of the French Society for the Prevention of Cruelty to Animals and founder of a hospital for underprivileged and sick women, Mme. du Gast ran her greatest race in the Paris–Madrid of 1903. In a ferocious appearing 30-h.p. de Dietrich she battled against dust, rocks and unbanked turns, pressing crowds and masculine resentment, with buoyant cheeriness and irresistible grace. But she did more than that. As the race approached Bordeaux in the final section, a stretch of terror and disaster because the spectators crowded the roads and did not leap to safety until the drivers were almost upon them, the Yorkshireman, J. E. Stead, hurtled into a ditch while avoiding a triple collision.

While spectators stood by dumbly, Mme. du Gast dashed up in her car. She jammed on her brakes, leaped out and, with the aid of her mechanic and a few bystanders, she pulled Stead out from under his wrecked machine, gave him emergency first aid and made him safe and comfortable before going back to the race. She finished far behind her original position when the race was finally stopped at Bordeaux by the government.

Mme. du Gast went on to other thrills, including a dramatic victory in the Algiers–Toulon motor-boat race, in which she effected another rescue and was rescued in turn herself. She was a fine horse-woman, and her stable of black Orloffs was famous in its day. And, to complete the well-rounded life, she also was an excellent pianist, giving many success-ful professional concerts. By the time she died in 1942 she had accumulated many honours, including having a street named after her. But her greatest satisfaction came from the knowledge that she had opened the field of motor racing to women.

*   *   *

The French women drivers have carried on in the grand tradition of Camille du Gast. There was Hellé Nice, bright and lovely, who took her driving seriously, but managed to amuse her fellows by wearing overalls with shortened sleeves that were touched up with saucy little bows; Lucy Schell, Harry's mother, who was always among the leaders in rallies and earned a creditable record in racing; Odette Siko, the first woman to drive at Le Mans, and her companion, Mme. Mareuse, who raced well and repeatedly finished high in Monte Carlo rallies.

Among the unforgettable is Anne Itier, a piquant redhead who vied valiantly at Le Mans five times. She finished eighth in an M.G., fifth in a FIAT, tenth in an M.G. and fifth in a SIMCA. The only time she failed to finish was in a temperamental Adler.

It was she who echoed Carles Jarrott's long-ago idea of the perfect race by proposing a match between three English and three French women drivers using six cars of the same make, of equal speed and with pit crews of equal ability. The idea—a handicapper's dream—has won the hearty approval of almost everyone, but where and how to get such motor cars and such crews has not been solved to this day.

High on the list toward racing greatness is Gilberte Thirion, who started serious competition in 1952. In that one year this is what she did: a class second in the Paris–St.-Raphael rally with a Porsche; first in the Belgian Wolverthem speed trials; first in the Rally Soleil–Cannes; a fifth in the Tour de Belgique and a spectacular demonstration of top-notch driving on the Nürburgring during the German Grand Prix, in which she came in fifth.

Courtesy of the A.-C. de Nice]

Gilberte Thirion

In the ensuing years the record grew impressively. After rallies she went to racing and in the 1954 Mille Miglia she came in second in her class with a Gordini. In rallies she is regarded by many, including Sheila Van Damm, as formidable.

GWENDA HAWKES

The career of Gwenda Hawkes is interesting chiefly for the perennial debate it invokes about the virtues of track driving versus sports-car racing. The daughter of Maj.-Gen. Sir Frederic Manley Glubb, a highly decorated and distinguished soldier, and the sister of Glubb Pasha of Arab Legion fame, Mrs. Hawkes sought first and foremost to establish track records. She began with motor-cycles and went on to 3-wheeled Morgans, gaining undisputed honours in her field. Driving a Derby Special (a very much modified

American Miller built for Indianapolis), she did a lap at Montlhéry at 149 miles an hour. In 1935 at Brooklands she was matched against Kay Petre's giant Delage and brought her 2-litre Derby Special to 135·95 miles an hour—the fastest lap ever recorded by a woman at this track.

Although frankly cool toward competitive car-against-car racing, she was persuaded in 1934 to enter a Derby at Le Mans. Her car went out on the 16th lap. The following year, she and the Derby tried again and lasted 87 laps before engine trouble forced the car to be retired.

ELISABETH JUNECK

Mme. Elisabeth Juneck, a compact little woman whose face was forever burnished by the wind and the sun, won only one major race, the German Grand Prix of 1927, when the leading Bugatti was disqualified. Yet those who knew her—including Ettore Bugatti, whose cars she drove, and W. F. Bradley, who recorded the stirring motor-car events of the day—called her the greatest of women drivers. Stranger still, she earned this accolade in only two races, both at the Targa Florio.

S. C. H. Davis declares on a note of regret: "It was a pity the small, cheery woman, with her big Bugatti, white cap and dark overalls, could not have taken part in more races, for she had something which so many lack. But the Targa Florio was her choice; to succeed in it her ambition."

She went to Sicily for the first time in 1927 from her native Czechoslovakia with her husband, a banker, who had purchased a 2300-c.c. straight-eight Bugatti. Both were frankly addicted to high-speed driving and both were eager to take part in the wild and challenging mountain race. What they faced was Etna scowling over picture-book hills and vales through which snaked 67 miles of rugged, grinding roads flanked by cliffs and chasms. These 67 miles were to be circuited five times for a total of 335 miles, which included more than 1000 corners, curves and esses that would torture car and driver to the utmost. There was only one straight, five miles long, near the seacoast at Campo Felice. The roads consisted mainly of loose stones, many of them razor-sharp, or abrasive dust that rose in choking clouds to clog machinery.

The Junecks set about studying the course with calculated determination. First they took an ordinary touring car and went over the entire circuit. Then they did it again, slowing down, stopping and observing. And then they did something no one had ever done before at the Targa Florio. They covered the entire circuit on foot, 12 miles each day, memorizing every bend, gradient and *nuance*. They argued and discussed, made notes and revised them, and, when they seemed satisfied, took their Bugatti around the course the full five laps, trying, as Mme. Juneck recounted later, to find out at what speeds certain sections could *not* be taken.

Good sportsmanship, when prevailing within a family, makes for a happy combination of marriage and racing. Juneck proved this when he agreed that his wife should drive the first three laps, he the fourth and she the fifth and final one.

She began the race with excellent speed, finishing the first lap 70 seconds behind the leader. She was fourth behind such famous professionals as Minoia, Dubonnet and Materassi, and she was doing better than holding her position when the steering box cracked. The car hurtled off the road, struck a wall and lost a wheel. The body suffered considerable damage and the car was out of the race. Mme. Juneck suffered nothing but chagrin.

The following year she was back at the Targa, cheerful and ready to pit herself against such veterans as Divo, Fagioli, Dreyfus, Minoia, Chiron, Conelli, Maserati, Foresti and Campari, and one other woman driver, the German Countess Margot d'Einsiedel, who was there with a 1500-c.c. Bugatti.

That day at the Targa Florio, marked by many other thrilling incidents, will for ever be remembered for the breathtaking battle between the little woman from Czechoslovakia and the hardened professional, Albert Divo. The excitement began when Mme. Juneck, in her yellow and black car, saw the tiny blue spot that was Divo's car in the distance and she decided to catch him.

With a verve that seemed to border on recklessness, Mme. Juneck hurled her car into corners within inches of disaster and roared flat out on the milder bends, gaining perceptibly. Divo's mechanic looked back, saw the streaking threat and warned the driver. The duel was on.

For 270 throbbing miles the contest continued, neither driver slackening the headlong pace. Those lucky enough to catch glimpses of the roaring machines wondered how soon one car or the other would run out of road. At one point Juneck's Bugatti was dead astern of Divo's, with paper-thin space between them, but neither yielded. Divo's greater experience showed to his advantage on the bends, but on the small straights between curves Juneck's faster machine gained. She remained in his slipstream with some advantage, and although Divo, sportsman that he was, gave her every opportunity to pass, she never managed to overtake him.

The Targa Florio is a race that tests a driver's stamina like no other. In the final lap it showed. Divo's endurance made itself evident. The tiny woman, weary of brain and muscle, continued bravely, but she was falling back. When the race was over she was fifth, ahead of such excellent drivers as Minoia, Fagioli, Dreyfus and Lepori.

Her history thereafter is sketchy. Her husband was killed while practising for a race in Germany. She appeared as a guest in the observation car at the Targa in 1929 and then quietly faded from the scene. Since the war there have been unconfirmed stories of her remarrying and working as a mechanic in a tyre factory near Prague, and an unsubstantiated promise that she might return to racing. There are unconfirmed reports that she lives in Switzerland. Political conditions in that section of the world have made information difficult to obtain. Nothing, however, can obliterate the memory she left with those who saw her in Sicily. As Bradley sums it up: "Mme. Juneck never succeeded in her ambition to win the Targa Florio, but she proved herself superior to many male drivers and is undoubtedly the most brilliant female driver of this or any other period."

DOROTHY LEVITT

Dorothy Levitt, a tall, attractive girl of wealth and position, showed the women of Britain and the rest of the world that motor cars were not the sole domain of men. It is true that she had a Svengali in the publicity-conscious Selwyn Edge, who controlled Napier and whose philosophy was to burgeon to its fullest many years later in New York's Madison Avenue.

Miss Levitt came to him in the rôle of stenographer because she felt it was one way to get into the motoring field. Edge was immediately inspired by the thought that a woman driver would attract more attention than a man. In 1903, under the skilful manipulation of Edge, Miss Levitt started racing in a fully equipped Gladiator at the Southport speed trials and obtained a first in her class. Then she entered that year's 1000-mile trial and made an impressive showing.

She created quite a stir a year later when she entered the Hereford 1000-mile trial in a de Dion against the best men of the day. To the great delight of Edge and the press photographers, Miss Levitt made the run in a highly attractive creation especially designed to be worn somewhere between a garden party and a

[Courtesy of D. Napier & Son Ltd.

Dorothy Levitt

motor race. She was accompanied by her pet Pomeranian, a truculent little beast, which snapped and yapped and created general furore among the Victorians and made excellent copy. On the following day every male driver appeared with a toy dog (ugliness being the criterion) strapped to his bonnet. That night Miss Levitt was not invited to a special concert given to the drivers. She captured the evening, however, by sending to the concert an emissary solemnly bearing a gift of dog biscuits for each of the drivers and properly inscribed by the donor.

Miss Levitt scored a series of triumphs in hill-climbs, trials and races. Even though she took some time away from her beloved cars to race motor boats and fly biplanes, she fulfilled the hope of Edge to prove that motor cars were not the unique province of men. In a way she bridged the gap between the daring and spectacular Camille du Gast and the more timid ladies of the Edwardian era. She gave driving what Edge, had he known the phrase, might have called the Hollywood touch.

DENISE McCLUGGAGE

Denise McCluggage, America's foremost woman sports-car racing driver, states with understandable frankness that she'd rather wind up fifth in a man's race than win against a field of women. She is an excellent driver and can be well matched against most men, although she admits readily that the male in a race possesses the superiority of physical strength and an emotional impulsion to prove himself which the average female lacks.

On the question of sheer muscle, the power of the man shows itself in the twisting and turning of the car, the pulling of the wheel, the constant changing of gears. The actions will tire the female sooner, she declares. She recalls a race at Lime Rock where her fastest time was just one second slower than the male leader's, but, whereas he was able to continue the steady tussle with road and machine, she fell behind because of sneaking fatigue.

In the realm of emotions, Miss McCluggage continues, the male races biologically. He must prove his masculinity not only in skill but in daring. Every bend and every straight is another dragon to slay. Women drive with calculated caution, she feels. She calls it a sort of cultural approach to speed. To avoid generalities, however, she speaks for herself when she says: "I do not enjoy being frightened." Her whole attitude toward driving and her several other sports is that of the smooth and easy approach. The word *caution* must be defined on her personal terms. She hurls her car into a corner with the minimum amount of caution required to get the maximum result. Instinctively (because she is a woman) she leaves an assuring margin of safety going through that corner as close as possible without touching the verge and then actually smiling quietly to herself as she leaves the point of peril and goes flat out.

[*Bahamas News Bureau photograph*

Denise McCluggage

"Men regard the motor car as an instrument," Miss McCluggage says. "I feel it is an extension of my personality and an expression of a single will. In that sense driving at speed is not merely a craft, it becomes an art to be understood and respected. My way is to avoid fear, so I avoid frightening situations the best I can. As my driving improves, however, the margin of safety may be narrower, but, as I follow a method of increasing improvement, there will be less need for avoiding fear. The area of fright will become smaller but the philosophy will remain constant: to approach a dangerous sport cautiously."

No matter how she approaches danger, Miss Mc-Cluggage approaches it often. As the former sports-car editor of the *New York Herald Tribune* and a magazine writer on any interesting subject, she has plunged from a plane at 2300 ft. in a parachute; skied on perilous slopes and canoed in white water (rapids). By way of rounding out her activities, she swims, "one toe at a time"; finds fencing fascinating and goes flat out in a pool room or a table tennis match. After watching a horse show, she was enchanted by the jumpers and, if she can find time, will surely see how it feels.

Her plans for sports-car racing, however, show it to be her first love. She began at Montgomery in 1956, when she won a ladies' race in a Jaguar XK-140MC convertible. She promptly entered a men's race and came in eighth. During the same year she tried the Great American Mountain Rally with Louise King Collins in a Volvo and got the Worst Luck Award. She went on to win most of the ladies' races she entered. She tried an O.S.C.A. for the first time in the Nassau Ladies' Race, spun three times in five laps and finished fifth. Having won the first heat in

a Porsche, however, she finished second over-all. The following year at Nassau, after leading Jack McAfee for a lap and following him for another, she eased off, remembering she still had to compete in two ladies' races. Her fastest lap with the men that day was 3:03, yet she could not do better than 3:06 with the women.

With Ruth Levy she drove at Elkhart Lake and at Caracas in the Grand Prix of Venezuela. They were eighth over-all; second in class after 2 hours and 30 minutes at Elkhart when they broke a valve finger. At Caracas for the 1000-kilometre, they were 13th over-all and fourth in class. "We would have been third," Miss McCluggage recalled, "if I hadn't clobbered some dirt banks."

In 1957 she drove a FIAT Abarth at Sebring and came second in her class. She went to the Nürburgring in an Alfa Romeo Sprint the following year and finished second in her category, doing a 14-mile lap in 11:50. It was a man's race and she was the only woman. She drove brilliantly at Nassau and her eyes are frankly on Le Mans.

She has driven a varied number of cars, but there is another side to Denise. As editor and publisher of *Competition Press*, dedicated to purveying motor-sport news in a hurry, she became a recognized authority on racing as well as a highly articulate commentator.

Like every commentator (of any sport), Miss Mc-Cluggage selected a dream team. First, she created a car—the 3-litre (purely) Mythical, which was a "doozy". The Mythical was good for grand prix and sports, and her drivers were Stirling Moss, Phil Hill, Tony Brooks, Mike Hawthorn, Jean Behra—but who was number six? She considered many: Harry Schell, Masten Gregory, Olivier Gendebien, Wolfgang von Trips, Maurice Trintignant, Carroll Shelby, Joakim Bonnier, Ed Crawford, Chuck Daigh, Walter Hansgen and Dan Gurney.

As a chronicler of the sport, Miss McCluggage can be freely analytical of everyone she has mentioned, but she speaks especially hopefully of Gurney, whom she regards as the young driver with the greatest potential for international competition. She feels that Lance Reventlow, with or without his Scarab, will make history, and she agrees with Harry Schell and Briggs Cunningham that American builders and American drivers like the many she has mentioned are the hope of continued competition on international tracks.

She likes to drive the large cars for experience, but prefers racing the small and fast ones such as Porsche and O.S.C.A. She likes long-distance races "because you can learn so much driving them". She is pert and lovely in her racing costume, which is topped by a polka-dot helmet. Why? "Because I am a show-off," she replies mischievously.

Miss McCluggage admits she finds it difficult to equate so-called sportsmanship with hot competition. The incidents of sportsmanship are reported with such fanfare, she reflects, that there might be less to it than meets the eye. "I am very competitive," she says, "and drive my best trying to catch someone." It is not unlikely that her career as a topnotch driver may inspire discussions in sports-car circles about the compulsion of the female driver. She would be happy to lead such a discussion.

EVELYN MULL

Evelyn Mull, the fastest grandmother on four wheels, traded in a horse for a sports car (so to speak) in 1953 and since then has amassed almost 60 trophies, causing it to be said that she has cornered silver as far as American women drivers go.

The cheerful, vivacious lady from Malvern, Pa., for a long time favoured a dashing, scarlet A.C.-Bristol, which she handled with impeccable skill and enviable enthusiasm. She entered her first race at Thompson in an XK-120 Jaguar coupé and came second. With a beginning of this nature it was not astonishing that on June 28, 1958, she became the first woman to win a major race at Watkins Glen. Among her cherished souvenirs is the checkered flag, autographed by the starter, which she got as an extra reward that day.

Mrs. Mull, called Evie, is a hobbyist of action sports. Born in New York City, she attended Foxcroft in Virginia and easily followed the family tradition of the fox hunt. Her mother, riding side-saddle, was at one time the only woman in the Meadowbrook, L.I., Hunt. Evie went to Aiken, S.C., and became one of the few women during the 1930s to take part in big drag hunts. Some years later, when she was in Philadelphia to visit her best friend, she met John Mull, Master of the Hounds at Whitelands.

"I married the farmer boy next door", she recalls, referring to Mull, in whom she found a fellow-enthusiast. This word is inclusive of not only the hunt but photography and motor racing. One summer the Mulls took time out from racing to attend a photography school, thus opening a new field for their adventures.

This includes excellent films of Le Mans, the Mexican Road Races and a dangerous documentation of a trip through the Grand Canyon in a cataract boat. Exhilaration of this kind must be modified by something more sedate, so Evie became a cooking enthusiast and, leaving nothing to chance, earned her *Cordon Bleu*.

She has raced at Nassau, where on one occasion the pace was so fast that Ruth Levy flipped, Suzy Dietrich flipped and Isabel Haskell went out with engine trouble. Mrs. Mull has had the usual tussles with nearby wings, hay bales and other obstacles, but had managed to remain intact.

The Mulls' love for sports cars (John drives an O.S.C.A.) has diminished their attention to horses. However, they still maintain their ranch, El Desterrio, near Santa Fé, where they still have horses and alfalfa.

Photograph by the authors]

Evelyn Mull

In an account of the Mulls' activities in *The Spokesman*, published by the Philadelphia Region of the Sports Car Club of America, Emmie K. Heed makes the point that Mrs. Mull's life on horseback and "more recently behind the wheel has never been dull. And the Mulls' horse van still trundles off to the races, but as a ponderous symbol of the changes in their lives and the only modification in their stable, the van is now fully equipped with two sports cars—one of them the A.C.-Bristol."

Well aware that women were becoming increasingly active in sports-car racing and rallying, she felt that they should be told of the women who had preceded them. The swiftest, most direct way was a book. She is the author of *Women in Sports Car Competition*.

KAY PETRE

Kay Petre, pert, petite and persistent, earned the affectionate title of "girl ace" from the men at Brooklands after she lapped the historic and bumpy course at 132·24 m.p.h. Her maiden name was Defries, she was born in Canada and early in life she became an excellent ice skater. It was at a winter sports event that she met the quiet and gentle Henry Petre, who appreciated her newest interest—motor cars.

At Brooklands he allowed her to race his beloved Invicta, but when, to save his car, he presented her with a Wolseley Hornet, friends knew this was a solid marriage. Kay, dark-haired and bright-eyed, was like a sprite. She was lovely and feminine in every endeavour except when racing. Then she became the grim and determined competitor—a change that enabled her to amass a record of which any male driver would have been justifialby proud. Her racing

[*Courtesy of Ruth Sands Bentley*

Kay Petre

career began in earnest when she got a 2-litre super-charged Bugatti in 1933. The car served her well throughout her career although she used many other machines.

In 1934 she won the women's cup in the Relay Race and also took a 12-cylinder 10,500-c.c. Delage around at 129·58. With her reputation definitely on the rise, Kay became a member of the Riley team with Dorothy Champney for the great Le Mans race. The girls were placed 11th, a good showing for a 1½-litre car. The following year she teamed with Eisie (Bill) Wisdom as part of the Riley outfit. The weather was frightful, but the girls did nobly until a bearing in the engine gave up at the 38th lap.

Like all drivers Kay had many close brushes with disaster and at least one that might have made an excellent comic strip. During the Nuffield Trophy a cracked oil line flooded the cockpit and Kay so thoroughly that she had to pull into the pits before she was scalded to death. She decided to change her saturated blue overalls but no ladies' dressing room was available in the pits. She saw and seized an over-sized coat and crawled under it. The startled crowd noted with wonder the gyrations of a headless and bodyless garment for several minutes and then, emerging from it, Kay, neat and clean in a set of over-alls several sizes too large.

Kay continued to race at Donington, the South African Grand Prix and often at Brooklands, where on a sad September day in 1937 during practice for the British Racing Drivers' 500-mile run she was struck by Parnell's car. Persistence and faith brought her through partial paralysis and plastic surgery. She pulled through and did some racing afterward, but other interesting fields, like journalism, beckoned and Kay responded.

DOROTHY TURNER

Dorothy Stanley Turner was raised at the wheel of a sports car. Her father, an R.A.F. wing commander, had been an intimate of Jarrott and Edge and most of the other drivers of the pioneer era, and when his little girl showed the inclination he started instructing her himself. Her first contact with real speed was as navigator in a trial with Mrs. Cecil Kimber.

Saucy and spirited, wearing blue overalls to match her eyes, Dorothy made a striking picture when she entered her first big contest, the Nuffield Trophy in 1937, in a supercharged Q-type M.G. It was an unhappy beginning: a stone hurled by the rear tyre of another car struck her in the eye. The injury was serious and painful, but Dorothy continued to drive until she was flagged down on the 16th lap by worried officials.

With Enid Riddell she entered the 1937 Le Mans in a PB M.G. and gave an exhibition of driving and sportsmanship the memory of which still wells in the hearts of all good sentimentalists. The M.G. was second to an Aston Martin and both were making fantastic speeds when suddenly the Aston failed to pass its pit. The news came that it was stopped on the back stretch. Miss Turner knew the Aston firm wanted the car to finish at all costs. On the other hand, if it did not go on, she would win the Rudge Cup for M.G.

"The M.G. manager was asked if he could help", S. C. H. Davis, who was there, recalls. "Now that raised a curious problem. Was it fair to ask Dorothy to help a rival? Looked at one way, it was the luck of racing. Looked at another way, a win for Astons might mean the difference between survival and disappearance, while Dorothy was running privately and, if she finished her first real road race second, she would be luckier than most. Yet second is second and first is first. It was very difficult."

Miss Turner did not hesitate. On her next time round, she stopped and told the Aston driver that his pit wanted him to continue by any means if the car would run. He started up, one cylinder missing because of a bent valve. Aston Martin won the cup.

There were many other races, rallies and hill-climbs in which Miss Turner distinguished herself. When the war came she followed family tradition and won a commission in the W.A.A.F. But there her concern was not motor cars: it was barrage balloons. And, when the war was over, she married an air commodore.

SHEILA VAN DAMM

How does one get to be Queen of the Rallies? There must be an infinite number of means and methods toward that end, but if we examine the real queen—Sheila Van Damm—we find the desire, the devotion, the temperament and the skill. She began her career at the steering wheel in the worst possible way.

Her father, Vivian, head of the Windmill Theatre in London, a sort of respectable burlesque house, took her out for a spin when she was 18 and at one point stopped the car and asked her to take the wheel. Frightened and bewildered, she obeyed because "father ruled as a benevolent despot with the family's consent and no one questioned his orders". She managed to drive the car safely and adequately and not until it was over did her father find out that she had never driven before. The girl who later became Women's European Champion and won in her class in the Mille Miglia in 1956 admits that no assignment at the wheel was ever so trying.

When the war came, Miss Van Damm did a great deal of driving for the Women's Auxiliary Air Force and increased her determination to continue in sports cars when it was over. By 1951 she was sixth in her class with a Hillman in the British Rally; she won the Ladies' Cup of the *Daily Express*; a year later she was in the Monte Carlo with Bill Wisdom and in another year was second in the Coupe des Dames at Monte. That same year she won the Ladies' Prize in the British and the Coupe des Dames in the Alpine in addition to an Alpine cup for having a clean run right through without loss of marks. This was followed by a victory in the Scottish Rally.

The list grew. In 1954 she won the Coupe des Dames in the Dutch Tulip Rally, the Austrian Alpine Rally, the Viking Rally and the Geneva Rally and was second among the women in the British and Lisbon Rallies. She went to America for the Great American Mountain Rally with the Sun-

[*Courtesy of Rootes Motors Ltd.*

Sheila van Damm

beam team and was one of three drivers who won the team prize for the 1100-mile grind from New York through the New England hills and passes and back to New York.

Miss Van Damm's face is frank and friendly and, when she smiles, which is often, she has baby dimples. Her figure is comfortably plump and her eyes look upon the world with warmth and honesty. She is an accomplished aeroplane pilot and a competent business woman. Running the Windmill Theatre is encroaching upon her prime love, the sports car.

Perhaps she sums up her career in sports cars and her responsibilities to the theatre in her book with the philosophical title *No Excuses*. Her father, who in the long ago was a mechanic for Clément-Talbot when it was making history with Percy Lambert, wanted her to make good in the theatre as well as on the course.

"He told me not to spend all my time at the theatre," Miss Van Damm recalls. " 'Enjoy yourself while you've the chance,' he said. 'One day you'll be tied down here and you won't find it so easy then. Go and have fun.' "

Sheila was ready to stick to her duty, but as an afterthought her father asked: "When do you propose to tell me that you are going on the next Monte?"

ELSIE WISDOM

Some sage once said that marriage is fine especially if there are interests to be shared. What greater interest can there be, then, if it is shared in a pit or the cockpit of a speeding car or in twin cots in a hospital? This is virtually the entire story of Elsie Wisdom and her husband, Tom.

Elsie will henceforth be referred to as Bill, a name she acquired as part of the honorary rank of male while riding as rear ballast on the several motorcycles of her several brothers. She was the only girl in the family. It was not long after becoming competent at motor-cycling that she got her first car—an unusual marque made by the Messrs. Grice, Wood and Keiller (G.W.K.), on which she managed to attain an exhilarating 70 m.p.h.

Bill had graduated to Lea-Francis when she met an irrepressible young man named Tom Wisdom, sometimes known as Tinker. They fell in love with each other and a noisy Frazer Nash. They were married in 1930 and as a honeymoon gesture of affection Tom persuaded Bill to enter the Ladies' March Handicap at Brooklands. Qualms, doubts and fears notwithstanding, she brought the car up to a 95·05 lap and won. After beating her husband's time by one second at the Shelsley Walsh hill-climb (no recriminations), Bill got some valuable experience in the Junior Car Club's Double-Twelve in 1931 and then Tommy decided she should go for the women's lap record. They purchased a Leyland, large, fast and difficult to master—so difficult that officials would not permit Bill to drive the car unless an experienced

Elsie Wisdom

driver would vouch for her. The man who was to observe before vouching was John Cobb.

Bill had two obstacles to overcome. First: Cobb was known to cherish the opinion that woman's place is in the home. Second: the car was skittish. Several men had tried to purchase it but had turned it down because of its temperament. They said the car was not to be driven. It had to be coaxed on the straights and wheedled on the turns. Tommy watched with a mixture of apprehension, hope and confidence as his wife took the throbbing beast round the track at a brisk speed. Cobb also watched, his expression revealing nothing. When the trial was over and Bill

came up to Cobb, he said: "Bill, you will drive that car at the next meeting."

In 1932, with the Australian, Joan Richmond, she won the 1000 miles at Brooklands in a Riley— the first time women had done this. The car had borne up magnificently during the gruelling run and, when a reporter asked her what she thought of it, Bill patted it as if it were alive and said: "It's a darling." In 1933 she drove at Le Mans with Mortimer Morris-Goodall as a partner and had to quit when the car gave out. This happened to her again in 1935 when she and Kay Petre tried their luck and skill at Le Mans and their Riley broke down after 38 laps. During all that time Bill managed also to be Mrs. Wisdom, running a home, bringing up a family and having a full social life.

She and Tommy, after several races together, entered the 1937 Mille Miglia in an M.G. They were making wonderful time when Tommy twisted the car hard to avoid striking a woman leisurely crossing the road. There were flames and sparks and a procession of trees. Tommy and Bill wound up in a hospital, her face in bandages and his leg broken. They were astonished that they were in the hospital so quickly until they found out that they had actually crashed into its gates.

After another attempt at Le Mans in 1938 with an M.G., which quit after 48 laps, Bill slowed down somewhat. Tommy had joined the R.A.F. and Bill managed to add to her laurels the Ladies' Cup for the Bouley Bay Climb in Jersey and Maloga in Switzerland. At Monte Carlo, where she ran with a feminine crew, she was outstanding as the only driver who remained on speaking terms with her crew.

The second serious crash came in 1951 in the Alpine Rally, when the Wisdoms were struck head-on by an American car that was not supposed to be there. After damaged arms and ribs were repaired they returned to racing, but in 1953 at Le Mans Tommy's car caught fire and he was grievously injured. Bill was in the pits waiting and the friends who shared those dreadful minutes with her recall her outward calmness and efficiency in helping her husband. As one pit crew member tells it: "She seemed to know how to do the right thing at the right time."

VENUES: RACES, RALLIES, HILL-CLIMBS

The world's first automobile competition was the Paris–Rouen Trial of July, 1894, which was easily won by de Dion's steam car at a speed of 12·5 m.p.h. for the 80 miles. It would be called a rally rather than a race today, with its set interval for lunch and fixed arrival times. It was held, as all purists believe all sports-car competitions should be held, on ordinary public roads.

Paris–Rouen set the precedent for the great city-to-city races that were to criss-cross Europe and to survive into our own time: Paris–Bordeaux–Paris, Paris–Vienna, Paris–Berlin, Paris–Madrid, the Gordon Bennett, Paris–Marseilles–Paris, Peking–Paris, New York–Paris, St. Petersburg–Moscow, Riga–St. Petersburg–Riga, Le Mans and the Mille Miglia. The Monte Carlo Rally, the Alpine Trials and the Liège–Rome–Liège Rally—which are so nearly races rather than rallies that it is hard to classify them—are also survivals of that heroic epoch. In the United States and the United Kingdom, early racing was much different: American road racing, while it was allowed, was shunted away from main arteries; the British had to take ship to the Isle of Man or Northern Ireland to see automobiles compete in their appropriate *milieu*.

The petrol engine came into its own in the Paris–Bordeaux–Paris race some four months after Paris–Rouen, when a Peugeot won first prize despite a Panhard's faster 732-mile average of 16·875 m.p.h. because the rules stipulated that first prize must go to a four-seater. Every race, virtually, brought forth new rules of eligibility. Sometimes these related to vehicle weight—minimum or maximum—sometimes to engine size, sometimes to body capacity or dimensions. There was then no centralized body like today's Fédération Internationale de l'Automobile to determine vehicle classifications and racing rules that would be universally applicable.

The Gordon Bennett Cup Races that began in 1900 were the first annual events. James Gordon Bennett had donated a cup to be awarded on strict conditions, and the contestants were nations rather than individuals. Each competing nation could enter three cars, but every component of each car had to be built within the sponsoring country, and replacements *en route* could be made only with such components. Elimination heats were employed in each country to select its three representatives, and the nation that won in one year was to be host to the race in the next year. For the first three years of its short existence, the Gordon Bennett was a race within a race: that is, it was part of some already scheduled road race. These were the monopoly of the various national automobile clubs.

The first Gordon Bennett, run in 1900 within the 351-mile Paris–Lyons Race, attracted entries from many countries, including the United States; among them was Belgium's "Red Devil", Camille Jenatzy, the first man to drive a car at a mile a minute and one of the rarest winners among all the great drivers. Panhard won the trophy for France with the help of Ferdinand Charron, and this meant that the 1901 trophy would be contested on French roads. Only two cars qualified, a Panhard and a Mors, both entered in the Paris–Bordeaux. The Panhard won.

In 1902 the Gordon Bennett was merged with the famous Paris–Vienna that S. F. Edge won. This meant that in 1903 the race must be run in the United Kingdom. But in Great Britain it was impossible to race on public roads; while Continental races were held on open highways, Bennett considered this an unnecessary hazard and so he introduced closed-circuit racing. Tracks were unknown; this meant simply that public roads must be used but that they would be barred to other traffic. Great Britain remaining adamant in its prohibition, the locale was changed to Ireland, whose Parliament obligingly amended a law or two to make the race possible.

The course chosen was roughly in the form of an 8 on roads that included hard turns, poor surface and some hills, making brakes, suspension and steering quite as important as power and speed—in essence it was the forerunner of today's sports-car racing terrain. The list of drivers was a contemporary hall of fame: Edge, de Knyff, Gabriel, Jenatzy, Baron Pierre de Caters of Belgium, J. W. Stocks of England, Henry Farman of France, Foxhall Keene of the United States (driving for Germany). According to the universal practice of the time (which survived into our own day in some European races), the cars were sent off individually at intervals of about a minute, rather than together, so that he who finished first was not necessarily the winner. For once, in this Gordon Bennett, the gentle Jenatzy was a victor, with a 49·2-m.p.h. average in his Mercedes.

Gordon Bennett was delighted with the success of this first all-independent contest; he did not know that its death sentence was already being phrased. The great automobile clubs resented his infringement of their monopoly; since the manufacturers worked with the clubs and the clubs' members were the financial and social leaders of their various countries, the outcome was assured: when open agreement could not be openly arrived at, the manufacturers could be persuaded to be unable to deliver the cars, or governments could be influenced to enact last-minute legislation that could make the race impossible.

Nevertheless, Bennett persisted, and in 1904, Mercedes having won in Ireland, the site was Germany, among whose Taunus Hills near Frankfurt-am-Main the circuit was laid out on fine roads. A

Richard-Brasier won the cup—poor Jenatzy returned to his more accustomed position of second—and for 1905 the race was scheduled for France. The area chosen was in the Auvergne, full of gradients and bad curves that militated against any speeds like the 54·5 m.p.h. of the 1904 winner. Mercedes did not enter, and the major rival of the French was F.I.A.T., which, however, lost to the 48·4-m.p.h. Brasier. This meant that the next race would also be held in France.

But there was to be no next race. Virtually all the French makers agreed that thereafter they would boycott Gordon Bennett's competition and restrict themselves to the Grand Prix that had just been inaugurated by the Automobile-Club de France. The club, to double assurance, scheduled its second G.P. for a 1907 date much earlier than the normal Gordon Bennett spring date. Thereupon the German and Italian manufacturers decided that it would be a waste of effort for them to vie for the trophy. Thus the Gordon Bennett Cup became a relic in the year that gave birth to the Targa Florio, a prize that is still contested.

Europe was by far the busiest racing arena in the world, and the most important, in 1906. That *parvenu*, the Isle of Man Tourist Trophy Race, was only a year old; America's Vanderbilt Cup Race was twice that age and had already earned the respect of the Continental builders and drivers, but it was the only important *épreuve* in all the United States. Mr. and Mrs. H. F. Locke-King were still studying the contractors' bids that, a year later, were to bring to too short a life—and to undying legend—their £250,000 dream, the Brooklands track near Weybridge, in Surrey. The rolling inferno of the 1903 Paris–Madrid Race, which the French Government had had to stop at Bordeaux because of its astronomical toll, was a very living memory, and the two freak races across Asia had not yet been planned. But the foundation had been firmly cemented for the annual contests that have so enriched motoring tradition. In 1906, too, the small car came into its own with its first real race, the *Coupe des Voiturettes* at Rambouillet.

Formula racing had in effect been begun by the Gordon Bennett with its 1000-kg. weight maximum; the *Coupe des Voiturettes* attempted to initiate engine limitations by setting a maximum bore of 106 mm. for single-cylinder engines and 90 mm. for twins; but nothing was said about stroke or cubic capacity, and several monsters resulted before the trend was established—by Bugatti, Delage, Hispano and Isotta—that led directly to the modern Alfa Romeo Giulietta and Porsche. In addition, many other racing fixtures of that time, forgotten today, were flourishing, such as Germany's *Kaiserpreis* and Belgium's *Circuit des Ardennes*.

In this formative period of motor sport there were still to be two outstanding cross-country races: Peking–Paris in 1907 and New York–Paris in 1908. While they were officially designated as races, they resembled very closely the much shorter "reliability trials" that had become popular not only in Europe but also in England and America, where, since they were not speed contests, they were legal. The London–Edinburgh–London trial was typical of both the British and American events (such as the first Glidden Tours): tests of hill-climbing ability, top-gear potential, fuel economy, durability of components, braking and acceleration competitions and, without any changes in the contesting cars, one or more laps of a speed track. In contrast, the later Prince Henry Trials on the Continent returned much nearer to the spirit of the old Paris–Berlin and Paris–Vienna races, in which the ratio of time to distance was the paramount criterion.

Both the trans-Asiatic races were sponsored by *Le Matin* of Paris: it underwrote Peking–Paris alone, but it enlisted the help of *The New York Times* and *The Chicago Tribune* the second time. Glory was the chief reward in 1907; entrants had to make a substantial deposit, returnable at the Peking starting line. De Dion-Bouton entered two 10-h.p. 2-cylinder cars; Contal of France entered a 6-h.p. tricycle. From The Netherlands there was the almost unbreakable 15-h.p. Spyker. The giant of the race—and the eventual winner—was Principe Scipione Borghese's 50-h.p. 7½-litre Itala, capable of 50 m.p.h. No one could guess the appalling conditions that would be encountered; but the route as laid down —Peking to Mongolia, skirting the Gobi Desert to the Siberian border, then to Lake Baikal, along the Trans-Siberian Railroad to the Urals and then via Nizhni-Novgorod to Moscow and on to Germany, Belgium and Paris—specifically permitted deviations. It was the only race in history in which the course was not categorically set forth and the distance was merely estimated—8000 to 9000 miles.

Supply depots were prepared in advance—the needs of the automobile being carried by camel caravan. The race began at 8.30 a.m. June 10, and no one hurried: at the last minute all the competitors had agreed to stick together as long as possible. As soon as the cars were out of Peking, 10 m.p.h. became an impossible speed. Despite the gallant accord, the Itala was soon far in front, frequently pulled by coolies and/or mules. In the first week it covered 150 miles, handicapped by frozen ruts, quagmires, rows among the coolies, brigands, unanticipated fuel consumption, tyre trouble. Through the Gobi the route was barely a track, its borders outlined by bleaching bones. The hero of the expedition revealed himself as the Prince's chauffeur, Ettore Guizzardi, an orphan brought up on Borghese's estate who, in other circumstances, might have been a second Porsche. Completely unschooled, he had set up a machine shop on the estate and invented heating and laundering devices as well as caring for the Prince's car, which he was to rebuild more than once during the race. He was also an exceptional driver.

There were times when the Itala bumped along the Trans-Siberian's rail track until it had to turn off to let a train go by. Once a bridge collapsed and dumped the Itala upside-down into a stream; an hour later it stood on its wheels on the far shore, through the efforts of peasants and oxen. It was July 13 before the Itala could approach its maximum speed: that day it ran along at 45 m.p.h. A wooden wheel splintered; Borghese and the chauffeur repaired it but the repairs failed, and a village smith repaired it. In Kazan new springs had to be made; they were gone by the time the car reached Moscow. From that point until the triumphal entry into Paris on August 10, just two months from the start, the Itala ran fast and free of trouble, slowed only by the wild receptions in the cities it had to traverse. Borghese won a goblet from *Le Matin* and a new car from Itala; Guizzardi went back to his shop on the Prince's estate.

The New York–Paris Race was much more grim because of the bitter rivalries. There were three French cars—de Dion, Motobloc and Sizaire-Naudin; an Italian Züst, a German Protos and an American Thomas Flyer. At 11.14 a.m. on Lincoln's Birthday, 1908, they took off from Times Square, their crews dressed some in summer walking clothes, some in Alaskan tundra garb. Every car was festooned with picks, shovels, ropes, spare tyres and canvas bundles of gear and clothes. The Protos held 176 gallons of petrol; the de Dion's frame was filled with wood wrapped in felt and covered with rubber, and similar treatment had been applied to all other esposed metal parts. Its seven fuel tanks were independent of one another. Food for a month was carried with the cooking kits. Steel rims, flanged for use on railway tracks, were also strapped aboard. The Marquis de Dion had offered a $2000 prize for the first American car to reach Paris, which the Thomas seemed certain to win since two other American entries had backed out.

The de Dion's crew included a M. de l'Autran, mechanic for the marque in the Peking–Paris, and Capt. Hans Hansen, an Arctic explorer. Baron Charles Godard, driver of the Motobloc and one of the company's founders, had finished third in the 1907 race on a de Dion. The Sizaire's driver had started the Peking race on the Contal tricycle and been forced to withdraw in the middle of the Gobi. His name was Paul Pons; he was the father of the Metropolitan Opera soprano, Lily Pons. Montague Roberts and Charles Schuster were the Thomas's co-drivers. That car carried a winch to pull itself out of holes and wheels designed to be driven on the bare rims if necessary.

A month was allowed to reach San Francisco. No one went farther than 116 miles the first day; some went only 80. Crossing the United States in the winters of that period was a fine training for Siberia, except that there were motor clubs all along the route that were always ready to send aid to the disabled. The Sizaire had dropped out 98 miles out of New York with a broken differential. During a week's rest in Chicago, Hansen left the de Dion to join the Thomas; the Italians charged the Thomas with unfair modifications *en route*; the Germans lost two of their crew by resignation.

The trip to San Francisco was a nightmare for all the contestants. The Thomas got there first and was put aboard ship for Seattle and Alaska while the Züst's men were shooting hungry wolves in Death Valley. Early thaws thwarted the plan of driving through Alaska; the Thomas was shipped back to Seattle and thence to Yokohama. The other cars eliminated the Alaskan leg and sailed for Yokohama, except the Protos, which had to be sent by train to Seattle and put aboard ship for Vladivostok. The charges and counter-charges that ensued from these various infractions of the rules were voluminous and venomous. The Germans were penalized 15 days, while the others were hiring teams of 48 men and women each to haul the cars up Japanese grades at 2s. 2d. per person per haul. At one point men with axes had to chop away part of a house to enable the cars to negotiate a turn.

The Thomas was the last to arrive in Vladivostok, where the others had spent their time refurbishing their cars. De Dion decided to withdraw, having proved a year earlier that his cars could cross Asia, and his driver, M. de St.-Chaffray, enraged because the Thomas would not sign him on, bought up all the petrol in Vladivostok. When this extortion failed, he gave up and went home. The other contestants' trip across Asia was a repetition of 1907, with additions. The Thomas lost second gear riding the railway track, but one of its crew welded in new teeth in a blacksmith's shop; they held until a new gear arrived. Far ahead was the Protos, followed by the Züst. A ferry sank under the Thomas, but it survived.

Ultimately the Protos reached Paris first, on July 26, and claimed victory. But the Thomas, arriving four days later, was awarded the laurels when *Le Matin* disqualified the Germans for cutting out difficult parts of the route. The committee also noted that, violations aside, the Germans were 26 days behind the Americans in elapsed time for the 21,000 miles. The Thomas was shipped to its factory and certified completely original except for the new second gear; not even a sparking plug had been changed.

Both the Itala and the Thomas are preserved today. Restored to the state in which it started the 1907 race, the Itala is in the Museo dell'Automobile in Turin. The Thomas, exactly as it looked when it reached the works in Buffalo, is now in Austin Clark's Long Island Automotive Museum.

This final year of the ultimate in city-to-city races was the third year of the Targa Florio, which was the single-handed creation of Cavaliere Vincenzo Florio, who died early in 1959 in Épernay-les-Bains. Florio and his elder brother, Ignacio, were orphaned quite young and inherited some of the greatest estates in Sicily. Both, but especially Vincenzo, were passionate sporting motorists, and Vincenzo had acquired by 1905 a stable of the world's finest cars. He loved racing but Sicily had virtually no roads then, and few of his friends owned cars. It was therefore Florio's custom to invite his friends for visits and to lend each a car with which to race over the roads he had laid out on his vast estate. Florio's chauffeurs were also on the entry list, with stringent instructions not to hold back for any of the gentry, including their own employer. Whenever he got the chance, Florio raced against professionals on the Italian mainland. On one occasion, his brother, speeding by train to prevent him from running at Brescia, passed a level crossing at which the race cars were stopped. Looking anxiously out the window, Ignacio was saluted with a wave by Vincenzo, busily reparing his Mercedes, which had hit a dog. Vincenzo Florio finished third in that race—Lancia won it—and Felice Nazzaro on a Panhard was fourth.

In 1904, two years before he initiated the Targa Florio and drove a Mercedes in the French G.P., Vincenzo Florio offered the annual Coppa Florio, which was first put in contention the next year at Brescia and has since had a number of venues, sometimes being run in conjunction with the Targa and sometimes held as far afield as France. Like the Targa, the Coppa Florio is still run; but the Targa is the only point-to-point road race of the heroic era that has survived into our own day.

The *targa* for which the drivers were to compete was a great gold plate commissioned from a Parisian goldsmith in 1905. The next step was to find a course in an island almost devoid of roads. Florio retained engineers and surveyors who finally reported that they had found the route. It began at the seashore near the village of Cerda, 30 miles east of Palermo, and then climbed arduously into the mountains, reaching 3670 ft. before it dropped back to sea level and a short straight that returned it to Cerda. The whole circuit, according to W. F. Bradley, was "more than 90 miles of the most crazy highway it was possible to imagine, with the road struggling painfully to attain altitude, twisting, doubling back on itself as if giving up in despair, then resolutely attacking the vertical mass in a rage of determination to reach the fortified village towering above it. The road had been engineered . . . by successive generations whose very existence depended on reaching some dominating point and entrenching themselves there: no scattered farms, no isolated buildings, but compact groups of dwellings cunningly constructed on ledges. From the high ground the shimmer of the sea was visible to the north; to the east Etna reared."

The surface was adequate for mule carts. While the starting line was gay with lemon blossoms and luxuriant vegetation, the Geraci ridge, 3670 ft. up, was as likely as not to be snow-covered. There was another hazard that was more imponderable: the

traditional, and very real, Sicilian brigands. With these Florio dealt as only the lord of the manor in a still-feudal society could. He called together their leaders, after many of the drivers he had invited to the first Targa Florio had spoken plainly about their reluctance to become moving targets for already practised marksmen, and for these chiefs who were a law—or a variety of laws—unto themselves Florio had a master stratagem. He outfitted them in impressive regalia and solemnly proclaimed them Stewards of the Course, in whose hands lay the safety of the contestants and the honour of the island. There being neither wire nor wireless contact between any two points on the course, these men and their followers were also to be the communications service.

The first Targa Florio began at dawn on a Sunday, May 6, 1906, the cars starting singly. Probably the drivers were unaware of the archaeological bonanza that had come to light when the excavations were made for the grandstands at the start; probably they would have been bored by the bronzes and the ceramics that were dug out of the earth to testify to a civilization that went far beyond the Christian era. They were undoubtedly more concerned with their own and their rivals' cars. Florio had decreed that these must be "standard"—at least ten of each should have been built. These included a great Itala (the eventual winner, driven by Alessandro Cagno, who still lives in Italy); Lancia's F.I.A.T.; a Berliet driven by Paul Bablot, who was later to enhance his reputation with Delage, and Henri Fournier's Clément-Bayard.

In that historic inauguration of the 277-mile Big Madonie Circuit the winner's average speed was 29·07 m.p.h. for the three laps. Fifty years later the winner's mark for eight laps—357·8 miles—of the Short Madonie Circuit was barely double the 1906 figure: impressive evidence of the inherent toughness of the course, and of the virtuosity of the tiny Mme. Juneck, who finished fifth there in 1928 against the greatest amateur and professional male drivers of her day.

The years after 1906 saw frequent variations in the circuit. Sometimes the race was only two laps, or even one; sometimes it was run round Sicily; at others it was run on sections of the original course known as the Medium and the Short Madonie Circuits. Florio himself never won his own race, though in 1909, when it was a one-lap affair, he drove a FIAT into second place just one minute behind the winning S.P.A.

When the Targa Florio became a one-lap 600-mile run round the whole island, it attracted some American cars—Fords and Overlands—in 1912, but they did not fare too well. The round-Sicily run continued for the next two years; then the war suspended the Targa until 1919, when it was given a new course, the Medium Madonie Circuit. This 67-mile route eliminated all the seaside run and most of the high-speed straightaways, retaining all the worst difficulties of the Big Circuit. René Thomas, a former motor-cyclist and aeroplane test pilot who had won at Indianapolis in 1914 despite a permanent limp resulting from his first car race, was first on a Ballot, covering four laps—268 miles—at 34·19 m.p.h. in his characteristic manner. To Thomas racing was no glorious sport but, to quote Bradley, "a hard, cruel business" in which Thomas remained constantly "cautious, calculating and painstaking". These qualities were of special value on any of the Madonie circuits, where there could be no pit manager to control or advise the driver anywhere but at the start–finish line.

The Medium Circuit continued to be used until 1931, when the race returned to the Big Circuit. But the weather made both these courses unpredictable, and in 1932 Florio enlisted Mussolini's influence in the construction of a loop road that would make possible the Polizzi Circuit, also known as the Short Madonie Circuit. Since Il Duce was a keen enthusiast, he acquiesced at once, and the new 44-mile course eliminated not only what had already been cut out by the Medium Circuit but also many of the heights that this had retained. This made it possible for the spectators to see the cars more often but Florio, who believed that drivers should always be kept at maximum stress, ordained eight laps on this circuit: 354·5 miles. It was here that Nuvolari won one of his most cherished victories over Varzi, emphasised by the arrival of Baconin Borzacchini—named by a politically idealistic father after the Russian theoretical anarchist, Mikhail Bakunin—in second place, fully five minutes ahead of Varzi.

In the years just before the Second World War the Targa was radically altered. From mountain driving it switched to the short, level and very speedy roads of the Favorita Park, on the western edge of Palermo. These races ranged from 106 to 196 miles and the terrain allowed winning averages as high as 88 m.p.h. But again the Targa Florio was interrupted by war, which Florio and his wife spent in Rome, where they were imprisoned by the Germans and by sheer good luck were released just an hour before a wholesale execution of hostages.

When racing resumed after the war, the Targa reverted to the round-the-island route, expanded to 671 miles, and Italian cars maintained their traditional superiority with a new name, Ferrari, and an old one, Alfa, until the race returned to the Short Madonie Circuit in 1951. In that year Frazer-Nash became the first British marque ever to win a race in which, according to Ettore Bugatti, "any manufacturer taking part regularly . . . acquires a mass of information which he could not secure elsewhere, even on the track or in the laboratory". Bradley, biographer of Bugatti and historian of the Targa, believes that, because the physical conditions of the Targa rule out all but the best proportioned and balanced cars, it has done more than any other race in the world to encourage the automobile's all-round development. In Florio's last active year, 1958,

he succeeded in having it made part of the sports-car championship roster.

Diagonally across Europe an equally legendary competition had got its start a year before the Targa. This was the Royal Automobile Club's Tourist Trophy, which, unlike the Sicilian race, has had two periods of closed-track existence. From 1905 through 1922 it was run on the roads of the Isle of Man; then it moved to Northern Irish highways through 1936. In 1937 and 1938 the T.T. shifted to Great Britain proper, which meant it had to be run on a private course: in this case, Donington Park in Derbyshire; after the war it returned to Ulster and continued there into the mid-1950s. Since then it has been run in England, on closed courses again.

The town of Douglas on the Isle of Man had been the scene of the eliminations for the 1904 Gordon Bennett, and the terrain, while it lacked the altitudes of Sicily's mountains, was almost as tortuous. If the Targo Florio was the race of the thousand corners, the T.T. was the race of the 900; and very little of it was on level ground. The 1905 race, which was based on fuel consumption, started on a slope above the town of Douglas, at about the middle of the island's east coast. This led to a tricky S and up 500 ft. to Ballasalla, then on to Castletown, where an acute right turn sent the drivers north-west toward Peel, climbing 700 ft. fairly slowly and then descending much more rapidly.

From Peel the course ran along the coast, through a tricky U-turn, to the flat northern plain, and then right to Ramsey, where a left-hand hairpin led into a three-mile climb to a height of 1350 ft., the descent from which was particularly hazardous in the early days when brakes were sketchy and drivers were inclined to coast in order to meet the fuel requirements. Through a number of deceptive corners the road led its seven-mile downhill course to the finish, a few miles short of the start. Its total of 52 miles included virtually every road condition that the tourist of that day might expect to encounter anywhere in the United Kingdom; like the Targa, the T.T. ran for the most part along narrow roads where passing was all but impossible and stone bridges, walls and lamp-posts offered a constant series of hazards.

For the first race the railroads, which had an abundance of level crossings, were subordinated to the drivers, and the island was thrown into temporary chaos. In the next year, consequently, the southern part of the course was eliminated, as well as the northern flats, the cars turning west shortly after leaving Douglas and starting east at Ballaugh, and the route measured only 40 miles. Two years later the coastal run from Peel to Kirkmichael was eliminated with its Devil's Horseshoe and the circuit turned north from Ballacraine. In this form it continued through 1922. The dust of the early years was mitigated by paving in some stretches, but the hump-backed bridges were never altered.

The 1905 race set a maximum chassis weight of 1600 lb.—the Targa Florio never adhered to any formula—with a minimum load of 950 lb. and a minimum wheelbase of 90 in.; as a corollary, a chassis minimum of 1300 lb. was imposed to prevent excessive chassis drilling, which was a favourite Edwardian device to reduce weight. Some contestants, to remain within the limit, resorted to such measures as removing spring leaves and fitting cardboard bonnets and running boards. The 1905 fuel formula was a maximum rate of 25 miles per gallon: just before the race it was relaxed to 22·54 miles. This brought on, in all the first three T.T. races, an anguish of tuning, measuring, arguing and evading—some entrants exhausted their imaginations in concealing petrol tanks and lines. Seals were placed on carburetters and tanks. Bodies had to be ordinary touring models; the cries of "non-standard" were raised by rivals then as now. The cars were sent off singly at one-minute intervals. According to the classic formula, all spare parts and tools had to be carried in the car and only the driver and his mechanic might work on it. There were, of course, no pits. The 1905 race—four laps, 208 miles—was won by a flat-twin Arrol-Johnston at 33·9 m.p.h.

The 1906 formula lengthened wheelbase by 6 in. and specified widely spaced gear ratios. It was run on the shortened 40·25-mile course—four laps, 161 miles—and the Hon. C. S. Rolls won on a Rolls-Royce at 39·43 m.p.h., using the wire wheels that had been looked at so fearfully the year before. The 1907 race added a lap and a class: heavy touring, for larger cars required to carry a one-ton load, to get at least 16 miles per gallon and to mount a huge screen whose 5×8 ft. was to simulate the frontal area of a limousine body and was slotted for rear vision—a foreshadowing of the Mercedes 300SLR's Le Mans air brake in 1955.

One of the most controversial of all T.T.s was the "Four-Inch" of 1908, so named because its formula limited cylinder bore to 4 in. Four cylinders were the maximum allowed; 1600 lb. was the minimum weight, quite high for the 25·6 h.p. by R.A.C. rating that the formula allowed. However, the rules said nothing about stroke length or body design. Pits were provided for the first time, near Ramsey, and there the drivers' womenfolk prepared refreshment for them to bolt while the mechanics checked the cars. The Napier-based 102×182 Hutton won under the new formula, with the highest speed to that date: 50·25 m.p.h. for nine laps of the 37·5-mile circuit, a total of 339·5 miles.

There was a six-year hiatus after the Four-Inch; the 1914 race produced still another formula: 3310-c.c. maximum volume and 2400 lb. minimum weight. Another innovation was cash prizes: £1000 for the winning driver, £250 to the next man and a £300 team prize. The 1908 course was used, but 16 laps were to be made for a total of 600 miles, divided into two days' running. Many of the cars were capable of better than 90 m.p.h. and the predominantly untarred roads were most inadequate. German Adlers were far from standard touring cars, but

protests were faint if they existed. Kenelm Lee Guinness, who had run perseveringly in the Isle of Man, won at last in a Sunbeam at 56·44 m.p.h., defeating his brother, Sir Algernon, on the same marque.

War broke into the T.T. almost immediately thereafter, and it was eight years before the race could resume. The 1922 contest marked the début of the Bentley in road racing. Initially the formula called for 3-litre engines and a minimum of 1600 lb. Even more than in 1908 and 1914 the "touring" pretence was dropped—only the Bentleys resembled touring cars. Still entries were so few that a new class was set up: under 1500 c.c. and over 1000 lb. This drew Talbot-Darracqs and Bugattis, as well as an Aston Martin driven by H. Kensington Moir. The roads were unchanged from their pre-war condition. There being, it is said, no rain like Manx rain and no mud like Manx mud, most of the drivers were handicapped by having dispensed with front wings, windscreens and wipers; but in spite of this conspiracy of weather and terrain lap times of 70 m.p.h. were recorded by Sunbeam, which was to win this last Isle of Man race at 55·78 m.p.h. for 302 miles. The under-1500 winner, a Talbot-Darracq, averaged 53·3, a full mile an hour more than the Bentley that finished second in the big-car race. But what *The Autocar* had called "a Grand Prix in miniature" was over.

Once again the T.T. was interrupted, to resume again in 1928 on a road route in Northern Ireland that Richard Hough calls "the best road-racing course ever used in the British Isles". For the next eight years this 13·67-mile Ards circuit, with "every conceivable kind of corner, interesting gradients, hazards ranging from the famous butcher's shop in Comber to level-crossings and the formidable Town Hall in Newtownards, and a genuine hairpin, which brought every car down to 20 m.p.h. or so and first gear", was to bring out the best in the finest cars of Britain and the Continent. Prince Chula of Siam found it ideal because "it had all the features of a long road which one would meet on a tour"; Caracciola said: "The course is difficult but with an excellent road surface." S. C. H. Davis found that "each curve needs just a little difference in approach, a slight variation in method. . . . The circuit is one of the most interesting in the world, tricky, requiring accurate judgment above all things, yet fast, and with a nice sprinkling of those curves which give sheer joy when taken exactly right, and everywhere wide enough to make passing easy."

The circuit began just east of Dundonald, in County Antrim, and led directly into a 90-degree left turn, after which the road curved constantly as it ran east by north up, then down hills to Newtownards. It took the cars right through town, with a 90-degree right turn at the Town Hall followed by a very long straight that ultimately became a sweeping left curve up a hill into Comber, southwest of Newtownards. Thence another long stretch, up-hill at first, then down, led through a whole series of relatively mild corners to the famous Dundonald Hairpin, where a 45-degree right turn debouched into a straight past the start–finish line and the pits.

On this circuit the cars, though they ran together, were grouped by classes based on engine displacement not dissimilar to present practice. Engines of 5000–8000 c.c. were class B; 3000–3500 c.c., C; 2000–3000 c.c., D; 1500–2000 c.c., E; 1100–1500 c.c., F; 750–1100 c.c., G; 500–750 c.c., H. The 1928 race brought the entries back to something like touring cars, in that they had to be regularly catalogued models carrying starters, dynamos, wings, windscreens and hoods. As in the early Le Mans races, the hood had to be erected and used: at Ards, it was for the first two laps. Spares and tools had to be carried aboard, and no others could be used. Cars in classes B to E had to carry 264 lb. of ballast to simulate the weight of two passengers in addition to driver and mechanic; in class F 132 lb. had to be carried; the smallest cars were exempt. The start was like Le Mans': each driver stood in a circle across the road from his car and, at the signal, sprinted to it, erected the hood, jumped in, started the engine and took off—by all odds the most exciting start to watch. In that first race the starters included such names as Tim Birkin, Malcolm Campbell, Lord Howe (then Viscount Curzon), Baron d'Erlanger, Kaye Don, George Eyston and Sammy Davis. They had to cover 30 laps—410 miles. Despite the competition of a blown Mercedes-Benz, Bentleys, Stutz, Austro-Daimler, Bugatti, Lagonda and O.M. in the first four classes, the outright winner was Kaye Don's class F—1496-c.c.—Lea-Francis at an average of 64·06 m.p.h. The fastest lap was that of the Mercedes—74·39 m.p.h.

Caracciola won the 1929 race—often called the best of all T.T.s—in a blown Mercedes. The handicap system confused not only him but Neubauer, who was of course managing the pit, and Caracciola felt deprived of the thrill of close rivalry; certainly he had no means of knowing he had won until he was told. On the other hand, intrigued by the bookmakers' presence at the course, he found the odds against him were 60 to 1, and he resolved to make a little present to his manager by winning if he could. Neubauer had made substantial bets on his driver, and he went back to Germany with a tidy bundle of sterling. Both Germans were rather less intrigued by the R.A.C.'s ban on even the mildest alcoholic indulgence. The outstanding feature of the race itself was the rain, which was not steady but would cease and then resume in torrents, during all of which Caracciola performed the unheard-of feat of increasing his rate of overtaking the smaller cars that had shot out ahead of him at the start. He won at 72·82 m.p.h. despite handicap credits of as much as five laps for the smallest cars. In succeeding years, varying methods of handicapping resulted in the trophy's sometimes going to a car that was by no

means the fastest, as in 1931, when an M.G. averaging 67·9 m.p.h. was the winner over an Alfa that averaged 79·05.

Scrutineering—known in America as technical inspection—was most exacting at all the Ards races. Strict conformance to standard specifications was demanded: no accessories were permitted that were not available to the ordinary customer. Every cylinder head was removed to check the bore. Ards in its last year was notable, too, for allowing women on the course with men for the first time in modern racing in the United Kingdom. And, of course, in all the T.T.s as in every other British race and most Continental competitions with the notable exception of some in Germany in the early years, there was no question of amateurs as against professionals: anyone who was qualified and could get a car drove, whether for a living, for extra income or for sheer fun.

It was a tragedy for which the victims were to blame that ended racing at Ards. A large crowd was gathered in a prohibited area in Newtownards when a Riley came out of the railway bridge into a fast left-hand turn on Regent Street and started a front-wheel slide that could not be controlled. The car flattened a lamp-post and broadsided into the crowd, killing eight and injuring 15.

For the next two years the T.T. was a closed-course race, on the 3·125-mile Donington Park circuit of which today's 1·5-mile Lime Rock course in Connecticut is almost a miniature copy. The start–finish line was midway along a short straight that led into a hard left followed by a sweeping right, a relatively straight piece, a rather wide hairpin to the right, two more rights, a long straight broken by one or two mild corners and then a 15-m.p.h. hairpin that straightened on a steep grade to the starting line. This was a French Talbot course in 1937—they took first and second, listed in British records as Darracqs to avoid confusion with Britain's own Talbot—and the winner's average was 68·7 for the 100 laps—312 miles. Delage won the next year, and then war again interrupted the T.T.

It was 1950 before the race was resumed, and then it went back to the highways of Ulster. This last road circuit was 7½ miles long, with 14 right- and seven left-hand corners; the right-hand hairpin of less than 30 degrees was an authenic all-brakes-and-first-gear corner. A much faster course than any of its predecessors, despite a nice admixture of up- and down-grades with a range of 500 ft., it was also tenanted by much faster cars, and Stirling Moss won the first race there—34 laps, 225½ miles—at 97·47 m.p.h. in a Jaguar. This was to be the best winning average ever at Dundrod, whose original surface was later replaced by one of "razor-like granite chips", to quote Hough. The longest race there was that of 1953—111 laps, or 823·176 miles. Then, in 1955, not long after the holocaust of Le Mans, the T.T. had another fatal accident that took it off the highways for good: it is now run at Goodwood, owned by the Duke of Richmond and

Gordon, who, as the Earl of March, was a prominent driver and designer of the 1930s. In the 1955 race, studded with limited- and non-production specials, six cars piled up on the blazing wreck of a Cooper between the hard, high banks that flanked the narrow road at Deer's Leap, on the straight leading into Cochranstown. There were a number of deaths—all among the drivers—and the authorities would not relent again.

It is not inapposite to quote Hough here: "Dundrod is a victim of the modern sports/racing car, that logical but unhappy development of the true production sports car which is at present [1957] fast ruining sports-car racing in Europe and as quickly writing its own death sentence. Sports-car racing runs in cycles . . . competitors' persuasion results in the progressive abandonment of fixed screens, wings, fuel restrictions. And, if no wings, why carry lamps? And surely no one can object to fuel injection? And, if disc brakes are becoming commonplace, then why not assist deceleration by raising a panel of the bodywork before each corner?"

What Hough calls the first step in the return to normality that, he says, is inevitable if true sports-car racing is to survive was made in 1956 at Le Mans, when the sponsoring Automobile-Club de l'Ouest stipulated that every open car in the race must have a full-width windscreen. That this requirement should have been set by the A.C.O. is only fitting, for it was this club that was responsible for inaugurating the 24 Hours of Le Mans in 1923 as a test of the endurance of standard touring cars.

Three men created *le Grand prix d'endurance des 24 heures du Mans*. Charles Faroux, the dean of French motoring journalists, had long been concerned with the inadequacy of automotive electrical equipment, and one night in October, 1922, he suggested among his friends that a night race be organized with the aim of stimulating the perfection of these accessories. Georges Durand, secretary-general of the A.C.O., rejoined: "Why not a 24-hour race?" Faroux and Émile Coquille, managing director of the French branch of the Rudge-Whitworth wire-wheel firm, doubted whether the authorities would agree to so long a closing of public roads; but Durand and Marcel Canit, one of the directors of the A.C.O., undertook these negotiations. Two months later all was arranged; the inaugural race was set for May 26, 1923.

The rules were simple but strictly enforced. All entries must be cars that conformed in every respect to catalogue specifications of the current year, with full touring coachwork including wings, running boards, headlights, parking lights, tail lights, hood, horn and rear-view mirror; they were subject to examination by a jury and each manufacturer was to present ten cars, from which the officials would choose at random the two or three that would represent the marque. Cars with electric starters were to carry their cranks in the tool boxes, and these were to be of normal complement according to the catalogue. The driver was to make all repairs and pit help was limited to laying out what he needed. All cars except those of 1100 c.c. and less were to have four-seater bodies; the smaller cars had to have two-seater coachwork. A bag of sand or a lead ingot had to be carried to represent the weight of a co-driver. Minimum distances were set for each class to cover, from 571·6 miles (a 23·6-m.p.h. average) for the smallest to 994·2 (41·4 m.p.h.) for the biggest. Distance checks were set at 6-hour intervals: elimination was ordered for any cars that had fallen 20 per cent below their minima in six hours, 15 per cent in 12 hours or 10 per cent in 18 hours. All finishers would qualify for the Rudge-Whitworth Triennial (later Biennial) Cup.

In later years limits were set on time at the wheel for any one driver, area and dimensions of wings, width of oil and petrol fillers, shielding of auxiliary lights to prevent blinding of competitors, headlight bulbs—only the standard yellow prescribed for French highway use was admissible—and on many smaller details. Seals were placed on fillers, crankholes, batteries, dynamos, etc., and these could be broken only with official approval. But in the first race there was only one restriction relating to extra petrol and oil: these must be put in only at the pits; the seal regulations, however, were effective even then.

The circuit chosen was substantially the roads used earlier by the Automobile-Club de France for its G.P., a 10·726-mile course, roughly triangular, that was to be retained through 1931. The start–finish line was midway in the most irregular leg of the triangle, a wiggling straight along which the drivers rode right into Pontlieue, a suburb of Le Mans two miles from the start. There the triangle had its apex in a 30-degree angle necessitating a right turn into a five-mile stretch to Mulsanne, broken only by a sweeping S. At Mulsanne the circuit took a 60-degree right turn that led to a 90-degree-left-90-degree-right at Arnage, a mile away; two miles later, along the wiggling straight, the cars passed the starting lines and the pits. In that initial Le Mans, Chenard et Walcker covered the greatest distance—1371·9 miles—but Bentley had the fastest lap—66·69 m.p.h.

The second race brought changes in the rules governing hoods. All open-car drivers were to come into the pits after five laps, erect the hoods and cover 20 laps before coming in again to have their hoods checked: the slightest fault meant immediate disqualification. Today's fairground atmosphere within the circuit got its start then, with a boxing match and a circus. Other amenities were sparse, but the crowds seemed not to mind. The A.C.O. was already planning to buy all the land within and bordering on the roads that made up the circuit, but this took several years. In 1925 refuelling under 155·3 miles was prohibited; the next year the grandstands and pits were improved and a huge scoreboard was erected. Infield parking had already been admirably organized, and now bars, restaurants, shops and lavatories sprang up where they were most needed. The open-car regulation was altered, requiring the drivers to raise their hoods at the start as at Ards, run 20 laps and then lower them. Changes were made, too, in the minima for the various classes, which became the Index of Performance that is still applied at Le Mans and has spread to so many other races. Placement in the Index determined the winner of the Rudge Cup, which went to the marque showing the greatest proportionate excess over its stipulated minimum for three—later two—successive years.

Up to 1927 victory at Le Mans had been a French monopoly, which Bentley was to shatter. This year also marked a change in the repair rule, forbidding pits to keep any tools or parts and relief drivers to add to the supply aboard the car at the start. Such regulations made victory only more valuable, and "Le Mans" as a model designation sold extra cars for many a marque. A year later the Annual Cup for distance covered was established. All this time, contrary to the practice in most other competitions, there were no cash prizes. In 1929 the Pontlieue hairpin was eliminated by the use of a cross-road about a quarter-mile below it, shortening the course to 10·15 miles. The French, discouraged by Bentley's 1927 and 1928 wins, were outnumbered in 1929 by foreign marques; in 1930 only three of the 18 starters were French and one of these, a Bugatti, was driven by Mmes. Mareuse and Siko, the first women ever to race at Le Mans, open now to private as well as company entries. In that year, too, the lap record was raised twice: first by Caracciola in a 7-litre Mercedes, who turned 87·55 m.p.h., and then by Birkin's Bentley with 89·696.

In 1932 the circuit was altered to its present 8·38-mile route. From the start a short straight leads to a wide right turn and another straight ending in the abrupt left-right-right of the Tertre-Rouge corner, one mile from the start. Thence a barely broken 4-mile straight heads to the tight Mulsanne corner, unchanged from the original layout, and the old route is followed to the S ending at Arnage—its beginning is now called Indianapolis. The road is almost straight—the old wiggles have been eliminated —from Arnage to the sweeping right-left White House corner and straight again for almost a mile past the starting line. But this shortening and accelerating of the course seemed only to intensify the trend of many drivers to forget that Le Mans is a long test of endurance: the records of all three circuits are full of the names of those who pushed too hard too soon and broke up their cars. In 1931, for instance, only six of 26 starters were still going 24 hours later. The 1932 lap record for the new course was Minoia's 88·5 m.p.h., but at the very start of the next year's race Nuvolari's Alfa clocked 90·96 from rest. One of the added incentives to speed, especially in the absence of official prize money, was the awards that by now innumerable manufacturers and sellers of petrol, oil, tyres, sparking plugs and other components

were offering to the drivers who made the best time using their products. It was not until 1949 that the A.C.O. itself offered cash as well as trophies to the victors on Index, on distance and in the Rudge Biennial, as well as hourly bonuses for leaders on distance (these had been instituted in 1939) and lesser awards for every starter, including those who finished last or withdrew. The mechanics of the cars that finished first and second in distance were also rewarded.

Part of this huge purse—there were two top prizes of 1·5 million francs each and a host of smaller ones, down to the 15,000 francs for each of those who covered less than 500 kilometres—came from the fines of 1000 to 10,000 francs imposed on entrants or crews who violated pit and course rules, as well as from entrance fees and the club's treasury. Regardless of reward—and in many cases drivers were paid by the builders of their cars—Le Mans' entry lists have always been a recapitulation of the world's greatest drivers side by side with such non-professional enthusiasts as Roger Labric, the writer, and Georges Ham, the painter, who were to collaborate on a magnificent history of Le Mans; Count Czaikowski; Pierre Louis-Dreyfus, the banker who concealed his identity, as so many have done, under aliases (one was Ano-Nyme; another was Heldé); Freddy MacEvoy; Prince Nicholas of Rumania, Charles Moran, Jr.— the list is virtually endless. The names of men of the heroic epoch appear there too: Louis Wagner, who had raced in America before the First World War; Victor Hémery, like Wagner a Vanderbilt Cup holder as well as the winner of innumerable European races.

The dramas of Le Mans were innumerable— the Bentley victory after the frightful White House crash, the priceless contributions that chewing gum and soap have made to various victories (after all, these were among the supplies carried aboard by some drivers, and they are both useful for sealing leaks in petrol tanks), Louis Rosier's one-man victory despite the loss of a full hour in replacing a rocker arm on his Talbot (the other 23 hours he was at the wheel), Pierre Levegh's heart-breaking defeat in the final half-hour after 23½ hours of solo driving to a seemingly unassailable lead over Europe's best men and machines, and of course the holocaust a few years later in which he and some 80 others were killed; the cars pushed half a lap to refuel at their pits, the incredible one-gear run to victory when a Delahaye's gearbox broke . . . Many of these feats can never be repeated, whatever the circumstances, under changes in the rules that limit a continuous turn at the wheel to 40 laps, forbid pushing under any circumstances and restrict repairs to the pit area.

Other changes have radically altered the character of the competition from those early days of 1923. When Le Mans reopened in 1949 after the Second World War and the reparation of the incredible damage inflicted on the course by the German occupant and the Allied air force, the A.C.O. dropped its insistence on series production cars and allowed the entry of prototypes "in view of present conditions . . . to assist a more rapid return to normal conditions in the automobile industry". In effect, a large part of any year's entries since have been prototypes, for sales of such more-racing-than-sports cars as Porsche RS, Ferrari Testa Rossa, Lister-Jaguar and Tojeiro are hardly large enough to constitute series production as the term is generally understood; yet real dual-purpose cars are on the course with them.

Admittedly, it would otherwise have taken much more than 25 years to raise the record for distance covered on the 8·385-mile course from the 1835·55 miles of 1932 to Jaguar's 1957 record of more than 2730, or the lap record from Minoia's 1932 figure to Hawthorn's 126·2 m.p.h.—less than four minutes —in a Ferrari in 1957. In a field of 60 cars—the maximum permitted by A.C.O. regulations—ranging down to 4CV Renault saloons, the presence of stark 180-m.p.h. machines that would oil up in five minutes of city driving has not only a certain incongruity but also a rather frightening potential on a course that requires 250 marshals and 60 scouts. Obviously one or the other category should be eliminated; to the believer in dual-purpose automobiles the solution would seem to be the return of Le Mans to actual series cars that can stand up to ordinary hack use (and 300SL's and potent Ferraris can meet the test) and the re-assignment of the sports/racing cars with their token "touring" equipment—tiny nominal windscreens, *pro forma* passenger seats and the sketchiest hoods—to their own new classification and separate events, if not grouping with the undisguised grand-prix machines. New meaning would be given—or, rather, the old significance would be restored—to the results based on the Index of Performance. This is calculated on distances set according to engine capacities in comparison to distance actually covered at or above the minimum speed computed on the basis of the set distance divided by 24 hours. Thus, a score of 1·5 on Index means that a car has covered one and a half times as much mileage as the rules required.

What has happened at Le Mans has happened as well in sports-car racing on the few closed tracks in Europe where it is held, such as Monza in Italy, Montlhéry in France and the Nürburgring in Germany. While these are all artificial circuits in that they are not closed-off public roads but courses specifically built as courses, they are not all alike. Monza and Montlhéry—more properly, Linas-Montlhéry—consist of two parts each: a traditional high-banked oval and a simulated road section connected with the oval. The Nürburgring, the world's longest racecourse designed as such, is really a 14·2-mile private road with 89 left and 86 right turns, including ten hairpins, among some of the most beautiful hills in Germany. All three circuits are used for grand-prix as well as sports-car racing; Montlhéry has in addition a number of sections

designed to simulate all kinds of adverse conditions of paving and drainage where manufacturers and laboratories can make exhaustive tests. Monza and the Nürburgring are available, between races, to anyone who wishes to test himself or his car for quite reasonable fees.

Montlhéry was created in 1924–5 by Alexandre Lamblin on a wooded 2500-acre estate west of the village of Linas, some 14 miles south of Paris. In 1939 it was bought by the War Ministry and has remained government property. After the war its management was entrusted to the *Union technique de l'automobile, du motocycle et du cycle*. The speedway is a 1·58-mile road with steeply banked turns, each straight being 196·2 yards. The normal roadway width of 59 ft. is increased 10 ft. on the turns. The surface, the angle of banking and the radius of the curves will allow a maximum of 155 m.p.h.

Leading out of the speedway and back into it, a 6·9-mile road course provides a reasonable simulacrum of normal driving conditions, with 25 flat turns, some of very short radius, and a number of inclines. There are in addition cross-roads that make it possible to vary the road course. Within the oval of the speedway are a number of special test tracks for proving-ground experiments. But only the speedway itself is used for competition and, though sports cars have set hundreds of records there, it is predominantly a grand-prix and motorcycle circuit. Access from the Paris highway is gained, fittingly, by way of the Avenue Georges Boillot.

Antedating Montlhéry by two years, the Monza course was built by the Automobile-Club di Milano, which still owns and operates it. Originally it was a 6·25-mile circuit consisting of a 2·9-mile track and a 3·35-mile road course, interconnected. From time to time it was improved with detours and chicanes (reverse turns). Like Montlhéry, it was and is used for motor-cycles as well as cars; but at Monza the road course as well as the track is part of the route of some competitions. Between 1938 and 1948 the course lay idle, and then war added to the effects of deterioration. However, the A.-C. di Milano undertook to restore it and in November, 1948, re-opened it in substantially its present form.

The speed track is the usual oval with high banked concrete curves—the rest of the surface is tarred. It measures about 2·6 miles and gives access to a road course (which in turn leads into another circuit used only for technical tests) that makes the total length 6·25 miles. At its narrowest, the track roadway is 39½ ft. wide and the maximum speed permissible on the banking is 175 m.p.h. The road course is narrower—the minimum is 30 ft.—widening to 79 ft. in front of the stands, where it is joined by the track straight. Banking on the road course is like the camber of normal good roads, and lap speeds on this circuit have exceeded 125 m.p.h. Within the oval is a whole village of shops and services, as well as a swimming pool and tennis courts. While Monza is chiefly used for G.P. racing, sports-car competitions are also held there. When there is no racing or pre-race practice, the course is available to any licensed driver at a moderate fee, and a certificate of lap time is issued to anyone asking for it.

One of the most interesting closed road venues in Europe is Zandvoort, along The Netherlands' North Sea coast. The Dutch had considered various racing circuits since 1913 and, before the Second World War, races had been held on public highways near Zandvoort, closed for the purpose. During the German occupation plans were made for a circuit on its own roads, and work actually began, under Burgomaster van Alphen, with the laying of the foundation, composed of rubble from bombings. His successor, Burgomaster van Fenema, completed the work and the first race was held on the 2·61-mile course in August, 1948. Under John B. Th. Hugenholtz, managing director of Zandvoort, spectator facilities were expanded and two new surfaces were laid. The average width of the road is 30 ft., though it increases somewhat at some turns and in front of the pits, which are permanent, like those at most major European circuits. The winding course has one straight, paralleling the beach, and two formidable hairpins; the grand-prix lap record of 97·15 m.p.h. (Vanwall) is not much higher than the sports-car figure of 85·92 m.p.h. (Porsche RS). Between races Zandvoort is open to private drivers at very low rates.

The most impressive closed course is the Nürburgring, which dates from 1927. Originally constructed as a public-works project after the catastrophic German inflation of the 1920s, it is as much a road course as any on public highways, and undoubtedly one of the most difficult as well as the most beautiful. It lies in a region formed by prehistoric volcanoes, near Luxembourg and Belgium, and is a constant succession of hills and twists. The longest straight is that at the start–finish line—one kilometre, or five-eighths of a mile; its lowest point is 1050 ft. above sea level, its highest 2034 ft., ascents running as steep as 17 per cent and descents to 11 per cent. At the start the track is 65·6 ft. wide, but for most of its route it averages 26·3 ft.

Some idea of the ordeal of the Nürburgring may be drawn from the fact that the fastest lap time ever clocked was Stirling Moss's 9 minutes 43 seconds in 1958, when he also scored the record winning average speed of 84·75 m.p.h. for 44 laps—624·8 miles of what amounts to continuous mountain driving in an Aston Martin DBR1/300. In the first race ever held on the circuit, the winning Mercedes-Benz averaged about 63 m.p.h. for 315 miles. When the Ring re-opened after the war there was some talk of staging a 24-hour race on this Black Forest course to rival those of Le Mans and Spa-Francorchamps in Belgium, but the plan was abandoned in favour of a 1000-kilometre race analogous to the Mille Miglia. When the Italian race became a rally in 1958, the importance of the Nürburgring's 1000-km. was

immediately increased. As a test of both car and driver it is probably unequalled. The rough surface is extremely variable—chipped by traffic, rumpled by frost—and this fact coupled with the unending succession of high-speed curves puts a premium on suspension: in 1957 the Ring shook to pieces two 4½-litre Maseratis like the one that had triumphed at Sebring. The hairpins can never be memorized any more than the 165 other turns—except, possibly, the famous Karrussell, which is an extremely tight 360-degree turn.

Had the Mille Miglia survived as a race the Nürburgring's future might be different, for the 1000-mile Italian run equalled or surpassed all the problems of the German circuit and added to them a number of tests of sustained high speed by reason of long straight stretches. But legislative qualms killed the Mille in its 30th year as a result of Portago's tragic accident. In those three decades the race had achieved as rich a reputation as Le Mans or the Targa Florio and had more than attained the objective for which it was originally organized.

The Mille Miglia was born in Milan on Christmas Eve, 1926, when the distinguished Italian motoring journalist, Giovanni Canestrini, was unexpectedly visited by two famous drivers who were among his friends: Aymo Maggi and Franco Mazzotti. With them were another motoring journalist, Renzo Castagneto, and Baron Monti. Maggi was the spokesman, and he poured forth a lament that had nothing to do with the season. The Italian motor industry, he told Canestrini, was completely indifferent to competition machinery and was letting its early fame be lost. The reason, according to Maggi, was that there was no longer any worthwhile racing in the peninsula. He and his companions had come to Canestrini to ask his help in remedying the situation.

The five men reviewed a number of ideas, none of which had not already been beaten to a platitudinous death. They studied maps, and one of them suggested a race from Brescia to Rome. None of the others was enthusiastic until one of them—Canestrini himself cannot recall which—suggested a race from Brescia to Rome and back to Brescia. This was much more interesting, though a number of objections were raised; it would cover about half the country, it would require seemingly impossible government co-operation on every level and it would cost an astronomical amount of money. Against these cogent arguments was the equally strong contention that such a race would have a very healthy propaganda value both at home and abroad.

Then came the question of a name for the race, if only a working title under which to initiate action. *Brescia–Rome–Brescia* was rejected as being too long and sounding like a railway excusion; *Tour of Italy* was found to be prosaic; *Sports-Car Trial* seemed too technical. Mazzotti asked Canestrini and Castagneto, who were studying the map again, how long they thought the race would be. "About

1600 kilometres," they told him. Mazzotti, just returned from a trip to the United States, replied: "That would be 1000 miles. Why not call it the Thousand-Mile Cup?" One critic found the designation too American for a metric nation; but another pointed out that the mile was used as a measure in Rome and hence they would be following the best Roman tradition. And so in 1927, despite the initial opposition of the Reale Automobile-Club d'Italia, the first Mille Miglia was run out of Brescia with the blessing of Mussolini himself, who donated a cup.

In the early races Le Mans rules applied almost *in toto*: the cars had to be production models out of the catalogue. Unlike Le Mans, they were started individually, at one-minute intervals before dawn, from a ramp that led into the street, and each carried a driver and co-driver. The original course was 8-shaped, running from Brescia through the Po Valley to Bologna, across the Apennines to Florence, down to Rome, then north again through the worst of the mountain passes and east to the Adriatic port of Ancona, up the coast to Venice and back to Brescia. The surfaces used were village lanes, major highways, mountain cuts, city streets laced with tram tracks. Minoia, in an O.M., won the first race with an average speed of less than 50 m.p.h. Twenty-eight years later Stirling Moss, in a Mercedes-Benz, was to cover the 1000 miles at 97·9 m.p.h., with bursts as high as 170 m.p.h. along the way. But by then, of course, the catalogue-production-model regulation had evolved exactly as it had done at Le Mans and Ulster.

The founders' objective had been to re-invigorate the Italian automotive industry. In the 24 Mille Miglia races—there was none in 1939 and another hiatus occurred during and after the war—only three non-Italian cars ever finished first over-all, and they were all German: Mercedes-Benz in 1931 and 1955 and B.M.W. in 1940. Only three non-Italian drivers took first prize: Caracciola and von Hanstein of Germany and Moss of Great Britain. In eight of the last 10 races the victor was Ferrari; Alfa Romeo won 11 of the 24 contests. Mercedes was the only other marque to win more than once. The one-race winners were O.M., B.M.W. and Lancia.

Driving in the Mille Miglia presented a hazard unique in road-racing: the crowd, Italian model. Every Italian loves motor racing: the authorities, until they cancelled the Mille, gave the drivers every possible privilege and extended this to everyone even remotely connected with the race; and the crowds adored the drivers, the mechanics, the messengers. But, while the police and the Carabinieri could keep the roads clear of traffic, they were helpless against the spectator. When the Mille Miglia route went through his village, the ordinary Italian did not even bother to shrug at the policeman's warning: he merely pressed as close to the curb or as far out in the roadway as he could to get the best possible view of each car and crew. Wherever the route lay—it was altered from time to time, sometimes for obvious reasons, as when Mantua, Nuvolari's birthplace, was included—the excitement and the heedlessness were the same. Spectator casualties were hence as expected as the toll of cars and crews that the Mille always exacted.

The magic of the Mille Miglia was as potent for the participants. As the years passed, the rules were altered to allow new classes of contestants to be organized and new types of machines to enter. Every manufacturer wanted to run his cars—or felt he must because his competitors had entered; every sporting owner who could qualify and raise the money to finance his entry sought a place on the starting ramp. The veterans of racing would forget their age, their failing health, the law of averages that insisted they could have no more incredible escapes, in order to drive that one race. Antonio Brivio, Targae Florio veteran, over whose head Varzi had launched his Alfa at 135 m.p.h. in Tripoli when Dreyfus' Bugatti towed Brivio's across Varzi's unscheduled path; Nuvolari, dying of heart disease after the war; Caracciola, hoping to repeat his 1931 victory a score of years later; Taruffi, beaten year after year; Fitch, who walked away from a 140-m.p.h. end-over-end crash at Rheims—every one of them lusted for the Mille Miglia and screamed out of Brescia along the mountain roads where an inch of misjudgment was literally fatal, pushing his car to the limit unmindful of the race's tradition: "Who leads at Rome will lose at Brescia." Every year, when the Mille Miglia was over, the roads were strewn with abandoned and damaged cars.

The Portago incident turned the Mille Miglia into an uninteresting rally, especially dull in relation to its past. In this respect it is most unlike the great traditional Continental rallies, which derive directly from the legendary city-to-city races of which the Mille Miglia was the last and from the reliability trials of the heroic age. Officially, the Monte Carlo Rally, the Alpine Rally, the Tour de France and Liège–Rome–Liège—to name some of the outstanding examples—are not speed contests but challenges to driving and navigational skill and to mechanical ingenuity and ruggedness. But the rules laid down for such competitions bring them to the very borderline of racing.

In principle, a rally requires a competitor to follow a set route at a prescribed speed, or within a prescribed time, from point to point, penalizing him for early and/or late arrival; it may also prescribe that, *en route* or at the destination, he prove his skill and his car's merit in various driving tests. There are variations: sometimes the driver is given only the starting and finishing points and the required time, the route to be chosen being left to his discretion and penalties being imposed for covering too much or too little mileage as well as for time errors. In the major European rallies, in which hazard is co-driver from start to finish, penalties are also imposed for damage to the car, as well as for violations of road laws. And virtually every European rally runs through the most difficult terrain under foul weather conditions, so that contestants who have lost time must take full advantage of the fact that in most of Europe there are no speed limits outside settled areas. In addition, many such rallies run past a circuit such as Monza or Zandvoort in Holland, and the course becomes a part of the rally, to be taken at racing speed. The presence of leading amateur and professional racing drivers in these rallies does not tend to ease the pace, and the ratio of finishers to starters is frequently lower than that of the toughest races.

Among the most punishing of contemporary rallies is the Alpine, whose ancestry goes back to the Alpine Trials of the Edwardian era. In those days the route generally led into Austria, but for various reasons, some of them economic and political, the post-war Alpine confines itself to France, Switzerland and Italy. The start is in Marseilles, where a Mille Miglia-type ramp sends the competitors off one at a time, and the rally is as much hill-climb as rally. The lowest average speed set for any leg was 37·5 m.p.h. in 1958, and four speed tests were included in the 2800-mile run. In France the police escort the cars out of the city and in the countryside they warn non-rally drivers to stay off the route—it is no longer possible to close the roads. Each car bears a large rally identification plate front and rear. One of the speed tests is held at Monza, where a 90-m.p.h. average must be maintained to avoid penalty; another is the 20-degree Stelvio Pass, with 72 hairpin corners, whose 14 kilometres must be covered at 45 m.p.h. In such rallies as this, computers and precision clocks are sheer waste: the money is better spent on converting the co-driver's seat into a bed, for these are non-stop runs. Unlike American rallies, the Alpine imposes no penalties for early arrival at a check-point.

One of the most famous as well as one of the most venerable rallies is the Monte Carlo, which was started in 1911 with 22 entries. By now its entry list has grown so unwieldy that applicants must be rigorously seeded to keep it to manageable proportions: in 1959 322 cars started from Glasgow, Stockholm, Warsaw, The Hague, Athens, Rome, Munich, Paris and Lisbon. This was the first time in decades that there had been a start in any of the Slavic countries; in the first rally St. Petersburg was one of the points of origin. From each starting point the route is always so laid out as to give everyone approximately the same total distance—1900 miles in 1959—and the same problems of weather and terrain. Since the rally is a January event, these are generally unendurable and never better than bad. Only grand-prix machines are ineligible for the Monte Carlo, and any year's entry list is a heterogeneous mixture of tiny economy cars, oversize American family saloons, gran-turismo cars and open sports cars, each bearing the front and rear rally plate that assures it a clear track with the authorities

in every country it crosses. The averages to be maintained are as high as those in the Alpine—in some parts the routes of the two rallies are the same—and penalties are assessed not only for lateness but also for damage to the car or its equipment. Wherever he starts, every contestant must go through the Alps, regardless of road conditions—fog, rain, ice and sudden changes in temperature are normal aspects of the run, which rouses special enthusiasm in Britain.

Since most of the participants are Europeans and the whole course lies within the Continent, everything is calculated metrically. Hence one of the most important accessories—and the number and nature of these are limitless—is a speedometer-odometer calibrated in kilometres to avoid dissipating time and nervous energy in converting from miles. Actual routes between specified points are generally optional. It is always surprising how many cars reach Monte Carlo without demerits for loss of time, detours, defects in equipment such as lights and windshield wipers, traffic violations or body damage incurred in crashes, slides, spins or other hazards. The rally is really won only after the touring phase has been completed: in the hill-climb and the speed test on the road circuit of the Grand Prix de Monaco. In 1959 so many cars arrived without penalty that hasty revisions were made and the regularity run was held at night over 267 miles of mountain roads.

Monte Carlo rules are precise. Every car must be a recognized catalogue model of which 1000 must have been produced in a year if it is a 2-litre or less, 500 if it is bigger. No major modification or accessory affecting performance may be employed unless it is readily available to any customer from the car maker's catalogue; the only accessories on which there is no limitation are those relating to comfort and driving ease: extra lights, special wipers for headlamps, extra window wipers and such interior appointments as map desks, sleeping comforts, coffee makers and chemical toilets. Extra tools, of course, are allowable, and one may use any kind of jack or wrench or tyre chain that one can find or invent. Cars up to 1100 c.c. must carry two people; the rest must have room for at least four, though the crew may vary from two to five people living together in the utmost confinement for three or four days under unremitting nervous strain.

On the final night of the rally, in some years, the driver of each car has had to choose his own average speed for the last leg and declare it to the control point before he leaves. He is then held to it and, to avoid a demerit, must arrive at the finish line to the precise second. This means the finest kind of calculation by his navigator and incessant checking of odometer against chronometer—as indeed has been the case from the minute the car started so many days and miles before.

Not the least of the hazards is the constant sight of wrecked or abandoned cars of less fortunate or less skilful competitors: these create a psychological handicap that varies from crew to crew but cannot be ignored by anyone. Throughout the constant driving under pressure every instrument must be watched for the first sign of malfunction, every sound must be heard and heeded. A plug may foul in a night of zero weather; an oil line may snap; a brake cylinder may seize. At once the whole crew must fall to and make the repair if the car is to finish. Many crews spend week-end after week-end, before the rally, practising every operation from the simple one of wiping muck off glass or changing a tyre to removing a rear wheel and repairing or replacing a brake cylinder. A wise crew carries a good number of spares, for a car is penalized if, on arrival at Monte Carlo, any component, such as the starter, fails to function.

In the final phase—the regularity tests—only the 100 leading competitors participate. These are the cars with the lowest number of demerits. The final winner of the rally is determined by performance in the hill-climb and the speed run on the Grand Prix circuit. In addition to the over-all winner, there are winners in each of four classes: over 1500 c.c., 1100–1500 c.c., 750–1100 c.c. and under 750 c.c. The prizes are both cash and trophies—and it is the trophies that mean the most even to the professional drivers. Besides the awards given by the Automobile-Club de Monaco and the International Sporting Club, which sponsor the rally, there are many other prizes based on nationality, club membership, etc. The outright winner receives the Prince Rainier Cup and 1,000,000 francs. Yet cash and trophy alike are forgotten when a competitor sees another in serious trouble: for example, 1932 and, in the Alpine, 1958.

In 1932 a Mrs. Vaughan was driving a Triumph from Umea, Sweden, with a medical student named Charlotte North. They were leading for the *Coupe des Dames* when, within 100 miles of the finish, they saw a multiple wreck in the pelting rain. Mrs. Vaughan, a surgeon, pulled up at once and, with Miss North, set four broken legs in a roadside ditch. With poetic justice, they won the Ladies' Cup after all. Twenty-six years later Robert Halmi and Richard Smith, two Americans driving another Triumph in the Alpine, snatched two dazed, bleeding men from an overturned A.C.-Bristol and, strapping them to the rear deck of their TR, rushed them to the nearest doctor.

Liège–Rome–Liège, sponsored by the Royal Motor-Union of Liège, was born in 1921 as Liège–Paris–Liège and grew year by year, running to Lyons, to Orléans, then to Bordeaux, to Milan, to Turin, Nice and Paris and finally, in 1931, to Rome. It was not until 1933 that non-Belgians entered and since then the rally has always been international. The route runs differently from year to year, increasing in difficulty. A recent Liège–Rome–Liège ran through Spa and across the Rhineland to Munich, over Austria and down the Adriatic along the beautiful Yugoslav coast, then into the interior and across

northern Italy into France without touching Rome; sometimes the route goes down the Italian side of the Adriatic and over to Rome via Perugia, then up the Ligurian coast through La Spezia and into France. Competitors who miss a check-point are disqualified at once, as are those who stop within a given distance of the control in order to avert penalties for early arrival; in addition, they are subject to fines for unsportsmanlike behaviour at any time during the four-day, 3355-mile run.

The modern Tour de France is of much more recent origin, having been organized in 1951 by the second oldest of the French automobile clubs, the A.-C. de Nice et Côte d'Azur, founded in 1896 and, in the heroic age, sponsor of the famous contests at La Turbie. It combines ordinary road motoring with hill-climbs and speed tests on such circuits as Rheims, Le Mans, Montlhéry, Rouen and Pau, and covers almost 4000 miles from the start in Nice, which is usually also the finish, a week later. During this period a single traffic violation results in disqualification. Like all the major Continental rallies, the Tour de France is a welcome change for the world's top racing drivers, who compete on equal terms with the amateurs. The route runs along France's eastern border, starting with the climb at La Turbie and going on to the Rheims circuit and Abbéville, then west via Rouen to Cherbourg and into Brittany, down the Atlantic and sharply inland to Le Mans and Montlhéry. Then the rally cuts south-west across country to reach the coast again at Bordeaux, whence it returns due east to the Auvergne circuit and turns south to include Mont-Ventoux. Thereafter it runs west again, winding up in 1958 at Pau, which had to be lapped 30 times. The Sarthe course, in contrast, was given only 10 laps.

The hill-climb, which is what most of the Alpine Rally consists of and which is so well represented in the Tour de France, was far more popular in the early days than it became between the wars and after the second one. While climbs have always drawn cars of all types, from purely courtesy performance machines to full grand-prix, their very nature demands such modifications to many dual-purpose cars that it is frequently cheaper and more effective to use a car designed for the task. The greatest of these changes, of course, are those to the gearbox, the final-drive ratio and wheels and tyres in order to obtain maximum thrust.

One of the oldest European hill-climbs is La Turbie, some six miles of craggy, twisting road that was for many years one of the championship courses. Another almost as old is Mont-Ventoux, one of the longest: its 13·4 miles were covered by a Panhard in 1902 at 29·6 m.p.h. and by a 2-litre Maserati in 1957 at better than 64 m.p.h. Italy's Aosta–St. Bernard climb winds 21 miles along the 1·5-mile-high mountain. Susa–Moncenisio, on the French-Italian border, was equally famous though it is barely 700 ft. high. All these, except the last, are true mountains rather than hills; like those of the Gaisberg in Austria and the half-mile-high Schauinsland in Germany, their narrow roads are largely loose gravel and dirt. The cars are sent off singly, watched by spectators clinging to rocks and rowans at every curve. Throughout Europe these contests are mountaineering competitions on wheels.

The contrary is true in Great Britain, where the climb has never lost popularity to the same degree but where nature makes the terrain seem merely pimpled in contrast to the European courses. The oldest, the most famous and the toughest British climb is Shelsley Walsh, 1000 yards of constant snaking ascent situate in the Midlands, with which Leslie Wilson, secretary of the Midland Automobile Club, has been associated since its inception in 1905, when a Daimler climbed fastest in 77·6 seconds. During the vintage period Shelsley Walsh inspired numerous competition "specials", which ousted the heavy tourers from front rank in the competition and were in turn outmoded on the 1-in-5 gradients by the racing car. The Shelsley Walsh record was shattered in 1954 by a pre-war racing car, Ken Wharton's E.R.A., with a time of 35·8 seconds.

Shelsley Walsh's great rival is Prescott, wholly owned by the Bugatti Owners' Club. This half-mile course was opened in 1938, when a 4·9 Bugatti made the best time—55·58 seconds—for the serpentine run, which includes three hairpins—one wide enough to be called a loop—as well as a succession of S-turns leading into that semi-circle, which debouches into the finish line. While a time of almost a minute for a half-mile seems singularly unimpressive—the best is 43·7 seconds—it must be remembered that on any climb there are virtually no straights and that both car and driver are constantly contending not only with unending changes of direction but also with increasing gravitational pull as the ascent grows steeper.

The longest climb in Britain is Scotland's 1425-yard Rest and Be Thankful, which rises 400 ft. in less than a mile, culminating in a hump and a hairpin just before the finish. It owes its name to an inscription made in 1748 by a working-party of soldiers cutting the road out of the mountainside. Since it was opened in 1949 the best time scored has been 53·75 seconds, in a Formula III Cooper. As in most climbs, each entrant is allowed two runs and judged on the better of the scores.

This type of competition obviously favours certain types of cars above others and the dual-purpose machine is frequently at a considerable disadvantage against the trailer-transported "specials" that climbing has inspired. Even more particularized is the trial, a peculiarly British form of motor sport— "from which", Stirling Moss says, "perhaps only an Englishman could extract any fun". It adds to the demands of the hill-climb the problems of mud, ditches and unploughed fields, for it is customarily run on unimproved hilly land in winter, which in Britain is extremely wet. Moss calls the trial the rodeo of motor sport, for which the ordinary sports car is quite unsuitable. The best trials cars locate

engine and driver as far to the rear as possible to obtain maximum weight over the driving wheels. A co-driver is essential because frequently he is required to thrust his weight still farther back.

Britain's rallies are far tamer than Europe's, partly because of geography—it is a congested island—and partly because of laws, which still forbid speed contests on public highways even when these have no speed limits. Many rallies, however, not only are intricate navigational problems confounded by enigmatic instructions and mathematical exercises that make a computer almost essential, but also frequently include a run on a recognized hill-climb or one of the closed circuits on which British racing is held.

The most famous of these no longer exists: the 2·75-mile Brooklands track in the shape of an egg, built by Mr. and Mrs. H. F. Locke-King to encourage motor sport and afford a proving-ground for the automotive industry. A hundred feet wide, the road-way had two straights of unequal length—the longer was only a half-mile—joined by sharply banked curves that were safe up to 120 m.p.h.

Brooklands was the world's first concrete automobile track. At the narrower end, whose curve was known as the Members' Banking, the so-called Finishing Straight connected the main straights and was intended for the use its name implies. This, however, proved impracticable when braking failed to keep pace with the improvement of road speeds. As speeds mounted, different coloured lines were painted along the course for cars of three different potentials, the fastest machines getting, of course, all the best of it. Those drivers who did not come off the Byfleet Banking (the larger curve) into the proper lane were disciplined without delay. Lap times of more than 100 m.p.h. were known before the First World War, by which time the circuit had been the scene of many famous record attempts. By 1920 Jean Chassagne had lapped at 112·7 in an Indianapolis Ballot.

Forceful complaints by people who built houses near the track and objected to the noise resulted in the creation of the famous "Brooklands silencer", an expansion chamber whose inlet and exhaust pipes were carefully aligned asymmetrically; the outlet had to be of the same diameter as the cylinder port adjacent to the exhaust valve, and it had to run all the way to the rear of the car and end in a fishtail whose size and capacity were meticulously calculated. It was generally a good deal louder than the standard Continental silencing system and, when carburation was even slightly off, it had a devastating effect on pistons because of the over-heating it caused in the combustion chamber.

While most Brooklands races were short, it was the site of such famous contests as the Junior Car Club's 200-mile Race, a 500-mile competition, a Six-Hour Race and the famous Double-Twelve, in which the cars ran for 12 hours (on handicap) on each of two successive days, being locked away from drivers and mechanics overnight. This, the last race of the season, was always driven with particular dash and was invariably faster than Indianapolis. The Finishing Straight was later incorporated into a new circuit within the oval. This was called the Mountain Circuit because it encircled the Members' Hill, sometimes termed the "Mountain", and utilized part of the banking of the outer circuit and measured 1·2 miles, on which the fastest lap time ever recorded was 84·31 m.p.h., against the 143·44 set up on the big course by a 24-litre Napier-Railton special in 1935.

The Junior Car Club introduced artificial chicanes at Brooklands with indifferent success, and in 1937 an effort was made to devise a new circuit, named after Sir Malcolm Campbell, that would more closely simulate road-racing conditions by twisting back and forth within the original oval and utilizing the Railway Straight and the Members' Banking, but it was never popular. In 1939 Brooklands was requisitioned for war uses and afterwards the stockholders voted to sell it. The detailed chronicle of its four dramatic decades has been lovingly and skilfully told by W. Boddy in his monumental book, *The Story of Brooklands*.

Since Brooklands closed, a number of other courses have been built in Britain, but none of them has the tradition or the nostalgia of the original. Some of these have been conversions of abandoned airfields, others are totally new creations much like American closed circuits. None is over three miles long and most of them are completely flat. Britain takes motor sport much more seriously than does the United States, and courses like Oulton Park, Brands Hatch, Crystal Palace, Snetterton, Silverstone and Goodwood are taxed to capacity by both entrants and spectators at every event. No distinction is made between professional and amateur drivers; many clubs, in fact, offer starting money to all qualifiers, or refund their entry fees, and in addition give cash prizes as well as trophies for winners over-all and in classes. One of the most interesting aspects of sports-car racing in the United Kingdom is the continued appearance of veteran and vintage machines in competition—in races and hill-climbs as well as in rallies. But there is much irony in the fact that British cars and drivers—ranking with the world's best—have almost always had to forge their finest achievements overseas.

It is no less ironic that the United States, which has so far out-stripped the rest of the world in automobile production and ownership, should have fallen so far behind in motor sport. While the Sports Car Club of America and such individuals as Briggs Cunningham and Alec Ulmann have been outstanding in reversing that trend, the United States remains proportionately laggard, in comparison to other countries, despite a very virile past in motoring competition. American racing began as far back as 1895 and developed on both road and track in such diverse places as Brighton Beach in Brooklyn and the beautiful winding roads of Philadelphia's vast natural Fairmount Park, as well as many tracks —board, dirt and paved—across the country. Some of the most notable of these were at Elgin, Ill., and Santa Monica, Calif. But the premier sporting contest was—for too few years—the Vanderbilt Cup.

William K. Vanderbilt, who donated the cup, was himself not only an ardent but also a highly able enthusiast, the first American to hold the world speed record: 76·08 m.p.h. on a Mors in 1902 and again, in 1904, 92·8 on a Mercedes. He had also finished third in the Circuit des Ardennes. When the American Automobile Association decided to hold a race in New York State in 1904—the A.A.A. was a virile organization when it was young and brave enough to scoff at the phobias of public relations counsel and trend-spotters—Vanderbilt put his wealth and position whole-heartedly into the venture, helping to overcome opposition generated by farmers and Long Island villagers, who objected to losing the use of some of their roads, and by such ecclesiastics as the Rev. Newell Dwight Hillis, who called the mere thought of the race "as foolish as a bullfight; as vulgar as reddening the sands in a gladiatorial contest; as revolting as bartering Christ's garments for a few pieces of silver".

The course lay on a 30-mile triangle of roads in Queens and Nassau Counties, partly macadam, partly dirt oiled for the occasion: a dubious benefit. Ten laps were to be covered, but two neutralized sections were not timed: through two populated areas the racers had to follow a bicycle at 14 m.p.h. for one and 8 m.p.h. for the other. In addition, each of five level-crossings had to be traversed at 10 m.p.h. The cars were sent off at two-minute intervals, at dawn October 8, 1904, before a huge crowd of farmers, enthusiasts and city folk who had thronged out to "the island" for this new diversion. The residents' opposition was finally overcome when they realized how much money they would make the next year by charging—and getting—$25 for every car parked on their lands.

The first Vanderbilt Cup Race was run by the cream of international drivers: Gabriel, who had won the Paris–Madrid; Christian Werner, long a Mercedes star; Albert Clément, son of the builder of the Clément-Bayard; Joe Tracy of Old 16 fame; George Arents of New York on a Mercedes (another George Arents runs now in a Ferrari). The American cars entered were Royal Tourist, Pope-Toledo and Simplex. George Heath, an American on a Panhard, won at an average of 52·2 m.p.h., despite burning-hot tyres that had to be doused with water at control points. This made the rubber brittle and much tyre-changing resulted. The whole atmosphere was more that of a circus than of a race, the American contestants playing to the grandstand in the fashion of press agents relying on "stunts". There were many accidents but, though the crowd was as undisciplined as any at the Mille Miglia, no spectators were casualties.

Lancia, Jenatzy, Nazzaro, Szisz and Hémery crossed the ocean for the 1905 race, which Hémery won with his Darracq at 61·28 m.p.h., though Lancia was lapping at 72 m.p.h. for a time and frequently topping 100 m.p.h. on a F.I.A.T. "The huge crowd", Purdy says, "showed symptoms of the strange mania, a sort of death-compulsion, that was to reach full flower the next year. Women and baby carriages cluttered the most dangerous points. . . . Men and small boys clung to overloaded trees fringing the roadway like starlings at roost. . . . Vendors sold thousands of sticks with feathers tied to the ends . . . to tickle the drivers as they sped past." In 1906, when Joe Tracy almost won on Old 16 but was beaten by Louis Wagner's Darracq at only a few decimals more than the 1905 speed, the course had 11 bad corners, which included two steep hills, a full U-turn and several S's. The crowd was completely out of control; Tracy locked his wheels at the stewards' stand to plead that the course be cleared, but neither Vanderbilt's own appeal nor the police meant anything to the 300,000 spectators, many of whom, having stayed up all night, were well fortified with strong waters. Wagner said he had never encountered such "an unruly mob. . . . It was the most nerve-wrenching race in history." About a half-dozen spectators were killed. There was no race in 1907; 1908 was the first year that this American race was won by an American car and driver: George Robertson on the Locomobile, Old 16, a 100-m.p.h. car that sailed 150 ft. through the air when it crossed a hump-backed bridge. Americans won the next two years, though the winning Alco was really a Berliet built under licence. In 1911 the Vanderbilt Cup moved to Savannah, where the Grand Prix of America had been organized as a rival event in 1908.

The Savannah course was also on the highways, and all the cars started together. This circuit was the particular favourite of David Bruce-Brown, a young American who had left Yale University to race, despite the entreaties of his wealthy widowed mother. It is said that she followed him to Savannah to plead with him once more to return to college but she arrived too late: the race had already begun and she had to watch and wait for her son to finish. By the time the race was half over, what she had seen had made her a more zealous enthusiast than David, and the subject of Yale was never brought up again.

The Lozier's victory at Savannah was the last American triumph in the Vanderbilt, which continued to be run, at Milwaukee, Santa Monica and San Francisco, until 1916. Twenty years later it was revived for two years on a specially built Long Island course for grand-prix cars only, and it went first to Nuvolari and then to Rosemeyer.

Even after Indianapolis opened as a dirt track in 1909 and re-opened as a paved course in 1911, Elgin, Ill., was the scene of an annual 300-mile race that was a minor classic, and in which all the major American and foreign marques and drivers competed. But the 500-mile Indianapolis became the country's premier race the first year it was run, and little by little other courses lost their attraction for driver and spectator alike. Indianapolis, however, was never really a sports-car course and the cars that ran there, once the racing car made its clean break from the sports, soon became *sui generis*, their steering, their braking, even their gearing being devised for that one type of competition. It was Indianapolis, however, that contributed the mirror to American racing, when Ray Harroun fitted one on his 1911 Marmon in a shell whose lines were as aerodynamic as those of many of today's racing mirrors. The mirror put an end to such primitive actions as that in the 1908 Vanderbilt Cup when Robertson told his mechanic, Glenn Ethridge, to throw a hammer at the slower car in front that would not make room because that machine's mechanic was not watching the rear as he should have been doing.

Motor sport in the British and Continental sense ended in the United States with the First World War. The leisurely Glidden Tours had been the nearest approach to rallies in the United States; nothing like the Herkomer or Prince Henry Trials or Britain's London–Edinburgh and 2000-mile Trials, in which cars were really tested for days on end under all possible conditions, was attempted there on any regular basis as a sport. Hill-climbs had achieved some prominence—notably Mount Washington in New Hampshire and Giant's Despair in Pennsylvania—but from the American entry into the war in 1917 until almost 30 years later there was no real motor sport in the United States.

The revival was as impetuous as it was sudden, and it spread with gratifying speed and range. Some of it was born of the nostalgia of men who remembered America's own heroic period, or who had heard about it from those who had been part of it; fresh momentum came from others who, as service men remaining abroad after VE Day, and seeing the sporting drivers of Britain and Europe turn to and put their sport back into action as soon as conditions permitted, were fascinated by a revelation. There were in addition a few who remembered the one pioneering sports-car competition effort made in America between the wars.

This began in 1933, when the Collier brothers—Barron, Jr., Sam and Miles—later to be prominently identified with the foundation of the S.C.C.A. and the real development of American sports-car competition, held a day of racing on some dirt roads in Westchester County, N.Y. The cars were J-type M.G.s (few of them), Amilcars, American and British Austins, Willys and various "specials"; scrutineering was concentrated on brakes and steering; seat belts, regulations governing lights and wings, helmets were all in the future. The sponsor of this race was the Automobile Racing Club of America, founded by the Colliers and George Weaver, later to create the

Thompson Raceway in Connecticut. In 1934 the A.R.C.A. expanded its activities to eight so-called national events—races and hill-climbs in Westchester and at Mounts Washington and Equinox, Alexandria Bay, N.Y., and Wayland, Mass., where a course was made on an old pasture. The A.R.C.A. flourished, though it was not widely known, until the war, and it was the nucleus for what has happened since.

The beginning of post-war American motor sport was a road race in the classic tradition at Watkins Glen, in the beautiful Finger Lakes region of New York State. The race was the creation of Cameron G. Argetsinger, and the co-operation of the Watkins Glen Chamber of Commerce under Donald Brubaker brought it to fruition, aided by Cunningham, Ulmann, Nils Mickelson, Charles Lytle, David Garroway, to say nothing of their co-operating families. A *concours d'élégance* preceded that first race in 1948, under the auspices of the newly formed S.C.C.A., and the *concours* has remained part of the Glen's tradition. The vintage race that was part of that *première* has unfortunately not survived; but in 1948 it drew Bugattis and Vauxhalls. The 52-mile Grand Prix was won by an Alfa at 63·7 m.p.h. over eight laps of a 6·6-mile course as winding, hilly and fast as any public road course in France or Ireland. Surfaces were, variously, cement, macadam, oiled gravel and just plain dirt, and the route wound through the town and out into open country as a proper road race should. For five years the circuit was the outstanding race in America, until in 1952, when the lap record stood at 72·08 for a Cadillac-powered Allard, a car brushed the crowd at a corner on the second lap of the Grand Prix, injuring seven people and killing a little boy. Sam Collier had been killed two years earlier when his Ferrari missed a corner, and the two fatalities were sufficient to end highway racing at Watkins Glen.

However, the S.C.C.A., the Chamber of Commerce and Argetsinger were not defeated, and by September of 1953 a new closed course was ready. The programme had grown to a number of events, of which the outstanding were the Queen Catherine Cup and the Grand Prix, the latter being 22 laps of the 4·6-mile circuit, or 101·2 miles. On the 1·3-mile downhill straight the fast cars reached 150 m.p.h., frequently becoming air-borne at little humps; the record winning average was 83·3 m.p.h. In 1956 the Watkins Glen Grand Prix Corp. built the present course, financed by a community bond drive. Less curvilinear than the original road circuit and less angular than the first closed one, this 2·3-mile course remains one of the toughest driving tests in the country for both sports and grand-prix machines, which have run there both under S.C.C.A. amateur rules and in the new out-and-out professional racing.

The example of Watkins Glen was followed at the other end of the state by Bridgehampton, where from 1915 to 1920 mild road racing had been a feature of the annual Firemen's Fair on a 3-mile course. In 1949 the old course was re-activated,

with some alterations, the hay-bales were put in place where they would be most effective in protecting both competitors and spectators, and for the next four years the eastern Long Island village was the scene of excellent racing despite the flatness of its terrain. But once again it was an unavoidable accident that halted road racing. However, the men who had been responsible for the 1949 revival returned again to the example of Watkins Glen and came up with a 2·9-mile closed course that overlooks Long Island Sound and takes advantage of what little rolling country there is in the area to provide a very tricky up-and-down track with a dozen deceptive turns. B. J. Corrigan of Bridgehampton, who used to drive racing Duesenbergs there in the early days; H. Austin Clark, Jr., of the Long Island Automotive Museum, Ulmann and Cunningham and many more devoted their efforts to the new Bridgehampton, which opened at the very end of the 1957 season. To say it has a tradition would be premature; but every tradition needs a start, and Bridgehampton has made a vintage-car race on opening day one of its annual fixtures. The fastest race average there stands at more than 85 m.p.h.

Today only one round-the-houses race remains in the United States: Put-In Bay, on an island in Lake Erie off the Ohio shore. Established in 1951 by the Cleveland Sport Car Club, the island race is run entirely on local roads of varying degrees of roughness. While it has only one left turn, an obtuse angle largely vitiated by the narrow road curbed on both sides, the 3-mile course is hard on both drivers and cars and in any given event it is expected that at least half the machines will be unable to finish. At no point is the road more than 25 ft. wide; most of it is only 15 ft. Four of the turns are tight 90-degree angles at street intersections, among open fields and at the top of a rise facing an iron-fenced cemetery. The back stretch is a succession of undulations that sends every car air-borne three or four times a lap. Because of the terrain and the road, the race is limited to cars of 2 litres or less (1½ litres if modified). It is not uncommon for contestants to bounce from tree to tree on a lawn or to scream down escape roads into a residential street or the local airport. Unlike virtually all other sports-car venues, which use either a Le Mans start or a standing start on the course, Put-In Bay employs the Indianapolis start, in which the contestants do one full lap behind a pace car—usually an outstanding vintage machine—which then takes an escape road as the starter, facing backward in the pace car, drops his green flag. Porsche Spyders have lapped this difficult circuit at close to 90 m.p.h. and can utilize maximum speed on the longest straight, 1·2 miles between ploughed fields.

But the rest of the United States' sports-car competition is on closed courses. One of the fastest is Riverside, a 3·3-mile circuit known as Southern California's Little Nürburgring, because of its curves and hills. Its straights permit speeds of 150 m.p.h. and better, as does the up-hill-level-down-hill straight of 3300 ft. past the pits at Bridgehampton. With Palm Springs and Pebble Beach, California was ahead of the east in racing circuits until the mid-1950s, when Thompson was revised from 1·5 to 2 miles, Lime Rock was opened and Cumberland and Marlboro in Maryland attained national prominence, followed by Bridgehampton and the Virginia International Raceway. These courses have replaced the airport circuits, like those in England, that were among the earliest venues, because the specially built courses can reproduce actual road conditions in infinite variety and provide far more severe tests of driver and car, as well as much more drama for the spectator, than the completely flat airstrips with their invariable square turns and synthetic chicanes composed of hay-bales or pylons.

Thompson and Lime Rock exemplify the best design in eastern United States courses. The 2-mile Thompson circuit has a pleasing and exciting alternation of straights and turns, with two tight loops. One of these is entered on a steep ascent and debouches into a fast downgrade with a deceptively wide left-hand curve; the other is preceded by a bottom-gear left turn immediately at the end of a flat-out straight. Elongated right-angled S's add to the challenge. Lime Rock's very shortness—1·5 miles—makes it at least as difficult and exciting. The pit straight, which is the longest, is barely a half-mile, ending in a hard right hairpin that in turn leads quickly to a 90-degree left and then a succession of S's culminating in an abrupt steep grade. A short straight goes into a wide 90-degree turn followed by a slightly arced straight that ducks suddenly downward into the extremely fast right-hand turn that ends in the pit straight. There are in all 12 turns on this short course, which puts a considerable premium on brakes as well as on gear changing and acceleration. The lap record exceeds 82 m.p.h. and the 150-mile winning average is 79·09 for 100 laps.

Midway between the two coasts is Road America, the only challenge to America's greatest, Sebring. Road America, at Elkhart Lake, Wis., formerly a highway-racing venue, is a 4-mile course compounded of straights, twists and hills where Ferraris and 300SL's can use all their horsepower. It is one of the few American courses where endurance races are regularly held, usually of four and six hours, as well as a 500-miler. But the great annual American endurance test is the 12 Hours of Sebring, which became a major international championship event within a few years of its inauguration by Alec Ulmann in 1952. It is the only American sports-car race to enjoy international status. At Sebring the dual-purpose car races, as it does today in so many foreign venues, in the *grand touring* category, while the *sports* is primarily what is ordinarily considered a sports/racing machine.

Ulmann is a lifelong automobile enthusiast whose love for fine cars, both old and new, is backed by encyclopaedic knowledge. It began when, at the age of 7, he saw Hémery's Benz win the St. Petersburg–Moscow Race. The son of a Russian college professor, Ulmann, who is multi-lingual, fled to Switzerland with his parents in 1917 and later graduated from the Massachusetts Institute of Technology; when he is not working on the Sebring programme, writing monographs on famous marques or helping newcomers in automobile sport, he is an internationally known engineering consultant in such diverse fields as aeronautics, rubber and textile machinery. Always dignified and at the same time always warm, he is among the best loved figures in the sport in the United States. It was Ulmann's direct intervention that won F.I.A. approval for Sebring and it is his energy each year that assures the availability of prize money to attract the world's top racing names. Fangio, Moss, Hawthorn, Musso, Castellotti, Behra, Cunningham, Fitch, Hill—the *élite* of motor sport has run at Sebring; and the *élite* of manufacturers sends its costly factory teams to the steaming Florida hinterland each year.

The cavalcade of historic machines that precedes each year's *grand prix d'endurance* is a review of motor-sport history—winners from Dieppe, the Isle of Man, the early Indianapolis, the Targa Florio—of which Sebring is a vital contemporary chapter. Ordinary roads have been linked to the old Sebring air strip to make a 5·2-mile course with 16 turns of every kind and a half-dozen straights ranging from 800 to 4705 ft., allowing the D Jaguar to reach 164 m.p.h. The Le Mans start is used and the race begins in mid-morning, so that a considerable amount of racing is done in night conditions after an interlude of treacherous twilight when headlamps have next to no value. While the perimeter of the racing area may be said to be a huge right triangle open at one end, much of the actual circuit twists about within the triangle and is brutal to brakes and gears. As in most endurance races, many drivers forget that the car must last 12 hours; and a Sebring peculiarity is the effect of the very high temperatures. In 1958, for example, 22 of the 44 sports/racing machines failed to finish, but 19 of the 21 gran-turismo cars lasted the 12 hours. Collins and Hill won with a Ferrari covering 200 laps—1040 miles—at 86·7 m.p.h. Many of those who hope and work for an all-American championship—car and driver—look to Sebring as the forcing-bed.

Many of the men of Sebring are also veterans of that strange short-lived town-to-town race, the Carrera Panamericana. Running the length of Mexico, it was created to celebrate the completion of the Pan-American Highway from the United States border to the Guatemalan, and the route ran from Juaréz to El Ocotdl, 2135 miles away. The rules combined those of Le Mans, the Mille Miglia, the old city-to-city Gran Premio de Argentina and various rallies. The total distance was divided into nine legs, to be completed in six days at an average no lower than 37·2 m.p.h. Only standard closed saloons were eligible, though this rule was modified to permit boring out older cars and removing various body fittings. The crews were forbidden to accept help from anyone. The rules defined standard cars as models of which 50 had been produced and 500 were on customer order in normal commerce; this ruled out many of the European marques and most of the 1950 entries were American cars and crews.

One Ismael Alvarez of Vera Cruz entered a 1937 Hudson that he had bought with his last $300 and patched together just before the race. He had never owned a car before. The Hudson survived into the third leg, when the transmission disintegrated. Troops patrolled the well-made road, shooting any animals that appeared. A 1950 Oldsmobile won the race and Enzo Ferrari determined to have revenge when the 1951 contest was run in the opposite direction. He got it with the help of Taruffi and Chinetti, whose 2·7 averaged 88·04 m.p.h. This was the overture to the admission of sports cars as such to the 1952 race, which set a minimum of 5000 sales for production saloons.

Once again the route lay from north to south, but alterations to the itinerary took it through treacherous mountains and over stretches where the paving chewed away tyres. All the major sports-car makers were represented, including Mercedes-Benz with Le Mans-type 300SL's, all of which were hastily fitted with prison-like bars over the windscreens after a vulture smashed the bullet-proof glass on Kling's car and knocked out his co-driver, Klenk. Glaring sunlight in the high peaks could not be combated, however, and caused many accidents. The 300SL's averaged 132 m.p.h. on the last leg, having changed from mountain tyres to thin treads, and won the race with an over-all average of 102·6 m.p.h. Fangio's Lancia raised this figure to 105·2 in the next year's south-to-north race despite a blinding snowstorm on the last leg. In this year six spectators were killed and in 1954, the Carrera's last year, eight died. Maglioli's Ferrari won at 107·96 and Porsches topped their class at 97·63 m.p.h. But 62 of the 149 starters failed to finish and, as in each of the preceding years, the reason was as often a damaging accident as a mechanical breakdown. The Carrera was more a spectacle than a test, however, for, despite the rules, few of the "production" cars that appeared would have passed any examination for departures from the catalogue norm.

During the five years of the Mexican road race, sporting motorists in the United States had rediscovered a form of competition that had enjoyed with their predecessors the same esteem accorded it abroad: the hill-climb. Mount Washington, just above the exquisite Notch region of New Hampshire's White Mountains, was first stormed by an automobile in 1899, when F. O. Stanley's steamer took 1 hour 46 minutes to climb the 10-mile shale road to the peak, more than a mile above sea level. Since then the same road, in the same condition, has been a perennial venue. The grade averages 16 per cent, though it reaches 22 per cent in places, and there are some 365 bumps and infinitely more turns and hairpins on a loose surface rarely wide enough for two cars. One side is mountain, the other is nothingness: not even the psychological assurance of a guard rail stands between the edge of the road and the depths below. Frequently the route is wrapped in impenetrable fog; the temperature at the base of the mountain is often in the 80's when it is below freezing at the peak. The road is barred to vehicles with automatic transmissions.

The American climb, like its foreign counterpart, has become the province successively of the "special" and the full race car: even in 1905 a Gordon Bennett Napier proved this with a climb in little more than 20 minutes. More than 50 years later the record set by a grand-prix Ferrari was 10 minutes 21·8 seconds. The same car with the same driver, Carroll Shelby of Texas, a veteran of many European climbs, was also the first to negotiate America's second oldest climb, Giant's Despair, in less than a minute.

Giant's Despair, within the city limits of Wilkes-Barre, Pa., is a switchbacked, S-turned serpentine that runs exactly one mile up a hill with grades of 22 per cent. Shelby's 58·768-second ascent came just 46 years after a FIAT set a record of 1 minute 28·4 seconds. The surface is properly paved but proportionately it is nonetheless quite as difficult as Mount Washington. The Giant's Despair competition is held annually in conjunction with the Berwick— formerly Brynfan Tyddyn—races, which until 1956 were run on a twisting, climbing 15-ft. public road surrounding an estate outside Wilkes-Barre; the longest straight on the 3·5-mile course is just one-sixth of that distance.

The third major American climb is Mount Equinox, near Manchester, Vt. The mountain, which is scaled by the only privately owned toll road in the United States, belongs to Dr. J. G. Davidson, the inventor of vinyl, who opens it once a year to the S.C.C.A. competition. Beautifully paved in concrete throughout its 5·2-mile length to the 3800-ft. peak, the road rises 500 ft. in every mile, with 36 coils and 10 switchbacks. While a D Jaguar has set a record of 4 minutes 44·6 seconds over this course, some of which, just before the peak, is almost perpendicular, the XK140MC has stormed it in 5 minutes 17·4 seconds. It is a course on which the turns are so close together and so contradictory that one must fight for traction every moment in order to make a creditable time.

For obvious reasons, neither race nor hill-climb bring out as many participants as the rally. Racing —and climbing is a form of racing—is the most expensive form that motor sport can take. To comply with S.C.C.A. safety regulations, cars must be equipped with approved tyres, roll-bars, seat belts and fire extinguishers; drivers must wear acceptable crash helmets and fireproof clothing. Preparing a car properly is costly; a single error of judgment can mean a new body, a new engine, a new gearbox or even, if the error is grievous enough, a new car —or no car. The error need not be one's own; it may be a competitor's. Rallying, however, imposes none of these burdens; even the installation of special calculating equipment is scorned by many of the most successful rallyists.

American rallies are much different from the European kind, and even from many of those in Britain that incorporate, whenever possible, exhaustive tests of car and driver in acceleration, braking and other reliability factors, though these are becoming more popular in the United States. The American rally is primarily a test of the navigator rather than the driver, for success depends entirely on reaching each check-point at the precise time set and within the mileage clocked by the organizers. Rallies are always run at average speeds well within the legal limits and hence can never become speed contests (in theory, at least; competitors who have lost the route as well as time will often find themselves in a kind of self-imposed time trial). Ultimately it is hoped that at least one rally each year will be run on the European model, covering perhaps 1500–2000 miles in a week and including timed runs on recognized hill-climbs and such circuits as Bridgehampton, Road America or Riverside, depending on the point of origin.

Every sports-car club, however small, runs at least one rally a month; in addition, the S.C.C.A. runs several major tests that count toward a national championship and its various regions have also established exacting rallies: the Rip Van Winkle Mountain Rally, the Appalachian, the Ohio 24, the Continental Divide. These are usually week-end affairs, covering up to 1000 miles or more, and such rallies as these are exceptions to the generalization. Running through mountain terrain and over all kinds of roads to elevations as high as 10,000 ft., they test driver as well as navigator with the infinite variations in average speed as well as in road, and reliability runs are the rule. On such long rallies some special equipment, such as flares in case of roadside emergency, are sometimes required, and often cars are subjected to a technical inspection almost as exacting as that before a race or a hill-climb: a precaution that is in the best interest of the contestant as well as the organizers. Unlike European rallies, the American competitions offer no cash prizes: only trophies are awarded to winners over-all, in class, in teams, in various marques, in phases of the rally, etc.

While the European rallies have attracted more and more Americans, the reverse has not been true. For a few years foreign entrants, both factory and private, appeared in the Great American Mountain Rally, which was not sponsored by the S.C.C.A. and in which both professionals and amateurs competed; but the G.A.M.R. was short-lived. Touring Britons and Continentals who occasionally turn out for American rallies as polite guests have been surprised to find that, despite the differences of geography and traffic laws that are in turn responsible for the variations from what the foreigner considers the rally norm, they have thoroughly enjoyed the American rally. Certainly it is within the reach of a far higher proportion of the sports-car public than the specialized quasi-races through the Alps. And major American racing drivers, like their colleagues abroad, are turning to the rally in increasing numbers between seasons on the circuits.

We have mentioned only the major competitions —race, hill-climb or rally—sponsored directly by the S.C.C.A. and its regions. It would be unjust to conclude without at least citing for a record whose limits of space unfortunately preclude anything further the hundreds of local sports-car clubs throughout the United States—and most other countries—that make it possible for members and non-members alike, week after week and year after year, to enjoy the challenge and the achievement of motor sport.

ACKNOWLEDGMENTS

The authors wish to acknowledge a special debt to those without whose help this book could never have been begun and whose contributions have been of so nearly equal value that the only just listing of their names is alphabetical:

Julian Apley of New York; the late Count Carlo Biscaretti di Ruffia, president of the Museo dell'Automobile, Turin; T. W. Carson, secretary of the Vintage Sports-Car Club of Great Britain; G. S. Cesari of Ambler, Pa.; H. Austin Clark, Jr., director of the Long Island Automotive Museum, Southampton, L.I.; Michael P. Clapham of Beauchief, Sheffield, England; Briggs Cunningham of Greens Farms, Conn.; S. C. H. Davis of Guildford, Surrey, England; René Dreyfus of New York; G. H. Fisher of Newcastle, Staffs., England; H. R. Godfrey of Guildford, Surrey; H. J. Harding of Nuffield Exports Ltd.; A. J. Hoe of Weston, Conn.; Col. W. A. Howkins of New York; M. Jean-François, *chef du service*, Automobile-Club de l'Ouest, Le Mans; Dipl.-Ing. Alfred Kempter, Rüsselsheim, Germany; Artur J. Keser of Daimler-Benz A.G.; René Le Grain-Eiffel, director-general, Union Technique de l'Automobile, and vice-president, Société des Ingénieurs de l'Automobile, Paris; R. Mailander of Daimler-Benz A.G.; Philip A. Mann, historian of the V.S.C.C.; Douglas McKee of McKee & Mouche, Paris; Pvt. Kurt H. Miska, A.U.S.; Lord Montagu of Beaulieu, chairman of the Montagu Motor Museum and editor of *The Veteran and Vintage Magazine*; Valerio Moretti, Scuderia La Manovella, Rome; Mr. and Mrs. Robert Morrison of Cleveland Heights, Ohio; Dott. G. Pestelli of FIAT, Turin; Mr. and Mrs. Everett L. Poorman, president and vice-president of International Motors Ltd., White Plains, N.Y.; Georges Roesch, London; D. W. H. Scott-Moncrieff, Leek, Staffs., England; Michael Sedgwick, registrar of The FIAT Register and curator of the Montagu Motor Museum; Robert Sicot, Régie Nationale des Usines Renault; Fred H. Sills of Byron, Ill.; Charles Stich of New York; A. E. Ulmann of New York and Sebring; Raymond K. Wright of London and Capt. H. Liston Young of Melton Mowbray, England, secretary of The FIAT Register.

We wish, too, to thank the hundreds of enthusiasts and organizations in a score of countries whose co-operation has also contributed to the making of this book:

AUSTRALIA
George H. Brooks, Mount Gambier
Ian Fraser, Editor, *Sports Car World*, Sydney
George G. Gilltrap, Gilltrap's Motor Museum, Coolangatta, Queensland
Helen Harvie, Heathmont, Victoria

AUSTRIA
Wolfgang Denzel, Vienna
Henry Goldhann, Vienna
Dr. Josef Nagler, director, Technisches Museum für Industrie und Gewerbe, Vienna
Hannes Pilz, Steyr

BELGIAN CONGO
Albert de Lay, Elisabethville

BELGIUM
M. Garot, administrator-secretary general, Royal Motor-Union, Liège

CANADA
Lt.-Col. Malcolm Moir, Trois-Rivières, P.Q.
A. L. Porter, Montreal

DENMARK
B. Mackeprang, secretary, Dansk Veteranbil Klub, Gentofte

EIRE
J. Ellis, Straffan

FRANCE
J. R. Broncard, director of public relations, S.A. des Automobiles Peugeot
Bernard Cahier, Paris
R. Cotton, Écurie Ile-de-France, Paris
Amédée Gordini, Paris
J. A. Grégoire, Asnières (Seine)
Tony Lago, Automobiles Talbot-Darracq S.A., Suresnes (Seine)
A. Lanardonne, S.A. André Citroën, Paris
François Landon, Régie Nationale des Usines Renault, Billancourt (Seine)
P. Manusardi, Automobiles Talbot-Darracq S.A., Suresnes (Seine)
Pierre Marco, secretary-general, Automobiles E. Bugatti, Molsheim
Claude Maurel, Automobiles Deutsch-Bonnet, Champigny-sur-Marne (Seine)
Edmond Mouche, Mouche & Cie., Paris
P. Moulin, adjutant director general, Société de Constructions Mécaniques Chenard & Walcker, Gennevilliers (Seine)
The late Baron Charles Pétiet, president, Chambre Syndicale des Constructeurs d'Automobile, Paris
J. Rédélé, Société des Automobiles Alpine, Paris
M. Riesinger, S.A. des Anciens Établissements Panhard & Levassor, Paris
P. G. Rossi, administrative secretary, Association Sportive de l'A. C. de Nice
Jacques Rousseau, St.-Mande (Seine)
The late Harry Schell, Paris
Gabriel Voisin, Paris

GERMANY
Arno Dietzel, Hannover
Benno J. Feit, Bous/Saar
V. Hoepner, Bayerische Motoren Werke, Munich
Horst Irmer, Hönigsen/Lehrte b. Hannover
Dr. W. Kornmesser, Gesellschaft für Nebenbetriebe der Bundesautobahnen m.b.H., Bonn
Alfred Neubauer, Stuttgart/Untertürkheim
Nürburgring G.m.b.H.
Dipl.-Ing. Max Rauck, Deutsches Museum, Munich
Hans Schimpke, Auto-Union G.m.b.H.

INDIA
M. R. M. Porter, Digboi, Assam

ITALY
Abarth & C., Turin
Renato Ambrosini, commercial director, S.I.A.T.A., Turin
Ing. C. Bacciagaluppi, manager, S.I.A.S., Monza
Dott. G. Bassi, O.M., Milan
Raffaele Breda, president, Automobile-Club di Pescara
Principe Filippo Caracciolo di Castagneto, president, Automobile-Club of Italy, Rome
Comm. Renzo Castagneto, director, Automobile-Club di Brescia
Comm. Enzo Ferrari, Modena
Ing. S. Florio, Lancia & C., Turin
Avv. D. Jappelli, Lancia & C., Turin

Dr. Ugo Pontiroli Gobbi, director, Automobile-Club di Belluno
Dr. Pietro Manci, manager, Automobile-Club di Milano
Bindo Maserati, Automobili O.S.C.A., Bologna
Comm. Giovanni Moretti, Moretti Fabbrica Automobili ed Autocarri, Turin
Dr. Paolo Sanguineti, Torino Motori, Turin
Dr. A. Della Seta, Lancia & C., Turin

JAPAN
Nissan Motor Co., Yokohama

KENYA
B. C. Edwards, Kericho

MEXICO
Enrique Martin Moreño, general manager, Asociacion Nacional Automovilistica, Mexico, D.F.

MONACO
Louis Chiron, Monte Carlo
Josette Notari, vice-consul in New York

NEW ZEALAND
W. B. Easterbrook-Smith, Lower Hutt

SWEDEN
H. G. Andersson, Svenska Aeroplan Aktiebolaget, Linköping

SWITZERLAND
Aug. Baumgartner, Geneva
Adrian M. Conan Doyle, Geneva

THE NETHERLANDS
J. B. Th. Hugenholtz, general manager, Circuit van Zandvoort
C. Poel, Jr., Westzaan
H. Visser, first secretary, Pionier Automobilien Club, Amsterdam

UNION OF SOUTH AFRICA
D. Exner Baumann, Cape Town
Bryan R. Smith, Johannesburg

UNION OF SOVIET SOCIALIST REPUBLICS
Mrs. Ninel Yuryeva, press department, Embassy of the U.S.S.R. in Washington

UNITED KINGDOM
J. D. Akers, secretary, Les Hommes à l'Hispano, London
L. G. Albertini, London
Dr. Clifford Allen, London
B. L. C. Angell, Harrow, Middx.
R. Angus, C.C. Wakefield & Co. Ltd., London
Buell B. Anthony, Worcester
Arthur Archer, Dunmow, Essex
P. F. Baker, Colwyn Bay, North Wales
R. F. E. Baker, London
J. R. D. Barker, Sheffield
Ronald Barker, *The Autocar*, London
R. O. Barnard, Chiddingfold, Surrey
Patrick Benjafield, Guildford, Surrey
C. D. Bennett, Lotus Engineering Co. Ltd., London
Air Vice-Marshal D. C. T. Bennett (ret.), director, Fairthorpe Ltd., Chalfont St. Peter, Bucks.
Julian Berrisford, London
Lt.-Col. C. H. D. Berthon, secretary, Bentley Drivers' Club, Aylesbury, Bucks.
P. F. Besley, Halesworth, Suffolk
J. G. Birch, D. Napier & Sons Ltd., London
Dr. Anthony T. Birmingham, registrar-historian, The Riley Register, St. Albans, Herts.
H. P. Blake, Fakenham, Norfolk
W. Boddy, editor, *Motor Sport*
Mrs. W. Boddy, S.-T.-D. Register, Fleet, Hants.
John Borthwick, Send, Surrey
C. C. Bown, Othery, Somerset

William Bradley, Worcester
Graham Broad, Brighton
Miles Brooking, Frodsham
Air Commodore N. R. Buckle, M.V.O. (ret.), president, Lancia Motor Club, Erlestoke, Wilts.
K. J. Campbell, London
Major F. E. Chubb, London
Barry Clarke, Wilton
F/Lt. C. G. Clarke, Cheltenham, Glos.
J. H. M. Cockaigne, press officer, The Bristol Aeroplane Co. Ltd., Bristol
Cecil Clutton, London
D. L. Somerville Cocks, Hove, Sussex
P. G. Cole, Byfleet, Surrey
J. O. Cooper, Benenden, Kent
Dudley Coram, chairman, Aston Martin Owners' Club, Ditchling, Sussex
Maurice Craig, London
E. G. Coushion, Whetstone, London
Alan Dakers, information officer, The David Brown Companies, London
J. C. G. Dancer, Gloucester
Basil H. Davenport, Macclesfield, Ches.
G. N. S. Davies, Cleeve Prior, Worcs.
Glyn Davies, Vauxhall Motors Ltd., Luton, Beds.
K. R. Day, secretary, Alvis Owners' Club, New Malden, Surrey
Brian Dearden-Briggs, Buxton
G. P. H. Dyson, Normanton, Yorks.
E. P. Ellis, Teddington, Middx.
Dr. Ian A. Entwistle, Hoylake, Ches.
J. Morton Entwistle, Hoylake, Ches.
Capt. G. E. T. Eyston, London
Arnold Farrar, secretary-treasurer, Riley Motor Club, Abingdon-on-Thames
G. D. Firkins, Wembley, Middx.
Arthur J. Firth, London
Douglas FitzPatrick, Sheringham, Norfolk
W. B. G. Fletcher, Solihull, War.
J. W. Frazer, Cullybackey, Northern Ireland
S. L. Fulker, Brighton
William Galbraith, Dundonald, Northern Ireland
John Geary, Hurstpierpoint, Sussex
John Eason Gibson, secretary, British Racing Drivers' Club, London
George H. Goodall, managing director, Morgan Motor Co. Ltd., Malvern Link, Worcs.
Kevin Gover, press officer, Austin Motor Car Co. Ltd., Birmingham
H. F. Gray, Beckley, Oxon.
K. A. Gregory, public relations officer, The Donald Healey Motor Co. Ltd., The Cape, War.
D. R. Grossmark, Shoreham-by-Sea, Sussex
D. W. Hale, Welwyn, Herts.
C. W. P. Hampton, Bolney, Sussex
Jeremy J. Hall, North Watford, Herts.
D. Dex Harrison, London
Jack Hart, Armstrong Siddeley Motors Ltd., Coventry
J. W. Haughton, Cullybackey, Northern Ireland
The late J. M. Hawthorn, Tourist Trophy Garage, Farnham, Surrey
Anthony S. Heal, Beaconsfield
Donald M. Healey, The Cape, War.
John Hebbard, Penzance
R. G. Henderson, A.C. Cars Ltd., Thames Ditton, Surrey

R. J. T. Hewitt, London

S. J. C. Hill, sales manager, Peerless Cars Ltd., Slough, Bucks.

Philip Hingley, Kidderminster

F/Lt. P. M. A. Hull, R.A.F., Oakington

Christopher Hurst, assistant publicity manager, Rolls-Royce Ltd., London

M. K. Johnson, secretary, Wolseley Hornet Special Club, Birmingham

William G. Johnson, Belfast

G. de Jongh, Forest Row, Sussex

Edgar Duggan Kehoe, Woking, Surrey

Cyril Kieft, Cyril Kieft & Co. Ltd., Wolverhampton, Staffs.

H. E. Kingsman, Clacton-on-Sea

P. J. D. Langriche, Beckenham, Kent

Derek Leigh, Longhope, Glos.

I. Linsdell, Chipping Norton, Oxon.

Thomas Lush, The Allard Motor Co. Ltd., London

Kenneth MacLeod, Parslow's Hillock, Bucks.

R. W. May, secretary, Allard Owners' Club, London

M. Meade, The J. Arthur Rank Organization Ltd., London

John K. Milner, Badminton, Glos.

John Mix, Enfield, Middx.

E. D. S. Mobsby, Rustington, Sussex

Donald Monro, president, Invicta Section, V.S.C.C., London

F. P. Morley, Enfield

Capt. D. C. Morrison, R.N., secretary, Veteran Car Club of Great Britain

Elizabeth Nagle, Woking

George Newman, London

K. Nightingale, secretary, Bugatti Owners' Club, Birmingham

N. Nightingale, director, Dellow Engineering Co. Ltd., Oldbury

Pilot Officer J. Noakes, R.A.F., Weston, Lancs.

W. H. Nock, Birmingham

Mr. and Mrs. C. A. Oakden, Poynton

Roy Pearl, managing director, Pearl, Cooper Ltd., London

R. A. Pilkington, Sutton Coldfield, War.

F. W. Pittuck, Kingston Hill, Surrey

Stanley Pollard, Blackburn, Lancs.

Major M. C. Polyblank, Hawkhurst, Kent

R. Radford, Weybridge, Surrey

J. Harris Reed, Corbridge, Northumberland

Peter Reeve, Carshalton, Surrey

Dr. C. G. Rexford-Welch, London

J. D. Rogers, Welling, Kent

J. F. Rowe, press officer, Rootes Motors Ltd., London

D. K. St. John, The Chequered Flag Ltd., London

Sir Francis Samuelson, Bart., Steyning, Sussex

T. L. Seccombe, Leominster, Herts.

John Shutler, Ringwood, Hants.

Alan Skerman, Sharon Grove, Yorks.

H. Slingsby, Jowett Engineering Ltd., Batley, Yorks.

Frank Smith, Stockport

Capt. G. T. Smyth, R.N., O.B.E., St.-Leonard's-on-Sea, Sussex

A. P. Southon, Phoenix Green Garage, Hartley Wintney, Hants.

John Stanford, Birmingham

Allan Staniforth, London

Patrick J. Stephens, Pearl, Cooper Ltd., London

A. J. Stephenson, secretary, Royal Scottish Automobile Club, Glasgow

G. W. Stevens, Kirlington, Oxon.

D. A. Thirlby, London

R. M. Tufnell, Harpenden, Herts.

J. H. Turner, managing director, Turner Sports Cars, Wolverhampton

Sheila Van Damm, London

E. B. Watson, Broadstairs, Kent

A. M. Watts, publicity officer, The Dolomite Association, Potters Bar, Middx.

B. Bruce Whitehouse, Campden, Glos.

M. H. Wilby, London

Leslie Wilson, secretary, Midland Automobile Club, Birmingham

G. H. Wiltsher, Alvis Ltd., Coventry

D. H. F. Woodford, Godalming, Surrey

Alan G. Woodland, registrar, Lea-Francis Owners' Club, Leamington Spa, War.

R. E. Wright, Wolverhampton

B. B. Wylam, Wincanton, Somerset

UNITED STATES

Andrew Adler, Millbury, Ohio

David R. Allen, public relations manager, Standard-Triumph Motor Co. Inc., New York

Mrs. Louise Alpert, Jaguar Cars North America Corp., New York

Parr Aplin, Portland, Ore.

Cameron B. Argetsinger, executive director, Watkins Glen Grand Prix Corp.

Gordon Ayer, Long Island Automotive Museum, Southampton, L.I.

William H. Baldwin, Larchmont, N.Y.

Henry Barber, South Salem, N.Y.

E. C. Barker, Salt Lake City

Paul C. Bastien, Grosse Pointe, Mich.

Fred O. Benson, Wheaton, Ill.

Mrs. Ruth Sands Bentley, New York

Alan F. Bethell, president, Standard-Triumph Motor Co. Inc., New York

Charles L. Betts, Jr., Yardley, Pa.

Tony Birt, Hambro Automotive Corp., New York

Sam Blackman, The Associated Press, New York

Al Bloemker, Speedway, Ind.

R. H. Blum, New York.

Frank M. Blunk, *The New York Times*

Dr. William R. A. Boben, Wilkes-Barre, Pa.

John R. Bond, publisher, *Road & Track*, Playa del Rey, Calif.

John Bott, Oyster Bay, L.I.

E. N. Brandt, senior editor, *The Saturday Evening Post*, Philadelphia

Winthrop Brubaker, public relations officer, Rolls-Royce Inc., New York

The late Hodge Brush, Greenwich, Conn.

Mr. and Mrs. William Caldwell, Larchmont, N.Y.

Anthony Calvacca, New York

John Campbell, Peekskill, N.Y.

John Caperton, Louisville, Ky.

Loring Chandler, Phillipston, Mass.

Fred A. Chapman, Automobile Manufacturers' Association, Detroit

William H. Collins, Standard-Vacuum Oil Co., White Plains, N.Y.

L. Oliver Cook, New York

Miles Coverdale, Manhasset, L.I.

Gordon F. Crafts, Riverside, Calif.

Walter Cronkite, New York

Shirley E. Day, The Carriage Cavalcade, Silver Springs, Fla.

Peter Dinella, librarian, *The New York Post*

Robert Donner, Jr., Colorado Springs

P. F. Dubé, president, Fergus Imported Cars Inc., New York.

John Dugdale, Society of Motor Manufacturers & Traders, New York

Henry E. Edmunds, archivist, Ford Motor Co., Dearborn, Mich.

Richard Elfenbein, Advertising Agencies Inc., New York

Robert Fabris, Waynesboro, Pa.

Henry G. Fanelli, New Rochelle, N.Y.

David C. Fenner, Falmouth, Mass.

Mortimer Feuer, New York

O. E. Filius, vice-president, Porsche of America Corp., New York

John Fitch, Lime Rock, Conn.

J. C. Fox, secretary-treasurer, Auburn-Cord-Duesenberg Club, Hampton, Iowa

C. R. Funk, Birmingham, Mich.

David Garroway, New York

J. E. Gebby, Dayton, Ohio

R. B. George, Philadelphia

William R. Gibson, librarian, Veteran Motor Car Club of America, Newton Centre, Mass.

William Gordon, New York

James F. Graham, Chatham, N.J.

K. R. Graham, Kansas City, Mo.

Norbert Guillaume, New York

Howard Hanna, Broomall, Pa.

Carl R. Hahn, Redwood City, Calif.

Bernard Haines, Valerie Motors Inc., Mamaroneck, N.Y.

Walter Hartman, 20th Century-Fox, N.Y.

Jack Hoins, National Broadcasting Co., New York

William Hooper, Elgin, Ill.

George W. Howard, Lafayette Hill, Pa.

Arthur Hurwich, Sea Cliff, L.I.

E. E. Husting, Boston

George K. Jepson, Hillsdale, N.J.

George Jessop, J. S. Inskip Inc., New York

Ben F. Johnson, Connersville, Ind.

Karl C. Killorin, Andover, Mass.

William C. Kinsman, Snyder, N.Y.

Mr. and Mrs. David Klein, New York

Dr. Louis H. Klinger, New York

Alix Lafontant, Penfield, N.Y.

Thomas J. Lester, Bedford, Ohio

E. A. Lindstrom, Portola Valley, Calif.

Francis H. Ludington, Rye, N.Y.

Karl Ludvigsen, editor, *Sports Cars Illustrated*

D. F. Mallalieu, Grand Prix Engineering Inc., Norwalk, Conn.

Carl O. Mamay, Brooklyn

Richard A. Manley, Dearborn

Edward P. Manning, Jr., Highland Park, Mich.

M. Jacob Markmann, Philadelphia

Sonya Markmann, New York

Clinton Martin, Verona, N.J.

V. F. Mashek, Chicago

Denise McCluggage, *Competition Press*, New York

Mavis McIntosh, McIntosh-McKee, New York

Charles J. McManus, Jr., Philadelphia

J. Bruce McWilliams, vice-president, SAAB Motors Inc., New York

Dr. Morton Milsner, New York

Herbert Miska, Flushing, L.I.

George A. Moffitt, New York

Charles Moran, Jr., chairman, Automobile Competition Committee for the United States (F.I.A.), Rye, N.Y.

D. B. Morren, Nisonger Corp., New Rochelle, N.Y.

George E. Morse, executive vice-president, Classic Car Club of America

Robert Muelke, Milford, Conn.

Evelyn Mull, Malvern, Pa.

Doris Leonora Muller, New York

Inga M. Naylor, New York

John H. O'Donnell, Westfield, N.J.

Mr. and Mrs. Robert Parrella, New York

Arthur G. Peck, Manhasset, L.I.

Charles R. Penninger, Chrysler Corp., Detroit

Leonard Peterson, Jr., Rockford, Ill.

George W. Pixley, Newburgh, N.Y.

William Pollock, president, Antique Automobile Club of America, Pottstown, Pa.

Leonard Potter, Vintage Car Store Inc., New York

Arthur Ralston, Mamaroneck, N.Y.

Jack Raymond, New York

John Reimer, New York

Joseph Remsen, Greens Farms, Conn.

Arthur Rosenstock, New York

Arthur H. Rosien, public relations director, Sports Car Club of America, Westport, Conn.

Edgar L. Roy, president, Vintage Sports Car Club of America, Boston

Robert E. Runser, chief, technology department, Detroit Public Library

Boris Said, Nisonger Corp., New Rochelle, N.Y.

Ray Saidel, Manchester, N.H.

George Sanderson, White Plains, N.Y.

Paul Sann, New York

John Sattler, Ford Motor Co., New York

Lloyd J. Schafer, Los Altos, Calif.

William Scholes, Cheltenham, Pa.

Lewis M. Schulz, president, S. & R. Service Inc., Hanover, N.J.

Myron E. Scott, assistant public relations director, Chevrolet—Central Office, Detroit

Daniel Serritello, British Travel Association

Hayden R. Shepley, Port Orange, Fla.

Mary Sherwin, New York

Richard Sherwin, Pittsfield, Mass.

Dr. Anthony Simeone, Philadelphia

Stanley B. Smith, vice-president, Antique Automobile Club of America, State College, Pa.

Col. Elliott White Springs, Fort Mill, S.C.

William E. Swigart, Jr., The Swigart Museum, Huntingdon, Pa.

Al Symonds, curator of transportation, Henry Ford Museum, Dearborn, Mich.

Walter Dorwin Teague, Jr., New York

Robert M. Theise, West Orange, N.J.

M. W. Thomas, Jr., curator, Henry Ford Museum, Dearborn, Mich.

James Vail, Lime Rock, Conn.

George Weaver, secretary-treasurer, Thompson Raceway, Thompson, Conn.

James A. Wechsler, New York

W. S. Weiant, Jr., Newark, Ohio

Herman Weiler, New York

John Weitz, New York

Stephen Wilder, technical editor, *Sports Cars Illustrated*
Mrs. Richard Williams, Garden City, L.I.
Eugene Williamson, North Caldwell, N.J.
R. A. Wolff, Milwaukee

Sonya Wolfson, 20th Century-Fox, Beverly Hills, Calif.
URUGUAY
Washington Baptista-Miralles, Montevideo

The authors have made every effort to omit no one from their thanks; should inadvertence have defeated their high intentions, they offer their apologies and the assurance of their gratitude to all who have helped.

BIBLIOGRAPHY

ALLEN, David R.
The Triumph Guide. New York, 1959
BEAUMONT, Charles, and NOLAN, William F. (ed.)
Omnibus of Speed. New York, 1958
BENTLEY, John
Great American Automobiles. Englewood Cliffs, N.J., 1957
The Devil Behind Them. New York, 1958
BENTLEY, W. O.
W. O. London, 1957
BERTHON, Darell
A Racing History of the Bentley. London, 1956
BISCARETTI di Ruffia, Count Carlo, and others
FIAT—A Fifty Years' Record. Verona, 1951
BOWMAN, Hank Wieand
Sports Cars in Competition. New York, 1952
BRADLEY, W. F.
Ettore Bugatti. London, 1948
Targa Florio. London, N.D.
CANESTRINI, Giovanni
L'Automobile: il Contributo italiano all'avvento e all'evoluzione dell'autoveicolo. Rome, 1938
Uomini e motori. Monza, 1957
CHULA of Siam, Prince
Road Racing, 1936. London, N.D. (privately printed)
CLUTTON, Cecil, and STANFORD, John
The Vintage Motor Car. London, 1954
CLYMER, Floyd
Treasury of Foreign Cars. New York, 1957
CORAM, Dudley (compiler)
Aston Martin: The Story of a Sports Car. London, 1957
DARBYSHIRE, L. C.
The History of Vauxhall. Luton, Beds., N.D.
DAVIS, S. C. H.
Atalanta. London, N.D.
Great British Drivers. London, 1957
ELBERT, J. L.
Duesenberg, the Mightiest American Motor Car. Arcadia, Calif., 1951
FRAICHARD, Georges
(translated by Louis Klemantaski)
The Le Mans Story. London, 1955
FREEMAN, John Wheelock
Sports Cars. New York, 1955

GRÉGOIRE, J. A.
L'Aventure automobile. Paris, 1953
24 heures au Mans. Paris, 1957
HALMI, Robert
Sports Cars of the World. New York, 1958
HAWTHORN, Mike
Challenge Me the Race. London, 1958
HENDERSON, R. G.
The History of A.C. Cars Ltd. Croydon, Surrey, 1952
HOUGH, Richard
Tourist Trophy. London, 1957
JENKINSON, Denis
The Racing Driver. London, 1958
KARSLAKE, Kent, and POMEROY, Laurence
From Veteran to Vintage. London, 1956
LABRIC, Roger
Les 24 heures de Mans. Le Mans, 1949
LANG, Hermann
Grand Prix Driver. London, 1958
LESSNER, Erwin
Famous Auto Races and Rallies. New York, 1955
LOWRY, Russell
Monte Carlo Rally. London, N.D.
MARIANO, Carlo
Appunti di storia. Bologna, 1958
MOSS, Stirling
In the Track of Speed. New York, 1958
Stirling Moss' Book of Motor Sport. London, 1955
MOTEURS-COURSES
Numéro spécial édité à l'occasion du cinquante-naire de l'Automobile-Club de l'Ouest. Paris, 1956
MULL, Evelyn
Women in Sports Car Competition. New York, 1958
NAGLE, Elizabeth
Old Cars the World Over. London, 1958
NICKOLS, Ian, and KARSLAKE, Kent
Motoring Entente. London, 1956
NITSKE, W. Robert
The Amazing Porsche and Volkswagen Story. New York, 1958
NIXON, St. John C.
Wolseley, A Saga of the Motor Industry. London, 1949
PARTRIDGE, Bellamy
Fill 'Er Up. New York, 1952

PURDY, Ken
   Kings of the Road. Boston, 1952
RAE, John B.
   The American Automobile. New York, N.D.
ROLT, L. T. C.
   A Picture History of Motoring. New York, 1956
ROSEMANN, Ernst
   The Big Race. Frankfurt-am-Main, 1955
ROUSSEAU, Jacques, and IATCA, Michel
   Histoire mondiale de l'automobile. Paris, 1958
ROYAL MOTOR-UNION
   Livre d'or de l'automobile et de la motocyclette.
      Liège, 1951
SCOTT-MONCRIEFF, D. W. H.
   Veteran and Edwardian Motor Cars. London, 1955
SCOTT-MONCRIEFF, D. W. H., NIXON, St. John, and
      PAGET, C.
   Three-Pointed Star. London, 1955

STANFORD, John
   The Sports Car: Development and Design. London,
      1957
TANNER, Hans
   Great Racing Drivers of the World. New York,
      1958
THORNLEY, Lt.-Col. John W.
   Maintaining the Breed (second edition). London,
      1956
ULMANN, A. E.
   A History of Hispano-Suiza. New York, N.D.
      (privately distributed)
   Mercedes: Pioneer of An Industry. New York, 1948
VAN DAMM, Sheila
   No Excuses. London, 1957
COMPILATION
   Vittorie Maserati, 1926–1954. Modena, N.D.

and the files of *Road & Track, Sports Cars Illustrated;
Motor Sport, The Autocar, The Motor, The Veteran
and Vintage Magazine; l'Automobile; l'Auto italiana,
Torino Motori; Das Auto, Motor und Sport.*